International Human Rights Law

Riccardo Pisillo Mazzeschi

International Human Rights Law

Theory and Practice

Springer

G. Giappichelli Editore

Riccardo Pisillo Mazzeschi
Department of Political and International Sciences
University of Siena
Siena, Italy

ISBN 978-3-030-77031-0 ISBN 978-3-030-77032-7 (eBook)
https://doi.org/10.1007/978-3-030-77032-7

Revised and updated translation of the Italian language edition: Diritto internazionale dei diritti umani - Teoria e prassi. Ristampa emendata by Riccardo Pisillo Mazzeschi, © G. Giappichelli Editore 2020. Published by G. Giappichelli Editore. All Rights Reserved.

This Springer imprint is published by the registered company Springer Nature Switzerland AG.
The registered company address is: Gewerbestrasse 11, 6330 Cham, Switzerland

To my little grandsons Marco and Alessandro, with the wish that they will grow up in a society more open to the universal values of equality and fraternity

Preface

This book has a didactic purpose, for the students of the specialized courses of international protection of human rights; but also of consultation for scholars and practitioners in the field of international law and human rights. I have tried to provide a sufficiently complete and systematic overview of the subject, as I think is necessary for a textbook, even though the field of international human rights law has now taken on such a large dimension that it is difficult to deal with it in a small volume. The book seeks to give an account of the most relevant practice and case-law, but also to deal with theoretical issues. Hence its title, which deliberately recalls the work of an authoritative scholar of international law.[1]

One might wonder what the reasons that led me to write a new book on human rights are, given the large number of manuals already published in recent decades, especially in English and French. There are, in summary, three reasons. The first consists in my desire to give a different approach and structure to this volume, trying to reconcile its didactic and scientific purposes. In fact, many of the existing textbooks, and, in particular, those of Anglo-American doctrine, privileging the didactic and expositive purpose of the subject, focus on the description of the institutional part of the international protection of human rights (conventional systems, organs, and procedures) or deal only with some human rights. In my opinion, this structural choice is not convincing. In fact, even if one wanted to place oneself in a predominantly didactic perspective, it must be considered that students do not need to receive much information and detailed descriptions, which they can easily find on the Internet and which they soon tend to forget, but rather to reflect on concepts, theories, and systematic framings. Only these reflections are formative for young jurists and help to understand how the law works, including international human rights law. In other words, for me, there is no conflict, but rather a necessary synergy, between the educational and scientific purpose of a textbook. Of course, this does not mean that my intention to combine theory, practice, and a certain completeness of the subject in the book has really succeeded.

The second, even more important, reason derives from my conviction that international human rights law should not be studied (as occurs in almost all manuals) as a specific legal regime, separate and autonomous from the overall

[1] O. Schachter, International Law in Theory and Practice (1991).

system of international law; but as a regime that is fully integrated into the international legal order, which follows the inspiring principles of the latter, and which has, in turn, had a strong impact on the structure and content of contemporary international law. This book has as its dominant theme the mutual relationship between international human rights law and general international law. Following this approach, I have chosen to devote little space to the institutional aspects (Part IV) and to deepen instead the themes of the impact of human rights on the entire international order (Part I), on the sources (Part II), on obligations (Part III), as well as the part of the book that deals with the content of "fundamental" human rights (Part V), without neglecting other rights (Part VI). I am aware that this choice may have had some negative effects on the homogeneity of the book, since it has led to a deeper study of some subjects and a more concise treatment of others.

Finally, the third motivation for this book is linked to my general conception of international law, from the point of view of the theory of law. The volume is the result of reflections I have been doing for a couple of decades on human rights; but which are linked to studies on more general themes of international law, which have led me to follow a *fil rouge* that has developed over time and which has come to be linked to a certain conception on the deontological foundation of law. This scientific path, influenced by my growing attention to human rights, has led me to a critical attitude towards the theory of formal positivism (while recognizing the rigor of its method) and to cultivate an interest in "anti-formalist" theories (e.g., the modern normative theory of law), which recover an openness to the ethical-political values of law. From this general approach also derived the idea that it is intellectually stimulating to study not only the law of rules and "what the law is," but also the law of principles and values and the direction towards which the law is moving;[2] and this especially in an area, such as international law, which has recently undergone strong processes of change. In fact, in my scientific path, I have proposed attempts to systematically relocate some classical institutions (breach of treaties, fault and due diligence, exhaustion of domestic remedies) and attempts to revisit, in a key that I believe is more modern, other general issues (theory of international obligations, State responsibility for violation of human rights, international subjectivity, new role of the individual, general principles of international law, international immunities, access to justice). Readers will note that many of these topics have inevitably ended up, albeit incidentally, in this book as well.[3]

I would like to thank Alessandra Viviani, Federico Lenzerini, Eugenio Carli, and Federico Travan for reading the book or parts of it and for their useful comments. Of course, I am solely responsible for any errors and omissions.

[2]Cf. A. Cassese, Self-Determination of Peoples. A Legal Reappraisal (1995), p. 3.

[3]I hope readers will forgive me if, in an attempt to provide further references on these topics, I have often cited my earlier writings.

Advisory Notice

A. *Searching for acts and documents*
Almost all international normative materials (judgments, decisions, treaties, and other acts) are officially published on their online sites. Therefore, to find them, please refer to the table of websites.

B. *Use of languages*
For official in-text citation of passages from judgments, treaties, or other normative acts, I have usually adopted the English version. When it was not possible, I usually gave my own English translation.

C. *Citations in the footnotes*
In the footnotes, the doctrine is quoted in abbreviated form (author's surname and year of publication), referring to the bibliography for a more complete indication. Cases are also cited in summary form, with reference to their table for more information. To distinguish cases with the same name, the date of their decision is cited.

Siena, Italy
January 2021

Riccardo Pisillo Mazzeschi

Contents

Abbreviations

Acronyms

ACHPR	African Charter on Human and Peoples' Rights of 27 June 1981
ACHR	American Convention of Human Rights of 22 November 1969
ACmHPR	African Commission on Human and Peoples' Rights
ACtHPR	African Court on Human and Peoples' Rights
ACtJHR	African Court of Justice and Human Rights
AP	Additional Protocol
AP I	Protocol Additional to the Geneva Convention of 12 August 1949 (Protection of Victims of International Armed Conflicts) of 8 June 1977
AP II	Protocol Additional to the Geneva Convention of 12 August 1949 (Protection of Victims of Non-International Armed Conflicts) of 8 June 1977
ArCHR	Arab Charter on Human Rights of 22 May 2004
ASEAN	Association of South-East Asian Nations
AU	African Union
CAT	Convention against Torture and Other Cruel, Inhuman or Degrading Treatment or Punishment of 10 December 1984
CCPR	International Covenant on Civil and Political Rights of 16 December 1966
CEDAW	Convention on the Elimination of All Forms of Discrimination against Women of 18 December 1979
CERD	International Convention on the Elimination of All Forms of Racial Discrimination of 21 December 1965
CESCR	International Covenant on Economic, Social and Cultural Rights of 16 December 1966
CFI	Court of First Instance of the European Communities
CJAU	Court of Justice of the African Union
CmHR	Commission on Human Rights

CoE	Council of Europe
CMW	International Convention on the Protection of the Rights of All Migrant Workers and Members of Their Families of 18 December 1990
CPPED	International Convention for the Protection of All Persons from Enforced Disappearance of 20 December 2006
CPPCG	Convention on the Prevention and Punishment of the Crime of Genocide of 9 December 1948
CRC	Convention on the Rights of the Child of 20 November 1989
CRPD	Convention on the Rights of Persons with Disabilities of 13 December 2006
CSCE	Conference on Security and Co-operation in Europe
CSPCA	International Convention on the Suppression and Punishment of the Crime of Apartheid of 30 November 1973
CSR	Convention relating to the Status of Refugees of 28 July 1951
CteeAT	Committee Against Torture
CteeED	Committee on Enforced Disappearances
CteeEDAW	Committee on the Elimination of Discrimination against Women
CteeERD	Committee on the Elimination of Racial Discrimination
CteeESCR	Committee on Economic, Social and Cultural Rights
CteeMW	Committee on Migrant Workers
CteeRC	Committee on the Rights of the Child
CteeRPD	Committee of the Rights of Persons with Disabilities
EC	European Community
ECCC	Extraordinary Chambers in the Courts of Cambodia
ECJ	European Court of Justice
EC Treaty	Treaty establishing the European Community (former Treaty establishing the European Economic Community of 25 March 1957)
ECHR	European Convention for the Protection of Human Rights and Fundamental Freedoms of 4 November 1950
ECHRB	European Convention for the Protection of Human Rights and Dignity of the Human Being with regard to the Application of Biology and Medicine of 4 April 1997
ECmHR	European Commission of Human Rights
ECML	European Charter for Regional or Minority Languages of 5 November 1992
ECOSOC	Economic and Social Council
ECOWAS	Economic Community of West African States
ECOWAS-CCJ	ECOWAS Community Court of Justice
ECPT	European Convention for the Prevention of Torture and Inhuman or Degrading Treatment or Punishment of 26 November 1987
ECteeSR	European Committee of Social Rights
ECtHR	European Court of Human Rights
EEC	European Economic Community

ESC	European Social Charter of 18 October 1961
ESCrev	European Social Charter revised of 3 May 1996
EU	European Union
EUCh	Charter of Fundamental Rights of the European Union
FAO	Food and Agriculture Organization
FCPNM	Framework Convention for the Protection of National Minorities of 1 February 1995
GA	General Assembly of the United Nations
GC	Geneva Conventions of 12 August 1949
GC I	Geneva Convention for the Amelioration of the Condition of the Wounded and Sick in Armed Forces in the Field of 12 August 1949
GC II	Geneva Convention for the Amelioration of the Condition of the Wounded, Sick and Shipwrecked Members of Armed Forces at Sea of 12 August 1949
GC III	Geneva Convention relative to the Treatment of Prisoners of War of 12 August 1949
GC IV	Geneva Convention relative to the Protection of Civilian Persons in Time of War of 12 August 1949
HCHR	United Nations High Commissioner for Human Rights
HRC	Human Rights Council
HRCtee	Human Rights Committee
IACAT	Inter-American Convention to Prevent and Punish Torture of 9 December 1985
IACmHR	Inter-American Commission on Human Rights
IACtHR	Inter-American Court of Human Rights
ICAO	International Civil Aviation Organization
ICC	International Criminal Court
ICJ	International Court of Justice
ICRC	International Committee of the Red Cross
ICSID	Convention on the Settlement of Investments Disputes between States and Nationals of Other States of 18 March 1965
ICTR	International Criminal Tribunal for Rwanda
ICTY	International Criminal Tribunal for the Former Yugoslavia
ILC	International Law Commission
ILO	International Labour Organization
IMT	International Military Tribunal of Nuremberg
IMTFE	International Military Tribunal for the Far East (of Tokyo)
ITLOS	International Tribunal for the Law of the Sea
ITU	International Telecommunication Union
IUSCT	Iran-United States Claims Tribunal
NATO	North Atlantic Treaty Organization
NGO	Non-Governmental Organization
OAS	Organization of American States

OAU	Organization of African Unity
OECD	Organization of Economic Co-operation and Development
OHCHR	Office of the High Commissioner for Human Rights
OSCE	Organization for Security and Co-operation in Europe
PCIJ	Permanent Court of International Justice
PSR	Protocol Relating to the Status of Refugees
Rome Statute	Rome Statute of the International Criminal Court of 17 July 1998
RSCSL	Residual Special Court for Sierra Leone
SADC	Southern African Development Community
SC	Security Council of the United Nations
SCSL	Special Court for Sierra Leone
SICTR	Statute of the International Criminal Tribunal for Rwanda of 8 November 1994
SICTY	Statute of the International Criminal Tribunal for the Former Yugoslavia of 25 May 1993
STL	Special Tribunal for Lebanon
TEU	Treaty on European Union
TFEU	Treaty on the Functioning of the European Union
UDHR	Universal Declaration of Human Rights of 10 December 1948
UN	United Nations
UN Charter	Charter of the United Nations
UNCC	United Nations Compensation Commission
UNHCR	Office of the United Nations High Commissioner for Refugees
UNDP	United Nations Development Programme
UNESCO	United Nations Educational, Scientific and Cultural Organization
UPR	Universal Periodic Review
VCLT	Vienna Convention on the Law of Treaties of 23 May 1969
WHO	World Health Organization
WTO	World Trade Organization

Journals, Periodicals, and Other Sources

ACDI	Annuaire de la Commission du droit international
AFDI	Annuaire français de droit international
AIDI	Annuaire de l'Institut de droit international
Am J Int Law	American Journal of International law
ASDI	Annuaire Suisse de Droit International
ASIL Proc	American Society of International Law Proceedings
AV	Archiv des Völkerrechts
Aust Yearb Int L	Australian Yearbook of International Law
Br Yearb Int L	British Year Book of International Law
CD	Collection of Decisions of the European Commission on Human Rights
Col JTL	Columbia Journal of Transnational Law
Com int	La Comunità internazionale

CS	Comunicazioni e Studi dell'Istituto di diritto internazionale e straniero dell'Università di Milano
DUDI	Diritti umani e diritto internazionale
ECR	European Court Reports
Eur J Int Law	European Journal of International Law
ED	Enciclopedia del Diritto
EPIL	Encyclopedia of Public International Law
ESIL Proc	European Society of International Law, Select Proceedings of the ESIL
German Yearb Int Law	German Yearbook of International Law
Georgia J Int Comp Law	Georgia Journal of International and Comparative Law
Hum Rights Q	Human Rights Quarterly
ICJ Rep	Reports of Judgments, Advisory Opinions and Orders of the International Court of Justice
ILM	International Legal Materials
ILR	International Law Reports
Int Comp Law Q	International and Comparative Law Quarterly
Ital Yearb Int Law	Italian Yearbook of International Law
J Int Crim Just	Journal of International Criminal Justice
J Int Disp Settlement	Journal of International Dispute Settlement
Leiden J Int Law	Leiden Journal of International Law
Mich J Int Law	Michigan Journal of International Law
Neth ILR	Netherlands International Law Review
Netherlands Yearb Int Law	Netherlands Yearbook of International Law
ÖZöR	Österreichische Zeitschrift für öffentliches Recht und Völkerrecht (Austrian Journal of Public and International Law)
PCIJ Publ	Permanent Court of International Justice Publications
Pol YIL	Polish Yearbook of International Law
RIAA	Reports of International Arbitral Awards
Riv int dir uomo	Rivista internazionale dei diritti dell'uomo
RBDI	Revue belge de droit international
RC	Recueil des Cours, The Hague Academy of International Law
RDI	Rivista di diritto internazionale
REDI	Revista española de derecho internacional
RGDIP	Revue générale de droit international public
Studi integr eur	Studi sull'integrazione europea
UNTS	United Nations Treaty Series
Virginia J Int Law	Virginia Journal of International Law
YILC	Yearbook of the International Law Commission
ZaöRV	Zeitschrift für ausländisches öffentliches Recht und Völkerrecht (Heidelberg Journal of International Law)

Part I

Human Rights in the International Legal System

1 The Foundation and Historical Development of International Human Rights

1.1 Concept and Foundation of Human Rights

The notion of "human rights" is apparently simple; but it is actually quite complex. In fact, these rights have been, in the history of juridical philosophy, gradually defined with different terms (natural, innate, original, moral, fundamental rights); their historical origin is situated at different times; their legal foundation has been explained from varying perspectives by naturalism, positivism, juridical realism, institutional law theory; and the very notion of "human rights" has progressively widened.

According to some authors,[1] human rights are those freedoms, immunities and benefits which, in conformity with accepted contemporary values, all human beings should be able to demand, as real rights, from the society in which they live. According to others, human rights are those that have the nature of fundamental and essential rights of the person and are therefore imprescriptible, inalienable, indispensable and universal.[2] According to others, human rights constitute an impassable minimum for every human being that the law must protect at any cost.[3]

These definitions are rather similar; however, they do not seem sufficiently precise to clearly distinguish human rights from other "ordinary" rights. Therefore, the problem of the legal basis of human rights opens up, especially from the point of view of the international legal order.

From one point of view, a certain right can be considered a "human right" when it corresponds to human nature, that is, to the reason and will typical of the human species. This view has a basic naturalistic law approach and has the disadvantage of leaving a margin of subjectivity in finding a definition of "human nature" that is universally accepted in the contemporary multicultural world.

[1] Henkin (1995), p. 886.

[2] Zanghì (2013), p. 5.

[3] Focarelli (2008), p. 342.

R. Pisillo Mazzeschi, *International Human Rights Law*,
https://doi.org/10.1007/978-3-030-77032-7_1

Other authors have supported the theory of the "self-evidence" of human rights. They would be so obvious and so immediate that they would not require a rational justification and legal basis. But even this view lends itself to different subjective interpretations by different groups of States with different traditions, religions and cultures.

The third theory, in my view the most convincing, is that human rights are based simply on consensus. In other words, human rights are those rights that are recognized as such in a given legal system on the basis of a general consensus of the subjects of that system. In the international legal order it will be the consensus of the international community to determine which rights can be defined as "international human rights". A different problem (the answer to which is more restrictive) is to ascertain which human rights are truly universal because they are well established in general international law.[4]

To this third theory another concept, in my opinion, can be added; namely that human rights are, of all rights, those that best express the essential and noblest function of law: that of a legitimate instrument in the fight against force, power and abuse. In international human rights, this function is realized above all in the opposition between the person and the State.[5]

1.2 Historical Precedents

1.2.1 Historical Development of Human Rights in National Legal Systems

If one wants to go back to ancient times, one can argue that the idea of certain human rights can be found in the Bible, in the Hammurabi Code, in the laws of Greek cities like Athens, as well as in some precepts of various religions or philosophies, such as Buddhism, Confucianism and Hinduism.

However, a more interesting development occurs many centuries later with some English national documents, such as the famous *Magna Charta Libertatum* of 1215, the *Habeas Corpus Act* of 1679 and the Bill of Rights of 1689. In modern times, some American declarations are of great importance, such as the Virginia Declaration of Rights of June 12, 1776,[6] the American Declaration of Independence of July 4, 1776,[7] and the Bill of Rights adopted in 1789 and ratified in 1791.[8] Finally,

[4] See below, Sects. 1.4 and 13.1–13.3.

[5] This contrast evokes, *mutatis mutandis*, the image of the State as Leviathan. See Hobbes (1651).

[6] Art. 1: "[. . .] all men are by nature equally free and independent, and have certain inherent rights [. . .]".

[7] "We hold these truths to be self-evident, that all men are created equal, that they are endowed by their Creator with certain inalienable Rights, that among these are Life, Liberty and the pursuit of Happiness . . .".

[8] These are ten amendments to the US Constitution of 1787.

French documents include the Declaration of Human and Citizen's Rights of 1789.[9] Subsequently, many States followed the examples of the USA and France in their constitutional charters.[10]

However, it should be noted that, in these instruments, beyond the universalistic language, human rights are essentially understood as citizens' rights; and that they are relevant to domestic constitutional law and not to international law. The idea that a State can assert the human rights of persons against another State, and especially against the State of nationality of the person, is in fact extraneous. In other words, human rights had no impact on international relations between States in the eighteenth and nineteenth centuries and little impact during the first half of the twentieth century.

1.2.2 The Role of the Individual in Classical International Law

According to the concept of classical international law, predominant until the middle of the twentieth century, individuals were not subjects of international law, their role was essentially irrelevant and they were submitted to the exclusive power of government of the State of which they were "subjects". International law formally regulated only relations between States. Also from a substantive point of view, international law dealt almost exclusively with interstate relations and therefore the way in which the State treated its subjects was a matter of "domestic jurisdiction" of that State. In reality, certain limits to the territorial sovereignty of States already existed in classical international law; but individuals derived only an indirect benefit from such limits and not true rights under international law. Let us look briefly at these limits.

1.2.3 Obligation to Protect Aliens and Their Property

Traditional international law has recognized since the early centuries of its development that States have an obligation to protect aliens who are on their territory or under their jurisdiction from offences relating to their person or property, through preventive and repressive measures that conform to certain minimum standards of civilization and justice. But this obligation, of a customary nature, was conceived only as operating between the territorial State and the State of nationality of the alien; the individual victim was considered only as a possible "*de facto* beneficiary" of this obligation. Therefore, when the foreign individual suffered a violation of this

[9] Art. 1: "Men are born and remain free and equal in rights. Social distinctions can only be based on common utility"; Art. 2: "The aim of every political association is the preservation of natural and inscribed human rights. These rights are freedom, property, security and resistance to oppression".

[10] See, for example, The Netherlands (1798), Sweden (1809), Spain (1812), Norway (1814), Belgium (1831), the Kingdom of Sardinia (1848), Denmark (1849), Prussia (1850).

obligation of protection by the territorial State, only the nation-State of the individual had the right to take international action against the offending State, according to the rules on diplomatic protection and those on international responsibility of States.

In essence, the individual was an "object" and not a "subject" of international law; and he did not even have a true right to receive from his own nation-State the reparation that the latter might have been able to obtain from the offending State.

1.2.4 Humanitarian Intervention

The doctrine of humanitarian intervention, already supported by some internationalists in the seventeenth century, recognized as legitimate the use of armed force by one or more States when it was necessary to stop the mistreatment of individuals in a foreign State, and when such mistreatment was so brutal and systematic as to offend the conscience of the community of States.[11] In fact, humanitarian intervention was used mainly in the nineteenth century by the European Powers to protect persecuted Christians in the territories of the Ottoman Empire. The doctrine was sometimes used in an abusive manner and as a pretext for the strongest States to occupy or invade the territory of weaker States.

However, the doctrine of humanitarian intervention highlighted the fact that there were certain limits to the freedom of States in the treatment of their subjects when it came to very serious violations of their human rights.

1.2.5 Treaties Against Slavery and on the Protection of Religious Groups

In the nineteenth century, the strictly interstate conception of international law was largely dominant; but there was the possibility, albeit in rare and isolated cases, that a State, through a bilateral or multilateral treaty, would assume obligations to grant certain rights to individuals. In this way the treatment of individuals became the subject of an international obligation between the States Parties and went beyond the sphere of the "domestic jurisdiction" of those States.[12] This process of "internationalization" of individual interests already had its start with the Congress of Vienna of 1815.

The Congress adopted a Declaration on the Slave Trade, which recommended its abolition to States, affirming that slavery was incompatible with the principles of humanity and international morality. Later, this objective was included in a series of bilateral treaties, in a multilateral treaty of 1842 between European and Latin-American States, in the Berlin Congo Act of 1885 and in the General Act of the 1890 Brussels Conference on the abolition of slavery. In the twentieth century, as we

[11] Buergenthal et al. (2004), p. 3.

[12] Buergenthal et al. (2004), p. 6.

shall see,[13] the subject was taken up in the important 1926 Slavery Convention of the League of Nations and other subsequent treaties.

Similar developments occurred with regard to the protection of religious minorities. As early as the seventeenth century, a number of treaties contained provisions protecting religious minorities. Thus, the Congress of Vienna imposed an obligation on some States to guarantee non-discrimination of religious minorities and the freedom to practice the Catholic religion in certain territories. Later, in the Treaty of Berlin of 1878 a special legal status was granted to certain religious groups.[14]

1.2.6 The Birth of International Humanitarian Law

International humanitarian law (originally called *jus in bello*) deals with the protection of the victims of armed conflict and the prohibition of certain means and methods of warfare considered inhuman, with the aim of "humanizing" armed conflict as far as possible through legal rules. Its origin is much older than international human rights law, although at present these two legal fields tend to be closer and complementary.

The birth of modern international humanitarian law dates back to the mid-nineteenth century, when the Swiss Henry Dunant proposed measures for the protection of war victims, which led to the creation of the International Committee of the Red Cross and the drafting of the 1864 Geneva Convention for the Amelioration of the Condition of the Wounded in Armies in the Field.[15] In the meantime, in 1863, US President Lincoln had issued the so-called "Lieber Code", which established a set of rules and instructions for military operations during the American Civil War. The next step in this development process was the St. Petersburg Declaration of 1868, which prohibited the use of certain weapons and in whose Preamble it was solemnly declared that "the only legitimate purpose that States should pursue during the war is to weaken the military forces of the enemy".

Subsequent developments, of great importance, were the Hague Conventions of 1899 and those of 1907. Particularly significant is the 1907 Hague Convention (IV) respecting the Laws and Customs of War on Land, whose Preamble contains the famous "Martens Clause", according to which, in the absence of a specific legal rule applicable to the case, the inhabitants and the belligerents:

> remain under the protection and the rule of the principles of the law of nations, as they result from the usages established among civilized peoples, from the laws of humanity, and the dictates of the public conscience.

---

[13] See below, Sect. 16.1.

[14] Buergenthal et al. (2004), p. 7.

[15] Kälin and Künzli (2009), p. 11.

It should be noted that these first norms of international humanitarian law were based on the principle of reciprocity and were structurally conceived within the framework of traditional international law of an interstate nature; and therefore did not attribute real rights to individuals under international law. However, most of these norms were, in fact, designed to protect individual interests as well, and thus represented a sign of the growing role of the individual in international law.

International humanitarian law was revised, updated and further developed in the twentieth century, especially after the Second World War.[16] There is no doubt that the legal position of the individual has changed substantially in contemporary humanitarian law.

1.2.7 The League of Nations and the System of Mandates

Some important developments in relation to specific human rights occurred after the First World War. US President Woodrow Wilson presented to Congress in 1918 his "Fourteen Points", an ambitious program aimed at creating a more peaceful and just international community. He called, among other things, for the realization of the principle of self-determination of peoples, albeit limited to Western States, through a redetermination of borders based on the principle of nationality and the recognition of statehood to nation-entities seeking autonomy. The principle was not accepted; but it exerted a certain influence on the League of Nations.

In reality the Covenant of the League of Nations, approved on April 28, 1919 and included in the Versailles Peace Treaty of June 28, 1919,[17] did not contain any general provisions dedicated to human rights. The idea that human rights, in general, should be protected at international level was not yet mature in the international community. However, the Covenant contained two provisions, Articles 22 and 23, which were intended to have an influence on the development of certain human rights.

Article 22 of the Covenant established the system of mandates of the League of Nations, which applied to the colonies and non-autonomous territories of the States that had lost the First World War and which transformed these colonies into Mandates of the League entrusted in administration to the winning Powers. The final purpose of the mandates was to achieve the self-determination of these colonies and territories over time. In the meantime, the Powers entrusted with the mandate undertook with the League to administer the territories promoting the material and moral well-being, and social progress, of the inhabitants. The Mandates Commission of the League gradually acquired more and more powers over time to control the administration of the mandates and the way in which the native populations were treated. However, the dissolution of the League of Nations put an end to this development. In its place, the United Nations established the Trusteeship System,

[16] See below, Sect. 2.4.1.

[17] The Treaty of Versailles was signed by 44 States and came into force on 10 January 1920.

which was entrusted with controlling powers over the remaining mandates and other non-autonomous territories.

1.2.8 Protection of Workers

The Versailles Peace Treaty recognized the need to protect workers, since it stated that world peace "can only be established if it is based on social justice". Article 427 of the Treaty set out a number of more specific objectives with regard to the protection of workers.[18]

Besides, Article 23 of the League of Nations Covenant dealt, inter alia, with issues relating to "fair and humane working conditions for men, women and children"; and provided for the creation of an international organization to promote this objective. In fact, the International Labour Organization (ILO) was created, which quickly managed to prepare and have adopted some important conventions, such as the 1919 Hours of Work Convention, the 1919 Maternity Protection Convention, the 1919 Night Work of Young Persons Convention, and the 1930 Forced Labour Convention.

1.2.9 The System for the Protection of Minorities

The League of Nations has also played an important role in the creation of an international system for the protection of minorities. This matter was not regulated by the League of Nations Covenant. However, some Central and Eastern European States, which had been created after the collapse of the Ottoman Empire and the Austro-Hungarian Empire, included ethnic, linguistic and religious minority groups on their territory. These groups had historical reasons to fear that the new States would not respect their cultural autonomy. Therefore, the victorious States of the First World War succeeded in imposing unilateral treaties or declarations on these States, which contained guarantees of protection for those minorities. One may recall the peace treaties with Austria, Bulgaria, Hungary and Turkey; the special agreements with Czechoslovakia, Greece, Poland, Romania and Yugoslavia; and the unilateral declarations of Albania, Finland, Estonia, Lithuania and Latvia.

These States were obliged not to discriminate against members of protected minorities and to guarantee them protection of life and personal security, freedom of religious belief and practice, and certain linguistic rights. In order to strengthen the fulfilment of these obligations, the States in question agreed that their obligations should be placed under the guarantee of the League of Nations. The latter exercised its monitoring function by developing a system for dealing with petitions from minorities who complained of violations of their rights. Petitions were examined by a committee of three members of the League Council to which the States

[18] See Kälin and Künzli (2009), pp. 12–13.

concerned could submit their observations; and, when appropriate, the Permanent Court of International Justice (PCIJ) was asked to give an advisory opinion on controversial legal issues.

This system of international protection of minorities was an interesting experiment at the time. However, it is also true that the treaties on the protection of minorities remained in line with traditional international law, since they only established obligations of States towards other States and the League of Nations, and did not create genuine substantive rights, at international level, either for minorities as collective bodies or for individual members of minorities. The latter only had the right to submit petitions to the League.

1.2.10 The Limits of the Above Historical Precedents

We have so far examined some historical precedents, indicating the existence of limits to the general principle of the "domestic jurisdiction" of the State in the treatment of its citizens and, at the same time, an increasing attention of international law to the interests and role of the individual.

However, three important limitations that characterized these developments must be stressed. The first is that they were very specific and sectoral in character. The second limitation is that many of the above-mentioned treaties actually pursued political or economic interests of States, rather than being motivated by humanitarian concerns. The third limitation is that the prevailing doctrine of positivist formation continued to interpret these treaties as formally regulating only relations between States, from which there were no real rights for individuals at the international level. This view was also endorsed by the Permanent Court of International Justice in its 1924 judgment in the *Mavrommatis* case, in which the Court formulated the notion of diplomatic protection in traditional terms, stating that:

> By taking up the case of one of its subjects and by resorting to diplomatic action or international judicial proceedings on his behalf, a State is in reality asserting its own right – its rights to ensure, in the person of its subjects, respect for the rules of international law.[19]

1.3 The Turning Point After the Second World War: Human Rights Theory Imposes Itself Internationally

In the post-World War II period, under the pressure of world public opinion, the efforts for an international protection of human rights, with a general and not only a sectoral aspect, are multiplying. Individuals are considered as human beings to be protected as such, and therefore also from their own nation-State. Therefore, the issue of human rights, as a whole, becomes a central issue on the international scene.

[19]PCIJ, *Mavrommatis Palestine Concessions*, p. 12.

The most important reason for this radical change is certainly the awareness on the part of the international community that the Nazi system and other totalitarian regimes had shown, before and during the war, an absolute contempt for the most essential human rights and that the protection of human rights through the constitutions of individual States was not sufficient. Instead, a new world order had to be created, based on peace and the international protection of human rights. These ideas were initially supported primarily by Western States, by virtue of their constitutional traditions; they were included in the Atlantic Charter of 1941; and they were taken up at the Dumbarton Oaks Conference in 1944, which proposed the establishment of the United Nations (UN).

Finally, the Western Powers, at the San Francisco Conference in 1945, created the United Nations, entrusting it with the promotion and protection of human rights as an important part of its mandate. The basic idea was to develop human rights principles to guide the work of the UN and its Member States, with the aim of gradually creating a comprehensive system of human rights protection in peacetime, through its progressive codification in a series of international treaties and guarantee mechanisms. This aim has been achieved over time, giving rise to the so-called UN human rights protection system.[20] It is a system that tends to operate at a universal level. Over time, it has been joined by a number of human rights protection systems operating at regional level, sometimes more advanced than the UN system.[21]

We can therefore speak today, in a more general and overall sense, of an "international system of protection of human rights". This international system has been progressively implemented through conventional norms and guarantee mechanisms (monitoring bodies and procedures), whose broad path of evolution I will discuss later on. For the time being, it is sufficient to note that the international movement for the protection of human rights, which has developed in a generalized manner, and no longer only in a limited and sectoral way, since the entry into force of the UN Charter, has taken the form, in legal terms, of the adoption of many acts of soft law, the conclusion of numerous treaties on a universal and regional scale[22] and also the creation of certain norms of general international law.[23] It may also be recalled that, thanks to the work of the international monitoring bodies set up by some of the above-mentioned treaties, there is now an extensive international, judicial and quasi-judicial practice in the field of human rights.

Ultimately, it can be said that the theory of human rights strongly characterized the phase of development of the international community that took place after the Second World War and that this theory led to the affirmation and progressive

---

[20] See below, Chap. 10.

[21] See below, Chaps. 11–12.

[22] These agreements contain both a detailed catalogue of human rights that States Parties are obliged to grant to all individuals under their jurisdiction and instruments of guarantee and control.

[23] These rules include customs, principles of international law and general principles of law recognized by civilized nations in domestic courts.

consolidation of a new, vast and important area of the international legal order, the so-called international law of human rights.

Moreover, it is worth pointing out that the theory of human rights has also exercised a wider role, since, by taking root deeply in the life of the international community, it has ended up producing a great influence on the general principles that regulate this community and therefore also, as we shall see,[24] an impact on the international legal order as a whole. In this sense, we can speak of a process of structural change in international law.

In my view, there are basically two related reasons for this. The first is that the theory of human rights is by its very nature "subversive" or "revolutionary"[25] with respect to the traditional structure of relations between States, because it runs counter to the principle of sovereignty, which is the basic principle of traditional international law and which has long prevented States from interfering in the internal organization of other States and in the way they treat their citizens. The second reason is that this theory focuses on the individual, who is no longer considered as an object of State sovereignty, but considered in him or herself, as a human person, and tends to assume an increasingly important and central role in the life of the international community. In this sense too, the theory of human rights is "subversive", because it runs counter to the traditional conception that only States and other sovereign bodies are the subjects of the international order.

In the next chapter, I will look more deeply at the impact of the human rights theory on the structure of international law.

1.4 General Aims of Human Rights

1.4.1 Dignity of the Human Person and Universal Values

At the beginning of this chapter I have dealt, in a nutshell, with the main theories on the notion and foundation of human rights. It is now appropriate to address the problem of the general objectives pursued by these rights in international law. In summary, it can be said that international human rights norms simultaneously pursue two general aims: (a) to protect the dignity of the human person and to defend it in relation to the State; (b) to become a universal value of the contemporary international legal order.

The first aim is very obvious. Under the pressure of various historical factors, which I have briefly described, the international community was convinced that it was necessary to create an *international* legal regime for the protection of the individual with regard to the State, and especially with regard to its own State. This also means that international human rights law tends to create a legal regime for the protection of *individual interests* which tend to take precedence over State

[24] See below, Chap. 2.

[25] Cf. Cassese (1984), p. 321; Id. (2003–2004), vol. II, pp. 83–84.

interests, simply because human rights are, in principle, rights which the individual has against the State. In this sense, in my view, the *principle of the primacy of the individual* (or human person) can be considered a guiding principle of international human rights law.

The second purpose is closely linked to the first. In fact, under the impetus of the protection of the essential interests of individuals, the international norms on human rights today also aim to realize a community interest of the States, which overrides their individual and "selfish" interests. This is because it is recognized that the protection of human rights pursues high objectives of humanity, civilization and morality, and constitutes a central and universal value for the contemporary international community. Therefore, the *principle of the universality of human rights* can be considered a second guiding principle of international human rights law.

However, this second conclusion is not taken for granted, since the very concept of universalism of human rights is controversial and has to deal with phenomena of particularism and multiculturalism that are present in the reality of the international community. The problem deserves some reflection.

1.4.2 The Problem of the Universalism of Human Rights in a Multicultural World

The problem of the universalism of human rights will only be addressed from a legal point of view.[26] In common language, it is often taken for granted that human rights are universal in the twofold sense that they belong to all people and are globally recognized. But in reality the question is more complex, and can be summed up and simplified into one question: is the universalism of human rights possible in a multicultural world[27]? And in a contemporary reality that sees the rebirth of nationalism and particularism? What exactly does universalism of human rights mean in international law?

In my opinion, the universalist *vocation* of human rights is sure and cannot be called into question, if one does not want to renounce belief in the very existence of international human rights. These are, by definition, rights that *should* belong to all human beings and that all States *should* recognize. The idea that all States should guarantee fundamental rights to all human beings, and to the same extent, is clear from Article 1 of the Universal Declaration of Human Rights, according to which:

> All human beings are born free and equal in dignity and rights [. . .].[28]

Moreover, as stated above, the idea of the central and universal value of the protection of human rights has also been affirmed in the international community of

[26] And therefore neglecting the philosophical, historical, social, cultural aspects.

[27] See, recently, Lenzerini (2014).

[28] UDHR, Art. 1.

States; and therefore it can be said that *the principle of universality* is a guiding principle that operates in the whole field.

However, this universalistic *vocation* of human rights must come to terms with a multicultural world in which there are different conceptions of what rights and values are truly fundamental; and with legal reality, for which only certain human rights are governed by general international law. In summary, there are two opposing trends or, if you like, *two conflicting principles*: universalism and multiculturalism/particularism. But, since, in human rights theory, multiculturalism is also recognized as a value to be defended,[29] there is a need to try to reconcile the two principles in some way. This need also responds to the requirement to harmonize the utopian aspects of universalism, which would like to achieve equality in respect and enjoyment of human rights for all States and for all human beings, with the more realistic aspects of particularism, which take into account the differences concretely existing in the international community. One could say, with a synthetic expression, that it is a matter of reconciling, in some way, the values of equality with those of diversity. In other words, it is a matter of conciliating a common heritage of humanity with a plurality and diversity of values and traditions.

In my opinion, this conciliation is possible if it is recognized that, in international law, a balance (or compromise) between universalism and multiculturalism has so far been achieved: the universalist *vocation* of human rights operates as the driving force of the whole area, but it has been fully realized, *from a legal point of view*, only in part; that is, for the limited number of human rights that are regulated by general international law (principles of international law, customary law, general principles of law recognized *in foro domestico*). In other words, this vocation has been realized for those human rights which enjoy the general consent of the international community, a consent which is expressed in different ways in the various above-mentioned sources of general international law.[30] Moreover, as we shall see,[31] this general consensus of the international community is also reinforced by the fact that human rights regulated by general international law almost always (but not always) end up coinciding with human rights regulated by *jus cogens*; that is, recognized as essential and peremptory values of the entire international community.

However, the legal universalism of human rights still has many limitations, because most human rights, as we shall see, are governed only by conventional international law; in other words, by norms that only bind States that have voluntarily accepted and ratified them. It is in this aspect that the principle of multiculturalism/particularism is expressed: it is clear that those human rights that are regulated only by treaties, and by treaties ratified only by a part of the existing States, cannot be considered concretely as universal, *from a legal point of view*. Those rights do not belong to all human beings and do not oblige all States. In other words, conventional

[29] Cf. Lenzerini (2014); Crawford (2013), pp. 325–341. See also the UNESCO Convention on the Protection and Promotion of the Diversity of Cultural Expressions, 20 October 2005.

[30] See below, Chaps. 3–5.

[31] See below, Sects. 13.3.4 and 13.3.5.

international law leaves States free, even on the basis of their own culture of human rights, to accept or not to be bound by the respect of certain rights. To give an example (though not edifying), if those treaty norms which establish the principle of equality between men and women are not accepted by the States of the Muslim world, this prevents them from becoming norms of general international law. A similar discourse could be made for other human rights that are accepted only by some States, such as, for example, the prohibition of the death penalty.

Furthermore, consider another aspect in which the relationship between universalism and multiculturalism/particularism is expressed; that is, the fact that the content of the customary norm on a given human right is not identical to that of the corresponding conventional norms on the same right. Usually, the content of the customary norm is more general, simpler and more essential, as we shall see later. For example, the right to life in customary law means, in essence, the prohibition of arbitrary deprivation of life.[32] On the other hand, in many conventional rules the right to life has more complex and detailed content, with restrictions and exceptions, as well as criteria for better defining the concept of arbitrariness. To give another example, the right of access to justice, in customary law, has a synthetic and essential content,[33] while in the conventional rules it is specified in detailed provisions on fair trial and effective domestic remedies, which establish a complex legal regime, with a series of substantive and procedural guarantees. And these treaty provisions vary according to the different treaties and different human rights systems, leaving room for particularism and regionalism.

But it should be noted that conventional human rights law does not only express the trend towards multiculturalism. It can also, in the difficult balance between the two trends, reflect the universalistic vocation. In fact, in the first place, some human rights treaties have been ratified by a very large number of States[34] and therefore they are "quasi-universal". Secondly, as we shall see,[35] treaty law can, under certain conditions, have a considerable impact on the progressive development of general international law (especially customary law). In the third place (and this point will be explored in more detail later[36]), the universalist principle exerts an influence on certain "special" features of human rights treaty law, since it tends to favor the widest possible participation by States in such treaties and to widen their scope of application.

In summary, in my view, the relationship between universalism and multiculturalism of human rights can be visually represented by two concentric circles: the largest represents all human rights, while the smallest, within the former, represents human rights governed by general international law, which I define, for the moment

[32]See below, Sect. 14.1.

[33]See below, Sect. 17.1.

[34]See, e.g., the Convention on the Rights of the Child (below, Sect. 10.4.2.7).

[35]See below, Sect. 3.1.

[36]See below, Sects. 4.2 and 4.3.

on a provisional basis, as "fundamental" human rights.[37] As the international law of human rights develops and progressively widens, the small circle tends to widen; and so it tends to decrease the difference between the dimensions of the two circles. In other words, universalism is strengthened at the expense of multiculturalism/particularism. But, obviously, it is a very slow process and not always linear and continuous; and probably the two circles will never end up coinciding.

References

Buergenthal T, Shelton D, Stewart DP (2004) International human rights in a nutshell, 3rd edn (2nd rep). West Group, St. Paul
Cassese A (1984) Il diritto internazionale nel mondo contemporaneo. Il Mulino, Bologna
Cassese A (Gaeta P ed) (2003–2004) Diritto internazionale, vol. I: I lineamenti, vol. II: Problemi della comunità internazionale. Il Mulino, Bologna
Crawford J (2013) Change, order, change: the course of international law. General course on public international law. RC 365:9–389
Focarelli C (2008) Lezioni di diritto internazionale, vol I. Cedam, Padova
Henkin L (1995) Human rights. EPIL 2:886–893
Kälin W, Künzli J (2009) The law of international human rights protection. OUP, Oxford-New York
Lenzerini F (2014) The culturalization of human rights law. OUP, Oxford
Zanghì C (2013) La protezione internazionale dei diritti dell'uomo, 3rd edn. Giappichelli, Torino

[37] For a closer examination of this notion see below, Chap. 13. As we shall see, it can be added that, within the smaller circle, there is another even smaller circle represented by human rights protected by *jus cogens*.

The Impact of Human Rights on International Law

2

2.1 Human Rights and the Modernization Process of International Law

As mentioned above, human rights theory has gradually taken on a central role in international law and has become deeply rooted in the dynamics of contemporary international society.

This means, in my view, that this theory has also produced a phenomenon of innovation and modernization both in some general and structural aspects of international law and in many specific areas of that law.[1] In this regard, a part of the doctrine has spoken of a process of "humanization" of international law, wanting to mean that classical or traditional international law, essentially formed by so-called "state-centric" norms (i.e., protective of interstate relations), while remaining largely current also in the contemporary world, has gradually and progressively left a space also for a "new" international law, formed by so-called "human-centric" norms (i.e., aimed at protecting also and above all, the human person).[2]

However, it must be warned that another part of the doctrine does not agree with the existence of such a process of modernization and "humanization" of international law; or at least it tends to diminish its importance.[3]

These two different opinions correspond, to a large extent, to two very different general theories on the coherence and completeness of the international legal order and on the related problem of the existence or non-existence of the so-called

[1]See, for classical works, Friedmann (1964), Jennings (1979), Simma (1994), Tomuschat (1993), Carrillo Salcedo (1997).

[2]See, in particular, Simma (1993), Meron (2003), Meron (2006), Pisillo Mazzeschi (2004a), pp. 16–36; Id. (2008), pp. 198–220; Sicilianos (2012); Pisillo Mazzeschi and De Sena (2018).

[3]See, e.g., Weil (1983), Weil (1992), esp. pp. 25–39 e 66–81; Combacau (1986), Combacau and Sur (2006), pp. 17–28; Pellet (2000).

R. Pisillo Mazzeschi, *International Human Rights Law*,
https://doi.org/10.1007/978-3-030-77032-7_2

self-contained regimes.[4] These theories also lead to different conceptions of the specific field constituted by international human rights law: is it a closed and isolated system, incapable of communicating and interacting with general international law and with other specific fields of such law (and therefore, in essence, it is a self-contained regime) or, vice-versa, is it a sector which communicates and interacts with the international legal order considered as a whole? As is clear, only the latter conception of international human rights law allows us to assume that it has produced the aforementioned phenomenon of modernization of the entire international order. It is therefore appropriate to go into the two general theories in question in greater depth.

2.2 International Human Rights Law as a Self-Contained Regime?

A part of the internationalist doctrine (composed mainly by authors specialized in single fields) adheres to the first of the two general theories indicated above; that is, it is based, already from the beginning, on a "particularistic" conception of international law, which considers this law as a set of normative subsystems poorly interconnected with each other, due to the lack of common superordinate principles.[5] This leads to favoring the general theory of self-contained regimes; and therefore also the idea that the international system of human rights constitutes, in whole or in part, a self-contained regime; that is, a special regime which is in itself closed and sufficient, which excludes recourse to norms other than those proper to the regime in question, and then also excludes the functioning of general international law or, at least, admits it only in exceptional and residual cases.

The idea that international human rights law constitutes a self-contained regime is also accepted, on a less theoretical and more pragmatic basis, by many human rights lawyers, who tend, probably also with sincere enthusiasm and optimism for the rapid developments in this field, to accentuate the importance of these developments and, consequently, the differences between the legal regime of human rights and general international law. In essence, this means that, for these authors, the peculiar characteristics of the human rights regime do not affect general international law. Therefore, this tendency also leads to "isolate" international human rights law from the overall system of international law. The main legal instrument, which can provide the theoretical basis for this "particularistic" approach, is, as mentioned above, the concept of a self-contained regime. This is, in my view, a paradoxical

[4]On the theory of self-contained regimes, see Simma (1985), Simma and Pulkowski (2006), Pisillo Mazzeschi (2014a), pp. 278–287; Crawford (2013), pp. 275–309; Treves (2019), pp. 339–373.

[5]On the problem of the so-called "fragmentation" of international law see ILC, *Fragmentation of International Law: Difficulties Arising from the Diversification and Expansion of International Law, Report of the Study Group of the International Law Commission (Finalized by Martti Koskenniemi)*, A/CN.4/L.682 of 13 April 2006; Koskenniemi and Leino (2002). For critical comments see Conforti (2007); Benvenisti (2008); Simma (2009).

result for human rights advocates, because it means, in a certain sense, closing this sector in a sort of "ghetto" and admitting that it cannot affect the entire international legal order.

On the contrary, in an inverse and opposite way, another part of internationalist doctrine (formed especially by so-called "generalist" scholars), starts from a very different basic conception about the very structure of international law and considers this law as a single legal system, and with strong characteristics of completeness and systematic coherence (a "universalist" conception of international law). This doctrine, to which I adhere, tends in principle to reject the concept of self-contained regimes, understood as systems totally closed to the outside world, and instead to accept only the possibility of special regimes, mainly of a conventional nature, which function within the framework of the normal relations between general law and special law. Moreover, the existence of a special regime, derogating from general international law, should result from sure elements; namely, from the fact that the States parties to a special treaty regime have clearly expressed this desire for derogation.

This general conception also applies to the specific field of human rights. The doctrine under examination shows the tendency not to "isolate" international human rights law with respect to general international law and other specialized areas of that law; and therefore to consider that international protection of human rights, while constituting in some respects a regime that may derogate from general international law, on the basis of the criterion of specialty, is nevertheless part of the general system and interacts with that system and other specific regimes, through the possibility of mutual influences, interactions and coordination. It is clear that this doctrine is much more inclined to admit that the above-mentioned process of "humanization" of international law has taken place. Therefore, it must be concluded that it is the generalist authors, rather than human rights specialists, who more easily recognize the innovative impact of these rights on the entire system of international law.

Ultimately, it must be stressed that, even beyond the theoretical and doctrinal premises of departure, it is the concrete examination of the reality of contemporary international law that demonstrates the correctness of the second theory described above. In fact, as we shall see immediately, it is very difficult to deny that the theory of human rights, transported to an international level, has produced a significant impact on the international legal order.[6] For systematic reasons, I will distinguish between two phenomena of change: (a) a real process of structural modification of the international system; (b) an impact on a number of specific areas of international law.

---

[6]See Pisillo Mazzeschi (2014b).

2.3 Influence of Human Rights Theory on the Traditional Structure of the International Legal Order

2.3.1 Extension of the Content and Scope of International Law

According to the classical or traditional definition, absolutely dominant until the middle of the twentieth century, international law is the legal system that governs relations between States (or between States and other sovereign entities). This statement is intended first of all to point out that international law, *in terms of subject matter*, regulates relations between States; i.e., that its *typical content* is that of regulating matters pertaining to interstate relations and legal questions, so to speak "external" and of typically diplomatic interest.

The theory of human rights has produced a considerable fracture with respect to this content, since it has transferred relations between the State and its citizens to international law and has given the individual a central role. In so doing, it has produced a significant *expansion of the content and scope* of international law.[7] In fact, contemporary international law no longer regulates only typically interstate relations, but also, and increasingly, a great many relations that take place within the various State communities, which exist between States and individuals, and which affect all internal legal operators and all individuals.[8] One could say, in short, that international law is no longer just a law for States, but *also a law for individuals*. In this process of change, the theory of human rights has played a primary and fundamental role, since it has internationalized the relations between the State and its citizens, which for centuries were matters of "domestic jurisdiction", excluded from the very scope of international law. This theory has also produced a dynamic impetus for the development of other areas of contemporary international law, which also regulate relations between States and individuals or inter-individual relations: just think of international criminal law and contemporary international humanitarian law.[9]

2.3.2 Enlargement of International Law Actors: The New Role of the Individual

A second element of the traditional concept of international law concerns its subjects or formal holders of international rights and obligations. In classical international law only States are considered as international subjects. Individuals are considered only "objects" or, at least, mere "*de facto* beneficiaries" of international norms. In

---

[7] *Ibidem*, p. 90. On the general theme of the expansion of international law see, recently, Treves (2019).

[8] Cf. Conforti (2006), p. 3.

[9] See below, Sects. 2.4.1 and 2.4.2.

more recent times, the international subjectivity (or personality) of international organizations has also become established.

The theory of international human rights has, according to the now dominant opinion, made a fundamental contribution to radically changing this traditional conception.[10] Today, it is admitted that contemporary international law *formally and directly* regulates (i.e. without the need to be incorporated into domestic law) also *some* relations between States and individuals (and other non-state entities) and *some* inter-individual relations. In other words, individuals are now *direct addressees* of certain primary, secondary and tertiary international norms, and therefore also holders of rights and obligations at the international level. The International Court of Justice (ICJ) itself has established that the 1963 Vienna Convention on Consular Relations contains rules that directly grant rights to individuals.[11]

International human rights norms are the main, though not the only, example of norms that impose obligations on a State to which *both the rights of other States and the rights of individuals* correspond. Indeed, it is worth repeating here what I have already said:[12] that the *principle of the primacy of the individual* dominates the whole area of international human rights law. As far as obligations are concerned, the norms of international criminal law are the main example of international norms which directly impose obligations on individuals.

In doctrine, since there is no unanimous agreement on the concept of international personality, it is still debated whether this change means that individuals are "subjects" of international law, or "partial or limited subjects", or only entities with certain capabilities.[13] In my opinion, it is now only a theoretical discussion, with little impact on reality, which consists in determining, concretely and in each case, who the *addressees* of each single international norm and the holders of each single international right or obligation are.[14] Alternatively, this solution, of a pragmatic nature, could be expressed, in more theoretical terms and borrowed from state law, arguing that individuals are international subjects, but have different *capabilities* (and sometimes no capabilities at all), depending on the individual areas and norms of international law.

In any case, it is clear that the theory of human rights, also on this aspect of international subjectivity, has radically modified a fundamental element that had characterized the traditional structure of international law for centuries. Today it can

---

[10] See Pisillo Mazzeschi (2004a), pp. 16–36; Id. (2014a), pp. 287–294.

[11] ICJ, *LGrand*, p. 466; *Avena*, p. 121; *Jadhav Case*, paras. 116–119. See also IACtHR, *The Right to Information on Consular Assistance*, para. 80.

[12] See above, Sect. 1.4.

[13] See Pisillo Mazzeschi (2014a), pp. 287–294. On the various theories on the subjectivity of individuals in international law see also Bartolini (2009), pp. 17–53; Peters (2016), pp. 167–193.

[14] See also Treves (2019), p. 110, according to which it is basically a question of doctrinal or political preference to consider individuals as subjects of international law or not.

be argued that the international community must be extended and interpreted in a broad sense, as it also includes individuals and other non-state actors.

2.3.3 Change in the Typical Nature of International Law

A third element of the traditional concept of international law concerns its *typical function and legal nature.*[15] Classical international law, especially customary law, had the typical function of regulating the coexistence of States within the framework of an equal and horizontal structure of international society. Consequently, it was based essentially on the principles of reciprocity and bilateralism and therefore had a typically "private" legal nature, i.e. it was intended to regulate the individual and "selfish" interests of individual States. This private nature concerned two main aspects: (a) the absence of collective interests of States; (b) the absence of fundamental values belonging to the entire international community. The first aspect is illustrated by the fact that traditional international norms, even when they were addressed to several States, operated in a bilateral and reciprocal manner. The second aspect is shown by the fact that almost all traditional customary norms had a dispositive nature, i.e. they could be derogated from by States by agreement. This confirms that classical international law did not recognize the existence of fundamental and peremptory values of the international community as a whole.

For a natural historical process, the expansion of the content and scope of international law has also produced an extension of its function and nature: the so-called international law of *coexistence*, all based on an individualistic and "private" conception of relations between States, on the principles of reciprocity and "bilateralism" in matters of State responsibility, while surviving, has gradually left room also for the so-called international law of *cooperation*, which has become increasingly open to the protection of collective, solidarity and even community interests of States.[16] In other words, there has been not only a phenomenon of a quantitative increase of cooperation between States, but also a progressive opening towards a "public" conception of the relations between States, at least at a normative level, if not yet at an institutional level.

This phenomenon of change has been caused by a complex series of factors; but it must be recognized that the theory of human rights has played a fundamental role, which is well highlighted by the two concepts of *erga omnes* obligations and *jus cogens*.

2.3.3.1 *Erga Omnes* Obligations and Collective Values

The first concept is linked to the emergence, in contemporary international law, of certain *collective and community interests* of States.

---

[15] See Pisillo Mazzeschi (2014b), pp. 90–92.

[16] See above, the literature cited in Sect. 2.1.

As already mentioned, in traditional international law, norms usually create bilateral links between States; i.e. they create reciprocal rights and obligations between them. In other words, such norms are "synallagmatic" in nature. This is the case not only for norms deriving from bilateral treaties; but also for norms deriving from multilateral treaties or customary law. In fact, even the latter two categories of norms, although addressed to a number of States, are liable to be broken down into a bundle of bilateral relations between States. This decomposition can be clearly seen in the case of violation of the norm, since only the injured State (i.e. the State whose subjective right has been violated and which has suffered damage) has an active legitimation to assert the relationship of responsibility (principle of bilateralism). There were, of course, also in traditional international law, some exceptions to the principle of reciprocity and to the rule of the "synallagmatic" nature of international norms. But they were, in fact, only isolated exceptions. The principle of reciprocity was dominant because it reflected well the equal and exclusively horizontal structure of the international community, the absence of intense juridical ties between States and the absolute prevalence of individual and selfish interests of States over those of a collective nature.

The situation has changed a great deal in contemporary international law, since there are now many examples of international norms which are not based on reciprocity, but on the opposite principle of solidarity. These are precisely the norms that establish solidarity obligations or, as is more often said, *erga omnes* obligations.[17] This term means that the obligation exists towards all the members of the international community (*erga omnes* obligations) or towards all the contracting parties to a multilateral treaty (*erga omnes partes* obligations); i.e., that its breach by a State affects all the other States or, at least, all the other States parties to a treaty. In other words, the solidarity of the obligation may derive both from a customary norm and from a treaty norm. It is clear that this evolution of contemporary international law is linked to the progressive emergence in this system of collective values of the international community. The norms that protect these values have a "public" rather than a "private" character, and therefore they are placed on a different level from the other norms of the system and tend to create obligations of a solidarity nature in the sense that they commit each State to every other State within the international community as a whole (or within a smaller group of States that share these collective values).

It should be stressed that the initial impetus and the decisive push for the development of the concept of *erga omnes* obligations came precisely from the area of human rights, as is demonstrated by the fact that the International Court of Justice, in the famous passage of the *Barcelona Traction* judgment in which it enucleates this concept, includes, above all, examples relating to human rights.[18]

---

[17]The bibliography on *erga omnes* obligations is very extensive. See, e.g., Simma (1994); Ragazzi (1997); Picone (2005); Tams (2005); Ronzitti (2007); Pisillo Mazzeschi (2008), pp. 249–256; Gaja (2014), pp. 97–136.

[18]ICJ, *Barcelona Traction*, Judgment of 5 February 1970, paras. 32–34.

In fact, customary norms and treaties on human rights are paradigmatic examples of norms containing *erga omnes* obligations, in the sense that they oblige each State towards all other States or towards all other States parties to a multilateral treaty.

This has important effects especially in the field of international responsibility, since the breach of *erga omnes* obligations infringes a right, or in any case a legal interest, of all other States or any other State party to the multilateral treaty.[19] Therefore, it is clear that the new concept of solidarity obligations, while coexisting with the traditional concepts of bilateral and reciprocal obligations, has introduced a considerable change in the function and nature typical of classical international law, since the recognition of solidarity values constitutes a strong push towards a "public" (or, according to some, "vertical" or "constitutionalist") nature of international law.

2.3.3.2 *Jus Cogens* and Fundamental Values

A similar argument can be made for the concept of *jus cogens*,[20] which originates from the development, in contemporary international law, of certain *essential, fundamental and peremptory values* of the entire international community. The legal concept of *jus cogens*, now universally recognized, must not be confused with that of *erga omnes* obligations, because the former does not concern the particular structure of the obligation, but rather the value, the legal force of resistance and (according to the preferable view) also the hierarchical rank of the norm. Moreover, the notion of *jus cogens* is more restrictive than that of *erga omnes* obligations. However, there are also strong affinities between the two concepts, since their basis is the idea that in contemporary international law there are "community" or "public" values, which must be protected.

Human rights theory has played an important role in bringing the concept of *jus cogens* to the forefront of international law and, in the practice, many peremptory norms correspond to customary norms (or general principles) on "fundamental" human rights, which also establish *erga omnes* obligations, such as, for example, the prohibitions of genocide, crimes against humanity, torture, slavery and racial discrimination.

Therefore, this theory has contributed, also through the concept of *jus cogens*, to change the function and legal nature of international law in the sense of their modernization: alongside the private dimension of international law, a public dimension has gradually developed and established itself. As we shall immediately see, the concept of *jus cogens* (like that of *erga omnes* obligations) has also had important effects in the field of State responsibility.

---

[19] See ILC, *Draft Articles on Responsibility of States for Internationally Wrongful Acts*, 1 August 2001, Arts. 48 and 54. See also below, Sect. 2.3.4.1.

[20] Even on the concept of *jus cogens* the bibliography is very extensive. See, e.g., Ronzitti (1978); Gaja (1981); Id. (2014); Hannikainen (1988); Kolb (2001); Orakhelashvili (2006); Picone (2008); and the work of the International Law Commission, in particular the reports presented by the Special Rapporteur: Tladi (2016); Id. (2017); Id. (2018); Id. (2019).

2.3.4 Modernization of the Regime of International Responsibility of States

The theory of human rights, along with other factors, has produced significant changes in the traditional area of State responsibility, affecting the fundamental elements of this area, which were the principle of "bilateralism" and the principle of the exclusively interstate character of responsibility. It has modernized these aspects, since the structural changes mentioned above (especially that relating to the new role of the individual and that relating to the new "public" nature of international law) have also affected the "pathological" phase of international law, represented by international responsibility.[21]

More specifically, these changes have: (a) widened the sphere of the States legitimated to invoke the responsibility of the State accused of a wrongful act; (b) established, alongside the ordinary regime of State responsibility, also a regime of "aggravated" responsibility; (c) paved the way for the possibility of international responsibility of States towards individuals. Let us look at these three aspects separately.

2.3.4.1 Invocation of Responsibility for Breach of *Erga Omnes* Obligations

With regard to the first aspect, it has already been seen that an important factor in the process of change in contemporary international law, through the decisive impetus given by the theory of human rights, concerns the growing role of the collective interests of States. This development is represented above all by the fact that there are now many international norms that establish *erga omnes* obligations. This applies especially to the field of human rights, since the very numerous conventional human rights norms in principle establish *erga omnes partes* obligations; and the less numerous customary human rights norms establish *erga omnes* obligations.

That said, the most important changes concern State responsibility for breach of *erga omnes* obligations. Generally speaking, it can be said that the solidarity of the obligation involves an extension of the States that are entitled to invoke the responsibility of the offending State. More specifically, it must be established in concrete terms which States are entitled to invoke the responsibility and what legal consequences of the offence they may invoke.

On this point, the well-known case-law of the ICJ, which first developed the concept of *erga omnes* obligations, does not provide much help. In its advisory opinion of 1951 on *Reservations to the Genocide Convention*[22] and in the *Barcelona Traction* judgment of 1970[23] the Court seems oriented to recognize that the breach by a State of an obligation *erga omnes* harms a *legal interest* and not a true right of

[21]See Pisillo Mazzeschi (2014b), pp. 93–98.

[22]ICJ, *Reservations to the Convention on the Prevention and Punishment of the Crime of Genocide*, p. 23.

[23]ICJ, *Barcelona Traction*, p. 32, paras. 33–34.

other States.[24] But the Court does not go into the merits of the forms and ways in which those States may react to the infringement.

These latter aspects were discussed at length, as is well known, during the ILC work on responsibility of States for internationally wrongful acts; where there was a rather different approach between the Draft adopted at first reading in 1996 and the final Draft of 2001.[25] The latter Draft makes a general distinction between injured States (Art. 42) and States other than an injured State but which are still entitled to invoke the responsibility of the offending State (Art. 48). Injured States may invoke all the legal consequences of the internationally wrongful act (cessation of the act, guarantees of non-repetition, reparation, countermeasures).

On the other hand, States that are not injured, but are entitled to invoke the responsibility for breach of *erga omnes* obligations, may claim only some of the consequences of the wrongful act (Art. 48(2)): cessation of the act and guarantees of non-repetition, as well as reparation for the injury, but only in the interest of the injured State (if there is an injured State) or of the "beneficiaries" of the obligation breached (e.g., individuals who are victims of human rights violations). Moreover, these States may take other "lawful measures" against the responsible State according to international law (Art. 54).[26] It seems to me that, when the breach of an *erga omnes* obligation does not involve also a serious violation of *jus cogens*, the concept of "lawful measures" should be interpreted in a restrictive way; that is, it should be limited to peaceful retaliations. Indeed, it is logical that the legal consequences of a simple breach of a solidarity obligation should be lighter than those resulting from a serious breach of *jus cogens.*[27]

Finally, a question has recently arisen concerning the standing of a State other than the injured State to claim a breach of an obligation *erga omnes* before an international court or tribunal.[28] Of course, the issue is simple when there is a human rights treaty that provides procedures for interstate appeals to bodies provided for in that treaty concerning violations of its provisions. In this case, each State party to the treaty has standing to bring a claim before such bodies for breach of *erga omnes partes* obligations.[29]

---

[24]Even in more recent cases the Court seems to maintain this position. See ICJ, *Questions relating to the Obligation to Prosecute or Extradite*, para. 69; *Application of the Convention on the Prevention and Punishment of the Crime of Genocide (The Gambia v. Myanmar)*, Order of 23 January 2020, para. 41.

[25]ILC, *Draft Articles on Responsibility of States for Internationally Wrongful Acts*, 1 August 2001.

[26]Art. 54 (*Measures taken by States other than an injured State*): "This chapter does not prejudice the right of any other State, entitled under article 48, paragraph 1, to invoke the responsibility of another State, to take lawful measures against that State to ensure cessation of the breach and reparation in the interest of the injured State or of the beneficiaries of the obligation breached".

[27]For breaches of *jus cogens* see below, Sect. 2.3.4.2.

[28]On this question see, e.g., IDI, Resolution "Obligations *erga omnes* in international law", Krakow Session-2005, in AIDI, vol.71-II (2006), p. 287 ff.; Gaja (2014), pp. 110–117; Treves (2019), pp. 273–277; Papa (2020), pp. 743–751, also for further references of doctrine.

[29]See also below, Sects. 4.1.1 and 4.1.2.

In contrast, the matter is more complicated when there is no such treaty and the standing of a State to enforce the breach of an obligation *erga omnes* is at issue. In this case, is there a coincidence between the substantive right (or interest) of that State to invoke the responsibility of the State accused of the breach and its procedural standing to claim that right? Or, on the contrary, is there no coincidence because the procedural standing requires, in addition, a "special juridical interest" of the claimant State[30] or a particular "jurisdictional link" between the two States[31]? The question has been brought before the International Court of Justice in the *Belgium v. Senegal* case[32] and in the recent *Gambia v. Myanmar* case.[33] The ICJ did not explicitly address the issue of the "jurisdictional link". However, in both cases, and more clearly in the second, the Court seems to have adopted the theory of the coincidence between the substantive right (or interest) to claim the breach and the standing of having such breach ascertained by an international court.[34] In my opinion, this solution is to be approved.

In conclusion, the extension of the sphere of States that can invoke international responsibility for breach of *erga omnes* obligations constitutes a significant change in the regime of State responsibility.

2.3.4.2 Aggravated Responsibility for Breach of Obligations Arising Under *Jus Cogens* Norms

The second change in the regime of international responsibility has been produced by the concept of *jus cogens*. As already mentioned, an important factor in the process of structural change in international law is the emergence and consolidation of the norms of *jus cogens*. From the point of view of State responsibility, the concept of *jus cogens* has contributed to the creation of the notion of "international crimes of States" in the framework of the relevant ILC works; but this notion was later replaced by that of "serious breaches of obligations arising under peremptory norms of general international law" (Art. 40 of the ILC final Draft).[35]

These particular breaches produce an "aggravated" responsibility of the offending State, since they produce some particular legal consequences (Art. 41), which are in addition to the normal consequences of the wrongful act, and which entail the

---

30 Treves (2019), p. 275.

31 See IDI Resolution, Art. 3.

32 ICJ, *Questions relating to the Obligation to Prosecute or Extradite*, paras. 69–70.

33 ICJ, *Application of the Convention on the Prevention and Punishment of the Crime of Genocide (The Gambia v. Myanmar)*, Order of 23 January 2020, paras. 39–42.

34 In fact, the Court, on the question of the standing of the Gambia, rejected Myanmar's arguments and adhered, in essence, to Gambia's arguments; but with some clarification (see para. 52 of the Order).

35 ILC, *Draft Articles on Responsibility of States for Internationally Wrongful Acts*, 1 August 2001, Art. 40 (*Application of this chapter*): "1. This chapter applies to the international responsibility which is entailed by a serious breach by a State of an obligation arising under a peremptory norm of general international law. 2. A breach of such an obligation is serious if it involves a gross or systematic failure by the responsible State to fulfil the obligation".

involvement of all States other than the offending State in certain obligations: that of cooperating to put an end, by lawful means, to the breach; that of not recognizing as lawful a situation created by the breach; and finally that of not rendering aid or assistance in maintaining the illegal situation.

In reality, these particular consequences, even if they contribute to aggravate the responsibility of the State that has seriously violated a norm of *jus cogens*, do not appear very incisive and are lighter than expected, bearing in mind that they should sanction serious infringements of fundamental values of the entire international community. However, it should be borne in mind that the ILC Draft provides for some general safeguard clauses, since it states that the Draft's articles are without prejudice to the rules on responsibility established by international law, either because they are special rules (Art. 55) or because they are not expressly provided for in the Draft (Art. 56) or because they are enshrined in the UN Charter (Art. 59).

In addition, for the serious violations of *jus cogens*, it seems to me that Article 54 of the Draft is also applicable. It affirms the right of any State, entitled under Article 48(1) to invoke the responsibility of another State, to take "lawful measures" against that State, in order to ensure cessation of the breach and reparation in the interest of the injured State or of the beneficiaries of the obligation breached. The Draft does not specify the concept of "lawful measures"; but, in the light of the Commentary on Article 54[36] and the aforementioned Articles 55, 56 and 59, one can assume that, in order to define this concept, recourse may be made to international law (even in its progressive development) and the UN Charter. Therefore, in my view, in the case of serious violations of *jus cogens* (e.g., gross violations of human rights), "lawful measures" against the offending State may include: (*a*) peaceful retaliation; (*b*) peaceful countermeasures; (*c*) measures not involving the use of force recommended or decided by the Security Council ex Article 41 of the UN Charter when serious violations of *jus cogens* determine one of the conditions established by Article 39 of the Charter; (d) measures involving the use of force decided or authorized by the Security Council, still in the cases provided for in Article 39 of the Charter.

In conclusion, the regime of aggravated responsibility for serious violations of *jus cogens* established in the ILC Draft appears to be little incisive, but it could be strengthened in the future through a dynamic interpretation of international law. Despite these flaws, it must be acknowledged that such a regime has created a significant modernization of the field of State responsibility.

2.3.4.3 State Responsibility Towards Individuals and Individual Right to Reparation

The theory of human rights, which has greatly contributed to the affirmation of the concept that the individual can be the *direct addressee* of certain international norms, has produced another change in the area of State responsibility, since it has

[36]ILC, *Draft articles on Responsibility of States for Internationally Wrongful Acts, with commentaries*, *YILC*, 2001, vol. II (2), pp. 137–139.

undermined the traditional principle of the interstate character of the relationship of responsibility. In fact, individuals can, *in certain circumstances*, be the addressees of *secondary* international norms;[37] and therefore they can invoke and assert the responsibility of a State. In other words, when the primary international obligation breached by a State has as its formal addressees not only other States but *also individuals*, that State assumes international responsibility not only towards other States but *also towards individuals*, who become active subjects of the relationship of responsibility.[38] These conclusions are very important for the area of human rights, where it is therefore possible today to conceive of a true *international responsibility of the State towards individuals*. In this regard, the most important novelties concern the legitimacy of individuals to invoke responsibility and their right to claim reparation.

The ILC Draft on State responsibility, unfortunately, deals only with the international responsibility of the State towards other States, and is therefore very conservative in this respect. However, the ILC has implicitly admitted that contemporary international law may contain norms on the responsibility of States towards individuals (Art. 33(2)).[39]

The right of an individual *to invoke*, at the international level, the responsibility of a State is demonstrated by the numerous cases in which an individual can bring an action before international (judicial or quasi-judicial) human rights monitoring bodies against the responsible State.

As for the right of the individual *to claim reparation*,[40] its existence in international law is demonstrated by numerous human rights treaty norms, which establish that the offending State has an obligation to ensure reparation to the individual victim. Moreover, the practice of international human rights monitoring bodies shows very clearly that the decisions of these bodies often establish reparation (restitution, compensation or satisfaction) which is *directly* in favor of the individual victim, even if the obligation to repair is borne in practice by the State responsible for the violation. In addition, in support of this conclusion, at least with regard to serious and systematic human rights violations, one can mention, inter alia, the ICJ advisory opinion on the *Consequences of the Construction of a Wall in Palestine*;[41] the 2005 UN General Assembly resolution on the *Right to a Remedy and Reparation for Victims of Flagrant Violations of Human Rights*;[42] the 2004 Report of the

[37]See ICJ, *LaGrand* and *Avena*.

[38]Pisillo Mazzeschi (2004b).

[39]ILC Draft, Art. 33(2): "This part is without prejudice to any right, arising from the international responsibility of a State, which may accrue directly to any person or entity other than a State". See also below, Sect. 17.2.1.

[40]See Pisillo Mazzeschi (1999b); Bartolini (2009). On the right to reparation for violation of fundamental human rights see also below, Sect. 17.2.

[41]ICJ, *Legal Consequences of the Construction of a Wall*, paras. 151–153.

[42]*Basic Principles and Guidelines on the Right to a Remedy and Reparation for Victims of Flagrant Violations of Human Rights and Serious Breaches of Humanitarian Law*, UN Doc. A/RES/60/147, 16 December 2005.

Commission of Inquiry on Darfur;[43] two resolutions adopted by the *Institut de Droit International* in 2009 and 2015;[44] and most recently the European Court of Human Rights' ruling in the *Naït-Liman* case.[45]

Therefore, it can be concluded that the individual today holds, under international law, a *true right* to obtain reparation for human rights violations. This is another important development in the area of State responsibility.

2.3.5 The Relationship Between International Law and Domestic Law: Towards Ever Greater Harmonization and Integration Between the Two Legal Orders

Finally, the theory of human rights, in my view, has also contributed to modify, at least partially, another distinctive element of the traditional notion of international law: that relating to its autonomy, resulting from a clear and absolute separation between international and domestic legal orders. This autonomy is well represented by the traditional dualist (or pluralist) conception of the relationship between international law and domestic law, according to which the two legal systems are separate and distinct because they differ in the origin of the sources, the norms, the typical content of the norms, and the formal addressees of the norms.

In reality, the contemporary majority doctrine has abandoned the old net theoretical positions in favor of dualism or monism; and one should in fact recognize that the clear and radical opposition of the past between the two conceptions no longer makes much sense, especially if they remain based only on rigid theoretical and abstract assumptions. Instead, the two different conceptions should be considered as methodological models of a general nature, expressing general trends in international reality. In this respect, one should admit that this reality today requires a review of at least certain aspects of the traditional dualist conception, because some of the differences indicated above between the two legal systems have disappeared and others are becoming much smaller.[46]

First of all, the distinction between the two legal orders, which was based on the diversity of their respective contents, has now largely disappeared. As we have seen, international law, which once governed only relations between States, now also regulates, to a large extent, relations between States and individuals and inter-individual relations: international human rights law is a paradigmatic example of this. Secondly, the distinction between the two systems of law, which was based on

[43] *Report of the International Commission of Inquiry on Darfur to the United Nations Secretary General, Pursuant to Security Council Resolution 1564 of 18 September 2004*, Geneva, 25 January 2005, paras. 595–599.

[44] IDI, *Resolution on the Immunity from Jurisdiction of the State and of Persons Who Act on Behalf of the State in Case of International Crimes*, Naples, 10 September 2009; *Universal Civil Jurisdiction with regard to Reparation for International Crimes*, Art. 1, Tallinn, 30 August 2015.

[45] ECtHR, *Naït-Liman v. Switzerland*, para. 108.

[46] See Ferrari Bravo (2002), pp. 99–150; Pisillo Mazzeschi (1994a); Id. (2004a), pp. 33–36.

the diversity of their respective formal addressees, has also come to an end. Today international law directly creates some rights and obligations for individuals as well. Thirdly, even in terms of norms, the differences between international and domestic law are becoming increasingly narrower. Fourthly, with regard to the application of international law within domestic law, it can be noted that methods of transformation or nationalization of international norms, inspired by a dualist model, coexist in the practice of States with methods of direct reception or incorporation of international norms, inspired by a basically monist model. Conflicts between international law and domestic law are also resolved, in the practice of States, sometimes with the prevalence of international law, in a more monist perspective, and sometimes with that of domestic law, in a dualist perspective.

In conclusion, some data of contemporary international reality conform more to a dualist vision of the relationship between international and domestic law, while other data are more suited to a monist vision. Other data, finally, have an ambivalent character. This confirms, as said above, that today there is no longer much point in wanting to interpret the relations between international law and domestic law according to a rigidly dualist or rigidly monist model.

On the other hand, dualism and monism can be conceived not only as two different conceptual models of interpretation of the relations between international law and domestic law, but also, and above all, as two different political models of international society, one based on *nationalism-pluralism* and the other on *universalism.*[47] In this sense, it must be admitted that the structure of today's international society is still essentially made up of States and that international law is still to a large extent centered on the principle of State sovereignty; and that, therefore, it does not for the time being leave a large space for a universal human community that can bind individuals across national barriers.

However, it is also true that this *universal human community* is now present on the international scene, is assuming an increasingly important role, and is exerting strong pressure on the community of States to ensure that international law is increasingly concerned with the interests of man and humanity. This pressure from the human community, which is largely based on the strength of the human rights theory, has produced, as we saw, a real revolution in the content and scope of international law, in its subjects, and is also producing structural changes in the function and nature typical of that law. Therefore, ultimately, if one looks at the trend lines of international law, one can see some signs of overcoming the absolute sovereignty of the State and the structure of the international community based only on the sovereign equality of States. However, one must admit that, recently, there are also worrying signs of the opposite nature, based on the rebirth of nationalism-pluralism.

---

[47]Here I understand the term "universalism" in the broad sense, referring to a political model of international society. Therefore in a different sense from the principle of universalism of human rights examined above, Sect. 1.4.

Finally, on the more legal level of the relationship between international law and domestic law, it can be seen that international law is increasingly invading the areas that were reserved for national legal experience and is exerting increasing pressure on national realities. In other words, today we are witnessing an evolution towards ever greater communication, harmonization and integration between the international and domestic legal systems. This is a natural evolution because, in the contemporary world characterized by interdependence and globalization, it is "inconceivable that the legal world can remain distributed in mutually impermeable cells".[48]

2.3.6 Influence of International Human Rights Law on International Sources and Obligations (Cross-Reference)

These issues will be dealt with later in Parts II and III.

2.4 Impact of Human Rights on Specific Areas of International Law

The theory of human rights, implanted in the system of international law, has produced not only changes of a general and even structural nature on that system, but also more circumscribed changes on the sources of international law and on certain specific areas of that law. Leaving aside the question of sources for now,[49] let us briefly examine the impact that the human rights theory has had on the content of the substantive (or material) norms of general international law, not only in the areas where the interests of individuals are most evident, but also in areas traditionally reserved for interstate interests.[50] I will give just a few examples, starting with international humanitarian law and international criminal law, which are the two areas that, because they are so closely related to human rights, have been most influenced by the latter.

2.4.1 International Humanitarian Law

I have already dealt with the birth and early development of international humanitarian law from the middle of the nineteenth century until the Hague Conventions of 1899 and 1907.[51] I pointed out that, in this first historical phase, international

[48]Ferrari Bravo (2002), p. 149 (my translation).

[49]See below, Part II.

[50]See Kamminga and Scheinin (2009); Pisillo Mazzeschi (2008), pp. 208–212; Id. (2014b), pp. 99–100.

[51]See above, Sect. 1.2.6.

humanitarian law (which at that time was called *jus in bello*) had the traditional interstate nature of international law, was based on reciprocity, and did not attribute real rights to individuals.

The general purpose of *jus in bello* was, and still is, to humanize war as much as possible and to enforce certain legal norms even during armed conflicts. Its pivotal principle is that of "military necessity"; that is, the prohibition of acts that are not strictly necessary to achieve the purposes of war. Every belligerent State has its own interest in prohibiting gratuitous acts of violence and in respecting a nucleus of legal norms, because the opposing States could also commit the same violations against it. After all, rules of humanity in war have existed since ancient times. However, it is also clear that the aim of humanizing armed conflicts produces not only a mutual advantage for the belligerent States, but also an advantage, albeit indirect, for individuals, combatants and civilians. Therefore, *jus in bello* has, since its origin, a relationship with the protection of the human rights of individuals.

Moreover, it should be pointed out that, in traditional international law, *jus in bello* was divided into two parts: law of war in the strict sense (also called "The Hague law") and humanitarian law (also called "Geneva law"). The first was related to the discipline of war violence between belligerents: prohibition of certain methods of warfare and certain weapons, so as to regulate the conduct of hostilities. The second was related to the victims of war: treatment of prisoners, the wounded, the sick, protection of civilians, etc. Therefore, even in the traditional and more ancient *jus in bello*, the humanitarian purpose of protecting the individuals involved in the war was clear.

In the first half of the twentieth century, there were some changes in the *jus in bello*. First, its humanitarian component (the Geneva law) was strengthened through the 1929 Geneva Convention on the Wounded and Sick and the 1929 Geneva Convention on Prisoners of War. Secondly, and consequently, the old distinction between law of war and humanitarian law was gradually blurring and there was an increasing tendency to abandon the definition of *jus in bello* and to speak in a unified and all-inclusive way of international humanitarian law. This tendency was strengthened after the Second World War, with the adoption of the four Geneva Conventions of 1949 and the two Additional Protocols of 1977.

It should also be emphasized that international humanitarian law has not lost importance in contemporary international law, despite the fact that, in the second half of the twentieth century, there have been important regulatory changes regarding the use of international force. In fact, the UN Charter (Art. 2(4)) and then international customary law have established the general principle on the prohibition of the threat and use of international armed force. But humanitarian law maintains its importance for three reasons: (a) because the prohibition of force provides for some exceptions (self-defense, armed actions authorized by the Security Council, perhaps humanitarian intervention); (b) because the prohibition does not apply in internal conflicts; (c) because the prohibition is often violated in concrete reality. Therefore, it is necessary even today that armed conflicts do not completely suspend the application of international law and that humanitarian law continues to operate.

Humanitarian law norms continue to serve today to ensure minimum protections for victims of conflict and to regulate the conduct of hostilities.

I said above that the old distinction, within the *jus in bello*, between law of war in the strict sense (The Hague law) and humanitarian law (Geneva law) is no longer satisfactory. And this for various reasons: (*a*) because the expression "law of war" referred to the classical concept of international war between States, while today the law of armed conflicts also includes civil wars, wars of national liberation and low-intensity armed conflicts; (*b*) because the most recent treaties, especially the 1977 Additional Protocols, jointly address both the conduct of hostilities and the methods or means of warfare, and the protection of victims; (*c*) because the entire field of the law of armed conflicts tends to accentuate the purpose of the protection of individuals involved in such conflicts and therefore the humanitarian aspect of protection of the person.

Therefore, more and more lines of convergence between international humanitarian law and international human rights law have occurred and the two areas have undergone reciprocal influences of a legal nature. After all, both areas are inspired by a common principle of respect for the dignity of the human person. Moreover, even the borders, which were once clear, between war and peace have become obscured in a series of conflicts and political-military or guerrilla tensions, where it is no longer easy to distinguish clearly between a state of armed conflict and a state of peace. Another sign of convergence is the development of international criminal law and international criminal tribunals, whose task is to repress both war crimes, established by international humanitarian law, and genocide and crimes against humanity, established by international human rights law. Finally, although international humanitarian law continues to be largely based on reciprocity, there are now some norms of this law that establish obligations *erga omnes* in a similar way to human rights norms,[52] as also recognized by the International Court of Justice in its two opinions on *Nuclear Weapons* and the *Wall in Palestine*.[53]

However, it should be noted that the two areas are still different, because they have different regulatory sources, different norms, different guarantees and also partly different purposes. But what is the precise relationship between international humanitarian law and human rights law today? On this issue, one can distinguish, in essence, three theories.[54]

The first theory, the oldest one, can be defined as the theory of *separation* between the two regulatory areas. International human rights law would apply *only* in times of peace, while international humanitarian law would apply *only* during armed conflicts, as a special law that *derogates entirely* from human rights law. In other words, the individual, in times of armed conflict, would be protected only by international humanitarian law. But this theory seems outdated today, since the ICJ

[52]Focarelli (2013), pp. 283–284.

[53]ICJ, *Legality of the Threat or Use of Nuclear Weapons*, paras. 79–80; *Legal Consequences of the Construction of a Wall*, paras. 155, 157–159.

[54]See Kälin, Künzli (2019), pp. 174–176.

has established that human rights must be respected even in times of armed conflict and that they can only be derogated from to a limited extent.[55] Moreover, there are norms of international humanitarian law which, in establishing the fundamental guarantees applicable to the victims of armed conflicts, expressly refer to human rights norms.[56]

The second theory, which is opposite to the first, can be called a theory of *convergence* between the two areas and is supported especially by some authors.[57] According to this view, the two regulatory areas are not separated at all, but on the contrary they constitute only two aspects of a single system of human rights protection. Therefore, they should be applied *cumulatively in all situations where this is possible*, so as to maximize the protection of human rights even during armed conflicts. This theory is interesting and in many respects desirable; but it does not seem to me to be confirmed by international practice.[58]

Finally, the third theory, of an intermediate character between the two previous ones, is the theory of *complementarity* between the two regulatory areas. According to this theory, which is vigorously supported by the ICRC, but seems also adopted by the ICJ, international humanitarian law and international human rights law, while remaining in principle separate fields, are complementary and both apply *in a coordinated manner in certain limited situations*. More specifically, this means that three different situations can occur:[59] (a) some cases are regulated only by international human rights law; (b) other cases are governed only by international humanitarian law; (c) other cases are regulated by both areas.

The most interesting situation is the third, in which the concept of complementarity is fully expressed. This situation usually concerns the application of certain "fundamental" human rights, which must also be applied during armed conflicts, but *interpreted* taking into account the norms of international humanitarian law. This last law is conceived as a *lex specialis*; but the specialty does not imply excluding the applicability of human rights but *only restricting or limiting their content* during armed conflicts. On the other hand, correspondingly, the theory of complementarity also implies that, if there is a violation of these "fundamental" human rights during armed conflicts, the victims can have recourse to the international monitoring bodies provided for by human rights treaties to assert the violation.

To illustrate this point, a few examples can be given. The human right to life is not derogated from during armed conflicts, but remains applicable. However, it must be interpreted in the light of the norms of international humanitarian law. This means

---

[55]ICJ, *Legality of the Threat or Use of Nuclear Weapons*, paras. 24–25; *Legal Consequences of the Construction of a Wall*, paras. 104–106; *Armed Activities on the Territory of the Congo*, Judgment of 19 December 2005, paras. 216–217. See also HRCtee, General Comment No. 29, 31 August 2001, para. 3; General Comment No. 31, 26 May 2004, para. 11.

[56]See, in particular, AP I, Art. 75 and AP II, Art. 4.

[57]Meron (1987), p. 28.

[58]However, for an interesting case in which the theory of convergence appears to have been applied, see IACtHR, *Case of the Santo Domingo Massacre v. Colombia*, esp. paras. 211 ff.

[59]Kälin and Künzli (2019), p. 175.

that the deprivation of life during armed conflicts is not arbitrary when it is allowed by humanitarian law.[60] However, if there is nonetheless a violation of the right to life, the relatives of the victims can take advantage of the remedies allowed under international human rights law. To give another example, the detention of prisoners of war does not exclude the applicability of human rights norms on the prohibition of arbitrary detention. But these norms must take into account the less rigorous content of humanitarian law norms on the detention of prisoners of war or civilians who pose a threat to security.[61]

In my opinion, this third theory is the one that most correctly reflects the relationship between international humanitarian law and human rights in contemporary international law.

In conclusion, it can be said that the norms of international humanitarian law have undergone significant changes since the second half of the twentieth century, due to the impact of human rights theory. These norms must today be interpreted and applied more and more in the new human rights perspective rather than the old interstate approach.

2.4.2 International Criminal Law

The theory of human rights has also had an important impact on the norms of international criminal law, which are much more recent than those of humanitarian law. In order to explain this, it is worth making some brief reference to the origin and development of international criminal law.

The expression "international criminal law" today refers to an area of international law that aims to define and repress "international crimes"[62] conceived as crimes of individuals, to impose on States the obligation to try and punish the perpetrators, and to establish the rules for the conduct of the relevant criminal proceedings at the international level.[63] The category of international crimes refers to a number of crimes committed by private individuals or, more often, by State officials, which also constitute serious violations of human rights or humanitarian law, and which give rise to international criminal liability of such persons.

It is worth remembering that the category of "international crimes" dates back to the London Agreement of 1945,[64] by which the International Military Tribunal of

---

[60] See HRCtee, General Comment No. 36, 3 September 2019, paras. 64–69. See also below, Sect. 14.1.2.1.

[61] See ECtHR, *Hassan v. UK*. But also below, Sect. 4.4.3, where I will highlight the different positions taken by the European Court of Human Rights in the *Hassan* case and by the UK High Court of Justice in the *Serdar Mohammed* case.

[62] See also below, Sect. 14.3.

[63] Cassese (2005), p. 11.

[64] Agreement by The Government of The United Kingdom of Great Britain and Northern Ireland, The Government of the United States of America, the Provisional Government of the French Republic and the Government of the Union of Soviet Socialist Republics for the Prosecution and

Nuremberg was set up to punish Nazi criminals.[65] At that time, international crimes were divided into three categories: (*a*) war crimes; (*b*) crimes against humanity; (*c*) crimes against peace.[66] The Nuremberg trial, and the parallel Tokyo trial against Japanese criminals, marked the beginning of a new sector of international law, later called international criminal law.

This area, after many years of rather slow development, largely entrusted to the practice of State military tribunals, had an accelerating process since the 1990s, with the institutions of the International Criminal Tribunal for the Former Yugoslavia,[67] the International Criminal Tribunal for Rwanda,[68] the International Criminal Court[69] and other so-called "mixed" or "hybrid" or "internationalized" criminal tribunals.[70] The three original categories of crimes have been updated, on the basis of the statutes of the International Criminal Court and other international criminal tribunals, which now provide for four types of crimes: (*a*) genocide; (*b*) crimes against humanity; (*c*) war crimes; (*d*) crimes against peace (which today are practically solved in the crime of aggression). In essence, genocide, which was previously included in crimes against humanity, has now acquired its autonomy.

That being said, it must be considered that international criminal law is a normative area of international law that is different from that of the protection of human rights. However, it is also evident that its norms are largely based on the logic of human rights and appear as a real parallel path taken by contemporary international law, with the aim of strengthening, through the instrument of individual criminal responsibility, the protection of fundamental human rights in times of peace and in times of armed conflict. Moreover, from the point of view of the content of its norms, international criminal law makes use of notions, principles and legal institutions that derive largely from human rights norms (in addition to those of humanitarian law and States' criminal law).[71]

Therefore, it can be concluded that the two areas of international criminal law and human rights law are closely linked and complementary in their function.

This relationship of connection and complementarity is also clear in the light of another important element. In fact, it must be emphasized that, very often, individuals committing an international crime are officials of their own State or of a parastatal entity, such as an insurgent movement controlling a territory.[72] This is

Punishment of the Major War Criminals of the European Axis, London, 8 August 1945, in *UNTS*, vol. 82, p. 279 ff.

[65]Charter of the International Military Tribunal, Annex to the Agreement for the prosecution and punishment of the major war criminals of the European Axis ("London Agreement").

[66]IMT Charter, Art. 6.

[67]International Criminal Tribunal for the Former Yugoslavia (ICTY).

[68]International Criminal Tribunal for Rwanda (ICTR).

[69]International Criminal Court (ICC).

[70]See, for example, the Special Court for Sierra Leone (SCSL) and the Special Court for Lebanon (STL).

[71]Cassese (2005), p. 17.

[72]See, for all, Conforti (2015), p. 221.

because only these entities are usually capable of producing those extensive and systematic attacks against a population or a group, which characterize the various categories of international crimes. Therefore, when international crimes are committed, a *dual* international responsibility usually arises: (*a*) that of the individual, which aims at his punishment according to the rules of international criminal law; (*b*) that of the State (or other entity with international human rights obligations[73]) that has committed or not prevented the crime, which is regulated by the norms on international human rights[74] and those on the international responsibility of the State.[75]

I will return to some of these concepts later on when I will deal with the prohibition of international crimes,[76] within the framework of those "fundamental" human rights that aim to protect the life and physical integrity of people.

2.4.3 Use of Force, Humanitarian Intervention and "Responsibility to Protect"

Another important area of international law on which human rights theory has had a significant impact is the use of force. I refer to the two legal notions of humanitarian intervention[77] and "responsibility to protect",[78] which have the common purpose of allowing States the use of armed force in certain exceptional situations, to protect fundamental human rights. However, as we shall see, I do not believe that there is a consensus on these two notions on the part of the whole international community. Therefore, their impact on the field of the use of force, although significant, has not ended up producing new customary norms.

The notion of humanitarian intervention refers to the use of military force by States to protect the population of a foreign State that is a victim of serious violations and abuses by its own government. It is a very ancient institution of international law, which in history has often been used by the strongest States against the weakest ones.[79] For this reason it has been questioned in the twentieth century, as limits to the use of military force were affirmed in international law.[80] The most important turning point came with the UN Charter, which, in Article 2(4), expressly prohibits the threat or use of international force by States, with the sole exception of individual

[73]See below, Sect. 7.1.

[74]And by the norms of international humanitarian law in the case of war crimes.

[75]And by the norms on international responsibility of international organizations.

[76]See below, Sect. 14.3.

[77]The literature on humanitarian intervention is very extensive. See, among the most recent monographs, Krieg (2013); Falk (2014).

[78]There is also a wide literature on the responsibility to protect. See, e.g., Orford (2011); Thakur (2011); Glanville (2014).

[79]Shelton (2014a), p. 278.

[80]See, in particular, the League of Nations Covenant and the Kellogg-Briand Pact of 1928.

or collective self-defense under Article 51 of the Charter.[81] It is commonly held that the prohibition of the use of force was then incorporated into general international law, either as a customary norm or as a general principle, also having the character of *jus cogens*.

However, as is well known, according to the creators of the UN Charter, the prohibition of the use of force by States was to be balanced and replaced by the functioning of the collective security system based on the Security Council acting under Chapter VII of the Charter. But this system worked poorly for a complex series of factors. This has caused, in the concrete reality of international relations, the attempts of many States to regain possession of the use of force, both through an extension, sometimes exorbitant, of the concept of self-defense, and through a series of new exceptions to the prohibition of force, such as intervention to protect citizens abroad, humanitarian intervention, the so-called "doctrine of the responsibility to protect", armed reprisals in times of peace, interventions against international terrorism and interventions for democracy.[82]

As can be seen, some of these exceptions, or alleged exceptions, pursue a purpose that can be defined, in a broad sense, humanitarian;[83] and therefore appear to be very much influenced by human rights theory. I will deal only with humanitarian intervention and the "responsibility to protect", because these are the most emblematic cases in which some basic principles of international law are confronted and clash: on the one hand, the old principle of State sovereignty and the new principle of the prohibition of force, and, on the other hand, the new principle of the protection of fundamental human rights.

As I said above, humanitarian intervention, considered illegal after the entry into force of the UN Charter and the affirmation of the general prohibition of the use of force, has found some feedback in the most recent practice, due to the inability of the Security Council to act in some situations of serious humanitarian crisis.[84] The best known case is that of the intervention of NATO States against the Yugoslav Republic (Serbia-Montenegro) in 1999, for the massacres in Kosovo. The military operation in Kosovo was justified by some NATO States, especially the United Kingdom and Belgium, as a humanitarian intervention; but it was contested by other States, such as Russia, China, India and the group of non-aligned States. Internationalist scholars are also divided on the legitimacy of this intervention. Subsequently, on the other hand, the Russian Federation justified its military intervention in Georgia in 2008 and the annexation of the Crimea in 2014 on humanitarian grounds; but this stance was met with opposition from many Western States. Other situations in which the legitimacy of humanitarian intervention has been invoked

[81]Use of force can be done by the UN, through the actions of the Security Council under Chapter VII of the Charter.

[82]On all these exceptions see, e.g., Focarelli (2015), pp. 1786–1801.

[83]Conforti (2018), p. 422.

[84]For a good summary of this practice see Focarelli (2015), pp. 1789–1791; Id. (2019), pp. 614–616.

include measures taken by the USA, UK and France to protect the Kurdish minorities in Northern Iraq in the 1990s, and military interventions by several States in Syria in 2017–2018 against the Assad regime, accused of using chemical weapons against part of the Syrian population.

At the diplomatic level, the strongest position in favor of the legitimacy of humanitarian intervention has been taken by the UK Government, first in 1992,[85] then in 2013,[86] and more recently in a Policy Paper of 2018,[87] which however maintains that humanitarian intervention must meet three conditions: (*a*) that there is convincing evidence of "extreme humanitarian distress on a large scale"; (*b*) that there is no viable alternative to the use of force to save human lives; (*c*) that the use of force is necessary, proportionate and strictly limited in time. However, the issue was then debated in the Security Council, where States took different positions among themselves.

The scholars in favor of humanitarian intervention[88] have invoked various theories, such as, for example, that of the *erga omnes* nature of human rights obligations, that of the *jus cogens* character of fundamental human rights norms, and that of the state of necessity. But these theories lend themselves to some legally well-founded objections.[89] Moreover, the decisive fact is the lack at present of a consolidated and uniform practice and *opinio juris* on which the legitimacy of humanitarian intervention can be based.

On the other hand, given the controversies regarding the legitimacy of humanitarian intervention, States have sought to develop the so-called doctrine of the "responsibility to protect"; that is, a new legal notion that seeks to reconcile in some way the said conflict between the principles of State sovereignty and the prohibition of force, on the one hand, and, on the other, the necessity to protect peoples from serious and systematic violations of fundamental human rights. The doctrine of the responsibility to protect was first enunciated in 2001 by an independent Commission established by the Canadian Government;[90] then it was taken up in 2004 by a *High Level Panel* established by UN Secretary General Kofi Annan;[91] and finally it was accepted, albeit with some modifications, by the UN General Assembly

[85]See the comment of the United Kingdom legal adviser A. Aust about the intervention of some States in northern Iraq in favor of the Kurds, in Br Yearb Int L 1992, p. 827.

[86]See *Chemical Weapons Used by Syrian Regime: UK Government Legal Position*, 29 August 2013.

[87]See the *Policy paper Syria action-UK government legal position*, published by the UK Government on 14 April 2018, https://www.gov.uk/government/publications/syria-action-uk-government-legal-position/syria-action-uk-government-legal-position.

[88]See, for example, Cassese (1999). But this author sets various conditions and limits for the legitimacy of humanitarian intervention.

[89]See, e.g., Focarelli (2015), pp. 1791–1792.

[90]International Commission on Intervention and State Sovereignty, *The Responsibility to Protect*, Ottawa, 2001.

[91]See GA, *Report of the High-Level Panel on Threats, Challenges and Change*, 2 December 2004 (UN Doc. A/59/565).

in the 2005 World Summit Outcome.[92] Subsequently, the UN Secretary General appointed a special adviser to further develop the doctrine. With regard to the practice of UN bodies, the Security Council invoked the doctrine of the responsibility to protect during the 2011 Libyan crisis, but only as one of the bases of its action under Chapter VII of the UN Charter.[93]

In its original formulation, the doctrine envisaged a responsibility of the international community to *prevent, react and rebuild* in situations where serious and systematic violations of human rights occur in a State and that State does not want to or cannot act to protect its own population. It also provided for the military intervention power of States, albeit subject to various conditions. Subsequently, the doctrine underwent some changes and softening. In the formulation accepted by the UN General Assembly in 2005, the basic concept is that all States have a responsibility to protect the people living in their territory and that, when there is a clear failure to do so, the international community, acting through the UN, should take collective action in the exercise of its responsibility to protect the people from atrocities. But the doctrine has been limited to genocide, war crimes, ethnic cleansing and crimes against humanity. Moreover, it has emerged from the debates in the UN that many States are opposed to including in the doctrine the power of military intervention, and that such power should in any case be expressly authorized by the Security Council under Chapter VII of the Charter.

In conclusion, the doctrine of the responsibility to protect, while pursuing a purpose very similar to that of humanitarian intervention, has a more vague and generic content, such as to make turning its affirmation into a binding norm of customary international law difficult. In any case, it does not seem to be sufficiently consolidated for the moment in the practice and *opinio juris* of the international community as a whole.

Therefore, as I had anticipated above, it can be argued that the two notions of humanitarian intervention and responsibility to protect, while showing important trends in contemporary international law, have not produced real legal changes in customary international law on the use of force.

2.4.4 Other Areas Influenced by Human Rights Theory

Human rights theory has also had an impact on other areas of international law.

A recently formed area is international environmental law. In addition to interstate norms, which were first established beginning in the 1960s, norms are now being developed that address relations between States and individuals and which aim to protect individual rights; such as, for example, the right of the individual to a

[92] GA, *2005 World Summit Outcome*, 24 October 2005 (UN Doc. A/RES/60/1).

[93] See, for example, Security Council resolutions No. 1970 of 26 February 2011 (UN Doc. S/RES/1970) and No. 1973 of 17 March 2011 (UN Doc. S/RES/1973).

healthy environment[94] and his or her right to be informed and to participate in certain State decisions which may have a harmful impact on the environment. Moreover, especially in relation to dangerous or ultra-hazardous activities, there are international treaties which tend to establish uniform rules of domestic law aimed primarily at individuals, such as, for example, rules on civil liability in the field of nuclear energy, maritime transport of nuclear material, oil pollution and maritime transport of dangerous and toxic substances.

The human rights theory has also had an impact on some older fields of international law. For example, customary norms on the treatment of aliens have been much influenced by that theory, so much so that some authors even believe that the norms on the treatment of aliens have been absorbed by human rights norms. I do not share this extreme position; but one should recognize that various customary norms on the treatment of aliens have changed a great deal.[95] For example, the norms on the admission and expulsion of aliens[96] have changed as a result of the rights of refugees, the principle of *non-refoulement*, the prohibition of extradition for political offences. Similarly, norms on the protection of aliens and their property have undergone changes as a result of the prohibition of discrimination and the right to an effective domestic remedy, which has essentially absorbed the old prohibition of denial of justice.

Secondary norms on the treatment of aliens, in particular those on diplomatic protection, have also undergone a process of modernization inspired by the idea of protecting individual interests, if not human rights.[97] The most significant signs of change come from some recent decisions of the International Court of Justice[98] and the Inter-American Court of Human Rights,[99] which expressly recognize that some international norms on the treatment of aliens impose *international* obligations on the territorial State not only towards the national State of the alien but *also towards the foreign individual himself*. This logically leads to the consequence that, in the case of an individual who has suffered an injury by a foreign State for violation of a norm on the treatment of aliens, a relationship of international responsibility arises not only between the offending State and the national State of the individual, but also between the offending State and the individual himself. It is clear that this conclusion is also bound to affect the traditional secondary norms on diplomatic protection, since it leads to the new concept that the nation-State, when resorting to action under diplomatic protection, asserts not only its own right, but *also the right of its own citizens*. Therefore the right to reparation also belongs to both the nation-State and the injured individual.

---

[94]See below, Sect. 25.4.2.

[95]See Pisillo Mazzeschi (2011).

[96]See below, Sects. 24.2, 24.3 and 24.4.

[97]Cf. Pisillo Mazzeschi (2009).

[98]ICJ, *LaGrand*; *Avena*; *Jadhav Case*.

[99]IACtHR, *The Right to Information on Consular Assistance*.

This may even lead to a change in the legal regime governing the relationship between the individual victim and his or her own nation-State. Indeed, one could maintain that the individual has, at least in certain circumstances, towards his or her nation-State, a right to be granted diplomatic protection, or at least a right to judicial review of the reasonableness of the State's decision as to whether or not to exercise diplomatic protection; and also a right to obtain reparation, if his or her nation-State has successfully exercised diplomatic protection. Some of these changes have been recognized, albeit as a progressive development of international law, in the well-known Article 19 of the ILC Draft on diplomatic protection approved in 2006.[100] The domestic jurisprudence of some States is also moving in this direction.[101]

Finally, as already said, the impact of the human rights theory has been felt not only in the areas of international law of greatest interest to individuals, but also in those traditionally dominated by State interests. One thinks, for example, of the set of customary norms concerning the immunities of States and the functional immunities of State agents. As is well known, there is a tendency in contemporary international law to provide for exceptions to these immunities in the case of "gross violations" of human rights.[102] Furthermore, in order to protect workers' rights, there is a tendency, in the most recent international practice, to exclude the jurisdictional immunity of foreign States in disputes relating to employment relationships that have taken place in the State of the forum.

Also various norms of international economic law appear now to be influenced by the theory of human rights: think, for example, of how the right of self-determination of peoples, the Declaration on the New International Economic Order with its Charter of Economic Rights and Duties of States and the Declaration on the Right to Development have affected the traditional regime of international law on the protection of foreign investments and nationalizations and the role of international economic institutions. Finally, the norms on the law of the sea and those on common spaces have also felt the impact of the ideology of human rights, despite the fact that they are normative areas quite far from the domain of individual interests: think only of the idea of the deep-sea-bed and certain common spaces as "common heritage of mankind".

In conclusion, as far as the content of substantive international norms is concerned, there is perhaps no area of international law that has escaped the impact of the human rights theory.

---

[100] ILC, *Draft Articles on Diplomatic Protection*, 8 August 2006, Art. 19 (*Recommended practice*): A State entitled to exercise diplomatic protection according to the present draft articles, should: a) Give due consideration to the possibility of exercising diplomatic protection, especially when a significant injury has occurred; b) Take into account, wherever feasible, the views of the injured person with regard to resort to diplomatic protection and the reparation to be sought; and c) Transfer to the injured person any compensation obtained for the injury from the responsible State subject to any reasonable deductions".

[101] See, for example, the case-law cited by Pustorino (2020), pp. 5–6.

[102] See below, Sects. 17.1.4.2 and 17.2.3.

References

Bartolini G (2009) Riparazione per violazione dei diritti umani e ordinamento internazionale. Jovene, Napoli
Benvenisti E (2008) The conception of international law as a legal system. German Yearb Int Law 50:393–405
Carrillo Salcedo JA (1997) Reflections on the existence of a hierarchy of norms in international law. Eur J Int Law 8:583–595
Cassese A (1999) *Ex iniura ius oritur*: are we moving towards international legitimation of forcible humanitarian countermeasures in the world community? Eur J Int Law 23–30
Cassese A (2005) Lineamenti di diritto internazionale penale: vol. I. Diritto sostanziale. Il Mulino, Bologna
Combacau J (1986) Le droit international: bric-à-brac ou système? Archives de philosophie du droit 31:85–105
Combacau J, Sur S (2006) Droit international public, 7th edn. LGDJ, Paris
Conforti B (2006) Diritto internazionale, 7th edn. Editoriale Scientifica, Napoli
Conforti B (2007) Unité et fragmentation du droit international: glissez, mortels, n'appuyé pas. RGDIP 111:5–18
Conforti B (2015) Diritto internazionale, 10th edn. Editoriale Scientifica, Napoli
Conforti B (Iovane M ed) (2018) Diritto internazionale, 11th edn. Editoriale scientifica, Napoli
Crawford J (2013) Change, order, change: the course of international law. General course on public international law. RC 365:9–389
Falk R (2014) Humanitarian intervention and legitimacy wars: seeking peace and justice in the 21th century. Routledge, Abington
Ferrari Bravo L (2002) Lezioni di diritto internazionale, 4th edn. Editoriale Scientifica, Napoli
Focarelli C (2013) La persona umana nel diritto internazionale. Il Mulino, Bologna
Focarelli C (2015) Trattato di diritto internazionale. Utet/Kluwer, Torino-Milano
Focarelli C (2019) Diritto internazionale, 5th edn. Kluwer/Cedam, Milano
Friedmann WG (1964) The changing structure of international law. Stevens, London
Gaja G (1981) *Jus Cogens* beyond the Vienna Convention on the law of treaties. RC 172:271–316
Gaja G (2014) The protection of general interests in the international community. General course on public international law (2011). RC 364:13–185
Glanville L (2014) Sovereignty and the responsibility to protect: a new history. University of Chicago Press, Chicago
Hannikainen L (1988) Peremptory norms (jus cogens) in international law. Historical developments, criteria, present status. Publishing Finnish Lawyers' Company, Helsinki
Jennings RY (1979) Treaties as legislation. In: Wilner GM (ed) Jus et Societas. Essays in tribute to Wolfgang Friedmann. Springer, The Hague, pp 159–168
Kälin W, Künzli J (2019) The law of international human rights protection, 2nd edn. OUP, Oxford
Kamminga MT, Scheinin M (eds) (2009) The impact of human rights law on general international law. OUP, Oxford
Kolb R (2001) Théorie du ius cogens international. Essai de relecture d'un concept. PUF, Paris
Koskenniemi M, Leino P (2002) Fragmentation of international law? Post-modern anxieties. Leiden J Int Law 15:553–579
Krieg A (2013) Motivations for humanitarian intervention: theoretical and empirical considerations. Springer, Dordrecht
Meron T (1987) Human rights in internal strife: their international protection. CUP, Cambridge
Meron T (2003) International law in the age of human rights. General course on public international law. RC 301:9–490
Meron T (2006) The humanization of international law. Nijhoff, Leiden-Boston
Orakhelashvili A (2006) Peremptory norms in international law. OUP, Oxford
Orford A (2011) International authority and the responsibility to protect. CUP, Cambridge

Papa MI (2020) La tutela degli interessi collettivi nell'ordinanza sulle misure provvisorie nel caso *Gambia c. Myanmar*. RDI 103:729–755
Pellet A (2000) 'Droits-de-l'hommisme' et droit international. Gilberto Amado Memorial Lecture, 18 July 2000, United Nations
Peters A (2016) Beyond human rights: the legal status of the individual in international law. CUP, Cambridge
Picone P (2005) Obblighi *erga omnes* e codificazione della responsabilità degli Stati. RDI 88:893–954
Picone P (2008) La distinzione fra norme internazionali di jus cogens e norme che producono obblighi erga omnes. RDI 91:5–38
Pisillo Mazzeschi R (1994a) La dottrina pura del diritto di Kelsen e la realtà del diritto internazionale contemporaneo. Diritto e Cultura IV:43–66
Pisillo Mazzeschi R (1999b) International obligations to provide for reparation claims? In: Randelzhofer A, Tomuschat C (eds) State responsibility and the individual: reparation in instances of grave violations of human rights. Nijhoff, The Hague, pp 149–172
Pisillo Mazzeschi R (2004a) Esaurimento dei ricorsi interni e diritti umani. Giappichelli, Torino
Pisillo Mazzeschi R (2004b) The marginal role of the individual in the ILC's articles on state responsibility. Ital Yearb Int Law 14:39–51
Pisillo Mazzeschi R (2008) Responsabilité de l'État pour violation des obligations positives relatives aux droits de l'homme. RC 333:175–506
Pisillo Mazzeschi R (2009) Impact on the law of diplomatic protection. In: Kamminga MT, Scheinin M (eds) The impact of human rights law on general international law. OUP, Oxford, pp 211–233
Pisillo Mazzeschi R (2011) The relationship between human rights and the rights of aliens and immigrants. In: Fastenrath U et al (eds) From bilateralism to community interest: essays in honour of Judge Bruno Simma. OUP, Oxford, pp 552–573
Pisillo Mazzeschi R (2014a) La protezione internazionale dei diritti dell'uomo e il suo impatto sulle concezioni e metodologie della dottrina giuridica internazionalistica. DUDI 8:275–318
Pisillo Mazzeschi R (2014b) Human rights and the modernization of international law. In: Lenzerini F, Vrdoljak AF (eds) International law for common goods: normative perspectives on human rights, culture and nature. Hart, Oxford, pp 89–101
Pisillo Mazzeschi R, De Sena P (eds) (2018) Global justice, human rights and the modernization of international law. Springer, Cham
Pustorino P (2020) Lezioni di tutela internazionale dei diritti umani, 2nd edn. Cacucci, Bari
Ragazzi M (1997) The concept of international obligations Erga Omnes. OUP, Oxford
Ronzitti N (1978) La disciplina dello *ius cogens* nella Convenzione di Vienna sul diritto dei trattati. CS XV, 243 ff
Ronzitti N (2007) Ius cogens. In: Flores M, Groppi T, Pisillo Mazzeschi R (eds) Diritti Umani. Cultura dei diritti e dignità della persona nell'epoca della globalizzazione: Dizionario, vol. II. Utet, Torino, pp 805–808
Shelton D (2014a) Advanced introduction to international human rights law. Edward Elgar, Cheltenham
Sicilianos LA (2012) L'influence des droits de l'homme sur la structure du droit international. RGDIP 116(5–30):241–274
Simma B (1985) Self-contained regimes. Netherlands Yearb Int Law 16:111–136
Simma B (1993) International human rights and general international law: a comparative analysis. In: Collected courses of the academy of European law, vol IV. Book 2. EUI, Florence, pp. 153–236
Simma B (1994) From bilateralism to community interest in international law. RC 250:217–384
Simma B (2009) Universality of international law from the perspective of a practitioner. Eur J Int Law 20:265–297
Simma B, Pulkowski D (2006) Of planets and the universe: self-contained regimes in international law. Eur J Int Law 17:483–529

Tams C (2005) Enforcing obligations Erga Omnes in international law. CUP, Cambridge
Thakur R (2011) The responsibility to protect: norms, Laws, and the use of force in international politics. Routledge, London
Tladi D (2016) First report on peremptory norms of general international law (*jus cogens*). A/CN.4/693, 8 March 2016
Tladi D (2017) Second report on peremptory norms of general international law (*jus cogens*). A/CN.4/706, 16 March 2017
Tladi D (2018) Third report on peremptory norms of general international law (*jus cogens*). A/CN.4/714, 12 February 2018
Tladi D (2019) Fourth report on peremptory norms of general international law (*jus cogens*) A/CN.4/727, 31 January 2019
Tomuschat C (1993) Obligations arising for states without or against their will. RC 241:195–374
Treves T (2019) The expansion of international law. General course on public international law (2015). RC 398:9–398
Weil P (1983) Towards relative normativity in international law? Am J Int Law 77:413–442
Weil P (1992) Le droit international en quête de son identité. Cours général de droit international public. RC 237:1–369

Part II

International Sources

It has been seen that the international system for the protection of human rights is an integral, and not autonomous, part of the entire and unified international legal order. It is therefore clear that the sources of international human rights law are the same as the sources of international law; namely custom, general principles of international law, general principles of law recognized by civilized nations *in foro domestico*, treaties and the sources envisaged in international treaties. Soft law, instead, is not a source in the strict sense of the word, but it plays an important role in the field of human rights.

It must be said at the outset that the most important source of international human rights law are treaties, especially many multilateral treaties of both universal and regional character. But, in this Part, I will follow the traditional order of hierarchy of sources, starting with general international law and continuing with conventional international law and then with the sources envisaged in treaties.

The most interesting problem, in my view, is whether the sources of international human rights law have elements of specialty or peculiarity with respect to the normal functioning of the sources of international law. I reiterate that here the term "specialty" does not mean a separate and autonomous regime, a self-contained regime, of sources, but only the possible existence of certain specific or particular rules which derogate from, or partially supplement the traditional rules on the functioning of sources of international law, according to the normal criterion of *lex specialis*. Indeed, it is the question of the "specialty" of sources that justifies an ad hoc Part in this book, which might otherwise simply refer to the chapter about sources contained in a general textbook of international law.

I will examine the above sources from this perspective. My theory, which I will try to demonstrate and which I anticipate here, is that in fact the sources of international human rights law present some special characteristics; and that this can be explained by the operation of two *general guiding principles* governing this normative sector, and which I have already spoken about: (*a*) the principle of the *primacy of the individual* (or the human person); (*b*) the principle of the *universality of human rights.*[1]

As already mentioned, these two principles are an expression of the fact that international human rights norms have a *dual purpose*: (*a*) to protect individuals, as the main addressees of the norms themselves; (*b*) to pursue also a community interest of States, which have become aware that the protection of human rights constitutes a central and universal value in the contemporary international order.[2]

This *dual purpose* of human rights norms (and thus implicitly the existence of the two principles mentioned above) is highlighted, in an exemplary manner, in the famous 1951 advisory opinion of the International Court of Justice on *Reservations to the Genocide Convention*, where the Court states, with regard to that Convention:

> The objects of such a convention must also be considered. The Convention was manifestly adopted for a purely humanitarian and civilizing purpose. It is indeed difficult to imagine a convention that might have this *dual character* to a greater degree, since its object on the one hand is to *safeguard the very existence of certain human groups* and on the other to confirm and endorse the most elementary principles of morality. In such a convention the contracting States do not have any interests of their own; they merely have, one and all, a *common interest*, namely the accomplishment of those high purposes which are the *raison d'être* of the convention.[3]

In my opinion, the Court's words on the "dual nature" of the Genocide Convention can be referred, *mutatis mutandis*, to all international human rights norms,[4] in which the universalist vocation coexists with that of protecting the human person.[5]

Having said that, it is now a question of verifying whether the two guiding principles mentioned above have also had an impact on the system of sources of international human rights law, such as to confer certain characteristics of "specialty" on that system compared with the traditional regime of sources of international law.

Reference

Russo D (2012) L'efficacia dei trattati sui diritti umani. Giuffrè, Milano

[1]See above, Sect. 1.4.

[2]But also see the limits of universalism: above, Sect. 1.4.2.

[3]ICJ, *Reservations to the Convention on the Prevention and Punishment of the Crime of Genocide*, p. 23 (emphasis added).

[4]On this point see also Russo (2012), p. 11.

[5]See above, Sect. 1.4.

General International Law

3

Part of the doctrine argues that in the field of international protection of human rights (and also in closely related areas such as international criminal law and humanitarian law) the processes of formation (or at least of identification)[1] of general international law have different and innovative features compared to traditional ones. Moreover, within the framework of this general doctrinal approach, several more specific theories can be distinguished, which concern: (*a*) customary law; (*b*) the general principles of law recognized by civilized nations *in foro domestico*; (*c*) the general principles of international law; (*d*) *jus cogens*. Let us examine these four sources separately.

3.1 Customary Law

3.1.1 A Modern Concept of Custom in the Field of Human Rights

As is well known, there are different conceptions in doctrine on the manner of formation and identification of the norms of customary international law.[2] Simplifying, one can distinguish between a "traditional" and a "modern" conception.[3]

In summary, the traditional approach requires two constitutive elements for the formation of a customary norm: the practice of States (so-called *diuturnitas*) and the conviction of States that this practice is legally binding (so-called *opinio juris*).

[1]In fact, I think that, in general international law, the line between the procedures of identification and those of formation of law is very thin. I shall henceforth speak of the formation/identification of customary law indifferently.

[2]On this topic see, recently, Treves (2019), pp. 141–147.

[3]These two concepts were recently described by Special Rapporteur Michael Wood in the ILC work on "*Identification of Customary International Law*". See Wood (2013), paras. 95–101 (with extensive references to the doctrine).

R. Pisillo Mazzeschi, *International Human Rights Law*,
https://doi.org/10.1007/978-3-030-77032-7_3

Moreover, a large part of the doctrine that shares this conception believes that, even within the framework of the dualist concept of custom, more importance should be given to the element of *diuturnitas*, because it is more certain and stable than the element of *opinio juris*;[4] and that *diuturnitas* should be understood in a restrictive sense as a "real" practice (i.e. concrete behavior of States) and not as a "written or oral" practice.[5]

On the contrary, the modern approach tends to question the classic dualist concept of custom and/or the way of interpreting *diuturnitas*. More specifically, a large part of contemporary doctrine, and especially that specialized in human rights, argues that the method of formation (or identification) of customary norms, in the areas of human rights, international humanitarian law and international criminal law, would be innovative compared to the traditional method. The novelty would concern two different but closely related aspects.

First of all, some authors maintain that there is a tendency to extend the concept of *diuturnitas*, in order to include not only the "real" practice of the States, constituted by their concrete behavior, but also the "written and oral" practice, consisting of a series of legal acts, as well as statements and declarations of States, such as, for example, official declarations by State agents, legislative acts, decisions of domestic courts and executive bodies, instructions to the armed forces, comments on draft treaties, pleadings before international courts, resolutions and declarations expressed within international organizations.[6] According to some scholars, written and oral practice has even become more relevant than real practice.[7]

Secondly, other authors believe that, in contemporary international law, there is also a tendency to give a more important role to the element of *opinio juris* and even to reverse the traditional logic in the ascertainment of custom, according to which the identification of *diuturnitas* is preliminary and fundamental, while the identification of *opinio juris* serves only to confirm the existence of custom. Instead, according to the doctrine under examination, the identification of *opinio juris* would be the most important step in the process of ascertaining custom.[8]

Actually, the two aspects mentioned above can be considered as complementary. In fact, the written and oral practice of States can have a double function: that of constituting evidence of both *diuturnitas* and *opinio juris*.[9] Therefore, the overall

---

[4]See Wood (2013) para. 96.

[5]See, among others, Thirlway (1972), p. 58. On the contrast between "real" and "oral" practice see Simma (1993), pp. 213–223; Simma and Alston (1992), pp. 88–100; Simma and Paulus (1999), pp. 307–308 and 316.

[6]See, for example, Schachter (1991), pp. 335–342; Meron (2006), pp. 360–366; Pisillo Mazzeschi (2008), p. 205; Id. (2014a), pp. 294–303.

[7]Wouters and Ryngaert (2009), pp. 115–118 and 123.

[8]See Abi-Saab (1985), pp. 3–4 and 13; Id. (1987), pp. 169–178; Id. (1988), pp. 729–738; Schachter (1991), pp. 338–342; Tomuschat (1999), pp. 333–334; Cassese (2000), pp. 213–215; Wouters and Ryngaert (2009), pp. 127–131.

[9]On the difficulty of rigidly distinguishing the conduct of States from their expressions of views, see Treves (2019), pp. 144–147. See also Dupuy and Kerbrat (2020), pp. 381–383.

result of the new method of formation/identification of custom is to privilege *opinio juris* over *diuturnitas*.

In my view, this modern method, which, albeit within the framework of the dualist conception of custom, favors "written and oral" practice and privileges the element *opinio juris*, must be generally approved. In any case, this method is especially convincing in the field of human rights, understood in a very broad sense, as including international criminal law and humanitarian law.[10]

This is confirmed by international practice. In fact, in support of the new method of formation/identification of custom, some important international judgments can be cited. The oldest precedents are two decisions by the Nuremberg military courts.[11] Subsequently, the new method finds important confirmation from the International Court of Justice in a different area of international law. In fact, in the *Nicaragua* case judgment of 1986, in relation to the customary norm on the prohibition of the use of armed force, the Court stated that it "must satisfy itself that the existence of the rule in the *opinio juris* of States is confirmed by practice".[12] Therefore the ICJ applied a method of ascertainment of customary law in which the identification of the *opinio juris* logically precedes the examination of *diuturnitas*. But the most significant example of the new method of identification of customary law is the famous decision of the Appeals Chamber of the International Criminal Tribunal for the former Yugoslavia in the *Tadić* case.[13] As is well known, the so-called *Tadić* method was then taken up in the 2005 study of the International Committee of the Red Cross on customary international humanitarian law.[14]

The question should now be asked why international practice in favor of the new method of formation of custom focuses in particular on certain areas of international law. In my opinion, there are two reasons, which explain the pre-eminence of the *opinio juris* element. First, in the areas of the protection of human rights and international criminal law, the norms of customary law are characterized by a strong *opinio juris* of the international community (which emerges from declarations of

---

[10]However, it should be noted that the doctrine in favor of the new method of formation/identification of international custom has found strong opposition in another part of the doctrine. Some authors (see, e.g., Simma and Alston 1992, p. 104) have argued that this method, favoring the so-called "paper practice" (i.e. the written and oral practice), over the real and concrete practice of the States, takes the form of a "strained, or even denaturated [sic], 'new' theory of custom" and ends up transforming the process of formation of customary law into an exercise of rhetoric. According to these scholars, the strongest argument, which opposes a very wide use of customary law in the field of human rights, would be the clear contradiction between the real practice and the *opinio juris* of States. In fact, it seems to me that this argument is a bit circular: since it starts from the premise that the only fundamental element of custom is real and concrete practice, it is led to conclude that, where this element is missing, there can be no custom.

[11]ITM, *The United States et al. v. Göring et al.*, spec. pp. 218–224; US Military Tribunal Nuremberg, *The United States v. von Leeb et al.* spec. pp. 485–491.

[12]ICJ, *Military and Paramilitary Activities*, Judgment of 27 June 1986, paras. 184–188.

[13]ICTY, *Tadić*, 2 October 1995, para. 99.

[14]Henckaerts and Doswald-Beck (2005), vol. 1, pp. xxxii–xxxviii. See also Wouters and Ryngaert (2009), pp. 116–117.

States, multilateral treaties, resolutions of international organizations, other acts of soft law, etc.) and, on the contrary, by a rather scarce or sometimes even contradictory "real" and interstate practice. The smallness of this practice depends, to a large extent, on the fact that in these areas, which mainly regulate relations between States and individuals, violations of the norms tend to occur within a State; and therefore other States are reluctant to react at the international level. However, it should be noted that in recent years there has been a significant increase in interstate complaints based on human rights violations.[15]

Secondly, in these areas of international law, the community interests of States and the fundamental values of the international community come to the fore; and the *opinio juris* has the merit of indicating, more clearly and immediately than *diuturnitas*, the collective consciousness or consent of the international community as a whole. In this aspect one can note the impact of the principle of the *universality of human rights* on the formation of customary law.

However, it must be admitted that the new method of formation/identification of custom is not neutral from the point of view of values and interests, since, by privileging *opinio juris* over *diuturnitas*, it ends up favoring the establishment of customary law and thus favoring the protection of human rights over the sovereignty of States. It could be added that, if the interpreter intends to favor the progressive development of the above-mentioned normative fields, he could and perhaps should re-evaluate, within the *opinio juris seu necessitatis*, the more dynamic element of the sense of social duty and expectation of legitimacy (*opinio necessitatis*), compared to the other more static element of the conviction of legality (*opinio juris* in the strict sense).

3.1.2 The Role of Human Rights Treaties in the Formation of Custom

Related to the general topic discussed above is the more particular theme of the role that human rights treaties may play in the formation of customary norms. More precisely, the question is whether the constant and uniform presence, in human rights treaties, of a provision of identical or similar content on a given right (e.g., the prohibition of torture) can have an impact, and what impact, in the formation of a customary norm with similar content.

---

[15]This increase has affected the European Court of Human Rights, the Committee on the Elimination of Racial Discrimination (cf. below Sect. 10.4.2.3), and even the International Court of Justice. For the latter see, in particular, ICJ, *Armed Activities on the Territory of the Congo*, Judgment of 19 December 2005, paras. 313, 317, 332–333; Separate Opinion of Judge Simma, paras. 16–41; ICJ, *Questions relating to the Obligation to Prosecute or Extradite (Belgium v. Senegal)*; ICJ, *Application of the International Convention for the Suppression of the Financing of Terrorism (Ukraine v. Russian Federation)*; ICJ, *Application of the Convention on the Prevention and Punishment of the Crime of Genocide (The Gambia v. Myanmar)*. On the topic see, inter alia, Ulfstein and Risini (2020).

Actually, the issue of the relationship between treaties and custom is very complex, it has given rise to an extensive doctrinal debate, and cannot be addressed here.[16] In short, it can only be said that it usually focuses on the problem of the relationship between treaties codifying international law, drawn up on the basis of Article 13 of the UN Charter, and custom. The dominant opinion, supported by international case-law, is that codification treaties can make a contribution to the process of formation of customary law, since they can express, albeit to varying degrees, both the *opinio juris* and the *diuturnitas* of States. More specifically, those treaties can produce three different effects on custom: (*a*) a "declaratory" effect of a pre-existing customary norm; (*b*) a "constitutive" effect of a new customary norm, that is, the starting point or an intermediate stage in the process of the formation of that norm; (*c*) a "crystallizing" effect of a customary norm which was already being formed.[17] Furthermore, "declaratory", "constitutive" and "crystallizing" rules may coexist within the same codification treaty.

As a matter of fact, human rights treaties cannot, strictly speaking, be classified as treaties codifying international law under Article 13 of the UN Charter. However, they do share many aspects of such codification treaties, especially when they are promoted by the United Nations and have a universal character. Indeed, their purpose is also to contribute to the clarification and progressive development of international human rights law. Therefore, it can be considered that human rights treaties, and the individual provisions contained in them, can produce the above three effects on custom. But also human rights treaties existing within the framework of regional systems can affect customary law, both because they too can express the *opinio juris* and *diuturnitas* of a substantial regional group of States, and because their application and interpretation has an influence on those of the universal treaties.

This process of mutual influence between universal and regional human rights treaties is greatly enhanced in treaties with international monitoring bodies, such as the UN Treaty-Bodies, the European Court of Human Rights, the Inter-American Court and Commission, the African Court and Commission.[18] Indeed, the case-law and practice in the application of the treaties by these monitoring bodies clearly demonstrates the existence of this mutual influence. In any case, although this practice cannot be classified as *diuturnitas* and *opinio juris* of States, it is very useful as an authoritative indication of how conventional norms affect customary norms.

Consider, moreover, what I have already said in the previous section about the fact that, in the field of human rights, there is little "real" and interstate practice, because States are reluctant to react internationally to violations of human rights norms, which tend to occur within a single State and only rarely affect the direct and material interests of other States. The scarcity of interstate practice inevitably ends up by giving priority to the element of *opinio juris* over the element of *diuturnitas* in

[16]Among the classic contributions, see Baxter (1965–66): Id. (1970); D'Amato (1971), pp. 103–166; Thirlway (1972). More recently, see Dinstein (2006); Crawford (2013), pp. 115–146.

[17]See also Pisillo Mazzeschi (1994b), spec. pp. 202–204.

[18]See below, Part IV.

the formation/identification of customary norms. And this scarcity, at the same time, ends up increasing the role of the practice of international monitoring bodies on human rights. Finally, let us add the significant interpretative weight of the General Comments of the UN Treaty-Bodies.

Ultimately, it does not seem risky to argue that human rights treaties (and the provisions with constant and uniform content contained in them), for the above reasons, produce an important contribution to the formation of customary norms, a contribution comparable to that produced by the treaties of codification and progressive development of international law.

3.2 General Principles of Law Recognized by Civilized Nations *in foro domestico*

The general principles of law recognized by civilized nations,[19] understood as principles that originate and are uniformly applied in domestic legal systems, can also play an innovative and original role in the field of human rights.

This theory has been supported by some distinguished scholars. Conforti[20] has argued, since 1976, that this category of sources of international law can include those principles, universally present in State legal orders, which aim to safeguard human dignity, such as, for example, the principles prohibiting apartheid, racial discrimination, torture, massacre, genocide, slavery and other inhuman methods of government. With this view, the illustrious author employed a new method for detecting the existence of certain fundamental human rights from general international law, without the need to resort to traditional customary law and therefore also to the element of a consolidated *diuturnitas* at interstate level.[21] In fact, the "internal" origin of *some* fundamental human rights seems more convincing than their "international" origin: think, for example, of the prohibition of torture which probably became established in the domestic systems of the great majority of States before it has become established at interstate level.

A similar, but not identical, theory was maintained by Henkin.[22] According to this author, there are norms of general international law on human rights which are not based on interstate custom or practice, nor on the consent of States, but which are "constitutional" in the sense that they derive from the rights contained in contemporary national constitutions. Cassese too, while considering that the general principles of domestic law are only a subsidiary source of international law, maintains that this category is useful for regulating new areas; and points out that the international

[19]See Art. 38(1)(*c*) of the ICJ Statute.

[20]Conforti (1976), pp. 27–28; Id. (2018), pp. 49–52.

[21]In the general principles recognized by civilized nations, *diuturnitas* would instead be constituted by the uniform application of those principles in State legal systems.

[22]Henkin (1995–96), pp. 31–45.

criminal courts have frequently used the general principles of criminal law recognized by the main domestic legal systems.[23]

It should be noted that the theory using the general principles of law applied *in foro domestico*, as a method of formation/identification of the general norms of international human rights law, has met with opposition from various scholars. They believe that the identification of such principles lends itself to uncertainties and subjective interpretations when they are not confirmed in interstate practice. In my opinion, this criticism affects, more than the method described above of using general principles, the very validity of this source of international law. In fact, if it is required that the general principles recognized in *foro domestico* must find confirmation in a constant and consolidated *interstate* practice, then any difference between these principles and customs is dropped: in essence, these principles are conceived only as means of proof of the process of formation of *diuturnitas* and *opinio juris*. Therefore, it should logically be excluded that such principles constitute an *autonomous* source of international law. But international practice and case-law disprove this view. Suffice it to think, in addition to the aforementioned case-law of the international criminal courts, of the case-law of the internal administrative tribunals of international organizations and the human rights case-law of the EU Court of Justice.

In conclusion, I believe that, once the old differences in content and scope between international law and domestic law have largely disappeared,[24] the general principles of law applied *in foro domestico* lend themselves to being used mainly in areas of international law that are new, that regulate internal matters and that contain norms that directly create *rights and obligations for individuals* and other non-state actors. In these areas, these principles, which do not take into account the traditional interstate *diuturnitas*, have considerable dynamic potential in international law. This is particularly true for international human rights law where the principle of the *primacy of the individual* suggests to the interpreter a broad use of the general principles of law recognized *in foro domestico*.

3.3 General Principles of International Law

The general principles of international law, i.e. the principles which do not derive from domestic legal systems but which originate directly in the international order, have always been a highly controversial subject in internationalist doctrine.[25] The most traditionalist authors deny the existence of such principles as autonomous

[23]Cassese (2013), pp. 293–295.

[24]See above, Sect. 2.3.5.

[25]This source is now admitted by prevailing doctrine. But part of it still denies the existence of these principles as an autonomous source of international law. On the subject see, recently, Pisillo Mazzeschi and Viviani (2018), pp. 113–161.

sources.[26] Others propose a number of conservative theories that tend to seriously limit the role of such principles. Among these latter views,[27] the one that prevails today is that these principles derive from customary norms that already exist, through a process of induction or abstraction or generalization.

However, the dominant view today is that the category of general principles of international law should be admitted among the autonomous sources of contemporary international law.[28] But the foundation, the method of identification and the functions of these principles remain to be clarified.[29]

In my view, the theory that the principles derive by abstraction from existing customary norms can be accepted; but *only with regard to some general principles* of international law, which are usually the oldest and those operating in the more traditional areas of international law. These include, for example, the principles of territorial sovereignty, formal equality between States, effectiveness, freedom of the seas, State responsibility for wrongful acts and self-defense. The interpreter draws a wide and general principle from specific customary norms or groups of such norms. In essence, these principles have the same nature as customary norms, but a more general and indeterminate content. Therefore, the difference between these principles and the customary norms from which they are "'abstracted" is relative, because the criteria of generality and vagueness are also relative.

However, *in addition* to these principles, there are also *other principles*, which are usually the most recent and which operate in newer areas of international law.[30] They are more interesting because they have a *different foundation and method of identification*, which has been highlighted by some authoritative scholars.[31] In particular, these principles are not based on existing customary norms, but on the fact that there is *general recognition and consensus* on them by the international community. Moreover, in my view, the international community should here be understood in a broad sense; that is, not limited to States and international organizations, but also including other "actors" such as non-governmental organizations, individuals, groups of individuals, legal entities, associations and

[26]See, e.g., Scelle (1934), pp. 312–315; Kelsen (1966), pp. 440, 539–540; Tunkin (1974), pp. 190–203.

[27]On the various theories see, recently, Pisillo Mazzeschi and Viviani (2018), pp. 123–137.

[28]See, among others, Simma and Alston (1992), p. 102 ff.; Simma (1993), pp. 221–223 and 224–229; Charney (1993), pp. 537–538 and 543–550; Simma and Paulus (1999), pp. 306–308; Tomuschat (1999), pp. 335–340; Id. (2018), pp. 192–194; Dupuy (2002), pp. 186–187; Cannizzaro (2012), pp. 125–131; Cassese (2013), pp. 289–290. See also, albeit with a more cautious approach, Gaja (1986), p. 533 ff.; Id. (2012), paras. 18–20.

[29]See Pisillo Mazzeschi and Viviani (2018), pp. 134–137.

[30]*Ibidem*, pp. 142–155.

[31]For older doctrine see Verdross (1968). Among the more recent authors see, e.g., Simma (1993), pp. 224–229; Simma and Alston (1992), pp. 102–106; Bassiouni (1990), pp. 768–769; Dupuy (2002), pp. 186–187; Tomuschat (1999), p. 356; Gaja (2012), paras. 18–20; Dupuy and Kerbrat (2020), pp. 390–395; Cançado Trindade, Separate Opinion, in ICJ, *Pulp Mills on the River Uruguay*, para. 39. See also, for a similar view, Charney (1993), pp. 543–551; Henkin (1995–96), pp. 37–39.

political movements representing civil society in various ways. It should be noted that this *recognition and consensus* does not depend on the classical elements of *diuturnitas* and *opinio juris* which characterize customary norms; but on the fact that the international community believes that these principles express shared international juridical values, and sometimes even fundamental and peremptory values. This conviction derives largely from the ethical-legal value of these principles and can be inferred from many elements of the behavior, including oral practice, of the aforementioned "actors" of the international community. Among these elements, the formulation of these principles in international forums, organizations or institutions, such as the UN General Assembly, the Human Rights Council or the assembly bodies of other international organizations, is of particular importance.

Some of these principles have a non-peremptory nature, for example the principle of peaceful settlement of disputes, that which prohibits the harmful use of State territory, or that declaring the resources of the deep-sea bed as common heritage of mankind. Other principles (more important for our purposes) have a peremptory (*jus cogens*) character, for example the principle prohibiting the threat or use of armed force, the principle of self-determination of peoples, the principles prohibiting genocide, gross violations of human rights and serious breaches of international humanitarian law.

As can be seen, many of these principles of a peremptory nature belong to the field of human rights, broadly understood. In fact, the main proponents of these principles believe that it is on these principles that a large part of general international human rights law is based.[32] This is confirmed by some important judgments and advisory opinions of the ICJ, concerning human rights and humanitarian law, which establish, more or less explicitly, the existence of these principles. One can recall: the 1975 opinion on the *Western Sahara* case (principle of self-determination of peoples);[33] the 1951 opinion on *Reservations to the Genocide Convention* (principle prohibiting genocide);[34] the judgments in the *Corfu Channel*,[35] *Barcelona Traction*[36] and *US Diplomatic and Consular Staff in Tehran*[37] cases (principle prohibiting gross violations of human rights); the 1986 judgment in the *Nicaragua* case[38] (principle prohibiting serious breaches of humanitarian law).[39]

---

[32]See Simma (1993), pp. 224–229; Simma and Alston (1992), pp. 102–106.

[33]ICJ, *Western Sahara*, p. 12.

[34]ICJ, *Reservations to the Convention on the Prevention and Punishment of the Crime of Genocide*, p. 15.

[35]ICJ, *Corfu Channel*, p. 22.

[36]ICJ, *Barcelona Traction*, p. 3.

[37]ICJ, *United States Diplomatic and Consular Staff*, p. 3.

[38]ICJ, *Military and Paramilitary Activities*, Judgment of 27 June 1986, paras. 219–221.

[39]According to some authors (Simma 1993, pp. 225–226; Simma and Alston 1992, pp. 103–108), a further argument in favor of general principles in the field of human rights would derive from the concept of *jus cogens*. *Jus cogens* would not consist of customary norms, but of general principles of international law. And since almost all fundamental human rights belong to *jus cogens*, a "strong" *opinio juris*, in the presence of which *diuturnitas* would no longer be necessary as a

These principles on human rights have a very broad content. But this is a distinctive character of all principles. Indeed, it should be reiterated that the general principles of international law must be kept distinct from customary norms, because the former characterize the entire international legal order or, more often, a specific area of it, as in the case of human rights. Moreover, the principles, usually but not always, are at the basis of a group of other more specific norms, have a higher degree of generality than customary norms, express general aims and values, and have a teleological and flexible content instead of establishing a precise and well-defined conduct.[40]

Moreover, the principles in question (those based on general recognition) often express the evolutionary trends in international law or certain areas of international law; they can therefore influence the formation of customary norms with a more precise and specific content. In the field of human rights, for example, the principle of the prohibition of gross violations of human rights has favored the formation of more specific customary norms, such as prohibitions of slavery and arbitrary deprivation of life. Similarly, the general principle of non-discrimination, which underlies the Universal Declaration of Human Rights, has influenced the formation of a more specific norm on the prohibition of racial discrimination and apartheid. The principle of self-determination of peoples, which originally arose with the UN Charter as a general principle, has also materialized in customary norms, which have specified it in some areas.[41]

In conclusion, it can be maintained that there are *two categories* of general principles of international law, which, in principle, have developed in different historical periods and in different ways. When the international community was small and consisted only of States, the values and general principles governing that community had to be affirmed through formal sources, and essentially through traditional customary law, which was a guarantee of stability and certainty, especially by virtue of its element of interstate *diuturnitas*. Thus these principles were derived by abstraction from existing customary norms. When, on the other hand, in more recent times the international community has extended to other "actors", the values and general principles of this community could also be expressed outside the formal sources and traditional customary law, and founded instead on *general and direct recognition and consent* by the social base of the legal system, that is, by the international community as a whole. This is a more modern category of principles.

In short, it can be said that the theory of human rights has played an important role in the creation and development of the "new" principles of international law; and therefore, more generally, in modernizing this source of international law and in

---

constitutive element of general international law, would be of decisive importance for their recognition. In my opinion, this theory is not completely acceptable, since *jus cogens* includes both some customary norms and some general principles of international law.

[40]On the distinction between principles and norms, in the general theory of law, see, e.g., Dworkin (1967); Id. (1977), chaps. 2 and 3; Guastini (1993), pp. 76–79 and 447–461; Alexy (2000); Id. (2002).

[41]See below, Chap. 19.

increasing its importance in the contemporary international order. Therefore, this theory has contributed to broadening the system of sources of general international law. In this sense, it can be argued that the guiding principle of the *universality of human rights* and, albeit to a lesser extent, the other guiding principle of the *primacy of the individual* have also had an impact in this area.

3.4 *Jus cogens*

The issue of *jus cogens* has already been addressed in Chap. 2, but only in relation to the impact that the concept has had on the function and legal nature of international law and on the regime of State responsibility.[42] It is now a question, instead, of dealing briefly with the subject from the point of view of its impact on the system of sources, with particular regard to human rights norms.

It must first be made clear that *jus cogens* is not, strictly speaking, an autonomous source of international law; rather, it is a special character that certain norms of general international law take on. As already said,[43] the norms of *jus cogens* (or peremptory) express *fundamental and essential values* of the entire international community. They are a rather narrow category of customary norms and (in my opinion) also of general principles of international law,[44] which are supported by a particular *opinio juris* (for customary norms) or by a particular conviction (for principles) on the part of the international community. The latter must be convinced that certain conduct is not only legally binding but *also peremptory*. The conviction that the norm can never be derogated from is the crucial point in order to affirm its peremptory character. Moreover, it should be remembered that peremptory norms contain *erga omnes* obligations; but that the notion of *jus cogens* is more restrictive than that of *erga omnes* obligations.

The effects of peremptory norms are manifold.[45] Firstly, according to their original meaning as laid down in the 1969 Vienna Convention on the Law of Treaties, these norms invalidate or extinguish treaties that are contrary to them.[46] Secondly, peremptory norms take precedence, in the event of conflict, over customary norms and principles of international law that are not peremptory. This is due to the fact that peremptory norms have a special legal force of resistance or (according to the best theory) even a higher rank, which places them at the top of international sources. This effect of *jus cogens* is particularly important for certain human rights.[47] Furthermore, peremptory norms have other interesting effects, such as invalidating sources envisaged in treaties, if they are contrary to them; preventing a State from

---

[42] See above, Sects. 2.3.3.2 and 2.3.4.2.

[43] See above, Sect. 2.3.3.2.

[44] See Pisillo Mazzeschi and Viviani (2018), pp. 142–150.

[45] On this point see the brief, but excellent, description by Ronzitti (2007).

[46] See Articles 53 and 64 of the Vienna Convention.

[47] See below, Sects. 17.1.4.2 and 17.2.3.

invoking a circumstance precluding wrongfulness in relation to conduct contrary to a peremptory norm; impeding the legitimacy of a situation (e.g., an apartheid regime) resulting from the breach of a peremptory norm. Finally, as already seen,[48] the breach of *jus cogens* creates an aggravated responsibility, involving particular reactions from other States.

All these aspects are very relevant to human rights. In fact, as already mentioned, there are some principles and customary norms on human rights which have the character of *jus cogens*.[49] Among the general principles are the self-determination of peoples,[50] the prohibition of gross violations of human rights, the prohibition of genocide and crimes against humanity.[51] Among the customary norms are the prohibitions of torture,[52] slavery and slave trade,[53] systematic racial discrimination and apartheid.[54]

Therefore, it can be concluded that the theory of human rights has also contributed in a very important way to the affirmation and consolidation of the concept of *jus cogens* in the international legal order. And the guiding principles of the *universality of human rights* and the *primacy of the individual* have played a role in this development.

3.5 Conclusions

From the analysis carried out so far, on the methods of formation/identification of general international law on human rights, some conclusions can be drawn, which I have in summary anticipated.

A first conclusion is that the element of international *diuturnitas*, especially understood in the classical sense as interstate and "real" practice, tends to weaken in favor of the elements of *opinio juris* (in customary law), of the general recognition/consensus of the international community (in the general principles of international law) and of national practice (in the general principles of law recognized *in foro domestico*). This tendency, which seeks in various ways to remedy the scarcity of interstate *diuturnitas* in the field of human rights, promotes the formation and identification of general international law in this area. It is therefore an effect of the guiding principle of the *universality of human rights*. The principle of respect for human dignity and its universal value, supported by its generalized recognition by the international community as a whole, has given and continue to give a propulsive impetus to the expansion of the scope of general international law in the human

[48]See above, Sect. 2.3.4.2.

[49]See also below, Sect. 13.3.5.

[50]See below, Chap. 19.

[51]See below, Sects. 14.3.1 and 14.3.2.

[52]See below, Sect. 14.2.

[53]See below, Sect. 16.1.

[54]See below, Sect. 18.2.

rights field. As I already said,[55] universalism is strengthened at the expense of multiculturalism/particularism.

A second conclusion is that the wider use of *opinio juris* and the "immediate" consensus of the international community are two factors that lend themselves not only to expanding general international law on human rights, but also to filling gaps in more specific norms, interpreting them dynamically, adapting them to individual cases and providing greater completeness and systematic coherence to the whole area of human rights law. These trends also respond to the guiding principle of the *universality of human rights*. In other words, the recognition, on the part of the international community as a whole, that the protection of human rights constitutes a universal value in the contemporary international order motivates this community to favor the progressive development of this normative sector, even with instruments that are different and complementary to that of the expansion of the scope of general international law.

A third conclusion is that the above trends also strengthen the guiding principle of the *primacy of the individual*, and therefore also of the prevalence of individual rights over State rights. In fact, the extension of general international law on human rights means a parallel restriction of the sovereignty of States. Moreover, the primacy of the individual is particularly evident for that nucleus of human rights which are protected by norms of *jus cogens*, which are taken away from the power of the "contractual will" of States.

In short, as already mentioned,[56] the old "State-centric" norms gradually leave a space also for the new "human-centric" norms, and international law, through a process of "humanization", becomes a law not only for States, but also for individuals. This process has, to a certain extent, also affected the sources of general international law.

References

Abi-Saab G (1985) Reflexions on the contemporary processes of developing international law. Ninth Gilberto Amado Memorial Lecture presented at the International Law Commission, 25 June 1985

Abi-Saab G (1987) Cours général de droit international public. RC 207:1–464

Abi-Saab G (1988) Entangled treaty and custom. In: Dinstein Y (ed) International law at a time of perplexity: essays in honour of Shabtai Rosenne. Nijhoff, Dordrecht, p 717 ff

Alexy R (2000) On the structure of legal principles. Ratio Juris 13:294–304

Alexy R (2002) A theory of constitutional rights. OUP, Oxford

Bassiouni MC (1990) A functional approach to 'general principles of international law'. Mich J Int Law 11:768–818

Baxter R (1965–66) Multilateral treaties as evidence of customary international law. Br Yearb Int L 41:275–300

Baxter R (1970) Treaties and custom. RC 129:27–105

[55] See above, Sect. 1.4.

[56] See above, Sect. 2.1.

Cannizzaro E (2012) Diritto internazionale. Giappichelli, Torino
Cassese A (2000) The Martens Clause: half a loaf or simply pie in the sky? Eur J Int Law 11:187–216
Cassese A (Gaeta P ed) (2013) Diritto internazionale, 2nd edn. Il Mulino, Bologna
Charney JI (1993) Universal international law. Am J Int Law 87:529–551
Conforti B (1976) Appunti dalle lezioni di diritto internazionale. Editoriale Scientifica, Napoli
Conforti B (Iovane M ed) (2018) Diritto internazionale, 11th edn. Editoriale Scientifica, Napoli
Crawford J (2013) Change, order, change: the course of international law. General course on public international law. RC 365:9–389
D'Amato A (1971) The concept of custom in international law. Cornell University Press, Ithaca-London
Dinstein Y (2006) The interaction between customary international law and treaties. RC 322:243–428
Dupuy P-M (2002) L'unité de l'ordre juridique international. Cours général de droit international public. RC 297:9–490
Dupuy P-M, Kerbrat Y (2020) Droit international public, 15th edn. Dalloz, Paris
Dworkin R (1967) The model of rules. Univ Chic Law Rev 35:14–46
Dworkin R (1977) Taking rights seriously. CUP, Cambridge (Mass)
Gaja G (1986) Principi del diritto (diritto internazionale). ED XXXV:533–546
Gaja G (2012) General principles of law. EPIL, online edn. OUP, Oxford
Guastini R (1993) Le fonti del diritto e l'interpretazione. Giuffrè, Milano
Henckaerts JM, Doswald-Beck L (2005) ICRC, customary international humanitarian law, 3 vols. CUP, Cambridge
Henkin L (1995–96) Human rights and state sovereignty. Georgia J Int Comp Law 25:31–45
Kelsen H (1966) Principles of international law, 2nd edn. Holt, Rinehart and Winston, New York
Meron T (2006) The humanization of international law. Nijhoff, Leiden-Boston
Pisillo Mazzeschi R (1994b) Trattati e consuetudine nella codificazione del diritto internazionale. Com int 49:196–222
Pisillo Mazzeschi R (2008) Responsabilité de l'État pour violation des obligations positives relatives aux droits de l'homme. RC 333:175–506
Pisillo Mazzeschi R (2014a) La protezione internazionale dei diritti dell'uomo e il suo impatto sulle concezioni e metodologie della dottrina giuridica internazionalistica. DUDI 8:275–318
Pisillo Mazzeschi R, Viviani A (2018) General principles of international law: from rules to values? In: Pisillo Mazzeschi R, De Sena P (eds) Global justice, human rights and the modernization of international law. Springer, Cham, pp 113–161
Ronzitti N (2007) Ius cogens. In: Flores M, Groppi T, Pisillo Mazzeschi R (eds) Diritti Umani. Cultura dei diritti e dignità della persona nell'epoca della globalizzazione: Dizionario, vol II. Utet, Torino, pp 805–808
Scelle G (1934) Précis de Droit des Gens. Principes et systématique, Deuxième partie. Recueil Sirey, Paris
Schachter O (1991) International law in theory and practice. Nijhoff, Dordrecht-Boston-London
Simma B (1993) International human rights and general international law: a comparative analysis. In: Collected courses of the academy of European law, vol IV, Book 2. EUI, Florence, pp 153–236
Simma B, Alston P (1992) The sources of human rights law: custom, jus cogens, and general principles. Aust Yearb Int L 12:82–108
Simma B, Paulus AL (1999) The responsibility of individuals for human rights abuses in internal conflicts: a positivist view. Am J Int Law 93:302–316
Thirlway HWA (1972) International customary law and codification. Sijthoff, Leiden
Tomuschat C (1999) International law: ensuring the survival of mankind on the eve of a new century. General course on public international law. RC 281:9–438

Tomuschat C (2018) General international law: a new source of international law? In: Pisillo Mazzeschi R, De Sena P (eds) Global justice, human rights and the modernization of international law. Springer, Cham, pp 185–204

Treves T (2019) The expansion of international law. General course on public international law (2015). RC 398:9–398

Tunkin GI (1974) Theory of international law (trans: Butler WE). George Allen & Unwin Ltd., London

Ulfstein G, Risini I (2020) Inter-state applications under the European Convention on Human Rights: strength and challenges. Eur J Int Law:Talk! 24 January 2020

Verdross A (1968) Les principes généraux de droit dans le système des sources du droit international public. In: Guggenheim P (ed) Recueil d'études de droit international en hommage à P. Guggenheim. Georg, Geneva, pp 521–530

Wood M (2013) First report on formation and evidence of customary international law. UN Doc. A/CN.4/663, 17 May 2013

Wouters J, Ryngaert C (2009) Impact on the process of the formation of customary international law. In: Kamminga MT, Scheinin M (eds) The impact of human rights law on general international law. OUP, Oxford-New York, pp 111–131

4 Treaties

4.1 Possible Reasons for the "Specialty" of Human Rights Treaties

Even in relation to human rights treaties, a large part of the doctrine argues that *different and innovative* rules apply compared to the traditional rules of the law of treaties. In this sense it maintains that human rights treaties are "special" compared to other treaties.[1] This "special" character is justified by different, sometimes alternative and sometimes cumulative opinions or motivations:[2] (*a*) the *erga omnes* character of the obligations undertaken by States Parties; (*b*) the "objective" character of the same obligations and their collective guarantee;[3] (*c*) the peremptory character of conventional human rights norms; (*d*) the theory that human rights treaties would have a "constitutional" nature; (*e*) the theory that human rights treaties would be formally addressed to individuals alongside States.

In my opinion, as I shall try to demonstrate, it is not correct to talk about the "specialty" of human rights treaties, in the sense that they are governed by a special, different, separate and autonomous regime of the law of treaties; in other words, by a self-contained regime.[4] Rather, it must be recognized that there are certain general principles[5] which characterize human rights treaties (but not only these) in comparison with other international treaties; and that they may give rise to certain *particular rules* which, on the basis of the *lex specialis* criterion, merely supplement, and sometimes derogate from, traditional international rules on the law of treaties. In essence, human rights treaties have certain *special features*.

[1] See, e.g., Focarelli (2013), p. 101.

[2] On these various opinions see the excellent analysis of Russo (2012), pp. 280–304.

[3] For this theory see Sudre (2006), pp. 58–60.

[4] See above, Sect. 2.2.

[5] See Sudre (2006), pp. 57 ff. and 189 ff.

R. Pisillo Mazzeschi, *International Human Rights Law*,
https://doi.org/10.1007/978-3-030-77032-7_4

My theory, which I anticipate here, is that these peculiar characteristics derive, here too, from the principle of the *primacy of the individual* and, to a lesser extent, from the principle of the *universality of human rights*. It is now time to explore the theme of the "specialty" of human rights treaties, examining, separately and critically, the various theories that try to explain this "specialty".

4.1.1 Non-Reciprocity and Obligations *Erga Omnes Partes*

According to a first theory, the difference between human rights treaties and other treaties would be the *lack of reciprocity* of the obligations assumed by States in the former. The theory of the lack of reciprocity of conventional human rights obligations, which seems to evoke in some respects the old and now obsolete distinction between law-making treaties and contractual treaties (traités-lois and traités-contrats) has been affirmed several times in international case-law. Already the International Court of Justice, in its 1951 advisory opinion on *Reservations to the Genocide Convention*, had supported a similar theory, stating that:

> In such a convention the contracting States do not have any interests of their own; they merely have, one and all, a common interest, namely the accomplishment of those high purposes which are the *raison d'être* of the convention. Consequently, in a convention of this type, one cannot speak of individual advantages or disadvantages to States, or of the maintenance of a perfect contractual balance between rights and duties.[6]

Even more clearly, after a number of years, the Human Rights Committee has stated in relation to human rights treaties:

> [. . .] such treaties, and the Covenant specifically, are not a web of inter-State exchanges of mutual obligations. [. . .] The principle of inter-State reciprocity has no place.[7]

The idea of non-reciprocity of conventional human rights obligations was also supported by the Inter-American Court of Human Rights, when it stated:

> The American Convention and the other human rights treaties [. . . .] have a special character that sets them apart from other treaties. The latter govern mutual interests between and among the States parties [. . .].[8]

Finally, the Commission and the European Court of Human Rights have also affirmed on numerous occasions the idea of the non-reciprocity of conventional human rights obligations, although they (as we shall see) prefer to use the similar but not identical concept of the "objective" nature of such obligations.

---

[6]ICJ, *Reservations to the Convention on the Prevention and Punishment of the Crime of Genocide*, p. 23.

[7]HRCtee, General Comment No. 24, 4 November 1994, para. 19.

[8]See, e.g., IACtHR, *Ivcher Bronstein*, para. 42.

As for the doctrine, it usually agrees that conventional human rights obligations are, in principle, characterized by a lack of reciprocity; but some authors rightly point out that such treaties, if they exclude reciprocity understood as an exchange of interests and tangible benefits between States Parties, do not exclude reciprocity understood as a legal commitment of reciprocal rights and obligations between States Parties.[9] In other words, one could say that conventional undertakings on human rights go beyond, but do not exclude, the element of reciprocity. In this sense, the European Court of Human Rights' statement in the case of *Ireland v. the United Kingdom* is exemplary:

> unlike international treaties of the classic kind, the Convention comprises more than reciprocal engagements between contracting States. It creates, over and above a network of mutual, bilateral undertakings, objective obligations.[10]

Actually, in my view, the theory of the lack of reciprocity in human rights treaties, despite its imprecise terminology, is, in substance, equivalent to the theory (more used in doctrine than in jurisprudence but more precise in terminology) according to which such treaties contain obligations *erga omnes partes.* This second theory is more correct, because it better expresses the fact that, in human rights treaties, by virtue of the solidarity of the obligations undertaken, each State Party is obliged towards all other States Parties to fulfil its obligations and that, in parallel, each State Party has a right to the performance of obligations by all other States Parties.[11] Finally, the concept of solidarity of obligations also better expresses the idea that these obligations are intended to protect collective and community values.[12]

It may be added that the concept of *erga omnes partes* obligations contains two elements which, at first sight, do not appear evident in the concept of non-reciprocal obligations: (*a*) the collective and joint purpose of States Parties which oblige themselves to respect the *rights of individuals* irrespective of their nationality; (*b*) the fact that the violation by one State Party *legitimizes* all other States Parties to invoke the responsibility of the first State; that is, the overcoming of the traditional principle of bilateralism in interstate responsibility. In fact, as already seen, the most important element of *erga omnes partes* obligations consists precisely in the extension of the legitimacy to invoke the responsibility of the offending State.[13] However, these two elements, although not apparent at first sight, are also implicit in the theory of the non-reciprocity of conventional human rights obligations.

In conclusion, the concept of *erga omnes partes* obligations is suitable, rather than the somewhat ambiguous concept of non-reciprocity, to define the particular nature of conventional human rights obligations. But this concept *alone* is not

[9]See Simma (1994), p. 369.

[10]ECtHR, *Ireland v. UK*, p. 90, para. 239.

[11]Simma (1994), p. 369.

[12]See above, Sect. 2.3.3.1.

[13]See above, Sect. 2.3.4.1.

sufficient to explain the difference between human rights treaties and other treaties. In fact, human rights treaties are certainly not the only treaties that contain *erga omnes partes* obligations.

4.1.2 Theory on the "Objective" Nature of Conventional Human Rights Obligations. Criticism

According to a second opinion, conventional human rights obligations would be characterized, compared to other treaty obligations, by the fact that they are "objective" in character or, with a similar expression, by the fact that they establish an "objective" legal regime. As mentioned above, this terminology is mainly used by the supervisory bodies of the European Convention on Human Rights.

The Commission and the European Court of Human Rights have used the concept of "objective obligations" since the famous 1961 decision in the *Austria v. Italy* case.[14] Some important passages of the decision read:

> [. . .] the Contracting States have not wished to grant each other reciprocal rights and obligations in pursuit of their respective national interests, but to achieve the aims and ideals of the Council of Europe [. . .] and to establish a community public order [. . .] the obligations undertaken by the Contracting States [. . .] are essentially of an objective nature [. . .] the objective nature of these undertakings is also reflected in the mechanism set up in the Convention to ensure compliance with them; [. . .] a Contracting State, when referring a matter to the Commission [. . .] should therefore not be regarded as acting to ensure respect for its own rights, but rather as submitting to the Commission a question which affects the public order of Europe.

Subsequently, the Strasbourg bodies repeated the same concepts many times, stating: (*a*) that the European Convention goes beyond the traditional reciprocity of conventional obligations, since it creates, over and above a bundle of reciprocal commitments, objective obligations; (*b*) that these objective obligations benefit from a "collective guarantee" mechanism, since it allows each Contracting State to bring an action before the supervisory bodies even if the violation by another State does not create an injury to one of its nationals; (*c*) that the Convention establishes "a constitutional instrument of European public order".[15]

The Inter-American Court of Human Rights has also sometimes used the notion of "objective obligations":

> The American Convention and the other human rights treaties are inspired by a set of higher common values [. . .] are endowed with specific supervisory mechanisms, are applied as a

[14] ECmHR, *Austria v. Italy*, pp. 18–19.

[15] ECtHR, *Loizidou v. Turkey (preliminary objections)*, Judgment of 23 March 1995, paras. 70 and 75; *Ireland v. UK*, para. 239.

> collective guarantee, embody essentially objective obligations, and have a special character that sets them apart from other treaties.[16]

In reality, the concept of "objective obligations" is not entirely clear and is often confused with those, examined above, of "non-reciprocal obligations" or "obligations *erga omnes partes*". But, in my view, the notion of "objective obligations" contains, compared to the other two concepts, a *quid pluris*, consisting of two elements, which are quite clear especially from the case-law of the ECHR bodies: (*a*) the common purpose of the States Parties to achieve, instead of their own national interests, the objectives and ideals of the Council of Europe, and therefore a "European public order"; (*b*) the existence of a collective guarantee mechanism, which is suitable to achieve this purpose.

These two elements are also present, *mutatis mutandis*, in other conventional human rights systems, such as, for example, the Inter-American system, the African system, the UN Treaty-Bodies system; but not in all human rights treaties. Therefore, it can be concluded that, while the "*erga omnes partes*" character of obligations is present, in principle, in all human rights treaties, the "objective" character of such obligations is present only in some more advanced conventional systems. In particular, it is present in those systems where: (*a*) the collective and solidarity-based purpose of the States Parties to protect the human rights of all individuals is also accompanied by the broader purpose of achieving the objectives of the international organization uniting States Parties; (*b*) the collective guarantee mechanism is not limited to the possibility for all States to react to the violation by one State by the traditional means of general international law; but extends to the standing of each State Party (and sometimes also of the individual victim) to claim the breach before judicial or quasi-judicial bodies against another State Party, even when it does not create an injury to the former State or one of its nationals. In other words, in "objective obligations" the collective guarantee of their compliance is more progressive and effective because it is institutionalized.

Therefore, it can be concluded that the "objective" nature of conventional human rights obligations is apt to define the particular nature of *certain* conventional human rights obligations; but it is *not* apt to explain the "specialty" of *all* human rights treaties.

4.1.3 Theory on the Peremptory Character of Human Rights Norms. Criticism

According to a third opinion, supported in doctrine by some authors, human rights treaties are characterized by other treaties because human rights norms represent universal values and therefore have the character of *jus cogens*.[17] This would be

[16] IACtHR, *Ivcher Bronstein*, para. 42.

[17] See McDougal (1980), p. 279; Suy (1983), p. 939; Mosler (1980), p. 19.

confirmed by the fact that some general treaties on human rights expressly provide that certain rights are non-derogable.

However, there are a number of objections to this view. First of all, the above mentioned treaties define some human rights as "non-derogable in time of emergency", but this concept, as we shall see,[18] does not correspond to that of "peremptory norms". Secondly, these treaties expressly state that *only some* of the protected rights are "non-derogable in time of emergency".

Thirdly, as we shall also see,[19] it must be observed, on the basis of prevailing practice and doctrine, that only the norms of general international law can have the character of *jus cogens*; and that only a limited nucleus of human rights has been incorporated into the norms of general international law. Moreover, there is also no coincidence between human rights incorporated into general international law and those protected by *jus cogens*. Finally, as already noted,[20] it is also impossible to accept that there is a coincidence between the norms of *jus cogens* and the norms containing *erga omnes* obligations (and even less so the treaty norms containing only *erga omnes partes* obligations).

In conclusion, the argument about the peremptory nature of all conventional human rights norms *cannot* be accepted.

4.1.4 Theory on the "Constitutional" Nature of Human Rights Treaties. Criticism

According to a fourth, rather recent doctrinal theory, international human rights law would not only be an area of international law, but would represent a constitutional dimension of that law, as such binding on States even beyond their permanent will to be bound. In this sense, human rights treaties would not be "normal" treaties between States, but would constitute an embryonic form of a *global constitution*. In other words, conventional human rights norms would assume, in the contemporary international order, a function similar to that performed by constitutional norms in domestic legal systems.[21]

The "constitutional" nature of human rights norms would be based on their link with fundamental moral values and on the fact that individuals are the main addressees of these norms;[22] but this "constitutional" nature would not coincide with that of *jus cogens*. The latter concept would be more restrictive and human rights norms that have a *jus cogens* character would represent only a limited and extreme example of the constitutional nature of human rights norms, with the effect of conferring a formal supremacy of *jus cogens* norms over other norms

---

[18]See below, Sects. 13.3.3 and 13.3.5.

[19]See below, Sects. 13.3.4 and 13.3.5.

[20]See above, Sect. 2.3.3.

[21]See Scheinin (2009), pp. 29–31, and the other authors cited by Russo (2012), p. 295, note 28.

[22]Scheinin (2009), p. 30.

(constitutional nature in the formal sense). Instead, the constitutional nature of all human rights norms, here under consideration, would only have the effect of giving special character to the rules governing the interpretation and application of human rights treaties (constitutional nature in the substantive sense).

The theory of the "constitutional" nature of human rights treaties, in my view, is not based on objective elements of international practice and case-law. The reference, sometimes made, to certain judgments of the European Court of Human Rights, in which the Court defines the European Convention as a "constitutional instrument of European public order"[23] can be explained, as we have seen,[24] within the framework of the concept of the "objective nature" of human rights obligations, which, however, concerns *only* certain conventional human rights norms incorporated into institutionalized systems. In any case, this reference is not sufficient to demonstrate the alleged "constitutional nature" of all human rights treaties. Moreover, as has also been pointed out by others,[25] it is difficult to argue that conventional human rights norms, which are included in a plurality of normative systems at the universal and regional levels,[26] constitute the expression of a substantive constituent power and give rise to a single system of protection for the individual. Therefore, the argument about the "constitutional" nature of human rights treaties *cannot* be accepted.

Nevertheless, this theory has the merit of capturing some important aspects. In the first place, as already seen, international human rights law has had a considerable impact on the process of (albeit partial) opening to a "public" dimension of international law, by increasing the protection of collective and solidarity interests.[27] This "public" aspect of the treaties on human rights is relevant; but it does not seem to me that it can even be equated with their "constitutional" function in the international order. Secondly, I share the view that human rights treaties have a link with fundamental moral values; at least in the sense that they pursue the aim of "universalizing" the protection of the human person. This means, in my view that the *principle of universality of human rights* also applies to treaties, and not only to general international law. And indeed, as I will discuss later,[28] the functioning of this principle explains some of the "special" effects of human rights treaties, which tend to favor their continuity and the widest possible participation of States in such treaties. Thirdly, as we shall see immediately, I share another aspect of this theory, namely the view that individuals are the main addressees of human rights treaties.

However, despite these aspects, the theory under examination is *not* convincing for the above reasons.

---

[23]See, for example, ECtHR, *Banković*, para. 80.

[24]See above, Sect. 4.1.2.

[25]Russo (2012), p. 295.

[26]See below, Part IV.

[27]See above, Sect. 2.3.3.

[28]See below, Sects. 4.2 and 4.3.

4.1.5 Individuals as Addressees of Human Rights Treaties

Finally, there is a fifth doctrinal theory, which serves to explain the difference between human rights treaties and other treaties. It argues that human rights treaties have individuals as their primary addressees (or at least as addressees beside States). This theory starts from the general assumption that individuals are, in the reality of contemporary international law, subjects or, if you prefer, *formal addressees* of international law.[29] It follows that human rights treaties impose obligations on States to which correspond both the rights of other States and the rights of individuals. In other words, these treaties have a "binary" character, creating two categories of addressees or rather two categories of legal relations: one that binds the contracting States among themselves (according to the scheme of *erga omnes partes* obligations) and one that binds each contracting State to the individuals who are the true recipients of protection.

This means that States Parties, after ratifying human rights treaties, are restricted in their power to act by virtue of the rights conferred on individuals. In other words, the recognition of individual rights, directly attributed at international level by human rights treaties, ends up creating a *legal regime for the protection of individuals* that tends to be unchangeable unilaterally by the will of the States Parties.

In my view, this is the most convincing and decisive theory to explain *certain particular features* of human rights treaties compared to traditional international treaties, which only establish obligations between States or between international organizations (or between States and international organizations). The presence of individuals as direct and formal addressees of conventional human rights norms explains and justifies, as we shall see, the existence and functioning of a number of particular rules, which derogate or partially supplement the traditional rules of the law of treaties, with the aim of favoring the maximum protection of individuals. This protection of *individual rights* takes the form, in practice, of a legal regime which, on the one hand, favors the stability, or at least the continuity, of human rights treaties[30] and, on the other hand, promotes an interpretation that is favorable to individual rights rather than State rights.[31]

Ultimately, this theory, which is based primarily on the assumption that human rights treaties have the purpose of creating a legal regime for the protection of individuals, is the one that most emphasizes the guiding principle of the *primacy of the individual.* It finds various confirmations in the case-law and practice of international supervisory bodies. The Human Rights Committee, for example, has stated that:

---

[29]See above, Sect. 2.3.2 and below, Sect. 7.2.2.

[30]Through special rules on reservations, State succession in treaties, causes of treaty termination and withdrawal. See below, Sect. 4.2.

[31]Through special rules on dynamic interpretation, autonomous legal notions, positive obligations, "horizontal effects" of human rights. See below, Sect. 4.3.

> The rights enshrined in the Covenant belong to the people living in the territory of the State party. The Human Rights Committee has consistently taken the view, as evidenced by its long-standing practice, that once the people are accorded the protection of the rights under the Covenant, such protection devolves with territory and continues to belong to them [. . .].[32]

In conclusion, in my view, the theory based on individuals as the main addressees of human rights treaties is the most appropriate, together with that of the solidarity character of obligations, to define the particular nature of conventional human rights obligations. But even such theory *alone and in itself* (such as the one on *erga omnes partes* obligations) is not sufficient to explain the "specialty" of human rights treaties compared to other treaties. In fact, human rights treaties are the main, but not the only, examples of treaties that have individuals as formal addressees.

4.1.6 Provisional Conclusions: Impact of the Principles of Primacy of the Individual and Universality of Human Rights

The examination conducted so far, of the various theories on which the so-called "specialty" of human rights treaties is based, has led us to some tentative conclusions, which will need to be verified below.

The first conclusion is that human rights treaties always possess two important characteristics: (*a*) they are also (and mainly) addressed *directly and formally* to individuals; (*b*) they establish (in their substantive provisions) obligations *erga omnes partes*. These are characteristics that distinguish them from traditional treaties; but they do not belong exclusively to human rights treaties. Moreover, *some* important human rights treaties, which result from an international organization and which have a judicial or quasi-judicial collective guarantee mechanism, can also be defined as treaties that create an "objective" legal regime; i.e. a *quid pluris* with respect to other human rights treaties. In my view, one cannot go beyond this conclusion; that is, one cannot adhere to the theory that all human rights treaties have a peremptory character or are "constitutional" in nature.

The second conclusion is that conventional human rights norms, as well as those of general international law, are inspired, influenced, and perhaps even directed by the two general guiding principles I have already discussed: (*a*) the principle of the *primacy of the individual* (which is mainly expressed in the fact that individuals are the main addressees of human rights); and (*b*) the principle of the *universality of human rights* (which is expressed primarily in the concepts of obligations *erga omnes partes* and "objective" legal regimes). Moreover, it should be noted that in the case of treaty norms, compared to those of general international law, there is a

---

[32]HRCtee, General Comment No. 26, 8 December 1997, para. 3. The Committee also seems to be based on principles such as good faith or the recognition of acquired rights or the territorial link between human rights treaties and individuals. On the analogy between the regime of acquired rights and the regime of human rights treaties see Mullerson (1993).

reversal of the importance of the two principles: the primacy of the individual is more relevant. This is logical, since the principle of universality can only play a limited role in treaty law (with the partial exception of the human rights treaties promoted by the UN).[33]

The question now is whether and how these two general principles and these two features of human rights treaties give rise to certain *special* rules, which supplement or derogate from the traditional rules of the law of treaties. That is, what are the concrete *effects* of the two principles?

Anticipating my conclusions here, the main effects of the two principles are as follows. Firstly, the principle of the primacy of the individual tends to create a legal regime for the protection of individuals, which promotes *stability* and *continuity* of human rights treaties. This stability/continuity effect is reinforced by the principle of the universal value of human rights, which tends to encourage the widest possible participation by States in human rights treaties. Secondly, these two principles have an effect on the *interpretation* of the treaties in the sense of fostering the greatest possible protection for individual rights, broadening their scope and strengthening their effectiveness.

Let us now examine these effects in more detail. I will first deal with those relating to the regime of stability and continuity of human rights treaties, and then with those relating to the regime of their interpretation.

4.2 Effects of the Two Principles on the Stability and Continuity of the Treaties

An overall examination of the implementing practice of human rights treaties reveals the existence of certain *special rules*, which have introduced innovations with respect to the traditional customary regime of the law of treaties, in the sense of influencing the stability and continuity of the treaties and the amplitude of the Contracting States. These particular rules concern: (*a*) reservations; (*b*) State succession in treaties; (*c*) causes of treaty termination.

4.2.1 Reservations

A first example of innovative practice, compared to the traditional law of treaties, is in the area of reservations in human rights treaties.[34] The traditional regime on reservations, as is well known, is based on the 1951 advisory opinion of the International Court of Justice on the UN Convention against Genocide[35] and on

[33]See below, Sect. 10.4.

[34]On the subject see, among others, Sudre (2006), pp. 65–75; Boerefijn (2009); Russo (2012), pp. 1–70.

[35]ICJ, *Reservations to the Convention on the Prevention and Punishment of the Crime of Genocide.*

Articles 19–23 of the 1969 Vienna Convention on the Law of Treaties. In summary, this regime provides that a State may make a reservation provided that it is not expressly prohibited or implicitly excluded by the treaty and provided that it is not incompatible with the object and purpose of the treaty.[36] In addition, where the reservation is not authorized by the treaty, it may be challenged by another Contracting State by manifesting a clearly contrary intention;[37] in such a case the objecting State may consider that the treaty does not enter into force in its relations with the State making the reservation. The Vienna Convention also provides for other detailed provisions, but these are not considered to codify customary international law.

Compared to this traditional customary regime, the practice of international human rights monitoring bodies has brought at least two important innovations.

First, in the traditional regime it was not clear which criterion prevailed between the subjective criterion of the objections and acceptances of the reservations by the Contracting States and the objective criterion of the contrariety of the reservation to the purpose and object of the treaty; nor it was clear who could decide whether or not the objective criterion was met. The innovation is that the Inter-American Court of Human Rights, the Commission and the European Court of Human Rights and also the Human Rights Committee have claimed their autonomous power to decide whether reservations in human rights treaties are valid or not.[38] The Strasbourg bodies have derived their competence to decide on the validity of reservations "from the very system of the European Convention" and the "objective" nature of the obligations contained therein. The Human Rights Committee took an even more radical stance, stating that:

> it necessarily falls to the Committee to determine whether a specific reservation is compatible with the object and purpose of the Covenant. [. . .] Because of the special character of a human rights treaty, the compatibility of a reservation with the object and purpose of the Covenant must be established objectively, by reference to legal principles, and the Committee is particularly well placed to perform this task.[39]

Secondly, another innovation, even more important in relation to the traditional regime, concerns the consequences of the established invalidity of a reservation. The international monitoring bodies of human rights treaties, particularly at the instigation of the Strasbourg Court[40] and the Human Rights Committee,[41] have stated that,

---

[36] Art. 19 of the Vienna Convention.

[37] Art. 20(4)(b) of the Vienna Convention.

[38] See Conforti (2018), pp. 109–110 and the practice cited therein. See also Russo (2012), pp. 42–64.

[39] HRCtee, General Comment No. 24, 4 November 1994, para. 18.

[40] ECtHR, *Belilos*, para. 60; ECtHR, *Weber*, paras. 38–40; ECtHR, *Loizidou (preliminary objections)*, Judgment of 23 March 1995, paras. 90–98.

[41] HRCtee, General Comment No. 24, 4 November 1994; HRCtee, *Kennedy v. Trinidad and Tobago*, para. 6. See also the practice cited by Russo (2012), pp. 53–60.

once a reservation has been declared invalid, particularly because it is contrary to the object and purpose of the treaty, the invalidity does not result in the State making the reservation extraneous to the treaty, but in the invalidity of the reservation alone. It is clear that this solution is highly innovative, if not conflicting, with the traditional regime of reservations, and that it greatly limits the consensualist principle typical of conventional international law.[42]

How is this innovative solution justified? The Strasbourg Court seems to explain its position both on the basis of an implicit willingness of the State making the reservation to participate in the ECHR in any event and on the basis of the aim of preventing the protection provided for by the ECHR from being subject to limits which hinder it from achieving its purpose and object. A similar position has been taken by the Inter-American Court of Human Rights, which refers to the need to protect a:

> set of higher common values [. . .] endowed with specific supervisory mechanisms, (that) are applied as a collective guarantee.[43]

The Human Rights Committee has taken a more radical stance, since it considers that the rule of the elimination of reservations declared invalid is automatically applicable, without needing to take into account the implicit will of the State making the reservation.[44]

In my view, the innovative practice under consideration here is influenced both by the principle of the *universality of human rights* and by that of the *primacy of the individual.* In fact, from the first point of view, it tends to favor the widest possible participation of States in human rights treaties by placing limits on the consensualist principle, while from the second point of view, it tends to favor the interest of individuals to enjoy all the rights guaranteed by the treaty over the interest of States to place reservations on some of these rights.

4.2.2 State Succession in Treaties

A second example of innovative practice, compared with the traditional customary regime of the law of treaties, takes place in the area of State succession in human rights treaties.[45] The traditional regime provides that, for the so-called "non-localizable" treaties, the *tabula rasa* rule applies; that is, the "successor" State is not, in principle, and with some specific exceptions, bound by the treaties concluded by the predecessor State.

---

[42]Conforti (2018), p. 110.

[43]IACtHR, *Hilaire v. Trinidad and Tobago (preliminary exceptions)*, paras. 93–94.

[44]HRCtee, General Comment No. 24, 4 November 1994, para. 19. See also Russo (2012), pp. 56 and 60.

[45]On the topic see, among others, Sudre (2006), p. 77; Kamminga (2009); Russo (2012), pp. 167–276.

Compared to this traditional regime, the practice of international human rights monitoring bodies has brought a novelty, because it shows a clear trend in favor of the continuity (i.e. automatic succession) of multilateral human rights treaties. In this sense, the Commission on Human Rights was the first, albeit not in a clear-cut manner, to express its opinion in three resolutions adopted in the 1990s,[46] in which it urged newly formed States to guarantee, as soon as possible after their independence, the succession of human rights treaties, understood as continuity in conventional obligations. In one of these resolutions, the Commission:

> Reiterates its call to successor States which have not yet done so to confirm to appropriate depositaries that they *continue to be bound* by obligations under international human rights treaties.[47]

The Human Rights Committee has clearly adopted the same position and has stated several times, in relation to specific cases, that continuity for the "successor" State in the obligations assumed by the predecessor State with the Covenant on Civil and Political Rights is automatic, because it is linked to the right of individuals who are on the territory of that State to maintain the protection of human rights recognized in the Covenant.[48] This position was then reiterated, in more general terms, in General Comment No. 26:

> [...] once the people are accorded the protection of the rights under the Covenant, such protection devolves with the territory and continues to belong to them, notwithstanding change in government of the State party, including dismemberment in more than one State or State succession or any subsequent action of the State party designed to divest them of the rights guaranteed by the Covenant.[49]

The Committee subsequently maintained the same position. A similar practice has been followed by the Committee on the Elimination of Racial Discrimination.[50] The European Court of Human Rights implicitly adopted the same position with regard to the succession of States in the European Convention, attributing to the Czech Republic or to Slovakia certain violations of the Convention committed by Czechoslovakia as a predecessor State.[51]

Finally, the issue of State succession in human rights treaties was brought before the International Court of Justice during a dispute over the *Application of the*

---

[46]See the resolutions of 5 March 1993, 25 February 1994 and 24 February 1995, cited by Russo (2012), p. 253.

[47]CmHR, Resolution No. 18 of 24 February 1995 (emphasis added).

[48]See the Committee's practice cited by Russo (2012), pp. 254–259.

[49]HRCtee, General Comment No. 26, 8 December 1997, para. 4.

[50]CteeAT, General Recommendation No. 12, 20 March 1993. See also the practice cited by Russo (2012), pp. 259–60.

[51]ECtHR, *Matter v. Slovakia*, para. 52; *Chovancik v. Slovakia*, para. 18; *Konečný v. Czech Republic*, para. 62.

Genocide Convention.[52] Bosnia-Herzegovina supported the existence of the rule of automatic succession in human rights treaties, while the Federal Republic of Yugoslavia denied the operation of this rule. The Court did not take a position on this issue, which was however addressed in the separate opinions of some judges, who were in favor of the automatic succession rule in human rights treaties.[53]

In conclusion, the innovative rule on State succession in treaties, which provides for continuity for the "successor" State in the conventional human rights obligations assumed by the predecessor State, seems to have become established in practice. The justification for this rule rests primarily on the argument that individuals are the main addressees of human rights treaties and therefore have a right to continuity of protection, regardless of the consent of the States. On a more general level, it seems clear to me that this rule is influenced by the guiding principle of the *primacy of the individual* in human rights treaties. The principle of the *universality of human rights* also plays a role, as the rule of automatic succession promotes the widest possible participation of States in the treaties in question.

4.2.3 Causes of Treaty Termination

Finally, a third example of innovative practice, developed in human rights treaties compared to the traditional law of treaties, occurs in certain rules relating to the causes of treaty termination. These are the rules concerning: (*a*) material breach of treaty by a State party; (*b*) the effects of armed conflict on the treaty; and (*c*) withdrawal not provided for in the treaty. Let me now briefly and separately examine these rules.

4.2.3.1 Material Breach of Treaty

Article 60 of the Vienna Convention on the Law of Treaties provides that a material breach of a treaty, bilateral or multilateral, by one of the States Parties shall entitle the other States Parties to terminate or suspend the treaty, in whole or in part. However, Article 60(5) provides for an exception to this rule:

> Paragraphs 1 to 3 do not apply to provisions relating to the protection of the human person contained in treaties of a humanitarian character, in particular to provisions prohibiting any form of reprisals against persons protected by such treaties.

[52] ICJ, *Application of the Convention on the Prevention and Punishment of the Crime of Genocide*, Judgment of 11 July 1996, p. 595.

[53] *Ibidem*, Separate Opinions of Judges Shahabuddeen (p. 635 ff.), Weeramantry (p. 640 ff.) and Parra-Aranguren (p. 656).

The general rule of Article 60 is regarded as a codification of customary international law by both the International Court of Justice[54] and unanimous doctrine.[55] The exception in Article 60(5), the genesis of which in the preparatory work for the Vienna Convention is well known,[56] is also regarded as part of customary law. However, the question has been discussed as to whether this exception should be limited, in a literal interpretation, to humanitarian law treaties alone or whether it should also be extended to human rights treaties.[57] This second, more extensive interpretation has now become established in international practice.[58]

This confirms that the purpose of the exception is to keep alive, through the exception to the rule of termination or suspension for material breach, those conventional provisions that protect the human rights of individuals. Again, the continuity and stability of human rights treaties depends, in my view, on the fact that individuals are the main addressees of these treaties. Therefore, the guiding principle of the *primacy of the individual* operates. Moreover, this continuity and stability also indirectly promotes the large participation of States in human rights treaties and is therefore also linked to the principle of the *universality of human rights*.

4.2.3.2 Effects of Armed Conflict

The need to ensure the continuity of conventional human rights norms also operates with reference to the rules of the law of treaties governing the effects of armed conflict on treaty termination and suspension.[59] In truth, the exact content of the customary rules is rather controversial, as these rules have changed over time.[60] In summary, on the basis of the dominant opinion, it can be said that, until the First World War, the rule of the termination of treaties prevailed in relations between belligerent States. In the period between the two World Wars, some exceptions to the rule of termination were established, in the sense that some treaties, such as those of a commercial nature, were only suspended and others, such as those of humanitarian law or those constituting permanent regimes, remained in force even during armed conflicts. The practice of the post-World War II period seems to be oriented towards a general regime that favors the suspension (instead of termination) of treaties between belligerent States.

---

[54]ICJ, *Legal Consequences for States of the Continued Presence of South Africa in Namibia*, para. 94; ICJ, *Gabčikovo-Nagymaros Project*, para. 46.

[55]However, it is controversial in doctrine whether the rule derives from the law of treaties or that of State responsibility or from one or the other area depending on the circumstances and the type of reaction to the treaty breach. See, among others, Simma (1970); Pisillo Mazzeschi (1984); Sicilianos (1993); Forlati (2005).

[56]See Pisillo Mazzeschi (1984), pp. 147–154.

[57]On this point see Russo (2012), pp. 88–90.

[58]ICJ, *Legal Consequences for States of the Continued Presence of South Africa in Namibia*, para. 122.

[59]See Russo (2012), pp. 106–122.

[60]See the doctrine cited by Russo (2012), pp. 106–109.

However, the even more recent practice, which emerges above all from the ILC codification work of the topic,[61] is oriented towards a "mixed" legal regime, based on the nature, object and purpose of each treaty. In essence, depending on their content, many treaties are suspended, some are terminated, and others remain in force between the belligerent States. It should be noted that the ILC expressly lists human rights treaties among those that remain in force during armed conflicts. According to the ILC, the rule of "continuity" of human rights treaties is clearly derived from the most recent practice. Indeed, this is also confirmed by two advisory opinions of the ICJ[62] and in positions taken by the Human Rights Committee.[63]

Therefore, it can be concluded that the rule of continuity of human rights treaties has gradually become established; and that it has innovated both with respect to the oldest general rule of the termination of treaties and with respect to the more modern rule of their suspension. In my view, there are also various legal and logical reasons for the rule of continuity in the field of human rights. Firstly, and again, since individuals are the main addressees of human rights treaties, there is no reason why their rights should be overwhelmed by a conflict that primarily affects relations between States. Secondly, the collective interest of the international community as a whole tends to favor the continuity of human rights treaties and to prevail over the individual interests of the belligerent States.[64] Ultimately, also with regard to the effects of armed conflict on treaties, the rules applicable to human rights treaties are inspired by the two guiding principles of the *primacy of the individual* and the *universality of human rights*.

4.2.3.3 Withdrawal Not Provided for in the Treaty

Many treaties, including some human rights treaties, expressly allow the right of withdrawal for States Parties. In such cases, of course, the legitimacy of withdrawal is not in question, even though, in practice, cases of withdrawal by a State from a human rights treaty, even if it did provide for that right, have so far been rare and have been criticized by other States Parties as well as by international human rights monitoring bodies.

Instead the problem arises with treaties that do not provide for an express right of withdrawal.[65] Among these, there are also some important human rights treaties, such as, for example, the two UN Covenants of 1966. In customary international law prior to the 1969 Vienna Convention, the existing rule excluded the right of withdrawal in the absence of a provision in the treaty, in accordance with the general

[61] See ILC, *Draft articles on the effects of armed conflicts on treaties*, 17 May 2011.

[62] ICJ, *Legality of the Threat or Use of Nuclear Weapons*, para. 24; ICJ, *Legal Consequences of the Construction of a Wall*, para. 106.

[63] HRCtee, General Comment No. 31, 26 May 2004, para. 11.

[64] It can also be noted that human rights treaties sometimes provide for the possibility of suspending certain human rights, but not fundamental ones, in situations of necessity and emergency, which may include armed conflict (see below, Sect. 4.4.3). This may mean that, outside the operation of such express clauses, the continuity of human rights norms is the general rule.

[65] See Russo (2012), pp. 137–165.

principle *pacta sunt servanda*. The 1969 Vienna Convention contains an ad hoc provision, Article 56, which confirms, in general terms, the rule excluding the possibility of withdrawal for treaties concluded for an indefinite period, which do not provide for such a possibility, unless: (*a*) it is established that the States Parties intended to admit the possibility of withdrawal; or (*b*) the right of withdrawal can be inferred from the nature of the treaty. In essence, Article 56 limits the right of withdrawal to cases where it results from the implicit will of the States or from the objective nature of the treaty. These two exceptions were probably, at the time of the Vienna Convention, attempts to progressively develop customary law. The most problematic exception is the one based on the nature of the treaty.

Can it be considered that the two exceptions to the traditional rule have now become part of customary international law? The answer is probably in the affirmative, and it must therefore be concluded that customary law now allows for cases in which a State has the power to withdraw from a treaty that does not expressly provide for that power. But the two exceptions should be interpreted restrictively. In particular, the exception allowing withdrawal when it can be inferred from the nature of the treaty should be interpreted as meaning that certain treaties are intended to regulate interests of an objectively temporary nature.[66]

With regard to human rights treaties, which do not expressly provide for the right of withdrawal, one must assume that this right is excluded. Firstly, this is confirmed by practice.[67] Secondly, the exception based on the implicit will of the States Parties appears impracticable for human rights treaties. The same conclusion applies to the other exception based on the nature of the treaty. Indeed, human rights treaties certainly do not regulate interests of a temporary nature. Moreover, as has been said several times, they are primarily aimed at individuals and at protecting universal values.

In conclusion, here too, many legal and logical factors militate in favor of the continuity and stability of human rights treaties and the widest possible participation by States in them. These factors amply justify the rule against the right of withdrawal.

4.3 Effects of the Two Guiding Principles on Treaty Interpretation

Let us now examine the effects produced by the two guiding principles of the *primacy of the individual* and the *universality of human rights* on the traditional customary regime of treaty interpretation. As we shall see, the implementing practice

[66]The ICJ judgment concerning the *Gabčikovo-Nagymaros* project can be interpreted in this sense, since the Court stated that the permanent nature of the treaty concluded between Hungary and Czechoslovakia excluded the possibility of withdrawal by Hungary. See ICJ, *Gabčikovo-Nagymaros Project*, para. 100.

[67]See the practice cited by Russo (2012), pp. 149–159. See also HRCtee, General Comment No. 26, 8 December 1997, paras. 3–4.

of human rights treaties reveals the existence of some particular rules that present innovative aspects with respect to the traditional rules of the law of treaties. These aspects concern: (*a*) the dynamic and evolutionary method of interpretation of human rights treaties; (*b*) the use of "autonomous" legal notions; (*c*) the concepts of positive obligations and "positive procedural" obligations of States; (*d*) the theory of the so-called "horizontal effects" of human rights.

It should be noted that the main conventional human rights systems, as we shall see further on,[68] have international judicial or quasi-judicial bodies and procedures for monitoring compliance with the treaties. Therefore, these systems have developed mainly through the case-law and practice of the monitoring bodies. For this reason, the methods of interpretation adopted by these bodies have assumed great importance, especially when these methods have innovative aspects.

4.3.1 Dynamic and Evolutionary Interpretation

First of all, the international human rights monitoring bodies have adopted a general method that provides for a *dynamic, teleological and evolutionary* interpretation, with the aim of making human rights treaties as *effective* as possible, and with a view to extending the rights of individuals and not limiting the obligations undertaken by States Parties.

The Commission and the European Court of Human Rights have shown this trend since the early years of their operation.[69] Already in the *Wemhoff* judgment of 1968, the European Court noted that the Preamble to the ECHR refers not only to the safeguarding but also to the development of human rights and stated a general criterion for interpreting the ECHR in the following terms:

> s'agissant d'un traité normatif, il y a lieu d'autre part de rechercher quelle est l'interprétation la plus propre à atteindre le but et à réaliser l'objet de ce traité et non celle qui donnerait l'étendue la plus limitée aux engagements des Parties.[70]

Even in the *Golder* judgment of 1975,[71] the European Court, while referring to the criteria for interpreting the treaties laid down in the 1969 Vienna Convention, reaffirmed its intention to favor a *dynamic and teleological* interpretation of the European Convention. Moreover, the Court has repeatedly stated that it wanted to use an *evolutionary* interpretation, since the Convention is "a living instrument";[72] that it "must be interpreted in the light of the conditions of contemporary times";[73]

---

[68]See below, Part IV.

[69]See, among others, Pustorino (1998), pp. 25–81; Sudre (2006), p. 230 ff.

[70]ECtHR, *Wemhoff*, para. 8.

[71]ECtHR, *Golder*, paras. 33–35.

[72]ECtHR, *Tyrer*, para. 31.

[73]ECtHR, *Marckx*, para. 41.

and that it "calls for a dynamic and evolutionary approach".[74] This method of interpretation by the European Court has subsequently been confirmed in a large number of cases, which cannot be mentioned here. It is only worth recalling that, since the 1970s, the Court has also interpreted the extra-territorial scope of the Convention in a dynamic and evolutionary way;[75] and then, since the early 2000s, it has developed the important innovative case-law on "general measures" for the enforcement of its judgments and the consequences of so-called "structural violations" of the Convention.[76]

This general method of interpretation adopted by the Strasbourg bodies has also greatly influenced other international human rights monitoring bodies. The Human Rights Committee, for example, stated that the Covenant on Civil and Political Rights must be interpreted "as a living instrument and that the rights it protects must be applied in the context and in the light of the situation of contemporary times".[77] The Committee on the Elimination of Racial Discrimination[78] and the European Committee of Social Rights[79] have expressed a similar view. Even more explicit is the practice of the bodies of the American Convention of Human Rights. Take, for example, the evolutionary interpretation given by the Inter-American Court to the right of property in various cases relating to the rights of indigenous peoples.[80]

4.3.2 "Autonomous" Legal Concepts

A second method of interpretation, adopted by international human rights monitoring bodies (which can also be considered as a specification of the dynamic and evolutionary interpretation described above), consists in the use of "autonomous" legal notions; i.e. in giving the terms, expressions and concepts contained in the treaty a "common" and "autonomous" legal meaning with respect to the meanings given in the domestic systems of the individual States Parties. This is in order to make up for the inaccuracies in some terms contained in the treaty, to remedy the differences in the individual domestic laws of the States Parties, and to allow a uniform legal definition of the provisions of the treaty and hence of the obligations of

[74]ECtHR, *Stafford*, para. 68; *Goodwin Christine*, para. 74.

[75]See below, Sects. 9.5 and 9.6. See also De Sena (2002), p. 45 ff.

[76]See below, Sect. 11.1.2. See also Cannone (2018); Saccucci (2018), pp. 17–69; Pustorino (2019), p. 51; Focarelli (2019), pp. 733–734.

[77]HRCtee, *Judge v. Canada*, para. 10.3.

[78]CteeERD, *Hagan v. Australia*, para. 7.3.

[79]ECteeSR, *FIDH v. France*, para. 27.

[80]See, for all, IACtHR, *Mayagna (Sumo) Awas Tingni (Merits)*, paras. 146–155. See also below, Sect. 25.2.

all States Parties.[81] In fact, this method also contributes greatly to strengthening the effectiveness of human rights treaties.

Obviously, there is a general rule of the law of treaties, also codified by the 1969 Vienna Convention,[82] which tends to avoid "unilateralist" interpretations of treaties; that is, to avoid that a norm contained in a treaty may have different meanings depending on the Contracting State to which that norm is to apply at any given time. But this rule takes on *particular force* in treaties governing matters of special interest to individuals, such as trade agreements, agreements on uniform private law, conventions on private international law and procedural law, and even human rights treaties. This is probably due to the fact that, in such matters, the intervention of domestic courts, which could jeopardize a uniform interpretation of the treaty, is more frequent. Moreover, the effectiveness of the rule is best ensured when the treaty provides for an international supervisory, judicial or quasi-judicial body.

The most important human rights treaty systems[83] have both these characteristics. In fact, the method of interpretation based on "autonomous" legal notions has taken on particular importance in these systems; and above all, it allows international monitoring bodies to arrive at a *substantive* and non-formal interpretation of the notions contained in human rights treaties and to give them a *broad* meaning. In this way, a double result is achieved: that of extending the scope of the provisions of the treaties protecting the human rights of individuals and that of strengthening the *effectiveness* of the treaty.[84]

The Commission and the European Court of Human Rights have used the "autonomous" legal concepts method since the early years of their operation.[85] The Strasbourg bodies have used this method, for example, to interpret the terms "law" and "quality of the law";[86] to interpret the notion of "victim" within the meaning of Article 34 of the European Convention;[87] and to interpret the notions of "charge in criminal matters"[88] and "civil rights or obligations"[89] in relation to Article 6 of the European Convention. It should be noted that, particularly with regard to the last two notions, the "autonomous" interpretation has enabled the European Court to extend the guarantees of Article 6 to a wide range of matters which, in many domestic legal systems, did not enjoy such guarantees. To give just one example, think of the extension of the criminal nature to such matters as military disciplinary

[81] See Sudre (2006), p. 234.

[82] See Articles 33 and 31(3) of the Vienna Convention.

[83] See below, Part IV.

[84] Sudre (2006), p. 236.

[85] See Pustorino (1998), pp. 135–144.

[86] ECtHR, *Kruslin*.

[87] See, e.g., ECtHR, *Klass and Others; Norris*.

[88] See, e.g., ECtHR, *Engel and Others; Ozturk*; *Adolf*; *Bloch*.

[89] See, e.g., ECtHR, *König*.

sanctions,[90] sanctions for breaches of competition law, administrative sanctions[91] and numerous tax sanctions.[92]

In a similar way, the Human Rights Committee has also applied the interpretative method of using "autonomous" legal concepts, again with a view to allowing a uniform legal interpretation of the provisions of the Covenant on Civil and Political Rights, and to broadening the scope of the Covenant in the interest of protecting human rights.[93] Finally, the monitoring bodies of the Inter-American human rights system have also used the same method of interpretation.

4.3.3 Positive Obligations and "Positive Procedural" Obligations

Another innovative element, developed from the interpretative practice of human rights treaties, is the theory of positive obligations.

In truth, it must be said that the distinction between negative and positive obligations (to which I shall return later)[94] applies to the general theory of international obligations, and is therefore not specific to the field of human rights. However, it is also true that, in the most important conventional systems on human rights, the international monitoring bodies have progressively made wider and wider use of the category of positive obligations,[95] always with a view to interpreting the conventional norms in a dynamic and evolutionary way and giving them the greatest possible effectiveness. Also in this practice, therefore, one can see the impact of the two guiding principles, cited many times, of the *primacy of the individual* and the *universality of human rights*.

In the area of human rights, negative obligations are conceived as obligations in which the State abstains or does not interfere in the sphere of individual rights and freedoms. Positive international obligations, on the other hand, require the State to intervene, by carrying out certain actions or certain services, in order to promote the realization of individual rights and freedoms. That said, it is easy to understand why, in the evolution of the international protection of human rights, the positive obligations of States have gradually increased compared to negative obligations. In the past, in the era of so-called first generation human rights, such as civil and political rights, there was a tendency to view the obligations of States mostly as negative obligations. Only more recently has the importance of positive obligations been understood in the area of first generation rights as well. But it is mainly with the

---

[90]ECtHR, *Engel and Others*.

[91]See, e.g., ECtHR, *Great Stevens and Others*.

[92]However, it should be pointed out that sometimes the European Court, when interpreting certain concepts not well defined by the European Convention, tries to check whether there is a "European consensus", to be identified by comparing different national legislations.

[93]See, for example, HRCtee, *Gordon C. Van Duzen v. Canada*, para. 10.2; *Wallmann and Others*.

[94]See below, Sect. 8.1.2.

[95]See Pisillo Mazzeschi (2008).

importance acquired by second and third generation human rights that the relevance of positive obligations of States has been better understood.

This means that contemporary international law is not limited to establishing norms on what States should not do against the human person, but also norms to determine what States should do in favor of the human person. In other words, the State's responsibility for the violation of human rights is realized not only when it actively interferes against a human right of individuals; but also when the State does not take the positive measures that the concrete and effective application of human rights requires; that is, when an unlawful omission by public authorities takes place.[96] It is clear that this has represented an important change of perspective in the area of human rights. On the other hand, it is also a particular aspect of a more general phenomenon which affects the whole system of international law and which has often been described as the shift from international law of coexistence to international law of cooperation or interdependence.[97]

This growing importance of positive obligations in the area of human rights, as mentioned above, is very clearly reflected in the practice of international human rights monitoring bodies.[98] Already in the *Airey* decision of 1979,[99] the European Court of Human Rights, with regard to the right of access to justice, argued that the European Convention intends: "protéger des droits non pas théoriques ou illusoires, mais concrets et effectifs"; and that this requires "mesures positives" on the part of the State "qui ne saurait se borner à demeurer passif". In the *Marckx* judgment of the same year, the Court, with regard to the right to private and family life, stated that Article 8 of the Convention:

> [. . .] ne se contente pourtant pas d'astreindre l'Etat à s'abstenir de pareilles ingérences: à cet engagement plutôt négatif peuvent s'ajouter des obligations positives inhérentes à un 'respect' effectif de la vie familiale. Il en résulte notamment que l'Etat [. . .] doit agir de manière à permettre aux intéressés de mener une vie familiale normale.[100]

The Inter-American Court of Human Rights, in the 1999 *Castillo Petruzzi* case, also stated that:

> [. . .] as part of the obligation to ensure human rights, the States parties are to adopt laws for effective protection of the rights and freedoms established in the Convention. As the Commission pointed out, 'this obligation implies positive action, in that States are obliged to adopt new measures' [. . .].[101]

---

[96]Sudre (2006), p. 240.

[97]See above, Sect. 2.3.3.

[98]See Pisillo Mazzeschi (2008), chaps. III, IV, V.

[99]ECtHR, *Airey v. Ireland*, paras. 24–25.

[100]ECtHR, *Marckx*, para. 31.

[101]IACtHR, *Castillo Petruzzi*, para. 202.

Subsequently, other human rights monitoring bodies have also developed a very extensive practice on positive obligations. This practice shows that positive human rights obligations include, in turn, a very diverse set of more specific obligations, which, depending on the content of the activities required of States' public authorities, may include the following categories:[102] (*a*) obligation to have legislation that respects human rights; (*b*) obligation to have an adequate machinery for the prevention of human rights violations and to take concrete preventive measures when circumstances so require; (*c*) obligation to have an adequate machinery for the investigation of human rights violations and to take concrete measures for the investigation of such violations; (*d*) obligation to have an adequate machinery of administration of justice to ascertain human rights violations; (*e*) obligation to grant reparation to victims of human rights violations; (*f*) specific obligations to adopt administrative or judicial acts or concrete measures for the protection of certain human rights; (*g*) obligations to act with a view to progressively ensuring the full realization of certain human rights.

A particular category of positive obligations, which is typical of the human rights field, is that of so-called "procedural"[103] obligations. It has been developed mainly by the Commission and the European Court of Human Rights and has been taken up by other human rights monitoring bodies and the doctrine. This category concerns situations in which a State is obliged to take certain positive measures of a procedural or instrumental nature, of a preventive or repressive character, to protect certain human rights, in particular the right to life and the prohibition of torture and inhuman or degrading treatment. The State's conduct of omission, which does not take the preventive or repressive measures necessary each time according to the concrete situation, constitutes an *autonomous violation* with respect to the substantive violations of the above-mentioned human rights, even if the two types of violations may sometimes coexist.

Moreover, in the breach of the "procedural" obligations, the wrongful omission by the State may be linked both to substantive violations by other State authorities or by individuals, based on the theory of the "horizontal effects" of human rights, which I will discuss later.[104] For example, a State can breach its "procedural" obligation to prevent a violation of the right to life, either by omitting the preventive measures of control over certain operations of its own security forces which have caused a violation of that right,[105] or by omitting the preventive control measures over certain dangerous activities by private individuals, which have then resulted in a breach of the right to life of other private persons.[106] The same goes for the

[102]See Pisillo Mazzeschi (2008), chaps. III, IV, V. See also below, Sect. 8.2 and Parts V and VI, *passim.*

[103]See Pisillo Mazzeschi (2008), pp. 228–230, 393–410 and 414–422; Bestagno (2003), pp. 75–146.

[104]See below, Sect. 4.3.4.

[105]See, e.g., ECtHR, *McCann and Others.*

[106]See, e.g., ECtHR, *Osman.*

repressive measures that the State has a "procedural" obligation to take in order to capture, prosecute and punish both State officials and private individuals who have violated the right to life.

4.3.4 Theory of "Horizontal Effects" of Human Rights

Closely linked to the theory of positive obligations of States is that of the so-called "horizontal effects" of human rights, or rather of certain norms contained in human rights treaties. These are norms that require States Parties to protect individuals against violations of their human rights by other individuals. The "horizontal effect", in essence, consists in extending the application of human rights norms (typically designed to regulate relations between States and individuals) to relations between private individuals. This effect is inspired by the theory of German origin of the *Drittwirkung*, according to which fundamental constitutional rights must be respected by both public authorities and private individuals among themselves.[107]

Here again, the theory of the horizontal effects of human rights norms was first developed by the Commission and the European Court of Human Rights,[108] and then taken up by other international monitoring bodies[109] and by doctrine.[110] In fact, there are many conventional human rights provisions that expressly envisage a horizontal effect for certain human rights. For example, Article 20 of the Covenant on Civil and Political Rights requires States to prohibit, even to private individuals, propaganda in favor of war and appeals to national, racial and religious hatred. Article 17(2) of the same Covenant establishes that the right to privacy must be protected by law and that, therefore, the State must provide legal protection against all interference in the private life of persons also by other individuals or private entities. Instead, many other conventional provisions on human rights do not expressly provide for horizontal effects, but have also been interpreted by international supervisory bodies as likely to produce horizontal effects. Meaningful examples include treaty provisions on the prohibition of torture and inhuman or degrading treatment.

The importance of the horizontal effects of human rights norms is quite clear. The practical *effectiveness* of a large number of human rights would be seriously threatened if States were not also obliged to control human rights abuses in the sphere of relations between private individuals.

The theory of the horizontal effects of human rights has often been considered as a novelty in international law. But in reality, in my view, it is, in most cases, only an application, to the new area of human rights, of a theory that had already developed in other more traditional areas of international law, such as, for example, the

[107]See, among others, Sudre (2006), pp. 244–245.

[108]See, among the first cases, ECtHR, *Young, James and Webster*; *X and Y v. The Netherlands*.

[109]For this practice see Sudre (2006), p. 247.

[110]See Pustorino (1998), pp. 48–50 and the authors cited therein.

protection of aliens; that is, the theory of State responsibility in connection with acts of private individuals. According to this last theory, now commonly accepted, if a foreign citizen suffers an injury in a State by private individuals, that State is responsible if and when its officials, which in the concrete circumstances had an obligation to prevent or repress the injury done by individuals against the alien, have committed an omission in their obligation.

Indeed, the theory of the horizontal effects of human rights is almost always based on the same assumption. Where certain human rights norms impose, explicitly or implicitly, positive obligations with horizontal effects on a State, the responsibility of that State arises only if it is shown that the organs of that State have failed to fulfil their obligation to protect, by preventive or repressive measures, the individuals to whom those obligations are addressed against unlawful acts by other private individuals. In this sense, this theory also includes, within its scope, the above-mentioned more restrictive theory of positive "procedural" obligations, that only applies to certain human rights.

However, there is also a different, rarer application of the theory of the horizontal effects of human rights, which does not presuppose omissive conduct by the State responsible for the violation. These are situations in which the State is responsible for human rights violations committed by individuals against other individuals, for providing the former with the means to carry out the violations; for example, when the domestic law of the State has legitimized or even favored such violations. In this respect, one can recall some judgments of the European Court of Human Rights on freedom of association,[111] freedom of information and the right to privacy.

In summary, the theory of the horizontal effects of human rights, although partly based on concepts already operating in other areas of international law, has had the effect of broadly expanding States' obligations under human rights treaties. Therefore it too is a method of *interpreting* these treaties that fits within the framework of the two guiding principles of the *primacy of the individual* and the *universality of human rights*.

4.4 Limits to the Two Principles: The Prerogatives of States

It has been seen so far that human rights treaties have certain *peculiar* characteristics compared to other international treaties; and that these characteristics are influenced by the two guiding principles of the *primacy of the individual* and the *universality of human rights*. These two principles have favored the development of a practice for the application of such treaties, which has ended up creating innovative, or at least supplementary, rules with respect to the traditional customary rules of the law of treaties. These innovative rules, on the one hand, favor the *stability and continuity* of

[111] ECtHR, *Young, James and Webster*; *Sigurjónsson*; *VgT Verein gegen Tierfrabriken*; *Pla and Puncernau*; *Sciacca.*

human rights treaties[112] and, on the other hand, encourage the *interpretation* of these treaties as favorably as possible to the rights of individuals.[113]

However, this does not mean that States, in setting up and then ratifying human rights treaties, have "abdicated" their sovereignty and have renounced the assertion of their interests in order to favor *only* individual interests. Such a conclusion would be utopian and totally unrealistic. On the contrary, it must be recognized that, in human rights treaties, there are some important limits to the functioning of the two guiding principles mentioned above. These limits, in my view, can be conceived as a protection of the *prerogatives* of States.

The main limits derive from: (*a*) the concept of *subsidiarity*, which governs the relationship between human rights treaties and State legal orders; (*b*) the existence in human rights treaties of *restriction clauses*, which allow national authorities to take measures that interfere with guaranteed rights in order to pursue certain public interests; (*c*) the existence in many human rights treaties of *derogation clauses*, which even allow national authorities to suspend the exercise of many guaranteed rights in more extreme cases of war or public emergency; (*d*) the jurisprudential notion of the so-called "margin of appreciation", which gives States a certain discretionary power to restrict or suspend guaranteed rights.

Let us see now, concisely, these limits.

4.4.1 Subsidiarity

The first limit is the concept (or principle) of subsidiarity. The idea of the subsidiarity of human rights treaties with respect to State legal systems means that it is primarily up to national authorities, and especially domestic courts, to ensure compliance with the human rights enshrined in the treaties. These treaties are therefore subsidiary or, if you like, complementary, from a substantive and procedural point of view, to State legal orders. Moreover, as has been pointed out,[114] the very concept of subsidiarity logically stems from the fact that a State, having ratified a treaty, has the primary obligation to ensure that it is respected in a timely manner and that the means of achieving human rights in practice depend essentially on national governments. Therefore, States take primary responsibility for compliance with human rights treaties and any international monitoring mechanisms only take over when national mechanisms have not worked.

Indeed, the principle of subsidiarity inspires all human rights treaties, even though it has found its broadest elaboration in the system of the European

[112] See (above, Sect. 4.2) the rules on reservations, on State succession, on the causes of treaty termination.

[113] See (above, Sect. 4.3) the rules on dynamic and evolutionary interpretation, on "autonomous" legal notions, on positive obligations and positive "procedural" obligations, on "horizontal effects" of human rights.

[114] Tomuschat (2014), p. 103.

Convention on Human Rights. The case-law of the Strasbourg bodies has, since the early years, expressly established this principle. For example, in the *Belgian Linguistic Case* of 1968, the European Court stated that:

> elle ne saurait se substituer aux autorités nationales compétentes, faute de quoi elle perdrait de vue le caractère subsidiaire du mécanisme international de garantie collective instauré par la Convention.[115]

Even more explicitly, in the *Handyside* judgment of 1976, the same Court said that:

> le mécanisme de sauvegarde instauré par la Convention revêt un caractère subsidiaire par rapport aux systèmes nationaux de garantie des droits de l'homme.[116]

Subsequent case-law of the European Court has confirmed the principle of subsidiarity many times.[117] Moreover, this principle was clearly reaffirmed in the 2012 Brighton Declaration[118] and in Protocol No. 15 to the European Convention.[119]

The EU Charter of Fundamental Rights also contains an explicit provision on the principle of subsidiarity (Art. 51(1)). The American Convention, while not containing an ad hoc provision on this principle, provides in Article 2 that the primary responsibility for the implementation of human rights shall be entrusted to the domestic systems of the States Parties. In the African system of protection of human rights, the so-called principle of complementarity performs similar functions to those of subsidiarity. Furthermore, the African Commission on Human and Peoples' Rights has adhered to the principle of subsidiarity, stating that the primary responsibility for the implementation of the African Charter lies with the States Parties.[120]

Finally, it should be noted that the most important human rights treaties provide for the rule of prior exhaustion of domestic remedies and the right of individuals who are victims of violations to obtain an effective domestic remedy. As we shall see immediately, this rule and this right are the clearest expressions of the principle of subsidiarity, from a procedural point of view.

4.4.1.1 Exhaustion of Domestic Remedies

Human rights treaties that provide for monitoring procedures, for the consideration of complaints concerning violations of the rights guaranteed therein, almost always

[115]ECtHR, *Belgian Linguistic Case*, para. 10 (Interprétation retenue par la Cour).

[116]ECtHR, *Handyside*, para. 48.

[117]See Tomuschat (2014), p. 103 and the case-law cited in note 46.

[118]Council of Europe, Committee of Ministers, Declaration of Brighton, 20 April 2012, paras. 3, 7–9.

[119]Art. 1 of Protocol No. 15 amending the Convention for the Protection of Human Rights and Fundamental Freedoms, Strasbourg, 24 June 2013.

[120]ACmHPR, *Garreth Anver Prince v. South Africa*, para. 50.

contain provisions on the prior exhaustion of domestic remedies.[121] These provisions are essentially similar in that they stipulate that international monitoring bodies will consider complaints only after all domestic remedies existing in the State accused of the violation have been exhausted, in accordance with generally recognized principles of international law. See, for example, Article 35(1) of the European Convention; Article 41(1)(c) of the Covenant on Civil and Political Rights and Articles 2 and 5(2)(b) of its Optional Protocol; Articles 46(1)(a) and 46(2) of the American Convention; and Articles 50 and 56(5) of the African Charter.[122]

The practice of the international supervisory bodies has built up a very extensive application of these provisions on the exhaustion of domestic remedies, so much so that, in my opinion, an ad hoc customary norm can now also be derived from this practice. This norm, although inspired by the oldest customary norm on the exhaustion of domestic remedies in the field of diplomatic protection, actually has its own autonomy and its own specific content, in part different from the older norm.[123]

Anyway, returning to the rules on prior exhaustion contained in the human rights treaties, there is no doubt that they are inspired by the above-examined principle of *subsidiarity* of these treaties with respect to State legal systems. In this respect, it is worth stressing the different foundation between the rule on prior exhaustion in the field of human rights and the similar rule on diplomatic protection. The latter rule concerns, as is well known, the exercise of diplomatic protection by the State claiming the offence suffered by its own citizen, natural or legal person, abroad. It means that a State cannot exercise international action to protect its own citizen, damaged by an offence committed by another State, before the injured person has exhausted the domestic remedies existing in the latter State without obtaining reparation. The rule, according to the dominant doctrine and practice, is based on the assumption that foreigners are subject to the sovereignty of the territorial State; and therefore also on the principles of sovereignty, domestic jurisdiction and non-interference. The main purpose is to grant the territorial State the possibility of repairing the offence caused to the alien before international claims between that State and the nation-State of the offended person come into play.

Instead, in the area of human rights, the foundation of the rule of prior exhaustion shifts decisively from the principle of sovereignty to that of *subsidiarity*. The practice of international human rights monitoring bodies has always avoided mentioning the principle of sovereignty and has instead often referred to the principle of subsidiarity. This fact is very significant. In matters of diplomatic protection, the absolute dominance of the principle of State sovereignty means that the rule of prior exhaustion is intended to protect above all State interests, especially those of the

[121]On the subject in general, see Pisillo Mazzeschi (2004a).

[122]See also Articles 11(3) and 14(7)(a) of the International Convention on the Elimination of All Forms of Racial Discrimination; Articles 21(1)(c) and 22(5)(b) of the 1984 Convention against Torture and Other Cruel, Inhuman or Degrading Treatment or Punishment; Article 4(1) of the Optional Protocol to the Convention on the Elimination of All Forms of Discrimination against Women.

[123]See Pisillo Mazzeschi (2004a), *passim* and esp. pp. 38–53.

territorial State and also, by extension, those of other States. The rule works within the framework of a strictly interstate logic and the interests of the alien who has been offended abroad are completely secondary, if not irrelevant.

On the contrary, in the field of human rights, the principle of subsidiarity shifts the general perspective for interpreting the rule of prior exhaustion. First of all, this principle does not necessarily privilege State interests over individual interests; it does not operate only within the framework of an interstate logic; it does not presuppose a clear separation between the international and domestic spheres; on the contrary, it aims to coordinate the two spheres in an appropriate manner and does not exclude the idea of a certain continuity between them. In other words, international human rights procedures can be conceived as a kind of continuation of internal procedures: the most important function of the rule, in matters of human rights, is to coordinate in a balanced and efficient way the level of international complaints and procedures with the level of national appeals and procedures. This coordination function differentiates the human rights rule, which is clearly procedural and not substantive in nature,[124] from the rule concerning diplomatic protection.

Secondly, the fact that the prior exhaustion rule, in human rights matters, is based on subsidiarity rather than sovereignty, introduces another general change of perspective in interpreting the aims and content of the rule. Indeed, in the practice of human rights monitoring bodies, the importance of the protection of individual interests as opposed to State interests has gradually increased. This has affected the content of the rule in various ways, for example in the regime of exceptions to the rule, which in practice have developed much more widely than those in the field of diplomatic protection.[125] The exceptions (i.e. cases in which the victim is relieved of the burden of exhausting domestic remedies), in the field of human rights, are the following: (*a*) inaccessibility of domestic remedies; (*b*) ineffectiveness or inadequacy of domestic remedies; (*c*) denial and delay of justice; (*d*) so-called "special circumstances"; (*e*) unlawful legislative measures or administrative practices; (*f*) serious and systematic violations of human rights.

This difference between the two rules logically reflects the fact that, while diplomatic protection is a means of settling disputes between States, human rights norms and procedures are primarily aimed at protecting individual rights. Thus, States parties to a human rights treaty, as noted above, must guarantee individuals protection of the rights recognized in the treaty first and foremost in their own domestic law and before their own domestic courts. An important consequence of this is that the rule of prior exhaustion, in human rights treaties, not only has the "negative" function of acting as a filter for claims before international monitoring bodies; it also has the "positive" function of verifying whether or not the domestic system of the member State has complied with its obligations under the treaty. In other words, the rule also serves to control the domestic implementation of human rights and to ensure *effective domestic remedies* for individuals. The "positive"

[124]See Pisillo Mazzeschi (2004a), pp. 81–94.

[125]See Pisillo Mazzeschi (2004a), chap. IV, pp. 171–194.

function of the prior exhaustion rule in the human rights field has been explicitly recognized by international monitoring bodies.[126] Once again, the influence of the principle of the *primacy of the individual* emerges clearly.

4.4.1.2 Right to an Effective Domestic Remedy

The last statement made above is confirmed by the fact that, in human rights treaties, alongside the provisions imposing on the individual victim the burden of exhausting domestic remedies, there are almost always other provisions, which guarantee the individual the right to an *effective remedy* before domestic courts, in order to claim the violation of human rights guaranteed by the treaty and to obtain redress.[127] Examples include Article 2(3) of the Covenant on Civil and Political Rights, Article 13 of the European Convention, Article 25 of the American Convention, Article 7 of the African Charter, Article 47 of the EU Charter of Fundamental Rights, Article 6 of the Convention against Racial Discrimination, Articles 13 and 14 of the UN Convention against Torture.

As already mentioned, in each of these treaties the rule of prior exhaustion of domestic remedies must be closely linked to the right of the individual victim to have an effective domestic remedy. This close link is very clear in the practice of international human rights monitoring bodies.[128] It means that a State party to a human rights treaty must fulfil the obligation to respect these rights in its internal legal system and the additional (and functionally linked) obligation to provide individuals with effective domestic remedies, so that they can effectively enforce these rights. If the State does not fulfil these two obligations, it can no longer use the shield of the prior exhaustion rule. This is for three reasons: (*a*) because the exception of the inaccessibility or ineffectiveness/inadequacy of domestic remedies occurs; (*b*) because the exception of denial of justice also occurs, at least in the most serious cases; (*c*) because the rule of prior exhaustion has not fulfilled its "positive" function in this case.

In essence, the principle of subsidiarity, in the field of human rights, is also implemented in the right to an effective domestic remedy. However, it should be noted that this principle, which still aims to give priority to national authorities over international ones in the task of ensuring compliance with the human rights guaranteed by treaties, has evolved in recent years in the sense of a rebalancing of State and individual interests in favor of the latter. In other words, today the weight of the balance shifts from the defense of State interests to that of the full realization of human rights. One could say that the weight shifts from the "negative" function of the rule of prior exhaustion towards its "positive" function and towards the

---

[126]For the case-law of the European Court, see, e.g., ECtHR, *Aksoy*; *Akdivar and Others*, Judgment of 16 September 1996; *Selmouni*; *Scordino and Others*, Decision of 27 March 2003.

[127]In my view, the right to an effective domestic remedy against human rights violations, now absorbed by the right of access to justice, is also protected by customary international law. See below, Sect. 17.1.

[128]See the practice cited by Pisillo Mazzeschi (2004a), p. 198, notes 190, 191, 192.

strengthening of the individual's human right to obtain effective domestic remedies. It follows that the latter right must now be interpreted extensively, because it is part of the broader human right of *access to justice*, understood as a fundamental procedural right, necessary to guarantee the concrete effectiveness of substantive human rights.[129]

4.4.2 Restriction Clauses

The second limitation to the two guiding principles of the primacy of the individual and the universality of human rights consists of the so-called *restriction clauses*.[130] This limitation, too, demonstrates that States, even with the ratification of human rights treaties, have not given up on asserting their own interests. The restriction clauses are often found in these treaties and mainly concern first generation human rights. In short, they allow national authorities to interfere in protected rights, and to restrict their substance, in order to satisfy certain public interests, which are considered worthy of particular protection. Therefore, these clauses, like the principle of subsidiarity, also highlight in an exemplary manner the dialectic relationship between the protection of individual rights and the defense of State public interests.

The restriction clauses do not apply to a limited number of rights which are sometimes defined as "absolute". This is a term that risks creating some confusion and which, in my view, should have a more restrictive meaning.[131] Anyway, most human rights enjoy only relative protection, as States may, in certain circumstances, restrict their enjoyment.

It should be noted that the restriction clauses have a partially different content in the various human rights treaties. Some clauses are formulated in a broad and generic manner, since they refer to the public interest or public order of the State. Others, equally generic, prohibit any "arbitrary" interference by the State with the human rights guaranteed by the treaty.[132] But many restriction clauses are more precise, since they set out what objectives the State can pursue in restricting the human rights in question. For example, Article 8(2) of the European Convention, on the right to private and family life, states that:

> There shall be no interference by a public authority with the exercise of this right except such as is in accordance with the law and is necessary in a democratic society in the interests of national security, public safety or the economic well-being of the country, for the prevention of disorder or crime, for the protection of health or morals, or for the protection of the rights and freedoms of others.

---

[129] See below, Sect. 17.1.

[130] On the topic see, among others, De Schutter (2010), pp. 288–364; Sudre (2006), p. 206 ff.; Tomuschat (2014), pp. 104–106.

[131] See below, Sect. 13.3.2.

[132] See, for example, CCPR, Articles 6(1), 9(1) and 17(1).

In more concise terms, Article 18(3) of the Covenant on Civil and Political Rights, on freedom of thought, conscience and religion, reads:

> Freedom to manifest one's religion or beliefs may be subject only to such limitations as are prescribed by law and are necessary to protect public safety, order, health, or morals or the fundamental rights and freedoms of others.

If one examines the practice of international human rights monitoring bodies, one can derive a *method*, widely used, for verifying the legitimacy of a State restriction or interference.[133] This procedural method involves four logically separate and successive steps.[134] First, the monitoring body must ascertain the existence of *interference* by the State in the exercise of the human right in question. The concept of interference means that the human right in question is limited or restricted in any way. Once the existence of interference has been established, it must be ascertained that it is based on a legal basis (*legality test*). Third, it must be verified that the interference pursues one of the legitimate grounds for limitation listed in the relevant provision of the treaty (*legitimacy test*). Fourth, it must be assessed whether the interference is "necessary in a democratic society" (*necessity test*). This expression means that such a measure must respond to a pre-eminent social need, i.e. "an actual need in that particular social context, at that particular moment in history".[135] It should be noted that the necessity test often also includes a judgment of *proportionality* of the interference. Sometimes, for the sake of clarity, the judgement of proportionality is kept separate and then constitutes a fifth phase of verification. This assessment means that the monitoring body, after having ascertained that the interference meets a pre-eminent social need, also makes an assessment of the proportionality of the interference to the objectives set by the State authorities.

As said above, the restriction clauses mainly concern first generation human rights. Instead, with regard to treaties or individual treaty provisions on second generation human rights (especially economic, social and cultural rights) and some third generation rights, the argument is partly different,[136] since States usually assume obligations that are not immediate, but "progressive";[137] i.e. they commit themselves to take measures in order to progressively achieve full realization of the rights recognized in the treaty. In this sense, Article 2(1) of the Covenant on Economic, Social and Cultural Rights is exemplary:

[133] See Tomuschat (2014), pp. 105–106 and the practice cited therein.

[134] For one of the first applications of this method see ECtHR, *Sunday Times*.

[135] The definition of the term "necessary" was provided by the European Court in the *Handyside* case. The Court specified that the adjective "necessary" does not mean "indispensable", but neither does it have milder meanings such as "permissible", "normal", "useful", "reasonable" or "appropriate". According to Tomuschat (2014), p. 105, the necessity test requires a "pressing social need" of the State.

[136] See Tomuschat (2014), p. 106.

[137] For obligations "of progressive realization", see below, Sect. 8.2.3.

> Each State Party to the present Covenant undertakes to take steps, individually and through international assistance and co-operation, especially economic and technical, to the maximum of its available resources, with a view to achieving progressively the full realization of the rights recognized in the present Covenant by all appropriate means, including particularly the adoption of legislative measures.

It is clear that, in relation to their "progressive" obligations, as we shall see further on,[138] States have more discretion and time to comply. Therefore, in these cases, human rights are subject to greater limits than those placed by restrictions clauses on human rights containing immediate obligations. But this does not mean that States Parties to treaties that provide for "progressive" obligations do not assume true legally binding obligations. In fact, such States still commit themselves "to take steps", "to the maximum of their available resources" and "by all appropriate means", in order to achieve the "full realization" of human rights.

Therefore, in the first place, the international supervisory bodies must verify the "adequacy" or "reasonableness" of the measures taken by States. This requirement is confirmed by Article 8(4) of the Optional Protocol to the Covenant on Economic, Social and Cultural Rights.[139]

Secondly, States Parties must comply with other obligations:[140] (*a*) they must not adopt regressive measures with respect to the objective of the full realization of the right in question; (*b*) they must not remain totally passive, i.e. avoid taking any action aimed at the above objective; (*c*) they must use the appropriate means to achieve the objective; (*d*) they must use reasonableness in balancing the means and resources used to implement the human right in question with those used to pursue other primary State interests; (*e*) they must ensure an essential minimum level of the human right in question.

4.4.3 Derogation Clauses

The third limitation to the two general principles repeatedly mentioned, which plays in favor of the prerogatives of States, consists of the so-called *derogation clauses*, which are present in the most important general treaties on human rights.[141] These provisions provide for the possibility that a State Party may derogate from many of

---

[138]Below, Sect. 8.2.3.

[139]Optional Protocol to the International Covenant on Economic, Social and Cultural Rights, 18 June 2008, Art. 8(4): "When examining communications under the present Protocol, the Committee shall consider the reasonableness of the steps taken by the State Party in accordance with part II of the Covenant. In doing so, the Committee shall bear in mind that the State Party may adopt a range of possible policy measures for the implementation of the rights set forth in the Covenant".

[140]On these obligations see Pisillo Mazzeschi (2008), pp. 429–489.

[141]On derogation clauses see, inter alia, Higgins (1976-77); Ergec (1987); McDonald (1997); Svensson-McCarthy (1998); Viarengo (2005); Cataldi (2006); Id. (2012); Id. (2019); Sommario (2018).

the rights guaranteed, *rectius* suspend those rights, when it is in a state of public emergency or even war. But the possibility of derogation is subject, as we shall see, to a number of procedural and substantive conditions. The derogation clauses must not be confused with the restriction clauses nor with the concept of rights established by norms of *jus cogens*.[142]

The most famous clause, which is the example of other provisions, is contained in Article 15 of the European Convention.[143] Article 15 states, in summary, that a State Party, in time of war or other public emergency threatening the life of the nation, may take measures derogating from the rights guaranteed by the Convention, to the extent that the situation so requires and provided that the measures do not conflict with other obligations under international law. Certain rights expressly specified are excluded from the possibility of derogation. Finally, Article 15 lays down a procedure whereby the State exercising the derogation must inform the Council of Europe of the measures taken and their termination. The European Court may review compliance with this norm.

Similar provisions are Article 4 of the Covenant on Civil and Political Rights, Article 27 of the American Convention, Article F (Part V) of the European Social Charter (revised), Article 4 of the Arab Charter. By contrast, there are no derogation clauses in other human rights treaties, for example in the Covenant on Economic, Social and Cultural Rights and the African Charter. This perhaps does not prevent a State party to these treaties from invoking, if the conditions laid down in general international law are met, the state of necessity as a circumstance precluding the unlawfulness of an act that violates a human right.

What is the purpose of these derogation clauses? It is to prevent States from suspending human rights with too much freedom or discretion, using the generic state of necessity of general international law, and to delimit and regulate more specifically the procedural and substantive conditions to be met by States in order to suspend the application of human rights; and all this under the control of international judicial or quasi-judicial bodies. In short, it is a question of striking the right balance between security of States and respect for human rights. Indeed, there is a practice, although not particularly extensive, of States applying derogation clauses. For example, in the framework of the European Convention, several States, including France, Greece, the United Kingdom and Turkey, have made use over time of the possibility of derogation under Article 15. Many of these derogations have been motivated by the need to tackle terrorism or separatist movements.

The main legal questions raised by the derogation clauses are three: (*a*) what is the precondition for the derogation; (*b*) what are the procedural conditions that the State

---

[142]For these concepts see also below, Sect. 13.3.

[143]Art. 15: "1. In time of war or other public emergency threatening the life of the nation any High Contracting Party may take measures derogating from its obligations under this Convention to the extent strictly required by the exigencies of the situation, provided that such measures are not inconsistent with its other obligations under international law [. . .]".

must comply with when requesting the derogation; (*c*) what are the substantive conditions justifying the derogation.

The first issue concerns, in essence, the precise definition of the concept of "public emergency". In the system of the European Convention on Human Rights, the Strasbourg bodies have defined this concept since the 1960s,[144] establishing that it means an emergency situation that constitutes a present or imminent threat to the organized life of the State community. The danger must be exceptional, in the sense that the normal measures permitted by the Convention for the maintenance of security and public order must be inadequate to deal with the situation. This initial definition of the concept of "public emergency" has not changed much in subsequent practice before the Strasbourg bodies; but there has been a tendency over time to interpret it more broadly.

In fact, for many years the derogation under Article 15 could not be invoked for preventive purposes only, but required the existence of violence already unleashed on the territory of the State or at least a current or imminent danger on that territory. However, the Strasbourg Court has recently interpreted more broadly the concept of imminent danger, since in the case *A. and Others v. UK*[145] it has stated that the fear of a terrorist attack is justified by the mere existence of international Al-Qaeda terrorism, even though that organization has not carried out any attacks in the United Kingdom. This is because the State can legitimately protect its population from future dangers.

Another interesting point, in the definition of the concept of "public emergency", concerns its spatial dimension. Article 15 of the European Convention seems to require that the emergency, in order to allow the derogation from human rights, should only affect the territory of the State requesting the derogation, but the practice has almost immediately extended the territorial scope of the emergency. For example, in the *Lawless* case, the Commission and then the Court admitted that the terrorist operations of the IRA, although they produced concrete effects only in Ireland, were destined to have consequences also in the United Kingdom.[146] Also in the above-mentioned case *A. and Others v. UK*, the Court ruled that the emergence of international terrorism justified derogation measures taken in the United Kingdom, even though the threat had not actually manifested itself on British territory.[147] In essence, it now seems sufficient that the emergence is likely to produce *effects* on the territory of the State requesting the derogation.

Recently, there has been a further widening of the spatial dimension of the concept of public emergency, leading to a real extraterritorial scope of Article 15. This provision seems to require that the emergency, in order to allow the derogation, must affect, directly or even indirectly (i.e. through its possible effects), only the

---

[144]ECmHR, *Lawless v. Ireland*, Report of 12 April 1960; ECtHR, *Lawless v. Ireland (No. 3)*, Judgment of 1 July 1961; ECtHR, *Greek case.*

[145]ECtHR, *A. and Others v. UK*, para. 216.

[146]ECmHR, *Lawless v. Ireland*; ECtHR, *Lawless v. Ireland (No. 3)*, paras. 27–30 and 36.

[147]ECtHR, *A. and Others v. UK*, para. 180.

territory of the State requesting the derogation. However, both the British High Court of Justice[148] and the Strasbourg Court[149] have recently stated that a State may invoke Article 15 even when the emergency takes place *in a foreign territory*, where that State carries out military operations, such as those undertaken by the United Kingdom in Afghanistan in the post-conflict phase or those conducted in Iraq during the international armed conflict.

Moreover, whereas in older cases the Strasbourg bodies had stated that the emergency should "affect the entire population" of the State requesting the derogation, in some subsequent cases (especially concerning Turkey) they admitted that the emergency could affect only part of the territory and therefore of the population of a State. Of course, in such cases the derogation measures must also have effects *limited* to that part of the territory.[150]

Coming to the Covenant on Civil and Political Rights, Article 4 has a rather similar wording to Article 15 of the European Convention, since it speaks of "public emergency which threatens the life of the nation". However, the Human Rights Committee, in its General Comment No. 29, tends to give a more restrictive interpretation of the concept of public emergency, as it stresses that:

> Not every disturbance or catastrophe qualifies as a public emergency which threatens the life of the nation [. . .] During armed conflict, whether international or non-international, norms of international humanitarian law become applicable and help [. . .] to prevent the abuse of a State's emergency powers. The Covenant requires that even during an armed conflict measures derogating from the Covenant are allowed only if and to the extent that the situation constitutes a threat to the life of the nation.

The second of the main issues raised by the derogation clauses concerns the procedural conditions to be respected by the State. The emergency measures must be officially declared by the State requesting the derogation, respecting the specific provisions laid down in the treaty in question, and notification of the derogation must be given to the international body established in that treaty. For example, Article 15 (3) of the European Convention provides that any State Party availing itself of the right of derogation must keep the Secretary-General of the Council of Europe fully informed of the measures it has taken and the reasons for them. It must also inform the Secretary-General when such derogating measures have ceased to operate and the provisions of the Convention are again fully applied. In a very similar way, Article 4(3) of the Covenant on Civil and Political Rights provides that any State Party wishing to exercise the right of derogation must immediately inform the other States Parties, through the intermediary of the UN Secretary-General, of the provisions of the Covenant it intends to derogate from and the reasons for doing

---

[148]High Court of Justice, *Serdar Mohammed*, paras. 155–158.

[149]ECtHR, *Hassan v. UK*, para. 101 ff.

[150]See, e.g., ECmHR, *France, Norway, Denmark, Sweden and The Netherlands v. Turkey*; ECtHR, *Sakik and Others* v. *Turkey*.

so. A further communication shall be sent on the date on which the State Party ceases to derogate. A similar rule is contained in Article 27(3) of the American Convention.

However, all the treaty provisions mentioned above are silent on the consequences for the State of its failure to communicate and provide the above information. In the event of such a failure, it must, in my view, be considered that the derogation measures taken are unlawful and that the State is responsible to other States Parties and treaty monitoring bodies for breach of the relevant treaty.

The third main issue, the most complex one, concerns the substantive conditions justifying the derogation. These conditions are basically similar, although not identical, in the various treaties mentioned above. For the sake of brevity, I will examine, in particular, those laid down in the European Convention.

Under Article 15 of the Convention, the first, and perhaps the most important condition required is that the derogation measures taken by the State respect the principles of *necessity* and *proportionality*. This follows from the letter of Article 15 which speaks of "measures [. . .] to the extent strictly required by the exigencies of the situation". In my view, a distinction must be made between the concepts of necessity and proportionality, which are different even though they are closely linked.[151] The first concept means that there must be a relationship of strict necessity of the measures taken in relation to the emergency situation. In other words, the State must demonstrate that different and less stringent measures were not sufficient to deal with the emergency. The requirement of proportionality, on the other hand, means that once it has been established that certain derogation measures are necessary, their practical application must be proportionate, i.e. the measures must not be excessive in relation to the purpose of dealing with the emergency. In other words, there must be a link of proportionality between the concrete measures of exercise of exceptional powers and the concrete needs posed by the individual emergency situation.

The second condition, which is supported especially in doctrine, is that of the *limited duration* in time of the derogation measures. It is said that the state of emergency does not usually last indefinitely and that therefore the derogation measures should also be temporary and provisional. From the temporary nature of the measures, the doctrine also deduces an obligation on the State in question to keep the emergency measures in force under continuous review for an ongoing adaptation process.[152] However, the Strasbourg Court recently questioned the limit of the

[151]However, various authors do not distinguish between necessity and proportionality. Even in case-law, the distinction is often not clear-cut.

[152]See, e.g., Cataldi (2012), pp. 558–559. The State's obligation to control derogation measures implicitly results also from some decisions of the European Court (ECtHR, *Ireland v. UK*; *Brannigan and McBride*). Moreover, from the temporary nature of the state of emergency and the derogation measures, the doctrine also deduces that Article 15 is by its very nature unsuitable for regulating situations in which a State often repeats declarations of derogation over time. In fact, many Member States of the European Convention have challenged the practice of Turkey which, in the 1980s, had many times repeated over time the declarations of derogation. In 1985, on the basis of an action brought by five States against Turkey, the Commission agreed that the continued use of

temporary nature of the measures, claiming that its case-law does not explicitly state this limit, even though the proportionality of the responses may be linked to the duration of the emergency.[153] The Court added that there is a possibility of a public emergency continuing for many years.

The third condition, which, on the other hand, is expressly provided for in the above-mentioned treaties, is that the derogation clauses cannot operate for *non-derogable human rights*. Article 15(2) of the European Convention contains a list of provisions which may under no circumstances be suspended because they provide for non-derogable rights in time of emergency.[154] These are the right to life, with one exception; the prohibition of torture and inhuman or degrading treatment or punishment; the prohibition of slavery and servitude; and the principle of non-retroactivity of criminal law. The prohibition of the death penalty and the *ne bis in idem* principle were subsequently added to this list. But the list of non-derogable rights in the European Convention is more limited than that contained in Article 4 of the Covenant on Civil and Political Rights,[155] which also includes the prohibition of discrimination, the prohibition of imprisonment for contractual debts, the right to recognition as a person before the law, and freedom of thought, conscience and religion. Even more extensive is the list of non-derogable rights contained in Article 27 of the American Convention.[156] Moreover, the doctrine considers that other human rights should be implicitly considered as non-derogable in time of emergency, for example the right to an effective domestic remedy. Therefore, the question arises as to exactly which human rights are non-derogable in time of emergency according to general international law; and practice and case-law are not unequivocal in this respect.[157]

The fourth condition, also expressly provided for in the above-mentioned treaties, is that the derogation measures must not conflict with *other obligations under international law*.[158] This means, according to an agreed interpretation, that the derogation measures must comply not only with the limits laid down in the treaty in question, but also with any limits laid down in other norms of international law applicable to the State. Therefore, the State must respect, even in an emergency, other human rights treaties and treaties of international humanitarian law to which it

---

Article 15 measures distorted the State's participation in the Convention (ECmHR, *France, Norway, Denmark, Sweden and The Netherlands v. Turkey*).

[153]ECtHR, *A. and Others v. UK*, para. 178.

[154]It should be noted that this concept of "non-derogation in time of emergency" does not correspond to the concept of peremptoriness of *ius cogens*. On this point see below, Sects. 13.3.3 and 13.3.5.

[155]ECHR, Art. 4(1) and (2).

[156]ACHR, Art. 27(1) and (2).

[157]See below, Sect. 13.3.3.

[158]See ECHR, Art. 15(1); CCPR, Art. 4; ACHR, Art. 27(1).

is a party,[159] as well as the norms of general international law.[160] With regard, in particular, to respect for international humanitarian law, it should be pointed out that the question has recently arisen as to whether this law can also interact in a different way, and in a certain sense the opposite way, with Article 15 of the European Convention; that is, by extending, rather than limiting, the right of States to suspend certain human rights. In other words, the question has been raised in case-law as to whether international humanitarian law can authorize a State, in situations of international or internal armed conflict, to adopt measures which do not respect certain rights protected by the European Convention (e.g. the right to personal liberty), measures which would not be permitted by the Convention itself in peacetime; and whether the State can adopt such measures without having to notify an exemption under Article 15. A positive answer, based on the special nature of international humanitarian law in relation to human rights law, was given by the Strasbourg Court in the famous *Hassan* case.[161] Instead a negative answer, which I believe is more convincing, was given by the British High Court of Justice.[162]

The fifth condition, on which, however, there is no agreement in doctrine, is that the derogation measures respect the *general prohibition of discrimination*.[163] This condition is expressly laid down in some treaties, such as the Covenant on Civil and Political Rights and the American Convention, but not in others, such as the European Convention. The question therefore arises as to whether or not the prohibition of discrimination applies in those treaties that do not expressly provide for it as a limit for derogation measures. The authors who answer in the affirmative argue that this prohibition is part of general international law;[164] and that therefore the condition that derogation measures must comply with the prohibition of

[159]According to Kälin, Künzli (2009), p. 146, the human rights lists contained in Art. 75 of Additional Protocol I and Art. 4 of Additional Protocol II to the Geneva Conventions are particularly relevant.

[160]On the norms of general international law of human rights, see below, Sect. 13.3.4.

[161]ECtHR, *Hassan*. In this judgment, which concerned the conduct of British military personnel in Iraq during an international armed conflict, the Court stated that, even if the United Kingdom had not submitted a formal derogation under Article 15, this did not prevent the interpretation of Article 5 of the European Convention, on personal freedom, taking into account the context of the armed conflict in Iraq and international humanitarian law. It therefore concluded that Article 5 had not been violated. See also above, Sect. 2.4.1.

[162]High Court of Justice, *Serdar Mohammed*. The British High Court of Justice, in this case which concerned the behavior of British military personnel in Afghanistan in the post-conflict phase, strongly rejected the idea that, in times of armed conflict, international humanitarian law could derogate from Article 5 of the European Convention. The Court said that Article 5, which prohibits arrest and detention except in certain listed cases, is a specific rule, which does not allow an exception under humanitarian law. It also rejected the argument that, during an armed conflict, humanitarian law, as a special law, may derogate from the European Convention. The Court therefore concluded that Article 5 had been infringed.

[163]See, e.g., De Schutter (2010), p. 547 ff. Article 4 of the Covenant expressly provides that derogation measures must not lead to discrimination. See also, in a similar sense, Article 27 of the American Convention.

[164]On the prohibition of discrimination see below, Sect. 18.1.

discrimination would already be implicitly included in that of compliance with the international obligations of the State. In my view, this argument can be accepted.

Finally, some authors argue that there is a sixth substantive condition required to make the derogation legitimate, namely that there are adequate *legal guarantees*, and especially judicial procedures, to control possible abuses in the application of the derogation measures. In the case-law of the Strasbourg Court, there are some cases in which the Court has attached importance to such safeguards,[165] and the Commissioner for Human Rights of the Council of Europe has also taken a similar position in his opinion on the derogation communicated by the United Kingdom in 2001 in relation to its anti-terrorism legislation. However, in my view, the practice in support of this sixth condition is too meagre to conclude that it is established by general international law.

In conclusion, the derogation clauses have the merit of laying down rather precise procedural and substantive rules to legitimize human rights derogation measures taken by States. However, they also have some critical aspects. The first concerns the mechanisms for monitoring that the measures respect the procedural and substantive conditions for their legitimacy. In fact, the mechanisms provided for usually operate *only after the event* and incidentally, when an appeal is made to the international judicial or quasi-judicial monitoring bodies provided for in each treaty. Instead, it would be preferable to have an international mechanism of continuous and effective control every time a State communicates that it intends to make use of the derogation clauses.

The second critical aspect stems from the fact that these clauses are designed to deal with exceptional emergency events and do not work well when a State is often in an emergency situation.[166] Furthermore, since the terrorist attacks of 11 September 2001, many States have adopted anti-terrorist measures that are intended to last, regardless of immediate and concrete emergencies. These long-term measures, as already mentioned, do not lend themselves well to falling within the scope of the derogation clauses contained in the main human rights treaties, even though the Strasbourg Court seems recently to be inclined to admit their legitimacy.

The third critical aspect consists in the fact that the mechanism for the operation of the derogation clauses is rather rigid and ends up discouraging its use by States. A recent demonstration of this is the pandemic emergency caused by Covid-19, which forced many States to adopt very restrictive measures of many human rights (freedom of movement and assembly, right to private and family life, etc.), without resorting to the derogation procedures provided by human rights treaties.[167]

All this suggests that perhaps the time has come to review and update the operation of the human rights derogation clauses.

---

[165] See, e.g., ECtHR, *Aksoy; Brannigan and McBride*.

[166] For example, in the case of Turkey.

[167] On this topic see Pustorino (2020), pp. 43–44.

4.4.4 State Margin of Appreciation

Finally, the fourth limitation, which also tends to favor State interests, consists of the so-called "margin of appreciation" of the States, which, in certain respects, could also be considered as an expression or consequence of the principle of subsidiarity.[168]

The legal concept of the margin of appreciation was first developed by the case-law of the Commission and the European Court of Human Rights and then taken up by other international monitoring bodies, such as the African Commission on Human and Peoples' Rights. The practice of the Human Rights Committee has also implicitly applied this notion in some infrequent cases.[169] In contrast, the concept plays a very limited role in the case-law of the Inter-American Court of Human Rights. The importance of this notion within the European Convention system has recently been confirmed, as it was expressly incorporated into the Preamble to the Convention by Protocol No. 15.[170] I will therefore refer mainly to the system of the European Convention.

The margin of appreciation is particularly relevant for human rights which are subject to restriction or derogation clauses by States. Indeed, through this notion, States are granted a certain measure of discretionary power to restrict or even derogate from human rights guaranteed by the treaties. More generally, the concept serves to define, in a flexible manner, the relationship between measures reserved for national autonomy and the competence of international bodies in their function of monitoring human rights treaties. In other words, it serves to strike a difficult balance between national autonomy and conventional international norms, which are, in principle, common to all States Parties.

What are the motivations behind the notion of the margin of appreciation?

First of all, international human rights monitoring bodies are often called upon to rule on *disputes of a sensitive nature*, which can either touch on basic elements of a State's constitutional philosophy[171] or affect the very security of a State. The question then arises of who should take the final decision when, on the basis of a restriction or derogation clause, a State has actually taken measures limiting or even suspending one or more human rights. This applies even though the international monitoring bodies, with a rather obvious style clause, have always stated that the restrictive or suspensive measures adopted by the State remain under their control.

[168] However, I think it is preferable to treat the notion of margin of appreciation separately, since it has its own characteristics and its own autonomy with regard to the principle of subsidiarity, although it has a link with the latter.

[169] See the practice cited by Tomuschat (2014), p. 109.

[170] Protocol No. 15 amending the European Convention for the Protection of Human Rights and Fundamental Freedoms, 24 June 2013, Article 1.

[171] See Tomuschat (2014), p. 107.

Secondly, there is a *practical motivation*;[172] that is, the fact that the national authorities have the best knowledge of the concrete circumstances and local conditions and needs for the application of the human rights norms in question. The European Court, for example, in the *Handyside* case, stated, with regard to a restriction on a freedom, that:

> [. . .] grâce à leurs contacts directs et constants avec les forces vives de leur pays, les autorités de l'Etat se trouvent en principe mieux placés que le juge international pour se prononcer.[173]

The Court has often repeated this motivation.[174]

The African Commission also expressed a similar, if not broader, concept when it said that the State:

> [. . .] has direct and continuous knowledge of its society, its needs, resources, economic and political situation, legal practices, and the final balance that needs to be struck between the competing and sometimes conflicting forces that shape its society.[175]

Thirdly, the margin of appreciation responds to an ideological need, linked to the principle of *pluralism* typical of a democratic society.[176] This motivation is particularly strong in the context of the European Convention. The principle of pluralism requires the Strasbourg Court to pay attention to the diversity of the European States that are parties to the Convention, especially the diversity of their legal cultures,[177] their cultural traditions[178] and the historical and political factors specific to each State.[179] In other words, the European Convention cannot impose "absolute uniformity"[180] of national legislation or a uniform European understanding of certain concepts, such as morality,[181] the meaning of religion in society[182] or the right to abortion.[183]

Finally, a fourth and final reason, which has sometimes emerged from the case-law of the European Court, is the *democratic legitimacy of national authorities*,

[172] See Sudre (2006), p. 217.

[173] ECtHR, *Handyside*, para. 48.

[174] See the case-law cited by Tomuschat (2014), p. 107, note 75.

[175] ACmHPR, *Garreth Anver Prince v. South Africa*, para. 51.

[176] See Sudre (2006), pp. 217–219.

[177] See ECtHR, *Sunday Times*, para. 61, where it is stated that the Court cannot "négliger les caractéristiques de fond et de procédure (des) droits internes respectifs".

[178] See ECtHR, *Casado Coke*, para. 54.

[179] See ECtHR, *Gitonas*, para. 39.

[180] ECtHR, *Sunday Times*, para. 61.

[181] ECtHR, *Handyside*, para. 48.

[182] ECtHR, *Otto-Preminger-Institut*, para. 50.

[183] ECtHR, *Open Door v. Ireland*, para. 63.

which may justify, especially in relation to certain human rights, a restriction of the Court's supervisory power in favor of the State's margin of appreciation.[184]

From these four motivations, which underlie the notion of the margin of appreciation, derive also the *criteria* that the European Court, and other international supervisory bodies, have usually employed to decide whether or not to grant a margin of appreciation to the State in individual disputes; and also to decide whether the State's margin of appreciation should be "wide" or "narrow".

A first criterion, the most important under the European Convention, is the absence or presence of a common denominator in national legal systems. The absence of a common denominator increases the State's margin of appreciation. This applies, in particular, to social issues which have typical national characteristics and which often concern aspects of ethics or morality.[185] Examples are the granting of parental rights to transgender people,[186] the right of access to adoption by homosexuals,[187] and the exhibition of religious symbols in schools.[188] On the contrary, the presence of common legal principles or interpretations between States Parties restricts the margin of appreciation of the State. In other words, if there is a broad European consensus on the content of a human right, there is no reason to leave a margin of appreciation, i.e. a discretionary power of autonomy to the individual State. One can take the examples of the right of equality between legitimate and natural children[189] or the protection of journalistic sources.[190]

A second criterion is the nature of the human right under consideration or the specific legal issues at stake. The international supervisory bodies grant States a margin of appreciation, or even a "wide" margin, when the human right in question affects aspects of morality, with particular regard to sexual morality, which also tend to vary from State to State and be contingent rather than permanent in character.[191] The same is true when the legal issues at stake are very technical and complex or when they are predominantly issues of legal policy, such as, for example, unfair competition[192] or town planning policy.[193] It should also be noted that, when it comes to applying the notion of the margin of appreciation with regard to derogations (and not restrictions) to human rights, the tendency is always to give States a wide margin of appreciation.[194] In fact, derogations bring into play the assessment of emergency situations or public security of the State, issues on which

[184]ECtHR, *Hatton*, para. 97.

[185]See the case-law cited by Tomuschat (2014), p. 108, note 77 and by Sudre (2006), p. 222.

[186]ECtHR, *X, Y and Z v. UK.*

[187]See ECtHR, *Fretté*, para. 41.

[188]See ECtHR, *Leyla Şahin*, paras. 109–110; *Lautsi and Others.*

[189]ECtHR, *Marckx.*

[190]ECtHR, *Goodwin.*

[191]This criterion is highlighted by Sudre (2006), p. 221.

[192]ECtHR, *Markt Intern Verlag GmbH and Klaus Beermann.*

[193]ECtHR, *Sporrong and Lönnroth.*

[194]See Svensson-McCarthy (1998), esp. pp. 313–319 and 324–325.

State autonomy is considered prevalent compared to the uniformity of conventional rules for all States Parties. On the contrary, the supervisory bodies tend to deny the margin of appreciation, or to apply a "narrow" margin, when the right subject to State interference affects the intimate and private sphere of the individual or his identity,[195] evidently considered as values on which conventional norms must prevail over State autonomy. The same applies when a right that is closely linked to the concept of democracy or the rule of law is at stake, such as, for example, freedom of expression or information on issues of public interest.[196] In these cases, too, the need to ensure uniform and common rules among all States Parties to the treaty must clearly prevail.

However, it should be noted that the case-law on the margin of appreciation of the European Court and other international human rights monitoring bodies is not always convincing; and sometimes the application of the margin of appreciation in favor of the State does not seem justified.

On a more general level, in my opinion, it can be concluded that the margin of appreciation theory has for many years been a useful instrument of flexibility in the relationship between national autonomy and international control. In the past, it was justified as a means of recognizing the differences between States Parties and their difficult progress towards more uniform human rights norms. But now, after many years of functioning of the international systems of human rights protection, I believe that the time has come for international monitoring bodies (primarily the European Court) to impose these uniform norms more clearly and courageously on States, and to avoid putting the decision on whether or not a human rights restriction or derogation is legitimate in the hands of governments. In other words, the progress of human rights requires the broadening of the sphere in which these rights must become the common heritage of States.[197] The notion of the margin of appreciation, especially when applied in a "broad" manner, is a serious obstacle to this progress and fuels a harmful relativism in the field of human rights.[198]

References

Benvenisti E (2018) The margin of appreciation, subsidiarity and global challenges to democracy. J Int Disp Settlement 9:240–253

Bestagno F (2003) Diritti umani e impunità. Obblighi positivi degli Stati in materia penale. Vita e Pensiero, Milano

Boerefijn I (2009) Impact on the law of treaty reservations. In: Kamminga MT, Scheinin M (eds) The impact of human rights law on general international law. OUP, Oxford, pp 63–97

[195] See the case-law cited by Sudre (2006), p. 220 and by Tomuschat (2014), p. 108, note 78.

[196] See the case-law cited by Tomuschat (2014), p. 109, notes 87, 88 and 89.

[197] This is even more true in the framework of regional human rights protection systems, where there is greater homogeneity among States Parties.

[198] See also Benvenisti (2018).

Cannone A (2018) Violazioni di carattere sistemico e Convenzione europea dei diritti dell'uomo. Cacucci, Bari
Cataldi G (2006) Le deroghe ai diritti umani in stato di emergenza. In: Pineschi L (ed) La tutela internazionale dei diritti umani. Norme, garanzie, prassi. Giuffrè, Milano, pp 752–772
Cataldi G (2012) Articolo 15. In: Bartole S, De Sena P, Zagrebelsky V (eds) Commentario breve alla Convenzione europea per la salvaguardia del diritti dell'uomo e delle libertà fondamentali. Cedam/Kluwer, Padova, pp 555–564
Cataldi G (2019) Sulla recente prassi in materia di comunicazioni di deroga alla Convenzione europea dei diritti dell'uomo. In: Sicilianos LA et al (eds) Regards croisés sur la protection nationale et internationale des droits de l'homme, Liber Amicorum Guido Raimondi. Wolf Legal Publishers, Tilburg
Conforti B (Iovane M ed) (2018) Diritto internazionale, 11th edn. Editoriale Scientifica, Napoli
De Schutter O (2010) International human rights law. Cases, materials, commentary. CUP, Cambridge
De Sena P (2002) La nozione di giurisdizione statale nei trattati sui diritti dell'uomo. Giappichelli, Torino
Ergec R (1987) Les droits de l'homme à l'épreuve des circonstances exceptionnelles. Etude sur l'article 15 de la Convention européenne des droits de l'homme. Bruylant, Bruxelles
Focarelli C (2013) La persona umana nel diritto internazionale. Il Mulino, Bologna
Focarelli C (2019) Diritto internazionale, 5th edn. Kluwer/Cedam, Milano
Forlati S (2005) Diritto dei trattati e responsabilità internazionale. Giuffrè, Milano
Higgins R (1976–77) Derogations under human rights treaties. Br Yearb Int L 48:281–319
Kälin W, Künzli J (2009) The law of international human rights protection. OUP, Oxford
Kamminga MT (2009) Impact on state succession in respect of treaties. In: Kamminga MT, Scheinin M (eds) The impact of human rights law on general international law. OUP, Oxford, pp 99–109
McDonald RSJ (1997) Derogations under Article 15 of the European convention on human rights. Col JTL 36:225–267
McDougal MS (1980) Human rights and world public order: the basic policies of an international law of human dignity. Yale University Press, New Haven
Mosler H (1980) The international society as a legal community. Sijthoff, Alphen aan den Rijn
Mullerson R (1993) The continuity and succession of states by reference to the former USSR and Yugoslavia. Int Comp Law Q 42:473–493
Pisillo Mazzeschi R (1984) Risoluzione e sospensione dei trattati per inadempimento. Giuffrè, Milano
Pisillo Mazzeschi R (2004a) Esaurimento dei ricorsi interni e diritti umani. Giappichelli, Torino
Pisillo Mazzeschi R (2008) Responsabilité de l'État pour violation des obligations positives relatives aux droits de l'homme. RC 333:175–506
Pustorino P (1998) L'interpretazione della Convenzione europea dei diritti dell'uomo nella prassi della Commissione e della Corte di Strasburgo. Editoriale Scientifica, Napoli
Pustorino P (2019) Lezioni di tutela internazionale dei diritti umani. Cacucci, Bari
Pustorino P (2020) Lezioni di tutela internazionale dei diritti umani, 2nd edn. Cacucci, Bari
Russo D (2012) L'efficacia dei trattati sui diritti umani. Giuffrè, Milano
Saccucci A (2018) La responsabilità internazionale dello Stato per violazioni strutturali dei diritti umani. Editoriale Scientifica, Napoli
Scheinin M (2009) Impact on the law of treaties. In: Kamminga MT, Scheinin M (eds) The impact of human rights law on general international law. OUP, Oxford, pp 23–36
Sicilianos LA (1993) The relationship between reprisals and denunciation or suspension of a treaty. Eur J Int Law 4:341–359
Simma B (1970) Reflections on Article 60 of the Vienna convention on the law of treaties and its background in general international law. ÖZöR 20:5–81
Simma B (1994) From bilateralism to community interest in international law. RC 250:217–384
Sommario E (2018) Stati d'emergenza e trattati a tutela dei diritti umani. Giappichelli, Torino

Sudre F (2006) Droit européen et international des droits de l'homme, 8th edn. PUF, Paris
Suy E (1983) Droits des traités et droits de l'homme. In: Festschrift für Hermann Mosler. Springer, Berlin, pp 935–947
Svensson-McCarthy AL (1998) The international law of human rights and states of exception. With special reference to the Travaux Preparatoires and case-law of the international monitoring organs. Nijhoff, The Hague
Tomuschat C (2014) Human rights: between idealism and realism, 3rd edn. OUP, Oxford
Viarengo I (2005) Deroghe e restrizioni alla tutela dei diritti umani nei sistemi internazionali di garanzia. RDI 88:955–996

Sources Envisaged in International Treaties 5

5.1 Binding Decisions of International Organizations

The most important sources envisaged in international treaties (sometimes also referred to as third degree sources) are currently the *legally binding acts of international organizations*. In fact, as is well known, in most cases international organizations do not have normative powers, but only those to issue recommendations or other legally non-binding acts (soft law) or to prepare draft treaties. There are, however, some rather exceptional cases in which such organizations have the power to adopt binding acts. The latter, when they are "organic" acts, i.e. issued by bodies authorized by the founding treaty of the organization, usually (but not always) take the name of "decisions" and are considered as "sources envisaged in treaties". The most important hypotheses of binding acts of international organizations are to be found in the framework of the United Nations and the European Union. Other examples can be found in some UN Specialized Institutes, in the WTO and in NATO.

The UN Charter provides that the General Assembly may take decisions under Article 17 concerning the approval of the budget and the distribution of expenditure among Member States. The Security Council, *ex* Article 94(2) of the Charter, may decide on measures to compel a State condemned by a judgment of the International Court of Justice to comply with the decision. Furthermore, and this is the most important hypothesis, the Security Council can take decisions under Article 41 of the Charter; i.e. take "measures not involving the use of armed force" and impose their observance on all Member States.

In the European Union system, legally binding acts adopted by the Institutions, which can be considered as sources envisaged in treaties, are the norm rather than the exception. The most important of these acts are, as is well known, regulations, decisions and directives,[1] usually referred to as "typical normative acts" of EU

[1]TFEU, Art. 288.

R. Pisillo Mazzeschi, *International Human Rights Law*,
https://doi.org/10.1007/978-3-030-77032-7_5

secondary legislation. Then there are the so-called "atypical acts" of the EU, such as, for example, decisions taken by the Council in the framework of the Common Security and Defense Policy.[2]

Furthermore, as mentioned above, some UN Specialized Institutes have the power to adopt binding acts against Member States; but especially on technical and specialized issues. The Treaty establishing the ICAO authorizes the Council to issue, by a two-thirds majority, in the form of "annexes" or "attachments", a series of acts relating to air traffic (called international standards or recommended practices), which enter into force for all Member States after a certain period, unless a majority of Member States have notified the Council of their opposition.[3] The Treaty establishing the WHO provides[4] that the Assembly may adopt, by a two-thirds majority, health "regulations" binding on all Member States except those States which notify the Secretary-General of the WHO of their rejection within a specified period.[5] The Statute of the ILO provides that Member States must submit draft conventions prepared by the Organization to their national authorities for ratification within a certain period.[6] Outside the Specialized Institutes, examples of binding acts can be found in the Statutes of the World Trade Organization (WTO)[7] and NATO.[8]

Having said that, the question now is whether international human rights law has influenced these sources of international law. Only the most important sources will be examined: the binding decisions of the Security Council under Article 41 of the UN Charter and EU secondary legislation.

5.1.1 Decisions of the UN Security Council

According to Chapter VII of the UN Charter, the Security Council (SC), before taking decisions under Article 41, must ascertain the existence of any "threat to the

[2]TEU, Arts. 28 and 29.

[3]Convention on International Civil Aviation, 7 December 1944, Articles 37–38. In practice, the annexes almost always become binding on all Member States.

[4]Constitution of the World Health Organization, 22 July 1946, Art. 21.

[5]*Ibidem*, Art. 22. In addition, Member States are obliged to submit draft agreements prepared by the WHO to their competent national bodies for ratification within a given deadline.

[6]The Treaty establishing the ITU, which has undergone several amendments over time, also provides that the bodies may adopt "regulations" and draft conventions. Periodic revisions of administrative regulations, adopted by simple majority, are binding on all Member States unless they express their opposition at the time of adoption or within a certain time limit thereafter. A "constitution" was adopted in 1992, followed by a "convention" and two "administrative regulations".

[7]The Statute of the WTO provides that the Ministerial Conference or the General Council may adopt, by a three-fourths majority, binding decisions by which such bodies provide a binding interpretation of the rules of the Statute and its annexes or even exempt, in exceptional cases and for a limited time, a Member State from compliance with the obligations set out in those rules. See Marrakesh Agreement Establishing the World Trade Organization, Art. IX (2) and (3).

[8]North Atlantic Treaty, Washington, 4 April 1949, Art. 9. See Focarelli (2015), p. 474.

peace, breach of the peace, or act of aggression" (Art. 39). After this determination, the Security Council may, among other things, decide which measures "not involving the use of armed force" (e.g. interruption of economic relations, trade embargo, freezing of assets and current accounts) should be taken by UN Members against the State or States responsible for one or more of the above-mentioned international offences.[9] These measures are usually defined as Security Council "sanctions".

A first effect of international human rights law on these decisions is that, in recent years, the Security Council has held on several occasions, sometimes with a considerable degree of discretion, that serious and repeated violations of human rights, even within a State, may constitute a "threat to the peace" and thus justify its taking decisions under Article 41. Therefore, the binding decisions of the Security Council can be used as sanctions against serious violations of human rights.[10]

A second effect of human rights occurred after the end of the Cold War, when the Security Council began to increasingly adopt measures not involving the use of armed force, especially economic sanctions, against various States. At the time, it was understood that such sanctions could produce serious damage, and also violations of fundamental human rights and economic and social rights, to the populations of the States affected by the sanctions and to those of third States that had trade relations with the former States. In other words, economic sanctions, as well as not always being effective against the States affected by them, have often ended up violating the human rights of innocent individuals and groups of individuals. To remedy this situation, it has not been sufficient introducing "humanitarian exemptions" in sanctions.

Therefore, the Security Council began to adopt so-called "targeted or smart sanctions";[11] i.e. measures directed against individuals or groups of individuals expressly named, for example, government authorities in office, suspected terrorists or terrorist organizations, insurgent groups, individuals who violate arms embargo measures, and even individuals who are qualified by a special Sanctions Committee as responsible for actions that threaten peace and security. Targeted sanctions also contain an "expiration clause", which provides for their automatic termination after a certain deadline if they are not expressly renewed. Finally, they usually concern individual sectors (e.g. embargoes on arms, diamonds and oil, freezing of certain assets or current accounts). However, even targeted sanctions have sometimes

[9]Article 41 lists the following measures, by way of example: a complete or partial interruption of economic relations and of rail, sea, air, postal, telegraphic, radio and other means of communication, and the severance of diplomatic relations. Other types of measures are also frequent in practice.

[10]It is true, however, as has been noted (Conforti 2015, p. 446), that the great discretion enjoyed by the Security Council in deciding when the conditions for its intervention under Chapter VII are met, means that the system of sanctions provided for therein, including Article 41, does not always guarantee a sanction against such violations.

[11]See Focarelli (2015), pp. 457–460.

violated, or threatened to violate, certain human rights of affected individuals, such as the right to a fair trial or the right to privacy.[12]

In conclusion, it can be said that international human rights law has produced certain effects on the Security Council decisions under Articles 39 and 41 of the UN Charter, both by broadening the Council's power of intervention through an extensive interpretation of the concept of "threat to the peace" and, in the opposite direction, by introducing certain limits to its power in order to protect human rights, through the practice of targeted sanctions. These effects have certainly not produced any structural changes to the binding decisions of the Security Council; but they have introduced some interesting *peculiarities* with respect to the normal functioning of such decisions.

5.1.2 Secondary Legislation of the European Union

Turning now to the acts of secondary legislation of the European Union, it should be noted at once that international human rights law has had an important influence on these acts. In fact, the three original Community Treaties did not contain any provisions aimed at ensuring that Community acts respected human rights (referred to as "fundamental rights" in the language of Community and then EU law).[13] Therefore, at an early stage in the process of European integration, until the end of the 1960s, this gap in the Community Treaties had led the Court of Justice to refuse to take into account possible violations of fundamental rights when assessing the legitimacy of a Community act.[14]

However, since the early 1970s, also because of the pressure exerted by the Italian and German constitutional courts,[15] the Court of Justice has gradually developed over time, through its case-law, a Community method of protection of human rights.[16] The Court has begun to affirm its competence to ascertain possible violations of human rights by the Institutions, on the basis of the argument that fundamental rights are part of the general principles of Community law.[17] Those principles on fundamental rights, according to the Court, derive from the constitutional traditions common to the Member States and from the international treaties on human rights that those States have ratified, with particular regard to the European Convention on Human Rights. This rather creative case-law of the Court of Justice

[12]On this issue see, e.g., ECtHR, *Nada v. Switzerland* and *Al-Dulimi and Montana Management Inc. v. Switzerland*. For the jurisprudence of the European Court of Justice see below, Sect. 11.2.2.

[13]On respect for human rights in EU law see, e.g., Villani (2017), pp. 48–60.

[14]See, e.g., ECJ, *Stork*.

[15]See Italian Constitutional Court, *Frontini*; Federal Constitutional Court (Bundesverfassungsgericht), "*Solange I* ".

[16]Daniele (2014), p. 185; Villani (2017), p. 49. This topic will be taken up and expanded upon below, in Sect. 11.2.

[17]The turning point in the case-law of the Court of Justice occurs with the well-known judgments *Stauder, Internationale Handelsgesellschaft, Nold*, and *Hauer*.

has been an important step forward, because it has in fact incorporated the protection of human rights into Community law (now EU law). However, it had some flaws: (*a*) that of developing slowly and sporadically by means of precedents; (*b*) that of leaving a margin of uncertainty as to the exact identification of human rights that belong to Community law; (*c*) that of referring only indirectly to human rights treaties, including the European Convention. In essence, there was a lack of a written and detailed catalogue of human rights belonging to Community law.

The subsequent evolution is well known: at first, the above-mentioned case-law of the Court of Justice was referred to in Article 6 of the Treaty on European Union (TEU), in its original version.[18] Then, the project was pursued to make the European Convention directly applicable in Community law through a formal accession of the European Community to that Convention. Once this project was arrested following an initial negative opinion of the Court of Justice,[19] it was decided to draw up an autonomous catalogue of fundamental rights. This was finally achieved by the EU Charter of Fundamental Rights, first proclaimed in Nice in 2000 and then made legally binding by the Lisbon Treaty in 2007. Currently, Article 6(1) TEU states that the Charter "has the same legal value as the Treaties".

What are the results of this long process of progressive affirmation of human rights in the EU legal order, especially with regard to the typical acts of secondary legislation?

Firstly, fundamental human rights belong to the general principles of EU law. These rights can be found in the constitutional traditions common to the Member States and in the human rights treaties ratified by them, and now also include those rights set out in the EU Charter of Fundamental Rights which are innovative compared to the former. The European Institutions are obliged to respect these rights, and therefore the legislative acts of the Institutions enacted in violation of them are unlawful and can be annulled by the Court of Justice.

Secondly, the fundamental rights referred to above are also binding on Member States when it comes to matters falling within the scope of EU law.[20] Therefore, in the context of such matters, the Court of Justice may find that a Member State has committed a violation of fundamental rights, for example, in respect of domestic legislation infringing freedom of expression in the context of the free movement of workers.

Thirdly, the question has arisen as to whether EU Member States are responsible when they violate fundamental rights through activities carried out to implement acts of EU Institutions, for example, to enforce a regulation or a directive. This issue has also arisen before the European Court of Human Rights and has been addressed in

[18]Treaty on European Union, Art. 6(2): "The Union shall respect fundamental rights, as guaranteed by the European Convention for the Protection of Human Rights and Fundamental Freedoms signed in Rome on 4 November 1950, as they result from the constitutional traditions common to the Member States, as general principles of Community law".

[19]ECJ, *Accession by the Community to the European Convention*, Opinion 2/94 of 28 March 1996.

[20]See, e.g., ECJ, *Wachauf*, para. 19.

several judgments. Of these, the 2005 decision in the *Bosphorus* case[21] is particularly important. The Strasbourg Court distinguished between two categories of cases. The first category includes cases in which Member States simply execute EU acts without any discretion. In these circumstances, the Court does not consider that its intervention is, in principle, necessary, since fundamental rights can be protected by EU law enforcement mechanisms, which are equivalent (unless there is evidence to the contrary in exceptional cases). The second category includes cases where Member States enjoy a certain margin of discretion in enforcing EU acts. In these circumstances, the Strasbourg Court argues that a State that violates fundamental rights must be held responsible under the European Convention. This seems logical, because in these cases the State has violated its obligations under the Convention without being required to do so by EU law.

More recently, the Strasbourg Court seems to want to extend its control over Member States' acts implementing EU law, by restricting the presumption of equivalent protection established in the *Bosphorus* case. In the *M.S.S. v. Belgium and Greece* judgment,[22] the Court condemned Belgium for violation of Article 3 of the European Convention for sending the applicant back to Greece, the country responsible for examining the asylum application under the so-called Dublin Regulation. The Court considered Greece as "unsafe" despite the presumption to the contrary enshrined in the Dublin system; argued that the Belgian authorities should have acted accordingly; and stated that the presumption of equivalent protection did not apply to the present case.

In conclusion, there is no doubt that the issue of human rights, originally outside Community law (now EU law), has currently acquired an important role in that law and has also had some important effects on its sources. In fact, human rights: (*a*) have led to a strong expansion of the content of the general principles of EU law; (*b*) as general principles, they are relevant for interpreting other sources of EU law;[23] (*c*) they operate as a parameter of legitimacy for the normative acts of the Institutions; (*d*) they also serve as a parameter of legitimacy for the behavior of the Member States in the hypotheses described above. In essence, it can be said that human rights have introduced many elements of "specialty" with respect to the traditional functioning of the sources of European Union law, including the acts of secondary legislation.

5.2 Conclusions

The examination conducted so far of the most important sources envisaged in treaties, although limited to Security Council's decisions under Article 41 of the UN Charter and EU secondary legislation, shows that international human rights law

[21]ECtHR, *Bosphorus*.

[22]ECtHR, *M.S.S. v. Belgium and Greece*, paras. 338–340.

[23]See Daniele (2014), p. 203; Villani (2017), p. 55.

has produced a significant impact on these sources. In relation to the Security Council's binding decisions, there has been a process of broadening their scope and, at the same time, a process of limiting and monitoring their content. In relation to EU's acts of secondary legislation, the monitoring of their compliance with general principles on human rights and the Charter of Fundamental Rights has become a very important factor. It has also affected the behavior of Member States that is required by the enforcement of EU legislation.

As mentioned above, this impact has not produced real structural changes on the sources envisaged in treaties; but has created some interesting effects or peculiarities with respect to the normal operation of such sources. Can it be argued that even these effects were ultimately produced by the influence of the guiding principles of the *primacy of the individual* and the *universality of human rights*? It seems to me that the answer is affirmative, especially with regard to the first principle: in fact, the value of the protection of the human person has ended up affecting the normative powers of important bodies and/or institutions of the United Nations and the European Union. In other words, the "new" value of human dignity has led to a *rebalancing* in the powers and functions of international organizations with respect to the "traditional" value of cooperation between States.

References

Conforti B (2015) Diritto internazionale, 10th edn. Editoriale Scientifica, Napoli

Daniele L (2014) Diritto dell'Unione europea. Sistema istituzionale-Ordinamento-Tutela giurisdizionale-Competenze, 5th edn. Giuffrè, Milano

Focarelli C (2015) Trattato di diritto internazionale. Utet/Kluwer, Torino-Milano

Villani U (2017) Istituzioni di Diritto dell'Unione europea, 5th edn. Cacucci, Bari

Soft Law

6

6.1 The Variety of Soft Law Acts

So far, with reference to human rights, the normative sources (custom, general principles of law *in foro domestico*, principles of international law, *jus cogens*, treaties and sources envisaged in treaties) have been examined. But it should be noted that, in addition to these sources, there are a multitude of international human rights acts that have been adopted as "recommendations", i.e. exhortative but not binding acts, and therefore cannot be framed among the sources. These acts are usually called "resolutions" or "declarations" or "final acts of conferences"; and sometimes, when they are formulated in a particularly solemn form by the UN General Assembly, they are called "declarations of principles". Taken as a whole, they are referred to as "soft law",[1] to indicate that they are not legally binding, as opposed to "hard law".

In the field of human rights, at universal level, it is worth recalling the numerous resolutions and declarations adopted by the UN General Assembly, the (former) Commission on Human Rights, the Human Rights Council. At regional level, various declarations by the Organization of American States (OAS),[2] the Council of Europe[3] and the European Parliament can be mentioned, among others. Some non-binding acts issued by non-governmental organizations or private initiatives should be added.[4] Finally, some agreements between States which are not binding are also defined by some authors[5] as soft law or, in any case, as acts of similar value

[1]On this topic see, inter alia, Boyle (2014), Shelton (2014b), Treves (2019), pp. 280–293.

[2]See, for example, the 1948 American Declaration of Rights and Duties of Man.

[3]Such statements are usually prepared by the Parliamentary Assembly and adopted by the Committee of Ministers in the form of a recommendation to the Member States.

[4]See, for example, the Islamic Declaration and the Helsinki Declaration on Ethical Principles for Medical Research involving Human Subjects, adopted at the 18th General Assembly of the World Medical Association (WMA) in 1964 in Helsinki, Finland.

[5]See Sudre (2006), p. 173.

R. Pisillo Mazzeschi, *International Human Rights Law*,
https://doi.org/10.1007/978-3-030-77032-7_6

to a recommendation: for example, the Helsinki Act adopted in 1975 by 35 States,[6] which also contains the so-called Basket III on cooperation in the humanitarian field. The Basket III was then expanded to include also the so-called "human dimension" of the CSCE (now OSCE), an expression which includes, but does not exhaust, that of "human rights".[7] However, it is not always easy to determine whether and when the OSCE commitments of States relating to the "human dimension" are legally binding.

It should be noted that some of the above recommendations are of a general nature, i.e. they tend to deal with international human rights in a general way; while others are of a sectoral nature, because they aim to establish rules or standards of behavior of States in relation to specific categories of people (e.g., women, children, refugees, minorities, indigenous peoples, disabled people, migrant workers, etc.) or specific rights or critical situations of violations (e.g., prohibition of genocide, racial discrimination, apartheid, torture, enforced disappearances, etc.).

6.2 Legal Value of These Acts

That said, two main legal problems arise: (*a*) the legal value, in general, of soft law; and (*b*) its possible "special" or "particular" value in the field of human rights.

The first problem concerns the value, *rectius* the *legal effects* of soft law acts. This is an issue that is very much dealt with in doctrine, and it is therefore sufficient to summarize it in a very synthetic way. One can talk about at least four effects produced by soft law acts within the framework of international law. A first effect, of a moral and political rather than legal nature, is that soft law induces States to comply with it, even if they have no legal obligation to do so.[8] In particular, recommendations issued by international organizations have an "exhortative" effect. In fact, in the field of human rights, the United Nations and regional human rights organizations have often pursued the strategic path of first issuing a declaration or recommendation, to gather the consensus of States on non-binding acts, and then to move on to the preparation of treaties that take up and specify in greater detail, and in a binding manner, the content of soft law acts.

A second effect concerns the function of interpretation and identification of international law. Soft law standards can help courts and other international supervisory bodies, national judges and legal practitioners more generally in the identification and interpretation of the content of international norms, written and unwritten.

[6] As is well known, this act gave rise to the Conference on Security and Cooperation in Europe (CSCE) and then the Organization for Security and Cooperation in Europe (OSCE).

[7] See Ronzitti (2016), pp. 343–346.

[8] Focarelli (2013), p. 78.

In the interpretative function of written law, soft law can be used as an aid to both objectivist[9] and subjectivist methods.[10]

A third effect may be the codification of general international law. In other words, sometimes certain acts of soft law reproduce, or reproduce in part, specifying better in writing, unwritten norms of general international law. As is well known, the codification effect occurs, in a significant way, for the "declarations of principles" of the UN General Assembly. However, for all acts of soft law, the codification effect should be properly verified on a case-by-case basis, comparing the content of soft law with that of general international law. Some examples of soft law acts on human rights, which are now regarded as reproductive of customary international law, are the Universal Declaration of Human Rights, in respect of *some* of the rights set forth therein;[11] the 1960 UN Declaration on the Independence of Colonial Peoples, with respect to the norm on external self-determination of peoples; the 1963 UN Declaration on the Elimination of All Forms of Racial Discrimination; the 1975 UN Declaration on the Protection of All Persons from Torture and Other Cruel, Inhuman or Degrading Treatment or Punishment.

Finally, the fourth effect produced by soft law, which is perhaps the most interesting, is that of contributing, sometimes in a very important way, to the progressive development of international law (i.e. hard law).[12] This effect has a legal character and it should not be confused (even if it is to some extent connected) with the first effect mentioned above, which is only of a moral and political nature.

In what way can soft law contribute to the progressive development of international law, and especially general law? As far as customary international law is concerned, first of all soft law, if it derives from a general consensus of States or international organizations, can express the element of *opinio juris ac necessitatis*, which can become stronger over time, especially if accompanied by other and subsequent manifestations of *opinio juris*. In the second place, soft law, since it derives from legal acts of States and international organizations, can also express the element of *diuturnitas*. This is all the more so today, when the opinion prevails that *diuturnitas* is made up not only of "material" practice but also of "verbal" practice.[13] Naturally, caution is needed in assessing the impact of soft law on *diuturnitas*, since it should be verified that *diuturnitas* is also detectable by a constant and uniform practice of States which is "external" with respect to acts of soft law. On the other hand, with regard to the general principles of international law, as already seen,[14] soft law can play an even more important role when it highlights a general consensus of the international community as a whole on some of these principles.

---

[9]Because it can help to establish the purpose and object of the international standard.

[10]Because it can help to establish the intention of States during the preparatory work on treaties and sources envisaged in treaties.

[11]See below, Sect. 10.2.

[12]Tomuschat (2014), pp. 45–46.

[13]See above, Sect. 3.1.1.

[14]See above, Sect. 3.3.

Coming to the second problem (that of a possible "particular" legal value of soft law in the human rights field), it seems to me that the answer is in quantitative rather than qualitative terms. In other words, the aforementioned four effects of soft law are particularly strong and significant in the field of human rights, for the reasons I have already set out when talking about customary law and general principles of international law.[15] The scarcity of a significant interstate practice and of interstate disputes on human rights and the pressure exercised by the guiding principles of the primacy of the individual and the universality of human rights lead the interpreter to attribute particular importance to the elements of *opinio juris* and the consensus of the international community. This ends up with greatly re-evaluating the role of soft law in the field of human rights.

References

Boyle A (2014) Soft law in international law-making. In: Evans MD (ed) International law, 4th edn. OUP, Oxford, p 118 ff

Focarelli C (2013) La persona umana nel diritto internazionale. Il Mulino, Bologna

Ronzitti N (2016) Introduzione al diritto internazionale, 5th edn. Giappichelli, Torino

Shelton D (2014b) International law and 'relative normativity'. In: Evans MD (ed) International law, 4th edn. OUP, Oxford, p 137 ff

Sudre F (2006) Droit européen et international des droits de l'homme, 8th edn. PUF, Paris

Tomuschat C (2014) Human rights: between idealism and realism, 3rd edn. OUP, Oxford

Treves T (2019) The expansion of international law. General course on public international law (2015). RC 398:9–398

[15] See above, Sects. 3.1 and 3.3.

Part III

International Obligations

The examination of international human rights sources, which I have done above, is important from the perspective of general concepts of international human rights law, because it gives us information on methods of normative production and knowledge of human rights. However, this examination does not tell us anything about other important conceptual and practical aspects, which mainly relate to obligations under international human rights law.

More specifically, the following questions arise. Who are the active and passive holders of these obligations? What is the content and nature (often very different) of the individual obligations? What is their "spatial" scope? Finding an answer to these questions is important, especially from the perspective of human rights violations and international responsibility. In fact, it is very relevant to understand who is obliged to respect human rights and to whom ("personal" scope of obligations); what the passive holder of the obligation has to do in order to respect a certain human right and when its violation occurs (content and nature of the obligation); finally, within what spatial limits the bearer of the obligation has to respect it ("spatial" scope of the obligation).

All of these issues require addressing and examining a real theory of international human rights obligations. To tell the truth, in a rather surprising way, the specialist doctrine of human rights has not dealt in depth with this topic and has so far conducted investigations on it mainly of a descriptive, and not of a theoretical-systematic nature. Moreover, as we shall see, even when it has attempted a more conceptual approach to the topic, it has, in my view, erroneously constructed a specific and autonomous theory of international obligations on human rights,[1] which, although it has had some success, is open to criticism and has no connection with the general theory of law and international law.

Furthermore, a general theory of international obligations is also rather lacking in the generalist doctrine of international law, since there are very few studies that deal systematically and organically with all the problems relating to this subject. In

[1] See below, Sect. 8.1.4.

reality, the debate on international obligations has had some development, albeit insufficient, not so much in the framework of studies of a general nature, but rather in some studies on State responsibility; and especially in those dedicated to the so-called objective element of the wrongful act, constituted precisely by the breach of an international obligation. But this has some logic, if one reflects on the fact that, in order to thoroughly investigate the international wrongful act, it is necessary, in advance, to clarify well the nature and the scope of the various international obligations to which States are bound.

This conclusion is evident with regard to the personal and spatial scope of obligations. But it also applies in relation to the nature and content of the obligations. In fact, the exact content of the conduct required of the State under international law in each case (and therefore also the possible assessment of its breach) does not depend on a particular primary norm but on any *specific obligation* imposed by that norm. In other words, each primary norm of international law may impose on the State *many obligations of a different nature and structure*, and their violation produces different forms of responsibility. This is also true in the field of human rights: for example, the norm on the right to life[2] includes a number of obligations of very different nature and characteristics. The same applies, to give another example, to the norm on the right to food[3] or that on the right to private life.[4] Therefore, for the purposes of State responsibility, the *really useful distinctions* should not be made between different categories of human rights, but between different categories of obligations.

In conclusion, a theory of international human rights obligations is necessary, both for theoretical and systematic reasons and for practical ones. But can one speak also for these obligations (as has been done for the sources) of their "specialty" with respect to the traditional obligations of international law? The answer, as we shall see, is only partly positive. It is positive with regard to the personal scope of the obligations and their spatial scope. On the other hand, the answer is negative with regard to the nature and forms of human rights obligations.

That said, I will first examine the question of the personal scope of human rights obligations; then the more complex issue of the content and nature of these obligations; and finally the question of their spatial (territorial and extraterritorial) scope.

---

[2]See below, Sect. 14.1.

[3]See below, Sect. 15.1.

[4]See below, Sect. 20.1.

7 Personal Scope of Obligations

7.1 Bearers of Obligations

The first question that arises is to establish who are the bearers (or passive holders) of international human rights obligations, i.e. on which entities these obligations are imposed.

7.1.1 States

It is clear that international human rights obligations are imposed first and foremost on States. Human rights arise, also at the level of domestic legal systems, as a limit to the potentially abusive exercise of the State's sovereign power over its subjects, which is accompanied by the State's monopoly on the use of force. Therefore, human rights are initially, and still largely, conceived as the rights of individuals vis-à-vis the State. Hence also the fact that human rights violations, due to the abusive exercise of power by the State, are particularly serious violations of the law and differ radically from violations of criminal or civil law committed by private individuals against other private individuals.[1]

The fact that the bearers of international human rights obligations are normally, and above all, States is also clear from the general provisions contained in the main human rights treaties. Article 1 of the European Convention on Human Rights declares that *States* Parties recognize the rights and freedoms contained in the Convention to every person under their jurisdiction. Article 2(1) of the Covenant on Civil and Political Rights declares that each *State* Party to the Covenant undertakes to respect and guarantee to all individuals within its territory and under its jurisdiction the rights recognized in the Covenant. Article 2(1) of the Covenant on Economic, Social and Cultural Rights establishes that each of the *States* Parties to

[1] Kälin and Künzli (2009), p. 78.

R. Pisillo Mazzeschi, *International Human Rights Law*,
https://doi.org/10.1007/978-3-030-77032-7_7

the Covenant undertakes to work towards progressively achieving the full realization of the rights recognized in the Covenant. The general provisions contained in other human rights treaties have similar content.

Therefore, the responsibility for fulfilling international human rights obligations rests primarily with States. But what is the concept of the State as a bearer of international obligations and as an entity possibly responsible for violating them? A first answer, of a very general nature, derives from the fact that, in international law, the State is taken into consideration as a State-government or State-organization and not as a State-community.[2] Therefore, the obligations of the State are, in principle, incumbent on all the bodies and authorities that make up the organization of the State.

However, a more precise answer to the above question now derives from the customary norms on State responsibility governing the subjective element of the international wrongful act (i.e. the attribution of the unlawful conduct to the State). As is well known, these norms are governed in detail by the ILC Draft Articles on State Responsibility adopted in 2001,[3] which, although not legally binding, are commonly recognized as being largely corresponding to customary international law. This Draft, which I cannot dwell on here, establishes that not only the conduct of its organs acting in the official exercise of their functions (*de jure* organs)[4] must be attributed to a State, but also other conducts, such as that of organs acting *ultra vires*[5] or individuals acting as *de facto* organs[6] or under the direction or control of a State.[7]

7.1.2 International Organizations

In recent years, there has been an increasing question as to whether international obligations relating to respect for human rights are imposed not only on States but also on international organizations.[8] This is due to the fact that States today tend to delegate a number of increasingly important functions to international organizations, such as, for example, the power to adopt binding acts against Member States;[9] the power to organize peace-keeping or peace-enforcing missions or even territorial administration missions; or the power to finance, organize and even administer operational projects or aid and relief missions in State territories. In exercising

[2]See, for all, Conforti (2018), pp. 13–14.

[3]ILC, *Draft Articles on Responsibility of States for Internationally Wrongful Acts*, 1 August 2001.

[4]Arts. 4 and 5.

[5]Art. 7.

[6]Art. 9.

[7]Art. 8.

[8]On this theme see, among others, Focarelli (2013), pp. 338–342; Tomuschat (2014), pp. 120–129; Buscemi (2020), pp. 67–94. See also, recently, on the responsibility of the European Union for human rights violations, Carli (2019), pp. 137–218.

[9]See above, Sect. 5.1.

these powers, international organizations may violate international law, especially in the field of human rights.

One could reply that international organizations do not have human rights obligations, because almost all human rights treaties have been signed and ratified only by States.[10] However, this is a rather formalistic objection, since, if the States Parties to a treaty establishing an international organization are bound by a given human rights treaty, it is difficult to argue that the organization, as the body that by definition pursues cooperation between States Parties, can ignore that treaty.

In any event, even if it were to be accepted that international organizations are not bound by human rights treaties to which they are not formally parties, it should still be concluded that international organizations, when they have international personality, are bound by general international human rights law, which applies to all members of the international community. I do not, instead, share the view that international organizations should be bound only by respect for human rights having a *jus cogens* nature.

That said, the norms on the international responsibility of international organizations, including those governing the subjective element of the international wrongful act, have recently been the subject of a draft codification of the International Law Commission: the Draft Articles on Responsibility of International Organizations, adopted in 2011.[11] This Draft tends to follow the general lines of the 2001 Draft on State Responsibility. Although not all the detailed provisions of the 2011 Draft may have acquired a customary nature, there can be no doubt about the existence of the general principle, set out in Article 3, for which every internationally wrongful act committed by an international organization entails its international responsibility.

7.1.3 Individuals

According to the rules on State responsibility, and in particular those on the attribution of unlawful conduct to the State, persons or groups of persons who have the status of private individuals are not bound by international human rights obligations, except in those rather exceptional situations where such persons act as *de facto* organs or under the direction or control of a State or where a State recognizes and subsequently adopts their conduct. But, in reality, in such cases, the conduct of persons or groups of persons is attributed to the State[12] and causes the latter's responsibility. Therefore, one cannot speak, in the proper sense, of international obligations directly bearing on such persons.

But it may be questioned whether, as an exception to this general rule, there are certain situations in international law in which individuals or private groups are

---

[10]For an exception, see the 2006 Convention on the Rights of Persons with Disabilities.

[11]ILC, *Draft Articles on Responsibility of International Organizations*, 3 June 2011.

[12]See above, Sect. 7.1.1.

directly bound by international human rights obligations and are themselves internationally responsible for breaches of those obligations.

At the present time, at least in general international law, this occurs only in relation to the obligations that individuals derive from international criminal law; that is, in relation to the prohibitions of individual international crimes (genocide, crimes against humanity, war crimes, aggression).[13] In this case, one can speak of real international obligations that are directly addressed to individuals, and whose breach creates individual criminal responsibility at the international level. Perhaps it can be considered that, by way of progressive development of international law, there is a tendency to consider also international terrorism (despite the continuing difficulties of a precise definition) as an individual international crime. A confirmation could come from the fact that there is a tendency of many States, in contemporary international law, to consider self-defense against groups of terrorists to be lawful, even when their conduct is not attributable to a State. Therefore, if this development will materialize, it will also be possible to talk about international obligations of individuals and groups of individuals relating to the crime of international terrorism. In any case, the carrying out of terrorist acts often results in the commission of offences which can be classified as international crimes, especially crimes against humanity, as in the case of extermination.

There are also certain situations in which private individuals are *indirectly* bound by human rights obligations under international law.[14] This occurs when an international treaty obliges States Parties to adopt domestic legislation that punishes violations of those human rights that are contained in the treaty in question. Examples include Article 4 of the 1965 Convention on the Elimination of All Forms of Racial Discrimination and Article 4 of the 1984 Convention against Torture. But, in reality, the obligations for individuals derive from domestic norms issued in implementation of the treaty and not directly from international law. The same can be said for situations in which a State, in order to fulfil its obligation to prevent and suppress violations of human rights protected by general international law or treaty law, enacts domestic civil or administrative law to enforce such obligation. Again, obligations for private individuals derive directly from national norms and only indirectly from international law.

7.1.4 Peoples, Minorities, Indigenous Peoples and Other Non-state Actors

One might wonder whether, alongside private individuals, there are also certain *groups* of individuals who are bearers of obligations relating to human rights.

For those groups of individuals consisting of peoples, minorities and indigenous peoples, the same conclusions apply in principle as those set out above for private

[13]See below, Sect. 14.3.

[14]Kälin, Künzli (2009), p. 83.

individuals. But it should be noted that the human rights norms *formally addressed* to these categories are less numerous than the norms formally addressed to individuals.[15] Moreover, even these norms are directed at establishing rights rather than obligations for these entities. Some obligations may arise for peoples, as we will see below, from the general norms of international humanitarian law in cases of armed conflict.

There are also other so-called non-state actors, for whom the problem is more complex and can only be mentioned here.[16]

Some of these entities, such as national liberation movements and insurgents, are recognized as having an international subjectivity, albeit limited, or, according to my preferred approach, entitlement to certain international rights and obligations. In the field of human rights and international humanitarian law, one can perhaps consider these entities as bearers of obligations deriving from the norms of general international law, and especially from those of *jus cogens*. In particular, national liberation movements and insurgents, when they actually represent peoples entitled to the right to "external" self-determination, are bearers of the same obligations as the peoples they represent. These are, as noted above, primarily obligations under the basic norms of international humanitarian law.

Finally, there is much talk, especially in the doctrine, of a presumed international responsibility of multinational enterprises, which would concern above all the violation of their obligations on the respect of human rights. In my opinion, it is difficult to configure this responsibility at the international level. This issue should not be confused with the different one of possible obligations of States to control multinational companies and their possible responsibility for omission.

7.2 Holders of Rights

7.2.1 States

It is clear that the human rights obligations assumed by a State, on the basis of international law, correspond to the rights of other States to demand compliance with these obligations. These are interstate relations typically governed by international law, which also operate in the area of human rights. Of course, this occurs on the basis of the different sources of international law. In fact, human rights treaties are entered into by States which oblige each other to respect these treaties; the norms of general international human rights law (be they customary rules or general principles of law or principles of international law) oblige all States among themselves to respect these norms; finally, the binding decisions on human rights taken by international organizations oblige among themselves the States to which such acts are directed.

[15]See below, Sects. 19.1, 25.1, 25.2 and 25.3.

[16]On the topic see, e.g., Pustorino (2020), pp. 228–231, 241–246.

That said, there are three situations in which one or more States may assert their right to respect for international human rights obligations undertaken by another State. The first situation, which is rather rare in practice, occurs when the obligation to respect human rights is only reciprocal in nature. One could take the example of a bilateral treaty that provides for the obligation of both States Parties to extradite or prosecute (*aut dedere aut judicare*) an individual accused of a serious human rights violation. If the State holding the offender does not intend to prosecute him, the other State has the right to obtain extradition.

The second, much more frequent, situation occurs when human rights treaties establish *erga omnes partes* obligations. As already said,[17] in this case each State Party assumes its obligations under the treaty in solidarity with all other States Parties. Therefore, each of them has the right[18] to the observance of conventional obligations by the State accused of their violation. In some of these treaties, as will be seen later,[19] this right can also be enforced through forms of collective guarantee, i.e. through interstate appeals before courts or other international human rights monitoring bodies.

Finally, the third situation occurs when there are norms of general international law on human rights, which establish obligations *erga omnes*, i.e. obligations of each State towards all other States of the international community. The latter are all entitled to compliance with these obligations by the State accused of the breach.

7.2.2 Individuals

There is no doubt, in my view, that the human rights obligations assumed by States correspond not only to the rights of other States but also and above all to *the rights of individuals*. In other words, the *main active holders* of human rights are individuals and, for certain human rights, groups of individuals, such as peoples, minorities and indigenous peoples. After all, the most common definition of human rights is that of rights that belong to all human beings.[20]

However, to be more theoretical, I can recall what I have already said; namely that, thanks to the innovative impulse of the human rights theory, contemporary international law *formally and directly* regulates (i.e. without needing to be incorporated into the domestic law of a State) *some* relations between States and individuals and *some* inter-individual relations. It follows that individuals are now direct addressees of certain international norms (primary, secondary and tertiary), as well as *holders of international rights and obligations*.[21] Obviously, in order for a single international norm to create rights or obligations for an individual, it must

[17]See above, Sects. 2.3.3.1 and 2.3.4.1.

[18]But, according to some authors, a mere legal interest.

[19]See below, Sects. 11.1, 12.1 and 12.2.

[20]Focarelli (2013), p. 122.

[21]See also above, Sect. 2.3.2, and the cited case-law of the ICJ: *LaGrand*; *Avena*; *Jadhav Case*.

have the appropriate characteristics (it must be addressed to the individual and be clear and precise). These characteristics should not be confused with the additional feature (justiciability) that the international norm must have, in order to create an enforceable right for an individual before the domestic courts.[22]

Almost all international human rights norms are typical examples of norms that impose obligations on a State to which both the rights of other States and the rights of individuals correspond. In this sense, it can be said that they have a "binary" character; that is, they create two categories of "active addressees". Of course, this does not mean that individuals have the same guarantees available to States (directly or indirectly injured) against the State to which the obligation applies.

As is well known, this conclusion is not accepted by a minority of doctrine, which continues to believe that individuals are neither subjects of international law nor direct addressees of international human rights norms. These norms should be constructed as norms directed *only* to States, which are obliged, in their national legal orders, to grant certain rights to individuals. Only within the framework of these domestic systems, and provided that such systems incorporate international norms, would individuals become true holders of the human rights recognized by international norms. In other words, individuals would be mere "*de facto* beneficiaries" of human rights norms.

This theory is formalistic and unconvincing today. Take, for example, a *primary* international norm on human rights: the prohibition of torture under Article 3 of the European Convention on Human Rights. There is no logical difficulty in believing that this norm directly creates an obligation of each State Party to the Convention not only towards all other States Parties, but *also towards the individuals* who are under the jurisdiction of States Parties; and that these individuals are therefore the direct holders of the right not to be subjected to torture, a right which is conferred on them *directly by international law*. Actually, this conclusion is the most natural and spontaneous one, if only one reflects on the fact that the obligation of States not to commit torture is assumed primarily in order to protect the individual.

This is confirmed by the fact that an individual, who has been subjected to torture within the meaning of Article 3 of the European Convention, can bring the matter before the Strasbourg Court and obtain a judgment stating that his right has been violated. It could be objected that the same individual cannot claim a breach of the prohibition of torture (which is not contained in a self-executing norm) before the domestic courts of a State which has not incorporated that prohibition into its national law (such as Italy until recently); and therefore that he does not have a "judicially enforceable" right before the domestic courts. But that does not mean that international law has not conferred the right in question on the individual; it merely means that the State which has not implemented that right in its domestic system has infringed international law.

A similar argument can also be made for *some secondary* international norms on human rights, for example, those relating to reparation for the injury caused by the

[22]On this point see Pisillo Mazzeschi (2008), pp. 256–267.

wrongful act. If a State violates a primary human rights norm that is *also* directed in favor of the individual, there is nothing to prevent the conclusion that the State is committing an offence and incurring international responsibility *also towards the individual victim*. And therefore the latter may benefit from certain rights deriving from secondary international norms, especially the right to claim reparation for injury. This conclusion was explicitly confirmed in the Resolution adopted on 16 December 2005 by the UN General Assembly on the right to a remedy and reparation for victims of serious violations of human rights and humanitarian law.[23]

Even in the case of international *tertiary* norms (which establish procedures of judicial or quasi-judicial assessment of international law), there is nothing to prevent individuals from being the direct addressees of *some* of these norms. The most obvious examples are the rights of individuals to resort to actions against States before international courts or monitoring bodies, such as the European Court of Human Rights, the Inter-American Commission on Human Rights, the Human Rights Committee, the UN Committee against Torture and other UN Treaty-Bodies. Confirmation that individuals may be entitled to rights under tertiary norms of international law can be found in Article 33(2) (and its Commentary) of the 2001 ILC Draft on State Responsibility;[24] and, even more explicitly, in Article 16 (and its Commentary) of the 2006 ILC Draft on Diplomatic Protection, which recognizes the right of individuals:

> [...] to resort under international law to actions or procedures other than diplomatic protection to secure redress for injury suffered as a result of an internationally wrongful act.[25]

7.2.3 Peoples, Minorities, Indigenous Peoples and Other Non-state Actors

Also with regard to the entitlement to international rights, one could wonder whether, alongside private individuals, there are certain *groups* of individuals or non-state actors who are holders of human rights. The issue is similar to the one, already discussed above, concerning the bearers of obligations.

Therefore, peoples, minorities and indigenous peoples enjoy in principle, in international law, the same legal position as individuals. Hence they are formal

---

[23] *Basic Principles and Guidelines on the Right to a Remedy and Reparation for Victims of Gross Violations of International Human Rights Law and Serious Violations of International Humanitarian Law*, GA Res. 60/147, 16 December 2005. See also above, Sect. 2.3.4.3.

[24] ILC, *Draft Articles on Responsibility of States for Internationally Wrongful Acts*, 1 August 2001, Art. 33(2): "This part is without prejudice to any right, arising from the international responsibility of a State, which may accrue directly to any person or entity other than a State". See also, in a similar way, ILC, *Draft Articles on Responsibility of International Organizations*, 3 June 2011, Art. 33(2).

[25] ILC, *Draft Articles on Diplomatic Protection*, 8 August 2006, Art. 16.

addressees of some international norms, as well as *direct holders* of some international rights. However, as we shall see later [26], these entities are only the holders of a limited number of legally binding human rights, especially from the point of view of general international law. In essence, their position is weaker than that of individuals.

With regard to other non-state actors, the issue of their entitlement to rights is similar to that, already dealt with, of the titularity of obligations. National liberation movements and insurgents enjoy the rights deriving from the general norms of international humanitarian law. Moreover, when they effectively represent the peoples, they can assert the latter's right to "external" self-determination.

References

Buscemi M (2020) Illeciti delle Nazioni Unite e tutela dell'individuo. Editoriale Scientifica, Napoli
Carli E (2019) La Politica di Sicurezza e di Difesa Comune dell'Unione europea. Profili di responsabilità internazionale. Giappichelli, Torino
Conforti B (Iovane M ed) (2018) Diritto internazionale, 11th edn. Editoriale Scientifica, Napoli
Focarelli C (2013) La persona umana nel diritto internazionale. Il Mulino, Bologna
Kälin W, Künzli J (2009) The law of International Human Rights Protection. Oxford University Press, Oxford
Pisillo Mazzeschi R (2008) Responsabilité de l'État pour violation des obligations positives relatives aux droits de l'homme. RC 333:175–506
Pustorino P (2020) Lezioni di tutela internazionale dei diritti umani, 2nd edn. Cacucci, Bari
Tomuschat C (2014) Human Rights: between idealism and realism, 3rd edn. Oxford University Press, Oxford

[26] See below, Sects. 19.1, 25.1, 25.2 and 25.3.

Content and Nature of the Obligations. Various Categories and Their Validity

8

After examining the topic of active and passive holders of human rights obligations, it is appropriate to address the content and nature of those obligations. But, first, it is worth making two premises on the broader issue of the conceptual framework of international human rights obligations.

The first premise is that, in my view, a theory on human rights obligations should not be confined within the specific and narrow field of international human rights law, but should instead be placed within the framework of a *general theory* on international obligations. Indeed, it is my firm belief that the international human rights obligations of States are not different in nature from other international obligations of States. They have the particularity of being directed, as addressees, not only to other States, but also to individuals, who become active holders of genuine rights under international law. But this particularity is not exclusive to the field of human rights today. On the other hand, I believe that doctrinal tendencies to separate and isolate the area of human rights (e.g., with the theories of self-contained regimes) from the rest of international law are wrong.[1] Instead, the normative field of human rights must be framed within the whole system of international law, with which it interacts and must be harmonised.

The second premise is that the theory of international obligations (and therefore also of human rights obligations) must include a wide range of categories and legal distinctions, which are different depending on the point of observation.[2] For example, from the perspective of the active holders of obligations, one can identify the categories of reciprocal obligations and *erga omnes* obligations; from the perspective of the domestic implementation of obligations, one can speak of self-executing and non-self-executing obligations; from the point of view of the judicial assessment of obligations, one can speak of judicially enforceable and non-enforceable obligations; and so on. Some of these categories have already been dealt with.

---

[1]See above, Sect. 2.2.

[2]See Pisillo Mazzeschi (2008), pp. 224–310.

R. Pisillo Mazzeschi, *International Human Rights Law*,
https://doi.org/10.1007/978-3-030-77032-7_8

In addressing the question of the content and nature of human rights obligations, priority should be given here to the way in which obligations in international law are fulfilled or violated. In other words, the most interesting aspect now is to understand *the content of the conduct required of the State* under international law on a case-by-case basis and thus to understand when there is a violation. It is clear that such conduct depends not on the general content of the primary norm, nor on the human right protected by that norm, but on *each specific obligation* imposed by the norm; and on the nature and structure of that obligation. In other words, as already said, each primary norm may impose on the State a number of obligations of different nature and structure, the breach of which corresponds to different forms of responsibility. This is also true in the field of human rights: each human right can impose on the State a spectrum of obligations of a different character. For the purposes of responsibility, *useful distinctions are not between categories of rights but between categories of obligations.*

It follows from these premises that I do not endorse (and find neither convincing nor useful) those doctrinal theories of human rights obligations that are based on a systematic organization made up of categories of rights,[3] nor those theories that are based on merely descriptive categories of obligations and that lack legal rigor and an adequate theoretical approach.

Having said that, let me, anyway, critically examine the best known theories which propose descriptive or inappropriate categories of obligations. Then I will propose the categories that seem to me useful and having conceptual-systematic value.

8.1 Categories Only Descriptive and of Low Conceptual-Systematic Value

8.1.1 Obligations Concerning Human Rights of First, Second, Third and Fourth Generation. Criticism

In the field of human rights, the distinction that has been used for a long time and is still the most famous is that between human rights of first, second, third and fourth generation (or dimension). Consequently, part of the doctrine has also developed a parallel distinction between first, second, third and fourth generation obligations on human rights. Civil and political rights are usually considered as belonging to the first; economic, social and cultural rights as belonging to the second; and certain collective rights (such as the right to development, to peace, to a healthy environment) as belonging to the third generation. Other human rights of a collective nature, more recently developed, such as the right to democracy, good governance and human security, are classified as belonging to either the third or fourth generation. Finally, certain new emerging rights, still in the process of being affirmed at

[3]See, e.g., Mowbray (2004).

international level, which are linked to the development of biotechnology, genetics and information technology, are considered as fourth generation rights.

This distinction between different generations of human rights has a mainly historical and socio-political basis: civil and political rights were the first to assert themselves internationally and within the framework of the United Nations thanks to the pressure of Western countries; economic, social and cultural rights were the second to develop internationally thanks especially to the pressure of socialist countries; while the human rights of the third generation are of more recent formation and are mainly due to the legal-political drive of developing countries. It is more difficult, instead, to attribute fourth-generation human rights to a particular "political" group of States.

However, the same distinction has also taken on a more technical-legal function from the outset, because various legal consequences have been drawn from it. The best-known ones concern the distinction between civil and political rights, on the one hand, and economic, social and cultural rights, on the other. Especially in the past, many jurists believed that the two groups of rights had a very different nature, in various respects.

Firstly, it was said that civil and political rights were negative in nature because they required abstention by the State, while economic, social and cultural rights were positive in nature because they required action by the State. Secondly, it was argued that first generation rights were immediately binding, while second generation rights were only programmatic. In other words, the enjoyment of the first generation rights could be achieved immediately, with the mere existence of certain norms in domestic law; while the enjoyment of the second generation rights presupposed that the State intervened, with not only legislative, but also administrative, organizational and technical measures, which required particular costs and a gradual implementation over time. Thirdly, it was said that first generation rights could be formulated in more precise terms, while second generation rights were more vague and generic. Fourthly, as a logical consequence, first generation rights were considered as "judicially enforceable" before the domestic courts once they were incorporated into the State's legal system; whereas second generation rights were not considered as "judicially enforceable". Fifth, the measures of control at the international level also had to be different: while for civil and political rights a form of judicial or quasi-judicial control over individual breaches could be envisaged; for economic, social and cultural rights only a political-diplomatic control over reports submitted by States was possible.

Actually, over time, many of these distinctions have proved to be inaccurate; and there is now a tendency to recognize that there are no such clear-cut differences between the two groups of rights. For example, it is now admitted that some of the economic, social and cultural rights lend themselves to being guaranteed and executed even before domestic courts; that, on the other hand, political rights and many civil rights are not immediately binding without intervention by the State apparatus; that the immediacy or gradual realization of rights depends more on pre-existing structures and mechanisms of the State than on the nature of the rights themselves; and finally, that international quasi-judicial monitoring measures can work for both categories of rights.

As far as third and fourth generation rights are concerned, doctrine usually considers that they are too vague and generic for the time being to give rise to real binding obligations for States and true rights for individuals. Therefore, they would be neither immediately binding nor merely programmatic, but would even lack normative force and would only be political action programmes. However, as we shall see later,[4] even this conclusion is not always valid.

What can one conclude about the distinction between first, second, third and fourth generation rights and the parallel distinction between the corresponding obligations?

In my opinion, this distinction is useful from a historical and socio-political point of view, as I already said. However, from a legal point of view, it is a distinction that is only descriptive and does not have much conceptual and systematic usefulness. So much so that jurists, in order to specify the differences between the above categories, resort to other distinctions, such as those indicated above, between binding norms, programmatic norms and political commitments without normative force; or between "judicially enforceable" and "judicially non-enforceable" rights; or between precise and vague rights, and so on. Moreover, it is clear that the distinction in question, being based mainly on historical reasons, is not destined to remain always clear in its essential characters, and indeed these characters tend to change over time.

Finally, the distinction in question is even less useful if it is transferred from the plan of rights to that of obligations and their breach. In fact, as already mentioned, it is not true that certain categories or certain generations of human rights always correspond to obligations of the same nature; on the contrary, each human right can impose on the State a *variety* of obligations of a different nature. To give just one example, the right to private and family life, which belongs to the first generation of human rights, imposes on the State negative obligations, positive and immediate obligations "of result",[5] positive and immediate obligations of "due diligence",[6] and finally obligations "of progressive realization" over time.[7] On the other hand, the right to work, which belongs to the second generation of human rights, can impose on the State negative obligations,[8] positive and immediate obligations of result,[9] and obligations "of progressive realization".[10] In other words, the fact that a first

[4]See, for example, certain aspects of the right to a healthy environment: below, Sect. 25.4.2.

[5]For example, enacting laws to protect the relationship between parents and illegitimate children or adopting a measure to admit an alien into the State for reasons of family reunion.

[6]For example, taking preventive measures to reduce pollution harmful to people's privacy.

[7]See below, Sect. 8.2, on the distinction between negative obligations, immediate and positive obligations of result, immediate and positive obligations of due diligence, and obligations "of progressive realization".

[8]For example, to allow freedom of trade union association.

[9]For example, enacting legislation on equal pay between the sexes.

[10]For example, eliminating *de facto* gender discrimination in employment.

generation right, such as the right to private and family life, or a second generation right, such as the right to work, is at issue does *not* in itself tell us anything about the differences in the way in which the State must fulfil the correlative obligation and therefore does not tell us anything about the nature and structure of the State's responsibility in the event of its violation.

In conclusion, the distinction between obligations on the basis of different generations of human rights is purely descriptive and does not help determine the exact content of the various obligations.

8.1.2 Precise Obligations and Vague Obligations. Criticism

A second distinction between obligations, which is sometimes used both in general legal theory and in international law as a whole, and finally in relation to the specific area of human rights law, is that between precise obligations and vague obligations. It refers to the precision with which the content of the individual obligation is described in normative terms.

This distinction is often associated, more or less explicitly, with the distinction between negative and positive obligations and the distinction between first, second and third (or fourth) generation human rights obligations. However, in my opinion, these are generalizations which can only have some element of truth; but which often prove to be inaccurate and approximate. In fact, it can often happen that a negative obligation has a more precise content than a positive obligation; but this does not always happen. One thinks, for example, of the rather vague content of the State's negative obligation not to interfere arbitrarily or illegally in a person's private life, under Article 17 of the Covenant on Civil and Political Rights, and instead of the rather precise content of the State's positive obligation to guarantee a fair salary and equal remuneration for work of equal value, under Article 7(a) (i) of the Covenant on Economic, Social and Cultural Rights.

Similarly, it may frequently occur that a first generation human right has a more precise content than a second generation human right and that this, in turn, is more precise than a third generation human right. But even this conclusion is sometimes inaccurate. For example, the right to life and the right to freedom of expression under Articles 6 and 19 of the Covenant on Civil and Political Rights, which are first generation rights, are no more precise than the right to join trade unions under Article 8 of the Covenant on Economic, Social and Cultural Rights, which is a second generation right. The right to be informed about environmental changes that may cause significant damage to the environment (which can be considered as a third generation right) is also more precise than some rights of first or second generation.

Actually, it must be concluded that the distinction between precise and vague obligations depends on a complex set of factors. Some of these factors are contingent in nature. For example, it is clear that the process of negotiating and drafting a human rights treaty, or a single norm of such a treaty, can lead to the formulation of provisions and individual obligations of a more or less precise nature, depending on the agreement between the negotiators, the degree of compromise needed, the opportunity to leave more or less room for an evolutionary interpretation of the norm, and so on. Other factors are of a historical nature. For example, many civil and political rights, at the time when they were internationally recognized, already had a long history in the domestic constitutional law of many States and also a long legal evolution in State legal systems. This has certainly fostered their degree of normative precision.

Even at international level, it is clear that if certain human rights obligations are first introduced into a treaty, their level of precision will usually be lower than other obligations that may be based on pre-existing treaties. This explains, for example, how many provisions of the Covenant on Civil and Political Rights are more detailed and more precise than corresponding provisions in the European Convention on Human Rights. Still at international level, the existence of judicial or quasi-judicial monitoring bodies on individual human rights violations tends, through the continuous interpretation given by these bodies, to make the meaning of certain rights more precise. From this point of view, the long jurisprudential elaboration of civil and political rights, which has occurred in the system of the European Convention, the American Convention and the Covenant on Civil and Political Rights, has favoured the process of clarifying these rights in comparison with economic, social and cultural rights.

In summary, therefore, it can be concluded that the distinction between precise and vague obligations is also descriptive in nature and not theoretical-systematic. But above all, this distinction is not rigorous and clear-cut, because there is a whole range or continuous spectrum of different levels of precision of an obligation, and not a real dichotomy between categories of qualitatively different obligations.

8.1.3 Obligations Without Cost and Expensive Obligations. Criticism

Another distinction between obligations, which is sometimes used especially in the field of human rights, is that between obligations without cost and expensive obligations, with reference to the measures for the implementation of the obligations that each State must take in its domestic legal system to fully achieve respect for human rights.

This distinction is also often linked to the distinction between negative and positive obligations, in the sense that the implementation of the former would be without cost while the implementation of the latter would be expensive. Or it is assimilated to the other distinction between human rights obligations of first, second and third (or fourth) generation, in the sense that the implementation of first generation human rights would be without cost, while the implementation of second and third generation human rights would be expensive. Indeed, there is some element of truth in these views and it can be admitted that the implementation of negative obligations often involves less expense than the implementation of positive obligations. Nor can it be denied that the implementation of many economic rights obligations involves more expenditure than the implementation of many civil rights obligations. However, these are generalisations in principle and do not correspond to an absolute rule; and it cannot be excluded that sometimes the opposite may happen.

But, above all, the criticism that must be made of the distinction in question is that it does not represent a real dichotomy between two categories of different obligations; and therefore has little theoretical-systematic value. And this occurs for several reasons. Firstly, the implementation of almost all human rights requires the State to use certain economic resources, if only to establish or maintain an adequate institutional structure. It is therefore difficult to configure human rights obligations that are without cost to the State. Secondly, it is clear that the implementation of each individual human rights obligation may involve different costs for the State. There is therefore no real dichotomy between cost-free and expensive obligations, but rather a continuous spectrum of more or less expensive situations. Thirdly, the higher or lower cost of implementing human rights clearly varies from State to State since it depends to a large extent on the institutional, legal, administrative and other structures already in place in each State when it has to fulfil that particular obligation.

Ultimately, it can be concluded that the distinction between obligations without cost and expensive obligations is imprecise and is not useful for the reconstruction of a legal and systematic theory on international obligations.

8.1.4 Obligations to Respect, to Protect and to Fulfil Human Rights. Criticism

Finally, one must also criticize, in my view, the classification of human rights obligations, which is currently the most popular in doctrine and has also been used by the Committee on Economic, Social and Cultural Rights, the African Commission and the UN High Commissioner for Human Rights. This classification, originally proposed by some scholars[11] and then supported with some variation by other human rights specialists, distinguishes between obligations *to respect*, obligations *to protect* and obligations *to fulfil* human rights. The Committee on Economic, Social and Cultural Rights also tends to distinguish, within the obligation to fulfil human rights, three different sublevels: (a) the obligation *to facilitate*; (b) the obligation *to provide*; and (c) the obligation *to promote*. It should be noted that this distinction, known as the "*tripartite typology*", has been studied and developed mainly with reference to economic, social and cultural rights; but that, in the intentions of its supporters, it is intended to apply to all human rights.

It is not easy to describe in a few words the exact content of each of these categories and subcategories; also because sometimes they assume, in doctrine, partially different meanings. However, with an effort at synthesis, it can be said that the obligation *to respect* human rights is predominantly negative and prohibits the State from acting in such a way as to directly and negatively affect the rights and

[11] See, especially, Shue (1980) and Eide (1984).

freedoms recognized to individuals; that is, in such a way as to deny or limit access to human rights. But it can sometimes also have a positive character, for example when it requires the State to recognize and register the property rights of certain individuals.

On the other hand, the obligation *to protect* human rights is mainly positive and requires the State to take a number of measures, legislative, administrative or otherwise, to prevent third parties from violating the rights or freedoms of others; and also to repress those violations that could not be prevented. This obligation therefore appears to correspond, essentially, to the category of positive obligations "with horizontal effects", which I have already dealt with.[12]

The obligation *to fulfil* human rights is the most difficult to define. In principle, it has a positive nature and requires the State to take more far-reaching and more programmatic measures; in particular to actively create the conditions for achieving certain results in the form of a more effective realization of recognized rights or freedoms. As for its three sub-levels, the obligation *to facilitate* the realization of human rights requires States to engage in activities designed to assist individuals in the enjoyment of human rights and to strengthen their capacity to access and use the resources available to them. The obligation *to provide* for the realization of human rights requires States to directly provide and ensure the enjoyment of a certain right when individuals or groups of individuals are unable, for reasons beyond their control, to achieve such enjoyment directly through the means at their disposal. Finally, the obligation *to promote* the realization of human rights requires States to take a number of different actions of a promotional nature, such as the study and research on human rights, the dissemination of information on human rights to their citizens, the management of human rights training programs, assistance to people in making well-informed choices about the enjoyment of human rights, and similar actions.

As has been said, this distinction into three main categories of obligations (but also in five categories if you consider the three sublevels of the obligation *to fulfil*), is now basically shared by many human rights scholars, although sometimes the terminology and certain nuances are different from author to author. It is not worthwhile entering into the merits of the small differences between the various doctrinal views; rather, it is worth evaluating the distinction accepted by the Committee on Economic, Social and Cultural Rights, which essentially ends up summarizing and incorporating the various doctrinal opinions mentioned above.

In my view, the merit of the distinction between obligations to *respect*, *protect* and *fulfil* (in its three sublevels) human rights lies in the fact that it has overcome the previous rather rough and approximate dichotomies. Above all, it has made it clear that each human right can impose a spectrum of obligations of a different nature, and therefore that the conduct of the State, especially from the point of view of responsibility, must be assessed on the basis of the individual and specific obligation that has been violated.

---

[12] See above, Sect. 4.3.4.

However, this distinction also has four serious flaws. First, it remains a purely descriptive distinction, since it merely and roughly groups together certain possible forms of behaviour of the State in relation to human rights, without going into the content, legal nature and structure of the obligations. For example, to say that the State has an obligation *to respect* human rights is, in some ways, a very obvious concept and, in other ways, a confused concept when it intends to include both negative and positive obligations. Equally, to say that the State has an obligation *to protect* human rights, through the prevention of their violations by private individuals, tells us nothing, from the point of view of legal theory, about the structure and nature of such obligations. Finally, to say that the State has the obligation *to fulfil* human rights, through a series of commitments of a very different nature aimed at facilitating or promoting their realization, or aimed at making up for people's inability, tell us nothing important and legally significant about the structure, content or nature of this obligation of fulfilment; that is, about the behaviour concretely required of the State for its exact compliance. In other words, the obligation *to fulfil* remains very vague and generic, and ends up even including commitments that are not binding, and therefore do not constitute real obligations (for example, that of informing and educating people about human rights).

Secondly, the "tripartite" distinction has the defect of being tailor-made only for human rights; and is therefore completely disconnected from the general theory of obligations in international law. This constitutes a very serious limitation, since it places the subject of human rights in isolation from other areas of international law and the general theory of law.[13] Of course, it is obvious that this second defect is linked to the first, since a distinction between obligations that is merely descriptive in character cannot contribute to a general theory of international obligations.

Thirdly, the distinction in question is not as innovative as it would appear at first sight, since it reflects, albeit roughly, old categories, already known and consolidated, of international obligations. The obligation *to respect* corresponds, for the most part, to the category of negative obligations.[14] The obligation *to protect* seems to have a very limited content, because it corresponds to the positive obligations of prevention with respect to private acts (or positive obligations with "horizontal effects").[15] The obligation *to fulfil*, instead, has a very ample content because it tries to unify in a vast category (which, however, remains heterogeneous) a series of obligations and non-binding political objectives which concern, above all, the realization of the second and third generation human rights.

Finally, the distinction in question, although it largely re-proposes old categories of obligations, has the defect of not being complete, because it neglects some important obligations: for example, the obligations of higher-ranking State agents to prevent and repress human rights violations committed by lower-ranking State

[13]See above, Chap. 2, for my criticism of the idea of a self-contained human rights regime.

[14]See below, Sect. 8.2.1.

[15]See above, Sect. 4.3.4.

agents,[16] the obligations of result and those of due diligence,[17] and the obligations "of progressive realization.[18]

In conclusion, the distinction between obligations *to respect*, *to protect* and *to fulfil* human rights, despite the growing support it enjoys in doctrine and also in the practice of some monitoring bodies, lacks legal rigour and therefore cannot be accepted in this book to identify true *legal* categories of obligations.

8.2 Useful Categories with Conceptual-Systematic Value

As has been seen, all the distinctions between categories of international obligations, that I have examined so far and which apply to the specific area of human rights, have considerable flaws and appear to be mainly descriptive, rather approximate and not legally rigorous. It is therefore appropriate to focus attention now on those distinctions between categories of obligations which have the merit of working for the entire international legal order, which are also fully applicable in the area of human rights, and which have juridical and conceptual-systematic value. Leaving aside now the category of *erga omnes* obligations, which I have already addressed.[19]

In my opinion, the most useful distinctions, again from the point of view of the content and nature of the obligations and the way they are fulfilled, are the following: *(a)* the distinction between negative and positive obligations; *(b)* that between obligations of result and obligations of due diligence; *(c)* that between immediate obligations and obligations "of progressive realization".

8.2.1 Negative and Positive Obligations

The first useful distinction is between negative and positive international obligations. Their respective definitions, both in general international law and in the field of human rights, are well known and it is sufficient here to recall them in extreme summary.

Negative international obligations are obligations in which the State (or another entity with international obligations) refrains from certain actions; i.e. obligations not to do or not to interfere. In the field of human rights, negative obligations are mainly obligations to abstain from the sphere of individual rights and freedoms. This category has its classic scope in many "fundamental" rights[20] (right to life, prohibition of torture and slavery, right to liberty and security of the person, etc.) and in many civil and political rights. However, it cannot be excluded that there are also

[16]See, e.g., below, Sects. 14.1.3.2, 14.1.3.3, 14.2.3.2 and 14.2.3.3.

[17]See below, Sect. 8.2.2.

[18]See below, Sect. 8.2.3.

[19]See above, Sects. 2.3.3.1, 2.3.4.1 and 4.1.1.

[20]See below, Part V.

negative obligations in relation to certain economic, social and cultural rights: for example, the obligation of the State to guarantee the right to strike, the freedom to form trade unions, the freedom of scientific research, the freedom of parents to make educational choices for their children.

Positive international obligations, on the other hand, are those obligations in which the State (or other entity) is required to perform certain actions or services; i.e. obligations to do or to intervene. In the field of human rights, positive obligations are mainly obligations of the State to promote the attainment of individual rights and freedoms. The scope of positive obligations, initially limited, has gradually widened and now extends to first, second, third and fourth generation human rights.

The distinction between negative and positive obligations works in the same way and equally well for both international law in general and the area of human rights. Moreover, this distinction is now also widely used in international practice and case-law.[21] This is logical because it is a distinction that belongs to the same general theory of law. However, it should be noted that it is only a very general distinction and that it is therefore possible, within each of the two broad categories, to configure other distinctions and other more specific categories.[22] It is hardly necessary to recall that the dichotomy between negative and positive obligations corresponds, in the case of their violation, to the dichotomy between commissive offences (and responsibility for action) and omissive offences (and responsibility for omission).

8.2.2 Obligations of Result and Obligations of Due Diligence

A second useful distinction, both in general international law and in the field of human rights, is that between "obligations of result" and "obligations of due diligence" (or of means or of conduct).[23] I am now talking about *immediate* obligations (i.e. those which operate immediately), which I will distinguish later on from obligations "of progressive realization".

It should be stressed that I do not in any way refer to the distinction between "obligations of specific conduct" and "obligations of result", elaborated in the past especially by a part of the Italian doctrine,[24] which mainly concerns the way in which international obligations require domestic implementation by the State.[25] On the contrary, I intend to refer to the distinction, which is very different although

[21]See Pisillo Mazzeschi (2008), chapters 3, 4 and 5. See also Id. (2018a), Sect. 4.3.3.

[22]See below, Sects. 8.2.2 and 8.2.3.

[23]See Pisillo Mazzeschi (1989); Id. (1992); Id. (2008); Id. (2018a). See also Kulesza (2016); Cassella (2018); Besson (2020a, b).

[24]See, above all, Ago (1938), p. 178 ff.; Ago (1939), p. 415 ff.; Ago (1977), paras. 2–46.

[25]According to this distinction, the "obligation of specific conduct" establishes the mode of domestic implementation that it requires (implementation which may be carried out through normative or administrative or judicial activity). On the other hand, the "obligation of result" does not specify the mode of domestic implementation required, but leaves the State free to choose the appropriate means and activities of implementation in order to achieve the ultimate purpose

similar in terminology, and which is widely used in the civil law of States with a Romanesque tradition. This distinction is also applicable in international law, where it has an ancient origin[26] but has only lately been consolidated. Recently, also the International Court of Justice, for instance in the case of *Bosnia and Herzegovina v. Serbia and Montenegro*, in relation to Serbia's obligation to prevent genocide, has expressly spoken of an obligation of means or conduct, as well as an obligation to use "best efforts" in prevention activities through a due diligence standard.[27]

In order to better understand the distinction in question, it should be noted that, on the basis of the general theory of law, in each obligation both the conduct of the obligated party and the result of that conduct have relevance; however, the two elements can have a very different weight and therefore sometimes the obligation is identified through the result and sometimes through the conduct of the obligated party. This characterizes two different categories of obligation: there is an obligation of result when the norm requires that the conduct of the obligor produces a result; there is an obligation of due diligence (or of means or of conduct) when the norm requires a certain conduct in itself, regardless of its outcome. For the obligation of result, the breach comes from the absence of the promised result; whereas, for the obligation of due diligence, the breach comes from the fact that the obligor did not use the due diligence required by the circumstances. In other words, the obligation of result is an obligation to "succeed", whereas the obligation of due diligence is an obligation to "strive", to use the "best efforts" in order to achieve the result.

The theoretical justification for the distinction rests mainly on the idea that the two categories of obligations are conditioned by a different *alea* (degree of risk). In the case of obligations of result, the realization of the object of the obligation does not encounter difficulties inherent in its nature, that is, it does not involve any particular risk. On the contrary, in the case of due diligence obligations, the fulfilment of the object and purpose of the obligation is by its very nature aleatory and therefore requires a special effort of diligence on the part of the obligor and the favourable play of certain objective risk factors. In the final analysis, it is the aleatory or not nature of the result sought by the rule that explains why certain obligations require only "efforts", while other obligations require "success".

This applies not only in general legal theory, but also in international law. In fact, the State, through its organs, is concretely able, in certain cases, to maintain active or passive conduct, which guarantees avoiding injury against other States (except for in the presence of certain circumstances precluding wrongfulness) and possibly also against individuals. Instead, in other cases, the State can only behave, with respect to the possible injury, in a way which, although usually sufficient to avoid the offence, cannot absolutely guarantee such a result, since it depends also on strongly aleatory

---

sought by the obligation. On this point see Pisillo Mazzeschi (2008), pp. 271–282; Id. (2018a), pp. 326–327.

[26]This origin probably goes back to the famous arbitration in the *Alabama* case of 1872. See *Alabama claims of the United States of America v. Great Britain.*

[27]ICJ, *Application of the Convention on the Prevention and Punishment of the Crime of Genocide*, Judgment of 26 February 2007, paras. 428–438, esp. 430–432.

factors. For example, with regard to the protection of aliens, international law can impose on State agents a negative obligation (of result) to refrain from the improper use of weapons against aliens. But it cannot require State agents to certainly avoid any misuse of weapons against aliens by private individuals nor to ensure the capture of those responsible: it must limit itself to requiring from State officials a positive behaviour of due diligence, i.e., to use their "best efforts" in the activities of prevention and repression.

This distinction has considerable theoretical and practical consequences. A first consequence is that the element of "diligence" is present in the content of certain international obligations, while it is absent in the content of other obligations. This characterizes differently the structure and content of two categories of international obligations, and also characterizes differently the way in which they are breached and thus the respective responsibility regime.

A second consequence is that it is easier for the victim to prove a breach of an obligation of result than an obligation of due diligence. In the first case, in fact, in order to prove the presence of the objective element of the wrongful act, i.e. the breach of the obligation, it is sufficient to show that the desired result of the obligation has not been achieved. And, since in this case the norm violated almost always clearly indicates such a result, the breach usually appears evident. In the second case, instead, the victim must demonstrate the lack of due diligence on the part of the alleged perpetrator of the offence; that is, the difference between the conduct concretely maintained by the perpetrator and that required by the standard of due diligence. It is then a question of comparing the content of the conduct actually carried out with that abstractly required by the norm and the problem is much more delicate. In other words, the relationship between the conduct held and the breach of the obligation (or, if you want the causal relationship) is more difficult to prove.

A third consequence of the distinction concerns the relationship between diligence and fault. This is a complex topic, which is not possible to go into here. In extreme synthesis, and referring only to international law, it can be said that the positive concept of diligence can be, in many respects, considered correlative to the negative concept of fault (in the strict sense of negligence); namely, that lack of diligence equals fault. But there are at least two elements of difference. First, while fault usually retains a psychological-subjective, or at least partly subjective, connotation, due diligence represents a standard of objective behaviour; and therefore a sort of "objective fault". Secondly, and this difference is more relevant: whereas fault is usually conceived as an element (necessary or not depending on the various theories) of the State's international wrongful act, and therefore within the framework of secondary norms on responsibility, due diligence is an element contained in primary norms, or *rectius* in primary obligations.

The practice of international human rights monitoring bodies shows that the distinction between obligations of result and obligations of due diligence is very important if we are to understand the exact content of the obligations undertaken by

States and thus to be able to ascertain with certainty in which cases they have committed a breach of these obligations.[28]

Finally, it is worth repeating that, when I talk about obligations of result and of due diligence, I have so far referred to *immediate and binding* obligations: that is, obligations that the State must perform immediately and in all their elements. However, there are also obligations relating to human rights which are different in nature from those examined so far, in the sense that they are not immediately and completely binding. To explain their nature, other legal categories must be used.

8.2.3 Immediate Obligations and Obligations "of Progressive Realization"

A third useful distinction, in fact, is that between immediate obligations (of result or of due diligence) and obligations "of progressive realization" (sometimes referred to more simply as "progressive obligations").[29] In reality, this distinction has been little studied in international law. The Committee on Economic, Social and Cultural Rights sometimes speaks of "progressive obligations", but has not explored this concept well. More recently, an attempt to clarify the distinction has been made by the UN High Commissioner for Human Rights.

In my view, the distinction between immediate and "progressive" obligations can be brought closer to the distinction, which is well known in the constitutional law of many States, between "preceptive" (or immediately binding) norms and programmatic norms. To tell the truth, even in international law there is sometimes talk of programmatic norms, precisely in relation to norms on economic, social and cultural rights; but the concept that prevails is that programmatic norms do not have binding effects, but merely exhortative effects. In other words, there is a tendency to contrast, in my view wrongly, the concept of a programmatic norm with that of a binding norm.

Instead, if one adopts the correct concept of a programmatic norm that has been established by comparative constitutional law today, the conclusion must be different. The programmatic norm has some binding effects and is capable of creating real obligations for those to whom it is addressed: not immediately binding obligations, but obligations that must be progressively realized over time and that are also capable, during the course of their full implementation, of producing certain legal effects.

More specifically, the constitutional courts have identified the following effects produced by the programmatic constitutional norms on social rights. First: a "negative" juridical effect of such norms is that of being able to invalidate laws that may be in absolute conflict with them. Second: a "positive" legal effect is given by the principle of reasonableness. This means that the legislator, in determining the

[28]On this practice see Pisillo Mazzeschi (2008), chapters III and IV.

[29]*Ibidem*, pp. 290–297 and chapter V.

implementation of social rights, must use due reasonableness in balancing this implementation with the other primary interests guaranteed by the Constitution and the needs of the budget. Thirdly, social rights, even if they are laid down in programmatic norms, cannot be so compressed as to affect certain "essential minimum obligations".

Returning now to international law and the field of human rights, it should be noted that the concept of "progressive obligations" finds normative confirmation in various treaties or individual treaty provisions on economic, social and cultural rights. Article 2(1) of the Covenant on Economic, Social and Cultural Rights (which is the fundamental norm of the Covenant) establishes that each State Party:

> [. . .] undertakes to take steps [. . .] to the maximum of its available resources, with a view to achieving progressively the full realization of the rights recognized in the present Covenant, by all appropriate means [. . .].

Article 26 of the American Convention on Human Rights (concerning economic, social and cultural rights) is entitled "progressive development", and prescribes that States Parties shall take measures:

> [. . .] with a view to achieving progressively [. . .] the full realization of the rights implicit in the economic, social, educational, scientific, and cultural standards [established in the OAS Charter].

Similar rules can be found in Article 4(2) of the UN Convention on the Rights of Persons with Disabilities, Article 4 of the UN Convention on the Rights of the Child, and Article 1 of the San Salvador Protocol. Analogous formulas are also contained in many more specific provisions of the Covenant on Economic, Social and Cultural Rights,[30] in the European Social Charter (revised)[31] and, albeit more implicitly, in certain principles on solidarity contained in the EU Charter of Fundamental Rights.[32]

Having said this, the nature of progressive obligations and the legal discipline of such obligations and their violations should now be better defined.

With regard to the first aspect, the concept of "progressive realization" of human rights can be inferred from the statement made by the Committee on Economic, Social and Cultural Rights, according to which Article 2(1) of the Covenant requires the State "to move as expeditiously and effectively as possible" towards the goal of full realization of human rights.[33] This is, in the final analysis, the real content of the obligation "of progressive realization": the State must produce a continuous and protracted effort, aimed at achieving a given objective, it *must move towards that goal*. The UN High Commissioner for Human Rights expressed the same concept when she said that States must:

---

[30]See, e.g., Articles 6(2), 11(1), 12(2), 15(2).

[31]See, e.g., Articles 2(1), 3(4), 12(3) of Part II.

[32]See, e.g., Articles 31(1), 33(1), 35, 36.

[33]CteeESCR, General Comment No. 3, 14 December 1990, para. 9.

> [. . .] undertake targeted measures to move as expeditiously and effectively as possible towards the full realization of economic, social and cultural rights.[34]

In my view, this is a *general and complex obligation*, for which the State must fulfil *several more specific obligations* over time: for example, that of legislating, that of adopting judicial or administrative measures, that of taking financial, technical, educational, promotional and social measures. These specific obligations can vary in nature, so they can sometimes be obligations of result and sometimes due diligence obligations. They can sometimes be imposed on the State as immediate obligations, during the path towards the full realization of the final objective to be achieved.

With regard to the legal discipline of "progressive obligations", it can be noted that all the treaty provisions on human rights which contain such obligations also establish *legal criteria* which regulate the forms, ways and timescale with which States must operate for their fulfilment. These criteria therefore place limits on the discretion of States. In brief, they are as follows: (*a*) States must use all "appropriate means" (i.e., adequate, reasonable and effective measures) to achieve the required objective; (*b*) States must also use "their own available resources", economic, human and technical, reasonably balancing the resources allocated to human rights and those allocated to other primary State interests.

It follows from this that any conduct by the State contrary to the various specific obligations and legal criteria that are part and parcel of the general "progressive obligation" will be unlawful. For example, an international wrongful act occurs: (*a*) if the State adopts *regressive measures* with respect to the objective of the progressive realization of a right; (*b*) if the State remains *totally passive* and does not adopt measures of any kind towards that objective; (*c*) if the State, while moving towards the objective of the progressive realization of a given human right, does not use the *appropriate means* or *available resources* (according to the criterion of reasonableness) to achieve that objective; (*d*) if the State does not respect the *minimum obligation* to meet the essential level of the human right that it is obliged to progressively realize.

These various hypotheses of violations of "progressive obligations" are confirmed, especially in the field of economic, social and cultural rights, by the practice of international human rights monitoring bodies.[35]

---

[34] *Report of the United Nations High Commissioner for Human Rights*, E/2007/82, 25 June 2007, para. 76.

[35] See Pisillo Mazzeschi (2008), Chap. V. See also above, Sect. 4.4.2.

8.2.4 Distinction Between Legal Obligations and Non-binding Political Objectives

Finally, it is possible that certain provisions contained in international human rights acts may not create true legal obligations on the States to which such provisions are addressed, but may only produce commitments or political objectives of a non-binding nature.

This is particularly the case for a limited number of collective human rights that belong to the third and fourth generations.[36] These rights are contained in several international acts of a different nature, but usually not legally binding, such as resolutions or declarations of principles of the UN General Assembly, resolutions of the Human Rights Council (formerly the Commission on Human Rights), and final declarations of international conferences. But sometimes they are also contained in international acts of a binding nature, such as the African Charter on Human and Peoples' Rights.

Collective human rights, as already mentioned,[37] usually include the rights to development, exploitation of natural resources, peace, a healthy environment, democracy, good governance, and human security. I will deal with these rights later.[38]

8.3 Conclusions on the Content and Nature of Human Rights Obligations

It is now appropriate to draw some conclusions on the various distinctions examined between categories of international human rights obligations. The first conclusion is that the distinction between negative and positive obligations, although in some cases it may not be entirely clear-cut, is nevertheless a distinction that has become firmly established both in general international law and in the field of human rights, and which has theoretical validity and practical utility. However, both categories are very broad and generic, and include within them subcategories of obligations of different nature and structure. In particular, the category of positive obligations only indicates that the State must in some way take action to comply with the obligation, but does not indicate the precise forms and ways for the fulfilment of individual positive obligations and consequently the forms and ways of their possible violation. Therefore, the distinction between negative and positive obligations can only be a starting point.

The second conclusion concerns those distinctions between international obligations which have been drawn up especially in the field of human rights, but with the claim that they have more general validity in international law. I have

[36]On this topic see, e.g., Tomuschat (2014), pp. 149–154.

[37]See above, Sect. 8.1.1.

[38]See below, Sects. 25.3 and 25.4.

defined them as "descriptive" distinctions, because it seems to me that they have in common the defect of having little technical-legal and conceptual-systematic value. They can only provide a description, apparently simple and effective but in reality very approximate, of certain characteristics (historical, economic or other) that tend to prevail in certain international obligations. Also the distinction between obligations *to respect*, *to protect* and *to fulfil* human rights, which has recently been successful in the doctrine specializing in human rights, is, in my view, very unsatisfactory from a technical-legal and theoretical point of view, and is also not really innovative with respect to some older distinctions.

The third conclusion, on the other hand, confirms the validity of the categories of (immediate) obligations of result, (immediate) obligations of due diligence and obligations "of progressive realization". They are valid both at the theoretical-systematic level and at that of the practice concretely operating in international law in general and in the specific field of human rights. They are the most useful categories for understanding the exact content of the various obligations and, therefore, the ways and timescales for their exact fulfilment by States and by other entities bearing such obligations.

Therefore, I will use these categories of obligations when, in Parts V and VI, I will examine the content and character of individual human rights.

References

Ago R (1938) La regola del previo esaurimento dei ricorsi interni in tema di responsabilità internazionale. Archivio di diritto pubblico, Padova, p 178 ff

Ago R (1939) Le delit international. RC 68:415–554

Ago R (1977) Sixième rapport sur la responsabilité des Etats. ACDI II-1:3 ff

Besson S (2020a) Due diligence and extraterritorial human rights obligations – mind the gap! ESIL Reflect 9:1–9

Besson S (2020b) La due diligence en droit international. RC 409:153–398

Cassella S (ed) (2018) Le standard de due diligence et la responsabilité internationale, SFDI Journée d'etudes du Mans. Pédone, Paris

Eide A (1984) The International Human Rights System. In: Eide A et al (eds) Food as a Human Right. The United Nations University, Tokyo, pp 152–161

Kulesza J (2016) Due diligence in International Law. Brill/Nijhoff, Leiden-Boston

Mowbray A (2004) The development of positive obligations under the European Convention on Human Rights by the European Court of Human Rights. Hart, Oxford

Pisillo Mazzeschi R (1989) "Due Diligence" e responsabilità internazionale degli Stati. Giuffrè, Milano

Pisillo Mazzeschi R (1992) The due diligence rule and the nature of the international responsibility of states. German Yearb Int Law 35:9–51

Pisillo Mazzeschi R (2008) Responsabilité de l'État pour violation des obligations positives relatives aux droits de l'homme. RC 333:175–506

Pisillo Mazzeschi R (2018a) Le chemin étrange de la due diligence: d'un concept mystérieux à un concept surévalué. In: Cassella S (ed) Le standard de due diligence et la responsabilité internationale, SFDI Journée d'etudes du Mans. Pédone, Paris, pp 323–337

Shue H (1980) Basic Rights: Subsistence, Affluence, and US Foreign Policy. Princeton University Press, Princeton

Tomuschat C (2014) Human Rights: between idealism and realism, 3rd edn. Oxford University Press, Oxford

Spatial Scope of Obligations 9

9.1 Introduction

The issue of the "spatial scope" of international human rights obligations of States is important,[1] because it serves to clarify the spaces, and consequently also the persons and concrete situations, that fall under the protection of human rights norms; and, therefore, it also serves to clarify when the conduct of a State is lawful and when, instead, it constitutes a violation of human rights capable of generating the international responsibility of the State.

Actually, the term "spatial scope" of human rights obligations is not often used; rather, the more technical "territorial application" or "jurisdictional application" of such obligations is preferred. But the latter two concepts are not identical. The term "territorial" has a precise and rather restrictive meaning: it refers to the power of government (or, in more traditional terms, of authority or domination) of the State over its own territory. On the other hand, the term "jurisdictional", in the Anglo-Saxon legal sense of "State jurisdiction", refers to the State's governing authority in the broadest sense, i.e. it includes executive, legislative and judicial power, and extends not only to the State's territory, but also sometimes outside the territory, including all spaces, objects and persons over which the State exercises, *de jure* or *de facto*, effective authority or control. This includes, for example, the diplomatic and consular missions of the State abroad or the missions and military occupations of the State in foreign territories. Therefore, to avoid confusion of terminology, I prefer to use the broader term "spatial scope".

States, in principle, when taking on human rights obligations, undertake to respect them both within their own territory and in other areas over which they exercise governmental authority or jurisdiction. However, the problem of the spatial scope of human rights obligations is rather complex, since, in the present reality,

[1]On this subject see, for all, De Sena (2002), Clapham and Kamminga (2004) and Milanovic (2011).

R. Pisillo Mazzeschi, *International Human Rights Law*,
https://doi.org/10.1007/978-3-030-77032-7_9

various situations of uncertain and controversial solutions may arise, especially when States operate outside their territory, sometimes together with other States or within the framework of international organizations. Moreover, it is not easy to reconstruct norms of general international law on the spatial scope of States' human rights obligations, since the most important multilateral treaties contain similar but not identical provisions on this point; and the practice of international human rights monitoring bodies is not entirely uniform. Nevertheless, as we shall see, I believe that some general norms can be established.

9.2 Provisions of the Treaties on Their "Spatial Scope"

The main human rights treaties, either explicitly or implicitly, establish the obligation for States Parties to respect the rights set out in the treaty in respect of all individuals, whether citizens or foreigners, who are present on their territory. This is the simplest situation. One could define these obligations of the State as "territorial" in the strict sense. However, during the preparatory work on these treaties, the question arose as to whether the conventional obligations of each State should also apply to conduct or acts *carried out* outside the territory or *having effects* outside the territory. It was then decided to include a number of ad hoc provisions to determine the "spatial scope" of the treaties.[2] These provisions do not all have the same wording; but they usually determine this scope either by using the two concepts of "territory" and "jurisdiction" cumulatively or by using only the concept of "jurisdiction" in the broad sense.

Among the treaties that use the two concepts, one can mention the Covenant on Civil and Political Rights, which adopts a precise formula, since it establishes, in Article 2(1), that each State Party undertakes to respect and ensure the rights recognized in the Covenant "to all individuals within its territory and subject to its jurisdiction". The Human Rights Committee has interpreted this expression in the sense that it also includes "extraterritorial" obligations; that is, that the Covenant also applies to actions and acts carried out by a State Party in foreign territories, provided that they are under the effective control of the State.[3] The International Court of Justice also supported this interpretation of the Covenant in its 2004 advisory opinion on the *Wall in Palestine*[4] and in its 2005 judgment on *Armed Activities on the territory of the Congo*.[5] The 1984 UN Convention against Torture adopts a formula similar to that of the Covenant, but less precise, since Article 2(1) provides that each State Party must take measures to prevent acts of torture "in any territory under its jurisdiction".

---

[2]See Tomuschat (2014), p. 94.

[3]HRCtee, *Celiberti*; *Lopez Burgos*; *Pereira Montero*. See also Focarelli (2013), p. 123.

[4]ICJ, *Legal Consequences of the Construction of a Wall*, paras. 109–113.

[5]ICJ, *Armed Activities on the Territory of the Congo*, Judgment of 19 December 2005, para. 216.

In contrast, other treaties use only the concept of "jurisdiction". Article 1 of the European Convention on Human Rights stipulates that States Parties "shall secure to everyone within their jurisdiction the rights and freedoms" provided for in the Convention. But in reality, as we shall see later, in the case-law of the Convention's supervisory bodies, the concept of "jurisdiction" of the State has been interpreted very broadly and includes several extraterritorial obligations of the State itself. The American Convention of Human Rights uses similar terminology, since Article 1 (1) provides that States Parties undertake to respect the rights and freedoms recognized by the Convention and to ensure "to all persons subject to their jurisdiction" the free and full exercise of those rights and freedoms. Again, the term "jurisdiction" has been interpreted broadly.[6] Similarly, the 1989 Convention on the Rights of the Child stipulates that States Parties must respect and ensure the rights provided for in the Convention "to each child within their jurisdiction".[7]

Finally, there are other human rights treaties which, in order to determine their spatial scope, do not refer either to the notion of "territory" or to that of "jurisdiction". One may recall, in this sense, the Covenant on Economic, Social and Cultural Rights,[8] the African Charter on Human and Peoples' Rights, and the 1965 Convention against Racial Discrimination. However, it must be considered that even in these cases the spatial scope of the treaty must be interpreted broadly. This interpretation is also confirmed by the position taken by the International Court of Justice in the case concerning the *Application of the Convention against Racial Discrimination*. In fact, the Court, in its order of 15 October 2008, after finding that there is no general restriction on the territorial application of the Convention and no specific territorial limit in the articles of the Convention whose infringement is alleged, stated:

> [. . .] the Court consequently finds that these provisions of CERD generally appear to apply, like other provisions of instruments of that nature, to the actions of a State party when it acts beyond its territory.[9]

Therefore, it can be concluded that States Parties to human rights treaties must respect the rights provided for therein with respect to individuals who are on their territory or under their "jurisdiction". However, it must now be explored how this general principle should be interpreted and applied more specifically.

---

[6]See the cases cited by Focarelli (2013), p. 124.

[7]CRC, Art. 2(1).

[8]With regard to the Covenant on Economic, Social and Cultural Rights, the International Court of Justice, in its advisory opinion of 9 July 2004 on the *Wall in Palestine*, said that the Covenant "guarantees rights which are essentially territorial". But this opinion has been criticized in doctrine: De Schutter (2010), p. 124; Ssenyonio (2009), pp. 42–46.

[9]ICJ, *Application of the International Convention on the Elimination of All Forms of Racial Discrimination*, Order of 15 October 2008, para. 109.

9.3 Three Different Forms of "Spatial Jurisdiction" of the State in Human Rights Matters

To examine how the spatial scope of the human rights treaties has been interpreted in the various contexts or situations that may arise in reality, I will distinguish, for systematic reasons, between *three different forms of spatial jurisdiction* that may be exercised by the State (i.e., between three categories of State obligations).

First of all, it will be worth dealing with the principle of *territorial jurisdiction*; that is, the obligations of the State relating to acts of possible human rights violations that *occur and have effects* on the national territory. As already mentioned, it is commonly accepted that the State is obliged to respect the human rights of all people on its territory. However, one has to wonder if this general rule suffers from exceptions when the State does not have effective control over its own territory (or part of it) and when agents of one State commit violations on the territory of another State without the latter being aware of the violations or having been able to prevent them.

Secondly, the so-called *extraterritorial jurisdiction* of the State will have to be examined; i.e. the State's obligations relating to acts of its agents who operate on foreign territory (or in areas not subject to the sovereignty of any State) and may commit human rights violations there. Within the large category of "extraterritorial jurisdiction", two different situations can be distinguished: (*a*) that in which military contingents or other agents of the State, usually in the framework of military or peace-building or State-building missions, occupy a foreign territory or exercise effective control over parts of a foreign territory; (*b*) that in which State agents operate on foreign territory, without having effective control of that territory, and commit human rights violations there. As we shall see, in this second situation, the question of the extraterritorial jurisdiction of the State is examined through the legal concept of "State agent authority and control".

Thirdly, one must consider *jurisdiction with extraterritorial effects*; i.e. the obligations of the State relating to acts carried out on the national territory, but which produce effects contrary to human rights outside that territory. This situation can occur when legislative, administrative or judicial acts of a State, carried out and executed in the national territory, or concrete behavior of agents of the State, also carried out in the national territory, cause violations of the human rights of persons who are on foreign territory. One thinks, for example, of a measure of the State which confiscates in its own territory property belonging to an alien or of an extradition measure which involves the violation of the rights of a person in foreign territory.[10]

I will now examine, in a separate and more analytical way, these three forms of spatial jurisdiction of the State related to human rights.

[10] See, e.g., ECtHR, *Soering v. UK*. See also below, Sect. 14.2.3.1.

9.4 Territorial Jurisdiction: Obligations and Responsibility of the State for Acts Performed on Its Territory

9.4.1 The General Rule Based on Territorial Sovereignty

As already said, there is no doubt that States must comply with their human rights obligations (under general or conventional international law) on their territory and that they are responsible, in principle, for violations of these rights occurring on their territory, provided, of course, that the violations are attributable to the State according to the rules on the attribution of internationally wrongful acts. After all, States, in accordance with the principle of territorial sovereignty, enjoy full power of government, subject to the limits dictated by international law, over their own territory and the human community there. Therefore, even when human rights treaties define their spatial scope with reference only to the concept of "jurisdiction", this concept, as we have seen, certainly includes also that of "territory".

The same general rule also applies to the obligations of the State relating to possible human rights violations occurring on board ships or aircraft of the nationality of the State. One could speak, in these cases, of "quasi-territorial" jurisdiction. However, beyond the terminology, it is clear that the exclusive power of government of the State, and its consequent responsibility, also applies in these circumstances.

That said, we must now see if this general rule is subject to exceptions.

9.4.2 Inability of the State to Control Its Territory

A first exception may occur when the State is unable to exercise its power of government, or in any case has lost effective control over the national territory or part of it. This situation may occur, for example, when the armed forces of another State have occupied the national territory, or when an insurgent movement has obtained full and effective control over part of the national territory, or when armed forces authorized by the UN Security Council have *de facto* occupied part of the national territory. The case-law of international human rights monitoring bodies seems to favor this exception; but with some caution. The most significant practices are those of the supervisory bodies of the European Convention system and the Inter-American system.

The European Court of Human Rights considers that there is a *relative presumption* that the territorial State exercises its power of government and control over events occurring on its territory; but that this presumption does *not* operate when it is shown that the State is materially incapable of exercising its power of government on its own territory or on parts of it.

A first decision, although not explicit, of the Court on this issue can be found in the 1995 *Loizidou* judgment,[11] in which the Court ruled that the responsibility of a

[11]ECtHR, *Loizidou*, Judgment of 23 March 1995, paras. 62–64.

State Party may arise when, as a result of military action, it exercises effective control over an area outside its national territory; and that this entails the obligation to respect human rights established by the Convention in that area. This conclusion was reiterated in the 1996 *Loizidou* judgment.[12] However, the first decision of the Court which explicitly addresses the issue of the inability of the State to control part of its territory is that of 10 May 2001 in the *Cyprus v. Turkey* case.[13] In that judgment the Court stated that, since Turkey had overall effective control over the territory of Northern Cyprus, it was also responsible for ensuring that the human rights of the European Convention were respected in that territory.[14] It also follows from the decision that, conversely, the Government of Cyprus did not have that responsibility. Indeed, according to the Court:

> Having regard to the applicant Government's [Cyprus] continuing inability to exercise their Convention obligations in northern Cyprus, any other finding would result in a regrettable vacuum in the system of human-rights protection in the territory in question by removing from individuals there the benefit of the Convention's fundamental safeguards and their right to call a High Contracting Party to account for violation of their rights in proceedings before the Court.[15]

This judgment takes a clear position in the sense that the "jurisdiction" of a State does not extend to its entire territory if, in certain parts of that territory, the State is *de facto* incapable of exercising its control for the effective protection of human rights.[16]

However, the Strasbourg Court, a few years later, in a similar case, took a more prudent and flexible stance. In its 2004 judgment in the *Ilaşcu* case, the Court stated that the Moldavian Government, the only legitimate government of the Republic of Moldova under international law, no longer exercised its governing authority in the part of its territory that had fallen under the effective control of the separatist movement called the Moldavan Republic of Transdniestra; but that it did not cease to have "jurisdiction" over the occupied territory and still had the obligation to take possible measures to protect the rights guaranteed by the Convention. In fact, the Court first acknowledged that the Moldovan Government:

> [. . .] does not exercise authority over part of its territory, namely that part which is under the effective control of the [Moldavan Republic of Transdniestra].[17]

[12]ECtHR, *Loizidou*, Judgment of 18 December 1996, paras. 52–57.

[13]ECtHR, *Cyprus v. Turkey*, para. 78.

[14]*Ibidem*, para. 77: "It follows that, in terms of Article 1 of the Convention, Turkey's "jurisdiction" must be considered to extend to securing the entire range of substantive rights set out in the Convention and those additional Protocols which she has ratified, and that violations of those rights are imputable to Turkey".

[15]*Ibidem*, para. 78.

[16]See De Schutter (2010), p. 133.

[17]ECtHR, *Ilaşcu and Others*, para. 330.

But then it added that:

> even in the absence of effective control over the Transdniestrian region, Moldova still has a positive obligation under Article 1 of the Convention to take the diplomatic, economic, judicial or other measures that it is in its power to take and are in accordance with international law to secure to the applicants the rights guaranteed by the Convention.[18]

Finally, the Court explained that, in such a situation, the scope of the "jurisdiction" of the legitimate Government is reduced:

> Where a Contracting State is prevented from exercising its authority over the whole of its territory by a constraining *de facto* situation [...] it does not thereby cease to have jurisdiction within the meaning of Article 1 of the Convention over that part of its territory temporarily subject to a local authority sustained by rebel forces of by another State. Nevertheless such a factual situation *reduces* the scope of that jurisdiction, in that the undertaking given by the State under Article 1 must be considered by the Court only in the light of the Contracting State's positive obligations towards persons within its territory.[19]

Therefore, it can be concluded that, according to the Strasbourg Court, when the State which has legitimate authority over a territory does not have the capacity to exercise concrete powers of control over that territory or part of it, its "jurisdiction" and relative responsibility for human rights violations, that occurred there, are not presumed; but it can nevertheless be demonstrated that the State had the power to influence the protection of the human rights of persons under the concrete control of another State or other para-State entities.[20]

The Commission and the Inter-American Court of Human Rights have also examined situations in which a State claimed to be incapable of exercising effective control over parts of its territory, and therefore could not be held responsible for human rights violations occurring in such parts of the territory.[21] One example is the *Ituango Massacres* case.[22] The Colombian Government claimed that the reported massacres were committed by paramilitary groups in a territory that could not in fact be controlled by the government army. The Inter-American Court, in a 2006 ruling, acknowledged that the paramilitary groups had committed armed raids and killed defenseless civilians; but held that Colombia was responsible for acts of omission, acquiescence and collaboration by Colombian agents. The Inter-American Commission has also reached similar conclusions in some reports on the human rights situation in Colombia.[23]

---

[18] *Ibidem*, para. 331.

[19] *Ibidem*, para. 333 (emphasis added).

[20] In this sense see also Focarelli (2012–2013), vol. I, p. 457. On the *Ilaşcu* case, see also Nigro (2005).

[21] On the case-law of the Inter-American system, see De Schutter (2010), pp. 138–141.

[22] IACtHR, *Ituango Massacres v. Colombia.*

[23] IACmHR, *Annual Report 1996*, 14 March 1997; *Report of the Human Rights Situation in Colombia*, 26 February 1999, Chap. IV. On these reports see also De Schutter (2010), pp. 139–141.

In conclusion, it seems to me that the practice of international human rights monitoring bodies has adopted a balanced solution, based above all on the criterion of *effective control of the territory*, as a key element of the principle of territorial sovereignty. This is not an absolute criterion, but a relative one; it therefore needs to be adapted to the specific and concrete circumstances of each individual case.

9.4.3 Inability of the State to Control Human Rights Violations Committed on Its Territory by Foreign Agents

According to some doctrine, a second exception, to the general rule based on the responsibility of the State for acts carried out on its territory, could occur when violations of human rights by foreign State agents have been committed on that territory, without the territorial State having *de facto* and concretely the possibility to know of the violations and/or to prevent them. One thinks, for example, of the acts of kidnapping, killing or extraordinary renditions carried out in the territory of a State by foreign secret service agents. The doctrine under examination considers that this exception is based on the same logic as the one just examined. Even in these circumstances, one should apply the rule of the inability of the territorial State to exercise effective control, but not generically on the territory but rather *on certain persons and certain situations*. Some authors say that the territorial State, because it loses *de facto* control over such persons or situations, is not directly responsible for the violations.[24]

However, in my opinion, this exception is problematic and cannot be assimilated to the previous one. In fact, in these circumstances, it cannot be argued that the principle of territorial sovereignty ceases to operate and that the State has lost effective control of its territory. What comes to the fore is another issue: the *concrete capacity of the territorial State to prevent offences* (human rights violations) by foreign individuals on its territory. Moreover, in the example I have given of abuses committed by foreign secret service agents, the violations are committed not by private individuals, but by officials of foreign States, who, because of their qualification, are usually subject to greater control by the territorial State.

Therefore, the problem must be brought back into the framework of the positive and due diligence obligations of the State relating to human rights; and, more precisely, the obligation to take concrete measures to prevent human rights violations.[25] It follows that we *cannot speak of an exception* to the general rule based on the responsibility of the territorial State. On the contrary, since that State should exercise a high degree of diligence in monitoring the actions of foreign agents on its territory, the same State has the burden of proving that, in the concrete circumstances of each case, it was absolutely impossible for it to prevent the

---

[24]Kälin and Künzli (2009), p. 132.

[25]See Pisillo Mazzeschi (2008), pp. 282–290 and 390–414.

human rights violations committed by foreign officials on its territory. Otherwise, the State incurs responsibility by omission.

9.5 "Extraterritorial Jurisdiction": Obligations and Responsibility of the State for Acts Committed on Foreign Territory

It is now worth considering the so-called "extraterritorial jurisdiction" of the State in matters of human rights, i.e. the obligations of the State in relation to acts of its agents operating abroad who may commit human rights violations there. It seems to me that only in this case can one correctly speak of "extraterritorial jurisdiction" and that it should be kept separate from the jurisdiction "with extraterritorial effects", which I will deal with later.[26]

Moreover, as already mentioned,[27] in the context of extraterritorial jurisdiction, a distinction must be made between two different contexts: (*a*) that in which a State occupies the territory of another State or otherwise exercises effective control over that territory;[28] (*b*) that in which the agents of one State act on the territory of another State without occupying or controlling that territory.[29] As we shall see, the second context may, in turn, include several situations.

9.5.1 Occupation or Effective Control of a Foreign Territory

Even in the contemporary world, despite the principle prohibiting the use of force, there are cases in which a State (sometimes together with other States or within the framework of missions authorized by international organizations) militarily *occupies* the territory (or part of the territory) of another State or, without reaching the extremes of occupation, exercises *effective control* over that territory. Examples include the Israeli occupation of the Palestinian territories, the occupation of Kuwait by Iraq in 1991, the occupation of Iraq by the USA and other States in 2003, and the control of Northern Cyprus by Turkey.

It is common ground that the concept of "jurisdiction" of the State, for the purposes of the applicability of its human rights obligations, extends, in principle, to cover these situations. It is irrelevant whether or not the occupation is lawful under international law. This rule, after all, is the one *inversely corresponding* to the rule already examined,[30] which exempts the territorial State from responsibility when it is incapable of effectively controlling its own territory.

[26]See below, Sect. 9.6.

[27]See above, Sect. 9.3.

[28]See below, Sect. 9.5.1.

[29]See below, Sect. 9.5.2.

[30]See above, Sect. 9.4.2.

International practice confirms this form of extraterritorial jurisdiction. In the framework of the European Convention on Human Rights, two important and classic cases, which have addressed the problem of extraterritorial jurisdiction in the case of control of a foreign territory, are the already mentioned *Loizidou* cases. In its 1995 judgment, the Strasbourg Court said:

> [. . .] the Court recalls that, although Article 1 [. . .] sets limits on the reach of the Convention, the concept of 'jurisdiction' under this provision is not restricted to the national territory of the High Contracting Parties [. . .] the responsibility of a Contracting Party may also arise when as a consequence of military action – whether lawful or unlawful – it exercises effective control of an area outside its national territory. The obligation to secure, in such an area, the rights and freedoms set out in the Convention derives from the fact of such control whether it be exercised directly, through its armed forces, or through a subordinate local administration.[31]

Then, in the subsequent *Loizidou* judgment of 1996, the Court stated:

> It is not necessary to determine whether [. . .] Turkey actually exercises detailed control over the policies and actions of the authorities of the 'TRNC'. It is obvious from the large number of troops engaged in active duties in northern Cyprus [. . .] that her army exercises effective overall control over that part of the island. Such control [. . .] entails her responsibility for the policies and actions of the 'TRNC' [. . .]. Those affected by such policies or actions therefore come within the 'jurisdiction' of Turkey for the purposes of Article 1 of the Convention [. . .]. Her obligation to secure to the applicant the rights and freedoms set out in the Convention therefore extends to the northern part of Cyprus.[32]

Therefore, for the Court, the main guiding criterion for determining the "jurisdiction" of the State under Article 1 of the Convention is that of the *effective overall control* that the State exercises over a foreign territory, regardless of whether or not there is formal sovereignty over that territory. This position was later confirmed also in the already mentioned *Ilaşcu* judgment of 2004, where the Court stated:

> The Court has accepted that in exceptional circumstances the acts of Contracting States performed outside their territory, or which produce effects there, may amount to exercise by them of their jurisdiction within the meaning of Article 1 of the Convention [. . .] It is not necessary to determine whether a Contracting Party actually exercises detailed control over the policies and actions of the authorities in the area situated outside its national territory, since even *overall control* of the area may engage the responsibility of the Contracting Party concerned.[33]

It should also be noted that, in recent years, the European Court has shown a tendency to broaden the concept of overall control that a State exercises on foreign territory. In this sense one can cite the *Catan* case of 2012 and the *Chiragov* case of 2015. In the *Catan* case, the Court held that a State can exercise control over a

[31]ECtHR, *Loizidou*, Judgment of 23 March 1995, para. 62.

[32]ECtHR, *Loizidou*, Judgment of 18 December 1996, para. 56 (emphasis added).

[33]ECtHR, *Ilaşcu and Others*, paras. 314–315 (emphasis added).

foreign territory, either directly through its armed forces, or indirectly through a subordinate local administration for whose actions the State remains responsible. Moreover, for the Court:

> It is a question of fact whether a Contracting State exercises effective control over an area outside its own territory. In determining whether effective control exists, the Court will primarily have reference to the strength of the State's military presence in the area [...] Other indicators may also be relevant, such as the extent to which its military, *economic and political support* for the local subordinate administration provides it with influence and control over the region.[34]

As can be seen, the Court has broadened the notion of control of the territory by a foreign State, stating that this may result not only from military occupation, but also from the influence that that State may exercise, from a political and economic point of view, over a geographical area of another State.[35]

The European Court's basic theory, founded on the guiding criterion of overall control on foreign territory, is shared by the UN Treaty-Bodies. The Human Rights Committee has stated that the norms of the Covenant on Civil and Political Rights are applicable, according to the principles of international law, in the Palestinian territories occupied by Israel;[36] and that the same norms are applicable in the Kuwait territories occupied by Iraq in 1991.[37] The Committee on Economic, Social and Cultural Rights has expressed the same position on the applicability of the Covenant to the Palestinian territories under the effective control of Israel.[38] Similar case-law emerges from the Inter-American human rights system.[39]

Finally, the most authoritative confirmation comes from the International Court of Justice. In its 2004 advisory opinion on the *Wall in Palestine*, the Court stated that:

> [...] the territories occupied by Israel have for over 37 years been subject to its territorial jurisdiction as the occupying Power. In the exercise of the powers available to it on this basis, Israel is bound by the provisions of the International Covenant on Economic, Social and Cultural Rights.[40]

The Court reached the same conclusion in relation to Israel's obligations under the Covenant on Civil and Political Rights and the Convention on the Rights of the

---

[34]ECtHR, *Catan and Others v. Moldova and Russia*, paras. 106–107 (emphasis added). Similarly, see ECtHR, *Chiragov and Others v. Armenia*, paras. 167–168.

[35]See Ronzitti (2016), p. 326.

[36]HRCtee, Concluding Observations: *Israel* (1999), para. 10; Concluding Observations: *Israel* (2003), para. 11.

[37]HRCtee, Concluding Observations: *Iraq* (1991), para. 652. See also HRCtee, General Comment No. 36, 3 September 2019, para. 63.

[38]CteeESCR, Concluding Observations: *Israel*, 23 May 2003, para. 31.

[39]See, for example, IACmHR, *Salas and Others v. USA*.

[40]ICJ, *Legal Consequences of the Construction of a Wall*, para. 112.

Child.[41] The Court subsequently reiterated this position, in more general terms, in its 2005 judgment in the case of *Armed Activities on the Territory of the Congo*, where it said that:

> [. . .] international human rights instruments are applicable 'in respect of acts done by a State in the exercise of its jurisdiction outside its own territory', particularly in occupied territories.[42]

9.5.2 Acts of State Agents Operating in Foreign Territory Without Effective Control Thereof. The Concept of "State Agent Authority and Control"

The second context to be considered is that which occurs when officials of one State act on the territory of another State *without there being effective occupation or control of that territory*, and commit human rights violations there. The question of whether or not the extraterritorial jurisdiction of the first State exists is usually assessed using the criterion of the so-called "State agent authority and control"; i.e., by examining whether State agents acting abroad could exercise, or did in fact exercise, effective control *over certain persons* (those affected by human rights violations) or *over certain concrete circumstances* (those in which human rights violations occurred).

It is therefore a very different situation from that of the effective control of a territory; and it is much more problematic and controversial, both in doctrine and in practice. In fact, also in this case the guiding criterion is that of the *effective control* exercised by the State through its agents; but this criterion, while it is rather easily applicable with respect to a territory or part of a territory, is more difficult to apply with reference to certain persons or certain concrete circumstances.

There are two problems in particular. The first is whether, in this context, the responsibility of the State derives only from the international rules on the attribution to the State of the wrongful conduct of its agents, or whether, in order to ascertain such responsibility, it is necessary to proceed in two distinct phases: (*a*) first, the problem of the attribution to the State of the conduct of its agents must be resolved; (*b*) then, it must be established whether the violation of human rights has occurred under the "jurisdiction" of the State.[43] This problem will be addressed later.[44]

The second problem is to better understand how the guiding principle of effective control should be used according to the "State agent authority and control" rule. That is: should the degree of control exercised by State agents be assessed on a *case by*

---

[41] *Ibidem*, para. 113.

[42] ICJ, *Armed Activities on the Territory of the Congo*, Judgment of 19 December 2005, para. 216.

[43] This problem is well highlighted by De Schutter (2010), esp. p. 147; and Focarelli (2012–2013), p. 457. In reality, the problem of the attribution of conduct and that of extraterritorial jurisdiction are conceptually distinct, although sometimes they tend to coincide in practice.

[44] See below, Sect. 9.5.2.3.

case basis[45] or should a distinction be made between *different situations* in which the rule works differently? This second solution, in my view, is adopted by international practice. More specifically, case-law shows that the investigation into State responsibility takes a different form depending on whether it derives from: (*a*) acts carried out by its diplomatic and consular agents abroad; (*b*) acts performed abroad by its agents on persons in custody or detention; (*c*) other categories of acts carried out abroad by its agents.[46] Let us now look at these three situations separately.

9.5.2.1 Acts of Diplomatic and Consular Agents

As already mentioned, the first situation does not give rise to uncertainty. According to practice, the State is responsible for human rights violations due to the acts or omissions of its diplomatic or consular agents.[47] It can be said that the criterion of effective control of the State is given as proven, with a presumption of absolute character.[48] Or, one could argue that these situations are included in the "quasi-territorial" jurisdiction of the State in matters of human rights,[49] by analogy with the rule on the jurisdiction of the State over ships and aircraft of its nationality.

9.5.2.2 Acts of State Agents on Persons in Custody or Detention

The second situation is more difficult to resolve; but help comes from practice, which is not univocal, but is sufficiently uniform. On the whole, it shows that the State has extraterritorial jurisdiction and is responsible for human rights violations committed by its agents abroad against persons who are under *arrest, custody or detention*. This solution must certainly be approved, because there is no doubt that the State (through its military or prison or police or security officers) exercises effective physical control over persons who are subject to these various forms of detention. Therefore, in this case, the satisfaction of the criterion of "State agent authority and control" must be *presumed*; but it is probably a relative and not absolute presumption.

The European Court of Human Rights has adopted this solution in several judgments, including the *Öcalan*, *Issa*, *Al-Saadoon*, *Medvedyev*, *Al-Jedda* and *Al-Skeini* cases. In the 2005 *Öcalan* case, the Court said that:

> [...] directly after being handed over to the Turkish officials by the Kenyan officials, *the applicant was effectively under Turkish authority* and therefore within the 'jurisdiction' of that State for the purpose of Article 1 of the Convention, even though in this instance Turkey exercised its authority outside its territory.[50]

---

[45] For this view see Kälin and Künzli (2009), p. 134.

[46] For a similar distinction in subcategories, see ECtHR, *Al-Skeini and Others.*

[47] See, e.g., HRCtee, *El Ghar*, para. 7.1 ff.

[48] See ECtHR, *Al Skeini and Others*, para. 134, where, however, the presumption does not seem to be absolute.

[49] Cf. UK High Court of Justice, *Al-Skeini and Others*, para. 270.

[50] ECtHR, *Öcalan*, Judgment of 12 May 2005, para. 91 (emphasis added).

In the *Issa* case,[51] the claim was based on the unlawful arrest, detention, ill-treatment and then the killing of some Iraqi citizens during a military operation conducted by the Turkish army in Northern Iraq in 1995. The Strasbourg Court held that, despite the scale of the military operation, Turkey had not exercised effective overall control over the whole area of Northern Iraq and that the principles which the Court had used in the *Loizidou* cases[52] were therefore not applicable. However, the Court also stated that, if it was established that Turkish soldiers had taken custody of Iraqi citizens before they were mistreated and killed, they would be subject to Turkey's extraterritorial jurisdiction on the basis of *the authority and control exercised over them by the soldiers*. In the *Al-Saadoon and Mufdhi* case,[53] the Court found that two Iraqi nationals held in military prisons controlled by British troops in Iraq fell under the "jurisdiction" of the United Kingdom, which exercised total and exclusive control over the prisoners. In the *Medvedyev* case,[54] French agents had exercised full and exclusive control over a ship and its crew intercepted in international waters. In the *Al-Jedda* case, the European Court confirmed the criteria used in previous cases, ruling that the plaintiff, who had been interned by British forces in a detention facility in Iraq controlled only by those forces, fell within the "jurisdiction" of the United Kingdom. In the words of the Court:

> The internment took place within a detention facility in Basra City, controlled exclusively by British forces, and the applicant was therefore within the authority and control of the United Kingdom throughout [. . .] The decision to hold the applicant in internment was made by the British officer in command of the detention facility [. . .] In conclusion, the Court agrees [. . .] that the internment of the applicant was attributable to the United Kingdom and that during his internment the applicant fell within the jurisdiction of the United Kingdom for the purposes of Article 1 of the Convention.[55]

In this context, the *Al-Skeini* case, which arose from more complex facts and gave rise to some divergent judgments by the English courts and a ruling by the European Court of Human Rights, is also very important. The case stems from an appeal made by relatives of some Iraqi citizens killed in Iraq in an area that was subject to occupation by the United Kingdom. Five of them had been killed in incidents with British military troops, while a sixth had died while held in a military prison by British troops. In a first judgment, in 2004, the UK High Court of Justice decided that the deaths of the five Iraqis resulting from military operations did not fall within the "jurisdiction" of the United Kingdom. On the contrary, the extraterritorial jurisdiction of that State existed in relation to the Iraqi citizen who died in prison. According to the Court:

---

[51]ECtHR, *Issa and Others*, paras. 72–81.

[52]ECtHR, *Loizidou*, Judgments of 23 March 1995, 18 December 1996 and 28 July 1998.

[53]ECtHR, *Al-Saadoon and Mufdhi*, Decision of 30 June 2009, para. 88.

[54]ECtHR, *Medvedyev and Others v. France.*

[55]ECtHR, *Al-Jedda v. UK*, paras. 85–86.

> [...] it is not at all straining the examples of extra-territorial jurisdiction [...] to hold that a British military prison, operating in Iraq with the consent of the Iraqi sovereign authorities, and containing arrested suspects, falls within even a narrowly limited exception exemplified by embassies, consulates, vessels and aircraft, and [...] a prison.[56]

This decision, which clearly confirms the "State agent authority and control" criterion on detained persons, was substantially confirmed by the UK Court of Appeal in a judgment of 2005.[57] But, subsequently, the House of Lords, in 2007, decided differently, stating that the 1998 Human Rights Act (which had implemented the European Convention on Human Rights in the United Kingdom) is not intended to have extraterritorial application, particularly with regard to the conduct of British forces engaged in peacekeeping operations abroad.[58]

Finally, the European Court of Human Rights intervened, with the *Al-Skeini* judgment of 2011,[59] which gave a different solution from those given in the three British judgments. The Court held that the "jurisdiction" of the United Kingdom, under Article 1 of the European Convention, existed in relation to *all Iraqi citizens* killed during the security operations conducted by British soldiers in the area and during the period in question. But it came to this conclusion, as we shall see, using a different criterion from that of the control over the persons detained or, if you like, giving a more extensive interpretation of the concept of "State agent authority and control".

Returning now to the criterion of effective control over persons in custody or detention, it can be said that the practice of other international human rights monitoring bodies also adopts this criterion. The Human Rights Committee believes that the State has "jurisdiction" and is responsible for human rights violations committed by its agents against persons in custody or detention. One may recall the two cases *Lopez Burgos*[60] and *Celiberti de Casariego*,[61] decided on the same day. Mr Lopez Burgos was first detained for several months in Uruguay and then accepted as a refugee in Argentina, where he was abducted by members of the Uruguayan security forces and secretly detained in Buenos Aires for about two weeks. He was then smuggled back to Uruguay, where he was held in a secret prison for three months. The Human Rights Committee stated that where Article 1 of the Covenant on Civil and Political Rights speaks of "individuals subject to the jurisdiction" of a State, it does not refer to "the place where the violation took place", but to "the relationship between the individual and the State".[62] Recently, the Committee confirmed its position in its General Comment No. 36 on the right to life:

---

[56]UK High Court of Justice, *Al-Skeini and Others*, para. 287.

[57]UK Court of Appeal, *Al-Skeini and Others.*

[58]House of Lords, *Al-Skeini and Others.*

[59]ECtHR, *Al-Skeini and Others v. UK.*

[60]HRCtee, *López Burgos v. Uruguay*, para. 12.3.

[61]HRCtee, *Celiberti de Casariego*, para. 10.1.

[62]HRCtee, *López Burgos*, para. 12.2.

> Given that the deprivation of liberty brings a person within a State's effective control, States parties must respect and protect the right to life of all individuals arrested or detained by them, even if held outside their territory.[63]

The Commission and the Inter-American Court of Human Rights adopt the same position. In the *Coard* case,[64] the Inter-American Commission decided that the United States had violated the American Declaration[65] and the American Convention because the US armed forces, after invading Grenada, had illegally detained and mistreated some citizens of Grenada.

Finally, there are cases in which acts of State agents on persons in custody or detention do not take place on the territory of other States, but in areas not subject to the sovereignty of any State, particularly on the high seas. It seems to me that the two situations can be assimilated. The Inter-American Commission, for example, in the *Haitian Interdiction* case[66] had to decide on the legitimacy of the US practice of intercepting boats of Haitian migrants on the high seas and returning them to Haiti, in possible violation of their rights of non-discrimination and asylum in other States. The Commission decided that the prohibition of *refoulement*, under Article 33(1) of the 1951 Geneva Convention on Refugees, has extraterritorial application and that the US had also violated the right of asylum under Article XXVII of the American Declaration. A similar situation has occurred more recently in the European system of human rights, in the well-known *Hirsi* case[67] of 2012. Italian military vessels had intercepted irregular migrants on the high seas and transferred them on board, returned to Libya and handed over to the Libyan authorities. The European Court of Human Rights condemned Italy, among other things, for violation of Article 3 of the European Convention and expressed no doubts about Italy's "jurisdiction" over migrants under Article 1 of the Convention.

In reality, it seems to me that these cases could even fall under what I have termed "quasi-territorial" rather than "extraterritorial" State jurisdiction. In any case, it is clear that these can also be considered as acts of State agents on persons in custody or detention.

9.5.2.3 Other Extraterritorial Acts of State Agents

Let us now examine the third situation indicated above: that relating to extraterritorial jurisdiction and the responsibility of the State for acts of its agents that do not fall within the categories already discussed. This is a situation of a *residual* nature. One thinks, for example, of acts carried out by military forces or other State organs during peace-keeping or peace-building missions in which there is no "effective overall control" on the territory; or executive or judicial functions exercised by bodies or

[63]HRCtee, General Comment No. 36, 3 September 2019, para. 63.

[64]IACmHR, *Coard et al.*, para. 57.

[65]American Declaration on the Rights and Duties of Man, 2 May 1948. See below, Sect. 12.1.

[66]IACmHR, "*Haitian Interdiction*", Decisions of 13 October 1993 and of 13 March 1997.

[67]ECtHR, *Hirsi Jamaa and Others.*

authorities of one State on the territory of another State with the consent of the latter; or isolated acts of individual State agents abroad, such as killings, kidnappings and other abuses (without the exercise of effective control over detained persons). In these cases international practice is not uniform.

A broad interpretation of the extraterritorial jurisdiction of the State seems to be the one accepted by the Human Rights Committee, which tends to apply the notion of "State agent authority and control" to all cases in which a person is subject to effective power or control by State agents, *regardless of the circumstances in which that power has been established and is exercised.* In fact, in its General Comment No. 31 of 2004, on Article 2(1) of the Covenant on Civil and Political Rights, the Committee writes:

> [...] a State party must respect and ensure the rights laid down in the Covenant to anyone within the power or effective control of that State Party [...] This principle also applies to those within power or effective control of the forces of a State Party acting outside its territory, *regardless of the circumstances in which such power or effective control was obtained*, such as forces constituting a national contingent of a State Party assigned to an international peace-keeping or peace-enforcement operation.[68]

This position was reaffirmed, and with greater breadth, by the Committee in its General Comment No. 36 of 2018.[69]

The Commission and the Inter-American Court of Human Rights also seem to adopt an extensive interpretation of the criterion of "State agent authority and control". For example, in the case of *Ecuador v. Colombia*, the Commission decided that Colombia had exercised its extraterritorial jurisdiction, under Article 1(1) of the American Convention, when its military forces had made incursions into the territory of the Ecuador, with the aim of capturing or killing members of the FARC insurgency movement. The Commission stated:

> [...] the Inter-American Commission has considered that it has competence *ratione loci* with respect to a State for acts occurring on the territory of another State, when the alleged victims were subjected to the authority and control of its agents. There would otherwise be a legal *lacuna* in the protection of those individuals' human rights that the American Convention seeks to protect, which would run counter to the object and purpose of this instrument. Thus, the following is essential for the Commission in determining jurisdiction: the exercise of authority over persons by agents of a State even if not acting within their territory, without

[68] HRCtee, General Comment No. 31, 26 May 2004, para. 10 (emphasis added).

[69] HRCtee, General Comment No. 36, 3 September 2019, para. 63: "In light of article 2, paragraph 1, of the Covenant, a State party has an obligation to respect and to ensure the rights under article 6 of all persons who are within its territory and all persons subject to its jurisdiction, that is, all persons over whose enjoyment of the right to life it exercises power or effective control. This includes persons located outside any territory effectively controlled by the State whose right to life is nonetheless impacted by its military or other activities in a direct and reasonably foreseeable manner".

> necessarily requiring the existence of a formal, structured and prolonged legal relation in terms of time to raise the responsibility of a State for acts committed by its agents abroad.[70]

The Inter-American Court expressed the same position in its advisory opinion of 15 November 2017 on transboundary environmental damage suffered by Colombia.[71]

Instead, the attitude of the European Court of Human Rights appears more cautious, at least initially. In the famous *Bankovic* case, the Court had to judge whether NATO Member States had violated the right to life of some people who had been killed by a missile launched by NATO forces on Serbian radio and television buildings in Belgrade in April 1999. In its 2001 judgment, the Court stated that sometimes extraterritorial acts may fall within the scope of the European Convention; but that the "jurisdiction" of the States Parties, under Article 1, is *essentially territorial*, while all other titles of jurisdiction are of an *exceptional* nature:

> The Court is of the view [. . .] that Article 1 of the Convention must be considered to reflect its ordinary and essentially territorial notion of jurisdiction, other bases of jurisdiction being exceptional and requiring special justification in the particular circumstances of each case.[72]

The Court then rejected the applicants' arguments that the NATO Member States had established their "jurisdiction" over the victims through the bombings. But this ruling generated a great deal of criticism.

Actually, in its subsequent case-law, the Strasbourg Court, while holding firm to the idea that the "jurisdiction" of the States under Article 1 of the European Convention is essentially territorial,[73] has in practice ended up extending the scope of the "exceptional" titles of jurisdiction. First, the Court recognized the exercise of extraterritorial jurisdiction by a Contracting State when, with the consent or acquiescence of the government of the foreign territory in question, it performs all or some of the public powers normally exercised by that government.[74] Secondly, the Court has broadened the interpretation of the concept of "State agent authority and control" over persons. In fact, in the already cited *Al-Skeini* judgment, the Court ruled that the United Kingdom had performed in Iraq some of the public powers normally

---

[70]IACmHR, *Ecuador v. Colombia*, paras. 98–99.

[71]IACtHR, *The Environment and Human Rights* (*Medio Ambiente y Derechos Humanos*). The Court has affirmed that: "[. . .] los Estados tienen la obligación de evitar daños ambientales transfronterizos que pudieran afectar los derechos humanos de personas fuera de su territorio. A efectos de la Convención Americana, cuando ocurre un daño transfronterizo que afecte derechos convencionales, se entiende que las personas cuyos derechos han sido vulnerados se encuentran bajo la jurisdicción del Estado de origen si existe una relación de causalidad entre el hecho que se originó en su territorio y la afectación de los derechos humanos de personas fuera de su territorio" (para. 101).

[72]ECtHR, *Banković and Others*, para. 61.

[73]See, e.g., ECtHR, *Al-Skeini and Others*, para. 131.

[74]See, e.g., ECtHR, *Gentilhomme, Schaff-Benhadji and Zerouki.*

exercised by a sovereign State, which justified its "extraterritorial jurisdiction". In particular:

> [...] the United Kingdom assumed authority and responsibility for the maintenance of security in south-east Iraq. In these exceptional circumstances, the Court considers that the United Kingdom, through its soldiers engaged in security operations in Basra during the period in question, exercised authority and control over individuals killed in the course of such security operations, so as to establish a jurisdictional link between the deceased and the United Kingdom for the purposes of Article 1 of the Convention.[75]

An even more extensive interpretation can be found in the 2014 *Jaloud* judgment.[76] The application concerned the death of an Iraqi citizen who was killed in Iraq in 2004 in an accident at a checkpoint held by Dutch soldiers. The Dutch Government claimed that it was not responsible for the events, as it was not among the "occupying powers" within the meaning of UN Security Council Resolution 1483. But the Court rejected this argument and held that there was Dutch jurisdiction over persons passing through the checkpoint. According to the Court:

> [...] Mr Azhar Sabah Jaloud met his death when a vehicle in which he was a passenger was fired upon while passing through a checkpoint manned by personnel under the command and direct supervision of a Netherlands Royal Army officer. The checkpoint had been set up in the execution of SFIR's mission [...] to restore conditions of stability and security conducive to the creation of an effective administration in the country. The Court is satisfied that the respondent Party exercised its 'jurisdiction' within the limits of its SFIR mission and for the purpose of asserting authority and control over persons passing through the checkpoint. That being the case, the Court finds that the death of Mr Azhar Sabah Jaloud occurred within the 'jurisdiction' of the Netherlands, as that expression is to be construed within the meaning of Article 1 of the Convention.[77]

Ultimately, in my view, the Strasbourg Court has ended up aligning itself with the extensive interpretation of the "State agent authority and control" criterion given by the Human Rights Committee and the Inter-American Commission and Court.[78]

In conclusion, in relation to the overall problem of the jurisdiction and responsibility of the State for acts of its agents operating in foreign territory without effective control of the same, I believe that the following answer can be given. When dealing with acts of diplomatic or consular agents and acts committed by State agents against persons in custody or detention, the existence of the criterion of "State authority and control" must be *presumed*. Instead, in the third and residual situation last described, the degree of effective control of State agents over persons and circumstances must be assessed in each individual case.

---

[75]ECtHR, *Al-Skeini and Others*, para. 149.

[76]ECtHR, *Jaloud.*

[77]*Ibidem*, para. 152.

[78]However, the European Court has again expressed some uncertainty about the scope of "exceptional" jurisdictional titles in the recent *Miller* case. Cf. ECtHR, *Miller v. UK*, para. 78.

With regard to the second problem that I raised,[79] that of the relationship between the rules on the attribution to the State of the conduct of its agents and the rules on the extraterritorial jurisdiction of the State, the solution seems clear. The acts of State agents operating abroad, without control of the territory, produce the violation of human rights and lead to the competence of international monitoring bodies if both conditions are met: (*a*) the acts must be attributed to the State according to the rules on the attribution of the international wrongful act; (*b*) there must be extraterritorial jurisdiction of the State in matters of human rights.

9.6 Jurisdiction "with Extraterritorial Effects": Obligations and Responsibility of the State for Acts Performed on Its Own Territory But That Have Effect Abroad

It is now appropriate to consider the third form of "spatial jurisdiction" of the State in matters of human rights, which can be defined as jurisdiction "with extraterritorial effects". The question is whether a State can be responsible for acts it performs *within its territory* but which produce *effects* contrary to human rights outside its territory. In principle, jurisdiction "with extraterritorial effects" is possible. The European Court of Human Rights, for example, has stated that:

> [...] acts of Contracting States performed outside their territory, *or which produce effects there*, may amount to exercise by them of their jurisdiction within the meaning of Article 1 of the Convention.[80]

However, it is not easy to establish exactly when the State is responsible for exercising its power of government with extraterritorial effects. In my opinion, the distinction between negative and positive obligations, combined with the guiding criterion of *effective control*, is useful.

On this basis, a first point is quite clear: a State has a (negative) obligation to refrain from violating the human rights of persons outside its territory, provided that they are subject to the control, or in any case to the power of government of the State.

This may occur in certain situations. Firstly, such violations could result from *concrete actions* by State agents that infringe the human rights of persons abroad. One could think, for example, of a soldier or a police officer of a State shooting at a foreigner trying to cross the border.

Secondly, violations may result from *laws or administrative or judicial decisions* of the State that affect persons abroad. For example, in the *Gueye* case, the Human Rights Committee had to decide on the claim of many Senegalese citizens and residents of Senegal who had served in the French army and whose pension was lower than that of French citizens in the same conditions. The Committee considered

[79]See above, Sect. 9.5.2.

[80]ECtHR, *Ilaşcu and Others*, para. 314 (emphasis added).

that the French legislation constituted discrimination in breach of the Covenant, even though the complainants were not normally subject to the jurisdiction of France:

> The Committee recalls that the authors are not generally subject to French jurisdiction, except that they rely on French legislation in relation to the amount of their pension rights.[81]

In essence, when the State has certain powers of control or government over people abroad, it must refrain from exercising these powers by violating the human rights of such people. There is a relationship between the State's power of control and its obligations. This is a concept which in some respects recalls the notion, examined above, of "State agent authority and control".

A similar situation occurs when certain administrative or judicial decisions of the State, such as extradition, expulsion or *refoulement* of certain persons, may lead to the violation of the human rights of such persons in another State; i.e., when the negative effects occur abroad. In this sense, one may recall the famous *Soering* case.[82]

But does the State also have positive obligations relating to its jurisdiction with extraterritorial effect? For example, does the State have an obligation to exercise due diligence in order to prevent violations of the human rights of individuals abroad *by other individuals*? And even more: does the State also have obligations of international assistance and cooperation with third countries to help them to realize certain economic, social and cultural rights on their territory[83]?

The Committee on Economic, Social and Cultural Rights, in some General Comments,[84] has argued that the States Parties to the Covenant should protect the enjoyment, in other States Parties, of the rights contained in the Covenant also through measures to prevent violations by private third parties

> [...] if they are able to influence these third parties by way of legal or political means, in accordance with the Charter of the United Nations [...].

Some authors, supporting this position of the Committee, argue in particular that States Parties to the Covenant should monitor the activities of private actors, especially their own multinational corporations, to ensure that such corporations do not violate human rights in foreign States.

However, the practice of other international human rights monitoring bodies and prevailing doctrine do not adhere to this broad interpretation of jurisdiction "with extraterritorial effects". The main argument is that positive extraterritorial human rights obligations of States have so far been established in situations where the State

---

[81]HRCtee, *Gueye et al.*, para. 9.4.

[82]ECtHR, *Soering v. UK.*

[83]These aspects are discussed in more detail by De Schutter (2010), pp. 162–178. See also, for a recent original position, Besson (2020a).

[84]CteeESCR, General Comment No. 14, 11 August 2000, para. 39; General Comment No. 15, 20 January 2003, para. 31.

exercises effective control over persons or concrete situations. And the criterion of effective control seems to be lacking in the situations mentioned above.[85] In my view, this criterion cannot be satisfied by the concept (suggested by the Committee on Economic, Social and Cultural Rights) of the capacity of influence, by political means, which a State can exercise over private actors acting abroad.

References

Besson S (2020a) Due diligence and extraterritorial human rights obligations – mind the gap. ESIL Reflections 9:1–9

Clapham A, Kamminga M (eds) (2004) Extraterrritorial application of human rights treaties. Intersentia, Antwerp

De Schutter O (2010) International human rights law. Cases, materials, commentary. CUP, Cambridge

De Sena P (2002) La nozione di giurisdizione statale nei trattati sui diritti dell'uomo. Giappichelli, Torino

Focarelli C (2012–2013) Diritto internazionale, vol I, 2nd edn. Cedam, Padova

Focarelli C (2013) La persona umana nel diritto internazionale. Il Mulino, Bologna

Kälin W, Künzli J (2009) The law of international human rights protection. OUP, Oxford-New York

Milanovic M (2011) Extraterritorial application of human rights treaties: law, principles, and policy. OUP, Oxford

Nigro R (2005) Giurisdizione ed obblighi positivi degli Stati parti della Convenzione europea dei diritti dell'uomo: il caso *Ilaşcu*. RDI 88:413–440

Pisillo Mazzeschi R (2008) Responsabilité de l'État pour violation des obligations positives relatives aux droits de l'homme. RC 333:175–506

Ronzitti N (2016) Introduzione al diritto internazionale, 5th edn. Giappichelli, Torino

Ssenyonio M (2009) Economic, social and cultural rights in international law. Hart, Oxford

Tomuschat C (2014) Human rights: between idealism and realism, 3rd edn. OUP, Oxford

[85]See Kälin and Künzli (2009), p. 141 and, more dubiously, De Schutter (2010), p. 162.

Part IV

Conventional Human Rights Systems: Treaties, Organs and Procedures

It has already been said that the theory of human rights has imposed itself at international level, in a generalized and not only sectorial way, since the Second World War; and that an "international system of protection of human rights" has been progressively realized.[1] This term usually refers to a set of norms, bodies and procedures, governed by conventional international law, which have been developed mainly by certain international organizations, with the aim of protecting human rights.

In fact, within this general normative evolution, it is necessary to distinguish between a system of protection of human rights of a "universal" nature (*rectius* tendentially universal), promoted and implemented by the United Nations,[2] and some systems of a "regional" nature. Among the latter, the European, Inter-American and African systems stand out for their importance. The European system for the protection of human rights, as we shall see,[3] is very complex, because it consists of norms and guarantee mechanisms that have been created within the framework of three different international organizations: the Council of Europe (CoE), the European Union (EU) and the Organization for Security and Cooperation in Europe (OSCE).

In this Part, I will try to draw a summary picture of these conventional systems from the prevailing viewpoint of the treaties, bodies and procedures that make up these systems; and therefore without going into the content of the human rights protected in them.[4] This part of international human rights law, which I could define as "institutional", is usually carried out very extensively in the textbooks dedicated to this law. Instead, in my opinion it can be treated in a synthetic way, since it is more descriptive than conceptual in nature.

---

[1]See above, Sect. 1.3.

[2]And also by some Specialized Institutes of the United Nations. See below, Sects. 10.6.1 and 10.6.2.

[3]See below, Chap. 11.

[4]On the content of individual human rights see below, Parts V and VI.

The United Nations System 10

10.1 The United Nations Charter

At the San Francisco Conference in 1945, a consensus emerged among the participating States on the inclusion of human rights provisions in the UN Charter, although different positions, supported by different groups of States, were discussed at the Conference, which made it necessary to reach a compromise.[1]

In the Charter, respect for human rights is included in the Preamble and in Article 1(3), among the general aims of the UN. Article 55(c) contains a programmatic norm, which commits the UN to promote universal respect and observance of human rights without discrimination. Article 56 provides that States undertake to act, collectively or individually, in cooperation with the Organization, to achieve the purposes of Article 55. However, this provision does not impose on each individual State a specific, immediate and binding obligation to act individually to ensure human rights. Articles 13, 62, 68 and 76 give the General Assembly (GA) and the Economic and Social Council (ECOSOC) the competence to deal with human rights issues. Finally, the Charter proclaims the right of peoples to self-determination, but only as a programmatic principle for the Organization (Arts. 1(2) and 55).

Therefore, the provisions on human rights in the Charter are few and generic. Moreover, the powers of UN bodies are subject to the general limit of the so-called "domestic jurisdiction" (Art. 2(7)), which could be interpreted in such a way as to severely restrict those powers in the field of human rights. Nevertheless, initially the GA and ECOSOC and then other main UN bodies have taken, with the help of a number of subsidiary bodies, many actions aimed at the protection of human rights. First of all, action of a normative nature was needed to clarify the content of human rights and to move from the general and programmatic obligations of the Charter to a

[1]Cassese (2003–2004), vol. II, pp. 87–88.

R. Pisillo Mazzeschi, *International Human Rights Law*,
https://doi.org/10.1007/978-3-030-77032-7_10

more precise and binding set of obligations. Secondly, institutional action was needed in order to create mechanisms for monitoring the behavior of States.[2]

Initially, UN action was limited to preparing draft treaties and general recommendations, but later became more courageous, calling on States to account for their conduct, at least in cases of serious human rights violations. In this way, the norms of the Charter on human rights, and especially Article 55, have gradually acquired greater normative value.

10.2 The Universal Declaration of Human Rights

The 1948 Universal Declaration[3] was born from the idea of approving an international document on human rights which, not being a treaty with detailed and binding obligations, could be more easily accepted by all UN Member States, inspired by very different legal traditions and political and ideological conceptions. It was therefore necessary to find an agreement capable of unifying these differences. The attempt was successful, even if the Declaration was approved with some States abstaining.

In terms of content, the Declaration consists of a Preamble and 30 articles. The Preamble indicates the aims and ideals of the Declaration. Subsequently, Articles 1 and 2 establish the concepts of freedom, equality and brotherhood and the principle of non-discrimination in the enjoyment of recognized human rights; Articles 3 to 5 affirm the fundamental rights of the person (right to life, liberty and security, prohibition of slavery and torture); Articles 6 to 21 deal with the classic civil and political rights of a liberal matrix; Articles 22 to 27 with some economic, social and cultural rights; finally, Articles 28 to 30 with the modalities of enjoyment and the limits of the listed rights. In reality, overall, the Western conception of human rights prevails, as more space is given to civil and political rights and less importance is given to economic, social and cultural rights. The right to self-determination of peoples is not included.

From the point of view of its legal nature, the Declaration, adopted by a resolution of the GA, is a non-binding act. However, over time, some authors have argued that the Declaration, being closely linked to the UN Charter, would in a certain sense concretize the commitment of Member States to promote respect for human rights (Article 56 of the Charter) and that therefore a breach of the rights listed in the Declaration would constitute a violation of the Charter. Others argued that the Charter and the Declaration, together with subsequent UN resolutions and declarations and the practice of States, would have ended up incorporating the rights listed in the Declaration into customary international law. In my view, these two arguments are not convincing. However, it must be admitted that *some* of the rights proclaimed in the Declaration have over time become part of general international

[2]*Ibidem*, pp. 88–89.

[3]Universal Declaration of Human Rights (UDHR), 10 December 1948.

law.[4] Furthermore, it must be recognized that the Declaration, despite its limitations, remains a fundamental instrument, which has formulated a universally recognized set of values for the international community and has given a very important impetus to the process of progressive formation of international human rights law.

10.3 Evolution Over Time of the United Nations' Action: The Different Generations of Human Rights

The United Nations' action on human rights has evolved progressively, both with regard to norms and to guarantee mechanisms. This evolution is due to the political majorities (which have changed over time) of the groups of States that have supported, especially in the General Assembly, such action. In this regard, it is common to distinguish between *four different historical phases* to which four so-called "generations" of human rights correspond.[5]

In the first phase, which goes from the adoption of the Charter until the end of the 1950s, one can see the predominance of Western States and their conception of human rights, which tends to privilege civil and political rights, which is not in favor of the principle of self-determination of peoples, and which prefers the preparation of human rights treaties with precise and detailed norms and the adoption of international control mechanisms to verify compliance with the norms. One speaks, in this sense, of a first generation of human rights.

The second phase, which runs from the late 1950s to around the mid-1970s, is characterized by the greater importance assumed by the group of Socialist States, which also had an influence on many developing countries. This group introduces in the UN a socialist conception of human rights, which tends to favor economic and social rights, which gives great importance to the principle of self-determination of peoples, and which does not favor the preparation of treaties with precise norms nor the adoption of international guarantee mechanisms. In this regard, one speaks of a second generation of human rights.

The third historical phase, from the mid-1970s to the beginning of the 1990s, sees a consolidation of the concept of human rights supported by developing countries. They tend to strengthen, for political, economic and cultural reasons, the authority of the State or of leaders with absolute powers, and they are unaware of the typically Western opposition between individual freedom and State power. Their conception of human rights tends (like the socialist one) to privilege economic and social rights; it puts in the foreground the need to radically change the international economic system as a priority with respect to the protection of human rights; it is interested in combating policies of racial discrimination and apartheid; and it prefers to promote the protection of human rights with soft law instruments. The concept of human rights in developing countries also brings significant innovations, favoring the

[4]See above, Chap. 3 and below, Sect. 13.3.4.

[5]See, e.g., Cassese (2003–2004), vol. II, pp. 88–93. See also above, Sect. 8.1.1.

creation of new rights of a collective nature (the so-called third generation human rights), such as the right to development, to peace, to a healthy environment, to the exploitation of natural resources and the rights of indigenous peoples. But many of these rights have a rather general character and are difficult to classify as rights with binding and "judicially enforceable" effects.[6]

Finally, in more recent years, one can speak of a fourth generation of human rights, which sees the development of some new collective rights, such as the right to democracy, to good governance and to human security. In addition, some rights linked to scientific and technological innovations (especially in the fields of biotechnology, genetics and information technology) are also emerging. But many of these rights are also non-binding political objectives, rather than legally enforceable rights.

In this period, there is also a sort of "reconciliation" between previous conceptions of human rights, since the UN, in a number of important resolutions, has repeatedly and solemnly affirmed that all human rights are universal, indivisible, interdependent and closely linked, on an equal basis and with equal importance. Actually, as we shall see,[7] these statements are more political than strictly legal in nature. Moreover, and this is more important, an essential nucleus of fundamental human rights, which are recognized by all States and which are now part of general international law, has become established.[8]

10.4 Treaties Promoted by the United Nations. Monitoring Bodies and Procedures (Treaty-Bodies and Treaty-Procedures)

As already mentioned, a first type of UN action, necessary for the development of a universal system of human rights protection, required the translation of the general principles of the Universal Declaration into legally binding international norms. This action, of a normative nature, was pursued in two different ways. On the one hand, it was necessary to prepare treaties with a universal vocation and with a *general content*, i.e. tending to include all human rights. On the other hand, it was appropriate to draw up other treaties, again with a universal vocation but of a *sectoral nature*, i.e. adopted for the protection of specific rights or certain categories of particularly vulnerable persons.

Furthermore, it was not enough to have a regulatory apparatus; it was also necessary to have bodies and procedures to monitor, at international level, the implementation of conventional norms by States. In fact, the UN proceeded to create, in a gradual manner, a set of international bodies and procedures for monitoring compliance with these treaties: the so-called "Treaty-Bodies" and "Treaty-Procedures". In addition to these guarantee mechanisms, other mechanisms were

---

[6]See above, Sect. 8.2.4, and below, Sects. 25.2, 25.3 and 25.4.

[7]See below, Sect. 13.1.

[8]See below, Sects. 13.2 and 13.3.

established, based on the UN Charter: the so-called "Charter-Bodies" and "Charter-Procedures".

10.4.1 General Treaties: The International Covenants of 1966

The first objective (to have human rights treaties with a general content) was largely achieved, after long negotiations, with the adoption of the two International Covenants on Human Rights, approved by the General Assembly in 1966 and entered into force in 1976. They aim, in essence, to specify in more detail and translate the principles of the Universal Declaration into binding norms.

As is well known, the initial idea was to draw up a single treaty, dealing with both first generation and second generation rights. But it was soon abandoned and it was decided to negotiate two separate treaties, because at the time the idea prevailed that there was a clear distinction between the two groups of rights. It was thought that civil and political rights required States to refrain from interfering in individual freedoms and rights and therefore were also self-executing and judicially enforceable before courts; and that, on the contrary, economic, social and cultural rights required States to take positive obligations and often also to take gradual action to implement them, and therefore they were not self-executing and judicially enforceable. Consequently, it was felt that the international monitoring mechanisms should also be different.

Two separate treaties were therefore prepared and then approved: the Covenant on Civil and Political Rights and the Covenant on Economic, Social and Cultural Rights. The two Covenants have so far achieved a very high number of ratifications and therefore constitute a considerable success on the part of the United Nations.

10.4.1.1 The Covenant on Civil and Political Rights

The Covenant on Civil and Political Rights[9] contains all the rights that derive from the liberal-democratic model of Western tradition, by taking up and specifying both the 1948 Universal Declaration and the 1950 European Convention on Human Rights.

In the Preamble, it is stated that the protection of rights derives from the inherent dignity of every human person. However, the Covenant opens, in Article 1, by establishing the right of peoples to self-determination and the free disposal of their natural wealth and resources.

Part II contains some general principles: very important is Article 2, which establishes that the States Parties undertake to guarantee to all individuals within their territory and subject to their "jurisdiction" the rights set forth in the Covenant without discrimination (para. 1); and which then requires the same States to adopt all legislative or other measures necessary to give concrete effect to these rights (para.

[9]International Covenant on Civil and Political Rights (CCPR), 16 December 1966.

2). Article 3 affirms the principle of equality between men and women in the enjoyment of the recognized rights.

Part III of the Covenant contains, first of all, the essential rights that are the object of protection: the right to life (Art. 6), freedom from torture and slavery (Arts. 7 and 8), personal liberty and security (Art. 9), the prohibition of arbitrary arrest (Arts. 10 and 11), the right to a fair trial and other judicial rights (Arts. 14 and 15). Then follow the classic civil rights, such as the right to personality (Art. 16), the right to private and family life (Art. 17), freedom of thought, conscience and religion (Art. 18), freedom of expression (Art. 19), freedom of assembly and association (Arts. 21 and 22). In addition, the catalogue also includes other rights, such as the right to enter and leave one's own country (Art. 12), protection for the family and children (Arts. 23 and 24), the right to participate in political life (Art. 25), and some minority rights (Art. 27). Article 26 reaffirms the principles of equality and non-discrimination. The rights provided for in the Covenant may be limited in emergency situations, but on the basis of well-defined procedures (Art. 4). But some rights are indicated as non-derogable even in emergency situations.

Part IV of the Covenant sets a procedure for monitoring compliance, establishing the Human Rights Committee[10] and determining the functions of this body. The Committee is composed of 18 individuals, competent in the field of human rights, who are elected and serve in their personal capacity and not as representatives of a State. The Committee exercises its functions through four typical procedures, which, as we shall see, have essentially been taken over by the other Treaty-Bodies. They will be briefly described.

The first procedure consists in examining the periodic reports transmitted by the Contracting States. The report is discussed with the representatives of the State in question and, at the end, the Committee in turn prepares a document, which contains "Concluding Observations", indicating positive developments, critical points and making appropriate recommendations to the State under examination. In reality, the Committee's conclusions are neither binding nor assisted by sanctions; however, they do exert an important political and diplomatic pressure on the States that have been monitored.[11]

The second procedure takes place through the examination of alleged violations of the rights contained in the Covenant by one Contracting State at the request of another Contracting State (so-called interstate claims). But so far this procedure has in practice remained inoperative.

The third procedure, which was established with the Optional Protocol to the Covenant,[12] is the most interesting and most effective. It consists in the examination of alleged violations of rights by a Contracting State at the request of individuals or groups of individuals who claim to have suffered a violation (so-called individual

[10]Human Rights Committee (HRCtee).

[11]On this point see also Zappalà (2011), p. 45.

[12]Optional Protocol to the International Covenant on Civil and Political Rights, 16 December 1966. This procedure operates only for States that have acceded to this Optional Protocol.

claims). This procedure has produced an important practice of the Human Rights Committee, which has ended up giving it a quasi-judicial function. In fact, the Committee examines the specific case, decides whether or not there has been a violation of one or more provisions of the Covenant and, if so, recommends the State to take remedial measures, which in reality are almost always carried out by the State. The procedure therefore does not end with a real judgment, but with opinions (*Views*), which are reasoned and which are very similar in form and content to real judgments.

Finally, the Committee has developed a fourth function, which consists in the practice of preparing *General Comments* on the provisions of the Covenant, in order to provide the Contracting States with an authoritative interpretation of their meaning.

10.4.1.2 The Covenant on Economic, Social and Cultural Rights

The Covenant on Economic, Social and Cultural Rights[13] contains a wide range of so-called "second generation" rights.[14] It is therefore a major innovation compared to the Universal Declaration, which provided for a very limited number of rights of this nature. The same conclusion also applies if we compare this Covenant with the European Convention on Human Rights.

The Covenant on Economic, Social and Cultural Rights also opens, in Article 1, recognizing the right of peoples to self-determination and the free disposal of their natural wealth and resources. Part II of the Covenant, by analogy with the Covenant on Civil and Political Rights, contains some general principles. But it must be emphasized that, with regard to the nature of the commitments required of the States Parties, the formulation of this Covenant is very different. This is clear from Article 2 (1) of the Covenant, which defines, in a general way, the nature of these commitments, which I have already defined as "obligations of progressive realization".[15] In fact, this provision establishes that each State Party commits itself to operate, with the maximum resources at its disposal, in order to *progressively* ensure, with all appropriate means, the full implementation of the rights recognized in the Covenant:

> Each State Party to the present Covenant undertakes to take steps, individually and through international assistance and co-operation, especially economic and technical, to the maximum of its available resources, with a view to achieving progressively the full realization of the rights recognized in the present Covenant by all appropriate means, including particularly the adoption of legislative measures.[16]

Part III of the Covenant contains the extensive and detailed catalogue of recognized economic, social and cultural rights. In summary they are: the right to

[13]International Covenant on Economic, Social and Cultural Rights (CESCR), 16 December 1966.

[14]See above, Sects. 10.3 and 8.1.1.

[15]See above, Sect. 8.2.3.

[16]On obligations "of progressive realization" see above, Sect. 8.2.3.

work (Art. 6), the right to enjoy just and favorable working conditions (Art. 7), the right to form (and join) trade unions and the right to strike (Art. 8), the right to social security (Art. 9), the right to family protection (Art. 10), the right to an adequate standard of living (Art. 11), the right to enjoy the highest possible standard of physical and mental health (Art. 12), the right to education (Arts. 13 and 14), the right to participate in the cultural life of the country and to enjoy the benefits and freedoms of scientific and artistic activities (Art. 15).

Part IV of the Covenant establishes a procedure for monitoring compliance with and implementation of the rights listed in the Covenant. This procedure was originally entrusted to ECOSOC and provided for neither interstate nor individual complaints, but only a system of reporting by States to ECOSOC. However, in 1985, ECOSOC set up the Committee on Economic, Social and Cultural Rights,[17] composed of 18 independent experts, which gradually developed a procedure for reviewing reports from States Parties similar to that adopted by the Human Rights Committee, as well as the practice of preparing General Comments on the interpretation of the Covenant's provisions. Finally, more recently, with the Optional Protocol of 2008,[18] the Committee was given the competence to receive (and decide on) individual and interstate communications. Therefore, currently the functions of this Committee are similar to those of the Human Rights Committee.

An overall evaluation of the operation of these two Committees will be made later, along with that of the other Treaty-Bodies.[19]

10.4.2 Sectoral Treaties

As noted above, the second regulatory objective of the UN, with a view to developing a universal system of human rights protection, was to establish a series of sectoral treaties, either for the protection of specific rights or for the protection of certain categories of particularly vulnerable people. This objective was only partially achieved and was conditioned by the priorities that were gradually privileged by the various groups of States exercising dominance within the General Assembly. In fact, the United Nations has promoted or adopted a large number of sectoral treaties relating to the protection of human rights.[20] However, only the *main ones* will be mentioned here, in chronological order. It should be pointed out that almost all of these treaties were preceded by a declaration of principles of the General Assembly. It is also worth noting that each of these treaties, with the exception of the two oldest,

[17]Committee on Economic, Social and Cultural Rights (CteeESCR).

[18]Optional Protocol to the International Covenant on Economic, Social and Cultural Rights, 18 June 2008.

[19]See below, Sect. 10.4.3.

[20]See https://www.ohchr.org/EN/ProfessionalInterest/Pages/UniversalHumanRightsInstruments.aspx.

provides for a committee of independent experts (*human rights treaty-body*), responsible for international monitoring of the application of the treaty by States Parties.

10.4.2.1 The Genocide Convention

Among the sectoral treaties, the 1948 Convention on the Prevention and Punishment of the Crime of Genocide[21] should be mentioned first and foremost. After the Second World War, as a reaction to the extermination of millions of Jews and members of other ethnic and religious groups during the Holocaust, the United Nations decided to dedicate an ad hoc convention to genocide. The content of the Convention will be further elaborated later and is only summarized here.[22]

The Convention declares that genocide, committed in times of peace or war, is a crime under international law, which States Parties undertake to prevent and punish (Art. 1). The crime of genocide and other related crimes are defined in Articles 2 and 3. Persons responsible for such offences must be punished "whether they are constitutionally responsible rulers, public officials or private individuals" (Art. 4). In addition, States Parties undertake to adopt internal norms, especially criminal ones, to implement the Convention. The jurisdiction to try persons accused of genocide lies with the courts of the State in whose territory the crime was committed (Art. 6).[23] However, the Convention takes account of the possibility that persons accused of genocide may be tried by "such international penal tribunal as may have jurisdiction with respect to those Contracting Parties which shall have accepted its jurisdiction" (Art. 6).[24]

As far as control and guarantee measures are concerned, the Convention is rather weak. It provides that each Contracting State may invite the competent UN bodies to take all appropriate measures to prevent and suppress acts of genocide (Art. 8). Moreover, Article 9 provides for the possibility of bringing before the International Court of Justice disputes between Contracting States concerning the interpretation, application or enforcement of the Convention. Indeed, as we shall see further on,[25] since the 1990s, especially the armed conflict in the former Yugoslavia has produced some genocide disputes before the International Court of Justice.

---

[21] Convention on the Prevention and Punishment of the Crime of Genocide (CPPCG), 9 December 1948. The Convention is, strictly speaking, part of international criminal law; but, in a broad sense, it can also be regarded as relevant to international human rights law.

[22] See below, Sect. 14.3.1.

[23] However, today it is believed that there is universal jurisdiction over the crime of genocide, i.e. the jurisdiction of the courts of all States to try those responsible.

[24] In fact, this possibility came about after many years with the creation of the International Criminal Tribunals and the International Criminal Court. See below, Sect. 14.3.

[25] See below, Sect. 14.3.1. See also, recently, ICJ, *Application of the Convention (The Gambia v. Myanmar)*, Order of 23 January 2020.

10.4.2.2 The Geneva Convention on Refugees

Another very important convention of a sectoral nature, promoted by the UN, is the 1951 Geneva Convention relating to the Status of Refugees,[26] later supplemented by the 1967 New York Protocol.[27] The issue of refugee protection came to the attention of the international community because of the large refugee flows that had occurred after the Second World War. The content of the Geneva Convention will be further elaborated on later and is summarized here.[28]

Chapter I of the Convention regulates its subjective and objective scope and the basic principles on the treatment of refugees. Leaving aside now the geographical and temporal scope of the Convention, it should be noted that the definition of the term "refugee" in Article 1 is very important: all those who, for a well-founded fear of being persecuted for reasons of race, religion, nationality, membership of a particular social group or political opinion, are outside their own State and are unable or unwilling to avail themselves of the protection of that State, are considered as "refugees".[29]

Chapter II of the Convention lays down certain provisions on the legal regime of refugees (Arts. 12-16), who are granted a number of rights in relation to personal status, property, freedom of association and access to justice. Chapter III regulates refugees' working activities (Arts. 17-19); Chapter IV (Arts. 20-24) provides for rights in the field of social assistance (housing, education, social security, etc.); and Chapter V (Arts. 25-34) deals with administrative and fiscal aspects relating to the refugee. Very important are Articles 32 and 33 on expulsion and *non-refoulement*, to which I will return later.[30]

The Geneva Convention does not provide for international measures to control or guarantee its implementation by States. However, a form of monitoring of the treatment of refugees is in fact carried out by the UN High Commissioner for Refugees.

10.4.2.3 The Convention Against Racial Discrimination

The fight against discrimination between human beings has always been at the heart of UN action for the international protection of human rights.[31] Of all forms of discrimination, racial discrimination is the most serious and hateful. It is therefore not surprising that the need to condemn racial discrimination has led the UN to

[26] Convention relating to the Status of Refugees (CSR), Geneva, 28 July 1951.

[27] Protocol relating to the Status of Refugees (PSR), New York, 31 January 1967.

[28] See below, Sect. 24.4.

[29] Art. 1(A): "For the purposes of the present Convention, the term "refugee" shall apply to any person who: [. . .] owing to well-founded fear of being persecuted for reasons of race, religion, nationality, membership of a particular social group or political opinion, is outside the country of his nationality and is unable, or owing to such fear, is unwilling to avail himself of the protection of that country [. . .]".

[30] See below, Sects. 24.2, 24.3 and 24.4.

[31] See below, Chap. 18.

promote an important multilateral treaty: the International Convention on the Elimination of All Forms of Racial Discrimination of 1965.[32]

The Convention prohibits not only racial discrimination in the strict sense, but also any distinction based on race, color, birth, national or ethnic origin, which has the purpose or effect of impairing the enjoyment of human rights (Art. 1(1)). The main obligations of the Contracting States are contained in Articles 2 and 5. Under Article 2, States Parties undertake, inter alia: to refrain from any act or practice of racial discrimination; not to encourage or defend such discrimination; and to take effective measures to repeal or change practices, laws or regulations which have the effect of creating racial discrimination. According to Article 5, States Parties undertake to prohibit and eliminate racial discrimination and to guarantee all people equality in the enjoyment of a specified set of civil, political, economic, social and cultural rights.

The procedures for monitoring the Convention are entrusted to the Committee on the Elimination of Racial Discrimination,[33] which is made up of 18 independent experts, whose task is to examine: *(a)* the periodic reports of the States Parties; *(b)* interstate complaints;[34] *(c)* individual complaints (only against States which have accepted this competence of the Committee). The practical application of these procedures does not differ significantly from that of the Human Rights Committee and other Treaty-Bodies.

Finally, it should be noted that the Convention provides, in Article 22, a procedure for the settlement of disputes between States Parties over its interpretation and application. Any dispute which is not settled by negotiation or by the procedures provided for in the Convention may be referred to the International Court of Justice.[35]

10.4.2.4 The Convention Against Apartheid

In the 1960s, a system of apartheid had spread in South Africa, against which the United Nations had led a long struggle. This brought the phenomenon to the attention of the whole international community and created the need for a regulatory response, which was realized with the adoption of the 1973 International Convention on the Suppression and Punishment of the Crime of Apartheid.[36]

The Convention aims to suppress and punish apartheid practices. It declares that apartheid is a crime against humanity and that acts resulting from apartheid policies

[32]International Convention on the Elimination of All Forms of Racial Discrimination (CERD), 21 December 1965.

[33]Committee on the Elimination of Racial Discrimination (CteeERD).

[34]Remarkably, the Committee has recently addressed three interstate communications: *Qatar v. Saudi Arabia*, *Qatar v. United Arab Emirates*, and *Palestine v. Israel*.

[35]See, e.g., ICJ, *Application of the International Convention on the Elimination of All forms of Racial Discrimination (Georgia v. Russian Federation)*, Order of 15 October 2008 and Judgment of 1 April 2011.

[36]International Convention on the Suppression and Punishment of the Crime of Apartheid (CSPCA), 30 November 1973.

or practices are crimes that violate the principles of international law (Art. I). Article II defines the crime of apartheid in detail. Article III is a key provision of the Convention, because it states that international criminal responsibility will apply to individuals, members of organizations or institutions and representatives of the State who commit the crime; but also to those who participate, incite or conspire or encourage, or cooperate in the commission of the crime.

Persons charged with the offence may be tried by a competent tribunal of any State Party which may acquire jurisdiction over such persons or by an international penal tribunal having jurisdiction with respect to those States which have accepted it (Art. V). This formula is similar to the one used in the Convention against Genocide.

10.4.2.5 The Convention Against Discrimination Towards Women

The principle of non-discrimination between men and women is contained in the UN Charter (Arts. 8 and 55), the Universal Declaration (Arts. 2 and 16), the Covenant on Civil and Political Rights (Arts. 2, 3, 23, 26) and many other human rights treaties, some of which are specifically dedicated to certain women's rights.[37] However, discrimination against women is a common and universal phenomenon and the United Nations considered it necessary to strengthen the fight against it and to promote an ad hoc convention aimed at ensuring equality between men and women in the political, civil, economic and social spheres. This action resulted in the 1979 Convention on the Elimination of All Forms of Discrimination against Women.[38]

The Convention seeks to eliminate discrimination against women, which is defined as any distinction, exclusion or restriction made on the basis of sex, which has the effect or purpose of impairing or nullifying women's enjoyment of human rights in the political, economic, social, cultural or civil spheres (Art. 1). States Parties undertake to pursue without delay a policy of elimination of such discrimination and, to this end, to adopt a range of laws and other measures, including sanctions, to ensure the practical implementation of the principle of gender equality (Art. 2). In addition, the Convention contains a number of very detailed provisions, including positive obligations on States Parties to remove discrimination against women in political and public life (Arts. 7-9), in economic, social and cultural life (Arts. 10-14), and in their legal, family and matrimonial regime (Arts. 15-16).

The control procedures are entrusted to the Committee on the Elimination of Discrimination against Women,[39] composed of 23 independent persons. Originally, the Committee was only responsible for examining periodic reports submitted by States Parties. However, with the adoption of the Optional Protocol to the

---

[37] See, e.g., Convention on the Political Rights of Women, 20 December 1952; Convention on the Nationality of Married Women, 20 February 1957; Convention on Consent to Marriage, Minimum Age for Marriage and Registration of Marriages, 7 November 1962.

[38] Convention on the Elimination of All Forms of Discrimination against Women (CEDAW), 18 December 1979.

[39] Committee on the Elimination of Discrimination against Women (CteeEDAW).

Convention,[40] which entered into force in 2000, provision was made for an individual complaint procedure and also an investigation procedure against States following information received on serious and systematic violations of the Convention. As part of the individual complaint procedure, the Committee may also indicate urgent precautionary measures.

10.4.2.6 The Convention Against Torture

Torture is one of the most serious human rights violations and has been officially banned by States since the nineteenth century. In today's world, no State officially admits or tolerates torture on its own territory or in the spaces under its "jurisdiction". However, it is well known, and many reports from non-governmental organizations indicate, that torture practices persist in many States. For this reason, in the 1970s, the United Nations considered that the fight against torture required special measures, including the adoption of an ad hoc convention. In 1984, the General Assembly adopted the Convention against Torture and Other Cruel, Inhuman or Degrading Treatment or Punishment.[41]

Article 1 of the Convention provides a restrictive and rather controversial definition of "torture",[42] since it: *(a)* is limited to acts inflicted by (or on the instigation, consent or acquiescence of) a public official or other person acting in an official capacity; *(b)* must be an intentional act; *(c)* cannot be committed without purpose (e.g. sadism), but must have the purpose of obtaining information or confession or other purposes expressly provided for; *(d)* does not include suffering or pain "arising only from [...] lawful sanctions".

The Convention also contains a number of obligations for States Parties, which include obligations of prevention (Art. 2), repression (Arts. 5-7 and 12), and reparation for victims (Arts. 13-14). But the most important objective of the Convention is the criminal repression of torture: all States Parties are obliged to recognize acts of torture in their domestic legislation as crimes and to provide for appropriate penalties for them (Art. 4). Moreover, the Convention provides for the principle of "universal jurisdiction" on acts of torture (Arts. 5(2) and 7(1)). Finally, it should be noted that many of the obligations of the Contracting States, and especially those of prevention, also apply to acts of cruel, inhuman or degrading treatment or punishment which do not amount to torture (Art. 16).

The international procedures for monitoring the implementation of the obligations under the Convention are entrusted, first and foremost, to the Committee against Torture,[43] which is composed of 10 independent experts. They have the competence to examine the periodic reports of the States Parties and to decide on

[40]Optional Protocol to the Convention on the Elimination of All Forms of Discrimination against Women (CEDAW-OP), 6 October 1999.

[41]Convention against Torture and Other Cruel, Inhuman or Degrading Treatment or Punishment (CAT), 10 December 1984.

[42]See Nowak (2003), p. 88.

[43]Committee against Torture (CteeAT).

interstate and individual complaints. The Committee may also carry out a confidential investigation against a State when it has received information on alleged torture practices. There is also a Subcommittee on the Prevention of Torture, which operates in accordance with the objectives and principles set out in the UN Charter, as well as in accordance with the norms of the United Nations relating to the treatment of persons deprived of their liberty. This body has 25 members and exercises three different functions.[44] First, members shall visit places where persons deprived of their liberty are, or may be, and make recommendations to States Parties regarding the protection of such persons. Secondly, the Subcommittee is responsible for the implementation of certain prevention mechanisms, mainly through advice and assistance to States, including with a view to establishing possible "national prevention mechanisms".[45] Thirdly, the Subcommittee shall co-operate on the prevention of torture in general, with relevant UN bodies and mechanisms, as well as with international, regional and national institutions or organizations whose objective is to enhance the protection of persons from torture and other cruel, inhuman or degrading treatment or punishment.

Finally, it is worth mentioning that this Convention, similar to the Convention against Racial Discrimination, provides a procedure for the settlement of disputes between States Parties over its interpretation and application (Art. 30). Disputes that cannot be resolved through negotiations will be submitted to arbitration, at the request of one of the Parties. If then, within 6 months, the Parties are unable to agree on the organization of the arbitration, any Party may refer the dispute to the International Court of Justice.[46]

10.4.2.7 The Convention on the Rights of the Child

The United Nations has always recognized the need to provide special protection for children and young people, as they are vulnerable and frequently exposed to exploitation, violence, carelessness and various forms of discrimination and exclusion. The rights of the child were already set out in the Universal Declaration (Arts. 25(2) and 26), in a GA Declaration of Principles of 1959[47] and in the two International Covenants;[48] but more specific and detailed protection was needed. Finally, after years of negotiations, the UN General Assembly adopted the Convention on the Rights of the Child in 1989.[49] It has been ratified by almost every State in the world.

The Convention defines the child as "any human being below the age of eighteen years unless under the law applicable to the child, majority is attained earlier" (Art. 1). By acceding to the Convention, the Contracting States assume the obligation to

---

[44] Cf. Optional Protocol to the Convention against Torture (CAT-OP), 18 December 2002, Art. 11.

[45] These are bodies with visiting powers for the prevention of torture and other cruel, inhuman or degrading treatment or punishment. See CAT-OP, Art. 3.

[46] See ICJ, *Questions relating to the Obligation to Prosecute or Extradite (Belgium v. Senegal).*

[47] Declaration of the Rights of the Child, GA Res. 1386 of 20 November 1959.

[48] CCPR, Art. 24 and CESCR, Arts. 10(3) and 13.

[49] Convention on the Rights of the Child (CRC), 20 November 1989.

grant children under their "jurisdiction" the rights provided for in the Convention (Art. 2); i.e. a very wide range of civil, political, economic, social and cultural rights, without any discrimination. The guiding principle of the Convention is that of the "best interests of the child"; i.e. the rule that, in all actions concerning children, the best interests of the child shall be the primary consideration. Therefore, the Convention seeks to satisfy all the different needs of children,[50] establishing not only special guarantees for their protection (e.g. from abuse, economic and sexual exploitation, violence in the family and at school); but also protecting children in the development of their identity and in their participation in social life. Finally, it imposes a number of positive obligations on States Parties to ensure that children have adequate standards of living and access to education, social security, etc.

It should be noted that, in order to strengthen the protection of children, two Optional Protocols were adopted in 2000: the Protocol on the sale of children, child prostitution and child pornography[51] and the Protocol on the involvement of children in armed conflict.[52]

The procedures for monitoring the 1989 Convention are entrusted to the Committee on the Rights of the Child,[53] which consists of 18 independent experts who are responsible for examining the periodic reports of the States Parties. Since 2014, with the entry into force of the third Optional Protocol on reporting procedures,[54] the Committee also has the competence to receive individual complaints concerning violations of the Convention and the two Optional Protocols of 2000, as well as to conduct investigations in the event of allegations of serious or systematic violations of the rights enshrined in these instruments.

10.4.2.8 The Convention on the Rights of Migrant Workers

In 1990, the UN General Assembly adopted the International Convention on the Protection of the Rights of All Migrant Workers and Members of Their Families.[55] The term "migrant worker" refers to a person who is engaged, is about to be engaged or has been engaged in a remunerated activity in a State of which he or she is not a national (Art. 2(1)). The guiding principle of the Convention is that of non-discrimination: States Parties undertake to ensure that all migrant workers and members of their families have all the rights contained in the Convention without discrimination (Art. 7). Then the Convention establishes a very detailed set of civil,

[50]See Nowak (2003), p. 93.

[51]Optional Protocol to the Convention on the Rights of the Child on the sale of children, child prostitution and child pornography, 25 May 2000.

[52]Optional Protocol to the Convention on the Rights of the Child on the involvement of children in armed conflicts, 25 May 2000.

[53]Committee on the Rights of the Child (CteeRC).

[54]Optional Protocol to the Convention on the Rights of the Child on a communications procedure, 19 December 2011.

[55]International Convention on the Protection of the Rights of All Migrant Workers and Members of Their Families (CMW), 18 December 1990.

political,[56] economic, social and cultural rights for such persons. Among these rights, in my view, the right of access to justice on equal terms with the citizens of the State in question (Art. 18) and the numerous procedural guarantees in case of expulsion (Arts. 22 and 23) are particularly important.

With regard to international control procedures, the Convention has established a special Committee,[57] composed of independent experts, which has the (mandatory) competence to review periodic reports from Member States and the (optional) competence to examine interstate and individual complaints. However, so far the Convention has not obtained a high number of ratifications, compared to other human rights treaties promoted by the United Nations.

10.4.2.9 The Convention on the Rights of Persons with Disabilities

Another category of vulnerable people, who need special protection, are people with disabilities. The Convention on the Rights of Persons with Disabilities was adopted in 2006.[58] The aim is to ensure the full enjoyment of all human rights by people with disabilities, which are defined as:

> [. . .] those who have long-term physical, mental, intellectual or sensory impairments which in interaction with various barriers may hinder their full and effective participation in society on an equal basis with others.[59]

The Convention, with an interesting and original provision (Art. 3), establishes that it is based on some general principles, such as respect for the dignity and autonomy of persons, non-discrimination, full and effective participation and inclusion in society, respect for differences, equal opportunities, accessibility, gender equality, and respect for the evolutionary capacities of children with disabilities. Then the Convention contains the usual detailed list of civil, political, economic, social and cultural rights that States must respect in relation to the beneficiaries.

For the international implementation and monitoring of the Convention, the Committee on the Rights of Persons with Disabilities is established,[60] which is responsible for examining the periodic reports from States Parties. The Optional Protocol to the Convention,[61] adopted in 2006, provides for the Committee's competence to examine complaints by individuals or groups of individuals against a State Party held responsible for a violation of the Convention.

---

[56]For regular migrant workers: see Articles 41 and 42 CMW.

[57]Committee on the Protection of the Rights of All Migrant Workers and Members of Their Families (CteeMW).

[58]Convention on the Rights of Persons with Disabilities (CRPD), 13 December 2006.

[59]Art. 1 CRPD.

[60]Committee on the Rights of Persons with Disabilities (CteeRPD). Cf. Art. 34 CRPD.

[61]Optional Protocol to the Convention on the Rights of Persons with Disabilities, 13 December 2006.

10.4.2.10 The Convention Against Enforced Disappearance

Finally, one must mention the 2006 International Convention for the Protection of All Persons from Enforced Disappearance,[62] which is the most recent sectoral human rights treaty adopted by the United Nations and equipped with an independent international monitoring body.

The Convention defines, in a rather laborious way, the concept of enforced disappearances (Art. 2). In brief, these are various forms of deprivation of liberty, which are kept hidden and which are carried out by State agents or persons acting with the help or acquiescence of the State. The right not to suffer enforced disappearance is absolute and non-derogable in time of emergency. In fact, according to Article 1, no one must be subject to enforced disappearance and no exceptional circumstances, be it a state of war or the danger of war or other public emergency, can justify enforced disappearance. Furthermore, the Convention states that an extensive and systematic practice of enforced disappearance constitutes a crime against humanity. Then the Convention lays down a series of obligations on States Parties, aimed in particular at the repression of such criminal acts: States must investigate (Art. 3); they must have adequate criminal provisions (Arts. 4 and 6); they must provide for adequate penalties (Art. 7); they must exercise their jurisdiction over those responsible (Arts. 9-10); and they must try or extradite those responsible (Arts. 11 and 13).

For the purpose of international control of the Convention, the Committee on Enforced Disappearances is established,[63] which has the (mandatory) competence to review the reports of Member States and the (optional) competence to examine individual and interstate complaints.

10.4.3 Overall Assessment of the Treaty-Bodies and the Opportunity for Their Reform

After examining the individual Treaty-Bodies and their procedures, it is advisable to make an overall assessment of their functioning and the opportunity for their reform.

The defects in the functioning of the Treaty-Bodies have been known for a long time and are getting worse over time: an excessive workload due to the growth of the system, a delay in the examination of State reports, a delay and often a failure of States to present their reports, an overlapping of competences and a lack of coordination between the various Treaty-Bodies and between them and the Charter-Bodies, the inadequacy of their economic resources, the lack of visibility of their work, and finally the problems of difficult internal implementation of their decisions and recommendations.

[62] International Convention for the Protection of All Persons from Enforced Disappearance (CPPED), 20 December 2006.

[63] Committee on Enforced Disappearances (CteeED). Cf. Art. 26 CPPED.

But the numerous attempts at reform by the UN, which have followed one another since 1988, have failed.[64] So far, only minimal procedural reforms have been adopted by some Treaty-Bodies. Even a more recent attempt, launched by the UN General Assembly with a Resolution of 2014, does not seem likely to produce major changes. Instead, in my view, radical reforms would be appropriate, aimed at strongly simplifying the system, making it more efficient, and greatly strengthening the protection of the human rights of individuals. But the idea, which had been proposed several times,[65] of merging all the Treaty-Bodies into a single body, has been rejected within the UN and it seems no longer available.

However, I still believe that one should at least try to obtain some more moderate and specific reforms for the two most important Treaty-Bodies' procedures: that of periodic State reports and that of individual complaints.

The State periodic reporting procedure is the oldest and least intrusive international mechanism for monitoring human rights treaties. As seen already when I dealt with the individual Treaty-Bodies, this procedure is not based on an assessment of the human rights violations committed by States, but rather on a dialogue between each UN Committee and representatives of the State under review, which aims to promote compliance with the treaties by the State itself. It has been rightly said, in this regard, that the principle of "constructive dialogue" governs the entire process.[66]

This procedure has shown, over time, to have certain effectiveness, because it obliges States to undertake self-examination of the human rights situation in their own internal legal system, which otherwise they would not make. Moreover, the political-diplomatic pressure exerted by the Treaty-Bodies on the governments of the States has sometimes resulted in improvements in the respect of human rights within those States.

However, the system of periodic State reports is the one that is most in need of reform. First of all, it suffers from a structural defect, since several States have the temptation, in their reports, to underestimate or even deny their internal problems regarding compliance with human rights.[67] The Treaty-Bodies do not have the necessary tools to discover these practices of underestimation. Secondly, the above mentioned difficulties of growth, duplication, non-observance and delay of States in their reports, and malfunctioning of follow-up mechanism, mainly concern this system.

Several reforms have been suggested to improve the system of State reports. Below I will talk about those that seem more important to me.

In the first place, each State under review could submit, instead of different reports to the different committees, a "Single State Report" that is valid for all

[64] Such attempts include reports by the independent expert Philip Alston (1988-1996); a proposal by the UN Secretary General (2002-2006); a proposal by the High Commissioner for Human Rights Louise Arbour (2006); other proposals by the High Commissioner Pillay (2012).

[65] See, in particular, the proposals made by Alston and Arbour.

[66] Shelton (2014a), p. 229.

[67] *Ibidem.*

treaties ratified by that State. The Single State Report could really simplify the system, harmonize the recommendations of the committees, greatly facilitate the obligations of the States Parties and encourage synergy with the Charter-Bodies and the Universal Periodic Review.[68]

Secondly, the synergy between the Treaty-Bodies and the Charter-Bodies should be improved, and especially that between the Treaty-Bodies' reporting procedure and the Universal Periodic Review. The suggested "Comprehensive Reporting Calendar for States" could be established, in order to promote such synergy.

A third appropriate reform would be to increase the participation of Non-Governmental Organizations (NGOs) in the reporting process. Currently this participation varies depending on the various Treaty-Bodies. Instead, uniform rules should be established in all committees, adopting those most open to the participation of NGOs.

A fourth reform should aim to give a more important role to national human rights institutions and civil society organizations. This would improve both the transparency and visibility of the reporting system and its efficacy. An absolute independence of national human rights institutions from their governments should also be guaranteed.[69]

A fifth reform should be aimed at creating a common follow-up mechanism for all Treaty-Bodies. Currently only a few Treaty-Bodies already have follow-up mechanisms.[70] These measures are important because they offer the possibility to maintain a more frequent and continuous dialogue between the committees and the States Parties. On the other hand, States, NGOs and national institutions could also benefit from a focal point within the committees to which they could turn for an opinion on the implementation of certain specific recommendations.

Finally, another possible initiative would be to link the national action plans to the recommendations of the committees. For example, following some UN World Conferences on Human Rights,[71] many States have developed strategies and action plans to implement the recommendations of these conferences. The final comments of the Treaty-Bodies in the reporting procedure could result in concrete national plans of action and the recommendations of the Committees could serve as indicators or reference points for such plans.

Let me now evaluate the procedure of individual complaints to the Treaty-Bodies. This procedure, in my view, currently works better than the reporting procedure; but it also needs reforms and should be much simplified and improved. It is a very important procedure, because it is the only mechanism that allows individuals who are victims of human rights violations to have universal access to justice. But it

---

[68]See below, Sects. 10.5 and 10.5.1.1.

[69]See, e.g., the Italian situation, which does not seem to respect these criteria of independence.

[70]See, e.g., the Human Rights Committee, the Committee against Torture and the Committee against Racial Discrimination.

[71]See, e.g., the World Conference on Human Rights (1993); the Fourth World Conference on Women (1995) and the World Conference on Racism (2001).

suffers from competition with the international courts operating in regional human rights systems, which are more effective and advanced, also because they can issue binding judgments. Moreover, the procedure of the Treaty-Bodies on individual complaints lacks visibility, because it is not well known in civil society.

Some specific reforms could improve this system.

First, the possibility of collective complaints could be established for all Treaty-Bodies, following the example of the European Committee of Social Rights. Currently, the possibility of complaints by groups of individuals exists under the Optional Protocol to the Covenant on Economic, Social and Cultural Rights. This possibility should be extended to all Treaty-Bodies.

Secondly, the rule of prior exhaustion of domestic remedies should be reviewed by means of uniform procedural rules or, at least, common guidelines. This rule constitutes a serious obstacle for victims of human rights violations; and should be less strictly interpreted and applied by the Treaty-Bodies. The rule should be more flexible and victim-oriented, rather than a shield for State sovereignty. In other words, the content of the rule should reflect that of the rule on domestic remedies which has gradually established itself in the practice of the regional human rights supervisory bodies; and which is very different from the traditional rule in the field of diplomatic protection. More specifically, with regard to the "horizontal" exhaustion of domestic remedies, one could adopt the criterion that it is sufficient for the victim to have "essentially" exhausted domestic remedies. With regard to "vertical" exhaustion, the following explicit exceptions should be established: (*a*) when domestic remedies are not accessible; (*b*) when they are ineffective or inadequate (the so-called "futility rule"); (*c*) when there has been a denial of justice or a serious delay in justice; (*d*) when there are illegal domestic laws or administrative practices; (*e*) when gross violations of human rights have occurred.

Thirdly, uniform guidelines or best-practices on reparation for violations could be established, encouraging the Treaty-Bodies to recommend that States responsible for violations take reparation measures other than and additional to monetary compensation for victims. Again, inspiration could be drawn from the practice of the regional human rights monitoring bodies. One thinks, for example, of the measures of *restitutio in integrum*, of satisfaction in favor of the victim and his family, of assurances and guarantees of non-repetition of the breach, which have been developed by the bodies of the Inter-American human rights system.[72] Other examples are the "individual measures" and the "general measures" of reparation, which have been developed by the European Court of Human Rights.[73]

Fourth, the prevention and investigation functions of the Treaty-Bodies and their power to take urgent measures in cases of serious and systematic human rights violations could be increased. Some of the Treaty-Bodies already have procedures

---

[72]See below, Sect. 14.1.3.4.

[73]See below, Sect. 11.1.1.2. "General measures" may imply, for the sentenced State, the use of legislative or administrative measures to remedy "structural" violations of human rights present in its national law.

for prevention, investigation and urgent action;[74] but these procedures are not uniform. Actually, there is a critical fragmentation and a gap in the prevention functions of the Treaty-Bodies; and the adoption of uniform rules would be desirable.

Finally, best-practices could be established, in order to foster greater interaction between the practice of the Treaty-Bodies and that of the regional human rights courts and commissions. For example, a single online collection of practice and case-law, organized on the basis of each human right, could be created.

10.5 Monitoring Bodies and Procedures Based on the UN Charter (Charter-Bodies and Charter-Procedures)

In addition to the international monitoring bodies that have been established by UN human rights treaties (Treaty-Bodies), which have been examined so far, there are also, within the UN, certain bodies and procedures that are based on the UN Charter, and are called Charter-Bodies and Charter-Procedures. Therefore, the human rights protection mechanism of Charter-Bodies is complemented by that of Treaty-Bodies. Within the Charter-Bodies, a distinction can be made between those specialized in human rights[75] and those (such as the main UN bodies) which have broader competences, including the protection of human rights.[76]

10.5.1 Human Rights Council

At present, the most important of the Charter-Bodies[77] is the Human Rights Council, which was established in 2006 by resolution 251/60 of the General Assembly, as a subsidiary body of the latter, and which replaced the previous Commission on Human Rights.[78] This Commission was a body of States, which had important functions in the field of the preparation of norms and the task of monitoring the respect of human rights by the Member States, through two procedures for controlling cases of serious and repeated violations of human rights[79] and a system of special procedures by territory (so-called *Country Procedures*) and by thematic areas (so-called *Thematic Procedures*).

The Human Rights Council was created to strengthen the UN human rights monitoring system and to replace the Commission, which had been accused of being inefficient and "politicized". It is a body composed of 47 States, elected by

[74]See, e.g., the Committee against Racial Discrimination and the Committee against Torture.

[75]See below, Sects. 10.5.1, 10.5.2 and 10.5.3.

[76]See below, Sect. 10.5.4.

[77]Human Rights Council (HRC).

[78]United Nations Commission on Human Rights (CmHR).

[79]See ECOSOC Resolutions 1235(XLII) and 1503(XLVIII).

the GA, with a distribution among the five regional groups in the UN system. The mandate of the States lasts 3 years and is not immediately renewable.

Actually, the Council has inherited the main functions of the old Commission, but with some significant innovations. Firstly, it has a higher status, since it is a subsidiary body of the GA and not of ECOSOC. Secondly, the elective procedure of its members and its composition has undergone some changes. Thirdly, the GA has the power to suspend a Council's Member State that has committed serious and systematic human rights violations. Finally, the Council meets much more frequently than the previous Commission and can also convene in special sessions to deal with urgent human rights issues.

The Council uses certain procedures and subsidiary bodies to carry out its mandate. It has maintained some procedures that were exercised by the Commission on Human Rights, although revised and updated; it has also established a new monitoring procedure, the so-called *Universal Periodic Review.*

10.5.1.1 Universal Periodic Review

In fact, the most significant novelty of the Human Rights Council concerns the establishment of the Universal Periodic Review, which was set up when the Council was created in 2006.[80] Subsequently, the members of the new Council passed a resolution on its "Institution-Building", in which they specified the mechanism of the UPR.[81] This mechanism was further refined by the Council.[82]

The UPR has two main purposes: (*a*) to periodically ascertain that all UN Member States respect their human rights obligations and commitments;[83] (*b*) to establish a mechanism for cooperation and interaction between the Human Rights Council and the States under review.[84] However, these two aims are to some extent contradictory, since in the first one the emphasis is placed on strict control over compliance with legal obligations, while in the second one the emphasis is put rather on cooperation and goodwill of the State under review and the understanding and tolerance of the Council towards the capacity building needs of that State.

From the point of view of its operation, the mechanism of the UPR provides, in summary, that each State must periodically submit a report on the human rights situation in its internal legal system. All the Council's Member States' comments

---

[80]GA Resolution 60/251 of 3 April 2006, Art.5(e).

[81]HRC Resolution 5/1 of 18 June 2007, which concluded the phase of the so-called "Institution Building".

[82]See, e.g., HCR Decision 6/102 of 27 September 2007 and HRC Resolution 16/21 of 12 April 2011.

[83]This purpose is linked to one of the main aims of the Human Rights Council, which is indicated in GA Resolution 60/251, para. 5(d): "[...] promote the full implementation of human rights obligations undertaken by States".

[84]See GA Resolution 60/251, para. 5(d): "the review shall be a cooperative mechanism, based on interactive dialogue, with the full involvement of the country concerned and with consideration given to its capacity building needs". *Ibidem*, para. 5(f): "contribute, through dialogue and cooperation, towards the prevention of human rights violations".

can be received on this report, which form a list of observations and recommendations to which the State under review must respond. The Council then, through the UPR Working Group which consists of the 47 Members of the Council, examines and discusses the reports of the States under review and presents observations on the human rights situation in those States. Each State review is assisted by groups of three States, known as "troikas", which serve as rapporteurs. Two rounds of reports have already been completed and the third is currently underway (2017–2021).

The most relevant aspects of the UPR mechanism are the following.

The legal and other sources underlying the revision are: (*a*) the UN Charter; (*b*) the Universal Declaration of Human Rights; (*c*) human rights instruments to which the State is party; (*d*) voluntary pledges and commitments undertaken by the State in the field of human rights; (*e*) applicable international humanitarian law.[85] No mention is made of general or customary international law on human rights.

The documents and information on which the review is based are: (*a*) information provided by the State under review; (*b*) a document prepared by the UN High Commissioner for Human Rights, based on information contained in the reports of the Special Procedures, of Treaty-Bodies and in other pertinent UN documents; (*c*) a summary of other "credible and reliable" information provided by other relevant stakeholders, such as National Human Rights Institutions and NGOs.[86]

The modalities of the review lend themselves to some critical considerations.[87] In fact, in my opinion, the review should have been designed in such a way as to reserve a role both for representatives of the States and for independent experts. Instead, the mechanism envisaged is totally reserved for States, while the role of the High Commissioner for Human Rights is minimal[88] and that of independent experts even tends to disappear. Finally, the presence of other relevant stakeholders appears rather formal.[89] Therefore, starting from this stage of the process, the UPR strongly accentuates its character as a mechanism of political and diplomatic cooperation and loses its connotations as an instrument of legal control over the fulfilment of obligations and commitments. In essence, the first of the two fundamental purposes of the UPR mentioned above loses relevance in favor of the second.

Following the review, a report is prepared by the troika with the involvement of the State under review. The "outcome report" provides a summary of the discussion and consists of the conclusions and recommendations made to the State under review

[85]HCR Resolution 5/1, Annex, I (A).

[86]HCR Resolution 5/1, Annex, I (D)(1).

[87]See HCR Resolution 5/1, Annex, I (D)(2).

[88]It is only established that the Office of the High Commissioner for Human Rights "will provide the necessary assistance and expertise to the rapporteurs" (HCR Resolution 5/1, Annex, I (D)(2)(18)(d)).

[89]It is only provided that "Other relevant stakeholders may attend the review in the Working Group" (HCR Resolution 5/1, Annex, I (D)(2)(18)(c)).

and the responses of that State.[90] However, the final outcome of the review also confirms the above mentioned nature of the UPR, which appears more characterized in a political-diplomatic than legal sense. In fact, as far as the content of the final outcome is concerned,[91] Resolution 5/1 does not speak of a legal control on the respect of obligations or commitments by the State under review; but merely of "assessment [...] of the human rights situation in the country under review", "challenges faced by the country", "sharing of best practices", "emphasis on enhancing cooperation" and "voluntary commitments and pledges made by the country under review ". In addition, throughout the whole process of adoption of the final outcome,[92] one notes many cautions in favor of the State under review, so much so that Resolution 5/1 goes so far as to declare that the State "should be fully involved in the outcome".[93]

Finally, the follow-up of the review also appears to be a rather weak mechanism.[94] The starting principle is that:

> The outcome of the review, as a cooperative mechanism, should be implemented primarily by the State concerned and, as appropriate, by other relevant stakeholders.[95]

A further confirmation of this weakness is given by the very limited role given, in the follow-up phase, to the international community, which, instead of being the guardian of respect for international law:

> [. . .] will assist in implementing the recommendations and conclusions regarding capacity-building and technical assistance, in consultation with, and with the consent of, the country concerned.[96]

In essence, the follow-up, in the absence of cooperation and voluntary implementation by the State concerned, is entirely entrusted to the Council, on the basis of rather vague and generic rules, which leave wide discretion to the Council itself.[97]

---

[90] HRC Resolution 5/1, Annex, I (E)(1).

[91] HCR Resolution 5/1, Annex, I (E)(2).

[92] HCR Resolution 5/1, Annex, I (E)(3).

[93] HRC Resolution 5/1, Annex, I (E)(3)(28). These cautions are particularly evident in the important final recommendations, where, with an ambiguous legal regime, a distinction is even made between those recommendations that enjoy the support of the State concerned, which will be "identified" as such, and the other recommendations, which, accompanied by the comments of the State concerned, will simply be "noted" (*Ibidem*, Annex, I(E)(3)(32)).

[94] HCR Resolution 5/1, Annex, I (F).

[95] HCR Resolution 5/1, Annex, I (F)(33).

[96] HCR Resolution 5/1, Annex, I (F)(36).

[97] See HRC Resolution 5/1, Annex, I (F)(37-38). In fact, the Council "will decide if and when any specific follow-up is necessary". Additionally "After exhausting all efforts to encourage a State to cooperate with the universal periodic review mechanism, the Council will address, as appropriate, cases of persistent non-cooperation with the mechanism". Therefore, specific follow-up measures are not indicated, not even by way of example.

Therefore, also from the follow-up phase, it is clear that the first fundamental purpose of the UPR (legal control on the compliance with obligations) has left ample room for the second purpose (mechanism of political-diplomatic cooperation).

In conclusion, it must be recognized that the UPR procedure constitutes an interesting development and progress in the traditional system of periodic State reports and that it has introduced some important innovations in this system. But is the UPR really able to contribute significantly to the general renewal of the Human Rights Council compared to the old Commission? Much will depend on its effectiveness over time. From this last point of view, some skepticism is justified by the fact that the UPR is a mechanism very much based on the good will of the States, and especially the States under review. Therefore, it is weak in legal terms, especially in its implementation, and has the structural defect of not being managed by independent bodies and of not providing effective sanctions for human rights violations. In essence, it constitutes a means of diplomatic pressure and solicitation towards the States.

In summary, it is clear that a jurist's preference goes spontaneously to the mechanisms of judicial or quasi-judicial control founded on precise and binding norms. Nevertheless, the role of those mechanisms that encourage respect for human rights and are based on diplomatic procedures inspired by the principle of "constructive dialogue" between States should not be underestimated too much. Actually, it must be recognized that the experience of these first years of operation of the UPR appears positive. So far, all UN Member States have submitted themselves to the procedure and have often accepted the recommendations they have received.

10.5.1.2 Special Procedures

The two procedures of the old Commission on Human Rights called "country procedures" and "thematic procedures" were basically maintained by the Human Rights Council and are now called "*Special Procedures*". They are led by independent human rights experts with a mandate to advice on human rights from a thematic or country-specific perspective. They constitute a central element of the Charter-Procedures and cover all human rights: civil, cultural, economic, political and social. The Special Procedures are formed by an individual (referred to as "special rapporteur" or "independent expert") or a working group of five members, one from each of the five regional groupings of the United Nations.[98] The special rapporteurs, the independent experts and the members of the working groups are appointed by the Human Rights Council and serve in their personal capacity.

With the support of the Office of the UN High Commissioner for Human Rights, the Special Procedures have the following functions: (*a*) to carry out visits to States; (*b*) to act on individual cases of alleged violations and on problems of a wider nature, sending communications to States; (*c*) to conduct thematic studies and convene expert consultations, contributing to the development of international human rights

[98] Africa, Asia, Latin America and the Caribbean, Eastern Europe and Western Group.

norms; (*d*) to engage in advocacy and public awareness raising and to provide advice for technical cooperation.[99]

10.5.1.3 Complaint Procedure

The so-called *Complaint Procedure*, which was already exercised by the Commission on Human Rights,[100] has also been maintained by the Human Rights Council. It may be initiated on the basis of communications submitted by individuals, groups of individuals or even NGOs; but it does not apply to individual human rights violations, but only to situations which appear to reveal "a consistent pattern of gross and reliably attested violations of human rights". In fact, this procedure, which had some success in the past, has lost much of its meaning today.[101]

10.5.1.4 Advisory Committee

Finally, it can be recalled that the Human Rights Council has a number of subsidiary bodies, among which the *Advisory Committee*, composed of 18 independent experts, stands out for its importance. This body makes its expertise available to the Human Rights Council, mainly in the form of studies and research on the promotion and protection of human rights. The Committee may also make further research proposals as part of the work plan defined by the Council.

10.5.2 High Commissioner for Human Rights

The function of the High Commissioner for Human Rights, created in 1993, is to promote respect for human rights; and he can also make recommendations, provide advice, technical assistance and cooperation. He heads the Office of the High Commissioner, which provides assistance, coordination and logistical and operational support for the Human Rights Council and the Treaty-Bodies. Among the various functions assigned to the High Commissioner, the most important is:

> [. . .] to play an active role in removing the current obstacles [. . .] to the full realization of all human rights and in preventing the continuation of human rights violations throughout the world.[102]

This very broad and general language can enable the High Commissioner to take an active role in the prevention of human rights violations;[103] in fact, he has intervened several times personally when it came to drawing attention to cases of serious human rights violations.

---

[99]The Special Procedures report annually to the Human Rights Council and sometimes also to the General Assembly.

[100]Established by ECOSOC Resolution 1503 (XLVIII).

[101]See Nowak (2003), p. 109.

[102]GA Res. 48/141, para. 4(f).

[103]See Buergenthal et al. (2004), p. 121.

10.5.3 Other Charter-Bodies Specializing in Human Rights

There are other international human rights monitoring bodies which are based on the UN Charter. Unlike those examined so far, these bodies are quite sectoral in nature, in the sense that they deal with specific human rights or certain categories of people. These include the Commission on the Status of Women,[104] the Commission on Crime Prevention and Criminal Justice,[105] the UN High Commissioner for Refugees,[106] the former Commission on Human Settlements now absorbed by the Government Council of the UN-Habitat Programme,[107] the Permanent Forum on Indigenous Issues,[108] the Special Adviser on the Prevention of Genocide,[109] and the Special Adviser on the Responsibility to Protect.[110]

10.5.4 Main Organs of the United Nations and Their Human Rights-Related Tasks

As already mentioned, the main UN organs also have, among their broad functions, that of addressing human rights issues. However, as these bodies do not specialize in human rights, they will be examined here in a very concise manner.

10.5.4.1 General Assembly

The General Assembly (GA), in accordance with Article 13 of the Charter, may, among other things, initiate studies and make recommendations for the purpose of:

---

[104]The Commission on the Status of Women is a body dedicated to the promotion of gender equality and the promotion of women.

[105]The Commission on Crime Prevention and Criminal Justice is one of ECOSOC's operational commissions and the main policy-making body within the UN on crime prevention and criminal justice.

[106]The United Nations High Commissioner for Refugees (UNHCR) is the United Nations agency specializing in the management of refugees, to which it provides international protection and material assistance, also pursuing durable solutions for their condition.

[107]The Commission on Human Settlements was one of ECOSOC's operational commissions, and then incorporated into the Government Council of the UN-Habitat Programme.

[108]The Permanent Forum on Indigenous Issues is a consultative body of the Economic and Social Council, which has the task of dealing with indigenous issues, including human rights issues.

[109]The Special Adviser on the Prevention of Genocide has the task of advising the Secretary General on matters related to his mandate, through early warning and mediation activities, also in collaboration with regional and sub-regional organizations. These activities are aimed at increasing the capacity of the UN to analyze and manage information on genocide and crimes against humanity.

[110]The Special Adviser on the Responsibility to Protect has the task of carrying out early warning activities with regard to situations of genocide, war crimes, ethnic cleansing and crimes against humanity. It works to develop the conceptual, operational and political aspects related to the concept of "responsibility to protect" and to promote its implementation, in cooperation with the Member States, civil society and the UN system; furthermore, its action is aimed at increasing the capacity of the UN to prevent and respond to such crimes.

> [...] assisting in the realization of human rights and fundamental freedoms for all without distinction as to race, sex, language, or religion.[111]

In practice, the GA can hold public discussions on general issues concerning certain human rights, but also on critical human rights situations in a specific State. It may adopt resolutions or declarations of principles, and it may also make appeals to the State concerned to cease the human rights violations attributed to it. In addition, the GA may directly negotiate and approve human rights treaties, which must then be ratified by States. Within the GA, it is its Third Commission which usually deals with human rights issues and which, every year, holds a discussion on these issues, based on reports received from the High Commissioner and other specialized human rights bodies.

10.5.4.2 Economic and Social Council

The Economic and Social Council (ECOSOC) has specific competence in the field of human rights under Articles 62(2) and 68[112] of the Charter and has in the past prepared various regulatory instruments on human rights. However, it is currently more concerned with coordinating the initiatives of other bodies, with particular regard to economic and social rights, and its role in human rights matters has become hardly significant.

10.5.4.3 Secretary General

The Secretary-General has no competence in human rights matters under the UN Charter. However, he can exercise his autonomous functions of conciliation, good offices and mediation in cases of interstate disputes and even internal State crises, in matters of human rights. In addition, he has an indirect competence, since, when conducting peace-keeping or peace-enforcing or peace-building operations, he must ensure that such operations are carried out with respect for human rights. Finally, the Secretary General has appointed a number of his special representatives[113] and has taken an initiative, called the *Human Rights Up Front Initiative*, to respond to serious and widespread human rights violations.

10.5.4.4 Security Council

According to the UN Charter, the Security Council (SC) also has no explicit competence for the protection of human rights. However, over the years, the peacekeeping functions (which are typical of the SC) and the protection of human rights have come closer together, so much so that serious and systematic violations of human rights can sometimes be considered a "threat to the peace" within the

[111] Art. 13(1)(b).

[112] Art. 62(2): "It may make recommendations for the purpose of promoting respect for, and observance of, human rights and fundamental freedoms for all".

[113] See, e.g., the Special Representative for Children and Armed Conflict, the Special Representative on Sexual Violence in Conflict, the Special Representative on Violence Against Children.

meaning of Article 39 of the Charter,[114] and therefore fall within the competence of the Security Council. And, in reality, the Security Council has concretely had the possibility of intervening in situations of serious violations of human rights, which constituted a threat to the peace, with measures not involving the use of force under Article 41 of the Charter,[115] or by authorizing States or groups of States to armed interventions, or with operations of peace-keeping, peace-enforcing and peace-building. Finally, the Council has used Chapter VII of the Charter as the legal basis for establishing the International Criminal Tribunal for the Former Yugoslavia[116] and the International Criminal Tribunal for Rwanda.[117]

10.5.4.5 International Court of Justice

The International Court of Justice does not have very extensive case-law on human rights, because individuals do not have the right to bring actions before the Court and, on the other hand, because disputes between States concerning human rights violations are not frequent. Nevertheless, especially in recent years, the situation is changing and the Court has issued some important judgments and advisory opinions on human rights.[118]

Among the less recent judgments, one can mention: the 1970 judgment in the *Barcelona Traction* case,[119] where the Court made the famous distinction between reciprocal and *erga omnes* obligations, indicating among the latter those relating to certain fundamental human rights; the 1980 judgment in the case of *US Diplomatic and Consular Staff in Tehran*,[120] where the Court declared that the unlawful detention of persons is incompatible with the fundamental principles of the Universal Declaration; the 1986 judgment in the case of *Military and Paramilitary Activities in Nicaragua*,[121] where the Court questioned whether certain US actions were in conformity with fundamental principles of humanitarian law. More recently, the Court has issued decisions on human rights matters in the *LaGrand*[122] and *Avena*[123] cases; in the case on the *Legality of Use of Force*;[124] in the cases on

[114]See Nowak (2003), pp. 129–130.

[115]Examples of measures taken under Article 41 of the Charter include economic sanctions against Iraq, Somalia, Haiti, Former Yugoslavia, East Timor, Sierra Leone and Afghanistan.

[116]International Criminal Tribunal for the Former Yugoslavia (ICTY). See below, Sect. 14.3.

[117]International Criminal Tribunal for Rwanda (ICTR). See below, Sect. 14.3.

[118]See above, Sect. 3.1. It has already been noted that, recently, the increase in interstate complaints regarding human rights violations has also affected the European Court of Human Rights and the Committee on the Elimination of Racial Discrimination.

[119]ICJ, *Barcelona Traction*, para. 33.

[120]ICJ, *United States Diplomatic and Consular Staff*, para. 91.

[121]ICJ, *Military and Paramilitary Activities*, Judgment of 27 June 1986, para. 220.

[122]ICJ, *LaGrand*, para. 126.

[123]ICJ, *Avena*, para. 124.

[124]ICJ, *Legality of Use of Force*, para. 41 ff.

Armed Activities on the Territory of the Congo;[125] in the case on *Questions relating to the Obligation to Prosecute or Extradite*;[126] in the cases on the *Application of the Genocide Convention*;[127] and in the cases on the *Application of the Convention against Racial Discrimination.*[128]

The Court's advisory opinions include: the opinion on *Reservations to the Genocide Convention,*[129] the opinion on *Western Sahara,*[130] the opinion on the *Legality of Nuclear Weapons,*[131] and the opinion on the *Construction of a Wall in the Occupied Palestinian Territory.*[132]

10.6 Specialized Institutes and Conferences on Human Rights

In addition to the international control mechanisms mentioned above, which operate within the framework of the UN, there are other international organizations, linked to the UN system, the so-called Specialized Institutes, which have competence in the field of human rights and have developed procedures for monitoring compliance with them. Here I will mention only the main ones, among these Institutes, which are the International Labour Organization (ILO) and the United Nations Educational, Scientific and Cultural Organization (UNESCO). Finally, the conferences on human rights organized by the UN are worth mentioning.

10.6.1 International Labour Organization

The International Labour Organization (ILO) focuses on human rights related to the right to work and working conditions, including trade union rights and strike and social security rights. It seeks to protect these rights through the preparation of draft conventions and the adoption of recommendations. ILO Member States, which have an obligation to submit draft conventions to the competent internal bodies for ratification (but not an obligation to ratify them), must submit reports on their outcome and the conventions they have ratified.

[125] ICJ, *Armed Activities on the Territory of the Congo*, Judgment of 19 December 2005, para. 181 ff. and Judgment of 3 February 2006.

[126] ICJ, *Questions relating to the Obligation to Prosecute or Extradite.*

[127] ICJ, *Application of the Convention on the Prevention and Punishment of the Crime of Genocide*, Judgment of 26 February 2007; Judgment of 3 February 2015; Order of 23 January 2020.

[128] ICJ, *Application of the International Convention on the Elimination of All Forms of Racial Discrimination*, Order of 15 October 2008 and Judgment of 1 April 2011.

[129] ICJ, *Reservations to the Convention on the Prevention and Punishment of the Crime of Genocide.*

[130] ICJ, *Western Sahara.*

[131] ICJ, *Legality of the Threat or Use of Nuclear Weapons*, paras. 24, 29.

[132] ICJ, *Legal Consequences of the Construction of a Wall*, para. 89 ff.

The ILO has established various monitoring procedures and expert committees to monitor compliance with the labor principles and standards contained in the numerous conventions and recommendations adopted by the Organization. First, there is a Committee of experts, composed of 20 independent persons, which examines the reports of States and, if it finds problems, can make "observations" to the State concerned. Secondly, there is a Committee on the application of conventions and recommendations, composed of representatives of governments, employers and workers. The ILO has also developed complaint procedures. Among these, one procedure which is reserved for freedom of association is important: the ILO Committee on Freedom of Association receives complaints directly from workers or workers' associations, examines them and, if it finds a violation, may ask the State concerned to continue to report on the matter or refer the case back to the Committee of Experts or the Conciliation and Inquiry Commission on Freedom of Association.

10.6.2 United Nations Educational, Scientific and Cultural Organization

UNESCO has a mandate to promote education, science and culture and, as part of that mandate, can take action to protect human rights. In fact, it prepares draft conventions and adopts recommendations on human rights which are linked to the subjects of its mandates. Again, Member States must submit draft conventions to their internal bodies responsible for ratification. Among the conventions that have been promoted by UNESCO and relate to human rights, the best known are the 1954 Convention for the Protection of Cultural Property in the Event of Armed Conflict,[133] the 1960 Convention against Discrimination in Education,[134] and the 2005 Convention on the Protection and Promotion of the Diversity of Cultural Expressions.[135]

UNESCO has established certain monitoring procedures. The most interesting is a complaint procedure open to individuals and NGOs, which, however, is confidential. The victim or other person, who is aware of the violation of a human right relating to education, science or culture, can submit a complaint to UNESCO. The complaint is examined by the Committee on conventions and forwarded to the Government concerned, which may respond. The parties may be heard by the Committee. Finally, the latter may propose to the State to take specific measures. Alternatively, the Director General of UNESCO may conduct consultations with a view to reaching an amicable solution. In reality, this procedure, even if it has some quasi-judicial features, aims to encourage a diplomatic and conciliatory solution to the dispute.

[133]Convention for the Protection of Cultural Property in the Event of Armed Conflict, 14 May 1954.

[134]Convention against Discrimination in Education, 14 December 1960.

[135]Convention on the Protection and Promotion of the Diversity of Cultural Expressions, 20 October 2005.

10.6.3 Human Rights Conferences

The first world conference on human rights was organized by the United Nations in Tehran in 1968, to celebrate the 20th anniversary of the Universal Declaration. The second major conference was held in Vienna in 1993 and produced, as a final document, the famous *Vienna Declaration and Programme of Action of the World Conference on Human Rights*, which presented a common plan to strengthen human rights worldwide. The Vienna Conference, after extensive discussion, also declared the principle of the universality, indivisibility and interdependence of all human rights.[136] Subsequently, the human rights conferences organized by the United Nations became more frequent; but they focused on more specific issues in turn. These conferences include, among others, the *International Conference on Population Development* (Cairo, 1994), the *World Conference on Women* (Beijing, 1995), the *World Conference against Racism, Racial Discrimination, Xenophobia and Related Intolerance* (Durban, 2001), the *World Conference on Indigenous Peoples* (New York, 2010), and the *World Conference on Disaster Risk Reduction* (Sendai, 2015).

In fact, the final results of the conferences usually consist of statements or other documents that are not legally binding. However, these conferences have played a role in shaping and developing UN human rights programmes.

References

Buergenthal T, Shelton D, Stewart DP (2004) International Human Rights in a Nutshell, 3rd edn. West Group, St. Paul. (2nd rep)

Cassese A (Gaeta P ed) (2003-2004) Diritto internazionale, vol. I: I lineamenti, vol. II: Problemi della comunità internazionale. Il Mulino, Bologna

Nowak M (2003) Introduction to the International Human Rights regime. Nijhoff, Leiden

Shelton D (2014a) Advanced introduction to international human rights law. Edward Elgar, Cheltenham

Zappalà S (2011) La tutela internazionale dei diritti umani. Il Mulino, Bologna

[136]But, for a criticism, see below, Sect. 13.1.

11 The European System of Human Rights

11.1 Council of Europe

The norms and mechanisms for ensuring respect for human rights that exist at regional level are often more advanced and effective than the (tendentially) universal ones examined above. This is due to a greater political, cultural and social homogeneity of States, which favors a common understanding of human rights and therefore also the possibility of more effective control mechanisms. It is now appropriate to examine these regional systems in a concise manner.

As is well known, the most advanced system of regional protection of human rights is that created within the framework of the Council of Europe (CoE). The main achievements of the CoE have been the conclusion of the European Convention on Human Rights of 1950, the European Social Charter of 1961 (revised in 1996), the European Convention against Torture of 1987, the Framework Convention for the Protection of National Minorities of 1995, and the European Commissioner for Human Rights established in 1999.

11.1.1 The European Convention on Human Rights

The European Convention on Human Rights is well known, so I can confine myself to its essential aspects.[1] The Convention was signed in Rome in 1950 and entered into force in 1953. The Member States of the Council of Europe can accede to it. The Convention is made up of two parts: the first part, which is of a substantive nature, lists the rights guaranteed, the second part, which is of a procedural nature, lays down the guarantee bodies and mechanisms. Over time, the Convention has been

[1] In fact, the ECHR is the subject of many specific manuals and ad hoc university courses. That is why I consider it unnecessary to explore this topic in depth in this book, which has a broader content.

R. Pisillo Mazzeschi, *International Human Rights Law*,
https://doi.org/10.1007/978-3-030-77032-7_11

supplemented and amended by 16 Additional Protocols, which have increased the rights guaranteed (the so-called Supplemental Protocols) and amended the guarantee mechanisms (the so-called Amending Protocols).

The most important changes are those that have transformed the guarantee mechanism. Originally, it was very complex and was based, until 1998, on three bodies: the Commission and the European Court of Human Rights and the Committee of Ministers of the Council of Europe. The Commission could examine both interstate complaints lodged by one State Party against another State Party and individual complaints lodged by private persons against a State Party. It decided on the admissibility of the complaint (application) and, if so, instructed it and attempted a friendly settlement of the dispute. If the attempt was unsuccessful, the Commission would draw up a report (giving an opinion on possible violations of the Convention) and forward it to the Committee of Ministers. Then, under certain conditions, both the Commission and a Member State could take the case to the European Court, which would decide whether or not there were violations of the Convention.

This system was radically reformed by Protocol No. 11, which entered into force in 1998, establishing a single, permanent Court, which essentially took over the functions previously performed by the Commission and the (previous) Court. Before the (new) Court, any natural or legal person can lodge an application directly. Indeed, it is precisely the possibility of individual actions before a court that is the central focus of the European Convention system. In essence, it gives the individual a genuine right of action at international level to assert the rights recognized by the Convention.[2] It should be noted that the individual right of complaint, which was previously provided for by an optional clause, is now automatically compulsory for all Member States. Other important changes were introduced with Protocol No. 14, which entered into force in 2010 and streamlined the procedure before the Court, and with Protocol No. 16, which allows the highest courts and tribunals of the States Parties to request an advisory opinion from the Strasbourg Court on questions relating to the interpretation and application of the Convention.[3]

It should also be stressed that the Convention contains obligations *erga omnes partes*. One consequence of this is that any State Party may bring an action against another State Party, which has committed a possible violation of the Convention, even if the first State Party has not suffered direct injury from the breach,[4] for example even if the individual victim of the violation is not its own citizen. This means that interstate complaints are based on the "concept of a collective guarantee by the Contracting States of the rights and freedoms defined in the Convention".[5] Interstate complaints, for a long time few in number, have increased in more recent years.

---

[2]See Zagrebelsky et al. (2019), p. 30.

[3]Protocol No. 16 is in force, but has not yet been ratified by Italy.

[4]See Ronzitti (2016), p. 324.

[5]See, for example, ECmHR, *Austria v. Italy*.

11.1.1.1 The Rights Guaranteed

As regards the substantive part of the European Convention, Article 1 establishes the general obligation of the Contracting States to secure the rights guaranteed therein "to everyone within their jurisdiction". We have already seen how this provision, which defines the spatial scope of the Convention, has given rise to interesting case-law and not always unambiguous interpretations by the Strasbourg bodies.[6]

As for the list of protected rights, most of them belong to the so-called first generation of human rights, consisting of "fundamental" rights and civil and political rights. This is because the Convention is inspired both by the Western tradition of human rights and, for the period in which it was drafted, by the Universal Declaration.

All the rights guaranteed by the European Convention and its Additional Protocols cannot be listed here. These include the right to life (Art. 2), the prohibition of torture (Art. 3), the prohibition of slavery and forced labor (Art. 4), the right to liberty and security (Art. 5), the right to a fair trial (Art. 6), the right to respect for private and family life (Art. 8), the freedom of thought, expression, assembly and association (Arts. 9, 10 and 11), the prohibition of discrimination (Art. 14), the right to property (Art. 1 of Protocol No. 1). Many of these rights are not absolute, but are restricted, and many rights may be derogated in time of war or public emergency (Art. 15). The content and character of these rights will be discussed in more detail later.[7]

Two important concepts must also be stressed. Firstly, the case-law of the Strasbourg bodies has made it clear that the rights provided for do not only impose negative obligations to abstain, but also positive obligations to act. Secondly, the substantive norms of the European Convention are formally addressed not only to States Parties, but also directly to individuals, giving them true rights at international level. Therefore, under the Convention, individuals have many substantive human rights and the procedural right to assert them before an international court.

11.1.1.2 Bodies and Procedures

The procedural part of the European Convention is the most interesting and innovative one, and in fact it also had an influence on other regional human rights protection systems, such as the Inter-American and African systems.

The European Court of Human Rights consists of a number of judges equal to that of the States Parties to the Convention. They sit individually and are independent of the States Parties. The Court is divided into four formations: (*a*) Single judge; (*b*) Committees of three judges; (*c*) Chambers of seven judges; (*d*) Grand Chamber of 17 judges. These formations have different competences, of increasing importance.[8]

---

[6]See above, Sects. 9.4, 9.5 and 9.6. See also Ronzitti (2016), pp. 324–326.

[7]See below, Parts V and VI.

[8]See ECHR, Articles 26–31.

The Court, as mentioned above, is competent to hear and determine both inter-state complaints (Art. 33) and individual complaints (Art. 34).[9] The latter may be filed by natural persons, legal persons and associations or trade unions; but such persons must prove that they are "victims" of the violation of one of the rights guaranteed by the Convention or the Additional Protocols. The question is sometimes complex. The Court has in the past demonstrated a restrictive attitude, which it now seems to want to review, about complaints coming from organizations that represent collective interests but are not directly affected by the violation. On the other hand, applications by indirect victims, such as family members of the "direct" victim, or by potential victims, are permitted. An example of potential victim is when the applicant complains that the State has adopted a law which has not yet been enforced against him or her, but is very likely to be enforced in the future and to cause him or her direct harm.[10]

The litigation procedure can be divided into three main phases: (*a*) that of admissibility (or inadmissibility) of the application; (*b*) that of examination, investigation of the facts and attempt at a friendly settlement of the dispute; (*c*) that of the decision by judgment.

In the first stage, which functions as a kind of preliminary filter, the Court decides on the admissibility of applications (Art. 35). The main condition of admissibility is the prior exhaustion of domestic remedies by the applicant individual or by the individual victim of the violation alleged by the State lodging the application. I have already dealt with the rule of prior exhaustion.[11] Another condition of admissibility is that the application must have been lodged within 6 months of the date of notification of the final domestic decision.[12] Furthermore, in individual applications, it is required that the complaint not be anonymous, not concern a matter already submitted to the Court or other international supervisory body, not be manifestly unfounded and that it not constitute an abuse of the right of application. Finally, a condition of admissibility which was added recently is that the applicant must have suffered a "significant disadvantage".[13]

If the application is admissible, a second stage of the procedure shall be opened, in which the Court shall examine the case with the parties' representatives and may conduct investigations, in which the Contracting States undertake to cooperate. Moreover, at any stage of the procedure, the Court makes itself available to the parties with a view to reaching a friendly settlement of the dispute (Art. 39). If settlement is successful, the application is removed from the Court's list and the

---

[9]The Court also has an advisory function: it may, at the request of the Committee of Ministers, give an advisory opinion on questions relating to the interpretation of the Convention and its Protocols. See also above, Sect. 11.1.1, Protocol No. 16.

[10]See, e.g., ECtHR, *Dudgeon v. UK*.

[11]See above, Sect. 4.4.1.1.

[12]The deadline has been reduced to 4 months after the entry into force of Protocol No. 15 to the European Convention.

[13]This condition of admissibility was included in Protocol No. 14; and is sometimes criticized in doctrine. See, for example, Citroni and Scovazzi (2013), pp. 97–99.

solution reached is set out in a decision that is forwarded to the Committee of Ministers, which supervises its execution.

If a friendly settlement is not reached, the third stage of the procedure is opened, in which the Court decides on the merits by a judgment, the function of which is to determine whether or not there has been a violation of the Convention or of the Additional Protocols. This is a judgment of mere assessment, which is limited to deciding whether or not the measure taken by the State complies with the Convention.[14] If the Court establishes that there has been a violation, it may grant the injured party "just satisfaction" (Art. 41),[15] which may consist of monetary compensation for material and non-material damage or *restitutio in integrum*. The Court's judgments are mandatory for the Member States (Art. 46), even if they are not directly enforceable in domestic law and thus leave the sentenced State a certain margin of discretion in deciding domestic enforcement measures.

However, the Strasbourg Court has recently developed new types of judgments through interesting case-law.[16] First of all, the Court, in the so-called cases of "structural violations" of the European Convention, does not limit itself to establishing whether the State has violated the Convention, but indicates to the State the measures, including legislative ones, which should be adopted to avoid repeated or continuous violations. In this regard, there is talk of "pilot judgments" of the Court and of "general measures" that it establishes against the State. In the second place, the Court has sometimes issued judgments that establish "individual measures", i.e. that leave no margin of appreciation to the States on their implementation (for example, the review of a particular criminal trial); and sometimes also "warning judgments", in which the Court, while not establishing a violation, warns the State that it could change its position in the future.

It is also worth remembering that, during the litigation procedure, the Court may adopt "provisional measures" of a precautionary nature, the purpose of which is to avoid serious and irreparable damage to the applicant; that is, damage which cannot be avoided when the judgment is delivered. Examples of provisional measures are the suspension of the expulsion of a person to a country where he or she risks being subjected to acts of torture or the suspension of the execution of a death penalty pending the judgment of the European Court.

The Committee of Ministers of the Council of Europe is responsible for monitoring the implementation of the Court's decisions. Protocol No. 14 reinforced this role of the Committee, as it created a kind of "judgment for failure to comply" with judgments. If the losing State fails to comply with the Court's judgment, the Committee of Ministers may refer the matter to the Court for a declaration of

[14]See Ronzitti (2016), p. 332.

[15]The term "just satisfaction" is rather unusual in international law; but it is essentially equivalent to the term "reparation".

[16]There is a vast body of literature and case-law on this subject. See, recently, Cannone (2018); Saccucci (2018), pp. 17–69; Pustorino (2020), pp. 55–58 and 67–71.

non-compliance.[17] If the Court issues such a declaration, it shall refer the matter back to the Committee of Ministers "for consideration of the measures to be taken" (Art. 46(5)). In fact, the measures that the Committee may take are not specified; but, in theory, a persistent failure to comply with a judgment of the Court could also lead to a suspension of the State from the Council of Europe, pursuant to Article 3 of its Statute.[18]

11.1.2 The European Social Charter

As the European Convention on Human Rights dealt only marginally with economic, social and cultural rights, the Council of Europe drew up the European Social Charter, signed in 1961, and subsequently supplemented by three Protocols. In addition, a new version of the Charter was adopted in 1996, called the Revised European Social Charter.

The Charter is an original legal instrument, which is flexible and differentiated between Member States. There is a distinction between Part I of the Charter, which contains 31 rights and principles, formulated in a very general way, and Part II, which contains 31 more detailed articles, each of which includes several numbered paragraphs. Each Contracting State undertakes to regard Part I of the Charter as a declaration of the objectives it will pursue by all appropriate means. In addition, it undertakes to be bound by at least six of the nine articles in Part II which are expressly mentioned; and also by an additional number of articles or paragraphs in Part II, of its choice, provided that the total number of articles or paragraphs to which it is bound is not less than 16 articles or 63 paragraphs (Part III, Art. A). This system confirms that Part I of the Charter does not contain immediately binding legal obligations; and that each State is left a fairly wide discretion in choosing the binding obligations contained in Part II. This mechanism favors a more generalized accession by the CoE States, which have very different internal situations in the economic and social fields.

The catalogue of protected rights includes, in summary, the right to work, in its various specifications; the right to health; the right to medical and social assistance; the economic protection rights of the family, women and children; the right to non-discrimination; the right to housing.

It is also worth mentioning the guarantee mechanisms. There are two control procedures, which are based, in the traditional way, on the submission of periodic reports by the States Parties. But there is also, since 1998, a more interesting procedure, of a quasi-judicial nature, which consists in the submission of collective complaints by international organizations of employers and workers, or certain

[17]See the resolution of 7 December 2017, by which the Committee of Ministers, after ordering Azerbaijan to enforce the judgment in the *Mikayil Mammadov* case, brought an action before the Court to enforce the non-implementation of the judgment.

[18]See Citroni, Scovazzi (2013), p. 102.

non-governmental organizations, or national organizations of employers and workers of the State accused of violating the Charter. These complaints are examined by the European Committee of Social Rights[19] (a body of independent experts), which decides first on admissibility and then, if necessary, on the merits. The Committee then prepares a report with its conclusions on whether or not the Charter has been violated and forwards it to the Committee of Ministers, which addresses a recommendation to the State that has committed a violation and monitors its compliance.

11.1.3 Other Human Rights Treaties of the Council of Europe

The Council of Europe has adopted a number of treaties dealing, more or less directly, with human rights, with reference, for example, to the rights of children, migrant workers, refugees and victims of crime. Below I will briefly examine only those that I consider to be the most significant.

11.1.3.1 The European Convention for the Prevention of Torture

As we have seen, the 1984 UN Convention against Torture focuses primarily on the *repression* of acts of torture and inhuman or degrading treatment or punishment. In the framework of the Council of Europe, however, it was considered important to create a legal regime aimed at the *prevention* of such acts. On this basis, the Council of Europe adopted, in 1987, the European Convention for the Prevention of Torture and Inhuman or Degrading Treatment or Punishment.[20]

This Convention is based on the assumption that the greatest risk of being subjected to such abuses occurs during the arrest and detention of persons by police officers, prison officers or other State authorities. It has therefore set up a body of independent experts, the European Committee for the Prevention of Torture and Inhuman or Degrading Treatment or Punishment,[21] which has the power to visit places of detention, to monitor the treatment of detainees (including through private interviews) and, if necessary, to make recommendations to the State concerned with a view to strengthening the protection of detainees. The Committee makes regular visits to States Parties to the Convention, but may also organize ad hoc visits. It also prepares reports, which are in principle confidential; but which are usually published with the consent of the State concerned.

[19]European Committee of Social Rights (ECteeSR).

[20]European Convention for the Prevention of Torture and Inhuman or Degrading Treatment or Punishment (ECPT), 26 November 1987.

[21]European Committee for the Prevention of Torture and Inhuman or Degrading Treatment or Punishment. Cf. Art. 1 ECPT.

11.1.3.2 The European Charter for Regional and Minority Languages

In the 1990s, the problem of national minorities became important again in Europe, with the re-emergence of numerous ethnic conflicts. The first response from the Council of Europe was the adoption, in 1992, of the European Charter for National or Minority Languages.[22] The aim of this agreement is to protect linguistic diversity and, in particular, regional and minority languages that have a historical tradition in Europe, and to respect the right to use them in public and private life. The Charter is structured in a similar way to the European Social Charter, as it first sets out a number of aims and principles and then a number of more specific measures. Each State Party undertakes to commit itself to a minimum number of articles in the Charter, which are explicitly set out. The monitoring mechanism is limited to a simple procedure of periodic reporting by States Parties.

11.1.3.3 The European Framework Convention for the Protection of National Minorities

After a short time, the Council of Europe adopted a more general treaty on the protection of minorities: the 1995 European Framework Convention for the Protection of National Minorities.[23] It contains rather vague norms and most of them are of a programmatic nature, due to the lack of unequivocal positions of the Contracting States on the matter. The concept of "national minorities" also remains undefined.

The first part of the Convention sets out some general principles; the second part states a number of more precise principles covering many aspects relating to the protection of persons belonging to national minorities. These topics can be grouped into five main areas: (*a*) rights relating to non-discrimination and the protection of cultural, linguistic and religious identity (Arts. 4–6); (*b*) issues related to language rights and the use of language in public and in private (Arts. 10–11); (*c*) rights in the educational sphere (Arts. 12–14); (*d*) rights relating to participation in decision-making (Art. 15); (*e*) issues relating to cross-border cooperation in the promotion of the rights provided for in the Convention. However, these minority rights do not correspond to precise positive obligations on the part of States. Part Four of the Convention establishes a monitoring mechanism, entrusted to the Committee of Ministers, assisted by an advisory committee of independent experts, to which States Parties submit regular reports.

11.1.3.4 The Convention on Human Rights and Biomedicine

With the Convention on Human Rights and Biomedicine, adopted in 1997,[24] the Council of Europe has sought to protect the human rights of people from the risks that may arise from new developments in biomedicine and biotechnology. In fact, some traditional human rights, such as the right to life, the right to personal integrity

---

[22] European Charter for Regional or Minority Languages (ECML), 5 November 1992.

[23] Framework Convention for the Protection of National Minorities (FCPNM), 1 February 1995.

[24] European Convention for the Protection of Human Rights and Dignity of the Human Being with regard to the Application of Biology and Medicine (ECHRB), 4 April 1997.

and the right to private life, already set limits to the excesses of modern medicine's interventions in people's dignity.[25] However, it was felt that more specific norms were needed. The Convention contains a number of principles and prohibitions on bioethics, medical research, prior and informed patient consent, organ transplantation, assisted reproduction and similar issues. However, some authors have pointed out that many of the core provisions of the Convention are only new formulations of principles that were already inherent in human rights, especially the right to private life.[26]

11.1.4 Council of Europe Commissioner for Human Rights

The Council of Europe established its own Commissioner for Human Rights in 1999.[27] His mandate is to: (*a*) promote effective observance of human rights and assist Member States in implementing the human rights norms of the Council of Europe; (*b*) promote and disseminate human rights education; (*c*) identify gaps and shortcomings in the legislation and practices of CoE Member States and make recommendations to them; (*d*) facilitate the work of national institutions and other human rights structures; (*e*) provide advice and information on human rights protection in the region. The activities of this institution focus on three main, closely related areas: country visits and dialogue with national authorities and civil society; thematic reporting and advice on the systematic implementation of human rights; and awareness-raising activities. The Commissioner cannot act on individual complaints, but can draw conclusions and take broader initiatives on the basis of reliable information on human rights violations suffered by individuals.[28]

11.2 European Union

The Treaties establishing the European Communities originally contained only very few provisions dealing with human rights, but these were only rights instrumental to the realization of the common market. This was justified by the fact that the Communities were predominantly economic in nature and that it was felt at the time that the Community Institutions could not have an opportunity to affect people's human rights.

---

[25] Nowak (2003), p. 181.

[26] *Ibidem*, p. 183.

[27] Council of Europe Commissioner for Human Rights.

[28] The Commissioner also cooperates with a wide range of national and international institutions and human rights monitoring mechanisms. The Office's most important intergovernmental partners include the United Nations and its Specialized Institutes, the European Union and the OSCE. The Office also works with major NGOs, universities and human rights think-tanks.

However, since the end of the 1960s, the protection of human rights has slowly and gradually established itself in Community law (now EU law),[29] mainly through case-law, thanks to the European Court of Justice. Under the impetus of some important rulings by the Italian and German Constitutional Courts claiming control over Community norms contrary to constitutional principles, the Court of Justice stated that the protection of human rights was part of the Community's objectives. More specifically, the Court of Justice, starting with the famous *Stauder*, *Internationale Handelsgesellschaft* and *Nold* cases,[30] affirmed that fundamental rights are part of the general principles of the Community legal order. The Court added that these principles on human rights can be derived from: (*a*) the constitutional traditions common to the Member States; (*b*) the human rights treaties to which the Member States are parties, with particular regard to the European Convention on Human Rights. However, this action of the Court of Justice, while having the great merit of filling a gap in the Community legal order, had the limitation of advancing fundamental rights only through case-law and therefore in a slow and fragmented manner, and of being able to establish, by referring to the constitutional traditions *common* to all the Member States, only minimum standards of protection.

But the situation later changed, through the inclusion of some explicit human rights norms in the subsequent treaties on the Communities and the European Union. A first important step forward was taken with the 1992 Maastricht Treaty on European Union, which expressly stated that the Union respects fundamental rights as guaranteed by the European Convention and as they result from the constitutional traditions of the Member States, as general principles of Union Law.

Subsequently, after the Commission's failure to accept that the Communities should accede to the European Convention due to a negative opinion of the Court of Justice in 1996, the Amsterdam Treaty of 1997 marked a further step forward: it established that the Union is based on respect for human rights; that such respect is a requirement for the accession of new States; and that serious violation of these rights by a Member State may be sanctioned by the suspension of some of its rights.

11.2.1 The Current Normative Framework

Following the entry into force, in 2009, of the 2007 Lisbon Treaty, the legal framework is as follows. Article 2 of the Treaty on European Union (TEU) lists, among the values on which the Union is founded, respect for human dignity, freedom, democracy, equality and human rights. Article 6(3) states that:

> Fundamental rights, as guaranteed by the European Convention for the Protection of Human Rights and Fundamental Freedoms and as they result from the constitutional traditions common to the Member States, shall constitute general principles of the Union's law.

[29] This topic has already been concisely discussed, above, in Sect. 5.1.2.

[30] ECJ, *Stauder* (1969); *Internationale Handelsgesellschaft* (1970); *Nold* (1974).

Article 7 TEU provides that a serious and persistent breach by a Member State of the values referred to in Article 2 may result in the suspension of the rights deriving from the application of the Treaties to that State.[31] Article 49 states, as a requirement for the accession of a new European State to the EU, that such State "respects the values referred to in Article 2 and is committed to promoting them".

In the meantime, the idea had emerged that the EU should have its own written catalogue of fundamental rights. This idea was first realized with the drafting of the EU Charter of Fundamental Rights and its proclamation as a non-binding document at the Nice European Council in 2000. Later, with the entry into force of the Lisbon Treaty, the Charter (with minor readjustments) finally took on the same binding legal value as the Treaties. This is expressly enshrined in Article 6(1) TEU.

The Charter takes over and updates the catalogue of rights of the European Convention on Human Rights, and reaffirms all the rights that the Court of Justice's case-law had progressively identified. The rights established by the Charter are grouped, in a rather innovative way, under six Titles: "Dignity", "Freedoms", "Equality", "Solidarity", "Citizens' Rights", and "Justice". However, it should be noted that Article 51 of the Charter states that it applies to the Institutions of the Union and the Member States "only when they are implementing Union law" and that it "does not extend the field of application of Union law beyond the powers of the Union or establish any new power or task for the Union".

Finally, Article 6(2) TEU now enshrines the EU's commitment and competence to accede to the European Convention on Human Rights. But the Court of Justice, in a new opinion of 18 December 2014, considered that the draft agreement drawn up by the Commission was not compatible with EU law.

11.2.2 The Competence of the Court of Justice in the Field of Human Rights

In this legal framework, it is worth mentioning the competences of the Court of Justice in the field of human rights. The Court certainly has jurisdiction to protect human rights which are part of European Union law, in relation to acts of the Institutions. On the contrary, the Court cannot judge the conformity with human rights of acts or norms of Member States in matters which are outside the scope of EU law.[32]

The problem is more complicated as regards a possible review by the Court of Justice of Member States' acts or norms *implementing* EU law. One could, for example, suppose that a national tribunal were to refer a question to the Court of Justice for a preliminary ruling on the compatibility of national legislation with the human rights protected by EU law.[33] It should be noted that such cases are very

[31]See also, in a similar sense, TFEU, Art. 354.

[32]See, e.g., ECJ, *Meryem Demirel.*

[33]Ronzitti (2016), p. 342.

thorny, as the jurisdiction of the Court of Justice risks conflict with that of the European Court of Human Rights. Indeed, the latter Court has declared itself competent, in numerous judgments, to rule on the conformity with the European Convention of the acts of the Member States implementing EU law.

The Strasbourg Court has also tried to resolve the problem of the possible conflict of competences. In the already mentioned *Bosphorus* case,[34] the Court distinguished between: (*a*) cases where Member States limit themselves to implementing EU acts; (*b*) cases where Member States enjoy a certain margin of discretion in implementing EU law. In the first category of cases, the Court considers that its intervention is not, in principle, necessary, since the EU is capable of protecting human rights in a manner, substantive and procedural, at least equivalent to that of the European Convention.[35] In the second category of cases, on the contrary, the Strasbourg Court considers that it has full jurisdiction to rule on possible violations of the European Convention by States in their implementation of EU law. This situation is likely to change if the planned agreement on EU accession to the European Convention is concluded and enters into force.[36] But some writers believe that potential conflicts between the Court of Justice and the European Court of Human Rights will increase.

Another problem concerns the competence of the Court of Justice to review, on the basis of respect for human rights protected by EU law, EU acts implementing UN Security Council decisions. This issue arose in the well-known *Kadi* cases,[37] where the legitimacy of an EU regulation implementing certain Security Council decisions, restricting the property rights of some individuals and entities associated with Osama bin Laden, the Al-Qaida network and the Taliban, was discussed. The Court of Justice has stated that, although the UN Charter obliges States to respect the decisions of the Security Council, the implementation of such decisions in EU law must respect the principles of that law, including fundamental human rights.[38]

11.3 Organization for Security and Cooperation in Europe

The Organization for Security and Cooperation in Europe (OSCE) was established at the Helsinki Conference in 1975 as a Diplomatic Conference (CSCE),[39] which was subsequently equipped with a number of bodies and operated for several years

[34]ECtHR, *Bosphorus*, paras. 149–165.

[35]But that is just a relative presumption. See also ECtHR, *M.S.S. v. Belgium and Greece*, paras. 338–340; *Michaud v. France*; *Avotiņš v. Latvia*. On the principle of equivalent protection see Marchegiani (2018).

[36]See, on the point, Daniele (2014), p. 191.

[37]CFI, *Kadi*; EGC, *Kadi*; ECJ, *Kadi and Al Barakaat*; ECJ, *European Commission and Others v. Kadi*.

[38]On the problem of the possible violation of human rights by Security Council resolutions see also ECtHR, *Nada*; *Al-Dulimi*, and above, Sect. 5.1.1.

[39]Conference on Security and Co-operation in Europe (CSCE).

through biennial conferences. In 1994, it became a permanent organization and took on its present name of OSCE.

One of the main aims of the OSCE is the protection of human rights, which is broadly defined as the "human dimension" of the Organization. This expression has a wider meaning than "human rights", since it applies not only to human rights in the strict sense, but also to relations between institutions: the concept of democracy, democratic institutions, the rule of law, minority rights, disarmament and conflict prevention.[40] In fact, the notion of "human dimension" has now become autonomous with respect to that of "human rights", although obviously the two topics are linked. This autonomy derives from several factors: (*a*) OSCE commitments are essentially political in nature, while human rights are mostly protected by legally binding norms; (*b*) OSCE commitments do not need ratification, unlike human rights treaties, or formal implementation in State legal systems; (*c*) OSCE guarantee mechanisms operate at the interstate level and are not open to recourse by individuals.

Indeed, various guarantee mechanisms have also developed within the OSCE, based mainly on negotiation, mediation and conciliation procedures.

The so-called "human dimension mechanism" is a procedure aimed at ensuring compliance with the human rights provisions contained in OSCE documents. It consists of four stages: a denunciation of non-compliance by one State against another; a reply by the second State and possible bilateral meetings; a referral of the matter to all participating States; and finally a discussion of the matter at a meeting of the OSCE Human Dimension Conference. Since 1991, experts and *rapporteurs* have also participated in the procedure. However, this mechanism has lost importance since the establishment of the OSCE Permanent Council,[41] within which discussions on the observance of human rights by States take place.

In 1992, the OSCE created the Office of the High Commissioner for National Minorities,[42] which has an independent conflict prevention task, when minority issues may pose a danger to international peace and security. Its functions consist of so-called "early warning" and "early action". The High Commissioner may carry out missions on the ground, with the consent of the territorial State, and then prepare reports. In 1997, an OSCE Representative on Freedom of the Media was established.[43]

Finally, the Stockholm Convention was signed in 1992 and entered into force in 1994, creating the OSCE Court of Conciliation and Arbitration.[44] To date, however, only 34 States, of the 57 OSCE Members, have ratified the Convention. The Court

[40]See Ronzitti (2016), p. 344.

[41]Permanent Council. See https://www.osce.org/permanent-council.

[42]OSCE High Commissioner for National Minorities. See https://www.osce.org/hcnm.

[43]OSCE Representative on Freedom of the Media. See https://www.osce.org/representative-on-freedom-of-media.

[44]Court of Conciliation and Arbitration within the OSCE. See https://www.osce.org/cca. On the Court's conciliation functions see, recently, Tomuschat et al. (2016); Tomuschat and Kohen (2020).

has in fact a very broad jurisdiction, since it can intervene in all interstate disputes (between States Parties to the Convention and, in certain cases, also between States Parties to the Convention and States that are only parties to the OSCE), which affect any matter; and therefore also in disputes relating to respect for human rights. It may act through a conciliation procedure, sometimes also on unilateral appeal, or through an arbitration procedure. However, the Court, for a rather complex set of reasons,[45] has not yet decided on any cases.

References

Cannone A (2018) Violazioni di carattere sistemico e Convenzione europea dei diritti dell'uomo. Cacucci, Bari

Citroni G, Scovazzi T (2013) La tutela internazionale dei diritti umani, Parte III del Corso di diritto internazionale (Scovazzi T ed). Giuffrè, Milano

Daniele L (2014) Diritto dell'Unione europea. Sistema istituzionale-Ordinamento-Tutela giuri sdizionale-Competenze, 5th edn. Giuffrè, Milano

Marchegiani M (2018) Il principio della protezione equivalente come meccanismo di coordinamento tra sistemi giuridici nell'ordinamento internazionale. Editoriale Scientifica, Napoli

Nowak M (2003) Introduction to the international human rights regime. Nijhoff, Leiden-Boston

Pustorino P (2020) Lezioni di tutela internazionale dei diritti umani, 2nd edn. Cacucci, Bari

Ronzitti N (2016) Introduzione al diritto internazionale, 5th edn. Giappichelli, Torino

Saccucci A (2018) La responsabilità internazionale dello Stato per violazioni strutturali dei diritti umani. Editoriale Scientifica, Napoli

Tomuschat C, Kohen M (eds) (2020) Flexibility in international dispute settlement. Conciliation revisited. Brill/Nijhoff, Leiden-Boston

Tomuschat C, Pisillo Mazzeschi R, Thurer D (eds) (2016) Conciliation in international law. The OSCE court of conciliation and arbitration. Brill/Nijhoff, Leiden-Boston

Zagrebelsky V, Chenal R, Tomasi L (2019) Manuale dei diritti fondamentali in Europa, 2nd edn. Il Mulino, Bologna

[45] See Tomuschat et al. (2016).

12 Other Regional Human Rights Systems

12.1 The Inter-American System

The Inter-American system of human rights protection was born, in 1948, with the adoption of the Charter of the Organization of American States (OAS) and the American Declaration on the Rights and Duties of Man,[1] a non-binding document. In 1959, the Inter-American Commission on Human Rights[2] was established, which became a body of the OAS and was entrusted with the task of monitoring compliance with the American Declaration. The Commission is based in Washington and consists of seven members, independent experts who sit in their personal capacity and who are elected by the General Assembly of the OAS.

Considerable progress was made with the approval, in 1969, of the American Convention of Human Rights,[3] which came into force in 1978, ratified by the most important countries of South America and Central America (but not by Canada and the United States).

The Convention, in its Part I, establishes the human rights that States Parties are obliged to recognize, with a catalogue that is largely inspired by the European Convention on Human Rights and the UN Covenant on Civil and Political Rights. The content of many of these rights will be further elaborated later.[4] Part II of the Convention establishes the Inter-American Court of Human Rights[5] and regulates its functions. The Court has its seat in San José (Costa Rica) and consists of seven judges, who sit in their personal capacity and are elected by the States Parties to the Convention. But the American Convention also confers further powers on the

[1]American Declaration on the Rights and Duties of Man, 2 May 1948.

[2]Inter-American Commission on Human Rights (IACmHR).

[3](Inter)-American Convention of Human Rights (ACHR). For an extensive discussion of the Convention see, most recently, Medina Quiroga (2016), Zanghì and Panella (2019), pp. 376–410.

[4]See below, Parts V and VI.

[5]Inter-American Court of Human Rights (IACtHR).

R. Pisillo Mazzeschi, *International Human Rights Law*,
https://doi.org/10.1007/978-3-030-77032-7_12

Commission, limited to the States Parties to the Convention. Two Additional Protocols were subsequently adopted.

As regards the guarantee mechanisms of the Inter-American system, they are entrusted to the Commission and the Court, with a binary system inspired by the (original) European Convention on Human Rights. However, while the Commission functions both as a body of the OAS and as a body of the American Convention, the Court has competence only under the Convention. Indeed, the Inter-American system is founded on two different legal regimes: the first is based on the OAS Charter and binds all the Member States of the OAS; the second is based on the American Convention and binds only the States Parties to it. The two regimes interact and overlap in various ways, sometimes making it difficult to keep them separate.[6]

12.1.1 The Inter-American Commission

The Commission carries out its mandate through various procedures.[7] A distinction should be made between those which operate in relation to the OAS Member States and those which operate in relation to States Parties to the American Convention.

With regard to the OAS Member States, the Commission has a more limited role.[8] It may, inter alia, address recommendations to governments, prepare studies and reports, request reports from States on human rights measures they take, provide advice to States, and conduct field visits to States. In addition, with respect to OAS Member States which are *not* parties to the American Convention, the Commission may receive petitions from individuals who complain of violations by OAS Member States of the rights proclaimed in the American Declaration.[9] This system of individual petitions based on the OAS Charter, although it has been strengthened over time,[10] remains weak, because it ends with a report by the Commission, which contains conclusions and recommendations and is forwarded to the General Assembly of the OAS; but it cannot be forwarded to the Court for instituting contentious proceedings, nor does it have effective means of enforcement against States that do not comply.

Instead, with regard to the States Parties to the American Convention, the role of the Commission is more effective.[11] It has, in addition to the above-mentioned

[6]See Buergenthal et al. (2004), pp. 222–223.

[7]See Arts. 41–51 of the ACHR and Arts. 18–20 of the Commission's Statute.

[8]See Art. 41(a), (b), (c), (d), (e), (g) of the ACHR, which codifies the pre-existing functions of the Commission as a body of the OAS, and Article 18 of the Commission's Statute.

[9]See Art. 20 of the Commission's Statute.

[10]Before, the Commission could only examine violations of certain "preferred" human rights contained in the American Declaration. This limit has been overcome with the adoption of the new Statute of the Commission.

[11]See Art. 41 and Arts. 42–51 of the ACHR and Art. 19 of the Commission's Statute.

pre-existing powers as a body of the OAS, a number of important functions in a complaints mechanism for violations of the Convention (Arts. 44–51). In this mechanism, which should not be confused with the one mentioned above, the Commission can examine both individual and interstate complaints. In the former, the Commission receives "petitions" from individuals or groups of individuals complaining of a breach of the Convention by a Contracting State (Art. 44). In the latter, the Commission receives, on the basis of an optional clause, "communications" in which a State Party accuses another State Party of violating the Convention (Art. 45).

The procedure is quite complicated. In a first stage, the Commission decides on the admissibility of the complaint (Arts. 46–47). The requirements are similar to those found in the European Convention on Human Rights system: the main one is the prior exhaustion of domestic remedies. If the complaint is admissible, a second stage is opened, in which the Commission examines the complaint on the merits in a quasi-judicial procedure, gathering information, conducting investigations and examining the parties' observations (Art. 48). At this stage, the Commission also seeks to facilitate a friendly settlement of the dispute. If such settlement is successful, the Commission draws up a report which is published (Art. 49).

If the friendly settlement is not successful, the Commission draws up a preliminary report of a confidential nature, containing proposals and recommendations, and sends it to the States concerned (Art. 50). Within three months of the transmission of the preliminary report, if the case has not been resolved or submitted by the Commission itself or by the State concerned to the Inter-American Court, the Commission draws up a final report, in which it sets out its conclusions on the matter, adopts recommendations and sets a deadline within which the State must take measures to remedy the situation (Art. 51). After that deadline, the Commission decides whether the State has taken the appropriate measures and whether to publish its report. As can be seen, this procedure ends with a report that has no binding force or with the case being referred to the Inter-American Court.

12.1.2 The Inter-American Court

The Inter-American Court of Human Rights has contentious and advisory jurisdiction. Under the former, the Court has competence to hear and determine actions already submitted to the Commission, at the request of the Commission or of the States concerned, subject to acceptance of its jurisdiction by those States. Individuals may not bring direct actions before the Court; however, since 2001, following a reform of the Regulation, complainants have been able to take part in the various stages of the proceedings.

The contentious proceedings before the Court have a judicial character, with an oral and written procedure, based on the adversarial principle. The judgment of the Court, which is reasoned and may be accompanied by concurring or dissenting opinions of the individual judges, determines whether or not there has been a violation of the American Convention, and also decides on possible reparation measures. It is final and irrevocable.

Enforcement of the judgments is monitored by the Court itself, which receives and examines reports submitted by the parties and may also convene appropriate hearings. It then makes an annual report to the OAS General Assembly, if necessary indicating the cases in which a State has not executed its judgments and making recommendations in this regard. In fact, the Court can exercise a rather incisive control over compliance with its rulings. As has been noted,[12] this system of monitoring the enforcement of judgments, being largely entrusted to a court rather than a political body, seems more effective than that of the European Convention on Human Rights.

As regards its advisory powers, the Court may, at the request of the Member States of the OAS or of certain bodies of that organization, adopt advisory opinions on the interpretation of the American Convention or other human rights treaties applicable in the American States. In addition, at the request of any Member State of the OAS, the Court may give opinions on the compatibility of national laws with the Convention and the above-mentioned treaties.

12.2 The African System

12.2.1 The African Union

In more recent times, the African continent has also equipped itself with norms and institutions on the protection of human rights.[13] In 1981, the African Charter on Human and Peoples' Rights[14] was adopted in the framework of the Organization for African Unity (OAU), today replaced by the African Union (AU). The Charter is inspired by the other regional treaties on human rights, but differs in part from them because it provides, in addition to rights, also the duties of individuals and especially the rights of peoples. The latter include the rights to equality, self-determination, exploitation of natural resources, development, peace and security, and a favorable environment for development. Part II of the Charter establishes and regulates the functioning of the African Commission on Human and Peoples' Rights.[15]

An Additional Protocol was adopted in 1998, establishing the African Court on Human and Peoples' Rights.[16] A further development took place in 2008, with the

[12] Pustorino (2019), p. 66.

[13] On the African human rights system see, e.g., Kamto (2011), Zanghì and Panella (2019), pp. 413–446.

[14] African Charter on Human and Peoples' Rights (ACHPR).

[15] African Commission on Human and Peoples' Rights (ACmHPR).

[16] African Court on Human and Peoples' Rights (ACtHPR).

adoption of a Protocol on the Statute of the African Court of Justice and Human Rights.[17]

12.2.1.1 The African Commission on Human and Peoples' Rights

The Commission, composed of 11 members acting in their individual capacities and based in Banjul (Gambia), has a very broad mandate: it can interpret the provisions of the African Charter, carry out studies on human rights issues, organize conferences, disseminate information, make recommendations to States, and formulate norms and guiding principles for national legislation (Art. 45 of the Charter). Above all, the Commission exercises the functions of monitoring compliance with the Charter through two procedures: (*a*) the traditional procedure of reviewing periodic reports from States Parties on measures taken to implement the Charter (Art. 62); (*b*) that of examining communications relating to specific violations of the Charter (Arts. 47–59).

Under the latter procedure, the Commission examines communications submitted by a State Party accusing another State Party of violating the provisions of the Charter (Arts. 47–49). After ascertaining that domestic remedies have been exhausted (Art. 50), the Commission takes the information it deems necessary and attempts to reach an amicable solution (Arts. 51–52). It then draws up a report which it sends to the States concerned and to the Assembly of Heads of State and Government, making any recommendations it deems useful (Arts. 52–53). The Commission may also decide to examine communications submitted by persons other than States Parties (e.g. individuals, groups of individuals or non-governmental organizations) (Art. 55), provided that they meet certain conditions of admissibility (Art. 56). It should be noted, however, that there is no condition that these complaints be lodged by the victim of the violation; in fact, most of the complaints have been lodged by non-governmental organizations. When the communication reveals the existence of a series of massive violations of human rights, the Commission informs the Assembly of Heads of State and Government, which may request the Commission to prepare a report with its conclusions and recommendations (Art. 58).

As can be seen, this procedure follows that of other regional human rights systems; but it is weaker, since the Commission's recommendations are not legally binding.

12.2.1.2 The African Court on Human and Peoples' Rights

The lack of effectiveness of the control mechanisms focused on the African Commission led African States to adopt the Protocol establishing the African Court on Human and Peoples' Rights. The Court, composed of 11 independent judges and based in Arusha (Tanzania), has advisory and contentious powers.

The Court, on the basis of its contentious competence, may examine the complaints lodged by: (*a*) the African Commission; (*b*) the State Party which has

[17] Protocol on the Statute of the African Court of Justice and Human Rights, 1 July 2008.

lodged a complaint with the Commission; (*c*) the State Party against which a complaint has been lodged with the Commission; (*d*) the national State of the victim; (*e*) all African intergovernmental organizations; and finally (*f*) also individuals and non-governmental organizations, but only when the State accused has accepted this competence of the Court (Arts. 5 and 34(6) of the Protocol). The competence *ratione materiae* of the Court is interesting, since Article 7 of the Protocol states that the Court:

> [...] shall apply the provisions of the Charter and any other relevant human rights instruments ratified by the States concerned.

This means, as has been noted,[18] that the Court can also deal with violations by Member States of provisions contained in universal human rights treaties, such as the two UN Covenants of 1966. This was in fact the case in a recent judgment of the Court against Mali.[19]

The Court's procedure follows the traditional rules of other international human rights monitoring bodies. There is a phase relating to the admissibility of complaints (Protocol, Art. 6), a phase relating to the attempt at an amicable settlement of the dispute (Art. 9), and finally a stage of assessment through hearings in adversarial proceedings between the parties (Arts. 10 and 26). The Court then delivers a judgment on the merits of the case, determining whether or not there has been a violation, and may order the sentenced State to take appropriate measures to remedy the breach, including fair compensation or other forms of reparation (Arts. 27–28). Judgments are recognized as mandatory by the States Parties to the Protocol. Their enforcement is supervised by the Court itself (Arts. 30–31) and the AU Council of Ministers (Art. 29(2)). However, it is not specified what sanctions may be taken by the Council if a State refuses to comply with the Court's judgments.[20]

12.2.1.3 The African Court of Justice and Human Rights

In 2008, the Assembly of Heads of State and Government of the African Union adopted a Protocol on the Statute of the African Court of Justice and Human Rights,[21] which has not yet entered into force.[22] This Court should become the main judicial body of the African Union and should concentrate on itself the competences hitherto attributed to the African Court on Human and Peoples' Rights and the Court of Justice of the African Union.[23] The new Court should be divided into two chambers, one with general jurisdiction and the other with human rights jurisdiction. It would constitute an international court with rather original features,

[18] Pustorino (2019), pp. 67–68.

[19] ACtHPR, *APDF & IHRDA v. Republic of Mali.*

[20] See Citroni and Scovazzi (2013), p. 108.

[21] See above, Sect. 12.2.1.

[22] It has so far been ratified by 8 States and should enter into force upon ratification by 15 States.

[23] Cf. Protocol of the Court of Justice of the African Union, 1 July 2003.

combining the jurisdiction of a generalist court of an international organization with that of a regional court specializing in human rights.

However, the replacement of the African Court on Human and Peoples' Rights, which is working well, could be risky. Furthermore, it must be considered that the new Court, which would also have competence over international crimes, defined in a very broad way, could also end up limiting for African States the current role of the International Criminal Court.[24]

12.2.2 The Economic Community of West African States and Its Court of Justice

The Economic Community of West African States (ECOWAS)[25] is an international organization made up of 15 States, which set up, in 1991, its own Court of Justice,[26] which has some interesting aspects.[27] The Court has advisory and contentious powers. The latter are very broad and include, among other things, the power to decide on cases of human rights violations that occur in each Member State.[28] The Court can therefore deal with human rights violations that are protected by numerous international instruments applicable to ECOWAS Member States.[29] In addition, both States and individuals or groups of individuals may bring actions before the Court; and without the filter of prior exhaustion of domestic remedies.[30]

12.3 Other Regional Initiatives

Asian States have not, for a long time, created binding regulatory instruments and guarantee mechanisms for the international protection of human rights. This is due to various reasons: the lack of cultural homogeneity among Asian States; the challenge of the principle of the universality of human rights by a group of such States;[31] the lack of a regional international organization of a "generalist" nature, comparable to the Council of Europe or the Organization of American States or the African Union. However, some sub-regional organizations have taken initiatives on human rights, which could be strengthened in the future.

---

[24] See Aja Agwu (2014).

[25] Economic Community of West African States (ECOWAS).

[26] The ECOWAS Community Court of Justice (CCJ).

[27] See Focarelli (2013), p. 276.

[28] See Supplementary Protocol, 1 May 2005, Art. 3(4): "The Court has jurisdiction to determine cases of violation of human rights that occur in any Member State".

[29] See CCJ, *Hadijatou Mani Koraou*.

[30] *Ibidem*.

[31] One thinks, for example, of the theory of the prevalence of Islamic law (*sharia*) over international law or the theory of the priority of "Asian values". See Nowak (2003), p. 253.

Within the Organization of Islamic Cooperation (OIC) (formerly called the Islamic Conference), an international organization established in 1969 and comprising 57 Member States, the Cairo Declaration on Human Rights in Islam was adopted in 1990.[32] It is a non-binding document, inspired by the Universal Declaration, but also contains certain collective rights of peoples, such as the right of self-determination against colonial repression and the right to a healthy environment. However, it should be noted that, on the basis of Articles 24 and 25 of the Declaration, all rights and freedoms contained therein are subject to Islamic Sharia law, which is also the only source of interpretation of the Declaration.[33]

More interesting are the initiatives that have been taken within the framework of the Arab League, an international organization established in 1945, which currently includes 22 Member States. The Arab League Council adopted the Arab Charter on Human Rights in 1994, which was revised in 2004[34] and entered into force in 2008. The Charter is a binding treaty, largely inspired by the European Convention on Human Rights and the Covenant on Civil and Political Rights; but it also contains "newer" rights, such as the right to development (Art. 37) and the right to an adequate standard of living, ensuring a decent life, including food, clothing, housing and a healthy environment (Art. 38). However, the Charter strongly criticizes Zionism, equating it with racism and viewing it as a threat to international peace and security (Preamble and Art. 2(3)). Finally, it establishes an Arab Human Rights Committee (Arts. 45–47),[35] with the task of examining the periodic reports submitted by the States Parties (Art. 48). In 2014, the Statute of the Arab Court of Human Rights was approved, but it has not yet entered into force.[36]

As far as the other Asian States are concerned, action for the international protection of human rights has so far been very limited. The most important initiative has been taken by the Association of Southeast Asian Nations (ASEAN), created in 1967 with the signing of the ASEAN Declaration. In 2008 the ASEAN Charter, which provided a legal status and institutional framework for ASEAN, was adopted. Subsequently, in 2012, the Heads of State and Government of the Member States of this organization adopted the ASEAN Human Rights Declaration.[37] It is, again, a non-binding document, inspired by the Universal Declaration, from which it takes many principles.

However, the ASEAN Declaration, having been adopted more than 60 years after the Universal Declaration, sets out in more detail the content of these principles. More particularly, taking into account the experience of the African Charter, it also contains some third and fourth generation human rights, such as the right to a safe,

---

[32]Cairo Declaration on Human Rights in Islam, 5 August 1990.

[33]See also Tomuschat (2014), pp. 39–40.

[34]Arab Charter on Human Rights (ArCHR), 22 May 2004.

[35]Arab Human Rights Committee.

[36]Statute of the Arab Court of Human Rights, adopted by the Council of the League of Arab States on 7 September 2014.

[37]ASEAN Human Rights Declaration, 19 November 2012.

clean and sustainable environment (Art. 28), the right to development of persons and peoples (Arts. 35–37), and the right to peace (Art. 38). Finally, the Declaration states that all persons should act towards one another in a spirit of humanity (Art. 1), and that the enjoyment of human rights "must be balanced with the performance of corresponding duties as every person has responsibilities to all other individuals, the community and the society where one lives" (Art. 6).

References

Aja Agwu F (2014) The African Court of Justice and Human Rights: the future of international criminal justice in Africa. Africa Rev 6:30–43

Buergenthal T, Shelton D, Stewart DP (2004) International Human Rights in a Nutshell, 3rd edn (2nd rep). West Group, St. Paul

Citroni G, Scovazzi T (2013) La tutela internazionale dei diritti umani, Parte III del Corso di diritto internazionale (Scovazzi T ed). Giuffrè, Milano

Focarelli C (2013) La persona umana nel diritto internazionale. Il Mulino, Bologna

Kamto M (ed) (2011) La Chartre africaine des droits de l'homme et des peoples. Bruylant, Bruxelles

Medina Quiroga C (2016) The American Convention on Human Rights. Crucial rights and their theory and practice, 2nd edn. Intersentia, Cambridge

Nowak M (2003) Introduction to the international human rights regime. Nijhoff, Leiden

Pustorino P (2019) Lezioni di tutela internazionale dei diritti umani. Cacucci, Bari

Tomuschat C (2014) Human rights: between idealism and realism, 3rd edn. OUP, Oxford

Zanghì C, Panella L (2019) La protezione internazionale dei diritti dell'uomo, 4th edn. Giappichelli, Torino

Part V

"Fundamental" Human Rights

This part and Part VI of this book will deal with the content of individual international human rights. I believe that this topic is very important for a textbook on international human rights law and that it cannot be overlooked.[1] However, given the impossibility, for reasons of space, to provide a complete and in-depth picture of the content of all human rights, I have made a methodological choice, which seeks to reconcile the need for systematic completeness of a textbook with the need not to limit it to a superficial summary of the subject. I will therefore try to give an overall picture of the content of human rights, but only those rights that I consider most important and representative of the whole picture will be examined in greater depth.

This choice also requires, for systematic reasons, somehow classifying human rights into categories. Whereas my choice is largely subjective and discretionary, I have decided to adopt a wide *bipartition* between: (*a*) human rights that I define as "fundamental", and (*b*) other human rights. The main reason for this solution, as will be seen more fully below,[2] is that only the former are governed by general international law and thus effectively realize the principle of universality of human rights.

Furthermore, within each of these two broad categories, I have identified a number of human rights' subcategories (or groups), based mainly on the *protective function* exercised by the group in question, that is to say, the nature of the human activities that each group aims to protect. In other words, on the basis of the principles and values which inspire each group of human rights. This *classification*, which only has the purpose of giving a logical and systematic order to individual human rights, seems to me more appropriate than other more traditional ones, such as the classification by different historical generations of human rights. I have already explained why I believe this last distinction is outdated.[3]

[1] On the contrary, the most frequent choice in human rights textbooks is to give up dealing with the content of individual human rights. This is, in my view, a major shortcoming.

[2] See below, Sects. 13.1–13.5.

[3] See above, Sects. 8.1.1 and 10.3.

Therefore, within the category of "fundamental human rights", I will distinguish between: (*a*) protection of the life and physical integrity of the person; (*b*) protection of his basic needs; (*c*) protection of his liberty and security; (*d*) essential judicial protection of the person; (*e*) protection of his essential identity; (*f*) protection of the identity of peoples. Similarly, within the category of "other human rights", I will distinguish between: (*a*) protection of private and family life; (*b*) protection of intellectual and cultural activities; (*c*) protection of political activities; (*d*) protection of economic activities; (*e*) protection of freedoms of movement; (*f*) protection of collective human rights.

Distinctions Between Human Rights Categories 13

13.1 The Problem of a Hierarchy Within Human Rights

My choice to classify human rights on the basis of categories and subcategories poses three problems in the following order: (*a*) is it possible to distinguish between different categories of human rights or should it be considered that all human rights form a unitary and indivisible whole[1]? (*b*) if it is possible to distinguish between categories of human rights, is it also permissible to establish a hierarchy between different categories? (*c*) finally, is a category of "fundamental" human rights justified and what, if any, is its content? These are important issues which should be addressed before dealing with the substantive content of individual human rights.

Within the framework of the United Nations, especially since the 1990s, the idea has been asserted that human rights constitute a *unique and unitary category* of rights,[2] that they have common characteristics and, above all, that they have equal legal dignity on the basis of the principles of universality, indivisibility and interdependence. These principles were solemnly affirmed in the Vienna Declaration of 1993 and subsequent international human rights instruments adopted within the United Nations. An important consequence of this approach is the *lack of a normative hierarchy* within international human rights.

However, while from a "normative policy" perspective the idea of the unity and equal dignity of all human rights is understandable and perhaps strategically useful, it must be recognized that, from a more strictly legal and conceptual point of view, this idea is not convincing, because in reality human rights differ from one another in many ways.[3]

---

[1]On this point see, inter alia, Tomuschat (2014), p. 136 ff.

[2]See Focarelli (2013), p. 128.

[3]*Ibidem*; Dupuy and Kerbrat (2020), pp. 283–291. But see also, for a defense of the concepts of indivisibility and independence of human rights, Pustorino (2020), pp. 17–19.

R. Pisillo Mazzeschi, *International Human Rights Law*,
https://doi.org/10.1007/978-3-030-77032-7_13

These differences have always been highlighted by doctrine, which has over time identified different categories of human rights, and also human rights obligations, adopting different perspectives, some of which have already been described. The most famous distinction is between civil and political rights, on the one hand, and economic, social and cultural rights, on the other. From a mainly historical perspective, this distinction has been partly taken up and absorbed by the distinction between first, second, third and fourth generation human rights. From another point of view, i.e. in relation to the holders of rights, a distinction has often been made between individual and collective human rights.[4] Other distinctions have been proposed between "judicially enforceable" and "judicially non-enforceable" rights,[5] or between "absolute" and non-absolute rights, or between "derogable" and non-derogable rights, or between "fundamental" and non-fundamental rights. As already seen, various categories, partially overlapping, have also been proposed by doctrine in relation to the human rights obligations of States.[6]

If one reflects on the doctrinal distinctions indicated above, one can conclude that some of them appear outdated today, but others undoubtedly retain their validity. It is, for example, undeniable that some human rights are "judicially enforceable" and others are not; that some human rights lend themselves to immediate implementation by States while others require progressive realization; that some human rights admit neither restrictions nor limits nor exceptions and are therefore "absolute" and others admit restrictions, limits and exceptions by States; that some human rights are non-derogable even in time of war or public emergency and others are not; that some human rights, being established by norms of *jus cogens*, have a higher hierarchical rank, or at least a greater force of normative resistance, than others; and so on. As one can see, these are legally important differences, which *contradict* the idea of the unity and equal legal value of all human rights.

Moreover, the idea of the lack of hierarchy among human rights does not convince even from the point of view of the different values that underlie the different human rights norms. In fact, it is clear that all human rights norms express important values; but it must also be recognized that these values may have different degrees of importance. In fact, even from a purely logical point of view, it is common sense to believe, for example, that the right to life, the prohibition of torture or the prohibition of genocide embody more important values than those expressed by the right to respect for private life or the right to cultural life or the right to form trade unions.

Once the possibility of making distinctions between different categories of human rights is admitted, it is now appropriate to move on to justify my choice to distinguish between two broad categories of human rights and to explore in greater depth the category of "fundamental" human rights.

---

[4]These latter rights largely coincide with third generation human rights.

[5]In the past this distinction tended to coincide with that between first and second generation rights.

[6]See above, Sect. 8.1.

13.2 The Category of "Fundamental" Human Rights

In international law, in the first period of historical development of human rights, the expression "fundamental rights" had no precise legal meaning and did not refer to an autonomous and unitary category of rights. This is probably due to the influence of domestic legal systems, where since the eighteenth and nineteenth centuries, the expressions "fundamental rights" or "inviolable rights" or "inalienable rights" of the human person were used in an equivalent manner, to refer to an essential group of rights recognized to the human person as such.[7]

In fact, adapting to this rather imprecise terminology, in the early years of the development of international human rights law, the expression "fundamental rights", although not frequently used, was usually equated simply to the more common expression "human rights". Sometimes, to reinforce the concept, the hendiadys "human rights and fundamental freedoms" was used, as in the 1950 European Convention on Human Rights. Even in European Union law, human rights have always been defined as "fundamental rights",[8] showing a preference for the use of terminology typical of State constitutions rather than that of international law.[9]

However, leaving aside these improper or imprecise uses of the term "fundamental rights", one must now ask whether this term can have autonomous and substantial content; that is, whether it can be said that some human rights are, effectively, more fundamental than others.

Actually, the idea of a hierarchy of importance among human rights has often been supported, albeit with different terminologies and sometimes different contents.[10] For example, Henry Shue stated that there are a limited number of "basic rights" which prevail over "non-basic rights", and he identified, in the first category, the right to physical security, the right to subsistence and the right to liberty.[11] Other authors favor civil rights over all other rights. Still others have spoken of "fundamental" human rights[12] or an "essential and indispensable nucleus"[13] of human rights, with reference only to rights that protect people's lives and physical integrity. Another part of the doctrine, especially recently, uses the concept of "core rights";[14] and the European Court of Human Rights also uses, in

---

[7]See De Sena and Saccucci (2007), p. 376.

[8]See the case-law of the Court of Justice and the title itself of the EU Charter of Fundamental Rights.

[9]But it should be noted that, in domestic law, fundamental rights are usually protected at constitutional level and therefore enjoy a higher hierarchical rank, or in any case a stronger protection, within internal sources, than all other rights of persons. See De Sena and Saccucci (2007), p. 377.

[10]On the subject of the hierarchy of human rights see, inter alia, Shue (1980), Meron (1986), Sudre (1995), Carrillo Salcedo (1997), Iovane (2000), de Frouville (2004), De Wet and Vidmar (eds) (2012), Cassese (2012) and Scheinin (2013).

[11]Shue (1980), p. 18 ff.

[12]De Sena and Saccucci (2007), p. 378.

[13]Conforti (2015), p. 214.

[14]See, e.g., Scheinin (2013).

some of its official documents, the distinction between "core rights" and "other rights and freedoms".[15]

In these theories, the terminology (*fundamental rights, basic rights, core rights*) does not seem so important to me as the idea of a *bipartition* between human rights on the basis of their importance. Therefore, I believe it is correct, at least as a starting hypothesis, to make a division (adopting the simplest terminology) between "fundamental human rights" and "other human rights". The term "fundamental rights" seems to me the most simple and direct, and therefore preferable to other terms, such as "core rights", which, as we shall see, has a very uncertain meaning.

But what are the distinctive criteria for the category of "fundamental" rights? In other words, what human rights are included in this category? On the premise that the answer to these questions is of a relative nature since it derives from a subjective choice of mine, I will examine below, in a critical manner, some possible theories, and then propose the conclusion that seems to me more convincing and useful from a legal point of view.

13.3 Possible Distinguishing Criteria for the Category of "Fundamental" Rights

13.3.1 The Criterion of Rights Considered "Essential" or "Preeminent" in Human Rights Treaties. Criticism

According to some scholars, the criterion for identifying "fundamental" human rights could be derived mainly from the case-law and practice of some human rights monitoring bodies. In particular, the European Court of Human Rights, in its jurisprudence, has sometimes recognized as "essential" or "preeminent" certain human rights, which were neither non-derogable in time of emergency nor established by peremptory norms (*jus cogens*). These are, above all, the right to physical integrity, the right to liberty and security of the person, freedom of expression, freedom of thought, conscience and religion, the right to free elections and the right to a fair trial.

However, apart from the first two rights, the others are all first generation rights, linked to typically Western values and the concept of democratic society. Therefore, it does not seem to me that this rather vague criterion of "essentiality" or "preeminence" of these rights over all the others can be used to identify the category of "fundamental" rights that must obviously operate at a universal level.

The Human Rights Committee has also sometimes talked about "rights of great importance", for example with reference to the right to personal liberty and the rights of minorities. But even this practice, which is rather limited, does not in itself seem significant for the reconstruction of a universal category of "fundamental" human rights.

---

[15] See the Court's *Annual Reports*.

13.3.2 The Criterion of "Absolute" Rights. Criticism

Another criterion, sometimes suggested to identify the category of "fundamental" human rights, is that of "absolute" rights. The use of this terminology is not unambiguous; in my view, "absolute" rights should only be spoken of for those human rights that are subject neither to restriction clauses[16] nor to limits or exceptions.

In fact, there are a very limited number of human rights, which can be defined as "absolute"; and they include some very important rights. But there are equally important rights (in the sense that their violation constitutes a serious attack on human dignity) which nevertheless allow exceptions and restrictions. For example, "absolute" rights include the prohibition of genocide, the prohibition of torture and inhuman treatment, and the prohibition of slavery, that certainly do not allow limits or exceptions. But the right to life cannot be considered "absolute", because it allows limits (e.g. the lethal use of force in certain circumstances) and also exceptions in general international law (the death penalty is not prohibited everywhere). And it is difficult to argue that the right to life is less important than the prohibition of inhuman treatment or the prohibition of slavery. In other words, if the category of "fundamental" human rights is admitted, it is difficult to justify the fact that the right to life does not belong to this category. A similar argument can be made for the prohibition of discrimination, which, although it is a right that underpins the international protection of human rights and is therefore "fundamental", admits limits and restrictions.

From this it can be deduced that the criterion of "absolute" rights, even if it is useful to identify a category of rights that has certain characteristics, is not suitable to identify the category of "fundamental" human rights.[17]

13.3.3 The Criterion of Rights Defined as "Non-derogable in Time of Emergency". Criticism

As we have already seen, the most important human rights treaties identify, usually explicitly, certain rights that cannot be derogated from by States even in time of war, public danger or other emergency that endanger the security or life of the nation.[18]

It should be made clear at the outset that the category of "non-derogable rights in time of emergency" does not coincide with the category of "absolute" rights: the reasons for the two categories are different and the first category is broader than the second. Nor is there any coincidence, despite the misleading terminology, between "non-derogable rights in time of emergency" and rights covered by peremptory

[16]See above, Sect. 4.4.2.

[17]Such a conclusion is reached by Scheinin, in order to exclude that the absolute rights criterion might serve to identify the category of "core rights". See Scheinin (2013), pp. 531–532.

[18]See above, Sect. 4.4.3.

norms (*jus cogens*) of general international law. Also in this case it must be considered that the reasons justifying the character of "non-derogation in time of emergency" are different from those on which the peremptory nature of certain norms is based. This has also been recognized by the Human Rights Committee which, in its General Comment No. 29, stated that the "conventional non-derogation" of certain human rights does not coincide with the peremptory nature of the norms that regulate them.

That said, it should also be noted that the category of "non-derogable rights in time of emergency" is not well defined, as the catalogue of such rights contained in human rights treaties is not unambiguous. This can be deduced even from an examination of the three main human rights treaties of a general nature. Article 15 of the European Convention lists, among the non-derogable rights, the right to life (except in the case of killings resulting from lawful acts of war), the prohibition of torture and inhuman or degrading treatment or punishment, the prohibition of slavery or servitude, and the prohibition of retroactivity of criminal law. Article 4 of the Covenant on Civil and Political Rights also considers these rights to be non-derogable; but it also adds the prohibition of imprisonment for breach of contract, the right to recognition as a person before the law and even freedom of thought, conscience and religion. Article 27 of the American Convention of Human Rights greatly broadens the category of non-derogable rights in time of emergency, because, in addition to the rights listed as non-derogable in the European Convention, it also includes the right to a legal personality, freedom of conscience and religion, the rights of the family, the right to a name, the rights of children, the right to a nationality, the right to political participation, and finally the judicial guarantees essential for the protection of those rights. In addition, both the Covenant on Civil and Political Rights and the American Convention consider the prohibition of discrimination to be non-derogable, because they provide that, even in time of war or public emergence, the State may not take measures that involve discrimination on grounds of race, color, sex, language, religion or social origin.

Examination of these conventions reveals that there are significant differences between them as regards the catalogue of rights regarded as non-derogable, and that, taking into account the historical periods in which they were signed, there is a tendency to extend this catalogue over time. Moreover, it should be noted that the supervisory bodies of these conventions have manifested an interpretative orientation towards further widening the category of non-derogable rights. For example, the European Court of Human Rights seems to consider that the right to an effective remedy and the prohibition of discrimination are also non-derogable under the European Convention. The Human Rights Committee, in its General Comment No. 29, also seems to consider the prohibition of mass deportations, the respect of certain guarantees of fair trial and personal liberty to be at least partially non-derogable. The Inter-American Court includes among the non-derogable rights, under the American Convention, also the right to *habeas corpus*, the right to an effective remedy and some guarantees of a fair trial.

What conclusions can be drawn from this regulatory and interpretative framework?

In conventional international law, the fact that the list of non-derogable rights in time of emergency does not coincide in the three above-mentioned conventions, or in other human rights treaties, is not a problem. It is clear that each State will be obliged to comply with the provisions on non-derogation contained in the treaties it has ratified. In the case of ratification of more than one treaty, the State will have to apply the provision that provides for more non-derogable rights; in other words, the provision that is most favorable to the rights of individuals.[19]

As far as general international law is concerned, it seems to me to rule out the possibility that customary norms have been formed that have incorporated a precise list of rights that are "non-derogable in time of emergency", given the considerable differences that emerge from treaty law. At most, it can be assumed that there is a general consensus among States on the *minimum catalogue* of such rights laid down in Article 15 of the European Convention.

Ultimately, in my opinion, for the reasons set out above, I do not consider that the criterion of "non-derogation in time of emergency" can serve to identify the category of "fundamental" human rights.

13.3.4 The Criterion of Rights Established by General International Law

In order to give a precise content to the category of "fundamental" human rights, a more valid criterion than those discussed so far is that of human rights which have become established in general international law. As I already said, the principle of the universality of human rights can be said to be *truly* realized, *from a legal point of view*, only for those human rights which, by virtue of customary norms, principles of law generally recognized *in foro domestico* or general principles of international law, enjoy the consent or recognition of the entire international community.

But what are these human rights in practice? It has to be admitted that it is not easy to identify precisely which human rights have actually become established in general international law. This depends on various factors: (*a*) the well-known difficulty of identifying unwritten law; (*b*) the increased difficulty of identification in the field of human rights, where interstate practice is not abundant; (*c*) the diversity of existing theories on how to identify custom and on the importance (if not the existence) of general principles of law *in foro domestico* and the general principles of international law.

These factors explain why the doctrine does not offer an unambiguous answer to the above question and why authoritative international institutions and bodies can also come up with different answers. It is enough to compare the rather restrictive catalogue of human rights protected by general international law that can be found in

[19] See Cataldi (2007), p. 384.

the *Restatement of the Foreign Relations Law of the United States*[20] with the much more extensive catalogue that can be found in the General Comments of the Human Rights Committee.[21]

Despite these difficulties, I will try, when examining individual human rights, to express my opinion on whether or not they are recognized under general international law.[22] In any case, I now wish to reaffirm that the human rights protected by general international law can be defined as *truly* universal; that for this reason they can be considered more important than other human rights; and that therefore they are the most appropriate to represent the category of "fundamental" human rights. Taking up an image that I proposed in Chap. 1, these rights, in the relationship between multiculturalism and universalism represented by two concentric circles, form the smallest circle.[23]

Can it also be considered that human rights recognized by general international law, in addition to being of particular importance, also *rank higher in the hierarchy* than other human rights? In other words, can the "United Nations myth" of the lack of hierarchy among human rights be questioned? In order to answer this question, I must return to the role of *jus cogens* in human rights.

13.3.5 The Criterion of Rights Established by *Jus Cogens* Norms

Another criterion, which has sometimes been suggested to identify the category of "fundamental" human rights, is *jus cogens*. According to this criterion, human rights protected by *jus cogens* should be defined as "fundamental".[24]

In my opinion, this definition can be used, provided that it is made clear that human rights protected by *jus cogens* are not only "fundamental", but *also* "peremptory"; that is, they have, *as a further characteristic*, the typical elements of all peremptory international norms: non-derogation and hierarchical prevalence.

The general discussion of *jus cogens*, already briefly summarized in Chaps. 2 and 3, is complex and cannot be addressed here. Now I would just like to remind that the norms and principles of *jus cogens*, expressing some *essential, fundamental and peremptory* values of the entire international community,[25] indicate the tendency of contemporary international law to establish a normative scale of values at the top of which these norms are set.[26] In my view, this scale of values also applies to the field of human rights, and therefore, the norms of *jus cogens* have also formed a

[20] *Restatement of the Foreign Relations Law of the United States*, 1986, adopted and promulgated by the American Law Institute, 14 May 1986 (ALI Publ., Washington 1987), para. 702.

[21] See, for example, HRCtee, General Comment No. 24, 4 November 1994, para. 8.

[22] See also below, Sects. 13.3.4 and 13.3.5.

[23] See above, Sect. 1.4.2.

[24] De Sena and Saccucci (2007), p. 378.

[25] See above, Sects. 2.3.3.2 and 2.3.4.2.

[26] See, for all, Cassese (2006), p. 199.

normative hierarchy within the framework of human rights. The idea of a *normative hierarchy* in international human rights can now be affirmed in the light not only of general developments in international law, but also of developments in the field of human rights protection itself. Suffice it to recall what I have already said in relation to the impact that human rights theory has produced on international law and the progressive affirmation of a "public" or "constitutionalist" nature of that law.[27]

But, at this point, two questions arise: what are the human rights protected by *jus cogens*? And is there a coincidence between this category and that of human rights established by general international law? Even on these issues the doctrine is divided; and one can distinguish, in synthesis, two general theories.

According to a first group of authors, the two categories tend to coincide and include a very narrow nucleus of human rights.[28] In essence, this core is identified, or described, through the concept of the "prohibition of gross violations of human rights". Indeed, this concept is not always interpreted unambiguously, but usually refers to the prohibition of *serious, systematic and organized* violations of fundamental human rights (and of fundamental principles of international humanitarian law[29]). The "seriousness" refers to the particular attack on the dignity of the person; the "systematic character" refers to the number of victims and the duration of the violation; and finally the "organization" means that violations almost always presuppose a design implemented by a State or an organized entity or group of persons.[30] Starting from this approach, this doctrine usually includes in the category of *gross violations*: (*a*) the prohibition of genocide, crimes against humanity and war crimes; (*b*) the prohibition of practices of torture, inhuman treatment or punishment, slavery and slave trade, racial discrimination and apartheid; and (*c*) the violation of the right of self-determination of peoples. However, some authors tend to expand this catalogue, adding the prohibition of arbitrary deprivation of liberty and forced labor[31] and the general prohibition of discrimination.[32]

A second group of scholars argues, on the contrary, that there is no coincidence between the two categories of human rights. But this does not depend on the catalogue of rights protected by *jus cogens*, which is considered roughly the same as the one mentioned above; but on the catalogue of rights established by general international law, which would be wider than the former.[33] In other words, according to this theory, general international law protects not only all human rights recognized by *jus cogens* norms, but *also further rights*; and prohibits violations that are not necessarily "serious", "systematic" and "organized", but may also consist of

[27]See above, Sect. 2.3.

[28]See, e.g., Conforti (2018), pp. 216–217; Cassese (2006), pp. 205–206.

[29]See Cassese (2006), p. 206.

[30]See Iovane (2007), p. 675.

[31]Conforti (2018), p. 216.

[32]Cassese (2006), p. 205. See also Pustorino (2019), pp. 23–24, which tends to further extend the scope of *jus cogens* in the field of human rights.

[33]See, for example, Tomuschat (2014), pp. 42–45.

individual and isolated abuses and committed against single individuals. In essence, the category of human rights governed by general international law would go beyond the "prohibition of gross violations". On this basis, for example, general international law would also prohibit *individual and isolated acts* of torture or inhuman treatment or arbitrary killing or arbitrary deprivation of liberty, or racial discrimination, or deprivation of a subsistence right or denial of access to justice.[34]

In my view, this second theory is more convincing, and I will try to make it clearer when I will deal with the content of individual human rights. For the time being, it is worth repeating that this theory means, as I had anticipated, that there is a group (not very large, but not quite small) of "fundamental" human rights, which is made up of those protected by general international law; and that, within this group, there is a narrower nucleus of human rights that are also "peremptory", that is, that they possess the further and additional characteristics of "non-derogation" and "hierarchical superiority", which are generally proper to *jus cogens*. In other words, within the small circle of human rights protected by general international law there is an even smaller circle represented by the human rights covered by *jus cogens*.

13.4 The Concepts of "Core Rights", "Core Content" and "Core Obligations"

In recent times, some human rights monitoring bodies and some authors have begun to use the notions of *core rights*, *core content of human rights* and *core obligations*. The three concepts should be kept separate, even if they are sometimes confused.

The concept of *core rights* is used to "define *some* human rights as superior or more fundamental than other human rights".[35] If the notion has only this generic meaning, it can be accepted, since it is only a matter of terminology: the term core rights may, for some writers, be better than the term "fundamental rights", which I consider preferable.[36]

However, the real problem is that the supporters of the concept of core rights have not clarified the exact content of this concept; that is, what are the distinctive legal characteristics of the core rights category and what human rights are included in this category. The European Court of Human Rights uses the concept of core rights only in certain documents,[37] in order to keep them separate from other rights: core rights are those governed by Articles 2, 3, 4 and 5 of the European Convention. But the

[34]Some authors add other rights, such as the right to property or certain social rights or even those human rights that are included in the Universal Declaration, but have not been taken up by the Covenant on Civil and Political Rights. See, e.g., Pustorino (2019), p. 24; Tomuschat (2014), pp. 42–44 and the doctrine cited therein. In my view, these opinions tend to extend too much the catalogue of human rights recognized by general international law.

[35]Scheinin (2013), p. 527.

[36]See above, Sect. 13.2.

[37]See, e.g., ECtHR, *Annual Report 2017, Overview of the Court's case-law.*

Court does not go into the distinctive features of the category. The doctrine does not seem to have more precise ideas. One author,[38] for example, analyses and then rejects the three criteria that could be used to identify the category of core rights: (*a*) that of rights deriving from the dignity of the human person; (*b*) that of "absolute" rights; (*c*) that of "non-derogable rights in time of emergency". And then he challenges the idea of a hierarchy among human rights and, in essence, also the very concept of core rights.

In conclusion, the category of core rights remains for the time being very uncertain and indefinite in both doctrine and practice; and therefore I prefer not to use it in this book.

The concept of *core content of human rights* must be kept separate and distinct from that of core rights. The question of core content is whether, within human rights or certain human rights, it is possible to identify an essential and inviolable content.[39] This is an important issue, which cannot be reduced to a simple question of terminology. However, in my opinion, the concept of core content is not convincing.

A first element of strong perplexity concerns the very idea that a human right can be broken down or divided into two or more contents; and that therefore, within a right, an "essential" content and one or more "non-essential" contents can coexist. It seems to me that this idea must be cleared of two conceptual confusions.

Firstly, the question of the content of a right should not be confused with the very different question of the norms governing that right. In fact, it is possible that a certain human right is regulated by different norms, not only conventional, as is obvious, but also customary. And these norms may have a different content. For example, as we shall see further on, the provision on the right to life in the European Convention on Human Rights now excludes the exception of the death penalty, whereas the provision on the right to life in the Covenant on Civil and Political Rights provides for this exception. Or, to give another example, the customary norm on the right to adequate food, which emerges from human rights treaties, is different from the norm prohibiting the deprivation of food essential for people's subsistence, which emerges from international humanitarian law treaties. Secondly, the content of a right must not be confused with that of the obligations, corresponding to the right, which a norm may establish. It is clear, as already said, that a certain norm governing a particular human right can establish a wide range of obligations, even of a different nature, on a State.

A second element of perplexity, on the concept of core content of human rights, derives, also in this case, from the fact that the concept is very uncertain and indefinite, both in practice and in doctrine.

Firstly, the elements that characterize this concept are not clear. In particular, it is unclear whether the core content of human rights has an "absolute" character (i.e. it is not subject to exceptions, limits or restrictions); or has the character of "non-derogation in time of emergency"; or even the character of *jus cogens*. The Human

[38] Scheinin (2013).

[39] *Ibidem*, p. 532.

Rights Committee, which is the international monitoring body that has made the most use of the concept of core content, shows uncertainty on this point. In its General Comments No. 27 and No. 31, the Committee has used the notion of "essence" of a human right and has stated that *restrictions* on that right can never prejudice that "essence".[40] Instead, in its General Comment No. 34, the Committee, speaking of freedom of opinion and expression, stated that, even if freedom of opinion is not listed in the Covenant among the non-derogable rights in time of emergency, there may be elements in that right which are not subject to *derogations*.[41] But then, in a rather contradictory way, the Committee said that:

> Paragraph 1 of Article 19 requires protection of the right to hold opinion without interference. This is a right to which the Covenant permits no *exception or restriction*.[42]

In General Comment No. 32, the Committee seems to argue that, in certain cases, the right to a fair trial can be neither derogated in time of emergency nor restricted. In fact, it stated earlier that:

> States derogating from normal procedures required under article 14 in circumstances of a public emergency should ensure that such *derogations* do not exceed those strictly required by the exigencies of the actual situation.[43]

And then it added:

> The failure of a State party to establish a competent tribunal to determine such rights and obligations or to allow access to such a tribunal in specific cases would amount to a violation of article 14 if [. . .] the access left to an individual would be *limited* to an extent that would undermine the very essence of the right.[44]

Therefore, it seems that, for the Human Rights Committee, the core content of a human right is that essential minimum content which is subject neither to restrictions nor to derogations in time of emergency.

By contrast, the EU Charter of Fundamental Rights uses the concept of core content *only* with reference to its "absolute" character. Indeed, Article 52(1) of the Charter states that:

> Any *limitation* on the exercise of the rights and freedoms recognised by this Charter must be provided for by law and respect the essence of those rights and freedoms.[45]

[40] HRCtee, General Comment No. 27, 2 November 1999, para. 13; General Comment No. 31, 26 May 2004, para. 6.

[41] HRCtee, General Comment No. 34, 12 September 2011, para. 5.

[42] *Ibidem*, para. 9 (emphasis added).

[43] HRCtee, General Comment No. 32, 23 August 2007, para. 6 (emphasis added).

[44] *Ibidem*, para. 18 (emphasis added).

[45] Emphasis added.

Secondly, the concept of core content is uncertain and indefinite, because it is not clear whether it should apply to all human rights[46] or only to certain rights. The first solution is contradictory: a human right that is already "absolute" in itself (for example, the prohibition of torture) certainly has no need for "absolute" core content. Similarly, a human right that is in itself already "non-derogable in time of emergency" does not need a core content that has the same character. The same can be said for a human right that is of *jus cogens*: it does not make much sense to believe, for example, that the prohibition of genocide has its own core content.

In conclusion, the concept of core content is conceptually confused and has not been clarified by its supporters in its essential elements. Therefore, it cannot be accepted here.

Finally, I come to the concept of *core obligations*. The issue here shifts from the field of human rights of a person to that of the obligations of States that correspond to those rights. It consists of the question whether certain core obligations or minimum core obligations can be identified, that is, human rights obligations that are "more burning, more immediate, or more compelling"[47] than other obligations. The concept of core obligations has been introduced into international human rights law since the 1980s, particularly in relation to economic, social and cultural rights. The Limburg Principles[48] recommended that States, regardless of their level of economic development, should take on the obligations to "ensure respect for minimum subsistence rights". Subsequently, the doctrine developed the concept that each human right should correspond to an "absolute minimum entitlement"[49] and the notion of "minimum core obligations".[50]

It must be said immediately that the concept of core obligations is, in theory, more correct than that of core content examined above. In fact, as I said several times, it is conceivable and indeed very frequent, that a single human right corresponds to a plurality of obligations and also that some of these are more immediate or more binding than others.

The concept of core obligations has so far been used mainly by the Committee on Economic, Social and Cultural Rights. As I already said,[51] the CESCR provides for the States Parties, for the implementation of the rights contained therein, especially obligations "of progressive realization".[52] However, this does not rule out the existence of certain obligations of a different nature. In fact, the Committee has tried to identify these latter obligations, which are defined as "core obligations" or

[46]This seems to be the opinion of Scheinin (2013), pp. 532–535.

[47]Scheinin (2013), p. 536.

[48]*Limburg Principles on the Implementation of the International Covenant on Economic, Social and Cultural Rights*, Maastricht, 2–6 June 1985.

[49]Alston (1987), p. 352.

[50]See, e.g., Scheinin (2013), Forman (2016) and Forman et al. (2016).

[51]See above, Sect. 8.2.3.

[52]See Pisillo Mazzeschi (2008), pp. 290–297 and 429–489.

"minimum core obligations". For example, in its General Comment No. 3,[53] the Committee argues that States have a minimum core obligation which consists in ensuring "satisfaction of, at the very least, minimum essential levels of each of the rights". It therefore offers examples of essential food, primary health protection, basic housing and most basic forms of education.[54] Other subsequent General Comments have taken up this concept. For example, in General Comment No. 12, dedicated to the right to food, the Committee stated that:

> The right to adequate food will have to be realized progressively. However, States have a *core obligation* to take the necessary action to mitigate and alleviate hunger as provided for in paragraph 2 of article 11, even in times of natural or other disasters [. . .].[55]

But what are the exact characteristics of core obligations? Their most important character seems to be *immediacy*. While the norms on economic, social and cultural rights usually require States to assume progressive obligations, these norms may also, exceptionally, require States to immediately fulfil certain essential minimum obligations relating to the right in question. Are there other effects of core obligations? One view[56] argued that core obligations are judicially enforceable, do not allow States to take regressive measures and do not allow States to invoke the excuse of lack of resources. This argument is not convincing: in my opinion, the first of these effects does not work for all core obligations, while the other two effects operate for all the obligations "of progressive realization"[57] and not only for core obligations.

In conclusion, the concept of core obligations is the only one, among the three examined here, that can be accepted. But it works, as a kind of exception, only in the framework of human rights which usually provide for progressive obligations, and its only relevant characteristic is that of being an *immediate* obligation.

13.5 Conclusions

Based on what has been said so far in this chapter, my choice to adopt a general bipartition between the category of "fundamental" human rights and that of other human rights seems well justified. In my view, "fundamental" human rights are those recognized by general international law. Among them there is a narrower nucleus of human rights, which are established by norms or principles of a peremptory character; and therefore they also have the typical characteristics of *jus cogens*.

[53]CteeESCR, General Comment No. 3, 14 December 1990.

[54]*Ibidem*, para. 10.

[55]CteeESCR, General Comment No. 12, 12 May 1999, para. 6 (emphasis added).

[56]Scheinin (2013), pp. 536–538.

[57]See Pisillo Mazzeschi (2008), pp. 445–484. See also above, Sects. 4.4.2 and 8.2.3.

In this Part of the book, I will examine the "fundamental human rights", taking into account both conventional and general international law. In Part VI below, I will address the "other human rights", primarily on the basis of conventional law. Within the two categories, I will distinguish the rights according to the subcategories that I have already indicated.[58]

References

Alston P (1987) Out of the abyss; the challenges confronting the new UN Committee on economic, social and cultural rights. Hum Rights Q 9:332–381
Carrillo Salcedo JA (1997) Reflections on the existence of a hierarchy of norms in international law. Eur J Int Law 8:583–595
Cassese A (Gaeta P ed) (2006) Diritto internazionale. Il Mulino, Bologna
Cassese A (2012) A plea for a global community grounded in a core of human rights. In: Cassese A (ed) Realizing Utopia. The future of international law. OUP, Oxford, pp 136–144
Cataldi G (2007) Diritti inderogabili. In: Flores M, Groppi T, Pisillo Mazzeschi R (eds) Diritti Umani. Cultura dei diritti e dignità della persona nell'epoca della globalizzazione: Dizionario, vol I. Utet, Torino, pp 382–385
Conforti B (2015) Diritto internazionale, 10th edn. Editoriale Scientifica, Napoli
Conforti B (Iovane M ed) (2018) Diritto internazionale, 11th edn. Editoriale Scientifica, Napoli
de Frouville O (2004) L'intangibilité des droits de l'homme en droit international. Pedone, Paris
De Sena P, Saccucci A (2007) Diritti fondamentali. In: Flores M, Groppi T, Pisillo Mazzeschi R (eds) Diritti Umani. Cultura dei diritti e dignità della persona nell'epoca della globalizzazione: Dizionario, vol I. Utet, Torino, pp 376–382
De Wet E, Vidmar J (eds) (2012) Hierarchy in international law: the place of human rights. OUP, Oxford
Dupuy P-M, Kerbrat Y (2020) Droit international public, 15th edn. Dalloz, Paris
Focarelli C (2013) La persona umana nel diritto internazionale. Il Mulino, Bologna
Forman L (2016) Can minimum core obligations survive a reasonableness standard of review under the optional protocol to the international covenant on economic, social and cultural rights? Ottawa Law Rev 47:557–576
Forman L et al (2016) Conceptualising minimum core obligations under the right to health: how should we define and implement the 'morality of the depths'. Int J Hum Rights 20:531–548
Iovane M (2000) La tutela dei valori fondamentali nel diritto internazionale. Editoriale Scientifica, Napoli
Iovane M (2007) Gross violations of human rights. In: Flores M, Groppi T, Pisillo Mazzeschi R (eds) Diritti Umani. Cultura dei diritti e dignità della persona nell'epoca della globalizzazione: Dizionario, vol 1. Utet, Torino, pp 675–680
Kälin W, Künzli J (2019) The law of international human rights protection, 2nd edn. OUP, Oxford-New York
Meron T (1986) On a hierarchy of international human rights. Am J Int Law 80:1–23
Pisillo Mazzeschi R (2008) Responsabilité de l'État pour violation des obligations positives relatives aux droits de l'homme. RC 333:175–506
Pustorino P (2019) Lezioni di tutela internazionale dei diritti umani. Cacucci, Bari
Pustorino P (2020) Lezioni di tutela internazionale dei diritti umani, 2nd edn. Cacucci, Bari

[58]See above, Introduction to this Part. For the adoption of similar categories see Kälin and Künzli (2019), Part III.

Scheinin M (2013) Core rights and obligations. In: Shelton D (ed) Oxford handbook of international human rights law. OUP, Oxford, pp 527–540

Shue H (1980) Basic rights: subsistence, affluence, and US foreign policy. Princeton University Press, Princeton

Sudre F (1995) Droits intangibles et/ou droits fondamentaux: y a-t-il des droits préeminents dans la Convention européenne des droits de l'homme? In: Liber Amicorum Marc-André Eissen. Bruylant, Bruxelles, pp 381–398

Tomuschat C (2014) Human rights: between idealism and realism, 3rd edn. OUP, Oxford

Protection of Life and Physical Integrity of the Person 14

Within the framework of "fundamental" human rights, it is worth examining, to begin with, a first group of rights which aims to protect the life and physical integrity of persons. There is no doubt that this purpose is paramount in the system of international protection of human rights, and therefore the rights in this group deserve to be treated rather broadly. They include: (*a*) the right to life; (*b*) the prohibition of torture and inhuman or degrading treatment or punishment; (*c*) the prohibition of international crimes. The latter prohibition includes, in turn, certain subcategories.

14.1 Right to Life

14.1.1 Norms

The right to life is enshrined in the Universal Declaration of Human Rights in very general terms. Article 3 proclaims that:

> Everyone has the right to life [. . .].

The main human rights conventions contain more specific provisions. Article 2 of the European Convention states:

> 1. Everyone's right to life shall be protected by law. No one shall be deprived of his life intentionally save in the execution of a sentence of a court following his conviction of a crime for which this penalty is provided by law.
> 2. Deprivation of life shall not be regarded as inflicted in contravention of this Article when it results from the use of force which is no more than absolutely necessary: (a) in defence of any person from unlawful violence; (b) in order to effect a lawful arrest or to prevent the escape of a person lawfully detained; (c) in action lawfully taken for the purpose of quelling a riot or insurrection.

R. Pisillo Mazzeschi, *International Human Rights Law*,
https://doi.org/10.1007/978-3-030-77032-7_14

Note that Paragraph 1 sets out the right to life and regulates the cases in which life can be deprived in execution of a death penalty. Paragraph 2, on the other hand, establishes that deprivation of life is legitimate when death results from the use of force which is absolutely necessary in certain circumstances, which are expressly indicated.

The Covenant on Civil and Political Rights does not contain an equally specific provision on this last point, since Article 6 merely states that "No one shall be arbitrarily deprived of his life".[1] On the other hand, the Covenant contains more elaborate and complex provisions on the death penalty than the ECHR. The right to life is also established by Article 4 of the American Convention,[2] Article 4 of the African Charter, Articles 5–7 of the Arab Charter, and Article 2 of the EU Charter of Fundamental Rights. There are also a number of human rights treaties of a specific nature, which contain provisions on the death penalty.[3]

It should be stressed that all these norms establish the basic concept that no one can be arbitrarily deprived of life. This is the essential and common nucleus of all conventional norms on the right to life. It follows from the practice of the various international supervisory bodies that killings resulting from the legitimate use of

[1]CCPR, Art. 6: "1. Every human being has the inherent right to life. This right shall be protected by law. No one shall be arbitrarily deprived of his life. 2. In countries which have not abolished the death penalty, sentence of death may be imposed only for the most serious crimes in accordance with the law in force at the time of the commission of the crime and not contrary to the provisions of the present Covenant and to the Convention on the Prevention and Punishment of the Crime of Genocide. This penalty can only be carried out pursuant to a final judgement rendered by a competent court. 3. When deprivation of life constitutes the crime of genocide, it is understood that nothing in this article shall authorize any State Party to the present Covenant to derogate in any way from any obligation assumed under the provisions of the Convention on the Prevention and Punishment of the Crime of Genocide. 4. Anyone sentenced to death shall have the right to seek pardon or commutation of the sentence. Amnesty, pardon or commutation of the sentence of death may be granted in all cases. 5. Sentence of death shall not be imposed for crimes committed by persons below eighteen years of age and shall not be carried out on pregnant women. 6. Nothing in this article shall be invoked to delay or to prevent the abolition of capital punishment by any State Party to the present Covenant."

[2]ACHR, Art. 4: "1. Every person has the right to have his life respected. This right shall be protected by law and, in general, from the moment of conception. No one shall be arbitrarily deprived of his life. 2. In countries that have not abolished the death penalty, it may be imposed only for the most serious crimes and pursuant to a final judgment rendered by a competent court and in accordance with a law establishing such punishment, enacted prior to the commission of the crime. The application of such punishment shall not be extended to crimes to which it does not presently apply. 3. The death penalty shall not be re-established in states that have abolished it. 4. In no case shall capital punishment be inflicted for political offenses or related common crimes. 5. Capital punishment shall not be imposed upon persons who, at the time the crime was committed, were under 18 years of age or over 70 years of age; nor shall it be applied to pregnant women. 6. Every person condemned to death shall have the right to apply for amnesty, pardon, or commutation of sentence, which may be granted in all cases. Capital punishment shall not be imposed while such a petition is pending decision by the competent authority."

[3]See, e.g., CRC, Art. 37.

force, which also meets the requirements of necessity and proportionality, are not considered arbitrary. I will return to this aspect later.

In my view, this essential nucleus of the treaty norms on the right to life, namely the *prohibition of arbitrary killing*, has become established not only in international treaty law, but also in general international law. It seems doubtful to me, however, that this prohibition has become part of *jus cogens*. Of course, this does not apply when there are serious, systematic and organized violations of this ban: we are then in the field of *gross violations* of a fundamental human right and therefore within the scope of *jus cogens*.

14.1.2 Content of the Right

The right to life is often regarded as a "supreme"[4] human right or a right protected by one of the most fundamental norms[5] or the right having pre-eminent value in the human rights hierarchy.[6] In addition, it is usually included among the non-derogable rights in time of emergency, but only in peacetime.[7] However, it is not an "absolute" human right, because it admits some limits and two exceptions: (*a*) the execution of the death penalty legitimately imposed; (*b*) the killing that occurs during an armed conflict according to the rules of international humanitarian law.

14.1.2.1 Exceptions: Death Penalty and Armed Conflict

The first exception to the right to life is the death penalty, which is usually allowed in human rights treaties. This is because the death penalty, regrettably, was and still is provided for in many States, and it was therefore necessary to regulate it and frame it within certain legal limits.[8] In fact, in the main human rights treaties, the death penalty is subject to a number of substantive, procedural and personal conditions that apply to States that have not abolished it.[9]

These conditions are well specified in Article 6 of the Covenant on Civil and Political Rights: (*a*) the death penalty can only be imposed for the most serious crimes; (*b*) such crimes must be established in accordance with the law in force at the time when they were committed (principle of non-retroactivity of criminal law);[10] (*c*) the law providing for the death penalty must not be contrary to other human rights laid down in the Covenant (e.g. the prohibition of inhuman treatment); (*d*) the death

---

[4]HRCtee, General Comment No. 6, 30 April 1982, para. 1.

[5]ECtHR, *McCann and Others*, para. 147.

[6]See ECtHR, *Streletz, Kessler and Krenk*, para. 72.

[7]See Focarelli (2013), p. 131.

[8]See Zagrebelsky et al. (2016), p. 156.

[9]See Focarelli (2013), p. 134.

[10]See below, Sect. 17.3.

penalty can only be established by a final judgment rendered by a competent court of law; (*e*) the person sentenced to death must have the right to ask for forgiveness or a commutation of the sentence; (*f*) the death penalty may not be imposed on persons below the age of 18 years and may not be carried out on pregnant women. Similar conditions, although not identical and not so detailed, are also provided for in other human rights treaties.[11]

However, it should be noted that, in recent years, there has been a clear trend towards the abolition of the death penalty. Firstly, the death penalty has been abolished in some additional protocols. In the European Convention system, the death penalty was abolished first, in peacetime, by Protocol No. 6 of 1983 and then, in all circumstances and therefore also in wartime, by Protocol No. 13 of 2002. Similarly, Protocol No. 2 to the Covenant on Civil and Political Rights and Protocol No. 2 to the American Convention also abolished the death penalty. Secondly, the Strasbourg Court first held that the death penalty should be regarded as an inhuman treatment prohibited by Article 3 of the European Convention[12] and then held that Article 2 of the Convention must now be interpreted as prohibiting the death penalty in all circumstances.[13] Thirdly, there are some treaty provisions prohibiting States that have abolished the death penalty from reintroducing it into their legal systems.[14] Finally, the Human Rights Committee and the Inter-American Court also regard the abolition of the death penalty as a step forward in the enjoyment of the right to life and encourage States towards that abolition.[15]

The second exception to the right to life consists of those killings that occur during armed conflicts in accordance with the norms of international humanitarian law.[16] However, this exception has also changed over time. In fact, in traditional international law it was believed that the right to life, protected by human rights treaties, did not apply in situations of armed conflict. According to this view, in times of peace, individuals would be protected by international human rights law, whereas in times of armed conflict this protection would be weakened because individuals would only be protected by international humanitarian law. And, according to the latter, the loss of life attributable to legitimate acts of war would not be illegitimate. In other words, during armed conflicts, international humanitarian law would *totally* derogate, as a *lex specialis*, from international human rights law.

[11] See ECHR, Art. 2(1); ACHR, Art. 4(2-5); ArCHR, Arts. 6 and 7; CRC, Art. 37(a).

[12] ECtHR, *Öcalan*, 12 May 2005, para. 165.

[13] ECtHR, *Al-Saadoon and Mufdhi*, Judgment of 2 March 2010, para. 120.

[14] In this sense see Art. 4(3) ACHR.

[15] HRCtee, General Comment No. 6, 30 April 1982, para. 6; Id., Concluding Observations: *Suriname* (2004), para. 10; IACtHR, *The Right to Information on Consular Assistance*, para. 134 ff.

[16] On the subject see, for all, Kälin and Künzli (2019), pp. 270–277.

But this theory seems outdated today, as I discussed in Chap. 2.[17] In contemporary international law, these two areas of law have come closer together and have undergone mutual influences and convergence, so that their distinction is no longer as clear-cut as in the past, nor is the functioning of the principle of *lex specialis* so clear. In particular, the tendency of practice is that certain fundamental human rights, including the right to life, also operate during armed conflicts. This has also been confirmed by the International Court of Justice in its opinion on the *Legality of Nuclear Weapons*[18] and in its opinion on the *Construction of a Wall in the Occupied Palestinian Territory*.[19]

The main consequence of this approach is that those deprivations of life that are prohibited under international humanitarian law (e.g. killings of wounded people or prisoners, or killings resulting from indiscriminate attacks) *also* constitute violations of the right to life under international human rights law. From a practical point of view, this allows victims or relatives of victims to lodge complaints with international human rights monitoring bodies. In this respect, I can recall the judgments of the European Court of Human Rights in the *Isayeva and Others*,[20] *Isayeva*,[21] *Khatsiyeva and Others*[22] cases, relating to the armed conflict in Chechnya.

14.1.2.2 Scope of the Right: The Beginning and End of Life

Still with reference to the content of the right to life, there is the problem of defining the scope of application of the right, especially in relation to a number of issues related to the beginning and end of life.

In connection with the beginning of life, an important issue concerns the position of the unborn child with regard to the right to life and the legitimacy of abortion.[23] The European Convention, the Covenant on Civil and Political Rights and the African Charter make no reference to abortion. Instead, the American Convention contains a provision (Art. 4(1)), according to which the right to life must be protected "from the moment of conception".[24] This issue is addressed more specifically by the 2003 Protocol to the African Charter on the Rights of Women in Africa, which, in Article 14(2), obliges States Parties to authorize abortion in certain cases, such as rape, incest or situations involving a risk to the physical or mental health of the mother, or to the life of the mother or the fetus.

[17]See above, Sect. 2.4.1.

[18]ICJ, *Legality of the Threat or Use of Nuclear Weapons*, para. 25.

[19]ICJ, *Legal Consequences of the Construction of a Wall*, para. 106.

[20]ECtHR, *Isayeva v. Russia*, para. 172–201.

[21]ECtHR, *Isayeva, Yusupova and Bazayeva v. Russia*, paras. 168–200.

[22]ECtHR, *Khatsiyeva and Others v. Russia*, paras. 129–140.

[23]On the subject see Citroni and Scovazzi (2013), p. 308 ff.; Focarelli (2013), pp. 134–136; Zagrebelsky et al. (2019), p. 165 ff.

[24]On the moment of conception see IACtHR, *Artavia Murillo et al. v. Costa Rica*, para. 264.

In the practice of human rights monitoring bodies, the issue of abortion comes to the fore both from the point of view of the possible right to life of the fetus and from the point of view of the protection of the mother's right to life, which could be put at risk if she were forced to give birth.

The Commission and the European Court of Human Rights have had to rule on various complaints concerning abortion.[25] On the question of the ownership of the right to life by the unborn child, these bodies did not want to rule in an abstract way, noting the lack of a consensus of the States Parties to the European Convention. They therefore gave the States a margin of appreciation.[26] However, in some cases they have ruled out the possibility that the unborn child has an absolute right to life that would result in a ban on abortion even in the event of the mother-to-be being in danger.[27] The European Court has also touched on the subject of abortion in cases of applications by women who were denied therapeutic abortion and who claimed violations of rights other than the right to life, such as the prohibition of inhuman or degrading treatment or the right to private life. I can mention the cases *Tysiac v. Poland*,[28] *R.R. v. Poland*,[29] and *P. and S. v. Poland.*[30]

The European Court of Justice has also ruled on this issue;[31] but it has not taken a position on the ownership of the right to life by the fetus; and has therefore left each State free to regulate abortion. On the other hand, the Human Rights Committee seems to have taken a somewhat clearer stance in favor of women's right to life and health. Indeed, in some cases the Committee has noted that the ban on abortion cannot be absolute and that it must allow exceptions to protect women's right to life; and also that national legislation prohibiting certain therapeutic abortions is contrary to the Covenant on Civil and Political Rights.[32] The Inter-American Commission, despite the fact that the above-mentioned Article 4 of the American Convention states that the right to life must be protected from the moment of conception, has concluded that this formula is of a general nature and does not prevent States from derogating from it by legalizing abortion in exceptional cases.[33]

[25] See, in particular, for a detailed examination of this case-law, Citroni and Scovazzi (2013), pp. 312–317.

[26] See ECmHR, *W.P. v. United Kingdom*, paras. 12–24; ECtHR, *Vo v. France*, paras. 84–85.

[27] ECmHR, *H. v. Norway.*

[28] ECtHR, *Tysiąc v. Poland.*

[29] ECtHR, *R.R. v. Poland.*

[30] ECtHR, *P. and S. v. Poland.*

[31] ECJ, *Brüstle*; *The Society for the Protection of Unborn Children.*

[32] HRCtee, Concluding Observations: *Chile* (1999), para. 15; Concluding Observations: *Guatemala* (2001); *Queenan v. Canada*, para. 4.2; *Huamán v. Peru*, paras. 6.4–6.6; *V.D.A. v. Argentina*, para. 9.2.

[33] IACmHR, *Baby Boy Case.*

As far as the end of life is concerned, issues relating to euthanasia and so-called "assisted suicide" come to the fore. In fact, these issues are not expressly regulated by the main general human rights treaties. The question of interpretation that arises is whether the right to life also includes the right of the person to decide to end his or her own life.

The European Court of Human Rights has responded in the negative, stating that the right to die cannot be deduced from the right to life;[34] but it has recognized the legitimacy under the European Convention of State laws that allow forms of assisted suicide as long as they ascertain the will expressed by the person. In some cases, the Court has held that Article 8 of the Convention, on the right to private life, is applicable to this issue.[35] On the whole, the Court, while noting that there is no agreement between the Member States on the issue of assisted suicide,[36] does not seem to rule out the possibility that State legislation in this area may be compatible with the Convention in certain specific situations and with adequate safeguards to prevent abuse.[37]

The Human Rights Committee dealt with the issue of euthanasia with reference to a Dutch bill on euthanasia and assisted suicide. In its concluding observations of 2001 on the Netherlands,[38] the Committee said that States have a margin of discretion in this matter. However, when a State offers legal protection to acts deliberately intended to end a human life, the strictest precautions must be taken in determining when such acts are not punishable, in order to protect the right to life.

14.1.3 Obligations

The issue of obligations incumbent on States (and other human rights duty-bearers[39]) to protect the right to life is a very important one. I will distinguish between *negative* obligations and various categories of *positive* obligations (of prevention, repression and reparation). In dealing with these positive obligations, I will adopt the conceptual categories I have already proposed: (*a*) immediate obligations of result; (*b*) immediate obligations of due diligence; (*c*) obligations "of progressive realization".[40] It must be said from the outset that many of the observations I will make on obligations relating to the right to life will serve as a

[34]ECtHR, *Pretty v. UK*.

[35]ECtHR, *Haas v. Switzerland*, paras. 51, 55 and 61; *Koch v. Germany*, paras. 65–72.

[36]See, e.g., ECtHR, *Lambert and Others v. France*.

[37]See Focarelli (2013), p. 136.

[38]HRCtee, Concluding Observations: *Netherlands* (2001).

[39]See above, Sect. 7.1.

[40]See above, Sect. 8.2.

model, with appropriate variations, when I will deal with obligations relating to other human rights.

14.1.3.1 Negative Obligations

The right to life imposes, first of all, negative obligations on the State. The first obligation of the State is to refrain from arbitrary killing through the conduct of its organs. It could be defined as a prohibition of the arbitrary or excessive use of "lethal force" (i.e. that can cause death). The use of lethal force by police officers, security forces, prison officers or other State agents is justified in certain circumstances, such as those set out in Article 2(1) of the European Convention. But such use of force, if it is not to be arbitrary or excessive, must meet the criteria of necessity and proportionality; that is to say, it must be necessary to achieve the aim and must not exceed the appropriate and necessary means to achieve that aim. In other words, there must be a proportionality link between the aim and the means used to reach it.[41]

In the case-law of the European Court of Human Rights, the leading case is *McCann v. UK*,[42] in which the applicants challenged the legality, under the European Convention, of an anti-terrorist operation conducted in Gibraltar by British military security forces in which relatives of the applicants had lost their lives. In relation to the use of force, the judges stated that it must be strictly proportionate to the achievement of one of the objectives set out in Article 2 of the European Convention. The Court at first found that the British military forces had acted reasonably, believing that it was necessary to shoot the suspects to prevent them from activating a bomb placed in a car. However, since the identity of the three terrorists was known to the British authorities and, therefore, it would have been possible to arrest them beforehand once they entered Gibraltar, the Court went on to conclude that the use of force was "not absolutely necessary" and that the killing of the three suspects constituted a breach of Article 2.

Excessive use of force by police officers was also found to be contrary to Article 2, for example, in the *Makaratzis*,[43] *Nachova*,[44] *Nikolova and Velichkova*,[45] *Saoud*[46] and *Alikaj*[47] cases. Instead, in the *Ramsahai* case,[48] the Court held that the killing of a person by a police officer was "no more than absolutely necessary".[49] The Court

[41]On the principle of proportionality in international law, see Cannizzaro (2000).

[42]ECtHR, *McCann and Others v. UK.*

[43]ECtHR, *Makaratzis*, para. 55.

[44]ECtHR, *Nachova and Others*, Judgment of 6 July 2005, paras. 71–74, 96 and 107.

[45]ECtHR, *Nikolova and Velichkova.*

[46]ECtHR, *Saoud.*

[47]ECtHR, *Alikaj and Others.*

[48]ECtHR, *Ramsahai and Others*, para. 288.

[49]Ramsahai had stolen a scooter, after threatening the rightful owner with a gun. He later escaped and was chased by some police officers. Once caught up, he drew his gun and pointed it at a policeman who, in response, shot him in the neck, killing him.

came to the same conclusion in the *Giuliani* case,[50] which originated from the violent protests against the G8 in Genoa in July 2001. Giuliani was one of the protesters; in the excitement of the events, he, after having grabbed a fire extinguisher, had approached a jeep with three gendarmerie policemen ("carabinieri") on board. One of them drew his gun and fired shots towards the rear window of the vehicle, striking and killing the victim. The Strasbourg judges stated that the Italian authorities had not violated their obligation to do everything reasonably possible to ensure an adequate level of safety with respect to the execution of operations potentially involving the use of lethal force, such as those that occurred in this case. In particular, the possession and use of the gun, from which the shots that killed Giuliani were fired by an officer, were considered legitimate, just as the use of lethal force was considered "absolutely necessary in defence of any person from unlawful violence".[51]

In essence, in the case-law of the Commission and the European Court of Human Rights, the excessive use of force may infringe upon the right to life, even when the purpose of such use is legitimate and the lethal consequence is not intentional.[52] Moreover, the existence of other ways of achieving the aim pursued by the use of lethal force precludes that use from being necessary and proportionate.[53] However, the European Court has recognized that the standard of absolute necessity of lethal force can be applied with varying degrees of severity depending on the extent to which the authorities were in control of the situation.[54]

The practice of the Human Rights Committee also confirms that the right to life, under Article 6 of the Covenant, consists, first and foremost, in the right not to be arbitrarily killed by the authorities of the State. In the *Guerrero* case,[55] for example, the Committee condemned Colombia for the killing of alleged criminals by police officers. In 1978, the police raided a house in Bogotá, where it was believed that an ambassador, who had previously been kidnapped, had been locked up. The ambassador was not found, but the police still hid in the house waiting for the kidnappers to arrive. Seven people later entered the apartment and were shot dead by the police. The *modus operandi* of the officers, who gave no prior warning to the victims and, consequently, the possibility for them to surrender or explain their presence, led the Committee to judge the killing, although "legitimate" under Colombian law, as arbitrary, unnecessary and disproportionate and therefore contrary to Article 6 of the Covenant. In the Committee's view, even an attempted murder may cause a violation of Article 6. In the *Chongwe* case,[56] the applicant contested the

[50] ECtHR, *Giuliani and Gaggio*.

[51] *Ibidem*, para. 194.

[52] See Zagrebelsky et al. (2016), p. 152 and the cases cited therein.

[53] *Ibidem*.

[54] See ECtHR, *Finogenov and Others v. Russia*, paras. 208–216; *Tagayeva and Others v. Russia*, para. 481.

[55] HRCtee, *Suarez de Guerrero*, paras. 13.2–13.3.

[56] HRCtee, *Chongwe*.

authorization by Colombian authorities to use lethal force, without legitimate reason, which could have caused his death. The Committee considered that the State had violated Article 6.

The Inter-American human rights monitoring bodies follow similar criteria in relation to the right to life protected by Article 4 of the American Convention. It should be noted that most of the cases relating to the right to life decided by these bodies concern massive violations perpetrated by State officers and hasty and indiscriminate killings against individuals under State jurisdiction. Examples include the cases of *Paniagua Morales*,[57] *Barrios Altos*,[58] *The Street Children*,[59] *Montero-Aranguren*.[60] In fact, the case-law of the Inter-American Court is very interesting, because it has specified in some detail the criteria of the need to use force and the proportionality of the means employed. Furthermore, as we shall see later, the Court has also explored the content of the positive obligations of repression incumbent on the State with regard to the right to life.[61]

Another negative obligation of the State, relating to the right to life, is that the State cannot reject, expel or extradite a person to a country where he or she is in serious danger of being deprived of his or her life. This obligation, in my view, derives from (or has been influenced by) the so-called principle of *non-refoulement*. This principle will be discussed in more detail later on, with regard to the rights of movement of aliens and the protection of asylum seekers and refugees.[62] Here it is sufficient to note that this principle has its origin in Article 33 of the 1951 Geneva Convention relating to the Status of Refugees, which prohibits States Parties from rejecting refugees to the borders of a country where their life or freedom would be threatened on a number of specific grounds of discrimination.[63] However, the principle was then established in customary law; it extended its subjective scope of application from refugees alone to all aliens; and its objective scope not only to *refoulement* in the strict sense, but also to the expulsion and extradition of aliens.

Finally (and this is the most interesting point here) the principle has also expanded in relation to the causes that prevent *refoulement*, since it now protects not only against the dangers arising from the specific grounds for discrimination listed in the Geneva Convention, but also against the risk of suffering violations of the right to life and acts of torture or inhuman or degrading treatment. This stems from the fact that the principle of *non-refoulement* has had an impact over time on these rights, which have gradually been interpreted in a more evolutionary way. In particular, the right to life has been interpreted to mean that a State has an obligation

[57]IACtHR, *Paniagua Morales and Others*.

[58]IACtHR, *Barrios Altos*, Judgment of 14 March 2001.

[59]IACtHR, *The "Street Children"*, Judgment of 19 November 1999.

[60]IACtHR, *Montero-Aranguren et al.*, paras. 67–74.

[61]See below, Sect. 14.1.3.3.

[62]See below, Sects. 24.2, 24.3 and 24.4.

[63]The prohibition of *refoulement* allows an exception when the refugee constitutes a danger to the security of the State of refuge (Art. 33(2) of the Geneva Convention).

not to reject (nor expel or extradite) a person to a country where he seriously risks, *for whatever reason*, being arbitrarily deprived of life.[64] In essence, the principle of *non-refoulement* and the right to life have been mutually integrated.

As we shall see,[65] a similar development has also affected the prohibition of torture and inhuman or degrading treatment.

14.1.3.2 Positive Obligations of Prevention

Respect for the right to life also imposes many positive obligations on the State: those of prevention, repression and reparation.

Starting with the former, it should be noted at once that the *general* obligation of the State to prevent violations of people's right to life is very important and that it is made up, in turn, of a number of more specific obligations. To sum up, the State has: (*a*) the obligation to have an adequate regulatory apparatus for the prevention of violations; (*b*) the obligation to have an administrative apparatus for the same purpose; (*c*) the obligation to adopt the concrete measures, each time required, for prevention.[66]

The distinction between these three different obligations was well highlighted by the European Court of Human Rights in the famous *Osman* case of 1998.[67] The applicants, Mrs Osman and her son Ahmet, complained that the London police had not protected Mr Osman and Ahmet's life in the face of the danger posed by Ahmet's teacher, who had developed a form of obsession with the latter. In fact, the teacher had then, during a shooting, killed Mr Osman, injured Ahmet and also killed a third person. The European Court concluded that, in the case in point, police responsibility had not been proven and therefore there had been no breach of Article 2 of the European Convention. However, in its judgment, the Court makes some very interesting observations regarding the State's prevention obligations; and, more specifically, it distinguishes between three different obligations: (*a*) that of having criminal law rules for deterring offences against persons; (*b*) that of having a law-enforcement machinery for the purpose of preventing, suppressing and punishing violations of those rules; and finally (*c*) the additional obligation of the State authorities, in certain circumstances, to take preventive measures of an operational nature to protect an individual whose life is at risk of being subjected to criminal acts by another individual. Indeed, according to the Court:

> [. . .] the State's obligation in this respect extends beyond its primary duty to secure the right to life by putting in place effective criminal-law provisions to deter the commission of offences against the person backed up by law-enforcement machinery for the prevention,

---

[64] In addition, States that have abolished the death penalty, for example States that are Parties to the European Convention, also have the obligation not to return a foreigner to a country where he or she risks being subjected to the death penalty.

[65] See below, Sect. 14.2.3.1.

[66] For an in-depth examination of these three categories of prevention obligations, see Pisillo Mazzeschi (2008), pp. 334–344 and 390–414.

[67] ECtHR, *Osman v. UK*.

> suppression and sanctioning of breaches of such provisions. [. . .] Article 2 of the Convention may also imply in certain well-defined circumstances a positive obligation on the authorities to take preventive operational measures to protect an individual whose life is at risk from the criminal acts of another individual.[68]

It is now appropriate to examine these *three prevention obligations* separately, because they have different characteristics.

The State's *first obligation of prevention* is to have (or to equip itself with) a *regulatory apparatus* (especially criminal but also of another nature) that is suitable, in general and abstract terms, to prevent violations of the right to life. This is an immediate obligation of result.[69] In fact, the State is certainly able to ensure the result of adopting, amending or repealing legislation and cannot be limited to a simple effort of diligence in this direction.

The case-law of the European Court contains, in addition to the *Osman* case, other interesting cases, which clearly confirm the existence of such an obligation on the part of the State. In the three cases *Güleç*, *Oğur* and *Akkoç*,[70] for example, the Court ruled that Turkish criminal law and criminal procedure, relating to offences in which military or police forces were involved, did not guarantee an independent and effective procedure and therefore violated the State's obligation to protect the life of persons under Article 2 of the European Convention. In the aforementioned *Makaratzis* case,[71] police officers, who had fired on a motorist who had violated roadblocks and who had been accused of unauthorized use of firearms, were acquitted on the basis of a Greek law of 1943. However, according to the European Court, Greece, by failing to lay down the directives or the limits on the use of armed force necessary to guide such use correctly, had violated the positive obligation to protect people's lives laid down in Article 2 of the European Convention. One can also mention the *Mastromatteo* case,[72] in which the applicant's son was killed by criminals, who had been provisionally released from Italian prisons on bail on the basis of certain laws designed to facilitate the social reintegration of prisoners. The European Court wondered whether the Italian legislation violated the positive obligation of the State to guarantee sufficient protection to society in relation to possible attacks against people's lives; but concluded that it did not violate Article 2 of the European Convention. For the obligation of the State to have a civil legislation to compensate damages for manslaughter, one can cite the *Calvelli and Ciglio* case,[73] concerning the professional liability of physicians.

The case-law of the Inter-American Court and Commission also confirms that the State has an obligation to have a preventive regulatory apparatus, which derives from

---

[68] *Ibidem*, para. 115.

[69] See Pisillo Mazzeschi (2008), p. 311 ff.

[70] ECtHR, *Güleç v. Turkey*; *Oğur v. Turkey*; *Akkoç v. Turkey*.

[71] ECtHR, *Makaratzis v. Greece*.

[72] ECtHR, *Mastromatteo v. Italy*.

[73] ECtHR, *Calvelli and Ciglio v. Italy*, paras. 49–51.

Article 2 of the American Convention. For example, in the *Castillo Petruzzi* case, the Inter-American Court stated:

> The general duty under Article 2 of the American Convention implies the adoption of measures of two kinds: on the one hand, elimination of any norms and practices that in any way violate the guarantees provided under the Convention; on the other hand, the promulgation of norms and the development of practices conducive to effective observance of those guarantees.[74]

Similar principles have been affirmed in other judgements, for example in the *Barrios Altos* and *The Street Children* cases.

Finally, the Human Rights Committee, albeit more generally, has also stated that the general obligation imposed on States Parties by Article 2(2) of the Covenant on Civil and Political Rights requires States to adapt their domestic law to implement protected rights. Indeed, the Committee stated that:

> [. . .] unless Covenant rights are already protected by their domestic laws or practices, States Parties are required on ratification to make such changes to domestic laws and practices as are necessary to ensure their conformity with the Covenant.[75]

The *second obligation of prevention* for the State is to have an adequate *administrative apparatus*, in general and in the abstract, in order to prevent violations of people's right to life, whether such violations are committed by State agents or private individuals. One thinks, above all, of the police and security apparatus, but also of the penitentiary and sanitary systems. This is also an obligation of result, because it is not subject to aleatory outcome.

It is worth mentioning, first of all, certain cases involving the State *police and security apparatus*. In the case-law of the monitoring bodies of the European Convention, the *Mahmut Kaya*[76] and *Akkoç*[77] cases can be mentioned in addition to the aforementioned *Osman* case. In both cases, some people had been killed by unknown persons in the south-east of Turkey and their relatives accused the Turkish authorities of violating the right to life. The European Court noted, inter alia, that there were structural deficiencies in the criminal protection system in the south-east region of Turkey at the time of the murder; that this system was not effective; and that the government did not put in place general and appropriate protection measures in this area. Therefore, the Court found that there was a violation of an obligation of result with regard to the State administrative apparatus of prevention. The Court's statements in the *Perk* case, concerning the protection of the right to life during certain counter-terrorism operations, are even clearer. On the obligation of States to have an administrative apparatus of prevention, the Court said:

---

[74]IACtHR, *Castillo Petruzzi et al.*, para. 207.

[75]In this sense see also HRCtee, General Comment No. 31, 26 May 2004, para. 13.

[76]ECtHR, *Mahmut Kaya v. Turkey*.

[77]ECtHR, *Akkoç v. Turkey*.

> L'obligation de l'Etat à cet égard implique le devoir primordial d'assurer le droit à la vie en mettant en place un cadre juridique et administratif propre à dissuader de commettre des atteintes contre la personne et s'appuyant sur un mécanisme d'application conçu pour en prévenir, réprimer et sanctionner les violations.[78]

In the jurisprudence of the Inter-American human rights system, the existence of a general obligation of the State to *have* adequate administrative machinery for the prevention of human rights violations is clearly confirmed. In this respect, the following identical statements made by the Inter-American Court of Human Rights in the *Velásquez Rodríguez*[79] and *Godínez Cruz*[80] cases are a good example:

> The second obligation of the States Parties is to "ensure" the free and full exercise of the rights recognized by the Convention to every person subject to its jurisdiction. This obligation implies the duty of the States parties to organize the governmental apparatus and, in general, all the structures through which public power is exercised, so that they are capable of juridically ensuring the free and full enjoyment of human rights.

In the practice of human rights monitoring bodies, there are also several cases involving structural weaknesses in the State *prison apparatus*. The Inter-American Court has held that, in some cases, the objective and structural deficiencies of prisons or other detention institutions in a given State constituted a violation of the right to life protected by the American Convention. For example, in the "*Juvenile Reeducation Institute*" case,[81] the Court found such violations by Paraguay, since that Institute did not constitute an adequate infrastructure to host the internees, had an overpopulation of inmates, unhealthy cells and insufficient toilets, and finally did not provide adequate food and medical care.[82] The Court therefore concluded that:

> [. . .] the subhuman and degrading conditions of detention to which all the inmates of the Institute were exposed, necessarily entails an effect on their mental health, with unfavourable repercussions on the psychological development of their life and personal integrity.[83]

Lastly, there are some cases involving structural weaknesses in the State *sanitary system*. These are found especially in the case-law of the European Court of Human Rights. One can cite, for example, the case of *Cyprus v. Turkey* of 2001.[84] Cyprus claimed before the Court, inter alia, that the Turkish authorities in Northern Cyprus

---

[78] ECtHR, *Perk and Others v. Turkey*, para. 54: "The obligation of the State [. . .] entails the primary duty to ensure the right to life by establishing a legal and administrative framework to deter crimes against the person, supported by an enforcement mechanism designed to prevent, suppress and punish violations" (my translation).

[79] IACtHR, *Velásquez Rodríguez v. Honduras.*

[80] IACtHR, *Godínez Cruz v. Honduras.*

[81] IACtHR, *"Juvenile Reeducation Institute" v. Paraguay.*

[82] *Ibidem*, paras. 165–166.

[83] *Ibidem*, para. 168.

[84] ECtHR, *Cyprus v. Turkey*, Judgment of 10 May 2001.

had failed to provide adequate medical services to many hundreds of Greek and Maronite Cypriots still living in the northern part of Cyprus, thereby violating the right to life under Article 2 of the European Convention. The Court concluded that there was no breach of Article 2; but, albeit cautiously, it said that a State may be responsible for a breach of the right to life, if its medical system fails to provide an individual with life-saving medical care that the State promised to make generally available.[85] In a subsequent judgment, in the *Calvelli and Ciglio* case,[86] already mentioned, the Strasbourg Court stated that, even when medical care is entrusted to private services, the State maintains a supervisory function; and that the positive obligations of the State under Article 2 of the European Convention require the State taking appropriate measures to protect the lives of patients on hospitals.[87] In essence, in the case-law of the European Court, an obligation is emerging for the State to have a health system that guarantees at least a minimum level of preventive protection of the right to life.[88]

Finally, the *third obligation of prevention* for the State, probably the most important, is to take the *concrete measures* that are required, in each and every situation, to prevent violations of the right to life. This is a typical obligation of due diligence, since a large part of the preventive activities required of the State authorities, in given concrete circumstances, are not by their nature suitable to guarantee a secure result, but are instead subject to alea. Therefore, the State's obligation is usually only an obligation to use due diligence or its "best efforts" to achieve a certain result, in this case preventing violations of the right to life. This applies both to the activities that the State must carry out to prevent violations of that right by State agents and, even more clearly, to the activities aimed at preventing such violations by private persons.[89]

The practice of international monitoring bodies, regarding this obligation to take concrete measures to prevent violations of the right to life, is very rich. It mainly concerns the following aspects: (*a*) prevention of criminal acts by private individuals; (*b*) prevention and control of the lethal use of force by State agents; (*c*) prevention of serious damage to health.

---

[85]According to the Court: "[...] an issue may arise under Article 2 of the Convention where it is shown that the authorities of a Contracting State put an individual's life at risk through the denial of health care which they have undertaken to make available to the population generally" (para. 219).

[86]ECtHR, *Calvelli and Ciglio v. Italy*.

[87]*Ibidem*, para. 49.

[88]See also ECtHR, *G. N. and Others v. Italy*, para. 64; *Lopes de Sousa Fernandes v. Portugal*, paras. 186–188.

[89]See HRCtee, General Comment No. 31, 26 May 2004, para. 8: "[...] the positive obligations on States Parties to ensure Covenant rights will only be fully discharged if individuals are protected by the State, not just against violations of Covenant rights by its agents, but also against acts committed by private persons or entities [...] There may be circumstances in which a failure to ensure Covenant rights [...] would give rise to violations by States Parties of those rights, as a result of States Parties' permitting or *failing to take appropriate measures or to exercise due diligence to prevent*, punish, investigate or redress the harm caused by such acts by private persons or entities" (emphasis added).

The first aspect (i.e. the obligation of the State to take preventive measures to protect the lives of individuals from criminal acts committed by other individuals) is placed, from a systematic point of view, within the framework of the classic responsibility of the State in relation to acts of private individuals, where the failure of State organs to take preventive measures is causally linked to the injuries materially committed by those individuals. This is one of the areas in which, traditionally, the lack of due diligence on the part of State organs, in carrying out those preventive activities that were required by the concrete circumstances, plays an important role.

In most cases, preventive activities must be carried out by the *State police forces*. In the case-law of the European Convention, the *leading case* in this matter is the already mentioned *Osman* case. In its judgment, the European Court ruled that Article 2 of the Convention not only obliges the State to have criminal legislation and a prevention apparatus, but:

> [...] may also imply in certain well-defined circumstances a positive obligation on the authorities *to take preventive operational measures* to protect an individual whose life is at risk from the criminal acts of another individual.[90]

The Court has then clarified and limited the content of this obligation of prevention, with some important statements, which have subsequently been taken up in other cases, and which deserve to be widely reported:

> [f]or the Court [...] such an obligation must be interpreted in a way which does not impose an impossible or disproportionate burden on the authorities. Accordingly, not every claimed risk to life can entail for the authorities a Convention requirement to take operational measures to prevent that risk from materializing [...] In the opinion of the Court [...] it must be established to its satisfaction that the authorities knew or ought to have known at the time of the existence of a real and immediate risk to the life of an identified individual or individuals from the criminal acts of a third party and that they *failed to take measures within the scope of their powers* which, judged reasonably, might have been expected to avoid that risk [...] it is sufficient for an applicant to show that the authorities *did not do all that could be reasonably expected of them to avoid* a real and immediate risk to life of which they have or ought to have knowledge.[91]

The obligation of the police forces to protect persons subject to threats to their lives has also been taken up by the European Court in the *Kaya*, *Kiliç* and *Akkoç* cases.[92] In these cases, as already seen, the European Court found that there were structural shortcomings in the State criminal prevention apparatus, but found that the Turkish authorities had *also* breached a more specific duty of care in the concrete preventive measures required by the actual circumstances.

The obligation to prevent injury to the right to life by criminal acts committed by third parties is not only incumbent on the police, but also on other State authorities.

---

[90]ECtHR, *Osman v. UK*, para. 115 (emphasis added).

[91]*Ibidem*, para. 116 (emphasis added).

[92]ECtHR, *Kaya v. Turkey*; *Kiliç v. Turkey*; *Akkoç v. Turkey*.

In particular, the *prison authorities* have a responsibility to protect the lives of prisoners in certain situations of real and imminent risk, such as the danger of criminal acts by other prisoners.[93] A similar situation occurred in the *Edwards* case,[94] in which the Strasbourg Court reaffirmed the principles on the obligation of prevention already established in the *Osman* case, but added that this obligation is weightier when it is in favor of persons under State custody.[95]

The second aspect of the practice, relating to the obligation to prevent violations of the right to life, includes cases in which arbitrary deprivation of life by *security forces*, which have made improper use of lethal force, has been complained of. These are usually anti-terrorist operations or actions against revolts or riots and, sometimes, even military interventions conducted by a State in the framework of a civil war. In these cases, as is evident, it is not a matter of responsibility of the State in relation to acts of private individuals, but of "direct" responsibility of the State deriving from the conduct, active or omissive, of the same security forces which have acted or from the omission of measures of prudence and caution by the superior authorities which have planned and organized such operations. To be precise, the conduct of security forces should be kept separate from that of their superior authorities; but the practice of the human rights monitoring bodies often tends to confuse the two and bring them back into the conceptual framework of lack of due diligence.

As far as *anti-terrorist operations* are concerned, the leading case, in the jurisprudence of the European Court of Human Rights, is the already mentioned *McCann* case, concerning an anti-terrorist operation conducted by British military security forces. The judgment is famous because the Court for the first time clearly stated the principle that the right to life requires, for its effective protection, the positive obligation of the State to take all appropriate measures to prevent injury to that right. The Court found a breach of that obligation, due to a lack of diligence, both in the monitoring and organization of the security operation and in the concrete manner in which the action was carried out:

> [t]heir reflex action in this vital respect lacks the degree of caution in the use of firearms to be expected from law enforcement personnel in a democratic society, even when dealing with dangerous terrorist suspects, and stands in marked contrast to the *standard of care* reflected in the instructions in the use of firearms by the police which had been drawn to their attention [. . .] This failure by the authorities also suggests *a lack of appropriate care* in the control and organisation of the arrest operation.[96]

---

[93]It should be noted that prison authorities have an obligation to protect prisoners' lives even in the face of dangers arising from serious health problems. See ECtHR, *Velikova v. Bulgaria* and *Anguelova v. Bulgaria*.

[94]ECtHR, *Edwards Paul and Audrey v. UK*, paras. 54–55.

[95]*Ibidem*, para. 56: "In the context of prisoners, the Court has had previous occasions to emphasize that persons in custody are in a vulnerable position and that the authorities are under a duty to protect them. It is incumbent on the State to account for any injuries suffered in custody, which obligation is particularly stringent where that individual dies".

[96]ECtHR, *McCann and others v. UK*, para. 212 (emphasis added).

Another well-known example, in which the European Court found a violation of the right to life in connection with anti-terrorist operations conducted by State security forces, is the *Ergi* case.[97] Here too, the Strasbourg Court found that there had been negligence in the planning and conduct of security force operations.[98]

With regard to State *operations against riots or revolts*, the same principles apply. One may recall, for example, the judgment of the Inter-American Court of Human Rights in the *Neira Alegría* case,[99] which discussed, among other things, the proportionality of the use of force by the Peruvian military authorities in countering an uprising in the "San Juan Bautista" prison. The Court held that the force used was disproportionate to the actual danger and that no precautionary measures had been taken to reduce the cost of human lives in suppressing the uprising.[100]

Finally, there are some important cases involving real *military operations* conducted by a State during a civil war. In this regard, the cases of *Isayeva, Yusupova and Bazayeva v. Russia*[101] and *Isayeva v. Russia*,[102] concerning attacks by Russian military aircraft on civilians during the armed conflict in Chechnya, are famous. The European Court of Human Rights held that Russia had violated Article 2 of the Convention on the right to life, because military operations had not been planned and monitored with due diligence to minimize any risk to the lives of the civilian population. The Court, inter alia, stated:

> [. . .] it is necessary to examine whether the operation was planned and controlled by the authorities so as to minimise, to the greatest extent possible, recourse to lethal force. The authorities must take *appropriate care* to ensure that any risk to life is minimised. The Court must also examine whether the authorities were not *negligent* in their choice of action.[103]

The third aspect of this practice concerns cases involving the obligations of the State to prevent, by means of concrete measures, serious *damage to the health* of persons likely to cause their death. In the case-law of the Strasbourg Court, two interesting examples are the *Velikova*[104] and *Anguelova*[105] cases, both relating to the

[97]ECtHR, *Ergi v. Turkey*, paras. 79–81 and 86.

[98]It was an anti-terrorism ambush conducted in 1993 in Southeast Turkey, during which the applicant's daughter was accidentally killed by a gunshot. In particular, the Court said: "[. . .] the responsibility of the State is not confined to circumstances where there is significant evidence that misdirected fire from agents of the State has killed a civilian. It may also be engaged where they *fail to take all feasible precautions* in the choice of means and methods of a security operation [. . .] Having regard to the above considerations, the Court finds that the Turkish authorities failed to protect Havva Ergi's right to life on account of *the defects in the planning and conduct* of the security forces' operation" (emphasis added).

[99]IACtHR, *Neira Alegría et al. v. Peru.*

[100]*Ibidem*, para. 62.

[101]ECtHR, *Isayeva, Yusupova and Bazayeva v. Russia*, Judgment of 24 February 2005.

[102]ECtHR, *Isayeva v. Russia*, Judgment of 24 February 2005.

[103]*Ibidem*, para. 175 (emphasis added).

[104]ECtHR, *Velikova v. Bulgaria.*

[105]ECtHR, *Anguelova v. Bulgaria.*

death of persons arrested or detained by police authorities who failed to provide or request urgent medical treatment for such persons. In both judgments, the Court ruled that the authorities had been negligent and that their omission had violated the State's obligation to protect the lives of the people in its custody.[106] One can also mention the case *L.C.B. v. UK*, which concerned the possible failure of the UK authorities to prevent the risk to a person's health arising from nuclear substances. Before the Strasbourg Court, the applicant argued that the UK Government had violated the right to life by failing to warn his father about the possible health risk caused by his participation in certain nuclear tests carried out by the Royal Air Force on a Pacific island, and by failing to monitor the levels of radiation to which he was exposed. The Court, while considering that, in the present case, there had been no breach of Article 2 of the European Convention, stated that:

> The Court's task is [. . .] to determine whether, given the circumstances of the case, the State did all that could have been required of it to prevent the applicant's life from being avoidably put at risk.[107]

Finally, there are also some interesting cases concerning the obligations of the State to prevent serious damage to health resulting from dangerous activities or environmental disasters.[108]

14.1.3.3 Positive Obligations of Repression

As already said, the effective protection of the right to life requires the State not only to prevent, but also to repress violations. Within the framework of the *general* obligation of repression, two more specific obligations can be distinguished, in the following logical order: (*a*) that of investigating alleged violations of the right to life; (*b*) that of prosecuting and punishing those responsible. These two obligations are often defined, in the language of the human rights monitoring bodies, as "positive procedural" obligations[109] and are deemed necessary to ensure compliance with the obligations defined as "substantive".

The importance of these two obligations is clearly confirmed by UN General Assembly Resolution 60/147 of 16 December 2005, which adopted a set of principles and guidelines on the rights of victims of serious violations of human rights and humanitarian law.[110] Principle I states, among others, that:

---

[106] See also, more recently, ECtHR, *Panaitescu v. Romania*, paras. 27–38.

[107] ECtHR, *L.C.B. v. UK*, para. 36.

[108] See, e.g., ECtHR, *Öneryildiz v. Turkey*, para. 90; *Budayeva and Others v. Russia*, paras. 129–137.

[109] See above, Sect. 4.3.3.

[110] *Basic Principles and Guidelines on the Right to a Remedy and Reparation for Victims of Gross Violations of International Human Rights Law and Serious Violations of International Humanitarian Law*, GA Res. 60/147 of 16 December 2005, Annex, Art. II (3)(b).

> The obligation to respect, ensure respect for and implement international human rights law [...] includes, inter alia, the duty to: [...] investigate violations effectively, promptly, thoroughly and impartially and, where appropriate, take action against those allegedly responsible in accordance with domestic and international law.

I will examine separately the obligation to investigate and the obligation to prosecute and punish, in relation to the right to life.

The purpose of the State's obligation to investigate is to establish the facts relating to the alleged violation of the right to life and to identify, search and apprehend the possible culprits. It includes, in turn, two more specific obligations that are of a different nature: (*a*) the obligation of the State to have an adequate administrative and judicial apparatus to investigate violations of the right to life; (*b*) the obligation of the State to take the concrete and effective measures of investigation that are required by the circumstances.

The obligation of the State to possess an *administrative and judicial apparatus of investigation*, capable in the abstract of achieving the above mentioned purpose, is an immediate obligation of result. In fact, in the contemporary world, every State must have such an apparatus and certainly cannot limit itself to an effort of diligence to obtain it.

The case-law of the European Court of Human Rights includes many cases in which this obligation of States comes to the fore. Among others, one can mention the *Güleç*, *Oğur*, *Akkoç* and *Perk* cases.[111] In all these cases, in which Turkey was defendant, the Court concluded that the Turkish State had violated its obligation to investigate the circumstances and those responsible for certain killings, due to an *institutional* lack of independence on the part of the investigating bodies. This lack of independence was not regarded by the Court as a contingent factor, but as a structural factor of the State apparatus. In the *Oğur* case, for example, the Court said:

> At all events, serious doubts arise as to the ability of the administrative authorities concerned to carry out an independent investigation, as required by Article 2 of the Convention. The Court notes that the investigating officer appointed by the governor was a gendarmerie lieutenant-colonel and, as such, was subordinate to the same chain of command as the security forces he was investigating [...].[112]

Also in the *Kelly* case,[113] the European Court declared that the State authorities conducting the investigation must be institutionally and practically independent. The case-law of the Inter-American human rights system confirms, in a number of cases, the existence of the State's obligation to have adequate administrative and judicial machinery for investigation. Among others, mention can be made of the judgments

[111] ECtHR, *Güleç v. Turkey*, para. 77; *Oğur v. Turkey*, para. 88; *Akkoç v. Turkey*, paras. 87–88; *Perk and Others v. Turkey*, para. 55.

[112] ECtHR, *Oğur*, para. 91.

[113] ECtHR, *Kelly and Others v. UK*, paras. 95 and 114.

of the Inter-American Court in the *Velásquez Rodríguez*[114] and *Godínez Cruz*[115] cases and the decision of the Inter-American Commission in the *Garay Hermosilla* case.[116] In the practice of the Human Rights Committee, one can cite the *Rodríguez* case.[117]

The second specific obligation of the State, within the scope of investigation activities, is to take, on a case-by-case basis, *concrete measures to investigate* violations of the right to life. In fact, it is clear that the State cannot limit itself to having a suitable investigation apparatus; it must make it work when necessary and in a rapid and efficient manner, all the more so when there has been a violation of the right to life. This is usually an obligation of due diligence, because normally the concrete activities aimed at investigating the facts, and searching for and apprehending the persons guilty of the violations, are subject to alea as to their outcome. Therefore, the State is only required to make "best efforts" in its investigative activities.

On the obligation to take concrete measures to investigate violations of the right to life, the bodies of the European Convention on Human Rights have developed an extensive case-law. The first important example is the aforementioned *McCann* case, where the European Court has set out the principle that the State's obligation to guarantee the right to life, in order to be effective, also implies a procedural obligation to investigate possible violations of that right:

> The obligation to protect the life [. . .] requires by implication that there should be some form of effective official investigation when individuals have been killed as a result of the use of force by, *inter alios*, agents of the State.[118]

In a number of subsequent cases, the Court has made it clear that the State's obligation to investigate exists even when there is uncertainty about the responsibility of State agents for the killing[119] and when the perpetrators are mere private individuals.[120] The Court has also clarified the content and nature of the obligation to investigate in the *Kelly* case:

> The investigation must also be effective in the sense that it is capable of leading to a determination of whether the use of force used in such cases was or was not justified in the circumstances [. . .] and to the identification and punishment of those responsible. This is not an obligation of result, but of means. The authorities must have taken the reasonable steps available to them to secure the evidence concerning the incident [. . .].[121]

---

[114] IACtHR, *Velásquez Rodríguez v. Honduras*.

[115] IACtHR, *Godínez Cruz v. Honduras*.

[116] IACmHR, *Garay Hermosilla et al. v. Chile*.

[117] HRCtee, *Rodríguez v. Uruguay*.

[118] ECtHR, *McCann and Others v. UK*, para. 161.

[119] ECtHR, *Ergi v. Turkey*, para. 82.

[120] ECtHR, *Yaşa v. Turkey*, para. 100.

[121] ECtHR, *Kelly and Others v. UK*, para. 96. See also ECtHR, *Mahmut Kaya v. Turkey*, para. 108.

The Commission and the Inter-American Court have also produced extensive case-law on the obligation to investigate violations of the right to life. It follows the principles applied by the Strasbourg bodies. The best known examples are, once again, the *Velásquez Rodríguez* and *Godínez Cruz* cases. In both cases, the Inter-American Court made the following specific observations:

> The duty to investigate, like the duty to prevent, is not breached merely because the investigation does not produce a satisfactory result. Nevertheless, it must be undertaken in a serious manner and not as a mere formality preordained to be ineffective. An investigation must have an objective and be assumed by the State as its own legal duty, not as a step taken by private interests that depends upon the initiative of the victim or his family or upon their offer of proof, without an effective search for the truth by the government [. . .].[122]

These principles were then taken up by the Court in several subsequent cases. Finally, the same conclusions can be drawn from the Human Rights Committee's practice. The *Mojica, Laureano* and *Bautista de Arellana* cases[123] can be mentioned.

I now come to the second obligation of repression. If the investigation of violations of the right to life and the search for the alleged perpetrators is successful, the State has the *obligation to try and possibly punish* those responsible or allegedly responsible. This is a natural corollary of the general obligation of repression. In my view, this is an immediate obligation of result, since every State must have a judicial system that is capable of ensuring that human rights violations are ascertained and that criminal justice is administered, both in general and abstract terms and in individual cases.[124] Therefore, the bringing to trial of those responsible for violations of the right to life, whether they are State officials or private individuals, cannot be an activity that is subject to aleatory factors.

Furthermore, it should be noted that the State's obligation to try and punish offenders is not only a "procedural" obligation, which serves to ensure the effectiveness of the substantive right to life; it is also closely linked to the State's obligation to ensure that victims have access to justice for the assessment of violations. This close connection is also reflected in the above-mentioned UN General Assembly Resolution 60/147, which, immediately after indicating the obligation of States to take action against those responsible for serious human rights violations, also proclaims their obligation to give victims "equal and effective right to justice".[125]

---

[122]IACtHR, *Velásquez Rodríguez*, para. 177; *Godínez Cruz*, para. 188.

[123]HRCtee, *Mojica v. Dominican Republic*, para. 5.5; *Laureano v. Peru*, para. 8.3; *Bautista de Arellana v. Colombia*, para. 8.6.

[124]See Pisillo Mazzeschi (2008), pp. 352–365.

[125]*Basic Principles and Guidelines on the Right to a Remedy and Reparation for Victims of Gross Violations of International Human Rights Law and Serious Violations of International Humanitarian Law*, Principle VII, para. 11(a).

The existence of the obligation to try and punish those allegedly responsible for violations of the right to life is clearly confirmed by the practice of human rights supervisory bodies.[126]

14.1.3.4 Positive Obligations Concerning Reparation

Finally, the State has an obligation to make reparation to victims of violations of the right to life.

This obligation is the necessary complement to the other obligations of the State that I have described so far: those of prevention, those of investigation and those of judicial assessment and of punishment of the guilty. It is clear that, in the case of a lack of prevention of arbitrary killing, the identification of those responsible through the activities of investigation and the assessment of violations through the judicial function do not, in themselves, make much sense if, in the end, the victims of violations and/or their relatives do not obtain reparation. This conclusion is unavoidable, even from a strictly legal point of view, if one believes, as I do, that individuals are now *direct addressees* of international human rights norms, including the secondary norms on reparation of the offence.[127] It follows that those individuals who are victims of human rights violations have a true right to reparation, which derives *directly* from international law.[128]

This conclusion is confirmed by the aforementioned Principles on the Rights of Victims of Serious Violations of Human Rights and Humanitarian Law. Principle VII (*Victims' rights to remedies*) states that remedies for such violations include, inter alia:

> [. . .] the victim's right to the following as provided for under international law:
> a) Equal and effective right to justice
> b) Adequate, effective and prompt reparation for harm suffered
> c) Access to relevant information concerning violations and reparation mechanisms.

That said, the nature of the obligation to provide reparation for violations of the right to life must now be clarified. On this point it is difficult to give a unitary response, because reparation, in international law in general as well as in matters of human rights violations, can take three different forms: (*a*) monetary compensation; (*b*) restitution (*restitutio in integrum*); (*c*) satisfaction.

The obligation of the State responsible for the violation to give monetary compensation to the relatives of the victims, and possibly to other States, is an immediate obligation of result. In fact, the payment of a sum of money is not subject to alea.

Instead, the situation is more complex as regards *restitutio in integrum*, i.e. the restoration of the factual and legal situation existing before the breach. Restitution is

---

[126]See Bestagno (2003), pp. 200–214 and the practice cited therein.

[127]See above, Sects. 2.3.2, 4.1.5, 7.2.2.

[128]See Pisillo Mazzeschi (2004b) and Bartolini (2009). Cf. also ICJ, *Legal Consequences of the Construction of a Wall*, paras. 147, 152–153.

in principle the preferred and primary form of reparation in international law; but, in the case of a violation of the right to life, it is unfortunately impossible. One could perhaps envisage, as a particular form of restitution, the abolishment of a law providing for the death penalty or an administrative measure cancelling the execution of the death penalty imposed on a person. In such cases, the State's obligation to remedy a violation of the right to life would be an obligation of result.

Finally, there is the obligation of the State to repair the offence through satisfaction. This is a form of reparation used especially for moral damages, and it may consist, in international law, in the recognition of the violation, or expressions of regret or official apologies or other forms appropriate to the circumstances.[129] Satisfaction can sometimes involve an obligation of result and sometimes an obligation of due diligence.[130]

In any case, it should be noted that satisfaction, which in traditional international law is of little relevance, can instead play an important role in violations of human rights, and especially fundamental rights such as the right to life. Indeed, the relatives of victims of arbitrary deprivation of life may be interested, rather than in monetary compensation for damages, in forms of moral satisfaction. In this respect, the case-law of the Inter-American Court of Human Rights is very interesting. This Court has made a habit of imposing on the State held responsible for violations of the right to life a detailed series of satisfaction measures, such as, for example, its official apology,[131] the publication of the judgment condemning the State in widely circulated newspapers,[132] the construction of statues or other memorials,[133] the dedication of a school or hospital to the memory of the victims,[134] and other symbolic acts of this kind. In these cases, satisfaction is an obligation of result.

[129]See ILC, *Draft Articles on Responsibility of States for Internationally Wrongful Acts*, 1 August 2001, Art. 37.

[130]The payment of a symbolic sum of money, for example, is an obligation of result, while the obligation of the State to search the bodies of the victims or that of taking appropriate measures to prevent the repetition of offences are due diligence obligations. See Pisillo Mazzeschi (2008), pp. 370–372 and 423–424 and the case-law cited therein.

[131]IACtHR, *Bámaca-Velásquez*, para. 84; *Barrios Altos*, Judgment of 30 November 2001, para. 44.

[132]IACtHR, *Cantoral Benavides*, Judgment of 3 December 2001, para. 79; *Bámaca-Velásquez*, para. 84.

[133]IACtHR, *The "Street Children"*, Judgment of 26 May 2001, para. 103.

[134]IACtHR, *Trujillo-Oroza*, para. 122; *Aloeboetoe et al.*, Judgment of 10 September 1993, para. 116.

14.2 Prohibition of Torture and Inhuman or Degrading Treatment or Punishment

14.2.1 Norms

The prohibition of torture and inhuman or degrading treatment or punishment is set out in Article 5 of the Universal Declaration of Human Rights in the following terms:

> No one shall be subjected to torture or to cruel, inhuman or degrading treatment or punishment.

A similar formula is contained in Article 3 of the European Convention, Article 5 (2) of the American Convention and Article 4 of the EU Charter of Fundamental Rights. The African Charter (Art. 5) also contains the same prohibition. Article 7 of the Covenant on Civil and Political Rights establishes a similar prohibition and adds that:

> [...] no one shall be subjected without his free consent to medical or scientific experimentation.

More complex is the rule contained in the Arab Charter (Art. 8), which also provides for the obligations of the States Parties to prevent and suppress such abuses and to provide reparation for the victims.

The prohibition in question is laid down not only in the above-mentioned general human rights treaties, but also in a number of sectoral and specific treaties, among which one should especially note the UN Convention against Torture and Other Cruel, Inhuman or Degrading Treatment or Punishment of 1984,[135] which binds more than 150 States, and the European Convention for the Prevention of Torture and Inhuman and Degrading Treatment of 1987.[136] In addition, torture is prohibited by other sectoral human rights treaties (e.g. the Convention on the Rights of the Child[137]) and numerous international humanitarian[138] and criminal[139] law norms. Of course, human rights treaties and international criminal law treaties must be kept conceptually separate.[140]

---

[135]Convention against Torture and Other Cruel, Inhuman or Degrading Treatment or Punishment (CAT), 10 December 1984. See above, Sect. 10.4.2.6.

[136]European Convention for the Prevention of Torture and Inhuman or Degrading Treatment or Punishment (ECPT), 26 November 1987. See above, Sect. 11.1.3.1.

[137]CRC, Art. 37.

[138]See, e.g., GC, Common Art. 3(1)(a); GC III, Arts. 13, 17, 87, 89, 99.

[139]See, e.g., Rome Statute, Arts. 7(1)(f) and 8(2)(a)(ii).

[140]The former treaties impose the prohibition of torture on a State against individuals and other States (*erga omnes* obligation) and their breach produces international responsibility of the State. Instead, the treaties of international criminal law impose the prohibition of torture on individuals, and their breach produces international criminal responsibility of the individuals themselves. See below, Sect. 14.3.

Therefore, the prohibition of torture and inhuman or degrading treatment or punishment is firmly established in conventional international law. But it is commonly believed that this prohibition is also enshrined in a general norm of international law.[141] It is more difficult to determine whether this norm has the nature of *jus cogens*. International case-law seems to favor the peremptory nature of the prohibition of torture and inhuman treatment or punishment, not only in the case of abusive practices but also in the case of isolated acts.[142] More uncertain seems to me the peremptory nature of the prohibition of degrading treatment or punishment.

14.2.2 Content of the Prohibition

Turning now to the content and nature of the prohibition of torture and inhuman or degrading treatment or punishment (and the corresponding right not to suffer such abuses), it should be noted at once that the prohibition is absolute in nature, because it does not allow exceptions, restrictions or limitations, not even as a result of other potentially conflicting human rights, such as the need to protect an individual's life.

Furthermore, the prohibition is non-derogable in time of emergency; that is, it cannot be suspended by the State even in situations of war, emergency, national security or public danger. This is expressly laid down in the European Convention (Art. 15(2)), the American Convention (Art. 27(2)), and the Covenant on Civil and Political Rights (Art. 4(2)). These rules, by providing for clauses derogating from rights in cases of public emergency, expressly exclude the prohibition in question from the operation of these clauses.

The two characteristics, of "absoluteness" and "non-derogation in time of emergency", of the prohibition also result from international case-law.[143] One can cite, among others, the judgment of the Inter-American Court in the *Bueno Alves* case.[144]

That said, the legal concept of "torture" and its differences with the concepts of "inhuman or degrading treatment or punishment" must now be examined in greater depth.

14.2.2.1 The Notion of Torture

The Covenant on Civil and Political Rights and the main regional human rights treaties, as seen, prohibit torture but do not contain a precise and detailed definition of this notion. This is probably due both to the general nature of these treaties and to

---

[141] According to some authors, it is a customary norm, while, according to others, it is a general principle of law recognized *in foro domestico*.

[142] See ICTY, *Furundžija*, paras. 153–154; ECtHR, *Al-Adsani*, para. 61; House of Lords, "*Pinochet III*", opinion of Lord Browne-Wilkinson (para. 198) and opinion of Lord Hope of Craighead (para. 247); Id., *Jones and Mitchell*, para. 43; IACtHR, *Maritza Urrutia*; IACtHR, *Goiburú*; ICJ, *Questions relating to the Obligation to Prosecute*, para. 99.

[143] See Citroni and Scovazzi (2013), pp. 325–328 and the judgments cited therein.

[144] IACtHR, *Bueno Alves v. Argentina*, para. 76.

the fact that it was preferred not to freeze the notion over time, in order to avoid excluding a dynamic interpretation of it.[145]

By contrast, the UN Convention against Torture of 1984, mentioned above, contains a detailed legal definition of the concept of torture. Article 1(1) of this Convention provides:

> For the purpose of this Convention, the term 'torture' means any act by which severe pain or suffering, whether physical or mental, is intentionally inflicted on a person for such purposes as obtaining from him or a third person information or a confession, punishing him for an act he or a third person has committed, or intimidating or coercing him or a third person, or for any reason based on discrimination of any kind, when such pain or suffering is inflicted by or at the instigation of or with the consent or acquiescence of a public official or other person acting in an official capacity. It does not include pain or suffering arising only from, inherent in or incidental to lawful sanctions.

It follows from this definition that torture consists in the fact that a State official, or a private individual with instigation, consent or acquiescence of a State official, intentionally inflicts severe physical or mental suffering on a person for a number of specific purposes; to the exclusion of suffering that is the inevitable consequence of a legitimate punishment. It should be noted that this definition, by limiting torture only to acts committed, instigated or tolerated by State organs, is very restrictive from the point of view of the perpetrators of the violation.

Instead, the notion of torture, which emerges overall from the practice of the Human Rights Committee and the regional monitoring bodies on human rights, is broader, since it also includes acts of torture committed by private individuals.[146] International criminal law is moving in the same direction, especially in the case-law of the Tribunals for the Former Yugoslavia and for Rwanda.[147] Even the definition of torture contained in the Statute of the International Criminal Court does not limit torture to acts committed by State officials. However, the latter tendency towards a broad interpretation should not be overestimated, because it may also result from the different function of international criminal law, which aims to punish individuals and not States.

In any case, in accordance with international practice, in order for the prohibition of torture to operate, it is necessary to exceed a *minimum threshold of severity* in the suffering inflicted on the victim. The case-law of the European Court of Human Rights defines torture as a particularly cruel treatment, inflicting severe suffering on the victim.[148] Moreover, this case-law has evolved in the sense that the Court has over time lowered the minimum threshold of severity required to comply with the

---

[145] See Zagrebelsky et al. (2016), p. 161, with reference to Article 3 of the European Convention on Human Rights.

[146] See, e.g., IACtHR, *López Soto v. Venezuela*, paras. 137–150. See also Kälin and Künzli (2019), p. 311.

[147] See, e.g., ICTY, *Kunarac*, Judgment of 22 February 2001, para. 496; *Kvočka*, Judgment of 2 November 2001, paras. 137–141, and other judgments cited by Focarelli (2013), p. 89.

[148] See, e.g., ECtHR, *Labita v. Italy*, para. 113 ff.; *Cestaro v. Italy*, paras. 164–176.

notion of torture.[149] This is due to a dynamic interpretation of the European Convention, which leads to increasing protection of fundamental human rights. In 1978, for example, the Court, in the case of *Ireland v. UK*,[150] not following the Commission report, decided that certain interrogation techniques used by British security forces against detainees accused of terrorist acts in Ireland[151] did not constitute torture, but only inhuman and degrading treatment. The Court would now probably classify such abuses as acts of torture. Consider, for example, that the Court in 1999, in the *Selmouni* case, characterized as torture a series of ill-treatments carried out by French agents against a foreigner in custody prior to deportation; and stated that:

> certain acts which were classified in the past as 'inhuman and degrading treatment' as opposed to 'torture' could be classified differently in the future.[152]

Then the Court added:

> [. . .] the increasingly high standard being required in the area of protection of human rights and fundamental liberties correspondingly and inevitably requires greater firmness in assessing breaches of the fundamental values of democratic societies.[153]

The Inter-American Court of Human Rights has also shown a similar trend towards a dynamic interpretation of the concept of torture. In the *Cantoral Benavides* case, for example, the Court cited with approval the jurisprudential developments of the European Court and said:

> [. . .] according to international standards for protection, torture can be inflicted not only via physical violence, but also through acts that produce severe physical, psychological or moral suffering in the victim [. . .] International jurisprudence has been developing the notion of psychological torture.[154]

Finally, the Human Rights Committee considered that the lack of medical or psychiatric care for prisoners, which had caused serious suffering, constituted inhuman treatment equivalent to torture.[155]

---

[149] Zagrebelsky et al. (2016), p. 162.

[150] ECtHR, *Ireland v. UK*, paras. 165–168.

[151] They consisted of keeping the inmates hooded, subjecting them to deafening noises, keeping them standing against the wall with their body weight on their fingers, depriving them of sleep, reducing food and water.

[152] ECtHR, *Selmouni v. France*, para. 101.

[153] *Ibidem*, para. 101 ff.

[154] IACtHR, *Cantoral Benavides*, Judgment of 18 August 2000, paras. 100–102. See also IACtHR, *Maritza Urrutia*, para. 91 ff.

[155] HRCtee, *Rouse v. The Philippines*, para. 7.8.

14.2.2.2 Differences Between Torture and Inhuman or Degrading Treatment or Punishment

As we have seen, human rights treaties usually contain a single provision prohibiting torture, inhuman treatment or punishment and degrading treatment or punishment. However, the differences between the three hypotheses, and also between the concepts of punishment and treatment, are not expressly defined. They must therefore be derived from the practice of international monitoring bodies, which is not always clear and unambiguous. The doctrine, in order to define these differences, has drawn two interpretative models from the practice: (*a*) the first is based on the levels of severity of suffering inflicted; (*b*) the second is founded on the aim pursued by those who violate the prohibition.[156]

The model based on the levels of severity of the suffering inflicted on the victim is the most traditional. According to this approach, torture is the most serious form of abuse, involving particularly harsh and cruel conduct on the part of the perpetrator, and producing a high degree of suffering for the victim. Inhuman treatment is a less serious form of abuse, but it can be qualified as inhuman because it still produces physical or mental suffering for the victim. It can be considered an abuse that is at an intermediate level between torture and degrading treatment. Finally, degrading treatment is at the lowest degree of severity. It consists of conduct that has the effect of deeply degrading or humiliating the victim, sometimes, but not always, even in front of other people. In essence, in this hypothesis, the suffering of the victim consists above all in the degradation and debasement of his dignity. The European Court, in the *Pretty* case, said:

> Where treatment humiliates or debases an individual, showing a lack of respect for, or diminishing, his or her human dignity, or arouses feelings of fear, anguish or inferiority capable of breaking an individual's moral and physical resistance, it may be characterised as degrading [. . .].[157]

This traditional model of distinguishing between the three forms of abuse, which dates back to the *Ireland v. UK* case,[158] has been maintained over time, especially by the European Court. For example, in the *Aksoy* case, the Court stated:

> In order to determine whether any particular form of ill-treatment should be qualified as torture, the Court must have regard to the distinction drawn in Article 3 [. . .] between this notion and that of inhuman or degrading treatment. As it has remarked before, this distinction would appear to have been embodied in the Convention to allow the special stigma of "torture" to attach only to deliberate inhuman treatment causing very serious and cruel suffering [. . .].[159]

---

[156] See, in particular, Kälin and Künzli (2019), pp. 312–314.

[157] ECtHR, *Pretty v. UK*, para. 52. See also ECtHR, *Jalloh v. Germany*, para. 68.

[158] ECtHR, *Ireland v. UK*, para. 167.

[159] ECtHR, *Aksoy v. Turkey*, para. 63. But in recent times the European Court has also given some space to the model that is based on the purpose of the abuse.

However, the interpretative model based on the levels of severity of the victim's suffering is not without problems, especially because it is often difficult to distinguish between these levels[160] and because different criteria can be used to qualify the severity of the abuse and suffering inflicted.[161]

The second interpretative model, to distinguish between torture, inhuman treatment or punishment and degrading treatment or punishment, is based on the aim pursued by the perpetrators. According to this view,[162] torture, in addition to being a conduct that produces serious physical or mental suffering, should be: (*a*) deliberate; and (*b*) have one of the purposes set out in Article 1 of the 1984 Convention against Torture; that is, to force the will of the victim to obtain information or confessions or to punish him. Degrading treatment or punishment, on the other hand, would occur when the purpose is to humiliate or degrade the victim. Finally, inhuman treatment would remain a more generic concept, encompassing abuses that produce serious physical or mental suffering: (*a*) caused in circumstances not covered by torture;[163] or (*b*) resulting from unlawful punishments. This second interpretative model is mainly applied by the Committee against Torture[164] and the most recent case-law of the Inter-American Court.[165]

But there are also some international monitoring bodies, such as the Human Rights Committee, which prefer not to attach great importance to the distinction between the three forms of abuse and simply to determine whether or not there has been a violation of the relevant provision of the Covenant.[166] In fact, from a practical point of view, this position makes sense, because the three abuses have the same legal consequences. However, the fact remains that the distinction is important from a theoretical point of view. Moreover, for the victim and his or her family, it may have a significant moral value that the State responsible and the material perpetrators of the abuse are affected by the strong stigma of torture rather than the weaker stigma of inhuman or degrading treatment.

Finally, it should be stressed again that not all cases of ill-treatment or behavior causing pain and suffering to people constitute breaches of the prohibitions on torture and inhuman or degrading treatment or punishment. The practice of international monitoring bodies is clear that, for such violations, a certain level of severity or intensity of the suffering caused must be reached. This level cannot be predetermined in general and in the abstract; it must be assessed in each specific case. The duration of the mistreatment, the harmful effects caused, the age and health of the victim, and other circumstances can be taken into account.

---

[160] Kälin and Künzli (2019), p. 312.

[161] Focarelli (2013), p. 139.

[162] See Rodley (1999), pp. 29 and 75; Kälin and Künzli (2019), pp. 312–313.

[163] For example, serious ill-treatment of prisoners or the mentally ill.

[164] On this point see Nowak and McArthur (2008), p. 51.

[165] See, e.g., IACtHR, *Bueno Alves*, para. 78 ff.

[166] See, e.g., HRCtee, *A. S. v. Nepal*, paras. 3.4 and 8.2.

14.2.2.3 Material Scope of the Prohibition: Main Abuses Prohibited in Practice

It is not possible to make a list of all abuses and mistreatments that are likely to be qualified as torture or inhuman or degrading treatment or punishment. I can only indicate, in summary, the main categories of situations that occur in the practice of human rights monitoring bodies. As we shall see, many of these situations concern ill-treatment of "vulnerable" people, such as prisoners, the mentally ill, and women.

A first category is *ill-treatment of detainees* and persons under arrest or in custody. People detained in prison retain, of course, their human rights, except those that are necessarily limited by the condition of detention.[167] Clearly, detention in itself cannot be considered unlawful mistreatment; but certain conditions of detention may be prohibited. Prison conditions, such as, for example, insufficient space or light or ventilation in the cells, may constitute inhuman or degrading treatment.[168] Personal searches of prisoners by prison guards can lead to degrading treatment. Absolute, and sometimes even relative, isolation may constitute inhuman treatment. Lack of medical care for sick or disabled prisoners or detainees with mental disorders can lead to inhuman or degrading treatment.[169] Force-feeding a detainee, when not necessary for his or her survival, may constitute torture. The execution of disciplinary measures in prison, if carried out with disproportionate force, may amount to inhumane treatment.

The practice of human rights monitoring bodies with regard to the treatment of prisoners is very extensive.[170] One of the most important judgments is that in the *Torreggiani* case, where the European Court stated that detainees may need special protection because of their situation of subjection to the authority of the State, and that therefore the State organs have:

> [. . .] une obligation positive qui consiste à s'assurer que tout prisonnier est détenu dans des conditions qui sont compatibles avec le respect de la dignité humaine, que les modalités d'exécution de la mesure ne soumettent pas l'intéressé à une détresse ou à une épreuve d'une intensité qui excède le niveau inévitable de souffrance inhérent à la détention [. . .].[171]

A second category of maltreatment is *abuse of mentally ill people.* These persons also are particularly vulnerable and therefore require special protection, because they are exposed to greater danger of being subjected to inhuman or degrading treatment. Indeed, a number of international instruments, albeit of a non-binding nature, have

---

[167] See, e.g., ECtHR, *Hirst v. UK (No. 2)*, paras. 69–70.

[168] See, e.g., ECtHR, *Sulejmanovic v. Italy*, para. 43; *Torreggiani and Others v. Italy*, para. 78.

[169] See, e.g., ECtHR, *Cara-Damiani v. Italy*, paras. 69–78.

[170] For an in-depth examination of the practice, see Citroni and Scovazzi (2013), pp. 353–382. See also, recently, ECtHR, *Provenzano v. Italy*, para. 147 ff.

[171] ECtHR, *Torreggiani and Others*, para. 65: "[. . .] a positive obligation to ensure that every prisoner is held in conditions that are compatible with respect for human dignity, that the manner in which the measure is carried out does not subject the person concerned to distress or hardship of an intensity that exceeds the inevitable level of suffering inherent in detention [. . .]" (my translation).

been adopted for the protection of these people, for example the *Principles for the protection of persons with mental illness*, approved by the UN General Assembly in 1991.[172]

The practice of human rights monitoring bodies confirms this approach.[173] The European Court of Human Rights has had to deal with many cases concerning the treatment of mentally ill people and has always stated that, for these people, a particular level of attention is necessary when assessing the existence of a violation of Article 3 of the European Convention. Among the various judgments,[174] one may note the *Keenan* case,[175] where the United Kingdom was condemned for lack of proper psychiatric supervision and care for a mentally ill and suicidal person. The Inter-American Court has also affirmed similar principles.[176] Finally, there is an interesting case decided by the African Commission,[177] which stated that Gambia's legislation on the mentally ill should be repealed because it was contrary to the prohibition on inhuman and degrading treatment.

A third category concerns *rape and sexual assault.*[178] The European Court held that rape is a form of torture since the 1997 judgment in the *Aydin* case.[179] This position has also been maintained in subsequent case-law.[180] The Commission and the Inter-American Court have also reached the same conclusions in some cases of rape and other forms of sexual violence. One can cite the *Raquel Martín de Mejía*,[181] *Miguel Castro*,[182] *Masacre de las Dos Erres*[183] and *Azul Rojas Marín*[184] cases. The practice of the African Commission follows the same principles.[185] Finally, it should be noted that the international criminal courts have developed interesting case-law on the crime of rape, which is equated with torture and considered, when the

---

[172]*Principles for the protection of persons with mental illness and the improvement of mental health care*, GA Res. 46/119 of 17 December 1991.

[173]See again Citroni and Scovazzi (2013), pp. 382–388.

[174]See ECtHR, *Herczegfalvy v. Austria*; *Rivière v. France*; *Filip v. Romania*; *Renolde v. France.*

[175]ECtHR, *Keenan v. UK.*

[176]IACtHR, *Ximenes Lopes v. Brasil.*

[177]ACmHPR, *Purohit and Moore v. Gambia.*

[178]See Citroni and Scovazzi (2013), pp. 341–350; Focarelli (2013), pp. 144–145.

[179]ECtHR, *Aydin v. Turkey*, paras. 83–86.

[180]See, e.g., ECtHR, *M.C. v. Bulgaria*; *Maslova and Nalbandov v. Russia*; *D.J. v. Croatia.*

[181]IACmHR, *Raquel Martín de Mejía v. Peru.*

[182]IACtHR, *Miguel Castro v. Peru*, paras. 310–312.

[183]IACtHR, *Masacre de las Dos Erres v. Guatemala*, paras. 139–141.

[184]IACtHR, *Azul Rojas Marín et al. v. Peru*, paras, 157–167.

[185]ACmHPR, *Malawi African Association and Others v. Mauritania*; *Institute for Human Rights and Development in Africa v. Guinea.*

conditions are met, as a crime against humanity. In this regard, one can mention the *Akayesu*,[186] *Delalić*,[187] *Furundžija*[188] and *Kunarac*[189] cases.

A fourth category is related to *excessive penalties and corporal punishment*. The European Court has ruled, for example, that the penalty of life imprisonment constitutes inhumane treatment where the applicable legislation excludes any possibility of release of the sentenced person;[190] and that a manifestly disproportionate penalty may constitute a violation of Article 3 of the European Convention.[191] On the question of corporal punishment,[192] the 1978 judgment in the *Tyrer* case is well known,[193] in which the European Court condemned the United Kingdom, establishing that the fustigation of a minor pupil as a punishment for assaulting another student was a degrading punishment within the meaning of Article 3 of the European Convention. The Inter-American Court, in the *Caesar* case,[194] stated that corporal punishment is now prohibited under international law and that the fustigation of an adult, naked and bound until he fainted, constitutes torture. The African Commission, in the *Doebbler* case,[195] described the penalty of flogging as a form of torture.

A fifth category of situations which recur in practice is given by the so-called "*extraordinary renditions*"; that is, those anti-terrorist measures which consist in the extra-judicial transfer of a person from one jurisdiction to another, for the purpose of detention and interrogation outside the normal legal system.[196] As has been appropriately noted in doctrine, extraordinary renditions constitute "a sort of secret circuit of torture by proxy which involves several States, linked by a relationship of complicity in the illicit act":[197] the State that organizes the circuit, the State that allows the victim to be captured in its territory, and the State that receives the victim and extorts the information by torture. It is clear that extraordinary renditions result in violations of many fundamental human rights, including, almost always, the prohibition of torture and inhuman and degrading treatment and the prohibition of arbitrary detention and enforced disappearance of people.[198]

---

[186]ICTR, *Akayesu*, Judgment of 2 September 1998, paras. 596–598.

[187]ICTY, *Delalić*, Judgment of 16 November 1998, para. 475.

[188]ICTY, *Furundžija*, Judgment of 10 December 1998, paras. 164–186.

[189]ICTY, *Kunarac*, Judgment of 12 June 2002, para. 185.

[190]ECtHR, *Kafkaris v. Cyprus*, paras. 95–99; *Vinter and Others v. UK*, paras. 103–118; *Öcalan v. Turkey (No. 2)*, Judgment of 18 March 2014, paras. 193–207.

[191]ECtHR, *Harkins and Edwards v. UK*, paras. 133–138.

[192]See Focarelli (2013), pp. 140–141.

[193]ECtHR, *Tyrer v. UK*, paras. 30–33.

[194]IACtHR, *Caesar v. Trinidad and Tobago*, para. 20.

[195]ACmHPR, *Curtis Francis Doebbler v. Sudan*, Decision of 4 May 2003, para. 42.

[196]See ECtHR, *Babar Ahmad and Others v. UK*.

[197]Citroni and Scovazzi (2013), p. 417.

[198]See below, Sects. 16.2 and 16.3.

Reports on the practice of extraordinary renditions have been prepared within the Council of Europe and the United Nations and numerous recommendations have been adopted by international bodies and organizations.[199] In the practice of human rights monitoring bodies, one can recall the *Alzery* case,[200] decided in 2006 by the Human Rights Committee, and the *Babar Ahmad* and *El-Masri* cases decided by the European Court.[201] In Italy, a well-known example of forced disappearance occurred in the *Abu Omar* case,[202] which gave rise to various rulings by domestic courts,[203] an intervention by the Italian Government which invoked the State secrecy defense, and then also a judgment by the European Court,[204] which ascertained numerous human rights violations by Italy.

Finally, it should be noted that other practices have been considered as violations of the prohibition of torture and inhuman or degrading treatment or punishment. Enforced sterilization, for example, was considered by the Strasbourg Court as a violation of Article 3 of the European Convention in some cases against Slovakia.[205] The disappearance of persons, accompanied by a lack of proper investigation by the authorities to find the missing persons, can also be considered as an inhuman treatment of family members of those persons. The European Court has reached this conclusion in some cases against Turkey and Ukraine.[206]

14.2.3 Obligations

The international norms on the prohibition of torture and inhuman or degrading treatment or punishment impose a number of obligations on States, which are similar to those already examined regarding the right to life. Thus, a distinction can be made between negative and positive obligations (of result and of due diligence). In addition, within the scope of positive obligations, those of prevention, repression and reparation can be identified. The analysis of these obligations will be brief, because the conceptual aspects of them have already been examined.

---

[199] For more details see Citroni and Scovazzi (2013), pp. 418–422.

[200] HRCtee, *Alzery v. Sweden.*

[201] ECtHR, *Babar Ahmad and Others v. UK*; *El-Masri v. FYRM.*

[202] There are numerous doctrinal contributions on the *Abu Omar* case. See Carpanelli (2013) and the doctrine cited therein on p. 316, notes 4 and 5.

[203] See, inter alia, Milan Court of Appeal, *Courtney et al.*; Id., *Abu Omar et al.*; Supreme Court of Cassation, *Nasr et al.*; Id., *Medero et al.*; Constitutional Court, Order No. 69 of 2013.

[204] ECtHR, *Nasr and Ghali v. Italy.*

[205] ECtHR, *V.C. v. Slovakia*; *N.B. v. Slovakia.*

[206] ECtHR, *Kurt v. Turkey*, para. 134; *Çakici v. Turkey*, para. 98; *Gongadze v. Ukraine*, para. 186.

14.2.3.1 Negative Obligations

The State has, first of all, the negative obligation to refrain, through its officials (even when they exceed their authority or contravene instructions),[207] from carrying out acts of torture or inflicting inhuman or degrading treatment or punishment.

With regard to this obligation, the practice of human rights monitoring bodies is very broad. In the jurisprudence of the European Convention, a classic example of the violation of negative obligations by a State is the aforementioned case of *Ireland v. UK*,[208] in which British security forces used five interrogation techniques against detainees suspected of being part of the IRA, which caused suffering to the victims. The European Court condemned the United Kingdom for violating the prohibition of inhuman treatment. In the more recent *Selmouni* case,[209] in which the applicant was subjected to very violent interrogations by French law enforcement authorities, the Court condemned France for acts of torture. In the case-law of the Inter-American system, reference can be made to the 1988 judgment of the Inter-American Court in the *Velásquez Rodríguez* case, in which the Court condemned Honduras for violation of Articles 7, 5 and 4, read in conjunction with Article 1(1), of the American Convention, and stated that:

> [...] under international law a State is responsible for the acts of its agents undertaken in their official capacity and for their omissions, even when those agents act outside the sphere of their authority or violate internal law.[210]

In certain circumstances, it may be difficult to obtain evidence of breaches of this obligation by the State. Examples include ill-treatment of persons in detention or custody. The practice of human rights monitoring bodies has often established that in such cases there is a reversal of the burden of proof: in the presence of physical signs of ill-treatment of persons in detention or custody, it is for the State to prove that such signs are not attributable to the conduct of its own officials.[211]

The obligation of States not to resort to torture and inhuman or degrading treatment or punishment is so important that it also entails, in certain circumstances, an obligation on States to prevent such abuses from being committed by other States and outside the territory or "jurisdiction" of the States themselves. In other words, there is also a negative obligation on States not to extradite, expel, return, or otherwise surrender a person to another State where there are reasonable grounds to believe that he or she may be subjected to such abuses. As already mentioned,[212] this interpretative development of the prohibition of torture has been influenced by

---

[207] See ILC *Draft Articles on Responsibility of States for Internationally Wrongful Acts*, Artt. 4–11.

[208] ECtHR, *Ireland v. UK*.

[209] ECtHR, *Selmouni v. France*.

[210] IACtHR, *Velásquez Rodríguez*, para. 170.

[211] See, inter alia, ECtHR *Aktaş v. Turkey*, para. 291; IACtHR *Juan Humberto Sánchez v. Honduras*, para. 100. See also Kälin and Künzli (2019), p. 334.

[212] See above, Sect. 14.1.3.1.

the principle of *non-refoulement* and has, in turn, ended up supplementing this principle.

In the case-law of the European Convention, this obligation was first stated in the well-known *Soering* case of 1989.[213] The plaintiff, a German citizen, was in prison in the United Kingdom awaiting extradition to the USA, where he was to be tried in the State of Virginia for aggravated murder, punishable by the death penalty. Mr Soering claimed that his extradition to the United States would result in his being sentenced and subjected in Virginia prisons to the so-called "death row phenomenon", which should be qualified as inhuman and degrading treatment prohibited by Article 3 of the Convention. The European Court accepted, in substance, that argument, stating that a State Party to the Convention must not extradite an individual if such a measure can produce, in a foreseeable manner, consequences contrary to Article 3. According to the Court:

> [. . .] It would hardly be compatible with the underlying values of the Convention [. . .] were a Contracting State knowingly to surrender a fugitive to another State where there were substantial grounds for believing that he would be in danger of being subjected to torture [. . .] this inherent obligation not to extradite also extends to cases in which the fugitive would be faced in the receiving State by a real risk of exposure to inhuman or degrading treatment or punishment [. . .].[214]

The principles established by the European Court in the *Soering* case have since been reiterated many times.[215] The Court also applied them when it came to the expulsion or extradition of individuals suspected or convicted of terrorist acts: the most well-known judgments are those in the *Chahal*[216] and *Saadi*[217] cases. It should be noted that in such cases the Court established that the prohibition of deportation applies absolutely, regardless of the dangerousness of the individual; and it has ruled out that a balance can be struck between the potential risks for the individual, if he were deported, and the dangers to public order deriving from his presence in the territory of the State.[218] It is also worth mentioning the 2012 judgment in the *Hirsi* case,[219] in which Italy was condemned for a violation of Article 3 of the European Convention, for having rejected migrants at sea and turned them back to Tripoli, exposing them to the danger of being mistreated in Libya and returned to Somalia or Eritrea and subjected to torture there. Finally, these principles have also been applied

---

[213]ECtHR, *Soering v. UK*.

[214]*Ibidem*, para. 88.

[215]See, for example, ECtHR, *Vilvarajah and Others v. UK*; *N.A. v. UK*.

[216]ECtHR, *Chahal v. UK*.

[217]ECtHR, *Saadi v. Italy*.

[218]However, this position is not "universally" accepted. The Canadian Supreme Court, for example, in the *Suresh* case, left room for the possibility of making this balance, albeit in exceptional cases. See Supreme Court of Canada, *Suresh v. Canada*.

[219]ECtHR, *Hirsi Jamaa and Others v. Italy*.

in the case of the removal from a country of a seriously ill individual who cannot receive adequate treatment in the country of destination.[220]

A practice in line with that of the European Court has also been developed by the Human Rights Committee.[221] Finally, it is worth noting that the 1984 UN Convention against Torture has expressly incorporated the principle in question (but limited to torture) in Article 3(1), according to which:

> No State Party shall expel, return ("refouler") or extradite a person to another State where there are substantial grounds for believing that he would be in danger of being subjected to torture.[222]

14.2.3.2 Positive Obligations of Prevention

The prohibition of torture and inhuman or degrading treatment or punishment imposes a *general* obligation on States to prevent such abuses, which in turn consists of a number of more *specific* obligations. This concept is expressed, albeit not in detail, in Article 2(1) of the 1984 UN Convention against Torture:

> Each State Party shall take effective legislative, administrative, judicial or other measures to prevent acts of torture in any territory under its jurisdiction.

Therefore, the State has, in the first place, the positive obligation (of result) to have (or to equip itself with) a *regulatory apparatus* of prevention, suitable to avoid in the abstract violations of the prohibition in question. This means, above all, introducing into its penal codes the crimes of torture and inhuman or degrading treatment, and providing for penalties appropriate to the seriousness of such crimes. This obligation is clearly set out by the Human Rights Committee in its General Comment No. 20,[223] and is confirmed in the case-law of other international supervisory bodies: for example, in the rulings of the European Court in the cases *A. v. UK* and *M.C. v. Bulgaria*[224] and the judgment of the Inter-American Court in the *Heliodoro Portugal* case.[225] Article 4 of the UN Convention against Torture also states that:

> 1. Each State Party shall ensure that all acts of torture are offences under its criminal law [. . .]
> 2. Each State Party shall make these offences punishable by appropriate penalties which take into account their grave nature.[226]

---

220 See, e.g., ECtHR, *Paposhvili v. Belgium*, paras. 172–193.

221 See, e.g., HRCtee, *Ng v. Canada*; *Maksudov and Others v. Kyrgyzstan and Uzbekistan*; *Kaba v. Canada*; *Warsame v. Canada*. For a detailed examination of these cases, see Citroni and Scovazzi (2013), pp. 410–415.

222 On Article 3 see, recently, CteeAT, General Comment No. 4, 4 September 2018.

223 HRCtee, General Comment No. 20, 10 March 1992, para. 8.

224 ECtHR, *A. v. UK*, paras. 23–24; *M.C. v. Bulgaria*, para. 166.

225 IACtHR, *Heliodoro Portugal v. Panama.*

226 Italy has not respected this obligation to legislate for a long time, despite having ratified the 1984 Convention. It has only recently adopted legislation on the subject: Law no. 110 of 14 July 2017. In

Secondly, the State has a positive obligation (of result) to have (or to equip itself with) an *administrative apparatus*, which is also capable, in the abstract, of preventing violations of the prohibition in question. This apparatus consists, above all, of the police, prison and armed forces structures and organizations. These institutions must have the degree of functioning and efficiency required of any modern State, in order to prevent acts of torture or inhuman or degrading treatment that may be carried out by State officials or private individuals. Also in relation to this obligation, one may cite the General Comment No. 20 of the Human Rights Committee, according to which:

> Article 7 should be read in conjunction with article 2, paragraph 3, of the Covenant. In their reports, States parties should indicate how their legal system effectively guarantees the immediate termination of all the acts prohibited by article 7 [. . .].[227]

Thirdly, the State has an obligation to take those *concrete measures* that are required, on a case-by-case basis, to prevent violations of the prohibition in question. This is an obligation of due diligence, because its fulfilment is by its very nature aleatory. The State must take action and take preventive measures, using its "best efforts", to avoid violations both by private individuals and by State officials subject to control by higher authorities.

The latter obligation is confirmed by a wide practice of international supervisory bodies. In the case-law of the European Court of Human Rights, there are many important cases. Some of them concern prevention obligations of specific State authorities with respect to acts committed by private individuals. In these cases, the principles already mentioned by the Court in the *Osman* case apply.[228] One may cite, for example, the *Z and Others* case,[229] in which some adolescents complained that the competent British authorities had not taken measures to protect them against inhuman and degrading treatment suffered by their parents. Other cases, instead, concern omissive conduct consisting of a lack of prevention on the part of the State bodies considered as a whole. I can mention, for example, the *Kaya* and *Ilaşcu* cases.[230] The Inter-American Court has also applied similar principles in numerous cases.[231]

14.2.3.3 Positive Obligations of Repression

The State also has a *general* obligation to repress violations of the prohibition of torture and inhuman or degrading treatment or punishment. Again, the general

---

the meantime, Italy's failure to comply with its obligation had led to condemnations by the Strasbourg Court: see, e.g., ECtHR, *Cestaro v. Italy*.

[227] HRCtee, General Comment No. 20, 10 March 1992, para. 14.

[228] See above, Sect. 14.1.3.2.

[229] ECtHR, *Z and Others v. UK*.

[230] ECtHR, *Kaya v. Turkey*, paras. 85–101; *Ilaşcu and Others v. Moldova and Russia*, para. 348.

[231] See, for example, IACtHR, *Velásquez Rodríguez; Godínez Cruz; Juvenile Reeducation Institute; López Soto*.

obligation consists of two more *specific* obligations: (*a*) *to investigate* rapidly and effectively, with a view to identifying and apprehending the perpetrators of the violations; (*b*) *to try and punish* the guilty. As already mentioned, some of these are obligations of result and others are due diligence obligations.

The practice of international monitoring bodies on these two obligations is very broad. For the European Court of Human Rights, one can mention, inter alia, the cases of *Assenov*, *Labita*, *Ilhan* and *Sakik*.[232] In the *Assenov* case, the Court said:

> [. . .] where an individual raises an arguable claim that he has been seriously ill-treated by the police or other such agents of the State unlawfully and in breach of Article 3, that provision, read in conjunction with the State's general duty under Article 1 of the Convention [. . .] requires by implication that there should be an effective official investigation. This investigation [. . .] should be capable of leading to the identification and punishment of those responsible [. . .]. If this were not the case, the general legal prohibition of torture and inhuman and degrading treatment and punishment, despite its fundamental importance [. . .], would be ineffective in practice.[233]

Similar conclusions have been reached by other supervisory bodies. The Human Rights Committee stated, in its General Comment No. 20, that any allegation of torture must be subject to a full, prompt and impartial investigation by the State;[234] and has since applied this principle in many cases.[235] The Committee against Torture, in the *Halimi-Nedzibi* case, followed the same principle.[236] For the Inter-American Court, one can mention the cases of *Velásquez Rodríguez*, *Godínez Cruz*, *Caballero Delgado* and *Vargas Areco*.[237] For the African Commission, the decision in the *Zimbabwe Human Rights NGO Forum* is an important example.[238]

Lastly, with specific reference to the obligation to execute sentences punishing those responsible for abuse, the *Bondonga* case[239] is interesting, in which the Human Rights Committee declared Congo responsible for a violation of Article 7 of the Covenant, because the Congolese authorities had not executed the judgment by which some soldiers had been sentenced by a Congolese military court for acts of torture and inhuman treatment against a person in custody.

14.2.3.4 Positive Obligations Concerning Reparation

Finally, the State has an obligation to ensure access to justice and adequate *reparation* for victims of torture and inhuman or degrading treatment and their families. As

---

[232]ECtHR, *Assenov and Others v. Bulgaria*; *Labita v. Italy*; *Ilhan v. Turkey*; *Sakik and Others v. Turkey*.

[233]ECtHR, *Assenov and Others*, para. 102.

[234]HRCtee, General Comment No. 20, 10 March 1992, para. 14.

[235]See, for example, HRCtee, *Rodríguez v. Uruguay*.

[236]CteeAT, *M. Qani Halimi-Nedzibi v. Austria*, para. 13.5.

[237]IACtHR, *Velásquez Rodríguez v. Honduras; Godínez Cruz v. Honduras; Caballero Delgado and Santana v. Colombia; Vargas Areco v. Paraguay*.

[238]ACmHPR, *Zimbabwe Human Rights NGO Forum v. Zimbabwe*.

[239]HRCtee, *Basongo Bondonga v. DRC*.

already seen, these two obligations are expressly provided for in the Principles on the Rights of Victims of Serious Human Rights Violations.[240] The Human Rights Committee, in its General Comment No. 20 on torture, also states that:

> States may not deprive individuals of the right to an effective remedy, including compensation and such full rehabilitation as may be possible.[241]

In addition, the Committee affirms that States Parties must indicate how their legal system guarantees adequate remedies for victims;[242] and that, in principle, amnesty laws for acts of torture are not admissible.[243] The concept that amnesty measures are incompatible with the norms on the prohibition of torture has also been affirmed by the Inter-American Court of Human Rights.[244]

In the practice of international monitoring bodies, the most common reparation measure for violations of the prohibition in question is, of course, monetary compensation, since restitution (*restitutio in integrum*) is not possible for such violations.

However, the most interesting form of reparation for the violations in issue is satisfaction, especially in the practice of the Inter-American human rights system. In fact, as we have already seen in relation to the right to life, the Inter-American Court has interpreted in an innovative way its power to decide on satisfaction measures against States condemned for violation of fundamental human rights; and this also applies, of course, to violations of the ban on torture and inhuman or degrading treatment or punishment. Sometimes the satisfaction measures decided by the Court also seem to have the function of guarantees of non-repetition of the wrongful act.[245]

The Court, for example, in the *González* case,[246] concerning the rape and disappearance of women, decided that Mexico should adopt, among other things, appropriate plans and investigation systems in cases of sexual violence, a database to identify missing women, and awareness programs for the population on violence against women. In the *Vargas Areco* case,[247] relating to acts of violence and the murder of a minor, the Court decided that Paraguay should: (*a*) take all necessary measures to identify, prosecute and punish those responsible for the killing of the

[240] See above, Sect. 14.1.3.3.

[241] HRCtee, General Comment No. 20, 10 March 1992, para. 15.

[242] *Ibidem*, para. 14: "The right to lodge complaints against maltreatment prohibited by article 7 must be recognized in the domestic law [. . .] The reports of States parties should provide specific information on the remedies available to victims of maltreatment and the procedure that complainants must follow [. . .]".

[243] *Ibidem*, para. 15: "Amnesties are generally incompatible with the duty of States to investigate such acts; to guarantee freedom from such acts within their jurisdiction; and to ensure that they do not occur in the future".

[244] IACtHR, *Barrios Altos*, Judgment of 14 March 2001, paras. 41–44; *Almonacid Arellano*, paras. 119–120.

[245] See ILC *Draft Articles on Responsibility of States for Internationally Wrongful Acts*, Art. 30.

[246] IACtHR, *González et al. v. Mexico.*

[247] IACtHR, *Vargas Areco v. Paraguay.*

boy; (*b*) hold a public ceremony to apologize and acknowledge the violations in the presence of the victim's family and the civil and military authorities; (*c*) affix a commemorative plaque; (*d*) ensure medical, psychological and psychiatric treatment for family members; (*e*) create human rights programs and courses for members of the armed forces; (*f*) publish the Court's ruling in the official gazette and in a nationwide newspaper; and finally (*g*) amend its laws on the recruitment of minors to the armed forces to bring them into line with international norms.

14.3 Prohibition of International Crimes

Within the framework of "fundamental" human rights which aim to protect the life and physical integrity of the person, the general prohibition of international crimes can also be placed. I have already spoken about these crimes when I dealt with international criminal law in brief.[248] In fact, it is important to remember here that the category of "international crimes" is commonly used in *international criminal law* in order to refer to certain crimes, committed by individuals, which also constitute serious violations of human rights or humanitarian law, and which produce an international criminal liability of such persons. In other words, "international crimes", *in the strict legal sense*, refer to individual international crimes, the international criminal liability of the *natural persons* responsible for such crimes and the regime of criminal repression that exists before some specialized international courts.

Actually, I do not intend to deal *directly* with international criminal law, because it is a different area than the protection of human rights, although obviously the two areas are closely linked and complementary.[249] However, as I already said, individuals who commit an international crime are very often organs of their own State or of a parastatal entity, because international crimes presuppose extensive and systematic attacks against a population or a group. Therefore, the commission of an international crime usually produces a *dual* international responsibility: (a) that of the *individual*, on the basis of international criminal law; (b) that of the *State* that committed or did not prevent the crime, on the basis of international human rights law (or humanitarian law).

I am now interested in this last aspect. Consequently, I will speak from now on of "prohibition of international crimes" with reference to the *norms that impose obligations on States* (or other entities with international human rights obligations).[250] However, it will also be necessary, albeit indirectly, to refer to the

[248]See above, Sect. 2.4.2.

[249]See above, Sect. 2.4.2.

[250]It must also be warned that, from a terminological point of view, it is not correct to speak of "international crimes of States", since this expression has not been recognized in the practice and *opinio juris* of the international community. The concept of "international crimes of States" was proposed by the Special Rapporteur Ago in the famous Article 19 of the Draft Articles on Responsibility of States for Internationally Wrongful Acts, adopted at first reading by the ILC in

norms of international criminal law, which have greatly clarified the content of international crimes.

That said, it should be remembered that the category of international crimes is constituted, in contemporary international law, by four types of crimes: (*a*) genocide; (*b*) crimes against humanity; (*c*) war crimes; (*d*) crimes against peace (which today are solved in the crime of aggression). It should also be noted that a State, if it violates one of the prohibitions mentioned above, commits a serious violation of fundamental human rights or basic norms of humanitarian law. Therefore, as we will see, it can also be considered, *usually but not always*, that the State has committed a violation of obligations established by norms of general international law and that have the character of *jus cogens*.

It is now convenient to examine separately the above four categories of international crimes.

14.3.1 Genocide

14.3.1.1 Norms

Genocide has probably been practiced often in human history. However, the legal term "genocide", which means the killing of an entire national group (*génos* in Greek), was first introduced into international law in 1944 by the Polish jurist R. Lemkin.[251]

But the word "genocide" was not used in the text of the Statute of the Nuremberg Tribunal or in the judgment of the Tribunal.[252] The genocide of the Jews was punished in Nuremberg as "acts of extermination and persecution", which fell into the broader category of crimes against humanity. However, after a short time, the legal concept of genocide was recognized by the UN General Assembly, which, in 1946, adopted a resolution defining genocide as "a denial of the right of existence of entire groups" and stating that genocide was a "crime under international law".[253]

Subsequently, genocide acquired autonomy and considerable importance in the 1948 Convention for the Prevention and Punishment of the Crime of Genocide, which I have already briefly discussed.[254] The Convention constitutes the reference legislation with regard to genocide in general. It considers genocide *both as an*

1976. But later, due to opposition from many States, this expression was removed. Article 40 of the ILC Draft approved in 2001 now speaks of serious breaches of obligations arising under peremptory norms of general international law.

[251] Lemkin (1944), p. 79.

[252] IMT, *United States et al. v. Goering et al.* But the indictment of the Nuremberg Tribunal referred to genocide: see *Trial of Major War Criminals before the International Military Tribunal, 1945-1946*, Nuremberg 1947, vol. 1, Indictment, Count Three, pp. 43–44. On the issue of the non-reference to genocide in the Nuremberg trial see also Barret (2010); Sands (2017), pp. 292, 297, 301, 306.

[253] GA Res. 96(I), 11 December 1946.

[254] See above, Sect. 10.4.2.1.

individual criminal act, involving the international responsibility of the individuals who perpetrated it, *and as an international wrongful act of the State*, to which the organs who committed acts of genocide belong. As already said, the two forms of responsibility must be kept separate.

Among the relevant international norms on genocide, the provisions contained in the statutes of international criminal courts should also be considered, even if they refer only to genocide as an individual crime. The most relevant provisions are Article 4 of the Statute of the International Tribunal for the Former Yugoslavia, Article 2 of the Statute of the International Tribunal for Rwanda, and Article 6 of the Statute of the International Criminal Court. In fact, the definitions of the crime of genocide contained in these Statutes take over, in an identical or very similar way, the definition contained in the 1948 Convention.

Finally, it should be noted that the prohibition of genocide is enshrined not only in the above-mentioned treaty norms, but also in a norm of general international law of a peremptory nature (*jus cogens*).[255] This is confirmed in some important judgments of the International Court of Justice.[256]

14.3.1.2 Content of the Prohibition

The content of the prohibition of genocide, also for the purposes of general international law, is derived mainly from the 1948 Convention against Genocide. Article II of the Convention defines the two constituent elements of this crime. The subjective element consists in the "intent to destroy, in whole or in part, a national, ethnical, racial or religious group". The objective element consists in the commission of one of the following acts:

> a) Killing members of the group; b) Causing serious bodily or mental harm to members of the group; c) Deliberately inflicting on the group conditions of life calculated to bring about its physical destruction in whole or in part; d) Imposing measures intended to prevent births within the group; e) Forcibly transferring children of the group to another group.

The most characteristic element of genocide is therefore the so-called "specific willful intent"; that is, the intention to physically destroy (in whole or in part) one of the four protected groups.

As can be seen, the Convention contains an accurate definition of the crime of genocide. In some respects the definition is broad, because it punishes the crime committed both in times of peace and in times of war; and because it also includes acts that do not involve the killing of persons (e.g. serious injuries). However, in other respects, the definition is restrictive, because it requires the difficult

---

[255] Some consider it to be a customary rule and others, instead, a general principle of international law. For this second view, see Pisillo Mazzeschi and Viviani (2018), p. 147.

[256] ICJ, *Armed Activities on the Territory of the Congo*, Judgment of 3 February 2006, para. 64; *Application of the Convention on the Prevention and Punishment of the Crime of Genocide*, Judgment of 26 February 2007, paras. 161–162; *Application of the Convention on the Prevention and Punishment of the Crime of Genocide*, Judgment of 3 February 2015, paras. 87–88.

demonstration of specific willful intent and because it excludes so-called political genocide (the destruction of an opposing political group) and so-called cultural genocide (the destruction of the cultural symbols of a group). The definition of Article II seems to exclude also so-called ethnic cleansing, i.e. the forced expulsion of an ethnic group from a certain geographic area to achieve local ethnic homogeneity.

Moreover, it must be noted that the definition of genocide in the Convention does not stipulate that the commission of the crime should be carried out within the framework of systematic or widespread practice. This means that, unlike crimes against humanity,[257] genocide does not require proof of a context of widespread violence or a concerted policy or plan of genocide. However, in reality, acts of genocide rarely constitute isolated or sporadic episodes and are usually part of a plan approved or tolerated by the State.[258] Therefore, as already mentioned, there is often a *double responsibility*: that of the State and that of its agents. Article III of the Convention is also important, since it provides for the punishability of other acts connected with the commission of acts of genocide, namely: (*a*) concertation aimed at committing genocide; (*b*) direct and public incitement to commit it; (*c*) attempt; (*d*) complicity.

The definitions of genocide contained in the statutes of the international criminal tribunals, as already said, are very similar to that established by the 1948 Convention.

As far as practice is concerned, a distinction should be made between genocide as an *international wrongful act of the State* and genocide as an *individual criminal offence*.

With regard to the first aspect, the application of the Genocide Convention has not given rise to a significant practice for a long time. It is only since the 1990s that the International Court of Justice has been called upon to rule on certain disputes relating to the *Application of the Convention against Genocide*.[259] In its judgment of 2007, the Court had the opportunity to clarify certain aspects of the content of the prohibition of genocide. The Court specified the concept of "protected group" for the purposes of genocide, arguing that the group cannot be defined in the negative, i.e. as a group of individuals who do not have certain characteristics; and that the term "in part" must refer to a significant part of the group. Furthermore, the Court held that the practice of ethnic cleansing may constitute a form of genocide, provided that the constituent elements of genocide laid down in Article II of the Convention are respected; that is, that there is intent to destroy a group and that one of the acts

[257] See below, Sect. 14.3.2.

[258] Cassese and Gaeta (2008), p. 189.

[259] See ICJ, *Application of the Convention on the Prevention and Punishment of the Crime of Genocide (Bosnia and Herzegovina v. Yugoslavia)*, *Preliminary Objections*, Judgment of 11 July 1996; ICJ, *Application of the Convention on the Prevention etc. (Bosnia and Herzegovina v. Serbia and Montenegro)*, Judgment of 26 February 2007; ICJ, *Application of the Convention on the Prevention etc. (Croatia v. Serbia)*, Judgment of 3 February 2015; ICJ, *Application of the Convention on the Prevention etc. (The Gambia v. Myanmar)*, Order of 23 January 2020.

referred to in Article II has been committed. Finally, the Court, as we shall see later, has also gone into the content of the State's obligations to prevent genocide.

On the other hand, with regard to genocide as *an individual criminal offence*, international law has made more progress, through the case-law of the international criminal tribunals.[260] However, I cannot go into the matter here because, as noted above, it only indirectly affects genocide as a wrongful act of States and thus international human rights law.

14.3.1.3 Obligations

The prohibition of genocide imposes negative and positive obligations on States (and other entities covered by the prohibition), which are not very different from those I have already examined in relation to the right to life and the prohibition of torture.

To summarize, the main negative obligation of the State is to refrain, through its own organs (acting *de jure* or *ultra vires*) or through individuals or groups acting as *de facto* organs or under the direction or control of the State, from committing acts of genocide. In this regard, as we shall see below, it can sometimes be difficult to solve the problem of whether or not to attribute to the State acts of genocide committed by armed, military or paramilitary groups, which are not organs of the State, but which are suspected of acting under the control of the State.

The main positive obligations of the State are to prevent and repress acts of genocide committed by private individuals or groups of private individuals. In the above-mentioned case *Bosnia and Herzegovina v. Serbia and Montenegro*, the International Court of Justice was called upon to ascertain, inter alia, responsibility for the massacre of thousands of Bosnian-Muslim people in Srebrenica in 1995 by Serbian military and paramilitary forces of the Autonomous Republic of Bosnia and Herzegovina (Republika Srpska). In its judgment,[261] the Court ruled that the acts of genocide could not be attributed to Serbia, since the military and paramilitary forces that had materially committed the genocide could not be considered as organs, either *de jure* or *de facto*, of Serbia. Nor, in the Court's view, was there any evidence of effective control by Serbia of the actions of those forces such as to justify the attribution of those actions to Serbia. However, the Court found that Serbia was responsible for the genocide, for breach of its positive obligations of prevention; that is, because Serbia had not exercised due diligence in preventing the massacre.[262]

The caution of the International Court of Justice, in assessing the element of effective control by Serbia over the military and paramilitary forces that had carried

---

[260]See, e.g., ICTR, *Akayesu*, Judgment of 2 September 1998; ICTR, *Kayishema et al.*, Judgment of 1 June 2001; ICTY, *Jelisić*, Judgment of 5 July 2001; ICTY, *Krstić*, Judgment of 19 April 2004.

[261]ICJ, *Application of the Convention on the Prevention and Punishment of the Crime of Genocide*, Judgment of 26 February 2007, paras. 385–450.

[262]In relation to the failure to prevent the Srebrenica massacre, see also, on the responsibility of The Netherlands, The Hague Court of Appeal, *Mehida Mustafić-Mujić et al v. The Netherlands*; Supreme Court, *State of the Netherlands v. Mustafić et al.* On these judgments see also Pustorino (2019), pp. 111–112.

out the Srebrenica massacre, has sometimes been criticized in doctrine. Furthermore, it should be noted that the International Tribunal for the Former Yugoslavia, in evaluating the *individual* international criminal responsibility of the soldiers who had committed the aforementioned massacre, established instead that there was global control by the Serbian authorities over those soldiers.

14.3.2 Crimes Against Humanity

14.3.2.1 Norms

The category of crimes against humanity was included in the London Agreement of 1945, which established the International Military Tribunal of Nuremberg (IMT) and then taken up in Article 6(c) of the Statute of the Tribunal. Its origin is due to the fact that the international law of armed conflict (*jus in bello*), which had already existed for a long time, applied only to relations between belligerents; and therefore the rules on war crimes, which were contained in that law, did not apply to crimes committed by German Nazis *against their own population* for political, religious or racial reasons (Jews, Gypsies, Communists, trade unionists, etc.) or the population of States allied to Germany. Therefore, to try Nazi leaders for such crimes before the Nuremberg Tribunal, one had to go beyond traditional international law.

In the Statute of the Tribunal, crimes against humanity were defined as:

> [. . .] murder, extermination, enslavement, deportation, and other inhumane acts committed against any civilian population, before or during the war, or persecutions on political, racial or religious grounds [. . .].[263]

In addition, it was made clear that such acts or persecutions could be judged by the Tribunal regardless of whether or not they constituted a "violation of the domestic law of the country where perpetrated".[264] However, such acts must have been committed "in the execution of or in connection with any crime within the jurisdiction of the Tribunal".[265] That is, the crimes against humanity had to be linked to a war crime or a crime against peace. It is clear that this condition placed a significant limitation on the jurisdiction of the Tribunal.

In any case, the most interesting aspect is that the category of crimes against humanity was an innovation in international law. This posed, on the one hand, the problem of respect for the principle of criminal legality (*nullum crimen, nulla poena sine lege*); and in fact this objection was raised by the lawyers of the Nazi leaders during the Nuremberg trial, but was overcome by the Tribunal. On the other hand, this new category of crimes represented an important advance in international law, because it meant that this law prohibited acts contrary to the fundamental values of

[263] IMT, Charter, Art. 6(c).

[264] *Ibidem.*

[265] *Ibidem.*

the human person, and this even if these acts had been carried out without violating (or even implementing) the internal law of the State.[266]

After the Nuremberg trial, the legal notion of crimes against humanity became established very quickly. In 1946, the International Military Tribunal of Tokyo[267] also adopted this notion.[268] Furthermore, the Allies concluded an agreement[269] in December 1945, which broadened the definition of crimes against humanity, because it omitted any reference or connection to the Second World War. In 1946, the UN General Assembly adopted a resolution[270] reaffirming the principles contained in the Statute and the judgment of the Nuremberg Tribunal. In 1950, the International Law Commission also adopted similar principles.[271]

More recently, the notion was reaffirmed in the *Draft Code on Crimes against the Peace and Security of Mankind*, presented in 1996 by the ILC to the UN General Assembly,[272] and then in the Statutes of the Tribunal for the Former Yugoslavia,[273] the Tribunal for Rwanda[274] and the International Criminal Court.[275] These Statutes, even if they are not completely uniform among themselves, have broadened the concept of crimes against humanity from that contained in the Statute of the Nuremberg Tribunal. In particular, it follows from the Statutes of the Tribunal for Rwanda and the International Criminal Court, and from the case-law of the Tribunal for the Former Yugoslavia, that crimes against humanity can also be committed in peacetime and that there is no longer a need for a link between such crimes and armed conflict.

It must now be asked whether the prohibition of crimes against humanity is enshrined in a general norm of international law and, if so, whether this norm has the character of *jus cogens*. In my view, the answer is positive to both questions. More specifically, it seems to me that the prohibition is established by a general principle of international law, rather than by a customary rule.[276]

---

[266] Cassese and Gaeta (2008), p. 182.

[267] Cf. Establishment of an International Military Tribunal for the Far East, Special proclamation by the Supreme Commander for the Allied Powers at Tokyo, 19 January1946; Charter of the International Military Tribunal for the Far East.

[268] IMTFE Charter, Art. 5(c).

[269] Control Council Law No. 10, 20 December 1945.

[270] GA Res. 95(I) of 11 December 1946: *Affirmation of the Principles of International Law recognized by the Charter of the Nuremberg Tribunal.*

[271] ILC, *Principles of International Law Recognized in the Charter of the Nuremberg Tribunal and in the Judgment of the Tribunal*, June–July 1950, in *YILC*, 1950, II, para. 97.

[272] ILC, *Draft Code of Crimes against the Peace and Security of Mankind with commentaries, 1996*, in *YILC*, 1996, II (2).

[273] ICTY Statute, Art. 5.

[274] ICTR Statute, Art. 3.

[275] ICC Rome Statute, Art. 7.

[276] Again, as with genocide, some writers argue that the general norm on the prohibition of crimes against humanity is customary in nature and others that it has the nature of a principle of

However, as I said, the conventional norms in this matter are *not* identical, especially with regard to individual prohibited acts. Therefore, it must be concluded that the *general principle* on the prohibition of crimes against humanity, which by its nature is broad and not detailed, has a content which corresponds, roughly speaking, to the *minimum common content of all the treaty norms* mentioned above. In other words, the content of the general principle cannot be considered to correspond precisely to the specific content of Article 7 of the Statute of the International Criminal Court or Article 5 of the Statute of the Tribunal for the Former Yugoslavia. In any case, the content of the *general* prohibition of crimes against humanity will now be addressed.

14.3.2.2 Content of the Prohibition

In contemporary international law, crimes against humanity consist, in their essential substance, of extensive or systematic and intentional attacks against the civilian population. This concept needs to be clarified.

First, attacks are "extensive" when they cause a high number of victims; and they are "systematic" when they are not isolated or sporadic in nature, but are part of a systematic and widespread practice, or a political plan approved or tolerated by a State or an authority exercising *de facto* control in the territory where the acts are perpetrated. According to the Tribunal for Rwanda:

> The concept of 'widespread' may be defined as massive, frequent, large scale action, carried out collectively with considerable seriousness and directed against a multiplicity of victims. The concept of 'systematic' may be defined as thoroughly organised and following a regular pattern on the basis of a common policy involving substantial public or private resources. There is no requirement that this policy must be adopted formally as the policy of a state. There must however be some kind of preconceived plan or policy.[277]

Secondly, the attacks must be "intentional"; i.e. the so-called subjective element (or *mens rea*) of the crime is required: the prohibited conduct must be carried out with the intent to commit the crime in question and awareness of the general context of the policy or systematic practice of violations.

Thirdly, "civilian population" means a group of people, whatever their nationality (including that of the perpetrators); but who are not "combatants".

Fourthly, it is also necessary the existence of the objective element (*actus rei*) of the crime; that is, of the individual material acts that are prohibited. In reality, they are multiple and, as already said, not always identical in the different conventional norms. Article 7 of the Statute of the International Criminal Court, for example, contains a much more detailed list of acts than Article 6(c) of the Statute of the Nuremberg Tribunal, because it also includes "gender crimes" and apartheid. This depends, of course, on the greater modernity of the former Statute.

---

international law. This second opinion seems preferable to me, both for the almost immediate nature of formation of the norm and for its broad and rather indeterminate content.

[277]ICTR, *Akayesu*, Judgment of 2 September 1998, para. 580.

Finally, it should be noted that, in crimes against humanity, the relationship between the *individual criminal offence* (on the basis of international criminal law) and the *international wrongful act of the State* (on the basis of international human rights law) is very close, since these crimes are usually part of a criminal policy of the government. This relationship also explains why the definition of a crime against humanity often refers to that contained in human rights norms.[278] One thinks, for example, of the prohibitions of torture, apartheid and enforced disappearance of persons, which constitute prohibited acts within the framework of crimes against humanity and, at the same time, are regulated by human rights norms.

14.3.2.3 Obligations

The prohibition of crimes against humanity (examined here from the perspective of human rights and therefore of State responsibility) imposes on States negative and positive obligations, in a similar way to those already discussed in relation to the other human rights concerning the protection of life and physical integrity of the person.

It can only be noted that, since such crimes are usually part of a systematic and widespread practice carried out or approved by a State, especially negative obligations come to the fore. The State must, first of all, refrain from making or endorsing those extensive and systematic attacks against the civilian population that constitute the essence of crimes against humanity. However, as with genocide, it cannot be excluded that sometimes these attacks come from entities or groups of people, who control, for example, part of the territory of the State, but whose acts are not attributable to the State. In such cases, the positive obligations of the State, especially those of prevention and repression, may come into play.

14.3.3 War Crimes

14.3.3.1 Norms

The category of war crimes is usually traced back, originally, to the so-called *Lieber Code*, a codification of the law of war adopted in 1863 by US President A. Lincoln. Subsequently, the Hague Conventions of 1899 and 1907 provided for the category of "violations of the laws and customs of war", a notion also taken up by some military manuals. However, this notion is too broad to be used as a legal concept of "war crimes".

In more modern times, the category of war crimes was included in the Statute of the Nuremberg Tribunal, which, after reaffirming that war crimes are "violations of the laws or customs of war", stipulated that such violations included, inter alia:

> murder, ill-treatment or deportation to slave labour or for any other purpose of civilian population of or in occupied territory, murder or ill-treatment of prisoners of war or persons

[278] See Focarelli (2013), pp. 305–306.

on the seas, killing of hostages, plunder of public or private property, wanton destruction of cities, towns or villages, or devastation not justified by military necessity.[279]

Actually, the Statute of the Nuremberg Tribunal continued to be largely inspired by the Hague Conventions of 1899 and 1907. But today the definition of war crimes contained in that Statute needs to be updated in the light of developments in international humanitarian law and international criminal law, which have taken place more recently. Suffice it to think, for the humanitarian law, of the four Geneva Conventions of 1949[280] and the two Additional Protocols of 1977[281] and, for international criminal law, of the statutes and practice of international criminal tribunals. I will return to this in relation to the content of the prohibition of war crimes.

As far as general international law is concerned, also in this case it can be said (as in the case of crimes against humanity) that the prohibition of war crimes is enshrined in a norm of general international law and of *jus cogens*. In my opinion this norm, given its long historical gestation, is a custom rather than a general principle of international law. However, the content of this norm is more generic and, at the same time, more limited than the detailed content of the above-mentioned conventional rules.

14.3.3.2 Content of the Prohibition

The question of the content of the prohibition of war crimes could be largely resolved by providing a precise legal definition of "war crimes". But this is a difficult problem, which has not so far given rise to a secure and generally accepted solution. However, I can try to establish certain criteria.[282]

Firstly, war crimes can only be committed in the context of an *armed conflict*, whether international or internal; i.e. in a context in which international humanitarian law applies. Secondly, there must be a *link* between the criminal conduct and the conflict. Third, it is also necessary that the *victim* (whether a combatant or a civilian) is identifiable with the "enemy" or the "adversary". It is not necessary for the perpetrator of the offence to be a military or a combatant.

Given these general criteria, what are the specific offences that constitute a war crime? An important definition, which may serve as a starting point, was provided by

---

[279] IMT Charter, Art. 6(b).

[280] Geneva Convention for the Amelioration of the Condition of the Wounded and Sick in Armed Forces in the Field (GG I); Geneva Convention for the Amelioration of the Condition of the Wounded, Sick and Shipwrecked Members of Armed Forces at Sea (GC II); Geneva Convention relative to the Treatment of Prisoners of War (GC III); Geneva Convention relative to the Protection of Civilian Persons in Time of War (GC IV).

[281] Protocol Additional to the Geneva Convention of 12 August 1949 (Protection of Victims of International Armed Conflicts) (AP I); Protocol Additional to the Geneva Convention of 12 August 1949 (Protection of Victims of Non-International Armed Conflicts) (AP II).

[282] See Cassese and Gaeta (2008), pp. 177–179; Henckaerts and Doswald-Beck (2005), Vol. 1: *Rules*.

the Appeal Chamber of the International Criminal Tribunal for the Former Yugoslavia in the interim decision made in 1995 in the *Tadić* case.[283] According to that decision, a war crime is committed when: (*a*) there has been an infringement of a rule of international humanitarian law "protecting important values" and the breach must "involve grave consequences for the victim"; (*b*) the rule is customary or, if it belongs to treaty law, it clarifies and develops customary law; (*c*) the violation entails, under international law, individual criminal responsibility of the person breaching the rule. In summary, it can be inferred from this decision that war crimes consist of serious violations of fundamental norms of the law of armed conflict; and that they also must involve individual responsibility. In my opinion, this definition, even if it pertains to *international crimes of individuals*, is also suitable for acts producing *international crimes of States*.

However, the problem remains to be resolved as to what are the above-mentioned fundamental norms of the law of armed conflict. This is an issue that requires the identification and interpretation of international practice. In this regard, the doctrine distinguishes between the legal regime of international armed conflicts and that of internal armed conflicts.

In the context of international armed conflicts, the norms on means and methods of warfare (so-called The Hague law) are of primary importance. In essence, it is a question of establishing which, among the provisions of the Hague Conventions of 1899 and 1907, have produced norms which are customary and which give criminal relevance to individual conduct. Secondly, the interpreter must examine the norms on the protection of those who do not participate, or no longer participate, in hostilities: i.e. the victims of war (so-called Geneva law). These norms are contained in particular in the four Geneva Conventions of 1949, which specify that certain violations are considered as serious infringements, which involve criminal sanctions. These are the so-called "grave breaches" of the Geneva Conventions (Art. 50 GC I, Art. 51 GC II, Art. 130 GC III, and Art. 147 GC IV).

Instead, with regard to the legal regime of internal armed conflicts, it has only recently been established that a serious breach of certain fundamental norms of that regime constitutes a war crime.[284] The dominant opinion is that serious violations of Article 3 common to the four Geneva Conventions of 1949, which lays down certain minimum rules of humanity to be respected during conflicts of all kinds, constitute war crimes. But many authors say that the main provisions of the Second Protocol to the Geneva Conventions, expressly dedicated to internal armed conflicts, should also be added.[285]

[283] ICTY, *Tadić*, Decision of 2 October 1995, paras. 94–136.

[284] See ICTY, *Tadić*, Decision of 2 October 1995, para. 134: "[. . .] customary international law imposes criminal liability for serious violations of common Article 3, as supplemented by other general principles and rules on the protection of victims of internal armed conflict, and for breaching certain fundamental principles and rules regarding means and methods of combat in civil strife".

[285] Cf. Abi-Saab, ICTY, *Tadić*, Separate opinion on the defence motion for interlocutory appeal on jurisdiction of 2 October 1995; Cassese and Gaeta (2008), p. 179.

The complex legal notion of "war crimes" outlined so far is, in principle, confirmed in Article 8 of the Statute of the International Criminal Court, which, however, constitutes an extremely detailed provision, which does not claim to codify customary international law. Article 8 provides for four general categories of war crimes and, within each category, a detailed list of more specific acts. The four general categories are: (*a*) the "grave breaches" of the 1949 Geneva Conventions; (*b*) other serious violations of the laws and customs applicable in international armed conflicts within the established framework of international law; (*c*) in non-international armed conflicts, serious violations of Article 3 common to the 1949 Geneva Conventions; (*d*) other serious violations of the laws and customs applicable in non-international armed conflicts within the established framework of international law.

One last point concerns the so-called subjective element of war crimes. Most of the provisions mentioned above require, expressly or implicitly, the willful intent of the person (State organ or private individual) who committed the crime. However, unless the provision explicitly excludes it, it seems that also gross negligence is sufficient.[286]

14.3.3.3 Obligations

International practice shows that the prohibition of war crimes entails not only negative obligations for States, but also, sometimes, positive obligations. In other words, responsibility can arise from both an action and an omission.

As usual, the primary negative obligation of the State is to refrain, through its own agents or other individuals or groups under the control of the State, from committing war crimes.

More interesting are the positive obligations of the State, particularly in cases of responsibility of the military leaders for war crimes committed by their subordinates.[287] The leading case in this matter is the *Yamashita* judgment of the US Supreme Court.[288] General Yamashita, who was head of the Japanese military forces in the Philippines from October 1944 until the end of the Second World War, was tried for the war crimes committed by those forces against the US military, first before a Military Commission and then before the US Supreme Court. Yamashita was not accused of committing, ordering or authorizing the criminal acts, but of failing to take appropriate measures to prevent them. Both the Military Commission and the Supreme Court established that the General was responsible because he had control over his own military forces and could not ignore their criminal acts.

The practice of the Allied Military Courts and the domestic courts of States, as well as the statutes of the international criminal tribunals, also confirm these principles about the omissive responsibility of military commanders and, more generally, of hierarchical superiors in relation to the conduct of subordinates. For

[286]Cassese and Gaeta (2008), p. 180.

[287]See, for a general examination of the judgment, Viviani (2005), pp. 203–324.

[288]U.S. Supreme Court, *In re Yamashita*.

example, Article 7(3) of the Statute of the International Criminal Tribunal for the Former Yugoslavia states:

> The fact that any of the acts referred to in articles 2 to 5 of the present Statute was committed by a subordinate does not relieve his superior of criminal responsibility if he knew or had reason to know that the subordinate was about to commit such acts or had done so and the superior failed to take the necessary and reasonable measures to prevent such acts or to punish the perpetrators thereof.

Very similar norms, although specified in greater detail, are contained in Article 28 of the Statute of the International Criminal Court.

14.3.4 Crimes Against Peace. Aggression

The category of crimes against peace also goes back to the London Agreement of 1945, which established the International Military Tribunal of Nuremberg, and the Statute of that Tribunal. Article 6(a) of the Statute defined the following acts as "crimes against peace":

> [. . .] planning, preparation, initiation or waging of a war of aggression, or a war in violation of international treaties, agreements or assurances, or participation in a common plan or conspiracy for the accomplishment of any of the foregoing.

It is clear that this provision did not provide a definition of the crime of aggression; but it did list a number of aggressive acts.[289] Also with regard to crimes against peace, the Nuremberg Tribunal argued that this was not a new legal notion and therefore did not violate the principle of legality of crimes and penalties. In fact, the Tribunal stated that aggression was the most serious of international crimes; and then condemned some of the defendants, after finding them guilty of crimes against peace.

Later, the International Military Tribunal of Tokyo[290] also condemned some defendants for crimes against peace. In 1946, the UN General Assembly adopted the aforementioned resolution in which it reaffirmed the principles contained in the Statute and the ruling of the Nuremberg Tribunal. In this way, as has been noted,[291] the States that were members of the UN at that time formally approved the notion of crimes against peace and the more specific notion of aggression. Subsequently, the two notions ended up, in practice, coinciding and the term "aggression" prevailed in use.

However, it should be stressed that the crime of aggression has found it more difficult to assert itself in international law than other categories of international

[289]See Focarelli (2013), p. 310.

[290]IMTFE Statute, Art. 5(a).

[291]Cassese and Gaeta (2008), p. 193.

crimes. These difficulties concerned both aggression as an *international wrongful act of the State* and aggression as an *individual criminal offence*. The reasons for the difficulties are clear. On the one hand, the strongest States (and especially the five permanent members of the Security Council) fear that an overly precise definition of the *State crime* of aggression may limit the discretion of the Security Council under Article 39 of the UN Charter[292] and their own discretion in interpreting international norms on the use of force. On the other hand, a strict definition of the *individual crime* of aggression could, in certain cases, lead to incriminating the supreme political and military leaders of States. In other words, this is a matter with a "high degree of politicization".[293]

This is demonstrated by the limited regulatory progress that the crime of aggression has achieved since the Nuremberg and Tokyo trials until today. With regard to aggression as a *wrongful act of the State*, the most relevant development is constituted by Resolution No. 3314 (XXIX) on the definition of aggression adopted by the UN General Assembly in 1974.[294] Article 3, in particular, lists in detail a series of acts which integrate the concept of aggression. However, the resolution has two important limitations. First, it expressly declares that it is not binding on the Security Council, which, with its discretion, may deviate from this definition (Art. 4). Secondly, it does not provide that acts of aggression may create both international responsibility of the State and international criminal responsibility of individuals; on the contrary, it seems to refer only to the responsibility of the State.[295]

Even in relation to aggression as an *individual criminal offence*, progress has not been significant. In the years from 1947 to 1954, the International Law Commission worked in an attempt to adopt a *Code of Crimes against the Peace and Security of Mankind.* A draft code, completed by the ILC in 1954, contained a provision (Art. 2), which grouped together all criminal offences and also mentioned aggression and the threat of aggression. But that draft code had no follow-up. After almost thirty years, in 1981, the ILC returned to deal with the topic; but it was only in 1996 that it completed a *Draft Code of Crimes against the Peace and Security of Mankind*,[296] which, however, was never approved by the United Nations. In any case, even this document lacks an accurate definition of the individual crime of aggression. Article 16 of the Draft Code, entitled "Crime of Aggression", merely provides that:

---

[292]UN Charter, Art. 39: "The Security Council shall determine the existence of any threat to the peace, breach of the peace, or act of aggression and shall make recommendations, or decide what measures shall be taken in accordance with Articles 41 and 42, to maintain or restore international peace and security".

[293]Cassese and Gaeta (2008), p. 196.

[294]GA Res. 3314 (XXIX) of 14 December 1974: *Definition of Aggression.*

[295]See also GA Res. 2625 (XXV) of 24 October 1970: *Declaration on Principles of International Law Concerning Friendly Relations and Co-operation among States in accordance with the Charter of the United Nations*, according to which: "A war of aggression constitutes a crime against the peace, for which there is responsibility under international law".

[296]ILC, *Draft Code of Crimes against the Peace and Security of Mankind*, 5 July 1996.

> An individual who, as leader or organizer, actively participates in or orders the planning, preparation, initiation or waging of aggression committed by a State shall be responsible for a crime of aggression.

Moreover, the individual crime of aggression does not usually fall within the jurisdiction of the international criminal tribunals; with the exception of the International Criminal Court, whose Statute provides that the Court has jurisdiction over such crime (Art. 5(1)). However, the Statute originally specified that the Court could not exercise such jurisdiction until an amendment to the Statute had been adopted, with a definition of the crime. Indeed, in 2010, a review conference of the Statute was held in Kampala (Uganda), which adopted an amendment containing a definition of aggression. Article 8-*bis*(1) states that:

> For the purpose of this Statute, 'crime of aggression' means the planning, preparation, initiation or execution, by a person in a position effectively to exercise control over or to direct the political or military action of a State, of an act of aggression which, by its character, gravity and scale, constitutes a manifest violation of the Charter of the United Nations.

Paragraph 2 specifies that "act of aggression" means the use of armed force by a State against the sovereignty, territorial integrity or political independence of another State or in any other way contrary to the UN Charter. Some specific forms of conduct are then listed which are considered as acts of aggression by GA Resolution No. 3314 of 1974. As can be seen, the definition of Art. 8-*bis* takes up, in substance, albeit with some variations and updating, the definitions that were contained in the Statutes of the Nuremberg Tribunal[297] and the Tokyo Tribunal.[298]

In conclusion, at least in relation to aggression as an international wrongful act of the State, it must be excluded that a norm with a sufficiently precise content has established itself in customary international law.[299] The main task of determining, with a large degree of discretion, whether and when an act of aggression by a State has occurred is therefore entrusted to the UN Security Council.

References

Barret JQ (2010) Raphael Lemkin and 'Genocide' at Nuremberg, 1945-1946. In: Safferling CM, Conze EA (eds) The Genocide Convention sixty years after its adoption. Asser Press, The Hague, pp 35–54

Bartolini G (2009) Riparazione per violazione dei diritti umani e ordinamento internazionale. Jovene, Napoli

Bestagno F (2003) Diritti umani e impunità. Obblighi positivi degli Stati in materia penale. Vita e Pensiero, Milano

[297] IMT Statute, Art. 6(a).

[298] IMTFE Statute, Art. 5(a).

[299] So also Focarelli (2013), pp. 311–312.

Cannizzaro E (2000) Il principio della proporzionalità nell'ordinamento internazionale. Giuffrè, Milano

Carpanelli E (2013) *Extraordinary renditions* e diritti umani: alcune riflessioni sul caso *Abu Omar*. DUDI 7:315–330

Cassese A, Gaeta P (2008) Le sfide attuali del diritto internazionale. Il Mulino, Bologna

Citroni G, Scovazzi T (2013) La tutela internazionale dei diritti umani, Parte III del Corso di diritto internazionale (Scovazzi T ed). Giuffrè, Milano

Focarelli C (2013) La persona umana nel diritto internazionale. Il Mulino, Bologna

Henckaerts JM, Doswald-Beck L (2005) ICRC, Customary international humanitarian law, 3 vols. CUP, Cambridge

Kälin W, Künzli J (2019) The law of international human rights protection, 2nd edn. OUP, Oxford-New York

Lemkin R (1944) Axis rule in occupied Europe: laws of occupation, analysis of government, proposals for redress. Carnegie Endowment for International Peace, Washington, D.C.

Nowak M, McArthur E (2008) The United Nations Convention against torture: a commentary. OUP, Oxford

Pisillo Mazzeschi R (2004b) The marginal role of the individual in the ILC's articles on state responsibility. Ital Yearb Int Law 14:39–51

Pisillo Mazzeschi R (2008) Responsabilité de l'État pour violation des obligations positives relatives aux droits de l'homme. RC 333:175–506

Pisillo Mazzeschi R, Viviani A (2018) General principles of international law: from rules to values? In: Pisillo Mazzeschi R, De Sena P (eds) Global justice, human rights and the modernization of international law. Springer, Cham, pp 113–161

Pustorino P (2019) Lezioni di tutela internazionale dei diritti umani. Cacucci, Bari

Rodley NS (1999) The treatment of prisoners in international law, 2nd edn. OUP, Oxford

Sands P (2017) La strada verso Est. Guanda, Milano

Viviani A (2005) Crimini internazionali e responsabilità dei leader politici e militari. Giuffrè, Milano

Zagrebelsky V, Chenal R, Tomasi L (2016) Manuale dei diritti fondamentali in Europa. Il Mulino, Bologna

Zagrebelsky V, Chenal R, Tomasi L (2019) Manuale dei diritti fondamentali in Europa, 2nd edn. Il Mulino, Bologna

Protection of Basic Needs and Subsistence Rights of the Person 15

When one talks, in relation to human rights, about the "basic needs" of the person, one usually refers to the rights to food, water, housing, health and, sometimes, the right to an adequate standard of living.[1] These rights are also, at times, defined as "subsistence rights".[2] This is because they have a connection with certain conditions necessary for the existence and subsistence of people. However, these definitions, even if partly appropriate, risk not being precise and creating some confusion if two clarifications are not made.

First of all, some of these rights are more general and others more specific and the relationship between them is rather complicated. For example, the right to an adequate standard of living could be considered as an autonomous human right, but it could also be considered, because of its very broad and indeterminate content, as a "right-container" (or perhaps only as a non-binding political objective) that includes the rights to food, water, housing and health. The right to health, which is less generic than the right to an adequate standard of living, could also be understood in a broad sense as including some of the more specific rights mentioned above, or in a narrow sense as an autonomous right. Caution should therefore be exercised when defining the scope of these rights and their mutual relations.

Secondly, and this is even more important, it does not seem to me that the individual rights in question have an univocal nature, so that they could *always* and indifferently be defined as "rights relating to basic needs" or as "subsistence rights". Instead, in my view, *a terminological and substantive distinction must be made between the two groups of rights.*

In fact, the rights to food, water, housing and health always concern basic needs of people. But if they are understood *in a broad sense*, they are economic and social rights, and are linked to *the right to an adequate standard of living*. In this case, as

[1]See, e.g., Focarelli (2013), pp. 211–213. I will not deal here, however, with the right to a healthy environment, which seems to me more relevant to collective human rights. See below, Sect. 25.4.2.

[2]See, e.g., Kälin and Künzli (2019), p. 290 ff.

R. Pisillo Mazzeschi, *International Human Rights Law*,
https://doi.org/10.1007/978-3-030-77032-7_15

we shall see, the rights in question are regulated by norms which, usually, do not have an immediate and binding character, but rather impose on States obligations "of progressive realization" or sometimes only non-binding political commitments or programs. Therefore, with regard to these rights understood *in a broad sense*, it is inappropriate, in my opinion, to speak of "rights of subsistence" and classify them among "fundamental" human rights.

On the other hand, the argument changes radically if the rights to food, water, housing and health are understood *in a strict sense*; that is, when they are linked, rather than to an adequate standard of living, to the *minimum survival and subsistence conditions of people*. In these situations, such rights, although autonomous, are functionally connected to the right to life, which means not only the right not to be killed arbitrarily, but also the right to enjoy the minimum conditions necessary for subsistence.[3] Therefore, in these hypotheses, the rights to food, water, housing and health can correctly be defined as *subsistence and survival rights* and be classified in the category of "fundamental" human rights.

How can this apparent contradiction between two different ways of understanding and interpreting these human rights be resolved? In my view, as I already mentioned, it is not a matter of identifying different contents within each right; that is, of distinguishing between one "core" content and one or more "non-core" contents, as the Committee on Economic, Social and Cultural Rights tends to do. Instead, it must be acknowledged that there are *different norms* governing each of these rights. For example, in relation to the right to food, as we shall see, there are certain norms which provide for *the right to adequate food for the well-being of people*, and other norms which establish *the right to food essential for people's subsistence and survival.* A similar situation also occurs for other human rights that are now under consideration.

Having said that, I will now separately examine the rights to food, water, housing and health, bearing in mind that I am primarily interested in the norms that consider them as "fundamental" rights. But it will also be inevitable to examine the norms that regard them as economic and social rights linked to the goal of an adequate standard of living. However, I will not consider this goal as an autonomous human right.[4]

15.1 Right to Food

15.1.1 Norms

The right to food is established by a number of conventional human rights norms, but also by several international humanitarian and criminal law norms, and perhaps even by a customary norm on humanitarian emergencies. However, an overall examination of these norms shows, in my view, an important *difference*: the norms of the first

[3]See IACtHR, *The "Street Children"*, Judgment of 19 November 1999, para. 139.

[4]But see, for a different view, Focarelli (2013), pp. 211–213.

group are broad and generic, and almost always conceive the right to food as an aspect of the right (or goal) to an adequate standard of living, while the norms of the other three groups are more precise and specific, and understand the right to food as an essential resource for people's subsistence and survival. In other words, the norms governing *the right to food adequate to people's well-being* should be distinguished from the norms governing *the right to food essential for people's subsistence and survival.* Let us now verify this distinction.

In the field of international human rights law, it is worth recalling, first of all, the Universal Declaration, which deals with the right to food in Article 25(1):

> Everyone has the right to a standard of living adequate for the health and well-being of himself and of his family, including food, clothing, housing and medical care [. . .].

As can be seen, the right to food is conceived only as a particular aspect of the right to an adequate standard of living.

The Covenant on Civil and Political Rights makes no mention at all of the right to food. Instead, the Covenant on Economic, Social and Cultural Rights contains an important provision on this right: Article 11. Actually, paragraph 1 of Article 11 merely takes up a formula similar to that of the Universal Declaration:

> The States Parties to the present Covenant recognize the right of everyone to an *adequate* standard of living for himself and his family, including *adequate* food, clothing and housing, and to the continuous improvement of living conditions. The States Parties will take appropriate steps to ensure the realization of this right, recognizing to this effect the essential importance of international cooperation based on free consent.[5]

This provision speaks of "adequate" food, as a specific and functional right, together with others, to realize the broader right to an "adequate" standard of living. Therefore, in my opinion, it can be said that this provision regulates *the right to food adequate to people's well-being*.

In truth, paragraph 2 of Article 11 seems to introduce, compared to paragraph 1, a different and more "courageous" meaning of the right to food, since it declares that the States Parties to the Covenant recognize "the fundamental right of everyone to be free from hunger". But, after this affirmation, the provision continues in a much more cautious way, indicating a series of measures and political programs, of a vague and non-binding nature that the States Parties undertake to take, individually and through international cooperation, in order to improve the production, conservation and distribution of food.

Many other human rights treaties contain provisions on the right to food; but this is always conceived, along the lines of the Universal Declaration and the Covenant on Economic, Social and Cultural Rights, as a *right to food adequate to people's well-being*. In this sense one can cite Article 12 of the San Salvador Protocol that states that everyone has the right to adequate nutrition, which guarantees the

[5]Emphasis added.

possibility of enjoying the highest level of physical, emotional and intellectual development.[6] Similarly, the Convention on the Rights of the Child mentions, indirectly and fleetingly, the right to food (*rectius* the issues of nutrition and malnutrition of children) within the framework of the child's right to the highest standard of health (Art. 24(2)(c)) and to a standard of living adequate for his or her development (Art. 27(3)). Similar and rather vague and generic norms are contained in the Arab Charter (Art. 38) and the Convention on the Rights of Persons with Disabilities (Art. 28(1)).

On the contrary, different norms can be found in the area of international humanitarian law. They aim to prevent States parties to armed conflicts from starving the victims of such conflicts (prisoners, civilians, etc.) or even depriving them of the *food essential for their survival*. One can mention the Third Geneva Convention of 1949 (Arts. 20 and 26), the Fourth Geneva Convention (Art. 55), the First Additional Protocol of 1977 (Art. 54) and the Second Additional Protocol (Arts. 5(1)(b) and 14). For example, Article 55 of the Fourth Geneva Convention states that:

> [...] the Occupying Power has the duty of ensuring the food and medical supplies of the population; it should, in particular, bring in the *necessary foodstuffs*, medical stores and other articles if the resources of the occupied territory are inadequate.[7]

Article 14 of the Second Additional Protocol provides that:

> Starvation of civilians as a method of combat is prohibited. It is therefore prohibited to attack, destroy, remove or render useless, for that purpose, *objects indispensable to the survival* of the civilian population, such as foodstuffs, agricultural areas for the production of foodstuffs, crops, livestock, drinking water installations and supplies and irrigation works.[8]

These norms do not deal with food that would be adequate for people's well-being or good standard of living, but with food as a resource essential to people's *survival*.

A similar situation occurs in international criminal law, where there are norms that even make it an international crime to deprive people, in certain circumstances, of food essential to their subsistence or survival. For example, Article 7(2)(b) of the Statute of the International Criminal Court considers as a crime against humanity, being extermination:

> [...] the intentional infliction of conditions of life, *inter alia* the deprivation of access to food and medicine, calculated to bring about the destruction of part of a population.

---

[6]Paragraph 2 of Article 12 adds: "In order to promote the exercise of this right and eradicate malnutrition, the States Parties undertake to improve methods of production, supply and distribution of food, and to this end, agree to promote greater international cooperation in support of the relevant national policies".

[7]GC IV, Art. 55 (emphasis added).

[8]AP II, Art. 14 (emphasis added).

Likewise, Article 8(2)(b)(xxv) of the same Statute considers as a war crime:

> Intentionally using starvation of civilians as a method of warfare [. . .].

Finally, there is another area of international law that deserves examination: that of humanitarian emergencies, which are due not only to armed conflicts but also to natural or other disasters. In fact, in recent times, the idea is emerging that a general norm of international law has been (or is being) formed, which obliges States to intervene in the event of humanitarian emergencies with activities to assist victims, through the distribution of food, water, makeshift accommodation, medicines and the provision of medical care.[9] In this regard, some speak of a "human right to humanitarian assistance". Here too, the right to food is an essential right for people's subsistence and survival.

In conclusion, as said above,[10] a distinction must be made between the norms governing *the right to food adequate to people's well-being* and the norms governing *the right to food essential for people's subsistence and survival.* It is true that the latter norms are to be found in humanitarian law and international criminal law; and this is quite logical, given the general aims of these normative areas. However, it seems to me that these norms can also operate, *by analogy*, in international human rights law, at least in particular situations of emergency, famine or natural disaster. In other words, they can operate in all cases where food provision is indispensable for people's survival. This is also confirmed by the existence (or at least the progressive development) of the above-mentioned customary norm on humanitarian emergencies. Furthermore, it should be remembered that, as I have said many times,[11] there has been considerable convergence in recent times between the area of human rights and those of humanitarian law and international criminal law, especially in relation to "fundamental" rights.

Can it be argued that the various conventional norms mentioned above on the right to food have, over time, also produced a customary norm? The answer seems negative with regard to *the right to food adequate to people's well-being*: the pertinent norms require States Parties to take on "progressive" obligations and non-binding political commitments that, in my view, are difficult to extend to all the States of the international community.

On the contrary, a positive response could be given, albeit with some caution, about the existence of a general norm of international law on *the right to food essential for people's subsistence and survival.* It is true that the practice, conventional and otherwise, is limited; but the interpreter could enhance the role of the *opinio juris*, the *ratio* of such a norm, its close link with the customary norm on the

[9]On this topic see Acconci (2001), p. 33 ff. Cf. also Institut de Droit International, Sixteenth Commission, "*Humanitarian Assistance*", Resolution of 2 September 2003, Bruges session; ILC, *Draft articles on the protection of persons in the event of disasters*, 2016, in *YILC*, 2016, II (2).

[10]See above, Sect. 13.4.

[11]See above, Sects. 2.4, 9.5.2.2 and 14.3.

right to life, and finally the recent development of the "human right to humanitarian assistance". All these elements could lead to the conclusion that there is a general consensus in the international community on the existence of such a general norm.

15.1.2 Content of the Right

The discussion on the content of the right to food also follows the same logic. In fact, the two groups of norms on the right to food, which I have indicated above, have a very different content. The norms on *the right to food adequate to people's well-being* usually have a very vague and indeterminate content, so much so that many aspects of this content seem to lack even binding legal value. On the contrary, the norms on *the right to food essential for people's subsistence and survival* have a more specific and binding content and a narrower scope, because they operate in situations of armed conflict or emergency or special urgency.

However, it should be warned that the Committee on Economic, Social and Cultural Rights does not follow this approach.[12] The Committee has tried, in some of its General Comments, to give a definition of the right to food;[13] but, in my opinion, not convincingly. Actually, the Committee, focusing on Article 11 of the Covenant on Economic, Social and Cultural Rights, merely distinguishes between a right to adequate food, vague and to be progressively realized, and a core obligation of States to act "to mitigate and alleviate hunger", which would derive from Article 11(2). In particular, in its General Comment No. 12, the Committee states:

> The right to adequate food is realized when every man, woman and child, alone or in community with others, have physical and economic access at all times to adequate food or means for its procurement. The *right to adequate food* shall therefore not be interpreted in a narrow or restrictive sense which equates it with a minimum package of calories, proteins and other specific nutrients. The *right to adequate food* will have to be realized progressively. However, States have a core obligation to take the necessary action to mitigate and alleviate hunger as provided for in paragraph 2 of article 11, even in times of natural or other disasters.[14]

From these words of the Committee, the actual realization of the right to food appears at least "utopian". And even the so-called core obligation is not well defined. Moreover, in the same Comment, the Committee, speaking again about the core content of the right to food, says that it would imply the availability of sufficient food to meet people's nutritional needs and access to such food.[15] Aside from my

[12]Perhaps also because the Committee's rule of reference is only Article 11 of the Covenant on Economic, Social and Cultural Rights.

[13]CteeESCR, General Comment No. 12, 12 May 1999; General Comment No. 15, 20 January 2003.

[14]CteeESCR, General Comment No. 12, 12 May 1999, para. 6 (emphasis in the original quotation).

[15]*Ibidem*, para. 8: "The Committee considers that the core content of the right to adequate food implies: the availability of food in a quantity and quality sufficient to satisfy the dietary needs of individuals, free from adverse substances, and acceptable within a given culture; the accessibility of

criticism of the very concept of core content,[16] it should be noted that even this definition of the core content of the right to food is too vague and extensive.

15.1.3 Obligations

The Committee on Economic, Social and Cultural Rights has also sought to define the obligations of States Parties to the Covenant, in relation to the right to food;[17] and has followed its traditional distinction between obligations to respect, to protect and to fulfil human rights. I have already criticized this "*tripartite typology*", because it has little conceptual value and little practical utility. Instead, I believe that, also with reference to the right to food, one should use the repeatedly mentioned categories of: (*a*) negative obligations; (*b*) immediate and positive obligations of result; (*c*) immediate and positive obligations of due diligence; (*d*) obligations "of progressive realization".

That being said, the norms on *the right to food adequate to people's well-being* contain some political programs and some "progressive" obligations. For the latter, the legal effects I have already described apply.[18]

Instead, the norms on *the right to food essential for people's subsistence and survival* contain immediate obligations. Firstly, the State has a *negative* obligation not to deny individuals or groups of individuals access to essential food that is already available, for example by destroying food or food supply infrastructure.[19] This prohibition is especially, but not only, relevant during armed conflicts.[20] State measures of a legislative nature that deny access to essential food may also form part of this prohibition. Secondly, the State has a *positive* and immediate obligation to provide essential food to the population during periods of armed conflict, famine or humanitarian disasters.[21] Finally, the State also has a *positive* and immediate obligation to prevent measures or actions by individuals aimed at denying other individuals access to food essential for their subsistence or survival.

---

such food in ways that are sustainable and that do not interfere with the enjoyment of other human rights".

[16] See above, Sect. 13.4.

[17] CteeESCR, General Comment No. 12, 12 May 1999, paras. 14–20.

[18] See above, Sect. 8.2.3.

[19] See ACmHPR, *Social and Economic Rights Action Center*, paras. 64–66; *Sudan Human Rights Organisation*, paras. 206–212. Cf. also Kälin and Künzli (2019), p. 306.

[20] See AP I, Art. 54(2); AP II, Art. 14.

[21] According to Kälin and Künzli (2019), p. 293, this would be an obligation to fulfil human rights. As I have already said several times, I do not agree with this category of obligations.

15.2 Right to Water

15.2.1 Norms

The debate on the right to water has many similarities with the one, just done, on the right to food. In fact, the right to water is also laid down, albeit less frequently, in some conventional human rights norms and some norms of international humanitarian law. And again a *difference* emerges: the norms of the first group are generic and indeterminate, while those of the second group are more specific and have a more restrictive content. In addition, it can be considered that the norm of general international law on humanitarian assistance in emergencies also applies to water.

Starting with the area of human rights, it should be noted that the right to water is not mentioned in the Universal Declaration, or in the Covenant on Civil and Political Rights, or in the San Salvador Protocol, or in the European Social Charter. In fact, not even the Covenant on Economic, Social and Cultural Rights explicitly provides for this right; but the relevant Committee has stated that the right to water is implicitly regulated by Article 11 of the Covenant, since it is a right "emanating from, and indispensable for, the realization of the right to an adequate standard of living".[22] Therefore the right to water, like the right to food, is also conceived by the Committee as a specific aspect of the broader right to an adequate standard of living.[23] In other words, one can speak of *the right to water adequate to people's well-being.*[24]

This view is reaffirmed in various sectoral human rights treaties, which are more precise because they explicitly mention the right to water. Examples include the Convention on the prohibition of discrimination against women (Art. 14(2)(h)); the Convention on the Rights of the Child (Art. 24(2)(c)); the Convention on the Rights of Persons with Disabilities (Art. 28(2)(a)); and some African continent agreements on the rights of children and women.[25] In the Convention on the prohibition of discrimination against women, for example, it is declared that States Parties shall take appropriate measures to ensure that women enjoy the benefits of rural development and, in particular, the right:

> To enjoy adequate living conditions, particularly in relation to housing, sanitation, electricity and *water supply* [. . .].[26]

[22]CteeESCR, General Comment No. 15, 20 January 2003, para. 3.

[23]In the Committee's view, the right to water should also be implicit in the right to food and the right to health.

[24]See also GA Res. 64/292, 3 August 2010, para.1.

[25]African Charter of the Rights and Welfare of the Child (Art. 14(2)(c)); Protocol to the African Charter on Human and Peoples' Rights on the Rights of Women in Africa (Art. 15(a)).

[26]CEDAW, Art. 14(2)(h) (emphasis added).

In the Convention on the Rights of the Child, States Parties are also required to combat malnutrition "through the provision of adequate nutritious foods and *clean drinking-water*".[27]

On the other hand, if one looks at international humanitarian law, one may observe that there are several norms that configure the right to water in a different way. These norms, like those examined above on the right to food, are intended to prohibit States parties to armed conflicts from making the victims of such conflicts thirsty or even depriving them of the water they need for their *subsistence or survival*. Articles 20, 26 and 46 of the Third Geneva Convention of 1949, Articles 89 and 127 of the Fourth Geneva Convention, Article 54 of the First Additional Protocol and Articles 5(1)(b) and 14 of the Second Additional Protocol can be cited. For example, Article 26 of the Third Geneva Convention states that:

> Sufficient drinking water shall be supplied to prisoners of war.

Article 5(1)(b) of the Second Additional Protocol provides that persons deprived of their liberty for reasons related to the armed conflict:

> [. . .] shall, to the same extent as the local civilian population, be provided with food and drinking water [. . .].

Moreover, as already seen, Article 14 of the same Protocol prohibits the attack or destruction of goods essential to the subsistence of the civilian population, including "drinking water installations and supplies and irrigation works".

In conclusion, also in relation to the right to water, as for the right to food, a distinction can be made between the norms governing *the right to water adequate to people's well-being* and the norms regulating *the right to water essential for people's subsistence and survival*. The latter norms operate in situations of armed conflict and consider the right to water as a "subsistence right", closely related to the right to life.

Again, I believe that these norms can also operate, by analogy, in the field of human rights, in emergency situations. And it does not seem too far-fetched to argue that a norm of general international law on *the right to water essential for people's survival* has also developed over time. Here too, as with the right to essential food, this conclusion is reinforced by the growing support for norms that oblige States to act in situations of humanitarian emergency.[28]

15.2.2 Content of the Right

The content of the right to water changes according to the two groups of norms mentioned above.

---

[27] CRC, Art. 24(2)(c) (emphasis added).

[28] See above, Sect. 15.1.1.

The norms dealing with *the right to water adequate to people's well-being* do not have a uniform content. As we have seen, sometimes this right only emerges implicitly as an aspect of the right to an adequate standard of living. Sometimes, instead, the right is functional to the rural living conditions of women, or to the social protection of the disabled, or to the health of children. The difficulty of giving a precise content to this right also emerges from the work of the Committee on Economic, Social and Cultural Rights. The Committee, for example, in its General Comment No. 15, starts from a very broad and ambitious definition of this right when it states that:

> The human right to water entitles everyone to sufficient, safe, acceptable, physically accessible and affordable water for personal and domestic uses.[29]

However, when the Committee has to clarify the legal content of the right, it merely says that it includes a series of "freedoms and entitlements",[30] which correspond to both general and specific obligations of the Member States. The Committee then goes on to deal with these obligations, neglecting to go further into the content of the right to adequate water.

Instead, the conclusions are different if one examines the second group of norms, i.e. those which govern *the right to water essential for people's subsistence and survival* and which derive from humanitarian law. Then one notes that their content is more precise, is immediately binding and, at the same time, their scope is more limited, because they only operate in situations of armed conflict or emergency or particular urgency. The considerations I have made about the right to essential food apply here.

In fact, even the Committee on Economic, Social and Cultural Rights seems to recognize, albeit from a different point of view than mine, that the right to water also has a different and "stronger" dimension than that merely linked to people's well-being and standard of living. Indeed, the Committee, albeit incidentally, has stated that this right "is one of the most fundamental conditions for *survival*"[31] and that it "should also be seen in conjunction with other rights [. . .] foremost among them the right to life and human dignity".[32] But then the Committee did not further develop the concept of the connection between the right to water and the right to life.

15.2.3 Obligations

Also in relation to the obligations arising from the right to water, it is useful to distinguish between the norms on *the right to water adequate to people's well-being*,

[29]CteeESCR, General Comment No. 15, 20 January 2003, para. 2.

[30]*Ibidem*, para. 10.

[31]*Ibidem*, para. 3 (emphasis added).

[32]*Ibidem*.

which contain political programs and "progressive" obligations, and the norms on *the right to water essential for people's subsistence and survival*, which contain immediate obligations.[33]

Some examples of the latter can be given. States have negative obligations not to prevent access of individuals or groups to essential water that is already available; not to destroy essential water services or infrastructure during armed conflicts or other states of emergency; not to disconnect or unjustifiably exclude people from essential water supply services. In addition, States have positive (and immediate) obligations to provide essential water to the population and to prevent measures by private individuals aimed at impeding the access of other individuals or groups of individuals to essential water.

In international practice, one must emphasize the importance of some decisions of the African Commission on Human and Peoples' Rights,[34] which highlighted the relevance of the obligation to provide essential water to the population. These decisions state that the right not to be deprived of essential water is a part of the right to health and of the right to a healthy environment, respectively protected by Articles 16 and 24 of the African Charter. In the *Free Legal Assistance Group* case,[35] the Commission stated that Zaire had violated Article 16 of the African Charter because it had failed to provide essential health services such as drinking water. In the *Social and Economic Rights Action Center v. Nigeria* case,[36] the Commission found that Nigeria had violated, inter alia, Articles 16 and 24 of the African Charter, because it had directly participated in, and in any case had not prevented, the pollution of water resources in the Ogoni territory.

15.3 Right to Housing

15.3.1 Norms

The right to housing is also established, more or less directly, by human rights norms and humanitarian law norms. And, again, these norms have different contents.

In treaties and other international human rights acts, there is a first, rather large group of norms that conceives the right to housing as a specific aspect of the right to an adequate standard of living. With reference to these norms, one can speak of *the right to housing adequate to people's well-being*. In this sense, one can recall Article 25(1) of the Universal Declaration; Article 11(1) of the Covenant on Economic, Social and Cultural Rights; Article 38 of the Arab Charter; Article 27(3) of the

[33]Instead, the Committee on Economic, Social and Cultural Rights, as usual, distinguishes between obligations to respect, to protect and to fulfil human rights. CteeESCR, General Comment No. 15, 20 January 2003, paras. 20–29.

[34]See Focarelli (2013), pp. 214–215.

[35]ACmHPR, *Free Legal Assistance Group and Others*, para. 47.

[36]ACmHPR, *Social and Economic Rights Action Center and Others v. Nigeria*, paras. 50–54.

Convention on the Rights of the Child; Article 28 of the Convention on the Rights of Persons with Disabilities; and Article 14(2)(h) of the Convention on the Elimination of Discrimination against Women. Article 31 of the (revised) European Social Charter, even if it provides for an *autonomous* right to housing, actually considers it in a similar way to the above mentioned provisions, by regulating it in essentially programmatic terms. In fact, Article 31 reads as follows:

> With a view to ensuring the effective exercise of the right to housing, the Parties undertake to take measures designed: 1. to promote access to housing of an adequate standard; 2. to prevent and reduce homelessness with a view to its gradual elimination; 3. to make the price of housing accessible to those without adequate resources.

A second group of norms conceives the right to housing in the same way; but it is *complementary* to the first group, because it merely establishes the principle of equality or non-discrimination in the enjoyment of that right. Examples include Article 5(e)(iii) of the Convention against racial discrimination; Article 21 of the Geneva Convention relating to the Status of Refugees; and Article 43(1)(d) of the Convention on the Rights of Migrant Workers. But these provisions are not relevant now, because the principles of equality and non-discrimination will be examined later.[37]

A third group of norms, again on human rights, actually deals with rights other than the right to housing, but which may have an indirect impact on that right. Examples include the right to health, the right to respect for private and family life, the right to property and the right to a healthy environment. But I will deal with these rights later.[38]

Finally, there are the norms of international humanitarian law on the right to housing, which are relevant here from the perspective of "fundamental" human rights. These norms, which admittedly are not numerous, conceive the right to housing as an *essential right for people's subsistence*. Exemplary in this sense is Article 69 of the First Additional Protocol to the Geneva Conventions, which regulates the essential needs in the occupied territories, and according to which:

> [...] the Occupying Power shall, to the fullest extent of the means available to it and without any adverse distinction, also ensure the provision of clothing, *bedding, means of shelter*, other supplies essential to the survival of the civilian population of the occupied territory [...].[39]

The following Article 70 provides that, when the supply of such goods is insufficient, relief actions of a humanitarian nature must be undertaken. Other relevant norms are, for example, those of the Fourth Geneva Convention which

[37] See below, Chap. 18.

[38] See below, Sects. 15.4, 20.1, 20.2, 23.2 and 25.4.

[39] AP I, Art. 69 (emphasis added).

prohibit pillage (Art. 33),[40] which prohibit the power occupying a territory from destroying property belonging to the civilian population (Art. 53), and which prohibit this power from requisitioning goods essential to the needs of this population (Art. 55).

In view of the above, the question must be asked, also with regard to the right to housing, whether all the aforementioned treaty norms have produced a customary norm. In my view, the answer is negative with regard to *the right to housing adequate to people's well-being*, for the same reasons as those already given with regard to the right to *adequate* food and water.[41]

It is more difficult to assess whether a norm of general international law has developed on *the right to housing essential for people' s subsistence*, and which can operate when there is no conventional ad hoc norm. On the one hand, a positive answer could be given, on the basis of the arguments I have proposed above in relation to the rights to food and water that are essential for people's subsistence; that is, by asserting the *ratio* of the norm, its link with the right to life and the growing consensus about a human right to humanitarian assistance. However, on the other hand, it must also be admitted that, with regard to the right to *essential* housing, the number of conventional norms is small. Moreover housing, compared to food and water, is more rarely an indispensable resource for people's subsistence or even survival. Therefore, on the whole, it seems to me that the formation of a norm of general international law should be excluded.

15.3.2 Content of the Right

Coming to the content of the two main groups of norms mentioned above, it is immediately apparent that the norms dealing with *the right to housing adequate to people's well-being* are vague and indeterminate. The Committee on Economic, Social and Cultural Rights also gives a very broad and extensive interpretation of this content when, for example, in its General Comment No. 4, it states that:

> [...] the right to housing should not be interpreted in a narrow or restrictive sense which equates it with, for example, the shelter provided by merely having a roof over one's head or views shelter exclusively as a commodity. Rather it should be seen as the right to live somewhere in security, peace and dignity.[42]

The Committee then adds that Article 11(1) of the Covenant refers not only to housing, but to adequate housing; and that it means:

---

[40]See also AP II, Art. 4(2)(g).

[41]Conventional rules on the right to adequate housing mostly contain "progressive" obligations or non-binding political commitments, which are not applicable to all States of the international community.

[42]CteeESCR, General Comment No. 4, 13 December 1991, para. 7.

> [. . .] adequate privacy, adequate space, adequate security, adequate lighting and ventilation, adequate basic infrastructure and adequate location, with regard to work and basic facilities – all at a reasonable cost.[43]

This very broad interpretation of the content of the right to housing, in my view, can only be accepted if it refers to a right that can be realized by States progressively in the rather indefinite future, or if it regards, rather than a real right, a political program that is not binding on States. After all, the Committee had to realistically admit that:

> [there] remains a disturbingly large gap between the norms set in article 11(1) [. . .] and the situation prevailing in many parts of the world.[44]

But the matter changes if one looks at the content of the norms governing *the right to housing essential for people's subsistence*. Let me recall the aforementioned Article 69 of the First Additional Protocol, which speaks of "supplies essential to the survival of the civilian population of the occupied territory" during armed conflicts. Here the right to adequate housing is not in question, with the criteria of privacy, space, security, lighting, ventilation and other similar criteria (indicated by the Committee on Economic, Social and Cultural Rights); but rather the much more limited "right to shelter". Once again, this is a *right to subsistence and survival*, closely linked to the right to life. It seems to me that the African Commission also expressed this concept of the right to housing, in the already mentioned *Social and Economic Rights Action Center* case, when it stated that:

> [. . .] the right to shelter obliges the Nigerian Government not to destroy the housing of its citizens and not to obstruct efforts by individuals or communities to rebuild lost homes [. . .] The government has destroyed Ogoni houses and villages and then, through its security forces, obstructed, harassed, beaten and, in some cases, shot and killed innocent citizens who have attempted to return to rebuild their ruined homes. These actions constitute massive violations of the right to shelter [. . .].[45]

However, the Commission considered that the right in question, although not explicitly provided for in the African Charter, derives from the combination of the Charter's provisions on the right to health, the right to property and the protection of the family.[46] Therefore, this decision also reveals the difficulty of basing *the right to housing essential for people's subsistence* on a norm of general international law, which could be applied when there is no ad hoc conventional norm. Indeed, the African Commission has preferred to infer this right from other human rights, expressly established by the African Charter.

---

[43] *Ibidem*.

[44] *Ibidem*, para. 4.

[45] ACmHPR, *Social and Economic Rights Action Center and Others v. Nigeria*, paras. 61–62.

[46] *Ibidem*, para. 60.

15.3.3 Obligations

The various norms on the right to housing examined above contain a number of different obligations on the part of States. Leaving aside the political commitments and the "progressive" obligations, to which the observations I made on several occasions apply, it is worth recalling the main treaty obligations which correspond to *the right to housing essential for people's subsistence.*

Firstly, States have a *negative* obligation, under international humanitarian law, to refrain from destroying or plundering the property of the civilian population; and a *negative* obligation to refrain from carrying out forced evacuations or deportations that are not justified by military necessity or the need to save the population. Secondly, States have a *positive* and immediate obligation to provide emergency accommodation for victims of armed conflict and natural or humanitarian disasters. In certain extreme cases, violation of this obligation may even constitute inhuman or degrading treatment.[47]

The Committee on Economic, Social and Cultural Rights considers that the right to housing also gives rise to *other obligations* for States, such as the prohibition of arbitrarily depriving people of their homes through illegal evictions or "forced evictions"[48] and the obligation to protect people from interference by private individuals suppressing the right to housing. In my view, these obligations exist, but they do not derive from the right to housing, but from other human rights, such as the right to property[49] and the right to respect for private and family life.[50]

15.4 Right to Health

15.4.1 Norms

The right to health[51] is enshrined in numerous international human rights norms, but also in various international humanitarian law norms aimed at protecting the health of combatants and civilians involved in armed conflicts. Finally, the general norm on the right to humanitarian assistance is also relevant.

International instruments on the protection of human rights include the Universal Declaration (Art. 25); the Covenant on Economic, Social and Cultural Rights (Art. 12); the Convention against Racial Discrimination (Art. 5(e)(iv)); the Convention on the Elimination of Discrimination against Women (Art. 12); the Convention on the Rights of the Child (Art. 24); the Convention on the Rights of Persons with Disabilities (Art. 25); the European Social Charter (revised) (Art. 11); the EU

[47]See ECtHR, *M.S.S. v. Belgium and Greece*, paras. 249–264.

[48]See CteeESCR, General Comment No. 7, 16 May 1997.

[49]See below, Sect. 23.2.

[50]See below, Sects. 20.1 and 20.2.

[51]On this right see, e.g., Acconci (2001) and Murphy (2013).

Charter of Fundamental Rights (Art. 35); the San Salvador Protocol (Art. 10); the African Charter (Art. 16); and the Arab Charter (Art. 39).

These provisions are not formulated in a uniform way; but their conception of the right to health is the same, namely *the right of people to enjoy a high level of health and well-being*. The Universal Declaration, for example, in Article 25(1), proclaims that:

> Everyone has the right to a standard of living adequate for the health and well-being of himself and of his family, including [. . .] medical care [. . .].

Article 12 of the Covenant on Economic, Social and Cultural Rights, instead, provides for an autonomous right to health; and begins (in paragraph 1) with a very broad definition of this right:

> The States Parties [. . .] recognize the right of everyone to the enjoyment of the highest attainable standard of physical and mental health.

But then Article 12 continues, in paragraph 2, listing a series of measures of a highly programmatic nature, which the States Parties should take in order to fully realize this right. Article 24 of the Convention on the Rights of the Child adopts the same formula as the Covenant (*the right to the enjoyment of the highest attainable standard of health*); but it is more elaborate and detailed in listing the measures that the States Parties should take. Much more concise, instead, are the provisions contained in the two conventions against discrimination, which are limited to prohibiting racial discrimination and discrimination against women in the right to medical and health care.

As for the regional instruments, Article 16 of the African Charter is very concise and is limited to the same formula as Article 12, paragraph 1, of the Covenant. Even "weaker" are the provisions contained in the European Social Charter[52] and the EU Charter of Fundamental Rights,[53] which even refers back to the laws and practices of domestic legal systems.

In contrast, the provisions contained in the San Salvador Protocol and the Arab Charter are more interesting. Article 10 of the San Salvador Protocol begins, in paragraph 1, with the usual formula that everyone has the right to health, understood as the enjoyment of the highest level of physical, mental and social well-being. But then it establishes, in paragraph 2, that the States Parties "agree to recognize health as

[52]ESCrev, Art. 11 (*The right to protection of health*): "With a view to ensuring the effective exercise of the right to protection of health, the Parties undertake, either directly or in cooperation with public or private organizations, to take appropriate measures designed inter alia: 1. to remove as far as possible the causes of ill-health; 2. to provide advisory and educational facilities for the promotion of health and the encouragement of individual responsibility in matters of health; 3. to prevent as far as possible epidemic, endemic and other diseases, as well as accidents".

[53]EUCh, Art. 38 (*Health care*): "Everyone has the right of access to preventive health care and the right to benefit from medical treatment under the conditions established by national laws and practices [. . .]".

a public good"; and that, in particular, they undertake to adopt several measures that are more precise in character than those provided for in other international instruments. Among these measures, the adoption of *primary health care*, i.e. health care accessible to all individuals and groups in the national community, is remarkable. The Arab Charter, in its Article 39, also recognizes the right to enjoy the highest attainable level of physical and mental health, and the right of citizens to enjoy *basic medical care* and access to medical services without discrimination.

In conclusion, the norms on the right to health contained in the human rights treaties usually provide for the right of all individuals to a high level of health and, sometimes, also for a series of programmatic measures for the progressive realization of this right. Only some treaties establish the more specific right of individuals to have access to basic or primary care.

Instead, the norms of international humanitarian law and those on emergencies and natural disasters are, once again, different.

In humanitarian law, the aim is not, of course, to achieve a high level of health and well-being for all people, but rather, much more limited but more urgent, to guarantee *medical assistance for people involved in armed conflicts*, with particular regard to the most vulnerable, such as the wounded, the sick, the infirm, prisoners and pregnant women. In other words, it is a question of providing *basic medical needs* for these people, and therefore their *right to an essential level of health care*.

Indeed, there are many norms of humanitarian law that pursue this aim. Only a few examples can be given here. Article 3(2) common to the four Geneva Conventions states that "the wounded and sick shall be collected and cared for". The Third Geneva Convention contains many detailed provisions to ensure adequate medical care for prisoners of war (Arts. 29–32). The Fourth Geneva Convention lays down similar norms for the wounded, sick, infirm and women who have recently given birth (Arts. 16–23); and states that, in the occupied territories, the occupying power must provide medicines, health services or hospitals and, where appropriate, relief actions in favor of the population (Arts. 55–57 and 59). The First Additional Protocol contains many provisions dedicated to treating and protecting the health of the victims of armed conflicts (Arts. 10–15), and an important provision dedicated to the relief of the civilian population (Art. 70). The Second Additional Protocol also contains rules on the protection of the wounded, sick and shipwrecked in non-international armed conflicts (Arts. 7–11).

Finally, on the subject of natural disasters, what I have already said about the right to food and water also applies here, regarding the existence of a norm of general international law on the *right to humanitarian assistance*. Actually, in relation to the right to health, the obligations of States to provide humanitarian assistance are even more relevant, since these obligations almost always have the primary purpose of responding to a health emergency.

15.4.2 Content of the Right

The content of the right to health varies according to the different groups of norms described above.

The norms of international human rights instruments, as already seen, tend to conceive of this right as "the right of everyone to the enjoyment of the highest attainable standard of physical and mental health".[54] It follows that the content of this right is vague and indeterminate. On the other hand, it is clear, even if only for logical reasons, that everyone's right to health cannot mean the right to be healthy, which obviously also depends on personal physical conditions and choices; but only the right to have the State commit itself to creating the conditions that favor the best standard of health for people.[55] This is also confirmed by the work of the Committee on Economic, Social and Cultural Rights. The Committee, in its General Comment No. 14, states that the right to health is not limited to the right to health care; but that it:

> [. . .] embraces a wide range of socio-economic factors that promote conditions in which people can lead a healthy life, and extends to the underlying determinants of health, such as food and nutrition, housing, access to safe and potable water and adequate sanitation, safe and healthy working conditions, and a healthy environment.[56]

The Committee also argues that the right to health:

> [. . .] contains both freedoms and entitlements. The freedoms include the right to control one's health and body, including sexual and reproductive freedom, and the right to be free from interference, such as the right to be free from torture, non-consensual medical treatment and experimentation. By contrast, the entitlements include the right to a system of health protection which provides equality of opportunity for people to enjoy the highest attainable level of health.[57]

Furthermore, in the Committee's view, the right to health, while having its own autonomy, has close interdependent relationships with many other rights, such as the right to life, the prohibition of torture and inhuman or degrading treatment, the right to personal liberty and security, the right to food, water, housing, etc. In many cases, therefore, there is an overlap between the right to health and other human rights. It is clear, for example, that when a serious lack of medical care causes death, the violation of the right to health can be absorbed by that of the right to life. One may recall the leading case *Lopes de Sousa Fernandes* of the European Court of Human Rights.[58]

---

[54] CESCR, Art. 12(1).

[55] Kälin and Künzli (2019), p. 303.

[56] CteeESCR, General Comment No. 14, 11 August 2000, para. 4.

[57] *Ibidem*, para. 8.

[58] ECtHR, *Lopes de Sousa Fernandes*, esp. paras. 162–196.

Instead, the norms of international humanitarian law, at least the conventional ones, have a more limited and more precise content, which is defined by each individual norm. However, a general principle can perhaps be drawn from them as a whole: that the States parties to an armed conflict have an obligation to provide *essential medical assistance* to those involved in armed conflicts, and especially to those who do not or no longer participate in hostilities. These people therefore have *the right to an essential level of health care.*

Finally, a right with a similar content is derived from the norms on humanitarian emergencies. Indeed, the emerging norm of general international law, which imposes an obligation on States to provide *humanitarian assistance* in situations of disasters or natural emergencies, has a broad content, since it provides for various relief and assistance activities; but, among these, the one aimed at responding to people's basic medical needs stands out. Therefore, also in this case one can speak of a right of the people involved in such emergencies to enjoy an *essential level of medical assistance.*

15.4.3 Obligations

With regard to the obligations of States, corresponding to the right to health, I can make a similar argument to that made in relation to the other rights that protect people's basic needs.

The right to the enjoyment of a high level of health and well-being is not, in principle, a binding and judicially enforceable right to which immediate obligations on the part of the States correspond. On the contrary, it requires political programs and "progressive" obligations from States. Moreover, it depends very much on the economic resources and effective means available to each State and therefore presupposes different norms of health protection in different countries.[59] However, it should be noted that some treaty norms, mentioned above, oblige States to adopt in favor of all individuals' primary health care (Art. 10, San Salvador Protocol) or basic medical care services (Art. 39, Arab Charter). Such obligations could be configured as positive obligations of due diligence. But they cannot be regarded as imposed on all States by a norm of general international law.

As for the obligations corresponding to *the right to an essential level of health care* (in situations of armed conflict or humanitarian emergencies), they have, in principle, the character of immediacy. For example, States have a negative obligation not to destroy, during armed conflicts, existing health care facilities and not to prevent people from having access to such facilities. They also have numerous positive obligations (both of result and of due diligence), which are set out in the various above-mentioned provisions of the Geneva Conventions and Additional

[59]Cf. CESCR, Art. 12(1): "[. . .] the right of everyone to the enjoyment of the *highest attainable* standard of physical and mental health" (emphasis added).

Protocols. Suffice it to mention, among others, the obligation of the Occupying Power to provide medicine and health services for the civilian population.

15.5 Right to a Healthy Environment (Cross-Reference)

The human right to a healthy environment is, in some respects, an individual right, but in other, more relevant respects, a collective right. Therefore I will deal with it later.[60]

References

Acconci P (2001) Tutela della salute e diritto internazionale. Cedam, Padova
Focarelli C (2013) La persona umana nel diritto internazionale. Il Mulino, Bologna
Kälin W, Künzli J (2019) The law of international human rights protection, 2nd edn. OUP, Oxford-New York
Murphy T (2013) Health and human rights. Hart, London

[60]See below, Sect. 25.4.2.

16 Protection of Liberty and Security of the Person

So far, I have talked about human rights which aim to protect the life and physical integrity of the person[1] and those which aim to protect the basic needs and sometimes even the very subsistence of the person.[2] There is no doubt that these goals are paramount under international human rights law. But another preeminent purpose is to protect the *liberty and security* of people. It is entrusted to certain rights of very ancient origin and which belong to the first generation of human rights. The most important are those arising from the prohibition of slavery, servitude and forced labor and the prohibition of arbitrary arrest or detention. More recently, norms have been added on the prohibition of enforced disappearance of persons.

16.1 Prohibition of Slavery, Servitude and Forced Labor

16.1.1 Norms

The prohibition of slavery, servitude and forced labor is provided for in numerous international human rights instruments. The Universal Declaration solemnly proclaims, in Article 1, that "All human beings are born free and equal in dignity and rights" and, in Article 4, states that:

> No one shall be held in slavery or servitude; slavery and the slave trade shall be prohibited in all their forms.

The main general human rights treaties include provisions supplementing the prohibition of slavery and servitude with the prohibition of forced or compulsory labor; and have a more specific and detailed content than the Universal Declaration.

[1]See above, Sects. 14.1, 14.2 and 14.3.

[2]See above, Sects. 15.1, 15.2, 15.3 and 15.4.

R. Pisillo Mazzeschi, *International Human Rights Law*,
https://doi.org/10.1007/978-3-030-77032-7_16

One can recall Article 8 of the Covenant on Civil and Political Rights, Article 4 of the European Convention,[3] Article 6 of the American Convention, Article 5 of the EU Charter of Fundamental Rights, and Article 10 of the Arab Charter. The African Charter, instead, limits itself to prohibiting slavery and the slave trade (Art. 5).[4]

There are also sectoral treaties dealing with these rights, such as the 1926 Convention on the Slave Trade and Slavery,[5] the 1956 Supplementary Convention on the Abolition of Slavery, the Slave Trade, and Institutions and Practices Similar to Slavery,[6] the 1930 ILO Convention on Forced Labour,[7] the 1957 ILO Convention on Abolition of Forced Labour,[8] the 2000 Additional Protocol to the Palermo Convention relating to Trafficking in Persons,[9] and the 2005 European Convention against Trafficking in Human Beings.[10]

Finally, it should be noted that reducing one to slavery is considered a crime against humanity and is punished by the Statute of the International Criminal Court.[11] In particular, when practices of enslavement, sexual slavery or forced prostitution are carried out as part of an "extensive or systematic attack" on the civilian population, in execution of a plan by a government or group, those responsible are liable to prosecution under international criminal law. Enslavement may also constitute a war crime.[12] Therefore, when these abuses are attributable to a State, the responsibility of that State for an international crime is also produced, in addition to that of individuals.[13]

[3]ECHR, Art. 4 (*Prohibition of slavery and forced labour*): "1. No one shall be held in slavery or servitude. 2. No one shall be required to perform forced or compulsory labour. 3. For the purpose of this article the term 'forced or compulsory labour' shall not include: a. any work required to be done in the ordinary course of detention imposed according to the provisions of Article 5 of this Convention or during conditional release from such detention; b. any service of a military character or, in case of conscientious objectors in countries where they are recognised, service exacted instead of compulsory military service; c. any service exacted in case of an emergency or calamity threatening the life or well-being of the community; d. any work or service which forms part of normal civic obligations".

[4]See also CRPD, Art. 27(2); CMW, Art. 11; ESCrev, Art. 1(2).

[5]Convention to Suppress the Slave Trade and Slavery of 25 September 1926.

[6]Supplementary Convention on the Abolition of Slavery, the Slave Trade, and Institutions and Practices Similar to Slavery of 7 September 1956.

[7]ILO Forced Labour Convention of 28 June 1930 (No. 29).

[8]ILO Abolition of Forced Labour Convention of 25 June 1957 (No. 105).

[9]Protocol to Prevent, Suppress and Punish Trafficking in Persons Especially Women and Children of 15 November 2000, supplementing the UN Convention against Transnational Organized Crime.

[10]European Convention on Action against Trafficking in Human Beings of 16 May 2005. It should be noted that "human trafficking" has to be distinguished from "migrant smuggling", although the two phenomena are often linked.

[11]Rome Statute, Art. 7(1)(c) and (g).

[12]See Rome Statute, Art. 8(2)(b)(xxii) and (e)(vi).

[13]See above, Sect. 14.3.

It follows from the numerous international norms prohibiting all forms of slavery or servitude and from the *opinio juris* of the international community that this prohibition has been incorporated into a customary norm of international law and that this norm has the nature of *jus cogens*.[14] I do not believe, instead, that the prohibition of forced or compulsory labor has acquired the character of a peremptory norm.

16.1.2 Content of the Prohibitions

The historical forms of slavery, that is, of individuals who are the property of other individuals, who have no personality or legal capacity, and who can be reduced to exploitable and marketable objects, have now disappeared. However, the international norms indicated above have not lost their meaning, since modern forms of slavery or servitude and forced labor survive in the world. Think, for example, of trafficking in human beings, especially women and children, for sexual exploitation; forced prostitution; the practices of forced marriages; the exploitation of child labor; and the use of child soldiers.

In order to clarify the content of the norms in question, the notions of slavery, servitude and forced labor should be better defined, bearing in mind that these notions have been interpreted in a dynamic and evolutionary way by the international human rights monitoring bodies.

Slavery is defined in Article 1(1) of the 1926 Convention as:

> [. . .] the status or condition of a person over whom any or all of the powers attaching to the right of ownership are exercised.

This definition was considered by the International Criminal Tribunal for the Former Yugoslavia as also valid for customary law. Instead, the Statute of the International Criminal Court defines slavery as:

> [. . .] the exercise of any or all the powers attaching to the right of ownership over a person and includes the exercise of such power in the course of trafficking in persons, in particular women and children.[15]

This provision poses the problem of the relationship between the notion of slavery and that of *trafficking in human beings*. In the Statute of the International Criminal Court, the latter concept is, in practice, included in the former. The

[14]See, among others, Zagrebelsky et al. (2016), p. 172.

[15]Rome Statute, Art. (2)(c).

European Court of Human Rights, in the *Rantsev* case,[16] also equated trafficking in human beings with slavery and applied Article 4 of the European Convention to it. The Human Rights Committee[17] considered that trafficking in women and forced prostitution, although not expressly provided for in Article 8 of the Covenant on Civil and Political Rights, actually violate this provision.

However, more often it is considered that the concept of trafficking in human beings has its own specificity and should be treated separately from the prohibition of slavery, especially with a view to criminal repression. For example, Article 5 of the EU Charter of Fundamental Rights expressly prohibits trafficking in human beings. The European Union has also adopted Directive 2011/36 on preventing and combating trafficking in human beings,[18] which specifies the concepts of trafficking and exploitation.

The concept of *servitude*, instead, refers to persons who have not lost their legal capacity, but who must submit their work or services to the discretionary will of another person. The above-mentioned Supplementary Convention of 1956 defines servitude as the condition of a person:

> [...] who is by law, custom or agreement bound to live and labour on land belonging to another person and to render some determinate service to such other person, whether for reward or not, and is not free to change his status.[19]

Furthermore, this Convention equates a number of practices which are listed in detail to servitude, such as debt bondage, matrimonial practices of exploitation of women, practices of exploitation of child labor. The European Court of Human Rights also considers servitude to be a concept close, but not identical, to that of slavery.[20] The Court, in the *Siliadin* judgment,[21] established that certain situations of domestic work by immigrant children, equated with servitude, were contrary to Article 4 of the Convention.

As for the concept of *forced or compulsory labor*, it is derived in particular from ILO Convention No. 29 of 1930, which speaks of:

> [...] all work or service which is exacted from any person under the menace of any penalty and for which the said person has not offered himself voluntarily.[22]

---

[16]ECtHR, *Rantsev v. Cyprus and Russia*, paras. 281–282.

[17]HRCtee, General Comment No. 28, 29 March 2000, para. 12.

[18]Directive 2011/36/EU of the European Parliament and of the Council of 5 April 2011 on preventing and combating trafficking in human beings and protecting its victims.

[19]Supplementary Convention on the Abolition of Slavery, the Slave Trade, and Institutions and Practices Similar to Slavery, Art. 1(b).

[20]ECtHR, *Seguin v. France.*

[21]ECtHR, *Siliadin v. France*, paras. 89 and 148.

[22]ILO Forced Labour Convention, Art. 2.

However, this notion has also been interpreted in a broad sense by human rights monitoring bodies. For example, the European Court of Human Rights has stated that the threat of returning immigrants employed as domestic workers may, in certain cases, constitute a hypothesis of forced labor.[23] The Inter-American Court of Human Rights, in the *Ituango Massacres* case, considered that the working conditions to which some shepherds in Colombia had been subjected, who had been forced to work in places far from home and threatened with death in case of escape, constituted forced labor.[24]

Finally, it should be noted that the prohibitions of slavery and servitude are absolute, i.e. they do not allow limits or exceptions; they are also non-derogable in time of emergency.[25] On the contrary, the prohibition of forced or compulsory labor provides for certain exceptions, and it can be derogated from, as will be seen below.

16.1.3 Derogations and Exceptions to the Prohibition of Forced Labor

The prohibition of forced or compulsory labor may be derogated in time of emergency. This can be deduced, for example, from Articles 8(3)(a) and 4(4) of the Covenant on Civil and Political Rights; Articles 4(2) and 15(2) of the European Convention; and Articles 6 and 27 of the American Convention.

Moreover, the prohibition in question is not absolute, because it provides for exceptions. In the main human rights treaties these exceptions are explicitly listed;[26] and they consist of: (*a*) work or services normally imposed on individuals who are regularly detained or on parole; (*b*) services of a military nature and, where conscientious objection is permitted, services imposed by law on conscientious objectors; (*c*) services imposed in situations of crisis or disaster or calamity, which threaten the life or well-being of the national community; (*d*) work or services which are part of normal civic duties.

The exact content of these exceptions raises a number of questions of interpretation, for the solution of which reference should be made to the practice of international supervisory bodies. The Human Rights Committee, for example, has considered that work carried out during detention can be considered "normally required" if its main purpose is the reintegration of detainees.[27] The European Convention on Human Rights does not provide for a right to conscientious objection; but the EU Charter of Fundamental Rights recognizes this right on the basis of the national laws governing its exercise. In relation to services of a military nature,

[23]ECtHR, *C.N. v. UK*, paras. 69 and 81. Se also, for a similar case, ECtHR, *Chowdury and Others v. Greece*, paras. 86–91.

[24]IACtHR, *Ituango Massacres v. Colombia*, paras. 154-166.

[25]See ECHR, Art. 15(2); CCPR, Art. 4(2); ACHR, Art. 27(2).

[26]See, e.g., CCPR, Art. 8(3)(c); ECHR, Art. 4(3); ACHR, Art. 6(3).

[27]See HRCtee, *Radosevic v. Germany*, para. 7.3.

the Strasbourg Court held, in the *Chitos* case,[28] that the plaintiff, a Greek citizen who had served in the army for 20 years and had been recalled to serve for a further 9 years on pain of paying a fee, was the victim of forced labor, not subject to the exception of services of a military nature.

With regard to civic duties, the Human Rights Committee has considered them to be "normal" if they are not exceptional measures, if they do not have a punitive purpose or effect, and if they are provided for by law to fulfil a legitimate purpose under the Covenant.[29] The Strasbourg monitoring bodies have stated that civic duties include that of a dentist in Norway who has to perform his profession as a public service for a period of 2 years; and that imposed by Austrian law on lawyers and notaries to provide free legal assistance to persons suffering from mental illness.[30]

16.1.4 Obligations

The prohibitions of slavery, servitude and forced labor entail a series of obligations for States similar to those I have already talked about in relation to the right to life, the prohibition of torture and the prohibition of international crimes.

Therefore, in summary, States have, first and foremost, a negative obligation to refrain from such abuses and to not adopt norms allowing them. Secondly, States are subject to several positive and immediate obligations of prevention, repression and reparation aimed at ensuring effective protection against the violation of these prohibitions by private individuals. In particular, States must have (or provide themselves with) adequate regulatory and administrative apparatus of prevention and must take concrete measures of prevention when necessary. In addition, they must have an adequate administrative and judicial apparatus of repression[31] and must take concrete investigative measures to identify and apprehend those responsible for violations. Finally, they have an obligation to prosecute and punish them[32] and to provide reparation to the victims of violations. As previously seen, some of these obligations are characterized as obligations of result and others as due diligence obligations. These positive obligations are well summarized by the Human Rights Committee in its Concluding Observations on Poland of 2016.[33] Finally, according to some authors,[34] the prohibitions in question would also impose some

---

[28]ECtHR, *Chitos v. Greece.*

[29]HRCtee, *Faure v. Australia*, para. 7.5.

[30]ECmHR, *Iversen v. Norway*; ECtHR, *Graziani-Weiss v. Austria*, paras. 41-42. See also Focarelli (2013), p. 153.

[31]See, for instance, Slavery Convention, Art. 6; Supplementary Slavery Convention, Art. 6.

[32]See, *e.g.*, ECtHR, *C.N. v. UK*, paras. 69 and 81.

[33]HRCtee, Concluding Observations: *Poland* (2016), para. 28.

[34]Kälin and Künzli (2019), p. 433.

non-immediate obligations on States, such as, for example, those relating to the rehabilitation and social reintegration of victims.

16.2 Prohibition of Arbitrary Arrest or Detention

16.2.1 Norms

The protection of personal liberty and security requires that every individual be free not only from slavery, servitude and forced labor, but also from powers exercised arbitrarily or illegitimately by the State (or other entities with human rights obligations). This necessarily implies the prohibition of arbitrary arrest or detention. Indeed, this prohibition dates back in history to the first national human rights documents, such as the *Magna Charta* of 1215, the *Habeas Corpus Act* of 1679, the *Bill of Rights* of 1689.[35]

In international human rights law, the close link between the protection of personal liberty and security and the prohibition of arbitrary arrest or detention is very clear.[36] From the *general* right of every human being to personal liberty and security derives the more *specific* right not to be subjected to illegal or arbitrary arrest or detention. In fact, Article 3 of the Universal Declaration provides that:

> Everyone has the right to [. . .] liberty and security of person.

And, in Article 9, that:

> No one shall be subjected to arbitrary arrest, detention or exile.

The Covenant on Civil and Political Rights makes this link even more explicit. Article 9(1) of the Covenant states that:

> Everyone has the right to liberty and security of person. No one shall be subjected to arbitrary arrest or detention. No one shall be deprived of his liberty except on such grounds and in accordance with such procedure as are established by law.

The prohibition of arbitrary arrest or detention is also provided for in Article 5 of the European Convention, Article 7 of the American Convention, Article 6 of the African Charter, and Article 14 of the Arab Charter. Other relevant provisions are Article 6 of the EU Charter of Fundamental Rights, Article 37(b) of the Convention on the Rights of the Child, Article 16 of the Convention on the Rights of Migrant Workers, Article 14 of the Convention on the Rights of Persons with Disabilities, and Article 7(1) of the Declaration on the Rights of Indigenous Peoples.

---

[35]See above, Sect. 1.2.1.

[36]For literature on the prohibition of arbitrary detention, see, e.g., Cornelisse (2010) and Favuzza (2018).

The essential nucleus of the prohibition of arbitrary arrest or detention is very well defined by the above-mentioned Article 9(1) of the Covenant on Civil and Political Rights. But it should be noted that the Covenant itself and many of the other norms mentioned above provide not only for the prohibition of arbitrary arrest or detention, but also for several *procedural guarantees* for those detained or arrested and for several *accessory rights* in their favor, which are closely linked to the main prohibition. In particular, these norms provide for: (*a*) their right to be promptly informed of the reasons for their detention; (*b*) their right to have recourse to a judge to decide on the legality of the detention and order their release if the detention has no legal basis; (*c*) their right to compensation if the detention is illegal. Moreover, those who have been arrested or detained on criminal charges have the right to be tried within a reasonable time or to be released.

It is clear that these procedural guarantees and accessory rights are important because they strengthen the main prohibition. However, since I am dealing here with "fundamental" human rights, I will only examine the basic prohibition of arbitrary arrest or detention. In my view, this prohibition is established not only by conventional norms, but also by a customary norm. This is derived from the centuries-old practice on the prohibition, the concordance of conventional human rights norms and the practice of international monitoring bodies. But this does not apply to the procedural guarantees and the accessory rights to the basic prohibition, which are too detailed in nature to be the subject of a customary norm; and therefore do not fall within my definition of "fundamental" human rights.

The opinion that the general prohibition of arbitrary arrest or detention is imposed by a customary norm is also maintained by the still active *Working Group on Arbitrary Detention*, which was created in 1991 by the (former) UN Commission on Human Rights.[37] In support of the customary nature of the norm, the *Working Group* cites, inter alia, the ICJ judgment in the case of the *US Diplomatic and Consular Staff in Tehran*.[38]

16.2.2 Content of the Prohibition

As already mentioned, the prohibition in question has the following content: no one may be arrested, detained, or otherwise deprived of his/her liberty, in an arbitrary or illegal manner. Often one speaks synthetically of "arbitrary" detention, including in this notion also "illegal" detention.

The first aspect to be clarified concerns the notion of "deprivation of liberty". It must be interpreted in a broad sense; and therefore includes all deprivations of a person's physical freedom of movement which, by their nature, degree, manner, duration and effect, are distinct from simple restrictions on freedom of movement

[37]See HRC, *Report of the Working Group on Arbitrary Detention*, UN Doc. A/HCR/22/44 of 24 December 2012. For a comment on the Report, see Bufalini (2013).

[38]ICJ, *United States Diplomatic and Consular Staff in Tehran*, para. 91.

which fall under the legal regime of freedom of movement of persons.[39] This distinction can sometimes be difficult to make; but the practice of international human rights monitoring bodies serves to clarify the criteria for distinguishing between the two situations. The European Court of Human Rights, for example, has stated that the difference lies in the level of severity of the restrictive measure.[40] The Human Rights Committee has argued that deprivations of people's physical liberty refer to more severe restrictions, and imposed in a more limited space, than mere restrictions on freedom of movement.[41]

Therefore, the forms in which "deprivation of liberty" can be achieved are manifold and are not limited to arrests or detentions related to criminal proceedings; but can include situations such as house arrest, personal searches, hospitalization in psychiatric hospitals, detention in identification and expulsion centers,[42] the obligation of migrants to remain in airport transit zones, arrests or imprisonments as disciplinary penalties for the military, exile to small islands without the possibility of social contact, etc.[43] The Human Rights Committee, in its General Comment No. 8, with reference to the purposes of detention, stated that Article 9 of the Covenant:

> [...] is applicable to all deprivations of liberty, whether in criminal cases or in other cases such as, for example, mental illness, vagrancy, drug addiction, educational purposes, immigration control, etc.[44]

The second aspect to be examined concerns the notion of "legality/illegality". First, in order to be allowed, deprivation of liberty must be legitimate under the procedural and substantive rules of State domestic law. Secondly, it is legal if it is based on one of the justifications allowed under international human rights law. On this point, for example, Article 5 of the European Convention, which specifically lists a number of situations justifying the deprivation of liberty,[45] is very clear.

---

[39] See Focarelli (2013), p. 154. On the freedom of movement of people see below, Chap. 24.

[40] ECtHR, *De Tommaso v. Italy*, Judgment of 23 February 2017, para. 80.

[41] HRCtee, *González del Rio v. Peru*, Views of 28 October 1992, para.5.1; *Karker v. France*, Views of 26 October 2000, para.8.5. See also HRCtee, General Comment No. 27, 1 November 1999, paras. 2, 11 and 13.

[42] On the deprivation of liberty of irregular migrants confined in a reception center see the important case *Khlaifia*: ECtHR, *Khlaifia and Others v. Italy*, paras. 88–108.

[43] See the practice cited by Kälin, Künzli (2019), pp. 452–453, and Favuzza (2018), *passim*.

[44] HRCtee, General Comment No. 8, 30 June 1982, para. 1.

[45] These situations concern: (*a*) who is lawfully detained following a conviction by a competent court; (*b*) who is lawfully arrested or detained for violation of a lawful measure taken by a court; (*c*) who has been arrested or detained for translation before the competent judicial authority when there are plausible grounds for suspecting that he/ she has committed a criminal offence; (*d*) the regular detention of a minor, decided to supervise his/her education; (*e*) the regular detention of a person in order to prevent the spread of a contagious disease, of an alienated person, of an alcoholic, of a drug addict or a vagrant; (*f*) the arrest or regular detention of a person in order to prevent him/her from illegally entering the territory or of a person against whom deportation or extradition proceedings are in progress.

However, the other human rights treaties do not contain this specific list, and therefore the practice of the international monitoring bodies must be used to identify the internationally legitimate grounds for deprivation of liberty. Thirdly, deprivation of liberty is illegal when it is the consequence of the exercise by an individual of his/her fundamental human rights[46] or when it constitutes a violation of the principle of non-discrimination.

Another important aspect concerns the notion of "arbitrariness", now understood *narrowly* as distinct from the notion of "illegality". A deprivation of liberty can be arbitrary, even if it is, or has been, legal. The concept of arbitrariness may refer: (*a*) to elements of unreasonableness, unpredictability and injustice; or (*b*) to the fact that detention, even if justified by a legally legitimate reason, ends up violating other human rights of the detainee,[47] especially some of his fundamental human rights; or (*c*) to the fact that it is linked to a serious violation of the right to a fair trial; or (*d*) to the fact that it is prolonged for an excessive or discretionary period.[48]

There is also the question of whether the prohibition of arbitrary arrest or detention is "non derogable in time of emergency". Some doubt may arise from the fact that, in human rights treaties, the provisions on this prohibition are not expressly mentioned as "non-derogable in time of emergency". However, this is not decisive since, as has been seen, this concept is not univocal and is not well defined in these treaties. Actually, the preferred view is that the prohibition of arbitrary arrest or detention is non-derogable in time of emergency. The Human Rights Committee also seems to agree with this conclusion, as it has stated that certain essential aspects of the right to personal liberty are mandatory.[49] The *Working Group on Arbitrary Detention* has reached the same conclusion. But it should be noted that this non-derogation does not extend to the procedural guarantees and the accessory rights to the basic prohibition.

Finally, it is worth remembering that the question of "derogation in time of emergency" should not be confused with that of the peremptory (*jus cogens*) nature of the norm on arbitrary detention; nor with that of the absolute character of the prohibition. Instead, the *Working Group on Arbitrary Detention* unfortunately makes a certain confusion between the three different concepts.

[46]According to the Working Group on Arbitrary Detention, these human rights are those set forth in Articles 7, 13, 14, 18, 19, 20 and 21 of the Universal Declaration.

[47]See Focarelli (2013), p. 155.

[48]See HRCtee, *A. v. Australia*, paras. 9.2-9.4; *C. v. Australia*, para. 8.2; *Baban et al. v. Australia*, para. 7.2.

[49]See HRCtee, General Comment No. 29, 31 August 2001, paras. 11 and 13. Indeed, the Committee seems to refer to the concept of *jus cogens* rather than to the concept of non-derogation in time of emergency. But it seems to maintain that the first concept includes the second. In my opinion, this is not correct: for my distinction between the two concepts see above, Sects. 13.3.3 and 13.3.5.

16.2.3 Obligations

The prohibition of arbitrary arrest or detention imposes, first of all, negative obligations on States. They concern, in a particular way, certain agents of the State, such as police and security officers, military and prison officers. But also important are the positive obligations, which require higher State officials (e.g. police chiefs, prison managers, high-ranking military personnel) to take action to prevent abuse by subordinate officials. Other positive obligations require State agents to prevent and suppress abuse by private individuals. Finally, the positive obligations of reparation towards the victims should not be overlooked.

16.3 Prohibition of Enforced Disappearance of Persons

16.3.1 Norms

The practice by States of the so-called "enforced disappearance" of persons constitutes a very serious and evident form of arbitrary detention, which, however, can be treated separately since it has acquired its autonomy in contemporary international law. This practice consists in the *secret* deprivation of a person's liberty by *State officials* or persons authorized by the State. Often this person is then killed. This practice, followed in the past in Latin America, has recently been resumed, even more seriously, with the already mentioned "*extraordinary renditions*", carried out within the framework of the anti-terrorist measures adopted by some States.[50]

General human rights treaties do not expressly mention the prohibition of "enforced disappearance"; but international human rights monitoring bodies consider such abuses to be violations of the prohibition of arbitrary arrest or detention. Indeed, the practice of the Human Rights Committee, the Inter-American Court and the European Court is very extensive.[51] In several cases, these bodies have considered that the practice of enforced disappearance also constituted a violation of the prohibition of torture and inhuman or degrading treatment. These include, among others, the judgments of the European Court in the *Kurt*, *El-Masri* and *Nasr and Ghali* cases,[52] the judgment of the Inter-American Court in the *Morales Zegarra* case,[53] and the decision of the Human Rights Committee in the *Sarma* case.[54] Finally, enforced disappearance may also violate the right to recognition as a person before the law.[55]

[50]See above, Sect. 14.2.2.3.

[51]For an accurate examination of this practice, see Citroni, Scovazzi (2013), pp. 286–308.

[52]ECtHR, *Kurt v. Turkey*, para. 124; *El-Masri v. The Former Yugoslav Republic of Macedonia*, paras. 191-193, 206, 223, 240-242, 262; *Nasr and Ghali v. Italy*, paras. 298–303.

[53]IACmHR, *Romer Morales Zegarra et al. v. Peru*, para. 62.

[54]HRCtee, *Sarma v. Sri Lanka*.

[55]See HRCtee, *Grioua v. Algeria*, para. 7.8.

There are also some important recent treaties dealing specifically with the prohibition of enforced disappearance. These are the 1994 Inter-American Convention on the Forced Disappearance of Persons[56] and the 2006 UN Convention for the Protection of All Persons from Enforced Disappearance.[57] Finally, it should be noted that Article 7(2)(i) of the Statute of the International Criminal Court considers enforced disappearance as a crime against humanity when it is committed as part of a widespread or systematic attack against the civilian population.

As far as general international law is concerned, the prohibition of enforced disappearance, being a very serious form of arbitrary deprivation of personal liberty, must be considered to be protected by a general and peremptory norm.

16.3.2 Content of the Prohibition

Article 2 of the above mentioned UN Convention of 2006 defines enforced disappearance as:

> [. . .] the arrest, detention, abduction or any other form of deprivation of liberty by agents of the State or by persons or groups acting with the authorization, support or acquiescence of the State, followed by a refusal to acknowledge the deprivation of liberty or by concealment of the fate or whereabouts of the disappeared person, which place such a person outside the protection of the law.

A very similar definition is contained in Article 7(2)(i) of the Statute of the International Criminal Court.

Therefore, the notion of "enforced disappearance" is precise and detailed; and the content of the prohibition is also clear. This prohibition must be considered as absolute and non-derogable even in times of emergency.

16.3.3 Obligations

With regard to the obligations imposed on States in relation to the prohibition of "enforced disappearance", the above considerations concerning the prohibition of arbitrary arrest or detention apply, with the clarification that State obligations of prevention and repression relating to acts of private individuals should be excluded, unless such acts involve State aid or acquiescence.[58]

---

[56] Inter-American Convention on the Forced Disappearance of Persons, 9 June 1994.

[57] International Convention for the Protection of All Persons from Enforced Disappearance (CPPED), 20 December 2006.

[58] This is because the acts of private individuals cannot, on their own, constitute a practice of enforced disappearance.

References

Bufalini A (2013) La natura del divieto di detenzione arbitraria secondo il *Working Group on Arbitrary Detention* del Consiglio dei diritti umani. DUDI 7:525–531

Citroni G, Scovazzi T (2013) La tutela internazionale dei diritti umani, Parte III del Corso di diritto internazionale (Scovazzi T ed). Giuffrè, Milano

Cornelisse G (2010) Immigration Detention and Human Rights. Rethinking Territorial Sovereignty. Nijhoff, Leiden

Favuzza F (2018) Security detention in times of armed conflict: the relevance of International Human Rights Law. Kluwer/Cedam, Milano

Focarelli C (2013) La persona umana nel diritto internazionale. Il Mulino, Bologna

Kälin W, Künzli J (2019) The law of International Human Rights Protection, 2nd edn. Oxford University Press, Oxford

Zagrebelsky V, Chenal R, Tomasi L (2016) Manuale dei diritti fondamentali in Europa. Il Mulino, Bologna

Essential Judicial Protection of the Person 17

One of the oldest aims of human rights, as we have seen, is to protect the individual from powers exercised arbitrarily or illegitimately by State authorities. The realization of this aim requires that the individual be provided with instruments of judicial protection at the internal level and, hopefully, also at the international level.

Furthermore, from a broader point of view, it should be considered that the existence of an adequate apparatus for the administration of justice in States, capable of ascertaining possible violations of human rights, is strictly and functionally necessary to achieve the general purpose of respect for human rights. In fact, it is clear that it is not sufficient for the State to seek to prevent human rights violations, and possibly to investigate to discover and apprehend those responsible, if the lack of an adequate apparatus for the administration of justice does not make it possible to ascertain violations impartially, to punish those responsible and to provide reparation to the victims.

As a result, many human rights have historically developed which relate to the judicial protection of people. Some of them are very precise and detailed. But here I will only deal with those rights that seem to me "fundamental": (*a*) the right of access to justice (in the broad sense); (*b*) the right of victims to reparation; (*c*) the rights of the accused that derive from the principle of criminal legality.

17.1 Right of Access to Justice

17.1.1 Norms and Their Historical Evolution

The right of access to justice is a difficult and controversial concept; and it is understood in international human rights law with different, sometimes restrictive and sometimes extensive meanings. This is probably also due to the fact that human rights treaties, as we shall see, do not usually use this term; but rather those of right to "effective remedy" or "fair trial" or "judicial protection". In reality, these different terms are intended to mean, at least originally, different concepts, but they have

R. Pisillo Mazzeschi, *International Human Rights Law*,
https://doi.org/10.1007/978-3-030-77032-7_17

come closer together over time. In particular, I believe that, in customary international law, the concepts of the right to an effective remedy and the right to a fair trial are now included in the broader *right to essential judicial protection*, which can also be called, for simplicity and because of a more recurrent terminology, the *right of access to justice* (in the broadest sense).

This historical process can be deduced if the relevant provisions of the major international human rights instruments are examined in chronological order. The Universal Declaration distinguishes between the right to an effective domestic remedy (Art. 8) and the right to a fair trial (Arts. 10 and 11). According to Article 8:

> Everyone has the right to an effective remedy by the competent national tribunals for acts violating the fundamental rights granted him by the constitution or by law.

Instead, according to Article 10:

> Everyone is entitled in full equality to a fair and public hearing by an independent and impartial tribunal, in the determination of his rights and obligations and of any criminal charge against him.

The European Convention also makes a clear distinction between the right to an effective domestic remedy (Art. 13) and the right to a fair trial (Art. 6). The second norm is very detailed, while the first norm is concise and states:

> Everyone whose rights and freedoms as set forth in this Convention are violated shall have an effective remedy before a national authority notwithstanding that the violation has been committed by persons acting in an official capacity.

The same distinction between the two rights is adopted by the Covenant on Civil and Political Rights, which contains very detailed provisions on both effective remedies (Art. 2(3)) and fair trial (Art. 14). The American Convention also deals with the two rights separately (Arts. 8 and 25). But it should be noted that here the right to an effective remedy (Art. 25) is referred to as the "right to judicial protection" and has a broader content than the similar right in previous human rights treaties. In fact, Article 25 speaks of the right of everyone to a "simple and prompt recourse" to "a competent court or tribunal" for protection against acts that violate his fundamental rights recognized "by the constitution or laws of the state concerned or by this Convention".

By contrast, sectoral human rights treaties usually contain provisions on the right to an effective remedy, but not on the right to a fair trial. These include, inter alia, Article 6 of the 1965 Convention against Racial Discrimination[1] and Articles 13 and 14 of the 1984 Convention against Torture.[2]

---

[1]CERD, Art. 6.

[2]CAT, Arts. 13 and 14.

It follows from these norms that, in this first historical phase, the right to an effective remedy has a *limited content.* It means the right of a person, who believes that he or she is a victim of a violation of his or her *human right* contained in a treaty,[3] to *take action* before a *State authority* (judicial or other) in order to obtain a decision; even if the alleged violation was committed by an individual-organ of the State. But the guarantee of effective remedy *is not autonomous* with respect to the violation of human rights. Moreover, these norms do not guarantee that the remedy has a *judicial character* in the strict sense of the term: the States parties to the treaties usually limit themselves to making a commitment to "develop" the possibilities of a judicial remedy in the future.[4] Finally, the right to an effective remedy does not include the guarantees pertaining to the phase of the procedure nor the guarantee of reparation for the victim in the event of an established breach. In essence, the right to an effective remedy is rather elementary at this early stage.

In contrast, the right to a fair trial is in some respects more restrictive, but in many others more extensive than the right to an effective remedy. It is more restrictive because it does not concern the phase of initiation and conclusion of the procedure, but only its intermediate phase. But it is broader, because it is not limited to proceedings relating to human rights violations, but *extends to all trials* in civil, criminal and (sometimes) administrative matters. In other words, the guarantees of fair trial *are autonomous* with respect to the violation of human rights. Moreover, conventional norms on fair trial usually require the national authority to be *judicial* in the strict sense of the word, to be pre-established by law, and to be independent and impartial. Finally, these norms provide for certain general principles of a procedural nature, such as equality of arms, reasonable trial time, as well as a very detailed set of guarantees of a more specific nature for criminal trials. In fact, the conventional provisions on fair trial are much longer and more detailed than those on effective remedy. One need only compare Articles 6 and 13 of the European Convention or Articles 14 and 2(3) of the Covenant on Civil and Political Rights.

It should be added that, at this historical stage, doctrine, when it speaks of access to justice in matters of human rights, usually tends to refer to the right to an effective remedy and not to the right to a fair trial. It therefore adopts a *restrictive interpretation* of the notion of access to justice.

However, over and above these differences between the two rights, there are also significant similarities, since both rights require the State to have an apparatus for the administration of justice that meets certain requirements or minimum operating standards established by international law. And indeed, as a result of these analogies, at a more recent historical stage, *the two rights have become closer and mutually complementary.* This is clear from the most recent human rights treaties. The African Charter, for example, contains only one provision (Art. 7), which includes rules on

---

[3]An exception, as seen, is contained in Art. 25 ACHR.

[4]See CCPR, Art. 2(3)(b); ACHR, Art. 25(2)(b).

the right to an effective domestic remedy and the right to a fair trial.[5] The Arab Charter also provides for the right of all persons to seek a legal remedy before independent courts (Art. 12) and detailed rules on fair trial (Arts. 13 and 16). Even more significant is Article 47 of the EU Charter of Fundamental Rights (*Right to an effective remedy and to a fair trial*), which states:

> Everyone whose rights and freedoms guaranteed by the law of the Union are violated has the right to an effective remedy before a tribunal in compliance with the conditions laid down in this Article. Everyone is entitled to a fair and public hearing within a reasonable time by an independent and impartial tribunal previously established by law. Everyone shall have the possibility of being advised, defended and represented.

As one can see, these treaties clearly show the complementarity between the two rights, which reinforce each other. In addition, there is a broadening of the content of the right to an effective domestic remedy, because this right becomes *autonomous* with respect to the violation of human rights contained in the treaty in question, and because it requires that the complaint be decided by a *judicial authority* in the strict sense.

Therefore, in my view, it can be concluded that, in human rights treaties, the distinction between the right to an effective remedy and the right to a fair trial still exists; but that the two rights tend to integrate. The practice of the international monitoring bodies of these treaties is also tending increasingly to re-evaluate and broaden the interpretation of the first right, to blur the differences between the two rights and to interpret them in a complementary way. From this practice emerges therefore the idea that, in contemporary international law, the right of access to justice must be understood *in a broad sense*, so as to encompass at least the *essential contents* of the right to an effective remedy and the right to a fair trial. One could speak of a "broad" and modern notion of access to justice.

It must now be asked whether this notion has also become established in general international law.

17.1.2 A Customary Norm on Access to Justice?

This broad notion of access to justice, in my view, has now been established in customary international law. This emerges from the whole of the conventional systems on human rights, from the practice of international monitoring bodies and from the *opinio juris* of the international community. According to this customary norm, the right of access to justice *includes* the right to bring proceedings before a court, which is predetermined by law, which is independent and impartial, which adopts the minimum procedural guarantees of a fair trial, which guarantees a decision within a reasonable time, and which ensures that the decision can be

---

[5] See ACHPR, Art. 7, para. 1 (a) (on effective domestic remedy), and Art. 7, paras. 1 (b), (c), (d) and 2 (on fair trial).

enforced in practice. This conclusion is well summarized in the following words of Judge Cançado Trindade:

> [. . .] the right of access to justice *lato sensu* comprises not only the formal access to justice (the right to institute legal proceedings) by means of an effective remedy, but also the guarantees of the due process of law (with equality of arms, conforming the *procès équitable*), up to the judgment (as the *prestation juridictionnelle*), with its faithful execution, with the provision of the reparation due.[6]

Further confirmation of the existence of this broad and modern notion of access to justice, at least for serious violations of human rights, can also be found in the UN General Assembly Resolution 60/147 on the Principles on the rights of victims of serious violations of human rights and humanitarian law, cited above.[7] Article VII proclaims that, among the rights of victims, there is an "equal and effective access to justice". Article VIII, entitled "Access to Justice", states that:

> A victim of a gross violation of international human rights law or a serious violation of international humanitarian law shall have equal access to an effective judicial remedy as provided for under international law [. . .] Obligations arising under international law to secure the right to access to justice and fair and impartial proceedings shall be reflected in domestic laws [. . .].

The customary nature of the right of access to justice for violation of human rights is also attested by the fact that, in international human rights law, a customary norm has been established requiring the individual victim to exhaust domestic remedies before he can appeal to international bodies.[8] This norm has, as a necessary corollary, the obligation of the State of the alleged violation to offer adequate and effective domestic remedies, to which the right of the individual victim obviously corresponds. Therefore, also through the affirmation of the aforementioned norm on the exhaustion of domestic remedies, the right to effective judicial protection for human rights violations has been affirmed.

Furthermore, on a more general level, it should be reiterated that the State's obligation to have an adequate apparatus for the administration of justice, to which victims of human rights violations may have access, is *functionally necessary* for the protection of human rights. After all, this State obligation has ancient roots, because it takes up and reproduces, in essence, in the field of human rights, the State's traditional customary obligation to protect aliens who have suffered offenses on its

---

[6]ICJ, *Jurisdictional Immunities of the State*, Dissenting Opinion of Judge Cançado Trindade, para. 221 (emphasis in the original quotation). It should be noted that Cançado Trindade also includes in the right of access to justice the right of the victim to obtain reparation in the event of a positive outcome of the procedure. I will return to this point below, in Sect. 17.2.

[7]*Basic Principles and Guidelines on the Right to a Remedy and Reparation for Victims of Gross Violations of International Human Rights Law and Serious Violations of International Humanitarian Law*, Annex, 16 December 2005.

[8]See Pisillo Mazzeschi (2004a). See also above, Sect. 4.4.1.1.

territory, including through access to its courts; i.e. the prohibition to commit a "denial of justice" in the treatment of aliens. It is logical that the customary obligation to give access to justice to aliens has then been reproduced, *mutatis mutandis*, also in favor of victims of human rights violations.

Finally, can the customary norm on the right of access to justice be regarded as *jus cogens*? Some element of the practice seems to tend in this direction. For example, the European Court of Justice, in the above-mentioned *Kadi* judgment of 2008,[9] has held that the right of access justice is indispensable even in the presence of a Security Council resolution which in fact limits it. However, in my view, the answer is in general negative, except when the individual seeks access to justice in order to assert the violation of human rights that are protected by *jus cogens*, such as acts of torture or crimes against humanity. In this case, the peremptory nature of the substantive human rights must logically extend to the procedural human right of access to justice. I will return to this point later.[10]

17.1.3 Content of the Right

The content of the right of access to justice, in customary law, has already been outlined above in its essential lines. But some questions remain to be clarified as to its scope.

The first question is whether this right, even if understood in a broad sense, operates only in the case of violation of human rights or also in the case of violation of other rights, for example, established by the civil, criminal or administrative law of the State in question. It has been seen that the right to an effective domestic remedy, even if it has broadened its scope over time, refers *only to the violation of human rights* (established by international law or the domestic law of the State). Instead, fair trial rights are *autonomous* with respect to the violation of human rights. Which of the two approaches ended up prevailing in the customary norm on access to justice?

In my view, on the basis of the practice of human rights monitoring bodies and the considerations made above, it must be concluded that the right of access to justice, *in customary international law*, only operates in the case of human rights violations. That is to say, it does not constitute an autonomous individual human right but rather a *procedural right* which exists only to the extent that there is a substantive human right to be asserted before a court.[11] One should therefore speak, to be precise, of the *right of access to justice for violation of human rights.*[12]

---

[9]ECJ, *Kadi*.

[10]See below, Sect. 17.1.4.2.

[11]In this sense, albeit in relation to a less extensive concept of access to justice, see Francioni (2007), pp. 30–33.

[12]In other words, it does not seem to me that the autonomous character of the right to a fair trial in conventional systems has also extended to customary international law.

The second question is whether the right of access to justice operates only before domestic courts or also before international courts or other international monitoring bodies.[13] The answer changes depending on whether reference is made to customary law or treaty law. As far as customary law is concerned, it is clear that there is no individual right of access to justice before all international courts and all quasi-judicial supervisory bodies existing under international law. Indeed, it is well known that many of these instances are not open to recourse by individuals. The answer is different, instead, from the point of view of conventional law. Many human rights treaties, as we have seen,[14] provide for their own control mechanisms, judicial or quasi-judicial, and, among them, more and more allow for direct access by individuals who are victims of violations of human rights covered by the treaty. In such cases, the individual right of access to justice must also be considered applicable at international level.[15]

However, it must be stressed that this limited capacity of the individual to access international procedural remedies does not mean that his or her national State cannot assert its own right and *also* the right of his or her citizen before courts or other international supervisory bodies against the State responsible for the violation, invoking the norms on the international responsibility of States. This is clear, inter alia, from the case-law of the International Court of Justice, which, for example in the well-known *LaGrand* and *Avena* cases,[16] has established that the national State of the victim can assert both its own rights and individual rights at the same time.[17]

Finally, as regards the nature of the right of access to justice, it should be noted that it is not, in principle, "non-derogable in time of emergency". Nor does it have an absolute character, because it admits certain exceptions or limits, as we shall see. However, in my opinion, it may become an absolute human right that is also non-derogable in time of emergency when it is functionally linked to substantive human rights that have the character of *jus cogens*. Let us now examine these issues in greater depth.

---

[13] Also on this point see Francioni (2007), pp. 41 ff.

[14] See above, Chaps. 10, 11 and 12.

[15] See also the cited UNGA Resolution 60/147, Annex, Art. VIII (12): "An adequate, effective and prompt remedy for gross violations of international human rights law or serious violations of international humanitarian law should include all available and appropriate international processes in which a person may have legal standing [. . .]".

[16] ICJ, *LaGrand*, pp. 466 ff.; *Avena*, pp. 121 ff. Cf. also IACtHR, *The Right to Information on Consular Assistance*.

[17] See also the cited UNGA Resolution 60/147, Annex, Art. VIII (12)(d): "[States should:] Make available all appropriate legal, diplomatic and consular means to ensure that victims can exercise their right to remedy for gross violations of international human rights law or serious violations of international humanitarian law".

17.1.4 Derogations and Limits

17.1.4.1 Derogations in Time of Emergency

The issue of derogation clauses in human rights treaties has already been dealt with in general terms.[18] It is now time to return to this issue with specific reference to the right of access to justice.[19] This is justified by the fact that this topic is controversial and is the subject of interesting practice. Furthermore, this is a current issue, since the growth of international terrorism in this century has led many States to adopt exceptional measures, which suspend many substantive human rights by virtue of these derogation clauses. The question must now be asked whether the suspension of the procedural human right of access to justice is also legitimate.

As has already been seen, human rights treaties that contain human rights derogation clauses, in time of war or public emergency, usually provide for an explicit list of rights that are excluded from the possibility of derogation.[20] But these treaties are not uniform as to whether or not the right of access to justice can be suspended. This right, for example, is not included in the list in Article 15(2) of the European Convention, nor in Article 4(2) of the Covenant on Civil and Political Rights. On the other hand, the American Convention, while not including the right to judicial protection under Article 25 in the list of non-derogable rights, expressly states in Article 27(2) that it is not possible to suspend "the judicial guarantees essential for the protection of such rights" (i.e. the non-derogable rights). Therefore, the American Convention establishes a *functional link* between non-derogable rights and their judicial protection: if a human right cannot be derogated from even in time of emergency, the judicial protection of that right must always be guaranteed and cannot be suspended. The Arab Charter provides an even higher level of guarantee for the right of access to justice: the list of non-derogable rights under Article 4 (2) includes the right to a fair trial under Article 13 (but not the right to an effective domestic remedy under Article 12). In addition, with a formula similar to that of the American Convention, the Arab Charter states that the "judicial guarantees required for the protection" of non-derogable rights may not be suspended (Art. 4(2)).

Despite this lack of uniformity between the various treaties, the application practice of the international supervisory bodies seems to be oriented to accept the most guaranteeing solution that is explicitly provided for by the American Convention and the Arab Charter. More specifically, three criteria are derived from this practice: (*a*) the criterion of the *importance* of substantive rights linked to the right of access to justice: the more important these rights are, the less possible is the suspension of their judicial guarantees. Usually, if substantive rights are non-derogable in time of emergency, their judicial guarantees cannot be suspended;

---

[18]See above, Sect. 4.4.3.

[19]On the subject see also Francioni (2007), pp. 43–47.

[20]One may cite ECHR, Art. 15(2); CCPR, Art. 4(2); ACHR, Art. 27(2); ArCHR, Art. (2). Instead, Art. F of the ESCrev provides for the possibility of derogations from rights in times of war or emergency, but does not contain a list of non-derogable rights.

(*b*) the criterion of preserving, even in time of emergency, the *essential* legal guarantees, such as access to an effective remedy and *habeas corpus*; (*c*) finally, also in relation to human rights that can be derogated from, the criterion of *proportionality* and the *balancing* between limitations to access to justice and the interest in the protection of public security must be respected: restrictions on the functioning of the judicial system must not go beyond what is strictly necessary to face the emergency.

These three criteria were explicitly accepted by the Inter-American Court in its two advisory opinions of 1987 on *States of Emergency* and *Habeas Corpus.*[21] The Court stated that:

> [...] the declaration of a state of emergency - whatever its breadth or denomination in internal law - cannot entail the suppression or ineffectiveness of the judicial guarantees that the Convention requires the States Parties to establish for the protection of the rights not subject to derogation or suspension by the state of emergency.[22]

It also added that:

> [...] the 'essential' judicial guarantees which are not subject to derogation, according to Article 27(2) of the Convention, include habeas corpus (Art. 7(6)), amparo, and any other effective remedy before judges or competent tribunals (Art. 25(1)).[23]

Finally, according to the Court, the criterion of proportionality must also apply in relation to the substantive rights that can be derogated from.[24]

The Human Rights Committee also believes that essential judicial guarantees must be respected in time of emergency. In its General Comment No. 29, it stated that even if access to justice is not included in the list of non-derogable rights under Article 4(2) of the Covenant on Civil and Political Rights:

> [...] the State Party must comply with the fundamental obligation under article 2, paragraph 3, of the Covenant to provide a remedy that is effective.[25]

The case-law of the European Court of Human Rights confirms this general approach. The Court held that the right to an effective remedy is also applicable in situations of armed conflict, when the victim complained of the violation of

[21] IACtHR, *States of Emergency*; *Habeas Corpus in Emergency Situations.*

[22] IACtHR, *Judicial Guarantees in States of Emergency*, para. 25.

[23] *Ibidem*, para. 1 of the operative part of the opinion.

[24] *Ibidem*, para. 21: "From Article 27(1) [...] comes the general requirement that in any state of emergency there be appropriate means to control the measures taken, so that they are proportionate to the needs and do not exceed the strict limits imposed by the Convention or derived from it".

[25] HRCtee, General Comment No. 29, 31 August 2001, para. 14.

fundamental human rights, such as the right to life[26] or the prohibition of torture.[27] According to the Court, the more serious the violation of the substantive right, the more important it is to protect the right of the victim to have access to judicial guarantees to assert the violation.

17.1.4.2 Restrictions and Limits. Conflict Between the Right of Access to Justice and International Immunities

It has been said above that the right of access to justice admits, in principle, restrictions or limitations; but not when it is functionally linked to substantive human rights of a "fundamental" nature. Let me now turn to this issue, which is very topical.

The right of access to justice may be subject to various restrictions, arising mainly from the need to protect some public interests of domestic legal systems. There may be limits to the jurisdiction of the State of the forum, or the obstacle of the judicially non-enforceable character of the dispute, or restrictions arising from theories followed by certain States, such as the doctrines of the "Act of State" or of the "*forum non conveniens*".[28] There may also be limits deriving from international law. Recently, for example, the problem has arisen of the possible conflict between the right of access to justice and the sanctioning measures adopted by the UN Security Council in the fight against international terrorism.[29]

It is not possible here to examine all these limits. I will be dealing with what I believe is the most important limitation on the right of access to justice, from the point of view of the victims of human rights violations. It is given by international immunities; that is to say, immunities from the jurisdiction of the State of the forum which foreign States, their organs, international organizations and their officials enjoy under international law. Indeed, as a result of these immunities, the victim of a violation cannot bring an action before his/her own national courts against such entities or persons who are held responsible for the violation.

In reality, the international norms governing immunities have a partially different and sometimes even controversial content (especially the immunities of State officials[30]). But, on the whole, simplifying, it can be said that all these norms have the common characteristic of constituting a limit to the right of access to justice. This limit to the *procedural* right of the victim can often also be resolved in a limit to the *substantive* human rights that the victim wants to assert in court, since, according to a general principle of justice, there is no effective substantive right in the absence of

[26] See, e.g., ECtHR, *Isayeva v. Russia*, paras. 226–230.

[27] See, e.g., ECtHR, *Ilaşcu and Others v. Moldova and Russia*, paras. 475–482. In fact, here the Court did not find a violation of Article 13, but of Article 34 of the European Convention, concerning the right of individual appeal to the Court itself.

[28] See Francioni (2007), pp. 42–43.

[29] See, e.g., ECtHR, *Bosphorus and Others*; CFI, *Kadi*; *Yusuf*; EGC, *Kadi*; ECJ, *Kadi*; *European Commission v. Kadi.*

[30] See Pisillo Mazzeschi (2014c).

remedies for its violation.[31] Therefore, it is clear that there is *a potential antinomy*, in contemporary international law, between the international norms on immunities (of States, State agents, international organizations and international officials) on the one hand, and the international norms on substantive human rights and on access to justice for violation of those rights on the other hand.

However, in *two hypotheses* this potential antinomy does not create particularly difficult problems. The first occurs when the individual victim, in order to overcome the barrier of immunity before the courts of the forum, has the possibility of *alternative and effective remedies* to assert the violation and obtain justice.[32] The criterion of "alternative remedies" is, after all, an application of the aforementioned principle of "equivalent protection" and responds to the same logic.[33] When the victim has alternative remedies, it can be argued that the potential antinomy between norms on immunities and (substantive and procedural) human rights norms does not result in a concrete and effective conflict. In other words, the victim's right of access to justice, and the substantive human rights he or she intends to assert, are not affected, or at least not substantially affected, by the norms on immunities.

The second hypothesis occurs when the antinomy between the norms on immunities and the norms on human rights is resolved in favor of the former norms, since they prevail, on the basis of the specialty criterion, over the latter. This is the case, in my view, when human rights norms do not protect "fundamental" human rights. One thinks, for example, of the hypothesis in which a foreign State, through nationalization, violates the right of ownership of an Italian citizen; that is, a human right that is not "fundamental". In this case, even if there is a concrete conflict between the right of the individual to sue the foreign State before the Italian courts and the norm on the jurisdictional immunity of States for acts *jure imperii*, the latter norm prevails, as *lex specialis*, both over the (substantive) norm on the right to property and over the (procedural) norm on access to justice in relation to the right to property.

Instead, the matter changes and the antinomy between the norms on immunities and those on human rights creates a difficult problem to solve when: (*a*) there is a *concrete and effective conflict* between the two groups of norms (because access to justice is not guaranteed by the "alternative remedies" rule); and furthermore: (*b*) human rights norms protect rights recognized as "fundamental" or even peremptory (*jus cogens*) by the international community. In essence, these two cumulative conditions occur when the norms on immunities *totally prevent* individuals who are victims from accessing justice against States, State agents, international

---

[31]See Pisillo Mazzeschi (2012), pp. 317–320 and 323–325. See also Italian Constitutional Court, Judgment No. 238 of 22 October 2014.

[32]When, for example, the individual may sue a foreign State before the courts of that State or bring an action against an international organization before an internal administrative tribunal of the organization or bring an action against a foreign diplomatic agent before the courts of the latter's national State.

[33]See above, Sect. 11.2.2.

organizations or international officials accused of committing violations of "fundamental" or even peremptory human rights.[34]

As is well known, some very important judgments have recently addressed and resolved this problem in very different ways. Examples include the three House of Lords judgments in the *Pinochet* case;[35] the House of Lords judgment in the *Jones and Mitchell* case;[36] the French Court of Cassation judgment in the *Gaddafi* case;[37] the Italian Court of Cassation judgment in the *Ferrini* case;[38] the Supreme Court of Canada judgment in the *Kazemi* case;[39] the decisions of the European Court of Human Rights in the *Waite and Kennedy,*[40] *Al-Adsani,*[41] *Stichting Mothers of Srebrenica*[42] and *Jones*[43] cases; the ICJ judgments in the *Arrest Warrant*[44] and *Jurisdictional Immunities of the State*[45] cases; and finally the judgment of the Italian Constitutional Court No. 238/2014.[46] In the latter ruling, the Court refused the internal execution of the ICJ judgment on *Jurisdictional Immunities of the State*, because it was considered in conflict with the fundamental human rights protected by the Italian Constitution.[47] This problem has also provoked a broad debate in internationalist doctrine, which has also maintained different positions.

What are the solutions proposed by doctrine and jurisprudence to solve the problem of this conflict?

In very general terms, there has been a contrast between a traditional and "State-centric" conception of international law, based on the central role of State sovereignty and interstate order, that has tended to oppose setting limits to the classical norms on international immunities, and, on the other hand, a more modern and "human-centric" conception of international law, aiming at giving a central role to the protection of the human person, which has been inclined to place increasing limits on international immunities when they are likely to undermine the protection of fundamental human rights.

[34]For my distinction between the category of "fundamental" human rights and the more restrictive category of peremptory human rights, see above, Sects. 13.3.4 and 13.3.5.

[35]House of Lords, "*Pinochet I*", Judgment of 25 November 1998; "*Pinochet II*", Judgment of 15 January 1999; "*Pinochet III*", Judgment of 24 March 1999.

[36]House of Lords, *Jones and Mitchell v. Saudi Arabia.*

[37]French Cour de Cassation, *Gaddafi.*

[38]Italian Court of Cassation, *Ferrini v. Federal Republic of Germany.*

[39]Supreme Court of Canada, *Kazemi Estate v. Islamic Republic of Iran.*

[40]ECtHR, *Waite and Kennedy v. Germany.*

[41]ECtHR, *Al-Adsani v. UK.*

[42]ECtHR, *Stichting Mothers of Srebrenica et al. v. The Netherlands.*

[43]ECtHR, *Jones and Others v. UK.*

[44]ICJ, *Arrest Warrant.*

[45]ICJ, *Jurisdictional Immunities of the State.*

[46]Italian Constitutional Court, Judgment No. 238 of 22 October 2014.

[47]See also, most recently, Italian Court of Cassation, *Toldo v. Federal Republic of Germany.*

More specifically, within the framework of this general opposition between theoretical conceptions and also ideological choices that differ greatly from the point of view of values and interests worthy of greater protection, various legal theories can be distinguished that support one or the other general conception.

Within the scope of the "State-centric" general approach, a first argument, of a radical nature, is that the clauses on "jurisdiction", contained in the human rights treaties,[48] should be interpreted as meaning that legal actions against foreign States or officials of foreign States are not subject to the "jurisdiction" of the State of the forum because of the functioning of international norms on immunities.[49] But this argument is not convincing, because, among other things, it does not explain why immunities should take precedence over obligations to respect human rights and judicial guarantees for their violation.[50]

A second argument, also in favor of immunities, is one that denies at the root the possibility of a conflict between the norms on immunities and those on human rights. The conflict could not exist because the two groups of norms would deal with different matters: the former would be procedural in nature and their assessment would be preliminary to the latter norms, which would be substantive in nature. As is well known, this theory has also been supported by the International Court of Justice, in its judgment on the *Jurisdictional Immunities of the State*.[51] In my opinion, this argument is very formalistic and unconvincing, because it runs counter to the general principle already mentioned that a substantive right does not exist in the absence of procedural remedies for its violation. It is clear that the victims of violations of fundamental human rights are concretely interested in having access to justice in order to obtain a decision and reparation for the harm suffered. Therefore, fundamental human rights are *functionally and necessarily linked* to the right of access to justice in the event of their violation. In partially different terms, one could object to the criticized argument that it overlooks the fact that the immunities are in conflict not only with substantive human rights, but also and above all with the procedural right of access to justice attached to those rights. There is therefore a conflict between groups of norms of the same procedural nature.

A third, more reasonable argument in favor of immunities starts from the premise that international norms on immunities are well rooted in international practice. Therefore, the problem would be solved only by determining whether, *within the regime of international immunities*, a new customary rule establishing an exception to immunities (the so-called "*human rights exception*") has emerged. This possible exception would concern only the violation of fundamental human rights, and especially international crimes. However, supporters of this argument argue that this alleged human rights exception is not confirmed by sufficient practice. Therefore it should be excluded, on the basis of practice and not on a logical argument, that a

---

[48]See, e.g., ECHR, Art. 1; ACHR, Art. 1; CCPR, Art. 2.

[49]See Voyiakis (2003), pp. 309 ff.

[50]Francioni (2007), p. 49.

[51]ICJ, *Jurisdictional Immunities of the State*, para. 93.

conflict could exist between the norms on immunities, on the one hand, and the substantive and procedural norms on fundamental human rights, on the other.[52]

In my opinion, even this argument is not convincing for two main reasons. The first is that it has the defect of being based on a "traditional" method of ascertaining customary norms, which is *outdated* for various reasons: (*a*) because it favors the element *diuturnitas* over the element *opinio juris*; (*b*) because it gives fundamental importance to a quantitative and arithmetical examination of *diuturnitas*; (*c*) because, in ascertaining *diuturnitas*, it goes back in time and does not favor the most recent developments; (*d*) finally, because it gives more importance to international case-law than domestic case-law on immunity.

The second reason is that this argument is based on a very restrictive method of interpretation, because it requires the interpreter to seek a possible human rights exception *only within the legal regime of immunities*. This leads to the regime of immunities being regarded as a kind of self-contained regime, which requires the interpreter to search only within the regime itself to find the general rule and the exception. On the contrary, I believe that the norms on immunities should not be interpreted in isolation and only within the scope of their own legal regime; they should be interpreted through a comparison with the norms and principles contained in other areas of international law. In essence, since the international legal order is unitary in character, there is nothing to prevent the interpreter from comparing norms belonging to different areas and thus providing a "systematic" interpretation of international law. From this point of view (as we shall see) *jus cogens* can constitute a very useful hierarchical criterion for resolving conflicts between customary norms of different sectors.

Let me now move on to the second general conception set out above; that is, the "human-centric" conception, which is inclined to justify a derogation from the norms on international immunities, or to interpret those norms restrictively, if they are in *concrete and effective conflict* with the norms on fundamental human rights.

Within this conception, numerous theories have been proposed. I cannot examine them all here. I merely mention that, according to a more radical theory, each State would be free to regulate any conflict between immunities and human rights at its own discretion, since immunities would not be governed by customary international law, but only by the different domestic laws for the purpose of regulating the external relations of each State.[53]

According to other more moderate theories, the "human rights exception" to immunities could be justified as an implicit waiver by States found in their accession to the UN Charter or to human rights treaties;[54] or as the exercise of a

[52]This view is supported by the International Court of Justice in the *Jurisdictional Immunities of the State* case, by the Supreme Court of Canada in the *Kazemi* case, and by the European Court of Human Rights in the *Jones and Others* case.

[53]See, for example, Brownlie (2008), pp. 323–333, expressing skepticism about the legal regime of immunities in customary international law. This opinion is still confirmed in the practice of some States of common law. On this point, see Francioni (2007), pp. 49–50.

[54]Gergen (1995–1996), pp. 783–787.

countermeasure by the State of the forum;[55] or as a consequence of the principle of universal jurisdiction over international crimes;[56] or through the instrument of *jus cogens*.[57] Finally, there is also the theory that the interpreter should, on a case-by-case basis, decide the conflict between immunities and fundamental human rights through a balancing between the interests, values and principles at stake. In my view, these last two theories are the most convincing, and it is worthwhile to explore them in more detail.

According to the theory that is based on *jus cogens*, the main normative instrument, in order to resolve the *real conflicts* between international norms on immunities, on the one hand, and international norms on the protection of fundamental human rights, on the other hand, is provided by the fact that this second group of norms belongs to *jus cogens*. This is conceived as a source *hierarchically superior*, or in any case endowed with superior normative strength, with respect to customary norms that are not peremptory, such as the norms on immunities. Therefore, the courts of the State of the forum may legitimately waive immunities and exercise their jurisdiction over foreign States and international organizations accused of violations of fundamental human rights or over officials of foreign States and international officials accused of the same violations or of individual international crimes. In jurisprudence, this theory has been argued several times. I can recall, for example, the judgments of the Italian Court of Cassation in the *Ferrini*,[58] *Milde*[59] and other cases; the dissident opinion of six judges in the *Al-Adsani* judgment of the European Court of Human Rights;[60] the opinions of two Lords in the *Pinochet III* judgment;[61] the dissident opinions of two judges in the *Arrest Warrant* judgment of the International Court of Justice;[62] the separate opinion of Judge ad hoc Dugard in the ICJ judgment on *Armed Activities on the Territory of the Congo*;[63] and the

---

[55]Bianchi (1997), pp. 414 ff.

[56]Gergen (1995–1996), pp. 792 ff.; Bianchi (1997), p. 427. See also ILA, *Final Report on the Exercise of Universal Jurisdiction in Respect of Gross Human Rights Offences, Report of the 69th Conference held in London*, 25–29 July 2000, London, 2000, p. 416.

[57]See, e.g., Bianchi (1999), p. 265; Kamto (2002), pp. 526–529; Robertson (1999), pp. 408–409; Van Alebeek (2000), p. 49.

[58]Italian Court of Cassation, *Ferrini*, paras. 9.1 and 11.

[59]Italian Court of Cassation, *Milde*, para. 3.

[60]ECtHR, *Al-Adsani v. UK*, Joint Dissenting Opinion of Judges Rozakis, Caflisch, Costa, Wildhaber, Cabral Barreto and Vajić.

[61]House of Lords, "*Pinochet III*", Opinion of Lord Browne-Wilkinson, para. 198; Opinion of Lord Hope of Craighead, para. 247.

[62]ICJ, *Arrest Warrant*, Dissenting Opinion of Judge Al-Khasawneh, para. 7; Dissenting Opinion of Judge ad hoc van den Wyngaert, paras. 27–28.

[63]ICJ, *Armed Activities*, Judgment of 3 February 2006, Separate Opinion of Judge ad hoc Dugard, paras. 3–14.

dissident opinion of Judge Cançado Trindade in the ICJ judgment on *Jurisdictional Immunities of the State.*[64]

But two important points must be stressed. The first, already highlighted, is that the norms on immunities may conflict not only with the substantive norms on fundamental human rights, but also, and indeed *more directly*, with the procedural norm on access to justice for victims of violations, when the rule of "alternative remedies" is not respected.

The second point is that the customary norm on access to justice, when it is linked to the violation of those human rights that are protected by *jus cogens*, also becomes a norm of *jus cogens*; and therefore, in the case of a real conflict, it prevails over the norms on international immunities that do not have a peremptory nature. This conclusion seems inevitable to me, even from a purely logical point of view. In fact, if the prohibition of violating certain human rights is established by a norm of *jus cogens*, it follows logically that the norm on access to justice for violations of that prohibition is also a norm of *jus cogens*, because it is *functionally and necessarily* linked to the former. In other words, the peremptory nature for the international community of the need to repress violations of *certain* fundamental human rights would have no real effect if access to justice for the victims of such violations were not protected by norms of the same peremptory nature. In case-law, this view was supported by the Inter-American Court in its judgment in the *Goiburú* case;[65] by the President of the Special Tribunal for Lebanon in its 2010 order in the *El-Sayed* case,[66] and by some judges of the European Court of Human Rights in the *Al-Dulimi* case.[67]

In conclusion on this point, I believe that the use of *jus cogens* as a hierarchical criterion, to resolve conflicts between customary norms on immunities and customary norms on fundamental human rights, should be approved. One advantage is that it provides a clear solution for such conflicts and ensures legal certainty. Another advantage is that it finally gives substance to the idea that the norms of *jus cogens*, incorporating essential and inalienable values of the international community, should prevail over customary norms that are not peremptory in nature. However, it must be recognized that international practice, even if it often admits in the abstract the existence of *jus cogens* in contemporary international law, has so far shown little willingness to apply this concept to concrete reality, especially to resolve antinomies between customary norms.

Finally, it is also worth evaluating the above mentioned theory that the conflict between international immunities and fundamental human rights should be resolved on the basis of a *balancing* between the values and principles at stake. This argument

[64]ICJ, *Jurisdictional Immunities*, Dissenting Opinion of Judge Cançado Trindade, paras. 117–120, 214–220 and 288–299.

[65]IACtHR, *Goiburú et al. v. Paraguay*, para. 131.

[66]STL, *El-Sayed*, para. 29.

[67]ECtHR, *Al-Dulimi and Montana*, Concurring Opinion of Judge Pinto de Albuquerque, joined by Judges Hajiyev, Pejchal and Delov, paras. 33–37.

has been put forward especially in relation to the immunities of State officials, but also in relation to the immunities of foreign States and international organizations.

With regard to the immunities of State officials, the criterion of balancing the principles at stake was explicitly proposed by Judges Higgins, Kooijmans and Buergenthal in their separate joint opinion in the *Arrest Warrant* judgment[68] of the International Court of Justice.[69] A similar criterion inspired, albeit less explicitly, the opinions of some Lords in the *Pinochet I* and *Pinochet III* rulings of the House of Lords.[70]

The balancing criterion was also supported in relation to the immunities of foreign States. In his dissenting opinion in the ICJ's *Jurisdictional Immunities of the State* judgment, Judge Yusuf stated that when jurisdictional immunities conflict with fundamental rights protected by human rights law or humanitarian law, a balancing between these different values is necessary, and that today a State's use of immunity to prevent access to justice and the right to an effective remedy can be considered "a misuse" of immunity.[71] Similar arguments have also been used by the Italian Court of Cassation in the *Ferrini* judgment[72] and, albeit with different results, by the Supreme Courts of Greece and Poland in their judgments in the *Margellos*[73] and *Natoniewski*[74] cases.

Finally, also in relation to the immunities of international organizations, some elements of international practice seem to use the balancing test. Although not explicitly, this criterion has been used by the Strasbourg Court in several well-known decisions (*Waite & Kennedy,*[75] *Beer & Regan,*[76] *Naletilić*[77]) in which the Court has balanced the immunity of international organizations with the right of access to justice for the victim. However, the Court has recently abandoned this

[68]ICJ, *Arrest Warrant*, Joint Separate Opinion of Judges Higgins, Kooijmans and Buergenthal, paras. 70–79.

[69]These judges criticized the fact that the majority of the judges of the Court did not strike an appropriate balance between the interests underlying the exercise of jurisdiction and those underlying the exception to immunity. They also said that the immunity norm evolves over time and that this makes the balancing test even more necessary. *Ibidem*, para. 75.

[70]See in *Pinochet I* the opinions of Lord Steyn (para. 115) and Lord Nicholls of Birkenhead (para. 110); and in *Pinochet III* the opinions of Lord Hutton (paras. 225, 262, 265), Lord Phillips (para. 290) and Lord Browne-Wilkinson (para. 65). They excluded the possibility that the functional immunity of Heads of State could cover acts of torture and similar serious international crimes, since such acts can never be regarded under international law as acts committed in the exercise of the official functions of a Head of State.

[71]ICJ, *Jurisdictional Immunities of the State*, Dissenting Opinion of Judge Yusuf, paras. 28–30 and 37.

[72]Italian Court of Cassation, *Ferrini*. On this point see De Sena, De Vittor (2005), pp. 89–116.

[73]Greek Supreme Court, *Margellos and Others v. Federal Republic of Germany*. Cf. De Sena (2016), p. 1020.

[74]Polish Supreme Court, *Natoniewski v. Federal Republic of Germany*.

[75]ECtHR, *Waite and Kennedy*, paras. 63–68.

[76]ECtHR, *Beer and Regan*, paras. 48–49, 53, 57–58.

[77]ECtHR, *Naletilić*, para. 1(b).

approach (e.g. *Mothers of Srebrenica*[78]) and has been reluctant to limit immunities.[79]

In my view, the criterion of balancing principles and values is an interesting attempt to address the general problem of antinomies and normative conflicts and the specific problem of conflicts between international immunities and fundamental human rights. By requiring the interpreter to assess the relative "weight" of the conflicting norms in each concrete case, it offers the advantage of flexibility over the hierarchical criterion of *jus cogens*. On the other hand, however, this method is today supported only by part of international doctrine and practice; and it is exposed to the criticism of those who fear the interpretative discretion of judges and prefer legal certainty.

17.1.5 Obligations

The right of access to justice (provided for by customary law) corresponds to a number of obligations on the part of States. I have already talked about them with reference to other "fundamental" human rights, so a brief mention will suffice.

The State has an obligation to possess, and to operate, an adequate apparatus for the administration of justice, in order to *ascertain* human rights violations; and the obligation that such apparatus ensure effective access to all victims of such violations occurring within its "jurisdiction". The adequacy of this apparatus should be measured with the criteria I have outlined above: (*a*) the existence of judges pre-determined by law; (*b*) their independence and impartiality; (*c*) their power to decide on the basis of law and within a reasonable time; (*d*) essential procedural guarantees of a fair trial. These are positive and immediate obligations of result, because every contemporary State must be able to guarantee such a system of justice on the basis of an international standard. These obligations are aimed at the judicial ascertainment of human rights violations and they must be kept separate from obligations aimed at investigating violations and apprehending the perpetrators.

Of course, the various and specific conventional rules governing the right of access to justice (in the forms of effective domestic remedy and fair trial) usually contain more detailed obligations, which are not part of customary law; but they meet the same general purpose.

---

[78] ECtHR, *Stichting Mothers of Srebrenica and Others*, paras. 161–165.

[79] See also, more recently, ECtHR, *Chapman v. Belgium*, paras. 50–57; *Klausecker v. Germany*, paras. 62–64, 72–76.

17.2 Right to Reparation

17.2.1 Norms

The right of the individual to obtain reparation, following the violation of his human rights, is, in my opinion, autonomous with respect to the right of access to justice, even though the two rights are obviously linked. The opposite view, which has authoritative followers,[80] is instead that the right of access to justice (for violation of human rights) already includes in its content the right to reparation (in case of ascertainment of the breach). In reality, this second view has the merit of making it clear that, for the individual victim, it is useless to obtain access to justice if, once the violation has been ascertained, he cannot obtain reparation.

However, for various reasons, the distinction between the right of access to justice (as a procedural right) and the right to reparation (as a substantive right) seems more correct.[81] First, in human rights treaties, the provisions on reparation are always separate and different from those on effective domestic remedy and fair trial. Secondly, the practice of international human rights monitoring bodies also confirms this separation. Finally, the UN General Assembly also considers that it should distinguish, within the rights of victims of human rights violations, between "effective access to justice" and "adequate, effective and prompt reparation for harm suffered".[82]

That said, it can be noted that the right to reparation is provided for in numerous provisions of human rights treaties. These include: Articles 5(5) and 41 of the European Convention, Article 3 of its Seventh Protocol, Articles 9(5) and 14(6) of the Covenant on Civil and Political Rights, Articles 10 and 63(1) of the American Convention, Article 27(1) of the 1998 Protocol to the African Charter, Article 14 (7) of the Arab Charter, Article 6 of the Convention on the Elimination of Racial Discrimination, and Article 14 of the UN Convention against Torture.

In reality, these norms have a different content. A first difference is that some of them provide for *general reparation*, i.e. in relation to all violations of the relevant convention. A famous example is Article 41 of the European Convention, according to which:

> If the Court finds that there has been a violation of the Convention or the Protocols thereto, and if the internal law of the High Contracting Party concerned allows only partial reparation to be made, the Court shall, if necessary, afford just satisfaction to the injured party.

[80] ICJ, *Jurisdictional Immunities of the State*, Dissenting Opinion of Judge Cançado Trindade, para. 221 (cited above in Sect. 17.1.2).

[81] See above, Sect. 2.3.4.3. For this view see also Buscemi (2020), p. 60.

[82] *Basic Principles and Guidelines on the Right to a Remedy and Reparation for Victims of Gross Violations of International Human Rights Law and Serious Violations of International Humanitarian Law*, Annex, Art. VII.

A similar, but more precise and detailed norm is contained in Article 63(1) of the American Convention.[83] The above-mentioned provisions of the Protocol to the African Charter, the Convention on the Elimination of Racial Discrimination and the Convention against Torture also belong to this category of norms. Instead, other norms have a more special nature, because they provide for *specific reparation*, i.e. only in relation to certain violations of the treaty, such as unlawful arrest or detention or a criminal conviction which has subsequently been annulled.[84]

A second difference is that, in conventional systems which have a *judicial* control body, the norms on reparation establish an *international* obligation of reparation by the State to the individual victim, since they provide that the reparation due by the State to the individual is expressly decided by a *judgment* of the international review body. By contrast, in treaty systems which have *quasi-judicial* monitoring bodies, the norms on reparation merely establish the State's commitment to provide reparation in its domestic law.

However, and this is an important point, the practice of the international supervisory bodies has, in practice, ended up mitigating these differences considerably.

In the first respect, even where the treaty did not contain a norm on *general reparation*, the supervisory bodies decided on reparation measures following the ascertainment of *any violation of the rights* contained in the treaty.[85] A paradigmatic case is given by the Human Rights Committee, which (in relation to individual complaints for breaches of the Covenant on Civil and Political Rights) has attributed itself the competence to indicate reparatory measures, beyond what is explicitly provided for in the Covenant, on the basis of an extensive interpretation of Article 2 (3) of the same Covenant.[86] Also other quasi-judicial monitoring bodies, in their decisions on individual complaints, indicate to the State guilty of a breach what reparation measures it should adopt in favor of the individual victims; and this in relation to *all the violations* of the treaty. In essence, the practice has established the existence of an implicit power of these bodies to decide a *general reparation*.[87] In a second respect, the decisions of these bodies on reparation measures, although not in theory binding, are generally respected by States. Therefore, the difference between the reparation decided by a true international court and that recommended by a quasi-judicial supervisory body has also blurred.

In fact, from an overall examination of the practice, it seems to me that another conclusion can also be drawn; that is, that a customary norm has now become established in contemporary international law, which requires the State that violates

[83]ACHR, Art. 63(1): "If the Court finds that there has been a violation of a right of freedom protected by this Convention, the Court shall rule that the injured party be ensured the enjoyment of his right or freedom that was violated. It shall also rule, if appropriate, that the consequences of the measure or situation that constituted the breach of such right or freedom be remedied and that fair compensation be paid to the injured party".

[84]See, e.g., CCPR, Arts. 9(5) and 14(6).

[85]See, for all, Bartolini (2009), Chap. II, esp. pp. 175 ff.

[86]Cfr. HRCtee, General Comment No. 31, 26 May 2004, para. 16.

[87]Bartolini (2009), p. 201.

human rights to provide reparation for the individuals who are the victims of the violation.[88] It is now appropriate to elaborate on the content of this norm.

17.2.2 Content of the Right

As has been said, the practice of human rights monitoring bodies shows that the decisions of these bodies establish reparation which is *directly in favor of the individual victims*, even though the obligation to give reparation is then in practice the responsibility of the State which is the author of the violation.[89] It can therefore be concluded that the individual has a true right to obtain reparation for human rights violations, which is conferred *directly* on him or her by international law and not only by domestic law implementing international law.[90]

It should also be noted that the ILC Draft Articles on State Responsibility do not exclude,[91] and indeed implicitly suggest, that individuals may have rights arising from State internationally wrongful acts.[92] For me, this conclusion is obvious, as I believe that individuals are *direct addressees* of international human rights norms, including the secondary norms on responsibility that are structurally applicable to individuals.[93]

Even if one were to accept a more restrictive theory on the content of the right of the individual victim to reparation, it should be at least admitted that this right has been established for *serious violations* of fundamental human rights and international humanitarian law. In this respect, as I already said,[94] the practice of international human rights monitoring bodies is well established. To this practice can be added: the ICJ opinion on the *Consequences of the Construction of a Wall in Palestine*;[95] the 2005 UN General Assembly resolution on the *Right to a Remedy*

[88]On this topic see Pisillo Mazzeschi (1999b), pp. 149 ff.; Id. (2003); Id. (2004b), pp. 39 ff.; Id. (2008), pp. 365–373 and 422–424; D'Argent (2005), pp. 27 ff.; Bartolini (2009); Buscemi (2020), pp. 61–67.

[89]On this practice see Bartolini (2009), Chaps. III and IV.

[90]See Pisillo Mazzeschi (1999b); Id. (2003); Id. (2004b), pp. 42–50.

[91]See above, Sect. 2.3.4.3.

[92]ILC, *Draft Articles on Responsibility of States for Internationally Wrongful Acts*, 1 August 2001, Arts. 33(2) and 48(2)(b). Cf. also UN Doc. A/56/10: *Report of the ILC on the Work of its Fifty-third Session (2001), Chapter IV, State Responsibility*, para. 4. See Crawford (2002), p. 27, who stated that the Draft Articles on State Responsibility did not wish to address the State's responsibility towards individuals; but implicitly admitted that such responsibility is configurable in contemporary international law. However, according to one author, the ILC did not provide a clear answer to the question of the existence of an individual right to reparation. Cf. Buscemi (2020), p. 53.

[93]See above, Sect. 7.2.2.

[94]See above, Sect. 2.3.4.3.

[95]ICJ, *Legal Consequences of the Construction of a Wall*, paras. 147, 152, 153.

and Reparation for Victims of Flagrant Violations of Human Rights;[96] the 2004 Report of the Commission of Inquiry on Darfur;[97] and two resolutions adopted by the *Institut de Droit International* in 2009 and 2015.[98]

17.2.3 Restrictions and Limits. Conflict Between the Right to Reparation and International Immunities (Cross-Reference)

The right to reparation for human rights violations is subject to derogations in time of emergency and to restrictions and limits, similar to those concerning the right of access to justice. Therefore, on these issues, I refer to what I have said about the latter right.[99]

17.2.4 Obligations

It is now necessary to determine the nature and structure of the States' obligations that correspond to the individual right to reparation. On this subject it is difficult to give a unitary response, because reparation, in matters of human rights as well as in international law in general, can take three classic forms: restitution (*restitutio in integrum*), monetary compensation and satisfaction.[100] Today there is a certain tendency to add, to these three forms, the guarantees of non-repetition of the wrongful act[101] and (in matters of human rights) the rehabilitation of the victim.[102] I will only deal with the three classic forms.

The obligation of the State responsible for the violation *to compensate* the damage, both to the individual victims and possibly to other States, is always a

[96] *Basic Principles and Guidelines on the Right to a Remedy and Reparation for Victims of Gross Violations of International Human Rights Law and Serious Violations of International Humanitarian Law*, UN Doc. A/RES/60/147, 16 December 2005.

[97] *Report of the International Commission of Inquiry on Darfur to the United Nations Secretary General, Pursuant to Security Council Resolution 1564 of 18 September 2004*, Geneva, 25 January 2005, paras. 595–599.

[98] IDI, *Resolution on the Immunity from Jurisdiction of the State and of Persons Who Act on Behalf of the State in Case of International Crimes*, Naples, 10 September 2009; *Resolution on Universal Civil Jurisdiction with regard to Reparation for International Crimes*, Art. 1, Tallinn, 30 August 2015.

[99] See above, Sect. 17.1.4.2.

[100] See above, Sect. 14.1.3.4.

[101] See ILC, *Draft Articles on Responsibility of States for Internationally Wrongful Acts*, Art. 30(b).

[102] See *Basic Principles and Guidelines on the Right to a Remedy and Reparation for Victims of Gross Violations of International Human Rights Law and Serious Violations of International Humanitarian Law*, Art. IX (21).

positive obligation of result, because its fulfilment does not depend on aleatory factors.

More complex is the situation regarding *restitutio in integrum*, which is obviously also the preferred form of reparation, when it is actually possible, both in international law in general and in the field of human rights.[103] When restitution results in the obligation to enact, amend or repeal legislation, it is an obligation of result. The same conclusion applies, in principle, when restitution requires the State to adopt or repeal an administrative or judicial measure. It is more difficult to evaluate the case where restitution requires the State to take a concrete measure, because then the answer may change depending on the type of measure requested. In fact, the execution of certain practical measures is not subject to alea (uncertainty) in the outcome, e.g. the release of a prisoner; whereas the execution of other measures may be subject to uncertainty, e.g. the discovery of a missing person. On the whole, it can be concluded that most of the obligations relating to *restitutio in integrum* are obligations of result.

A similar conclusion applies to the State's obligation to give *satisfaction*. When satisfaction consists of formal recognition of the violation, as is often the case with human rights, it surely constitutes an obligation of result. Classic examples are the numerous cases in which the international supervisory bodies have decided that the very issuing of a judgment establishing the violation by the State constituted satisfaction for the victim. The same conclusion applies to other State conduct, which does not contain the element of "diligence", such as apologies or symbolic monetary compensation or the construction of a monument in memory of the victim. Again, these measures are not subject to an aleatory outcome.

A different argument, however, can be made for those cases in which the international supervisory bodies have requested the State guilty of human rights violations, as satisfaction for the victims, to conduct further investigations to identify and punish those directly responsible for the offenses, or to find the bodies of the victims, or to take certain measures to prevent the recurrence of violations. In these cases, the obligation to give satisfaction is an obligation of due diligence.

Finally, it should be made clear that concrete reparation measures should be decided on a case-by-case basis, taking into account the effective needs of the victims and also their social and cultural requirements, in order to ensure a better level of realization of their rights.

[103]This does not apply when the violation of human rights results from continuing social conditions of iniquity. In such cases, *restitutio in integrum* would obviously be negative and the State must instead change these social conditions to prevent the repetition of violations.

17.3 Basic Rights of the Accused. Criminal Legality and Non-retroactivity of Crimes and Penalties

In international human rights law, there are many conventional norms that deal, even in detail, with the rights of defendants in criminal trials. They are usually contained in the provisions dealing with fair trial. However, I am now only interested in those rights that can be considered "fundamental", because they are founded, in addition to treaty law, on general international law. One could speak of "basic" human rights of the accused. These are, in my view, the rights that persons accused of criminal offences have under the principle of criminal legality and the related principle of non-retroactivity of crimes and penalties.

17.3.1 Norms

The principle of legality, in criminal matters, is expressed in the Latin brocardo "*nullum crimen sine lege, nulla poena sine lege*"; that is, in the norm that no one can be convicted of a crime or punished with a penalty that was not already provided for when the criminal act was committed. Furthermore, this principle also includes, logically, the other more specific principle of the non-retroactivity of criminal law: it means that no criminal law can be applied to an offence that was committed before the law came into force and that any more serious penalties established after the commission of an offence are not applicable to that offence. But retroactive effect is considered legitimate when the new law provides for lighter penalties than the old law (*lex mitior* rule).

These principles derive from a long historical tradition and are contained in many constitutional charters.[104] In Italy, for example, they are enshrined, in summary form, in Article 25 of the Constitution:

> No one may be withheld from the jurisdiction of the judge previously ascertained by law. No one may be punished except on the basis of a law in force prior to the time when the offence was committed [. . .].[105]

In international law, these principles are contained in the most important human rights acts and treaties. The Universal Declaration, in Article 11(2), proclaims that:

> No one shall be held guilty of any penal offence on account of any act or omission which did not constitute a penal offence, under national or international law, at the time when it was committed. Nor shall a heavier penalty be imposed than the one that was applicable at the time the penal offence was committed.

[104] According to one author, the origin of the principle of criminal legality derives from a general principle of domestic law. Cf. Pustorino (2019), p. 150.

[105] My translation. See also Articles 1 and 2 of the Italian Criminal Code.

The European Convention on Human Rights, in Article 7(1), takes up a formula almost identical to that of the Universal Declaration and adds the *lex mitior* rule. But then, in paragraph 2, it provides an important, but controversial "clarification" (or "exception") clause, according to which:

> This Article shall not prejudice the trial and punishment of any person for any act or omission which, at the time when it was committed, was criminal according to the general principles of law recognised by civilised nations.

The Covenant on Civil and Political Rights, in Article 15, contains a provision very similar to Article 7 of the European Convention; but, in the "clarification" clause, it speaks of criminal acts according to the general principles of law recognized "by the community of nations". Also worthy of note is Article 49 of the EU Charter of Fundamental Rights, which incorporates and specifies in greater detail the rules laid down in Article 15 of the Covenant on Civil and Political Rights; and adds the rule that the severity of penalties must not be disproportionate to the crime.

Other regional human rights treaties contain provisions which, while establishing the two basic principles (criminal legality and non-retroactivity of crimes and penalties), are more concise than those mentioned above; and above all, they are different because they do not include the "clarification" clause on criminal acts according to the principles recognized by civilized nations. In this sense, one can cite Article 9 of the American Convention, Article 7(2) of the African Charter, and Article 15 of the Arab Charter.

In my view, the principle of criminal legality and the connected principle of non-retroactivity of crimes and penalties have become established in general international law. The practice of international supervisory bodies confirms this conclusion. Therefore, the "basic" rights of the accused arising from these principles must be considered as "fundamental" human rights. It is more difficult, instead, to establish whether the same conclusion also applies to the "clarification" clause concerning crimes according to the principles recognized by civilized nations, which is contained only in some treaties. In reality, much depends on how this clause is interpreted, as we will see below.[106]

17.3.2 Content of the Rights

The principles of criminal legality and non-retroactivity of crimes and penalties give the accused rights which must be considered as non-derogable in time of emergency.

[106]See below, Sect. 25.4.2.

This is reflected in the main human rights treaties.[107] It seems to me that these are also absolute rights, as we shall see better below.[108]

Having said that, the main problems on the content of the rights in question are: (*a*) the qualification of the criminal nature of the offences and sanctions; (*b*) the requirements for compliance with the principle of legality; (*c*) the precise meaning of the "clarification" clause relating to crimes according to the principles recognized by civilized nations.

The first problem arises because the two principles apply to the area of criminal law and the concept of "criminal offence" may change depending on the different legal systems. But it is clear that international human rights monitoring bodies adopt an "autonomous" qualification of the concept of "criminal offence"; i.e. it is not (or not only) based on that of domestic legal systems. In particular, the European Court of Human Rights, in its case-law on Article 6 of the European Convention, has developed, since the well-known *Engel* case,[109] three criteria: (*a*) the qualification adopted by the domestic law of the State in question; (*b*) the nature of the offence, i.e. the fact that the norm violated has general addressees and a deterrent and punitive purpose; (*c*) the degree of severity of the sanction.[110] This "autonomous" qualification, which was carried out in practice and not on the basis of abstract legal assumptions,[111] has allowed the Court to consider as relevant to criminal law certain offences that, in domestic law, were qualified as administrative or tax offences.[112] This has provoked critical reactions from some State courts.

The second problem concerns the requirements for compliance with the principle of legality. The State must have criminal law norms that are *accessible, clear and predictable*, so that they can be easily known by all those to whom they are addressed.[113] These criteria apply not only to written norms, but also to interpretation of those norms by the courts.[114] It should be noted that the European Court of Human Rights, for the purposes of the applicability of Article 7 of the Convention, has held that the criteria of predictability and knowability of criminal law give rise to the need for an intellectual element (at least: conscience and will) in the conduct of the offender.[115]

---

[107]See, e.g., CCPR, Art. 4(2); ECHR, Art. 15(2).

[108]A different conclusion would have to be reached if one believed that the above principles suffer a real exception when acts considered as crimes are to be repressed on the basis of the general principles of law recognized by civilized nations. On this point see Pustorino (2019), pp. 153–154.

[109]ECtHR, *Engel and Others v. The Netherlands.*

[110]See Focarelli (2001), pp. 125–134. For other decisions of the European Court see Focarelli (2013), pp. 166–167; Zagrebelsky et al. (2019), pp. 256–260.

[111]Zagrebelsky et al. (2019), p. 248.

[112]See, e.g., on the rule *ne bis in idem* (Article 4 of Protocol No. 7 to the European Convention), ECtHR, *Grande Stevens and Others v. Italy*, paras. 94–101 and 222.

[113]See, e.g., ECtHR, *Vasiliauskas v. Lithuania*, paras. 153–162; *Drėlingas v. Lithuania*, paras. 108–110.

[114]See Pustorino (2019), p. 153, citing ECtHR, *Contrada v. Italy (No. 3).*

[115]See Zagrebelsky et al. (2019), pp. 260–261 and the case-law cited therein.

Finally, the third problem concerns the clause relating to crimes according to the general principles of law recognized by civilized nations (or the community of nations), which is provided for in the European Convention, the Covenant on Civil and Political Rights and the EU Charter of Fundamental Rights. This clause raises two questions of interpretation.

The first is whether the formula of "general principles" should be understood as a reference to existing international law (*rectius* to one of the sources of that law)[116] or to principles which are in the process of being formed or consolidated, but which cannot yet be considered as international law.[117] It seems to me that the first interpretation is preferable.

The second question is whether this clause should be interpreted as an *exception* to the principle of non-retroactivity of crimes and penalties[118] or whether it merely *clarifies* this principle, specifying that it also applies when it concerns crimes foreseen by a peculiar source and difficult to find and define, such as the general principles recognized by civilized nations.[119] The ambiguity of the clause probably derives from its original purpose, which was to avoid the repetition of the objections raised by the lawyers of the defendants during the Nuremberg Trial, concerning the accusation of crimes against humanity, judged contrary to the principle of non-retroactivity of criminal law. Therefore, the function of the clause was, and still is, to allow the conviction of perpetrators of international crimes committed during the war or during totalitarian regimes, even if such crimes were not foreseen as crimes by the State law in force at the time of their commission.

For these reasons, the clause, in my view, is not intended to be an exception to the principle of non-retroactivity of criminal law; rather, it is intended to *clarify and specify* that, among the sources of international law, the general principles of law recognized by civilized nations must also be included. The reference to this source allows for greater flexibility in the application of international law, especially considering that, in criminal matters, the contribution of principles deriving from State legal systems can be significant. This interpretation is confirmed by the practice. In fact, the Strasbourg Court and the Human Rights Committee, when faced with cases where the question of the retroactive application of criminal law came to light, have always said that States could judge the perpetrators of crimes, since they were provided for by international law at the time of their commission; and have therefore excluded the retroactive application of criminal law, albeit by

[116]For this view see, e.g., Focarelli (2013), pp. 167–168; Pustorino (2019), pp. 153–154.

[117]For this view, see Zagrebelsky et al. (2019), p. 272.

[118]This seems to be the opinion of Pustorino (2019), pp. 153–154.

[119]In this sense Zagrebelsky et al. (2019), p. 272. According to Focarelli (2013), p. 167, when it comes to international crimes, it must be assumed, in principle, that the crime, even if not provided for by domestic law at the time of commission, was foreseeable or provided for by international law.

way of exception. Examples include the *Streletz,*[120] *Kononov,*[121] *Maktouf*[122] and *Baumgarten*[123] cases.

17.3.3 Obligations

The "basic" human rights of the accused, which derive from the principles of criminal legality and non-retroactivity of crimes and penalties, correspond, as usual, to State obligations of various kinds. They are mainly the task of the courts and legislative bodies.

Those obligations include, first, the negative obligation of State organs (*primarily* the courts) to refrain from applying to defendants any existing criminal law which is contrary to those two principles. Secondly, there may be positive and immediate obligations (of result) of the legislative bodies, such as that of removing or amending regulatory provisions that conflict with the two principles. Furthermore, since the principle of legality, as has been seen, requires that criminal law norms be *accessible, clear and predictable* for all those to whom they are addressed, the State legislator will also have to ensure that these criteria are respected.[124] This obligation is also incumbent on internal judges when they are called upon to interpret and apply criminal law.

References

Bartolini G (2009) Riparazione per violazione dei diritti umani e ordinamento internazionale. Jovene, Napoli

Bianchi A (1997) Overcoming the hurdle of state immunity in the domestic enforcement of international human rights. In: Conforti B, Francioni F (eds) Enforcing international human rights in domestic courts. Nijhoff, The Hague, pp 405–439

Bianchi A (1999) Immunity versus human rights: the *Pinochet* case. Eur J Int Law 10:237–277

Brownlie I (2008) Principles of public international law, 7th edn. OUP, Oxford

Buscemi M (2020) Illeciti delle Nazioni Unite e tutela dell'individuo. Editoriale Scientifica, Napoli

Crawford J (2002) The ILC's articles on responsibility of states for internationally wrongful acts: a retrospect. Am J Int Law 96:874–890

D'Argent P (2005) Le droit de la responsabilité internationale complété? Examen des principes fondamentaux et directives concernant le droit à un recours et à la réparation des victimes de violations flagrantes du droit international des droits de l'homme et de violations graves du droit international humanitaire. AFDI 51:27–55

---

[120] ECtHR, *Streletz, Kessler and Krenz v. Germany*, paras. 75, 89 and 102 ff.

[121] ECtHR, *Kononov v. Latvia*, paras. 207 and 213.

[122] ECtHR, *Maktouf and Damjanović v. Bosnia and Herzegovina*, para. 72.

[123] HRCtee, *Baumgarten v. Germany*, para. 9.5.

[124] See, e.g., ECtHR, *Kafkaris v. Cyprus* and *Kasymakhunov and Saybatalov v. Russia*, where the Court found a violation of Article 7 of the European Convention for lack of clarity and precision in Cypriot and Russian criminal legislation respectively.

De Sena P (2016) Proportionality and human rights in international law: some ... 'Utilitarian' reflections. RDI 99:1009–1025

De Sena P, De Vittor F (2005) State immunity and human rights: the Italian Supreme Court decision on the *Ferrini* case. Eur J Int Law 16:89–116

Focarelli C (2001) Equo processo e Convenzione europea dei diritti dell'uomo. Contributo alla determinazione dell'ambito di applicazione dell'art. 6 della Convenzione. Cedam, Padova

Focarelli C (2013) La persona umana nel diritto internazionale. Il Mulino, Bologna

Francioni F (2007) The right of access to justice under customary international law. In: Francioni F (ed) Access to justice as a human right. OUP, Oxford, pp 1–55

Gergen JA (1995–1996) Human rights and the foreign sovereign immunities. Virginia J Int Law 36:765–800

Kamto M (2002) Une troublante 'Immunité totale' du Ministre des affaires étrangères. RBDI 35:518–530

Pisillo Mazzeschi R (1999b) International obligations to provide for reparation claims? In: Randelzhofer A, Tomuschat C (eds) State responsibility and the individual: reparation in instances of grave violations of human rights. Nijhoff, The Hague, pp 149–172

Pisillo Mazzeschi R (2003) Reparation claims by individuals for state breaches of humanitarian law and human rights: an overview. J Int Crim Just 1:339–347

Pisillo Mazzeschi R (2004a) Esaurimento dei ricorsi interni e diritti umani. Giappichelli, Torino

Pisillo Mazzeschi R (2004b) The marginal role of the individual in the ILC's articles on state responsibility. Ital Yearb Int Law 14:39–51

Pisillo Mazzeschi R (2008) Responsabilité de l'État pour violation des obligations positives relatives aux droits de l'homme. RC 333:175–506

Pisillo Mazzeschi R (2012) Il rapporto fra norme di *ius cogens* e la regola sull'immunità degli Stati: alcune osservazioni critiche sulla sentenza della Corte internazionale di giustizia del 3 febbraio 2012. DUDI 6:310–326

Pisillo Mazzeschi R (2014c) Organi degli Stati stranieri (immunità giurisdizionale degli). ED-Annali VII:735–794

Pustorino P (2019) Lezioni di tutela internazionale dei diritti umani. Cacucci, Bari

Robertson G (1999) Crimes against humanity: the struggle for global justice. Allen Lane/Penguin Press, London

Van Alebeek R (2000) The *Pinochet* case: international human rights law on trial. Br Yearb Int L 71:29–70

Voyiakis E (2003) Access to Court v. State Immunity. Int Comp Law Q 52:297–332

Zagrebelsky V, Chenal R, Tomasi L (2019) Manuale dei diritti fondamentali in Europa, 2nd edn. Il Mulino, Bologna

18 Protection of the Essential Identity of the Person

Another overriding aim, within the framework of the protection of human rights, is to protect the identity of the person when certain essential components of that identity, such as race, ethnic origin, sex, language or religion, are subjected to aggression through discriminatory treatment. That is to say, when a person is subject to exclusion measures, forms of prejudice or even hatred for reasons of belonging to a certain group or for innate reasons.[1] In such cases, the person is treated in a discriminatory manner not because of his behavior, but because of the characteristics he possesses as a human being.[2] Therefore, in these situations, there is a close link between the identity and dignity of the individual, and discrimination constitutes an assault not only on the identity of the person but also on human dignity.

18.1 The General Prohibition of Discrimination

18.1.1 Principles and Norms

The general prohibition of discrimination, in my view, derives, more than from a norm, from a true *general principle* that oversees the whole area of human rights; because at the basis of this system are both the idea of universalism (as a global recognition) of basic rights and the closely linked idea that States must guarantee these rights to *all human beings* without discrimination.[3]

Indeed, the principle of non-discrimination is expressly recognized as one of the main aims of the United Nations in Article 1(3) of the Charter, according to which:

[1] Kälin and Künzli (2019), p. 335.

[2] See, e.g., HRCtee, *Q v. Denmark*, para. 7.3.

[3] See above, Sect. 1.4.

R. Pisillo Mazzeschi, *International Human Rights Law*,
https://doi.org/10.1007/978-3-030-77032-7_18

> The purposes of the United Nations are: [. . .] To achieve international co-operation [. . .] in promoting and encouraging respect for human rights and for fundamental freedoms for all without distinction as to race, sex, language, or religion [. . .].

The same principle is reaffirmed in Articles 55 and 56 of the Charter, where respect for human rights by the UN and Member States is linked to the maintenance of peaceful and friendly relations between nations. The principle of non-discrimination also plays a prominent role in the Universal Declaration; but it is also accompanied by the *principle of equality*. In fact, Article 1 of the Universal Declaration proclaims that:

> All human beings are born free and equal in dignity and rights [. . .].

Immediately thereafter, Article 2 solemnly expresses the principle of non-discrimination:

> Everyone is entitled to all the rights and freedoms set forth in this Declaration, without distinction of any kind, such as race, colour, sex, language, religion, political or other opinion, national or social origin, property, birth or other status [. . .].

The subsequent Article 7 of the Universal Declaration reaffirms both principles.[4] Finally, as we shall see below, the general prohibition of discrimination is laid down in a large number of universal and regional human rights treaties; and it is confirmed by a copious body of case-law of the courts and other international human rights monitoring bodies.

However, it should be noted that both the principle of non-discrimination and that of equality have a rather broad and indeterminate content and scope. They are therefore, in my view, *framework principles*, the content of which can be clarified by more specific norms of a conventional or customary nature.

Having said that, it is now a question of gaining a better understanding of the relationship between the two principles, and then of verifying whether they have really taken the form of more specific norms in international human rights law. The issue of the relationship between the concept of equality and that of non-discrimination is not new, because it has also been raised in the general theory of law and in the constitutional law of States.

18.1.1.1 Equality

The legal concept of equality is complex and multiform, and its content is still controversial. Here I have to make an extreme simplification. The best known distinction is between formal and substantive equality. Formal equality requires equal treatment of equals, according to the well-known Aristotelian formula.

---

[4]UDHR, Art. 7: "All are equal before the law and are entitled without any discrimination to equal protection of the law. All are entitled to equal protection against any discrimination in violation of this Declaration and against any incitement to such discrimination".

Substantive equality, on the other hand, tends to change the *status quo* in order to remove the *de facto* obstacles that prevent effective and concrete equality. An example of the distinction between formal and substantive equality is provided by the two paragraphs of Article 3 of the Italian Constitution. The first paragraph reads:

> All citizens have equal social dignity and are equal before the law, without distinction of sex, race, language, religion, political opinion, personal and social conditions.[5]

The second paragraph states that:

> It is the Republic's task to remove the economic and social obstacles which, by effectively limiting the freedom and equality of citizens, prevent the full development of the human person and the effective participation of all workers in the political, economic and social organization of the country.[6]

It should be added that the principle of formal equality is embodied, in many legal systems, in the *two more specific norms* of "equality before the law" and "equal protection of the law". The first norm establishes in favor of the addressee the right to the same interpretation and application of the law; and therefore its respect is entrusted to the judge and the interpreter. Instead, the norm on equal protection of the law provides in favor of the addressee the right to be treated equally by the law; and therefore its respect is entrusted to the legislator.

In international human rights law, these two norms, which specify and concretize the principle of formal equality, can be found in some documents or treaties; but they are not numerous. As we have seen, Article 7 of the Universal Declaration contains both norms:

> All are equal before the law and are entitled without any discrimination to equal protection of the law [...].

An identical formula is contained in the first sentence of Article 26 of the Covenant on Civil and Political Rights; and similar formulas can be found in the American Convention (Art. 24), the African Charter (Art. 3) and the Arab Charter (Art. 11). By contrast, other treaties contain only the norm of equality before the law. For example, Article 20 of the EU Charter of Fundamental Rights states that:

> Everyone is equal before the law.

Finally, there are important treaties which contain neither the general principle of equality nor the two norms specifying it. The European Convention on Human Rights, which contains only provisions on the prohibition of discrimination, is exemplary in this respect.

---

[5]My translation.

[6]My translation.

What conclusions can be drawn about the principle of (formal) equality in general international law? It seems to me that the treaty provisions on the principle of equality, with its two corollaries of equality before the law and equal protection of the law, are rather limited in number. What is more, the few existing treaty provisions have a generic and indeterminate content. What does it mean in international law to say that everyone is entitled to the same interpretation and application of the law? Or that everyone has the right to be treated equally by the law? I think that these international norms on equality are incomplete, because in essence they refer to the domestic legislators and judges of the States for their application and interpretation. And different State systems can complement and specify these norms in different ways.

Therefore, in my view, the small number of conventional norms on equality and their indeterminate and incomplete content mean that a customary norm on equality, with its two corollaries, has not been established.

18.1.1.2 Non-discrimination

The argument, however, is different with regard to the general principle of non-discrimination (or general prohibition of discrimination). In fact, even this principle is controversial in the general theory of law and the constitutional law of States. In summary, it can be said that there are two different application models (or, if you like, two different interpretations) of the principle.

According to a first model, the principle of non-discrimination is seen simply as the negative aspect of the principle of equality. Therefore, it is usually said that unequal treatment of equals is prohibited, without objective and reasonable grounds. And, conversely, that it is forbidden to treat situations that are significantly different in the same way. In my view, the problem with this model is that it merely reproduces the generic and indeterminate content of the principle of equality.

Instead, on the basis of a second model, the principle of non-discrimination is more precise and complete than the principle of equality, since it presupposes that the *prohibited discrimination criteria* are established; that is, the grounds that cannot be invoked to justify unequal treatment. For example, it can be established that discrimination on grounds of race or sex, or on other grounds expressly mentioned, is prohibited.

It is this second concept that has been accepted in international human rights law. In fact, the prohibition of discrimination, as already mentioned, is contained in all the main documents and treaties on human rights; but it is *always* specified with an explicit list of prohibited discrimination criteria. In this sense, Article 1(3) of the UN Charter and Article 2 of the Universal Declaration have already been mentioned. The Covenant on Civil and Political Rights, using a formula very similar to that of the Universal Declaration, states in Article 2(1) that:

> Each State Party to the present Covenant undertakes to respect and to ensure to all individuals within its territory and subject to its jurisdiction the rights recognized in the present Covenant, without distinction of any kind, such as race, colour, sex, language, religion, political or other opinion, national or social origin, property, birth or other status.

Then Article 26 of the Covenant, after having established the principle of equality in the first sentence, goes on to specify that:

> In this respect, the law shall prohibit any discrimination and guarantee to all persons equal and effective protection against discrimination on any ground such as race, colour, sex, language, religion, political or other opinion, national or social origin, property, birth or other status.

Article 14 of the European Convention on Human Rights has almost the same content as Article 2(1) of the above Covenant.[7] And very similar is the content of the norms on non-discrimination contained in the other main human rights treaties, such as the Covenant on Economic, Social and Cultural Rights (Art. 2(2)), the American Convention (Art. 1(1)), the African Charter (Art. 2), the Arab Charter (Art. 3), the European Social Charter (revised) (Art. E), the EU Charter of Fundamental Rights (Art. 21(1)), and the Convention on the Rights of the Child (Art. 2(1)).

It should, however, be noted that most of these provisions lay down a so-called "ancillary" prohibition of discrimination; i.e. it only operates in conjunction with the other substantive human rights provided for in the treaty in question. In other words, there must be discrimination in the enjoyment of one of the rights guaranteed by the treaty. On the contrary, a smaller number of provisions establish a so-called "autonomous" prohibition of discrimination, i.e. that protects people from discrimination *also* in the enjoyment of rights other than those listed in the treaty in question. Examples are Article 21(1) of the EU Charter of Fundamental Rights and Article 1 of Protocol No. 12 to the European Convention of Human Rights, which supplements Article 14 of the Convention (which contained an only "ancillary" prohibition of discrimination).

With regard to the list of prohibited discrimination criteria, it should be remarked that the list is sometimes illustrative and sometimes exhaustive in the various treaties. The first formulation is preferable, because it allows the norm to adapt more easily to changes in the social context and new grounds for discrimination which may become relevant at international level. These include, for example, disability, age and sexual orientation. Moreover, there are some differences in the criteria laid down in the various treaties; but, on a comparative examination, it appears that some criteria are almost always provided for: they are race, color, sex, language, religion, political or other opinions, national or social origin, property, birth.

One important conclusion from this fact is that, in international human rights law, the prohibition of discrimination has a general and unitary purpose, which *does not* necessarily correspond to the prohibitions on discrimination laid down in State legal systems. This aim, as already mentioned, is to prohibit the different treatment of people *for reasons that are also part of their identity*. That is to say, to prohibit a person from being subjected to discriminatory measures because of his or her membership of a certain group or for innate reasons. In such cases, discrimination

[7]On the principle of non-discrimination in the ECHR see, e.g., Edel (2010) and Balboni (2017).

affects the person not because of his/ her behavior, but because of his/her character as a human being. Indeed, a person's identity depends largely on his/her race, ethnic origin, gender, language, religion, etc. These are the characters that define each individual. Therefore, as was said, given the close link between an individual's identity and his/her dignity, discrimination constitutes a serious assault on human dignity.[8] This explains the great importance of the prohibition of discrimination in international human rights law.

18.1.1.3 The General Prohibition of Discrimination As a Framework Principle

It is now necessary to address the question of whether the general prohibition of discrimination, contained in the above mentioned conventional norms, is also incorporated into a norm of general international law. In my view, the answer is affirmative; but, as said above, it seems to me more correct to speak of a general principle of international law, and more precisely of a framework principle that oversees and controls the area of human rights, rather than a customary norm. This is because its content, although more precise than that of the principle of equality, is still broad, including a wide range of discrimination criteria. However, as we shall see later, at least in relation to some of these criteria the *diuturnitas* and *opinio juris* of the States has ended up creating a specific customary norm.[9]

Anyway, this framework principle is useful because it gives unity to the more specific, conventional and customary norms on the prohibition of discrimination; and serves as a benchmark for their interpretation. In order to understand this, it is now necessary to elaborate on the content of the prohibition of discrimination and the way it works.

18.1.2 Content of the Prohibition

In order to clarify the content of the prohibition of discrimination, its constituent elements must be identified. Indeed, it would be wrong to think that any distinction between persons constitutes discrimination. On the contrary, the following conditions must be met.

Firstly, there must be *unequal treatment between equal persons or situations*, consisting, for example, of distinctions, limits, restrictions, exclusions, punishments or preferences.

Secondly, unequal treatment must create a *disadvantage* in relation to other persons who have the same characteristics or who are in similar situations.[10]

---

[8]See also Kälin and Künzli (2019), p. 336.

[9]See below, Sect. 18.2, on the prohibition of racial discrimination.

[10]It should be pointed out that discrimination can sometimes consist, instead of the different treatment of equal situations, in the equal treatment of very different situations. In this case the discrimination (so-called material discrimination) derives from the fact that certain distinctive

Thirdly, as already said, unequal and disadvantageous treatment must be given on the basis of one of the *prohibited grounds of discrimination*. But it should be noted that there is not always a direct and immediate link between unequal treatment and grounds for discrimination. In this respect, the distinction between *direct* and *indirect* discrimination is relevant. Direct (or formal) discrimination occurs when unequal treatment is directly related to one of the prohibited grounds of discrimination (e.g. sex). Instead, indirect discrimination occurs when unequal treatment is not explicitly linked to one of the prohibited criteria (e.g. sex), but, in fact, produces adverse effects only or predominantly for people who have those characteristics (e.g. women).

Fourth, before it can be concluded that treatment is discriminatory, it is usually necessary to verify whether or not it is *justified*. More precisely, it must be assessed whether the difference in treatment is objectively and reasonably justified because it pursues *a legitimate aim* and, if so, whether the difference is *proportionate*, i.e. necessary and not excessive to pursue that aim. The two conditions of legitimate aim and proportionality are clear from the practice of international human rights monitoring bodies. For example, the Human Rights Committee has stated that:

> [...] not every distinction constitutes discrimination, in violation of article 26, but that distinction must be justified on reasonable and objective grounds, in pursuit of an aim that is legitimate under the Covenant.[11]

The Strasbourg Court takes a similar approach. With a famous formula, in the *Belgian Linguistic Case*, the Court argued that:

> [...] the principle of equality of treatment is violated if the distinction has no objective and reasonable justification. The existence of such a justification must be assessed in relation to the aim and effects of the measure under consideration, regard being had to the principles which normally prevail in democratic societies. A difference of treatment in the exercise of a right laid down in the Convention must not only pursue a legitimate aim: Article 14 [...] is likewise violated when it is clearly established that there is no reasonable relationship of proportionality between the means employed and the aim sought to be realized.[12]

The Inter-American Court[13] and other international monitoring bodies also adopt such a test.

The question of justification is particularly relevant in the case of discrimination based on national origin, for example in the treatment of migrants. It is clear that a

---

elements of the situation are not taken into account, which instead would require consideration. See Zagrebelsky et al. (2016), p. 141.

[11]HRCtee, *Love et al. v. Australia*, para. 8.2. See also HRCtee, General Comment No. 18, 10 November 1989, para. 13: "[...] not every differentiation of treatment will constitute discrimination, if the criteria for such differentiation are reasonable and objective and if the aim is to achieve a purpose which is legitimate under the Covenant".

[12]ECtHR, *Belgian Linguistic Case*, para. 10 (The Law—B. Interpretation adopted by the Court).

[13]IACtHR, *Proposed Amendments of the Naturalization Provisions of the Constitution of Costa Rica*, paras. 56–57.

State can legitimately make differences in treatment between nationals and aliens, and that this does not in itself constitute discrimination; but differences in treatment must pursue a legitimate aim and be proportionate. Furthermore, "fundamental" human rights, such as the right to life, the prohibition of torture or inhuman treatment, subsistence rights, the prohibition of arbitrary arrest or detention, and the right of access to justice, must be guaranteed to foreigners without any restrictions.

18.1.3 Obligations

The general prohibition of discrimination imposes on States, in the first place, a negative obligation to refrain from discriminating against persons on any of the prohibited grounds and in an unjustified manner. Secondly, it also imposes a number of positive obligations of various kinds: for example, the obligation to prevent and repress discrimination against persons by other individuals and the obligation to take legislative and administrative measures in various areas of social life to eliminate discrimination.

Positive obligations may also include the obligation to adopt preferential protective treatment for disadvantaged persons or groups (e.g. women, people with disabilities, minorities) to remedy, on the basis of the principle of *substantive equality*, situations of structural disadvantage.[14] In this sense, one can cite, for example, Article 4(1) of the Convention on the elimination of discrimination against women:

> Adoption by States Parties of temporary special measures aimed at accelerating de facto equality between men and women shall not be considered discrimination as defined in the present Convention [...] these measures shall be discontinued when the objectives of equality of opportunity and treatment have been achieved.

18.2 The Prohibition of Racial Discrimination

The issue of the prohibition of racial discrimination, understood in a broad sense, as including discrimination based on race, color or ethnic origin, and as including apartheid policies, deserves special mention. The importance of this issue is confirmed by the fact that the international community has paid particular attention to it.

It should be remembered that discrimination against persons on the grounds of their identity as human beings is prohibited in international law. Therefore, such discrimination always constitutes an attack on the identity and dignity of persons. However, this does not mean that all discriminations are placed on the same level and that they all have the same seriousness. International practice and the consensus

[14]See, e.g., ECtHR, *Stec and Others v. UK*, paras. 50-65; HRCtee, *Jacobs v. Belgium*, paras. 9.3-9.5. Cf. also Focarelli (2013), p. 228.

of the international community indicate that certain forms of discrimination affect human dignity *in a particularly severe way*. This is especially true for discrimination based on race, color or ethnic origin. Apartheid is a systematic practice of racial discrimination.

The international community has led a special fight to eliminate racial discrimination. This battle has also taken place as a consequence of tragic historical experiences, dating further or less back, such as slavery, colonialism, the Holocaust and the apartheid regime in South Africa. The actions carried out within the framework of the UN include, among others, the first initiatives and then the subsequent developments in favor of the principle of self-determination of peoples, the firm condemnation of South Africa in the 1960s, the 1965 Convention against racial discrimination,[15] and the 1973 Convention against apartheid.[16] These two conventions are very important. I have already described, in summary, their content and I will limit myself here to highlighting a few aspects concerning the notions of "race" and "apartheid".

The 1965 Convention against racial discrimination seeks to eliminate such discrimination in all its forms and to combat racist doctrines.[17] It states in its Preamble that:

> [...] any doctrine of superiority based on racial differentiation is scientifically false, morally condemnable, socially unjust and dangerous [...].[18]

and that:

> [...] discrimination between human beings on the ground of race, colour or ethnic origin is an obstacle to friendly and peaceful relations among nations and is capable of disturbing peace and security among peoples [...].[19]

As can be seen, racial discrimination is even regarded as an obstacle to peaceful relations between States and a threat to international peace and security.

However, the notion of "race", when referring to human beings, raises several problems.[20] The biological conceptions of race, which were dominant for a long time, are today surpassed by science, which has shown that they are unfounded; since evolutionary biology has shown that there are no fixed or discontinuous racial groups that can be biologically defined. In essence, it is commonly believed today that racial categories are social constructs. In fact, the 1965 Convention seems to reject the biological conceptions of race and is instead influenced by the historical

[15]See above, Sect. 10.4.2.3. Cf. also Lerner (2015).

[16]See above, Sect. 10.4.2.4.

[17]CERD, Preamble, para. 10.

[18]*Ibidem*, para. 6.

[19]*Ibidem*, para. 7.

[20]See Kälin and Künzli (2019), pp. 355–357.

experiences of colonialism and the apartheid regime in South Africa.[21] If one follows this approach, the notion of "race" no longer depends on biological differences, but rather on a *social factor* of attribution of race and of exclusion and contempt for the one who is "different from himself". In other words, there is a tendency to associate the notion of race with a group of people *perceived as inferior* by other groups, due to certain evident or attributed physical and/or cultural characteristics.

This concept is more modern and correct, because it admits that all human beings are biologically equal and cannot be discriminated against on biological-genetic grounds. Paradoxically, however, it is no longer based on scientific factors but on social factors which are rather difficult to define, making it harder to identify people who are entitled not to be discriminated against on the grounds of race,[22] except in situations where there are widespread norms or practices in a State which explicitly marginalize certain groups, as was the case in the apartheid regime in South Africa. The Committee on the Elimination of Racial Discrimination has sought to resolve this problem, stating that the identification of an individual as a member of a particular racial or ethnic group should, if there are no grounds to the contrary, be based on *self-identification* by the individual concerned.[23] However, this criterion, being subjective in nature, does not seem very precise.

The 1973 Convention against apartheid (which was already a prohibited practice under the 1965 Convention) aims above all to punish this practice, expressly declared as a crime against humanity which violates the principles of international law and the UN Charter, and which constitutes a serious threat to international peace and security. The notion of apartheid is clearly easier to define than that of race, and in any case the 1973 Convention provides for a very detailed definition of this crime.[24]

The practice of international human rights monitoring bodies confirms that racial discrimination is regarded as the most serious and hateful form of discrimination, even affecting the concept of democracy, which presupposes a society open to diversity. The European Court of Human Rights, for example, in the *D.H. and Others* case, stated that:

> Racial discrimination is a particularly invidious kind of discrimination and, in view of its perilous consequences, requires from the authorities special vigilance and a vigorous reaction. It is for this reason that the authorities must use all available means to combat racism, thereby reinforcing democracy's vision of a society in which diversity is not perceived as a threat but as a source of enrichment [. . .].[25]

---

[21] See CERD, Preamble, para. 5.

[22] Kälin and Künzli (2019), pp. 356–357.

[23] CteeERD, General Recommendation No. VIII concerning the interpretation and application of article 1, paragraphs 1 and 4 of the Convention (Identification with a Particular Racial or Ethnic Group), 22 August 1990.

[24] CSPCA, Art. II.

[25] ECtHR, *D.H. and Others v. Czech Republic*, para. 179.

The same Court, in the *Nachova* case, concerning the obligation of States to investigate acts of racist violence, said that:

> [W]here there is suspicion that racial attitudes induced a violent act is particularly important that the official investigation is pursued with vigour and impartiality, having regard to the need to reassert continuously society's condemnation of racism and ethnic hatred and to maintain the confidence of minorities in the ability of the authorities to protect them [. . .] [W]hen investigating violent incidents [. . .] State authorities have the additional duty to take all reasonable steps to unmask any racist motive [. . .].[26]

Furthermore, the European Court, in the *Moldovan* case, held that racial discrimination by State officials may, in certain cases, also be regarded as a form of inhuman treatment and thus constitute a violation of Article 3 of the European Convention.[27]

The practice of the Committee on the Elimination of Racial Discrimination also confirms the seriousness of discrimination on the basis of ethnic and racial factors and the importance of the obligations undertaken by the States.[28] This is also corroborated by the recent interstate complaints before the Committee.[29]

On this basis, it seems to me that the practice and the *opinio juris* of the international community have, over time, produced the development and consolidation of a customary norm, which prohibits any discrimination on grounds of race, color or ethnicity; and that the prohibition of widespread practices of racial discrimination, reflecting essential and inalienable values of this community, has the nature of *jus cogens*.

18.3 The Prohibition of Discrimination Against Women and Customary Law

It has been mentioned above that the general prohibition of discrimination is established by a framework principle, which overrides more particular norms, conventional or customary, governing *specific prohibitions of discrimination*. But it seems to me that, among these particular norms, only the one on the prohibition of racial discrimination, which has just been examined, is regulated by customary law and therefore confers those "fundamental" human rights that are now under consideration.

However, because of its importance, the action of the international community to eliminate discrimination against women also deserves some mention here.[30] Of

[26]ECtHR, *Nachova and Others*, Judgment of 26 February 2004, paras. 157-158; *Nachova and Others*, Judgment of 6 July 2005, para. 160.

[27]ECtHR, *Moldovan and Others v. Romania (No. 2)*, para. 113.

[28]See, e.g., CteeERD, *Saada Mohamad Adan v. Denmark*; *Dawas and Shava v. Denmark*.

[29]CteeERD, *Qatar v. Saudi Arabia*; *Qatar v. United Arab States*; *Palestine v. Israel*.

[30]I will discuss later on the prohibitions of collective discrimination (against minorities and indigenous peoples). See below, Sects. 25.1 and 25.2.

course, the whole system of international protection of human rights is based on the assumption that these rights apply equally to men and women. But it is well known that, in the history of humanity and also in contemporary society, inequalities persist to the disadvantage of women. It is therefore logical that the international community has set itself the objective of acting to try to eliminate discrimination against women.

Initially, however, human rights acts and treaties only contained provisions on the general prohibition of discrimination, including sex among the prohibited grounds of discrimination. With this technique, as has been noted,[31] norms on the *prohibition of discrimination on grounds of sex* are created which operate *symmetrically*, i.e. in the same way for men and women; and which tend to obtain a *formal equality*, based mainly on the legislation of the States. A paradigmatic example of this approach is the combined provisions of Articles 2(1) and 26 of the Covenant on Civil and Political Rights.[32] However, this type of legislation, operating only at the formal level, is not effective to combat *de facto* discrimination against women rooted historically in society; i.e. to fight against situations of structural or systemic discrimination.

Subsequently, more effective action was taken within the framework of the United Nations with the 1979 Convention on the elimination of discrimination against women,[33] preceded by a similar Declaration of principles.[34] Here the emphasis shifts from the prohibition of discrimination on grounds of sex to the *prohibition of discrimination against women.* But it is not just a question of terminology: it is a question of providing protection *only in favor of women*; that is, legislation that operates *asymmetrically*[35] and tends to remove the obstacles that prevent women from achieving a *substantive equality* in the enjoyment of human rights, which is not only based on legislation, but also on social reality.

This aim, and this different approach to the problem, is clear from the whole 1979 Convention, the content of which I have already summarized earlier.[36] Here I merely point out that the Convention lays down several positive obligations for States Parties to eliminate discrimination against women in various areas of their private, public, economic and social life. It also provides that States may take *affirmative action*, i.e. special temporary measures favorable only to women, aimed at accelerating *de facto* equality between men and women.[37] The practice of the

[31] Kälin and Künzli (2019), pp. 346–348.

[32] See, e.g., HRCtee, *Aumeeruddy-Cziffra et al. v. Mauritius.*

[33] Convention on the Elimination of All Forms of Discrimination against Women (CEDAW), 18 December 1979.

[34] Declaration on the Elimination of Discrimination against Women, 7 November 1967.

[35] See Kälin and Künzli (2019), pp. 348–350.

[36] See above, Sect. 10.4.2.5.

[37] CEDAW, Art. 4: "Adoption by States Parties of temporary special measures aimed at accelerating de facto equality between men and women shall not be considered discrimination as defined in the present Convention [. . .]".

Committee on the Elimination of Discrimination against Women confirms this more modern and realistic approach to the problem.[38]

The idea that special protection should be provided for women, especially in their most vulnerable areas and situations, is also reflected in a number of sectoral international instruments, such as treaties on the protection of women in the field of labor, treaties against trafficking in women and prostitution, humanitarian law provisions designed to protect women, declarations and other acts aimed at protecting women from violence.

The last issue is also the subject of a recent and important treaty within the framework of the Council of Europe: the 2011 Istanbul Convention on violence against women and domestic violence.[39] The Convention is very broad and sets out a detailed set of obligations for States Parties, including prevention measures (Chap. 3), protection and support measures (Chap. 4), internal legislative amendments relating to civil and criminal investigations and trials against perpetrators of abuse (Chaps. 5 and 6), and international cooperation commitments (Chap. 8). There is also a monitoring mechanism, entrusted to a group of independent experts ("GREVIO"), which has the traditional task of examining the reports of the States Parties and adopting recommendations. The most innovative part of the Convention is given by the detailed provisions on investigations and judicial proceedings against those responsible for the violence and on compensation payable to victims. However, it is clear that these provisions, in order to be effective, require internal implementation by States Parties.

In conclusion, can it be argued that the prohibition of discrimination on grounds of sex and the prohibition of discrimination against women have become part of customary international law? It seems to me that, unfortunately, the answer must be negative: the persistence of historical traditions of inequality between men and women in many countries of the world still prevents the formation of the generalized and uniform practice and *opinio juris* of the international community that are necessary for the formation of a customary norm.[40] The same conclusion applies to the formation of a possible general principle of law recognized by civilized nations *in foro domestico*. However, it is also true that, at least on the prohibition of discrimination on grounds of sex, the consensus of the international community is increasingly growing.

[38]See, e.g., CteeEDAW, *The Vienna Intervention Centre against Domestic Violence v. Austria*; *J. I. v. Finland*.

[39]Council of Europe Convention on prevention and combating violence against women and domestic violence, Istanbul, 11 May 2011.

[40]The accession of a large number of States to the 1979 Convention loses much of its value when one considers the numerous important reservations made by many States, especially with regard to certain "key" articles of the Convention (Arts. 2 and 16).

References

Balboni M (ed) (2017) The European Convention on Human Rights and the principle of non-discrimination. Editoriale Scientifica, Napoli

Edel F (2010) L'interdiction de la discrimination par la Convention européenne des droits de l'homme. Les Editions du Conseil de l'Europe, Strasbourg

Focarelli C (2013) La persona umana nel diritto internazionale. Il Mulino, Bologna

Kälin W, Künzli J (2019) The law of International Human Rights protection, 2nd edn. Oxford University Press, Oxford

Lerner N (2015) The UN Convention on the elimination of all forms of racial discrimination. Brill/ Nijhoff, Leiden

Zagrebelsky V, Chenal R, Tomasi L (2016) Manuale dei diritti fondamentali in Europa. Il Mulino, Bologna

Protection of the Will and Identity of Peoples

19

So far, I have talked about individual human rights; in fact, the vast majority of human rights are characterized in this way, because they traditionally aim to protect individuals against the State (or other entities with human rights obligations). This *individualistic* character of human rights, which has its roots in the cultural heritage of the Western World, has often been criticized, but is still dominant.

However, there are also human rights which aim to protect a *group of persons* (peoples, minorities, indigenous peoples) against the State. One speaks, in these cases, of *collective* human rights. I will deal, in general, with these rights later on.[1] But it is appropriate here to examine a particular right of peoples, which can be included among the "fundamental" human rights, because it is protected by general international law. It is the right of peoples to self-determination, which has the essential function of safeguarding the *will and identity* of these collective entities.

It must be reiterated that, in international law, the people must be understood as an entity distinct from the State and that, when speaking of norms on the human rights of peoples, reference is made to "norms that deal with the people as opposed to the State, that deal with the governed as opposed to the governors, that tend [. . .] to protect the people from the apparatus that governs it".[2]

19.1 Right of Peoples to Self-Determination

19.1.1 The Principle of Self-Determination. Origin and Development

The principle of self-determination of peoples, whose importance in the overall system of international law goes far beyond the area of human rights, has a political and ideological origin and has subsequently acquired normative effectiveness. It was

[1] See below, Chap. 25.

[2] Conforti (2015), p. 27 (my translation).

R. Pisillo Mazzeschi, *International Human Rights Law*,
https://doi.org/10.1007/978-3-030-77032-7_19

first proclaimed at international level by Lenin in the Soviet Union and then by US President Wilson, albeit with partially different meanings and contents.[3] The political idea at the base of the principle was that of giving a role to the will and aspirations of the peoples in international relations, traditionally reserved exclusively to the will of the States; that is, to the governments. Self-determination was conceived as a democratic principle: peoples should be free from external oppression, especially from colonial domination, and they should be free to choose their own governance system and leaders.

It is clear that, conceived in this way, the principle of self-determination of peoples introduced dynamic and subversive elements into the traditional order of international relations, eroded the principle of territorial sovereignty of States and put colonial regimes in crisis.

In the period between the two World Wars, the principle was applied in Europe, but not in the colonies, where the Mandates System was largely in place within the League of Nations. However, the situation changed with the drafting of the UN Charter. The Charter enshrines the principle of self-determination of peoples in Articles 1(2), 55 and 56. Article 1(2) provides among the purposes of the UN:

> To develop friendly relations among nations based on respect for the principle of equal rights and self-determination of peoples [. . .].

Also Article 55 speaks of:

> [. . .] peaceful and friendly relations among nations based on respect for the principle of equal rights and self-determination of peoples [. . .].

Article 56 establishes that all Member States undertake to take action "for the achievement of the purposes set forth in Article 55". Indeed, in the Charter the principle of self-determination had a programmatic and not well specified content. But, in the following years, the intense action of the United Nations in favor of the decolonization process brought to the fore the importance of the principle, which had become an important part of the Organization's agenda. This was during the years when the Covenant on Civil and Political Rights and the Covenant on Economic, Social and Cultural Rights were being negotiated.

In fact, the principle of self-determination has been enshrined, in an identical manner, in Article 1 of both Covenants:

> 1. All peoples have the right of self-determination. By virtue of that right they freely determine their political status and freely pursue their economic, social and cultural development [. . .]
>
> 3. The States Parties to the present Covenant, including those having responsibility for the administration of Non-Self-Governing and Trust Territories, shall promote the realization of

[3]See, for all, Cassese (1984), pp. 154–155; Id. (1995), pp. 14–23.

> the right of self-determination, and shall respect that right, in conformity with the provisions of the Charter of the United Nations.

In the meantime, the principle was reaffirmed in some solemn declarations of principles of the UN General Assembly, such as the 1960 Declaration on the independence of colonial peoples,[4] the 1962 Declaration on permanent sovereignty over natural resources,[5] and the 1970 Declaration on friendly relations among States.[6] Therefore, the principle has progressively consolidated itself as legally binding in general international law. The International Court of Justice has also recognized this character of the principle in its 1995 judgment in the *East Timor* case[7] and in some important advisory opinions, such as those on *Namibia*,[8] *Western Sahara*,[9] the *Construction of a Wall in Palestine*,[10] *Kosovo*,[11] and the *Separation of the Chagos Archipelago*.[12]

However, as has been noted by the best doctrine,[13] the principle of self-determination is a *framework principle*, which has a general and indeterminate content and which does not indicate the various specific areas in which it must be realized. It has then been supplemented by some *customary norms*, which specify, in relation to individual areas, the regulatory content of this principle. It is therefore appropriate to examine these norms, first of all making a distinction between "external" and "internal" self-determination.

19.1.2 Right of "External" Self-Determination

The right of "external" self-determination means that peoples have the right to become an independent and sovereign State, or to associate or integrate with another independent State. This concept is well expressed in the following passage of the

---

[4] *Declaration on the Granting of Independence to Colonial Countries and Peoples*, GA Resolution 1514 (XV), 14 December 1960.

[5] *Permanent Sovereignty over Natural Resources*, GA Resolution 1803 (XVII), 14 December 1962.

[6] *Declaration on Principles of International Law Concerning Friendly Relations and Co-operation among States in accordance with the Charter of the United Nations*, GA Resolution 2625 (XXV), 24 October 1970.

[7] ICJ, *East Timor*, para. 29.

[8] ICJ, *Legal Consequences for States of the Continued Presence of South Africa in Namibia*, para. 52.

[9] ICJ, *Western Sahara*, para. 54.

[10] ICJ, *Legal Consequences of the Construction of a Wall in the Occupied Palestinian Territory*, para. 156.

[11] ICJ, *Accordance with International Law of the Unilateral Declaration of Independence in respect of Kosovo*, para. 79.

[12] ICJ, *Legal Consequences of the Separation of the Chagos Archipelago from Mauritius in 1965*, para. 155.

[13] Cassese (1995), pp. 126–133; Id. (2006), p. 136.

above-mentioned 1970 UN General Assembly Declaration on friendly relations among States:

> The establishment of a sovereign and independent State, the free association with an independent State or the emergence into any other political status freely determined by a people constitute modes of implementing the right of self-determination by that people.[14]

But it must be made clear that, in customary international law, the scope of application of this principle is much narrower than is commonly thought, because it meets three important limits.

The first limit derives from the fact that the principle applies only in *three situations* or, if you like, to three categories of peoples. In fact, if one examines the declarations of States and their actual practice, one must conclude that the principle applies only to: (*a*) peoples subject to colonial domination; (*b*) peoples of territories that have been conquered and occupied by force; (*c*) peoples subject to a regime of apartheid. In other words, customary norms have been formed which have specified the principle of "external" self-determination only in these three areas.[15] And they are norms of *jus cogens* and which establish *erga omnes* obligations.

A second limit is given by the *non-retroactive nature* of the principle, in the case of peoples of territories that have been acquired and occupied by force. Non retroactivity means that the principle does not apply when foreign domination dates back to a time when the principle did not yet exist; i.e. before the end of the 1940s.[16] This evidently has the aim of not calling into question the integrity of a great many States, which were historically formed before that period, also on the basis of war events, the use of force and processes of conquest.[17]

Finally, the third limit, more controversial in its content, derives from the *notion of people* and the relationship between "people" and "minorities". A first, more traditional, conception[18] considers that the notion of people, for the purposes of "external" self-determination, coincides substantially with the idea of *demos*, that is, of a group of people, general and indistinct, belonging to a certain territorial entity. In other words, the people would have a state-territorial character, and therefore

[14]*Declaration on Principles of International Law Concerning Friendly Relations and Co-operation among States in accordance with the Charter of the United Nations*, cit. (fourth paragraph of the principle of equal rights and self-determination of peoples).

[15]Moreover, the current scope of the principle is even more limited if one considers that two of these three hypotheses refer to historical phenomena that belong to the past.

[16]Actually, the International Court of Justice, in its Advisory Opinion on the *Chagos Archipelago*, seems to place the affirmation of the principle of self-determination in a more recent time. In fact, the Court states that the adoption of the AG resolution 1514 of 1960 represents a defining moment in the consolidation of decolonization practice. Cf. ICJ, *Legal Consequences of the Separation of the Chagos Archipelago from Mauritius in 1965*, para. 150.

[17]However, the theory of the non-retroactive character of the principle, although dominant in doctrine, is questioned, under certain circumstances, by authoritative scholars. See Crawford (2006), pp. 73 and 704–705.

[18]See Tancredi (2001), p. 624.

would be formed by the union of the inhabitants of a State or, if processes of change are underway which see the emergence of new entities entitled to self-determination, by the entire population of the territorial unit which was administered as a separate unit during its subjection to foreign domination. It is clear that, according to this conception, the notion of people and that of minorities, which coincides instead with the idea of *éthnos*, are sharply separated.

Instead, starting from a second conception, the notion of people should be expanded to include "people in the ethnic sense", identified on the basis of a subjective criterion (feeling of identification of individual members of the group) and an objective criterion (language, culture, religion, history, common traditions, etc.). This extensive notion of people would end up including minorities, or at least some minorities.

There is also an intermediate theory,[19] according to which the notion of people is predominantly ethnic in character, but should be supplemented and complemented by other elements, such as the size of the group aspiring to be a people, its recognition at constitutional level and the fact that this group has its own distinct legal status.

In reality, in my view, international practice, concerning "external" self-determination of peoples and attempts at secession, confirms that the international community recognizes and accepts the more traditional notion of "people" and intends to keep the concepts of people and minorities clearly separate.[20] As we shall see,[21] the argument is partly different with regard to "internal" self-determination. Therefore, it must be concluded that the principle of "external" self-determination cannot be invoked to legitimize secessionist claims by minorities or territorial districts ethnically distinct from the rest of the country (except in the case of apartheid). International law is not intended to favor secessions by minorities; and, at most, if secession in fact succeeds and stabilizes with a new State, this law can only take note of the new situation, on the basis of the principle of effectiveness.

In doctrine, some authors argue that this norm should suffer an exception in the case of the so-called *remedial secession*, i.e. when a minority within a country is subjected to serious violations of human rights. This argument has also been made before the International Court of Justice in the case of *Kosovo*,[22] but the Court has not ruled on this point. Instead, the Supreme Court of Canada, in the case of the *Secession of Quebec*, seems to be in favor of remedial secession, but only in

---

[19]See, for example, the definition of "people" that was given by UNESCO in a 1989 report: *Final Report and Recommendations, International Meeting of Experts on Further Study of the Concept of the Rights of Peoples*, 27–30 November 1989, para. 22.

[20]For this view, see also Cassese (1995), pp. 348–349. However, this author (*ibid.*, pp. 348–363) proposes, *de lege ferenda*, to extend to certain ethnic groups and minorities the rights of external and internal self-determination.

[21]See below, Sect. 19.1.3 and, for indigenous peoples, Sect. 25.2.

[22]ICJ, *Accordance with International Law of the Unilateral Declaration of Independence in respect of Kosovo*, para. 82.

exceptional cases, when the rights of the people are violated in a serious and massive way.[23] In my view, a customary norm on remedial secession has not yet been established in international law.[24]

19.1.2.1 Holders of the Right

A State that illegally governs a territory (or practices an apartheid regime) is obliged to allow the self-determination of the people therein. But a problem arises as regards the holders of the corresponding right. Can one really speak of a real subjective and international right of peoples to self-determination?

According to some authors,[25] the answer would be negative, since in this area relations under international law would only take place between States. This would be demonstrated by the fact that only other States can take sanctions against the State that violates this right and provide support to national liberation movements that want to exercise their right to self-determination.

However, it seems to me that this interpretation of the principle is reductive and suffers from a certain skepticism towards the international subjectivity of groups of individuals. In my view, the principle of self-determination is *formally addressed* not only to other States, but *also to peoples*. The fact that peoples do not have the possibility of activating international remedies in defense of their right does not affect the existence of that right. Even individuals do not, in many cases, have the possibility of asserting at the international level certain rights which are attributed to them by international law; but this does not affect the existence of such rights. This is because, as already said many times,[26] the holding of rights on the basis of primary norms of international law does not depend on the holding of means of enforcing those rights on the basis of secondary norms.

Therefore, the peoples, to whom self-determination is due, have a genuine subjective and international right towards the oppressing State and also towards third States, since the latter must refrain from assisting the former State.[27]

19.1.2.2 Obligations

The States that oppress the peoples, in the three situations in which the latter have the right of "external" self-determination, have a negative obligation not to impede the exercise of this right; and in particular to refrain from the use of threat or force against such peoples. On the other hand, third States, as mentioned above, also have a negative obligation: to refrain from helping or assisting the oppressing State.

---

[23] Supreme Court of Canada, *Re Secession of Quebec*, para. 138.

[24] This opinion also seems to be confirmed by the ICJ in its opinion on *Kosovo*. Cf. ICJ, *Accordance with International Law of the Unilateral Declaration of Independence in respect of Kosovo*, para. 82.

[25] Conforti (2015), p. 31.

[26] See above, Sects. 2.3.2 and 7.2.2.

[27] See Cassese (1995), pp. 143–145; Id. (2006), p. 137.

There are also other obligations of States, which derive from the principle of "external" self-determination of peoples, but which do not relate directly to human rights, because they concern other areas of international law on which this principle has had an impact. The main example is the legal regime of the acquisition of territorial sovereignty in violation of the principle of self-determination: the State responsible for the breach has the obligation to return the territory and all other States have the obligation to deny extraterritorial effects to acts of government issued in that territory.[28]

19.1.3 Right of "Internal" Self-Determination

So far I have spoken mainly about the right of "external" self-determination. However, even if the principle was born historically with such a connotation, in an essentially anti-colonialist key, over time an "internal" aspect of it has also become established. Therefore, today it is customary to speak also of a right of peoples to "internal" self-determination.

Actually, the content of this right is controversial. The most common meaning is that the peoples of a sovereign State have the right to a government that represents them or the right to freely choose their own government. This concept, in reality, also seems to emerge from Article 1(1) of the two United Nations Covenants of 1966. However, it is a concept that is apparently simple, but lends itself to different interpretations; and also the notion of "people" seems to be more flexible and extensive with regard to "internal" self-determination.[29] In summary, three interpretations of the principle can be identified.

According to a first, more moderate interpretation, "internal" self-determination should be understood as meaning that national and ethnic groups within a State would be entitled to be given importance and their aspirations duly taken into account by the government, through instruments such as plebiscites or referendums.[30] In a slightly different sense, the State, within which national or ethnic groups exist, should grant them a *high degree of autonomy and self-government in the political sphere*. It seems to me that this is the meaning that has been given to the right of "internal" self-determination by the Supreme Court of Canada in the *Secession of Quebec* case.[31]

There is also a second, more radical interpretation of the concept of "internal" self-determination, which has spread especially among Western States. This concept should be understood as an expression of the principle of democratic legitimation of

---

[28]See, for all, Conforti (2018), pp. 209–210. According to other authors, all States would have the more compelling obligation to disavow the illegitimate acquisition of sovereignty. See, e.g., Cassese (2006), p. 137.

[29]This notion would also include certain national and ethnic groups.

[30]See Cassese (1984), p. 158.

[31]Supreme Court of Canada, *Re Secession of Quebec*, para. 126.

governments. In other words, it would mean the right of the people to *a form of democratic government*, i.e. a true human right to democracy. But it is clear that such an interpretation of the principle of "internal" self-determination entails not recognizing true legal value to this principle, at least on a universal level, since there are still a great number of States that do not conform to democratic forms of government.

Finally, there is also a third meaning of the principle of "internal" self-determination, probably the one that most tends to diminish its value. According to this interpretation, the principle would attribute to the addressees of the principle only *individual human rights of political participation*, which could be enforced through international human rights monitoring bodies.[32]

In my opinion, the principle of "internal" self-determination should be understood in its first meaning; that is, as the right of "peoples" (and also of certain national and ethnic groups) within a State to obtain a high degree of political autonomy. However, it does not seem to me that this right has established itself as an international customary norm, except in the case of apartheid.[33] In addition, it can be argued that a customary norm is forming that grants the right of "internal" self-determination to indigenous peoples. But this topic will be dealt with later.[34]

References

Cassese A (1984) Il diritto internazionale nel mondo contemporaneo. Il Mulino, Bologna
Cassese A (1995) Self-determination of peoples. A legal reappraisal. CUP, Cambridge
Cassese A (Gaeta P ed) (2006) Diritto internazionale. Il Mulino, Bologna
Conforti B (2015) Diritto internazionale, 10th edn. Editoriale Scientifica, Napoli
Conforti B (Iovane M ed) (2018) Diritto internazionale, 11th edn. Editoriale Scientifica, Napoli
Crawford J (2006) The creation of states in international law, 2nd edn. Clarendon Press, Oxford
Focarelli C (2015) Trattato di diritto internazionale. Utet/Kluwer, Torino-Milano
Starita M (2011) I principi democratici nel diritto dell'Unione Europea. Giappichelli, Torino
Tancredi A (2001) La secessione nel diritto internazionale. Cedam, Padova

[32]See Focarelli (2015), p. 124. On political participation rights within the European Union, see Starita (2011).

[33]In other words, racial groups, who are denied full access to their country's government, are entitled to invoke both internal and external self-determination. See Cassese (1984), pp. 157–158.

[34]See below, Sect. 25.2.

Part VI

Other Human Rights

This part of the book will be devoted to human rights which, in principle, do not belong to the category of "fundamental" human rights, as I define them.[1] These are a large number of rights, and therefore I will limit myself to a synthetic examination of them, grouping them together, as I said,[2] on the basis of the nature of the human activities that each group of rights aims to protect.

However, even if these rights do not affect the crucial aspects of life, physical integrity, liberty, security and identity of the person or the will and identity of peoples, and do not usually have an absolute character, their relevance should not be underestimated. Indeed, they have, as a whole, the function of protecting important aspects of persons' private, social and public life. More specifically, individual rights are intended to protect: (*a*) private and family life;[3] (*b*) intellectual and cultural activities;[4] (*c*) political activities;[5] (*d*) economic activities;[6] (*e*) freedom of movement.[7] To these individual rights, certain collective human rights must be added,[8] particularly in favor of minorities and indigenous peoples.

[1]See above, Chap. 13, esp. Sects. 13.2 and 13.5.

[2]See above, Introduction to Part V.

[3]Below, Chap. 20.

[4]Below, Chap. 21.

[5]Below, Chap. 22.

[6]Below, Chap. 23.

[7]Below, Chap. 24.

[8]Below, Chap. 25.

Protection of Private and Family Life 20

The protection of the private and family sphere of persons from interference by the State or other entities or individuals, who are alien to that sphere, belongs to the classical tradition of civil liberties of Western origin. This tradition has then been extended to the whole system of international human rights law; but its importance is not the same in all the member States of the international community. In this area, two human rights, which are interlinked but which should be dealt with separately, are particularly relevant: (*a*) the right to respect for private life; (*b*) the right to family life. The latter also includes, as we shall see, the right to marry and to form a family.[1]

20.1 Right to Respect for Private Life

20.1.1 Norms

The most important international human rights acts and treaties provide for norms on the right to respect for private life, understood mainly as the right to privacy. In many cases, the relevant provision also deals jointly with respect for family life, always with a view to protection against undue intrusion.[2] But there are also treaties, more recent and with a more modern approach, which keep the two rights separate: for example, the Convention on the Rights of Persons with Disabilities contains a provision (Art. 22) on respect for private life and another (Art. 23) on respect for

[1]According to another approach, the right to private life could be considered as a broad concept, including the right to privacy, the right to family life and the right to marry and start a family. For this view, see Kälin and Künzli (2019), p. 376 ff. Still different is the opinion of those who believe that the right to private and family life is a kind of "container", that includes further rights arising from contemporary issues, such as, for example, the right to the protection of personal data, the right to oblivion, the rights of same-sex couples (cf. Pustorino 2019, p. 155 ff.).

[2]As we shall see, these treaties also contain other provisions which deal only with the protection of the family and/or the right to marry and found a family. See below, Sect. 20.2.

R. Pisillo Mazzeschi, *International Human Rights Law*,
https://doi.org/10.1007/978-3-030-77032-7_20

home and family. Finally, there are treaties that do not contain any norms on respect for private life: the most important example is the African Charter.

The right to respect for private life is contained in the Universal Declaration which, in Article 12, proclaims that:

> No one shall be subjected to arbitrary interference with his privacy, family, home or correspondence, nor to attacks upon his honor and reputation. Everyone has the right to protection of the law against such interference or attacks.

The Covenant on Civil and Political Rights establishes the same right, in Article 17, with a formula almost identical to that of the Universal Declaration. Article 8 of the European Convention on Human Rights speaks of respect for private life (rather than the prohibition of interference with privacy) and is more complete and detailed, because it also provides for legitimate restrictions to this right. According to this provision:

> 1. Everyone has the right to respect for his private and family life, his home and his correspondence. 2. There shall be no interference by a public authority with the exercise of this right except such as is in accordance with the law and is necessary in a democratic society in the interests of national security, public safety, or the economic well-being of the country, for the prevention of disorder or crime, for the protection of health or morals, or for the protection of the rights and freedoms of others.

Other provisions on the right to respect for private life, but with a rather concise wording, are contained in other general human rights treaties, such as the American Convention (Art. 11), the Arab Charter (Art. 21) and the EU Charter of Fundamental Rights (Art. 7); and in sectoral treaties, such as the Convention on the Rights of the Child (Art. 16) and the Convention on the Rights of Persons with Disabilities (Art. 22).

20.1.2 Content of the Right

The right to respect for private life can be derogated in time of emergency, and is not absolute, since it is subject to a number of limits and restrictions, which may vary according to the individual treaties. The most frequent restrictions are those for reasons of national security, public order, crime prevention, protection of the health, morals and reputation of others.[3]

The general purpose of this right is to guarantee the individual autonomy in matters concerning his or her private sphere. Therefore, its content is very broad and general. In fact, within this content, one can distinguish many different *aspects* of the life of individuals that fall within the scope of private life (individual and social), and which are highlighted by the practice of international supervisory bodies.

[3] See, for example, the list of restrictions established by ECHR, Art. 8(2).

A first, classic aspect concerns the freedom of the individual not to suffer unjustified *interference and intrusion* by the State or others.[4] Here, questions connected to forms of State surveillance of the individual, through telephone interceptions or video-surveillance techniques or the collection of private information by the police or intelligence services, come to the fore. This also includes respect for communications and the domicile of individuals, although these issues are sometimes considered to be the subject of related and autonomous rights.

A second aspect concerns the right to *confidentiality* (privacy in the strict sense). Many issues relating to the protection and retention of personal data are relevant here, with particular importance for health data. In principle, a use of personal data made by someone other than the interested person may constitute a breach of the right to confidentiality.[5] Issues related to the individual's right to access his or her own data, the right to be forgotten, the transfer of privacy, the undue disclosure of photographs or other images relating to the individual's private life are also considered.[6] It is clear that today, in the age of the Internet and social networks, the right to privacy has taken on a central importance and presents many problematic profiles.

A third aspect is the right to personal *honor and reputation*. This right is often highlighted in cases where it has to be balanced with other human rights, such as, for example, freedom of expression and freedom of the press. The right to reputation has also been invoked by some persons suspected of terrorist activities whose names have been published on the Internet in certain "black lists" prepared by the UN Security Council in the framework of "targeted sanctions" against terrorists. This affair has been the object of a well-known jurisprudential practice.[7]

A fourth very important aspect concerns the right to *a name and personal identity*.[8] The right to a name, as an essential element of identity, is expressly protected by certain specific conventional norms, and it comes to the fore in case-law especially in relation to the right to change one's name,[9] the right of parents to choose the name of their children,[10] the possible discriminatory treatment in the use of the names of the father and mother,[11] and the right to know one's biological origins as an essential element for one's identification.[12]

---

[4]For a recent important case concerning State responsibility in connection with employer video surveillance measures of workers, see ECtHR, *López Ribalda and Others v. Spain*, esp. paras. 87–91.

[5]Zagrebelsky et al. (2016), p. 256.

[6]ECtHR, *Vukota-Bojić v. Switzerland.*

[7]See, e.g., CFI, *Kadi*; ECJ, *Kadi*; EGC, *Kadi*; ECtHR, *Al-Jedda v. UK*; *Nada v. Switzerland*. See also Focarelli (2013), pp. 172–174.

[8]On the various facets of the right to personal identity see Viviani (2013).

[9]HRCtee, *Coeriel and Aurik v. The Netherlands.*

[10]ECtHR, *Guillot v. France*, paras. 21–22.

[11]ECtHR, *Burghartz v. Switzerland.*

[12]ECtHR, *Gaskin v. UK.*

The right to personal identity also includes the identity and *sexual orientation* of people. International practice has dealt with a number of cases involving persons who had undergone a surgical gender change and who wanted their new status recognized,[13] even for purely bureaucratic purposes.[14] The right to sexual identity also includes the right to respect intimate relationships between individuals, including consensual sexual relations between adults of the same sex. In the famous *Dudgeon* case,[15] the European Court of Human Rights condemned the United Kingdom for legislation punishing homosexual behavior between male and consenting adults in their private lives with criminal penalties. Recently, the same Court has condemned a State for its failure to prosecute individuals responsible for serious homophobic comments on Facebook against other individuals.[16] Cultural identity can also come within the scope of the right to private life. The European Court has dealt with this issue in some cases relating to the Roma.[17]

A fifth aspect, which falls within the sphere of private life, concerns the physical and mental *integrity and health* of people.[18] Here issues are highlighted relating to compulsory health treatment for children or imposed on adults without their consent, rights of access to information on health problems and medical treatment choices, freedom of choice for people on how to end life or assisted suicide. In some of these issues, other human rights may also be relevant,[19] such as the prohibition of inhuman or degrading treatment, or the prohibition of arbitrary detention. Abortion issues may also fall within the scope of the right to private life and other human rights, such as the right to life.

Finally, *environmental problems* can also be part of the content of the right to respect for private life. In particular, the European Court of Human Rights, even in the absence of the right to a healthy environment in the European Convention, ended up holding that Article 8 (right to private and family life) can give indirect protection in the area of environmental damage, in the sense that the introduction of fumes, noise and odors into an individual's private life and home can infringe upon Article 8. The Court also argued that from this provision it is possible to infer the right of individuals to be duly informed of the possible dangers arising from environmental pollution.[20]

---

[13]ECtHR, *A.P., Garçon and Nicot v. France*; IACtHR, *Gender identity, and equality and non-discrimination with regard to same-sex couples.*

[14]ECtHR, *Goodwin Christine v. UK*, Judgment of 11 July 2002.

[15]ECtHR, *Dudgeon v. UK*, paras. 47 and 60–61.

[16]ECtHR, *Beizaras and Levickas v. Lithuania*, esp. paras. 106–116.

[17]See, e.g., ECtHR, *Connors v. UK*.

[18]See Zagrebelsky et al. (2016), pp. 253–255, also for the case-law cited therein.

[19]See above, Sects. 14.2, 16.2 and 14.1.

[20]See below, Sect. 25.4.2.

20.1.3 Obligations

The very broad and diversified content of the right to private life corresponds to many obligations of a different nature on the part of States. The more traditional obligations are those, of a *negative* nature, which require States to refrain from interfering in the private sphere of persons, understood as physical and mental integrity, and also as freedom to establish and maintain relations with family members and other persons.[21] These obligations are linked, for example, to the aforementioned measures, by State authorities, of unlawful surveillance of persons or of communications or domicile, or of undue dissemination of photos, images or other private data. Other negative obligations relate to prohibitions of certain health treatments or measures likely to produce environmental damage that affect people's private life. Certain legislative measures may also be prohibited (and therefore subject to negative obligations), as demonstrated by the above mentioned *Dudgeon* case.

Moreover, in the most recent practice, effective protection of the right to private life has resulted in an increasing number of *positive* obligations (both of result and of due diligence) on States. A first group of such obligations concerns the measures (normative, administrative, judicial and executive) which must be taken by the State to prevent and repress violations of a person's private life from third parties (the so-called "horizontal" obligations of the State).[22] It is clear that, in contemporary society, illegitimate intrusions into the private life of individuals come more often from private actors than from State authorities. One thinks, for example, of violations of privacy or the right to personal image by newspapers, television, social networks or other media tools.[23]

A second group of positive obligations of States relates to other aspects of the right to privacy, which I have outlined above. The State must enact legislation that guarantees effective protection of this right or amend legislation that is deficient. For example, there may be regulatory obligations regarding the right to change the name or choose the name of children, or the right of persons to knowledge of their biological origins, or the right to change sex, or the right to access information on health issues, or the free choice of health care. In certain cases, the State must also take concrete or executive measures, such as, for example, those necessary to ensure a certain level of privacy for persons in custody or detention.

[21]See Kälin and Künzli (2019), pp. 394–395; Pustorino (2019), p. 157.

[22]See above, Sect. 4.3.4 and, more extensively, on prevention and repression obligations, Sects. 14.1.3.2 and 14.1.3.3. For a famous example of "horizontal" obligations of normative nature, see ECtHR, *X and Y v. The Netherlands*, para. 23.

[23]Focarelli (2013), pp. 170–173, rightly notes that sometimes people "sell" their privacy to organizations of political and economic interest in exchange for economic advantages. The problem then is no longer that, traditional in the logic of human rights, of the protection of the individual from the power of the State, but that of the inability of the State "to direct the conduct of individuals in a manner consistent with human rights for the good of the whole community" (my translation).

20.2 Right to Family Life

20.2.1 Norms

In treaties and other international human rights acts, the norms on the right to family life are more numerous than those on respect for private life. In fact, as mentioned above, there are many norms that deal *jointly* with respect for private and family life (in the prevailing perspective of the prohibition of undue interference). To these must be added a number of other provisions which are devoted *solely* to family life and, usually, from the different and broader point of view of the *protection of the family* and the right to marry and raise a family. For these reasons, I considered it appropriate to deal separately with the right to respect for private life and the right to family life. I will examine the latter, for the sake of brevity, only within the framework of the human rights treaties of a general nature.

The Covenant on Civil and Political Rights, in addition to Article 17 already mentioned, contains Article 23, according to which:

> 1. The family is the natural and fundamental group unit of society and is entitled to protection by society and the State. 2. The right of men and women of marriageable age to marry and to found a family shall be recognized. 3. No marriage shall be entered into without the free and full consent of the intending spouses. 4. States Parties to the present Covenant shall take appropriate steps to ensure equality of rights and responsibilities of spouses as to marriage, during marriage and at its dissolution. In the case of dissolution, provision shall be made for the necessary protection of any children.

The American Convention, in addition to Article 11, also contains Article 17 on family rights, which has a similar content to Article 23 of the Covenant on Civil and Political Rights. The same model is adopted by Articles 21 and 33(1) and (2) of the Arab Charter.

Then there are treaties, as already mentioned, which do not include provisions on respect for private life, but only on the protection of the family and marriage. One example is the Covenant on Economic, Social and Cultural Rights, which contains a very long and detailed norm (Art. 10) on the protection of the family. Another example is the African Charter. It is worth mentioning the first two paragraphs of its Article 18, which state that:

> 1. The family shall be the natural unit and basis of society. It shall be protected by the State which shall take care of its physical health and moral. 2. The State shall have the duty to assist the family which is the custodian of morals and traditional values recognized by the community.

20.2.2 Content of the Right

The right to family life may be derogated in time of emergency and is not absolute. In particular, the above-mentioned treaties provide for limits as regards the prohibition of interference with family life.

The purpose of the right to family life is, quite generally, to protect the family. Therefore, the content of the right is also very broad and its scope includes a number of manifestations, such as the right of a person not to be subject to intrusions into his family life, the right to marry and to found a family, personal and property relationships between spouses, equality between spouses, filiation, care, maintenance and education of children, adoption, etc. Again, the practice of international human rights monitoring bodies highlights this multiplicity of aspects.

Before giving a summary account of these aspects, there is a preliminary problem regarding the definition of the *concept of "family"* accepted by human rights treaties. This concept is not unique in all treaties. For the Human Rights Committee, since the Covenant on Civil and Political Rights has universal validity, it is more difficult to find a consensus on a precise concept of family within the meaning of Articles 17 and 23 of the Covenant. The Committee therefore tends to refer to the concept of the family that exists in the State legal system in question. Instead, the European Court of Human Rights has succeeded in giving a more autonomous definition of "family", believing that both the legitimate family and the natural family, as far as relations with children are concerned, fall within the scope of Article 8 of the European Convention. With reference to relationships between adults, the Court considers relevant both the formal marriage and the *de facto* relationships, for the latter taking into account the possible cohabitation, the duration of the relationship and the existence of a common commitment for the children.[24] More recently, there has been a debate as to whether or not a same-sex relationship constitutes a family. Other international human rights treaty monitoring bodies also tend today to see the family as not only formal but also factual.

Having said that, many different aspects of family life have been examined by the practice of international supervisory bodies. Let me here recall only the main ones. A first aspect concerns issues relating to *marriage*, the right to marry, equality between spouses, relations between unmarried couples.[25] A second aspect, which is very important, concerns issues relating to the name and surname of children,[26] *filiation*, choices regarding the birth of children, medically assisted forms of procreation,[27] *adoption* and custody of minor children in cases of parental crisis. These latter issues

[24]ECtHR, *B. v. UK*.

[25]On the protection of same-sex unions of a stable nature see, recently, ECtHR, *Vallianatos and Others v. Greece*.

[26]See, for example, ECtHR, *Cusan and Fazzo v. Italy*, on the prohibition of discrimination in State legislations on the naming of children.

[27]On the interesting topics of medically assisted procreation and surrogacy, see Pustorino (2020), pp. 109–116, also for cited case-law.

are very frequent and are the subject of a very extensive practice, in which the principle of the best interests of the child is becoming increasingly established.

A third aspect, which falls within the scope of the right to family life, concerns the principle of *family unity* and family reunification and the many questions that arise in relation to the entry, residence and expulsion of foreigners and migrants. As is well known, here there are usually problems of balancing the right to family life with the requirements of public order, public security and public health of the State. The practice of international supervisory bodies in this area is very abundant and rather complex. Finally, a fourth aspect, more specific but also important, concerns issues relating to the *family relationships of prisoners*. The state of detention evidently requires a number of limits and restrictions, but it does not affect the right of detainees to maintain links with their family members, through interviews, communications and correspondence.

20.2.3 Obligations

The norms on the right to family life impose obligations on States, both negative and positive, which are similar to those, examined above, which derive from the right to respect for private life. Therefore, I can refer to what I said in relation to these obligations, including the progressive extension of the scope of positive obligations in the practice of international supervisory bodies. This is logical because, as seen, the purpose, content and scope of the right to family life are also very broad and cover a multitude of aspects. The effective protection of the family, in all its manifestations, clearly requires States to adopt positive measures of various kinds.[28]

References

Focarelli C (2013) La persona umana nel diritto internazionale. Il Mulino, Bologna
Kälin W, Künzli J (2019) The law of international human rights protection, 2nd edn. OUP, Oxford
Pustorino P (2019) Lezioni di tutela internazionale dei diritti umani. Cacucci, Bari
Pustorino P (2020) Lezioni di tutela internazionale dei diritti umani, 2nd edn. Cacucci, Bari
Viviani A (2013) L'identità personale nel Sistema della Convenzione europea dei diritti dell'uomo. Editoriale Scientifica, Napoli
Zagrebelsky V, Chenal R, Tomasi L (2016) Manuale dei diritti fondamentali in Europa. Il Mulino, Bologna

[28]See also Pustorino (2019), p. 169.

21 Protection of Intellectual and Cultural Activities

One of the aims of international human rights law is to protect the intellectual and cultural activities of people. This protection is achieved through a series of human rights, which were born in Western civilization as civil rights and freedoms, but which have later extended to other parts of the world.[1] Among these rights, the most relevant are: (*a*) freedom of thought, conscience and religion; (*b*) freedom of expression and opinion; (*c*) the right to education; (*d*) the right to cultural life. Freedom of expression is sometimes also regarded as a right belonging to the political sphere.[2]

21.1 Freedom of Thought, Conscience and Religion

21.1.1 Norms

Freedom of thought, conscience and religion is proclaimed by Article 18 of the Universal Declaration in the following terms:

> Everyone has the right to freedom of thought, conscience and religion; this right includes freedom to change his religion or belief, and freedom, either alone or in community with others and in public or private, to manifest his religion or belief in teaching, practice, worship and observance.

Article 9 of the European Convention on Human Rights contains a similar but more complex provision, in paragraph 1, which takes up the content of the Universal Declaration, but then adds, in paragraph 2, the possibility of placing those limits on the freedom to manifest religion or thought which are prescribed by law and which

[1]However, these rights have not acquired, in all the member States of the international community, the high degree of importance that they have always had in Western States.

[2]For this opinion see Kälin and Künzli (2019), p. 492 ff.

R. Pisillo Mazzeschi, *International Human Rights Law*,
https://doi.org/10.1007/978-3-030-77032-7_21

are necessary in a democratic society to protect public security, public order, health, morals or the rights of others.[3]

The Covenant on Civil and Political Rights, in Article 18, largely reproduces the wording of Article 9 of the European Convention, but adds the prohibition of coercion that may undermine the freedoms established by the norm and the commitment of States to respect the freedom of parents to moral and religious education of their children. Furthermore, the Covenant contains a provision (Art. 27) on the cultural, religious and linguistic rights of persons belonging to minorities.[4]

Other relevant treaty norms are Article 12 of the American Convention, Article 8 of the African Charter, Article 30 of the Arab Charter, and Article 10 of the EU Charter of Fundamental Rights. The latter also contains a provision on the right to conscientious objection. Among the norms contained in the sectoral human rights treaties, one can cite Article 5(d)(vii) of the Convention on the Elimination of Racial Discrimination and Article 12 of the Convention on the Rights of Migrant Workers.

21.1.2 Content of the Freedoms

The general purpose of these norms is to enable people: (*a*) to think freely, without being influenced by the State or others; (*b*) to maintain and develop freely the beliefs of their conscience; (*c*) to have and manifest a religion or belief. It therefore seems that these norms are intended to regulate *three different freedoms*, rather than three different manifestations of the same freedom. But, in reality, the three freedoms are closely linked and it is often not easy to distinguish between them. This connection is also highlighted by the international monitoring bodies, which have stated that the freedoms of thought, conscience and religion guarantee ideological pluralism and therefore represent a pillar of democratic society.[5]

However, this does not mean that the three freedoms are non-derogable in time of emergency or absolute in nature. This last aspect is more complicated and needs to be clarified. In fact, in practice and doctrine, a distinction has been made between the so-called *forum internum*, that is, the processes strictly internal to the person, which produce his convictions of thought, conscience and religion, and the so-called *forum externum*, that is, the external manifestations of these convictions. It is believed that the exercise of the three freedoms in the *forum internum* of the person cannot be subjected to limits or restrictions by the State, which, for example, cannot force an

[3]ECHR, Art. 9: "1. Everyone has the right to freedom of thought, conscience and religion; this right includes freedom to change his religion of belief and freedom, either alone or in community with others and in public or private, to manifest his religion or belief, in worship, teaching, practice and observance. 2. Freedom to manifest one's religion or beliefs shall be subject only to such limitations as are prescribed by law and are necessary in a democratic society in the interests of public safety, for the protection of public order, health or morals, or for the protection of the rights and freedoms of others".

[4]See also below, Sect. 25.1.

[5]See, e.g., ECtHR, *Kokkinakis v. Greece*, para. 31.

individual to adopt or abandon a certain religious faith through the use of coercion or punishment, nor impose an oath of religious affiliation.[6] On the contrary, external manifestations of an individual's religion or belief may be subject to limits and restrictions. Article 9(2) of the European Convention on Human Rights makes this very clear.

In order to better understand the content of freedom of thought, conscience and religion, these *notions* must be clarified in the light of the practice of human rights supervisory bodies.

Firstly, this practice indicates that not purely personal ideas or judgements fall within the scope of the above norms, but those ideas which are characterized by a sufficient degree of cogency, seriousness, cohesion and importance[7] and those ideas which are consistent on certain fundamental problems.[8] The Strasbourg bodies, for example, considered that among the beliefs protected by Article 9 of the European Convention are pacifism[9] and the rejection of military force.[10]

Secondly, there is the more delicate problem of precisely defining the meaning of "religion" or "religious conviction". This problem does not arise for historical religions, practiced and recognized throughout the world, such as Christianity, Islam, Hinduism, Buddhism or Judaism; but rather for new or minority religions and for so-called "religious sects". The case-law of the European Court, while tending to avoid an autonomous notion of "religion" and therefore to refer to the State qualifications of this notion, has not renounced to exercise a certain degree of control over the matter, in order to guarantee respect for religious freedom.[11] For example, Jehovah's Witnesses, Scientology and the Osho movement have been recognized as religious in nature. The Human Rights Committee, on the other hand, accepted a broad notion of "religion", stating that Article 18 of the Covenant on Civil and Political Rights:

> [. . .] protects theistic, non-theistic and atheistic beliefs, as well as the right not to profess any religion or belief. The terms belief and religion are to be broadly construed.[12]

In addition, the Committee stated that:

> [. . .] the freedom to manifest religion or belief may be exercised 'either individually or in community with others and in public or private'. The freedom to manifest religion or belief in worship, observance, practice and teaching encompasses a broad range of acts.[13]

---

[6]See, e.g., ECtHR, *Buscarini and Others*, paras. 39–41.

[7]See, e.g., ECtHR, *Leela Forderkreis E.V. and Others*, para. 80; *Campbell and Cosans*, para. 36.

[8]See ECmHR, *X v. Federal Republic of Germany*, Decision of 10 March 1981.

[9]ECmHR, *Arrowsmith v. UK*.

[10]ECtHR, *Bayatyan v. Armenia*, paras. 110–111.

[11]Zagrebelsky et al. (2016), p. 291.

[12]HRCtee, General Comment No. 22, 30 July 1993, para. 2.

[13]*Ibidem*, para. 4.

Having said that, it is now worth mentioning the main *aspects* that fall within the scope of freedom of thought, conscience and religion and the most frequent questions that have arisen in the practice of international supervisory bodies.

A first aspect concerns the right not to adopt a certain religion and the right to change one's religion. In this regard, questions have arisen because certain States prohibit adherents of a certain religion from converting to another,[14] or because other States require people to adopt a certain religion.[15]

A second aspect relates to the right not to reveal one's philosophical or religious beliefs. It may constitute a violation of religious freedom, for example, if a person is forced to reveal his or her religious beliefs before a court[16] or in an identity document.[17]

A third important aspect concerns *conscientious objections* to military service or to certain medical practices, which are justified as an expression of freedom of conscience and religion. The European Court of Human Rights has recognized, in principle, a right to conscientious objection;[18] but not a right to refuse civilian services as an alternative to military service. Instead, the Human Rights Committee has changed its practice over time. At first, it stated that Article 18 of the Covenant on Civil and Political Rights does not recognize the right to conscientious objection,[19] but then came to diametrically opposed conclusions. In the *Aminov* case, the Committee stated that:

> [...] the right to conscientious objection to military service inheres in the right to freedom of thought, conscience and religion. It entitles any individual to an exemption from compulsory military service if such service cannot be reconciled with that individual's religion or beliefs. The right must not be impaired by coercion.[20]

A fourth aspect involves *religious signs* and clothing with religious significance. The issue of the so-called Islamic veil, which for some Muslim States is obligatory to wear and for some Western States is forbidden in public places, has been the subject of numerous decisions, not always uniform, by the international monitoring bodies. The Strasbourg Court has, as a norm, decided that a State ban on wearing the veil is legitimate if it pursues in a proportionate manner the aim of protecting public order, public security or the rights of others.[21] However, recently the Court seems to have

---

[14] HRCtee, Concluding Observations: *Yemen* (2002), para. 20.

[15] ACmHPR, *Amnesty International and Others v. Sudan*, paras. 74 and 76.

[16] ECtHR, *Alexandridis v. Greece*, para. 31 ff.

[17] ECtHR, *Sinan Işik v. Turkey*, paras. 37–53, 60; *Grzelak v. Poland*, para. 93.

[18] ECmHR, *X v. Germany*, Decision of 5 July 1977, para. 1; ECtHR, *Thlimmenos v. Greece*, para. 50; ECtHR, *Ebrahimian v. France*, para. 53.

[19] HRCtee, *L.T.K. v. Finland*, Decision of 9 July 1985, paras. 5.2–6.

[20] HRCtee *Matkarim Aminov v. Turkmenistan*, para. 9.7.

[21] See, e.g., ECtHR, *Şahin v. Turkey*; *Köse and 93 Other Applicants v. Turkey*. See also other decisions cited by Focarelli (2013), p. 192.

changed its stance.[22] The Human Rights Committee, on the other hand, has taken a more favorable attitude towards the freedom to wear the veil,[23] unless the ban is justified on public security grounds.[24]

A fifth aspect, which falls within the scope of the norms in question, concerns the importance given in a State to the majority religion, particularly in relation to the right of parents to educate their children according to their own convictions. For example, in the case of *religious instruction* in public schools, the Strasbourg Court considered it legitimate that the programs should give more space to the majority religion of the State in question.[25] The issue of the crucifix in public schoolrooms was of close interest to Italy in the controversial *Lautsi* case. The applicant complained about the presence of the crucifix in all the classrooms of the school attended by her two children, considering it contrary to the principle of secularity on which their education was based. In the first instance judgment of 2009, the Chamber of the European Court stated that the presence of the crucifix constituted a violation of the right to religious freedom.[26] In the subsequent ruling of 2011, the Grand Chamber overturned the conclusions reached in the first instance.[27]

Other questions that have been raised in the case-law of the European Court concerning school education in relation to religion are those of compulsory sex education in Denmark, considered by parents to be contrary to the Christian faith;[28] and the practice of corporal punishment in a Scottish school.[29] The Human Rights Committee's practice is more clear-cut, as it is strict that school education should be neutral and objective in relation to any religion.[30]

Finally, a sixth important aspect relates to *blasphemy*. In many cases, the right to religious freedom and respect for a person's religious beliefs may conflict with the right to freedom of expression of other people, as in the case of a film or a press article or satirical vignette[31] expressing an offensive opinion against a religion. The European Court has usually let the right to religious freedom prevail, considering justified the restrictive measures taken by the State that limited the expression of

---

[22]See ECtHR, *Lachiri v. Belgium*.

[23]HRCtee, *Hudoyberganova v. Uzbekistan*, para. 6.2.

[24]See, e.g., HRCtee, *Singh Bhinder v. Canada*, paras. 6–7, where the Committee found it legitimate to dismiss a Canadian railway worker who refused to wear the protective helmet imposed by law for safety reasons because his Sikh religion required him to always wear a turban.

[25]ECtHR, *Hasan and Eylem Zengin* v. *Turkey*, para. 63.

[26]ECtHR, *Lautsi v. Italy*, Judgment of 3 November 2009, paras. 54–55.

[27]ECtHR *Lautsi and Others v. Italy*, Judgment of 18 March 2011, paras. 72–76.

[28]ECtHR, *Kjeldsen, Busk Madsen and Pedersen v. Denmark*, para. 53.

[29]ECtHR, *Campbell and Cosans v. UK*, para. 41.

[30]In the case of *Leirvåg*, for example, the Committee considered that the compulsory teaching of a Christian religious current in Norwegian schools (the CKREE) violated Article 18(4) of the Covenant on Civil and Political Rights because it was not given impartially and objectively. Cf. HRCtee, *Leirvåg et al. v. Norway*.

[31]The case of the satirical vignettes against Muhammad published in Denmark in 2005 is well known.

critical or offensive opinions.[32] Instead, the Inter-American Court seems more in favor of allowing freedom of expression to prevail.[33]

21.1.3 Obligations

The freedoms of thought, conscience and religion correspond to obligations of States which are predominantly negative in character; that is, obligations to refrain from interfering in these individual freedoms. However, there are also some positive obligations: for example, the State must act with due diligence to prevent the free exercise of these rights from being impeded by third parties.[34] Furthermore, to give another example, if the State offers religious education based on a particular religion in schools, it is obliged to offer pupils the possibility of opting for alternatives or exempting them from that religious education.[35]

21.2 Freedom of Opinion and Expression

21.2.1 Norms

Freedom of opinion and expression is recognized in all human rights acts and treaties of a general nature and in many sectoral treaties. But the formulas used by the relevant provisions are not identical: sometimes they speak of freedom of opinion and expression, both of which include freedom of information; sometimes the latter is considered as only part of freedom of expression; sometimes freedom of expression includes both freedom of opinion and freedom of information.

In reality, these differences seem to me more terminological than substantive. Anyway, I will adopt the prevailing terminology, which speaks of freedom of opinion and expression and includes freedom of information in the latter.

The Universal Declaration, in Article 19, proclaims that:

> Everyone has the right to freedom of opinion and expression; this right includes freedom to hold opinions without interference and to seek, receive and impart information and ideas through any media and regardless of frontiers.

As can be seen, the Declaration speaks of a single right to freedom of opinion and expression, which also includes freedom of information. By contrast, Article 10 of the European Convention, with a different wording, provides for the right to freedom

[32]See, e.g., ECtHR, *Otto-Preminger-Institut v. Austria*, paras. 47–48 and 52; *Wingrove v. UK*, para. 64; *Dubowska and Skup v. Poland*, para. 2.

[33]IACtHR, *Olmedo Bustos et al. v. Chile*, Judgment of 5 February 2001, paras. 71, 73 and 79.

[34]ECtHR, *Members of the Gldani Congregation of the Jehovah's Witnesses v. Georgia*, paras. 133–134.

[35]See CCPR, Art. 18(4); CESCR, Art. 13(3).

of expression as a broader concept, including freedom of opinion and information. Indeed, Article 10(1) states:

> Everyone has the right to freedom of expression. This right shall include freedom to hold opinions and to receive and impart information and ideas without interference by public authority and regardless of frontiers [. . .].

Then, Article 10(2) specifies that the exercise of these freedoms may be subject to such formalities, conditions, restrictions or penalties as are prescribed by law and are necessary in a democratic society for the protection of a fairly broad range of public interests which are expressly listed.

The Covenant on Civil and Political Rights contains a norm which, in my view, is concise but complete and well worded. Article 19 of the Covenant distinguishes between the right of opinion, which is not subject to interference (para. 1), and freedom of expression, which includes the right to information (para. 2), and which is subject to the restrictions prescribed by law and necessary to protect the rights of others, national security, public order, public health and morals (para. 3). Article 20 adds that any propaganda of war and any support for national, racial or religious hatred that constitutes incitement to discrimination, hostility or violence must be prohibited by law.

Other relevant treaty norms on freedom of opinion and expression are Article 13 of the American Convention,[36] Article 9 of the African Charter, Article 32 of the Arab Charter, and Article 11 of the EU Charter of Fundamental Rights. With regard to sectoral human rights treaties, one can cite Article 5(d)(viii) of the Convention against Racial Discrimination, Article 13 of the Convention on the Rights of the Child, Article 13 of the Convention on the Rights of Migrant Workers, and Article 21 of the Convention on the Rights of Persons with Disabilities.

21.2.2 Content of the Freedoms

The freedoms of opinion and expression are derogable in time of emergency and do not have absolute character. In particular, they are subject to the restrictions specified in the various treaties. Significant are the different examples of restrictions contained in Article 10(2) of the European Convention and in Article 19(3) of the Covenant on Civil and Political Rights.

The general aims of these freedoms are clear. First, together they are one of the fundamental cornerstones for the protection of individuals' intellectual and cultural activities and for the development of their own personality. Secondly, they pursue a

[36] Article 13, however, is entitled "Freedom of Thought and Expression".

political aim, because they are one of the essential foundations of democratic and pluralist society[37] and one of the fundamental conditions for its progress.[38]

The link between these freedoms and democracy emerges clearly from the practice of international monitoring bodies: the basic idea is that they have an essential role in maintaining and developing a truly democratic system for two reasons: (*a*) because they contribute to the progress and development of every human person; (*b*) because they make it possible to control, judge and criticize the work of public authorities. With regard to this second aspect, the European Court of Human Rights has often described freedom of expression, very effectively, as the "watchdog" of democracy.[39] The issue of pluralism is closely linked: the European Court has often said[40] that, without pluralism, tolerance and open-mindedness, there can be no democratic society. In this way, a close and very important link has been established between three fundamental values: freedom of expression, democracy and pluralism.

Coming to the *notions* of the freedoms of opinion and expression, it should, first of all, be noted that the second (according to the prevailing concept I have adhered to above) also includes the *right to information*. The latter must be understood not only as the right to *communicate* information of various kinds and through any means, but also as the right to *seek and receive* information. This is a very important point, which has a major impact on the notion of freedom of expression. In fact, to the traditional concept of freedom of expression, as a human right of autonomy of the person, which must be protected against undue interference by the State (and which therefore imposes on the State negative obligations), a new concept of freedom of expression has been added over time, which is also understood as a human right of participation of the person. In other words, every person must be protected in his or her right to seek and receive information and opinions, and must have the cognitive tools to form his or her own independent and conscious opinion. This also imposes positive obligations on the State.

Secondly, in relation to the *forms and means* of expression and information, the above-mentioned conventional norms and their interpretative practice have made it clear that the rights in question include *any form* of expression of opinions, information or ideas and also *any means* by which they are disseminated,[41] for example the press,[42] radio, television, film and the Internet.[43] The State remains free to

[37]See, e.g., ECtHR, *Zana v. Turkey*, para. 51.

[38]ECtHR, *Handyside v. UK*, para. 49; *Hadjianastassiou v. Greece*, para. 67; *Perinçek v. Switzerland*, para. 196.

[39]See, e.g., ECtHR, *Thorgeir Thorgeirson v. Island*, para. 31; *Jersild v. Denmark*, para. 31; *Goodwin v. UK*, Judgment of 27 March 1996, para. 39.

[40]See, e.g., ECtHR, *Handyside*, para. 49; *Lingens*, para. 41; *Oberschlick*, para. 57; *Informationsverein Lentia and Others*, para. 38; *Janowski*, para. 30.

[41]See, e.g., ECtHR, *Oberschlick*; *Jersild*; *De Haes and Gijsels*.

[42]ECtHR, *Perna v. Italy*, para. 39.

[43]ECtHR, *Cengiz and Others v. Turkey*, para. 52.

regulate the various forms and means of expression and information in different ways.[44] It is clear that, given the technological advances made in recent decades in the forms and means of disseminating information, this aspect of freedom of expression has become considerably complicated and poses considerable problems in contemporary society.

A third, very important aspect of the content of freedom of expression concerns the *nature and content* of the information, opinions and ideas that are protected. The case-law of the international supervisory bodies has made it clear that protection covers *all* opinions, information or ideas, regardless of their objective relevance, taking into account in particular the social interest they hold; and that such ideas or information can take various forms: political speeches, journalism,[45] cultural and artistic expression, teaching, religious debates, etc.[46] In particular, the European Court of Human Rights has stated that protection also applies to opinions which are not shared, which offend, which are provocative and shocking, and which disturb the State or certain sectors of the population. In this regard, the Court has made some very remarkable statements, which have rightly become famous. In the *Handyside* case,[47] it said:

> The Court's supervisory functions oblige it to pay the utmost attention to the principles characterizing a 'democratic society'. Freedom of expression constitutes one of the essential foundations of such a society, one of the basic conditions for its progress and for the development of every man. Subject to paragraph 2 of Article 10 [...], it is applicable not only to 'information' or 'ideas' that are favourably received or regarded as inoffensive or as a matter of indifference, but also to those that offend, shock or disturb the State or any sector of the population. Such are the demands of that pluralism, tolerance and broadmindedness without which there is no 'democratic society' [...].[48]

However, although the scope of protection under the norms on freedom of expression is very broad, not all ideas and opinions can be expressed without consequences. Incitement to hatred, discriminatory acts and violence, for example, are not protected by freedom of expression. The same applies to racist discourses based on xenophobic, anti-Semitic, Islamophobic, religious or other intolerance.[49]

---

[44] It has already been seen, for example, that Article 10(1) of the European Convention on Human Rights provides that States may make broadcasting, cinematographic and television companies subject to an authorization regime.

[45] The European Court of Human Rights has developed extensive jurisprudence on source protection for journalists. See, recently, ECtHR, *Jecker v. Switzerland*, paras. 30–33.

[46] For example, in the *Kivenmaa case*, the Human Rights Committee made it clear that the right to express political opinions (in this case through the distribution of leaflets and the display of banners), including those relating to human rights, is protected by Article 19 of the Covenant on Civil and Political Rights. The Committee found no reason to accept the restrictions claimed by the State and laid down in Article 19(3). See HRCtee, *Kivenmaa v. Finland*, para. 9.3.

[47] ECtHR, *Handyside*, para. 49.

[48] For similar statements see ECtHR, *Lingens*, para. 41; *Oberschlick*, paras. 57–59.

[49] Some treaties are explicit on this point: see, for example, CCPR, Art. 20(2); ACHR, Art. 13(5).

More uncertain is the jurisprudence related to genocide denialist theories: the Strasbourg Court, for example, has sometimes made prevail the freedom of expression and sometimes has considered that such theories constituted an abuse of that freedom.[50]

21.2.3 Obligations

Finally, there is the question of the obligations of States, which correspond to the freedoms of opinion, expression and information. It has already been said that these freedoms, in their more traditional conceptions, mainly impose negative obligations on the State; but that, at present, they also require the State to fulfil a number of positive obligations. These include both intervening to ensure people's freedoms against injury by other individuals[51] and adopting rules and practices that are conducive to the exercise of those freedoms.

On the positive obligation to legislate, for example, one can recall the ruling of the European Court of Human Rights in the case *Centro Europa 7 v. Italy*, concerning concessions for television broadcasting on terrestrial frequencies. The Court declared that, in the audio-visual media sector, the State has, among other things, a positive obligation to create an adequate regulatory and administrative framework to ensure effective pluralism.[52] Another interesting example, which concerns the right to information, is the judgment of the Inter-American Court in the *Claude-Reyes* case.[53] The Court established that the refusal by the Chilean authorities to provide information to the three applicants, concerning a project involving deforestation of a region of Chile (which could have endangered the country's ecosystem and its economic development), had violated freedom of expression under Article 13 of the American Convention. The Court pointed out that freedom of expression also includes the right and freedom to seek, receive and distribute information of any kind, including information held by State authorities. Consequently, States have a positive obligation to provide such information.[54]

21.3 Right to Education

21.3.1 Norms

The right to education is also provided for in both general and sectoral human rights acts and treaties. Article 26 of the Universal Declaration states:

[50] See ECtHR, *Perinçek v. Switzerland*; *Williamson v. Germany*.

[51] See, e.g., ECtHR, *Young, James and Webster*, para. 55; *Dink v. Turkey*, paras. 106, 137–139.

[52] ECtHR, *Centro Europa 7 s.r.l. and Di Stefano*, para. 134.

[53] IACtHR, *Claude-Reyes et al. v. Chile*.

[54] *Ibidem*, para. 77 ff.

> 1. Everyone has the right to education. Education shall be free, at least in the elementary and fundamental stages. Elementary education shall be compulsory. Technical and professional education shall be made generally available and higher education shall be equally accessible to all on the basis of merit. 2. Education shall be directed to the full development of the human personality and to the strengthening of respect for human rights and fundamental freedoms. It shall promote understanding, tolerance and friendship among all nations, racial or religious groups, and shall further the activities of the United Nations for the maintenance of peace. 3. Parents have a prior right to choose the kind of education that shall be given to their children.

As can be seen, Article 26, with a broad and ambitious formulation, establishes three main components of the right to education: (*a*) the right to receive an education; (*b*) the general aims of education; (*c*) the right of parents to choose the type of education of their children.

The Covenant on Economic, Social and Cultural Rights regulates the right to education in Article 13, in a very extensive and detailed manner; and takes up the approach of the Universal Declaration, but with more prudent language. Paragraph 1 establishes, in principle, that the States Parties recognize the right of every individual to education and also the general aims of education, similar to those already indicated in the Universal Declaration. But paragraph 2, which is the most important because it clarifies and specifies the right to receive an education, is formulated in terms of State obligations "of progressive realization".[55] In fact, in it the States Parties make a series of commitments relating to the various stages of education of persons; but only "with a view to achieving the full realization of this right". The formula is the classic one, in matters of economic, social and cultural rights, which recalls the nature of the general obligations assumed by the States Parties under Article 2(1) of the Covenant.[56]

Actually, among the States' commitments related to the various stages of education, a distinction can be made. The only clear-cut commitment relates to the primary education stage, since Article 13 states that: "Primary education shall be compulsory and available free to all".[57] With regard to the other phases of education, the States' commitments are less strict.[58] Moreover, also the obligation relative to primary education, in the subsequent Article 14 of the Covenant, assumes the character of an obligation "of progressive realization", over a reasonable number of years, for those States which are not able to ensure the implementation of this obligation immediately.[59]

---

[55] See above, Sect. 8.2.3.

[56] Art. 2(1): "Each State Party to the present Covenant undertakes to take steps [. . .] to the maximum of its available resources, with a view to achieving progressively the full realization of the rights recognized in the present Covenant, by all appropriate means [. . .]".

[57] CESCR, Art. 13(2)(a).

[58] CESCR, Art. 13(2)(b) and (c).

[59] CESCR, Art. 14: Each State Party to the present Covenant which, at the time of becoming a Party, has not been able to secure [. . .] compulsory primary education, free of charge, undertakes, within two years, to work out and adopt a detailed plan of action for the progressive implementation,

Finally, paragraphs 3 and 4 of Article 13 establish the freedom of parents to choose schools for their children, but with a series of clarifications and limits to protect the rights of the State in matters of education.

The right to education, on the other hand, is regulated more succinctly by the European Convention on Human Rights. Article 2 of Protocol No. 1 to the Convention states that:

> No person shall be denied the right to education. In the exercise of any functions which it assumes in relation to education and to teaching, the State shall respect the right of parents to ensure such education and teaching in conformity with their own religious and philosophical convictions.

This right is also provided for in the San Salvador Protocol (Art. 13), the African Charter (Art. 17), the EU Charter of Fundamental Rights (Art. 14), and the Arab Charter (Art. 41).

In the framework of the sectoral human rights treaties, one may recall Article 5(e)(v) of the Convention against Racial Discrimination, Article 10 of the Convention on the Elimination of Discrimination against Women, Articles 28, 29(2) and 32(1) of the Convention on the Rights of the Child, Article 30 of the Convention on the Rights of Migrant Workers, Article 24 of the Convention on the Rights of Persons with Disabilities, Article 11 of the African Charter on the Rights and Welfare of the Child,[60] and Articles 12–14 of the Framework Convention for the Protection of National Minorities. The 1960 UNESCO Convention against Discrimination in Education should also be mentioned. Finally, there are a number of treaties of international humanitarian law that contain provisions on the right to education.[61]

Some of the above mentioned provisions are extensive and detailed, because they broadly follow the wording of Article 13 of the Covenant on Economic, Social and Cultural Rights. Examples are Article 13 of the San Salvador Protocol, Article 41 of the Arab Charter, and Articles 28, 29 and 32 of the Convention on the Rights of the Child. Other provisions, instead, are more concise. For example, Article 17(1) of the African Charter merely states that: "Every individual shall have the right to education".

21.3.2 Content of the Right

The right to education is derogable in time of emergency and does not have absolute character. Even the right to receive a primary education, as noted above, can be restricted if a State does not have sufficient resources.[62] The content of the right to

---

within a reasonable number of years, to be fixed in the plan, of the principle of compulsory education free of charge for all".

[60] African Charter on the Rights and Welfare of the Child, 1 July 1990.

[61] See GC III, Art. 38; GC IV, Arts. 50 and 94; AP I, Art. 52(3).

[62] CESCR, Art. 14.

education can be derived from the whole set of conventional norms mentioned above. These norms pursue the general purposes which were already clearly indicated in Article 26 of the Universal Declaration: (*a*) to guarantee all persons access to education; (*b*) to guarantee a free choice of education, especially by parents; (*c*) to ensure that education pursues aims which are not contrary to human rights.

From these purposes, it follows that the right to education consists of *three main elements*. The first element concerns *access to education*. Many treaty norms state that primary education must be compulsory and accessible for free to all. This has led some authors to argue that the right of access to primary education is the core content of the right to education.[63] For my part, I have already said that I do not share the view about an alleged core content of human rights. A different question, instead (which I will resume later) is to establish whether States have a minimum core *obligation* to guarantee access to primary education. Another important aspect of access to education concerns the right to receive it without discrimination.[64] This right does not imply an obligation on the part of the State to increase the availability of educational institutions;[65] rather, it must be understood as the right of non-discriminatory access to existing educational institutions.[66]

The second element of the right to education concerns the *free choice of education*. This means that every person (and parents for their children) is free to choose the education they prefer, and the State must respect that choice and ensure pluralism of educational pathways and services.[67]

Finally, the third element of the right to education concerns the commitment of States to ensure that education is directed towards the full development of the human person and *respect for human rights*. However, it should be noted that this element of the right to education is not present in all the treaties; and that it is rather vague and generic in nature.

21.3.3 Obligations

As for the obligations of States, which correspond to the various aspects of the right to education, they are, as usual, of various kinds. Some are negative obligations, such as not interfering in parents' free choices about their children's educational paths. Many are "progressive" obligations (as usually happens for cultural rights), for example the State's obligations regarding access to higher education.[68] But there

[63]See also Kälin and Künzli (2019), pp. 409–410.

[64]See Focarelli (2013), pp. 218–219.

[65]See ECtHR, *Leyla Şahin v. Turkey*, para. 137.

[66]See ECtHR, *Belgian Linguistic Case*.

[67]Focarelli (2013), pp. 218–219.

[68]See CESCR, Art. 13(2)(b) and (c).

are also some positive and immediate obligations (both of result and of due diligence).

The most interesting issue concerns the obligation of States to ensure primary education for all.[69] The Committee on Economic, Social and Cultural Rights argues that this obligation is a minimum core obligation and not a "progressive" obligation. Indeed, the Committee, in its General Comment No. 3, stated that:

> [. . .] a State party in which any significant number of individuals is deprived [. . .] of the most basic forms of education is, prima facie, failing to discharge its obligations under the Covenant. If the Covenant were to be read in such a way as not to establish such a minimum core obligation, it would be largely deprived of its raison d'être.[70]

It seems to me that this argument can be accepted in principle, if one considers that the defining characteristic of minimum core obligations is their *immediacy*. However, it should be noted that the Committee itself adds that any assessment of whether a State has fulfilled its minimum core obligation must also take account of the constraints imposed by the availability of resources.[71] A State can exclude its responsibility if it demonstrates that it has made every effort to use all the resources at its disposal in an attempt to fulfil such obligation as a matter of priority.

21.4 Right to Cultural Life

21.4.1 Norms

The right to cultural life is not among the most widely recognized human rights in the international community, perhaps also because of the complexity that derives from the many different definitions of "culture".[72] However, several treaties recognize the right of people to participate in cultural life and to enjoy the benefits of artistic and scientific creations.

Therefore, the right to cultural life has its own specificity in international human rights law, although it is clear that certain aspects of it are already protected by other human rights, such as the right to private life, freedom of thought, conscience and religion, freedom of opinion and expression, and the right to education. Hence, there is a complementary relationship between these different rights. It should also be noted that the topic of the human cultural rights of persons must be kept separate from the very broad topic of the protection of cultural property in international law, which is a different area from that of human rights. Here too, however, there are links and interactions between the two fields.

[69] See CESCR, Art. 13(2((a).

[70] CteeESCR, General Comment No. 3, 14 December 1990, para. 10.

[71] *Ibidem.*

[72] See Weissbrodt and de la Vega (2007), p. 177.

The right to cultural life is already provided, in its essential elements, by the Universal Declaration, whose Article 27 proclaims that:

> 1. Everyone has the right freely to participate in the cultural life of the community, to enjoy the arts and to share in scientific advancement and its benefits. 2. Everyone has the right to the protection of the moral and material interests resulting from any scientific, literary or artistic production of which he is the author.

The Covenant on Economic, Social and Cultural Rights contains a more complex and analytical norm. Article 15, in paragraph 1, takes up in almost identical terms the content of the Universal Declaration:

> The States Parties to the present Covenant recognize the right of everyone: a) To take part in cultural life; b) To enjoy the benefits of scientific progress and its applications; c) To benefit from the protection of the moral and material interests resulting from any scientific, literary or artistic production of which he is the author.

However, in the subsequent paragraphs 2, 3 and 4 of Article 15, the States Parties assume other obligations. But they are rather vague and generic, since these States undertake to take measures to achieve the full realization of the right to cultural life, including those relating to the conservation, development and dissemination of science and culture; they undertake to respect the freedom of scientific research; and finally, they recognize the benefits of international cooperation in these fields.

Other detailed norms on the right to cultural life, largely inspired by Article 15 of the Covenant, are contained in the San Salvador Protocol (Art. 14), the Arab Charter (Art. 42), and the Convention on the Rights of Persons with Disabilities (Art. 30). The other human rights treaties contain much more concise provisions. One may recall Article 17(2) of the African Charter, Article 13 of the EU Charter of Fundamental Rights, Article 13(e) of the Convention on the Elimination of Discrimination against Women, Article 31 of the Convention on the Rights of the Child, and Articles 43(1)(g) and 45(1)(d) of the Convention on the Rights of Migrant Workers. For example, Article 17(2) of the African Charter is limited to establishing:

> Every individual may freely take part in the cultural life of his community.

Finally, it should be remembered that, alongside the norms dealing with the cultural rights of individuals, there are those dedicated to collective cultural rights, which belong to minorities and indigenous peoples. But this issue will be dealt with later.[73]

---

[73] See below, Sects. 25.1 and 25.2.

21.4.2 Content of the Right

The content of the right to cultural life is inferred above all from Article 15 of the Covenant on Economic, Social and Cultural Rights and from the other conventional norms which are inspired by this provision. It comprises three main elements: (*a*) the right to participate in cultural life; (*b*) the right to enjoy the benefits of scientific research and to conduct such research; (*c*) the right to enjoy the protection of the interests derived by authors from their scientific, literary and artistic products.

The first element (right to participate in cultural life) protects both passive conduct of people, such as participation in cultural events, painting and sculpture exhibitions, musical, theatrical, cinematographic and similar performances; and active conduct, such as artistic and cultural creations of various kinds. But the right of artistic creation may be subject to restrictions and limitations, in order to defend other values, such as public order, morality, honor and reputation of other people. The European Court of Human Rights, for example, has stated that the limits set by Article 10(2) of the European Convention to freedom of expression also operate in relation to artistic creations and expressions, such as painting[74] or literature.

The second element (rights relating to scientific research) also protects both passive and active conduct of people. In fact, on the one hand, it safeguards people's freedom to be informed of the results of scientific research in order to benefit from them. This aspect is clear from Article 15(1)(b) of the Covenant on Economic, Social and Cultural Rights. On the other hand, the freedom to conduct scientific research is also protected, as reflected, inter alia, in paragraph 3 of the same Article 15, according to which States Parties undertake to respect "the freedom indispensable for scientific research".

Finally, the third element (authors' right to the protection of their scientific, literary and artistic products) was the subject of a General Comment by the Committee on Economic, Social and Cultural Rights.[75] The Committee has also deepened the normative content of this right.[76] "Authors" are to be understood as individuals or groups of individuals or communities; but not as legal persons. The benefits for authors must derive from "effective protection", but this does not necessarily reflect the level of protection found in legal regimes for the protection of intellectual property. The protection of authors' "moral interests" includes, above all, their right to be recognized as the creators of works and to oppose their modification. Finally, the protection of authors' "material interests" reflects the link between this right and the right to property; but it does not necessarily have to extend for the whole life of these authors.

[74]See, e.g., ECtHR, *Müller and Others v. Switzerland*, paras. 33–36.

[75]CteeESCR, General Comment No. 17, 12 January 2006.

[76]*Ibidem*, paras. 6–24.

21.4.3 Obligations

State obligations of various kinds correspond to the right to cultural life, in its many aspects. For example, a negative obligation is that of the State not to interfere in the right of persons to enjoy culture passively through books or films or performances or to enjoy it actively through the writing of books or the performance of artistic works. A positive obligation of the State is to protect people's right to culture from interference by other people. A "progressive" obligation of the State is to take measures to achieve the full realization of the preservation, development and dissemination of science and culture, as provided, for example, in Article 15(2) of the Covenant on Economic, Social and Cultural Rights.

References

Focarelli C (2013) La persona umana nel diritto internazionale. Il Mulino, Bologna
Kälin W, Künzli J (2019) The law of international human rights protection, 2nd edn. OUP, Oxford-New York
Weissbrodt D, de la Vega C (2007) International human rights law. An introduction. University of Pennsylvania Press, Philadelphia
Zagrebelsky V, Chenal R, Tomasi L (2016) Manuale dei diritti fondamentali in Europa. Il Mulino, Bologna

Protection of Political Activities 22

Another goal of international human rights law is to protect the sphere of political activities (in both the broad and narrow sense) of people. This is achieved through certain rights which, historically, are considered as belonging to the first generation of human rights. The most significant ones, which I will discuss below, are: (*a*) the freedom of assembly and association; (*b*) the right to participate in political and public life, which also includes the right to free elections and the right of access to public service.

22.1 Freedom of Assembly and Association

22.1.1 Norms

The freedoms of assembly and association are established in a unitary manner by Article 20 of the Universal Declaration in the following terms:

1. Everyone has the right to freedom of peaceful assembly and association
2. No one may be compelled to belong to an association.

Furthermore, Article 23(4) of the Declaration establishes the right of everyone to form and join trade unions for the protection of his or her interests. Article 11(1) of the European Convention on Human Rights resumes the content of the Universal Declaration, but mentions the two freedoms separately:

> Everyone has the right to freedom of peaceful assembly and to freedom of association with others, including the right to form and to join trade unions for the protection of his interests.

Then, paragraph 2 of the same Article 11 adds a provision on legitimate restrictions on the freedoms of assembly and association. Restrictions must be prescribed by law and necessary in a democratic society, for the protection of

R. Pisillo Mazzeschi, *International Human Rights Law*,
https://doi.org/10.1007/978-3-030-77032-7_22

national security or public safety, for the prevention of crime, for the protection of health or morals or the rights of others. In addition, it is specified that legitimate restrictions may be imposed on the exercise of the two freedoms by members of the armed forces, the police or the State administration.

The Covenant on Civil and Political Rights devotes two detailed, separate and distinct norms to freedom of assembly (Art. 21) and freedom of association (Art. 22). Each norm contains a list of legitimate restrictions, substantially similar to those provided for in the European Convention. The American Convention, in Articles 15 and 16, adopts the same approach as the Covenant. Other relevant provisions in the general human rights treaties are Articles 10 and 11 of the African Charter, Articles 24(5), (6) and (7) of the Arab Charter, Article 5 of the European Social Charter (revised), and Article 12 of the EU Charter of Fundamental Rights.

In the context of sectoral human rights treaties, one can cite Article 5(d)(ix) of the Convention against Racial Discrimination, Article 7(c) of the Convention on the Elimination of Discrimination against Women, Article 15 of the Convention on the Rights of the Child, Articles 26 and 40 of the Convention on the Rights of Migrant Workers, and Article 29(b) of the Convention on the Rights of Persons with Disabilities.

Finally, it should be noted that the right of private assembly in one's own home is guaranteed by the right to respect for private life and the right of religious assembly is specifically protected by freedom of religion.[1] The right to form and join trade unions is also provided for in certain treaties concluded within the framework of the International Labour Organization.

22.1.2 Content of the Freedoms

Freedoms of assembly and association can be considered as political rights in the broad sense, since they are essential for the protection of people's political and social activities in all forms of democratic and pluralist regimes. However, they are neither non-derogable rights in time of emergency nor absolute rights. Indeed, both freedoms are subject to several restrictions, as is clear from the above norms and from practice.[2]

It is appropriate to distinguish between the contents of the two freedoms, since, although they are mutually functional,[3] the behaviors to which they refer are different.

Freedom of assembly includes both private meetings and those held in public places, such as sit-ins, marches and parades, provided they are of a peaceful nature.[4] Meetings may be of a political, economic, social, sporting or artistic nature. The

---

[1]See Focarelli (2013), p. 208.

[2]See, e.g., HRCtee, *Kivenmaa v. Finland*, para. 9.2; *Zalesskaya v. Belarus*, para. 10.6.

[3]Zagrebelsky et al. (2019), p. 365.

[4]ECtHR, *Frumkin v. Russia*, paras. 97–98. See also HRCtee, General Comment No. 37, 17 September 2020, para. 6.

notion of "assembly" given by international supervisory bodies is usually broad and independent of the definitions given in the different national legal systems.[5] Freedom belongs both to the organizers of the assembly and to those who attend it.[6] In the case of violent meetings and demonstrations, intervention by the authorities is justified, but with forms and means that do not exceed the limits of necessity and proportionality.[7]

The notion of "association" is also broad and autonomous; and it implies a plurality of individuals, permanently and voluntarily associated. Associations also include trade unions,[8] political parties and NGOs. Freedom of association also includes, in positive terms, the right to found one, organize it and obtain legal recognition in order to operate effectively.[9] It also comprises, in negative terms, the right not to join any association and the right not to be forced to remain in one.[10] One may wonder whether freedom of association protects only individuals or also the associations themselves. The answer seems to vary according to the different treaties. For example, the rights protected by the European Convention can also be invoked before the Strasbourg Court by legal persons, whereas only natural persons can make individual complaints to the Human Rights Committee.[11]

In the practice, there have been some interesting cases concerning the prohibition or dissolution of political parties.[12] The European Court of Human Rights has, as a norm, held that the dissolution of a political party is a serious interference with freedom of association and is therefore justified only if the party poses a threat to the democratic life of the State.[13] However, in the *Refah Partisi* case,[14] it considered that the dissolution of a party by the Turkish Constitutional Court was legitimate because it was justified in order to protect national security, the rights of others and the prevention of crime.

---

[5]See, e.g., ECtHR, *Obote v. Russia*, para. 35, where the Court holds that a flash mob falls within the notion of a "peaceful assembly".

[6]ECtHR, *Djavit An v. Turkey*, para. 56.

[7]ECtHR, *Taranenko v. Russia*, paras. 80–97.

[8]On the right to form and join trade unions, see also CESCR, Art. 8, and below, Sect. 23.1.

[9]See HRCtee, *Korneenko and Others v. Belarus*, para. 7.2.

[10]See, e.g., ECtHR, *Sørensen and Rasmussen v. Denmark*, paras. 33 and 54–77. The Strasbourg Court condemned Denmark for infringement of Article 11 on the ground that the applicants, during the period of their service with a distribution company, had been obliged to join a specific trade union before or after recruitment. See also ECtHR, *Young, James and Webster v. UK*, paras. 64-65; *Sigurjónsson v. Iceland*, para. 41; *Gustafsson v. Sweden*, paras. 51–54.

[11]See Kälin and Künzli (2019), p. 508.

[12]See Focarelli (2013), pp. 210–211.

[13]See, e.g., ECtHR, *Case of United Communist Party of Turkey and Others v. Turkey*, para. 61; *Ouranio Toxo v. Greece*, paras. 40–41.

[14]ECtHR, *Refah Partisi (the Welfare Party) and Others v. Turkey*, paras. 67, 110–115, 119–123, 132–135.

22.1.3 Obligations

Again, the obligations of States, which correspond to the freedoms of assembly and association, are of various kinds. First of all, States have a negative obligation not to prohibit the freedoms of assembly and association of persons, and not to interfere in their exercise. Second, they have a positive and immediate obligation (of result) to enact norms and administrative practices (if they do not already exist) to protect these freedoms.

Thirdly, States also have a number of positive obligations to protect people, through preventive and repressive measures, from interference in their freedoms by third parties. As I have already said many times, these obligations are sometimes of result and sometimes of due diligence. Finally, it can be considered that States also have some positive obligations "of progressive realization", aimed at promoting over time those associations that pursue the development and knowledge of human rights.

22.2 Right to Participate in Political and Public Life. Free Elections and Access to Public Service

22.2.1 Norms

Article 21 of the Universal Declaration is worded as follows:

> 1. Everyone has the right to take part in the government of his country, directly or through freely chosen representatives. 2. Everyone has the right of equal access to public service in his country. 3. The will of the people shall be the basis of the authority of government; this will shall be expressed in periodic and genuine elections which shall be by universal and equal suffrage and shall be held by secret vote or by equivalent free voting procedures.

This provision clearly sets three different but closely related rights: (*a*) the right to participate in political and public life; (*b*) the right of access to public service; (*c*) the right to free elections. In reality, as we shall see, the second and third rights function as specifications of the first.

The Covenant on Civil and Political Rights takes up, in very similar terms, the content of Article 21 of the Universal Declaration, but specifying that the three political rights are reserved to citizens and that they allow restrictions, provided they are not "unreasonable". In fact, Article 25 of the Covenant reads:

> Every citizen shall have the right and the opportunity, without any of the distinctions mentioned in article 2 and without unreasonable restrictions: a) To take part in the conduct of public affairs, directly or through freely chosen representatives; b) To vote and to be elected at genuine periodic elections which shall be by universal and equal suffrage and shall be held by secret ballot, guaranteeing the free expression of the will of the electors; c) To have access, on general terms of equality, to public service in his country.

Other relevant provisions in the general human rights treaties are: Article 3 of Protocol No. 1 to the European Convention, Article 23 of the American Convention, Article 13 of the African Charter, Article 24(1), (2), (3) and (4) of the Arab Charter, and Articles 39 and 40 of the EU Charter of Fundamental Rights. However, these norms are not entirely uniform: for example, Article 3 of Protocol No. 1 to the European Convention includes only the right to free elections, whereas Article 13 of the African Charter does not include the latter right, and Articles 39 to 40 of the EU Charter of Fundamental Rights provide only for the right to vote in the European Parliament and in municipal elections. In the framework of sectoral human rights treaties, one can recall Article 5(c) of the Convention against Racial Discrimination, Article 7 of the Convention on the Elimination of Discrimination against Women, and Article 29 of the Convention on the Rights of Persons with Disabilities.

It should be stressed that these norms are not intended to guarantee a universally accepted concept of democracy, nor to promote a specific system of government over all others;[15] they merely establish certain rights for citizens to participate in the political life of their country.

However, a different argument applies to the European Convention on Human Rights, whose Preamble proclaims that human rights and fundamental freedoms "are best maintained [. . .] by an effective political democracy" and that European States "have a common heritage of political traditions, ideals, freedom and the rule of law". On this basis, the European Court of Human Rights has repeatedly stated that a democratic and pluralistic form of government is an essential component of European public order;[16] and that democracy is the only political model contemplated by the European Convention.[17]

22.2.2 Content of the Rights

As already said, three political rights emerge from the majority of the above mentioned treaty norms, which, although linked to each other, have different contents and fields of application. One of their common features is that they are derogable in time of emergency and do not have absolute character.

The first right is defined, in these treaties, sometimes as the right to participate in the government of one's own country,[18] sometimes as the right to participate in the conduct of public affairs,[19] and sometimes in both ways.[20] In my view, the most

[15]Weissbrodt and de la Vega (2007), p. 113.

[16]See, e.g., ECtHR, *Mathieu-Molin and Clerfayt v. Belgium*, para. 47; *Case of United Communist Party of Turkey and Others v. Turkey*, para. 45; *Sadak and Others v. Turkey (No. 2)*, para. 32.

[17]See, e.g., ECtHR, *Zdanoka v. Latvia*, Judgment of 17 June 2004, para. 78; *Zdanoka v. Latvia*, Judgment of 16 March 2006, para. 98; *Ahmed and Others v. UK*, para. 52.

[18]UDHR, Art. 21; ACHR, Art. 23; ACHPR, Art. 13.

[19]CCPR, Art. 25; ArCHR, Art. 24(2).

[20]CERD, Art. 5(c); CEDAW, Art. 7(b).

precise and complete definition is *the right to participate in political and public life*.[21] However, it must be admitted that this right has a very vague and general content. The Human Rights Committee, in its General Comment No. 25,[22] stated that the concept of "direction of public affairs", contained in Article 25 of the Covenant on Civil and Political Rights, is a broad concept, which includes the exercise of powers of government by all State bodies:

> The conduct of public affairs [. . .] is a broad concept which relates to the exercise of political power, in particular the exercise of legislative, executive and administrative powers. It covers all aspects of public administration, and the formulation and implementation of policy at international, national, regional and local levels. The allocation of powers and the means by which individual citizens exercise the right to participate in the conduct of public affairs protected by article 25 should be established by the constitution and other laws.[23]

The Committee also added that:

> Article 25 lies at the core of democratic government based on the consent of the people [. . .].[24]

But the Committee itself, in the *Marshall* case, was more cautious, because it said that:

> [. . .] article 25(a) of the Covenant cannot be understood as meaning that any directly affected group, large or small, has the unconditional right to choose the modalities of participation in the conduct of public affairs. That, in fact, would be an extrapolation of the right to direct participation by the citizens, far beyond the scope of article 25(a).[25]

It can therefore be concluded that paragraph *a*) of Article 25, despite its ambitious wording, does not guarantee every citizen a precise and specific right to participate directly in public affairs; but, at the most, the right that States, in their domestic legislation, should not place *unreasonable restrictions* or discrimination on him when he wishes to exercise his right of participation. Moreover, it seems to me that the right to participate in political and public life, in paragraph *a*) of Article 25 and in the other similar treaty norms governing it, functions as a kind of "framework right", which then finds specific applications in the right of access to public service and the right to free elections.

---

[21] See CRPD, Art. 29. In doctrine, it is sometimes referred to as the "right of political participation": see Weissbrodt and de la Vega (2007), p. 113.

[22] HRCtee, General Comment No. 25, 12 July 1996.

[23] *Ibidem*, para. 5.

[24] *Ibidem*, para. 1.

[25] HRCtee, *Marshall et al. and the Mikmaq tribal society v. Canada*, para. 5.5. In this case, the applicants complained of an infringement of Article 25 as they were not invited to attend the constitutional conferences of Canada as representatives of the aboriginal population of Mikmaq.

Indeed, *the right of access to public service* has a more precise and circumscribed content. However, this right must also be correctly interpreted: it does not guarantee people to obtain a job in the public service, but only the opportunity "on general terms of equality" to obtain one.[26] In addition, the right of access to public employment means that the processes of recruitment, promotion, suspension and leave in these jobs must respect criteria of objectivity and reasonableness, and above all must not be discriminatory.[27]

But it is the third political right, among those under consideration here, which is the most important. Although its definition is not identical in the treaty norms mentioned above, it can be defined, in short, as *the right to free elections*; that is, the right to have free elections held and to participate in them as an elector and as a candidate.

Indeed, one might wonder whether the aforesaid conventional provisions *directly* give the individual a genuine electoral right. Some doubt could arise, for example, from Article 3 of Protocol No. 1 to the European Convention, according to which:

> The High Contracting Parties undertake to hold free elections at reasonable intervals by secret ballot, under conditions which will ensure the free expression of the opinion of the people in the choice of the legislature.

The literal formula in Article 3 seems to provide only for a commitment to hold elections made by States among themselves.[28] However, the European Court of Human Rights has stated, from the very first judgments on the matter, that the provision in question also recognizes a *genuine individual right* to see elections called and to participate in them, both as a voter and as a candidate.[29] Furthermore, the concept of "elections" in Article 3 of Protocol No. 1, although it refers only to the election of the legislative bodies of the State, has been interpreted broadly by the Strasbourg bodies.[30] On the other hand, in other human rights treaties, the relevant norm is clear in giving individuals *directly* the right to vote and to be elected in free elections. Examples in this sense are Article 25(b) of the Covenant on Civil and Political Rights, Article 23(b) of the American Convention, and Article 24(3) of the Arab Charter.

It should also be noted that the right to be elected is just as important as the right to vote. On this point, the Human Rights Committee has stated that:

> The effective implementation of the right and the opportunity to stand for elective office ensures that persons entitled to vote have a free choice of candidates. Any restrictions on the

[26]See CCPR, Art. 25(b). Cf. also HRCtee, *Kall v. Poland*, para. 13.2.

[27]See, e.g., HRCtee, *Hinostroza Solís v. Peru*, para. 6.2. See also Kälin and Künzli (2009), p. 485.

[28]Zagrebelsky et al. (2016), p. 337.

[29]ECtHR, *Mathieu-Molin and Clerfayt v. Belgium*, paras. 46–51.

[30]This concept includes not only bodies exercising legislative functions in the strict sense, such as parliaments, but also bodies that have an important position in the normative process. See ECtHR, *Matthews v. UK*, paras. 50–54.

right to stand for elections, such as minimum age, must be justifiable on objective and reasonable criteria.[31]

Other important aspects of the content of the right to free elections concern the very notion of "free elections", the reasonable intervals between electoral periods, the principle of secrecy of voting and legitimate restrictions to this right. Elections are generally considered to be free if they are conducted with respect for other human rights, such as freedom of expression, assembly and association; and if their results are recognized and implemented by governments. The principle of secrecy of vote is fundamental to ensuring that elections are free. Finally, elections must be held at reasonable intervals.

The discussion is more complex when it comes to the legitimacy of *restrictions* on the right to vote in free elections. The treaty norms mentioned above do not provide for restrictions or limits to this right, other than that of its applicability to citizens only. However, the practice of the European Court, the Inter-American Court and the Human Rights Committee has recognized that there are other limits of an implicit nature, which States may place, provided that certain criteria are met.

For the European Court, restrictions on the right to vote must not be arbitrary or disproportionate or interfere with the free expression of opinion by the people. More specifically, according to the Court, as far as the active electorate is concerned, some people may be excluded from the right to vote on grounds of age or because they are convicted with a criminal sanction or detained. On the other hand, the exclusion of those who are under guardianship or treatment for mental illness, regardless of the seriousness of the illness, was not considered legitimate.[32] As for the passive electorate, there may be restrictions in some cases, provided that the criteria of proportionality and non-arbitrariness are respected. In the view of the Human Rights Committee, any restrictions, whether applied to the right to vote or the right to be elected, must be based on objective and reasonable criteria.[33] One can recall, for example, the *Yevdokimov and Rezanov* case, which concerned the absolute ban on voting imposed by Russia on all persons found guilty and sentenced to imprisonment while serving their sentence. The Committee condemned Russia for violation of Article 25(b) of the Covenant on Civil and Political Rights, considering that the restrictive measure adopted by Russia was not in conformity with the requirement of reasonableness.[34]

---

[31]HRCtee, General Comment No. 25, 12 July 1996, para. 15.

[32]See ECtHR, *Scoppola v. Italy (no. 3)*, paras. 81–110.

[33]See HRCtee, General Comment No. 25, 12 July 1996, para. 4. See also ECtHR, *Hirst v. UK (No. 2)*, para. 60.

[34]HRCtee, *Yevdokimov and Rezanov v. Russia*, para. 7.5. The criteria of objectivity and reasonableness also apply to the right to be elected. In the *Bwalya* case, the Human Rights Committee condemned Zambia for violation of Article 25(b) of the CCPR, since the applicant, a prominent member of a political party opposed to the former President, was unable to participate in the election campaign and stand for his party without reasonable grounds. HRCtee, *Bwalya v. Zambia*, para. 6.6.

22.2.3 Obligations

State obligations of various kinds correspond to the three human rights in question. With regard to the right to participate in political and public life, it seems to me, as noted above, that States have not assumed, at international level, binding and immediate obligations towards their citizens other than the general obligation not to place, in their internal legal systems, unreasonable restrictions or discrimination on this right. This obligation entails, above all, positive measures of a regulatory nature, since the State must eliminate domestic legislation containing unreasonable restrictions or discrimination.

The citizen's right of access to public service corresponds to somewhat more precise State obligations, which are directed to all the bodies of the State and not just the legislative ones. The States, as seen, undertake to respect objective, reasonable and non-discriminatory criteria in the processes concerning the recruitment, promotion, suspension and leave in such jobs of their citizens.

Finally, there are the obligations corresponding to the right of citizens to free elections. It has been noted that this right has a rather broad and complex content, as it includes various aspects of the right to vote and to be voted on. The corresponding obligations of States are also manifold and vary in nature: many of them relate to guaranteeing the requirements of the notion of "free elections" and are positive obligations for national legislative bodies.

References

Focarelli C (2013) La persona umana nel diritto internazionale. Il Mulino, Bologna

Kälin W, Künzli J (2019) The law of international human rights protection, 2nd edn. OUP, Oxford

Weissbrodt D, de la Vega C (2007) International human rights law. An introduction. University of Pennsylvania Press, Philadelphia

Zagrebelsky V, Chenal R, Tomasi L (2016) Manuale dei diritti fondamentali in Europa. Il Mulino, Bologna

Zagrebelsky V, Chenal R, Tomasi L (2019) Manuale dei diritti fondamentali in Europa, 2nd edn. Il Mulino, Bologna

Protection of Economic Activities

23

There are numerous norms, in international human rights law, which aim to protect people in the performance of their economic activities. In this regard, it is customary to talk of economic rights, a rather broad category of human rights, which are usually classified as second generation rights, with main reference to their historical development within the framework of the United Nations.[1] Actually, this classification is not always correct, because some of these rights, as we shall see, originated prior to the creation of the United Nations. Among the many economic rights, I will confine myself to examining those I consider to be the most important, namely: (*a*) the right to work;[2] (*b*) the right to property.

23.1 Right to Work

23.1.1 Norms

The right to work is understood here in a broad sense, as including a number of more specific rights that protect workers.[3] It is on this basis that it can be argued that the right to work has a longer historical origin than the United Nations human rights protection system.[4] In fact, the need to protect workers and their rights at the international level goes back, as has been said in Chap. 1, to the Versailles Peace Treaty, the Covenant of the League of Nations and the establishment of the International Labour Organization (ILO) in 1919.

[1]See above, Sects. 8.1.1 and 10.3.

[2]The prohibition of forced or compulsory labor has already been examined (above, Sect. 16.1).

[3]See Pustorino (2019), p. 189, who speaks of the right to work as a "container" in which more specific rights have merged over time.

[4]But see (above, Sects. 1.2.8 and 1.2.10) the limits of the system of worker protection in the period between the two World Wars.

R. Pisillo Mazzeschi, *International Human Rights Law*,
https://doi.org/10.1007/978-3-030-77032-7_23

Since then, the ILO has been very active and has over time produced numerous conventions and recommendations,[5] which have resulted in a broad set of international labor standards[6] covering a very wide range of aspects of working conditions. Many of these standards are very specific and detailed. Some of them are commonly regarded as "core labor standards" and were reaffirmed in the 1998 *ILO Declaration on Fundamental Principles and Rights at Work*. In fact, under the aegis of the ILO, a rather complex legal regime in the field of labor has emerged, which in turn is part of a broad area of international law, which is usually referred to as international labor law.

However, leaving aside from the ILO system, it is now appropriate to focus on the right to work and workers' rights *only from a strict human rights perspective*. Indeed, the right to work as a human right is already proclaimed in Article 23 of the Universal Declaration, according to which:

> 1. Everyone has the right to work, to free choice of employment, to just and favourable conditions of work and to protection against unemployment. 2. Everyone, without any discrimination, has the right to equal pay for equal work. 3. Everyone who works has the right to just and favourable remuneration ensuring for himself and his family an existence worthy of human dignity, and supplemented, if necessary, by other means of social protection. 4. Everyone has the right to form and to join trade unions for the protection of his interests.

In addition, the Declaration, in Article 24, states that everyone has the right to rest and leisure time, including reasonable limits on working hours and periodic paid leave. As can be seen, the Universal Declaration already enucleates the main components of the right to work: (*a*) free choice of work; (*b*) fair and favorable working conditions; (*c*) protection from unemployment; (*d*) non-discrimination in remuneration; (*e*) right to fair remuneration; (*f*) social protection of workers; (*g*) right to form and join trade unions.

The Covenant on Economic, Social and Cultural Rights deals extensively with the right to work, in its aforementioned components. The relevant provisions are Articles 6, 7, 8 and 9. Article 6 is dedicated to the *right to work in general* and to the *free choice of work*, and is formulated in a rather prudent way, in the prevailing view of State obligations "of progressive realization". In paragraph 1, the Contracting States recognize the right to work, which implies the right of every individual to obtain the possibility of earning a living by freely chosen or accepted work, and undertake to take "appropriate steps" to safeguard this right. In paragraph 2, the measures to be taken by States Parties to ensure the full realization of the right to work are described by way of example: they include programs of technical and vocational guidance and training, and the development of policies and techniques to ensure economic, social and cultural development and full productive employment.

[5] 189 conventions and 205 recommendations.

[6] See, in general, www.ilo.org.

Article 7 of the Covenant is dedicated to the right to enjoy *just and favorable working conditions*. The States Parties recognize this right and affirm that such working conditions should guarantee, in particular: (*a*) a remuneration that ensures all workers a fair wage and equal pay for equal work and a decent living; (*b*) safety and hygiene at work; (*c*) equal opportunities for promotion in work based on seniority of service and competence; (*d*) the right to rest, leisure, reasonable limitation of working hours and periodic paid leave.

Article 8 deals with the right to *form and join trade unions*. It is a specification, from the point of view of workers' rights, of the more general right of association, of which I have already spoken.[7] In Article 8, the States Parties also undertake to guarantee the right to strike, provided that it is exercised in accordance with the laws of each country. Finally, Article 9 is dedicated to *social security*: States Parties recognize the right of every individual to social security, including social insurance.

Among the regional human rights treaties, the European Social Charter (revised) and the EU Charter of Fundamental Rights are particularly important. The former contains numerous provisions regulating workers' rights in detail. These include, among others, the right to work (Art. 1), the right to fair working conditions (Art. 2), the right to safe and healthy working conditions (Art. 3), the right to equitable remuneration (Art. 4), the right to organize oneself (Art. 5), the right to collective bargaining (Art. 6), the right to social security (Art. 12), the right to equality in employment without discrimination on grounds of sex (Art. 20), and the right to participate in the improvement of working conditions (Art. 22). The EU Charter of Fundamental Rights regulates the right to work in Articles 27-32. In the context of the other regional systems, it is worth mentioning Articles 34(g) and 45(b) and (c) of the OAS Charter, Articles 6, 7 and 8 of the San Salvador Protocol, Articles 15 and 29 (6) of the African Charter, and Article 34 of the Arab Charter.

In addition, there are a number of sectoral human rights treaties containing provisions on the principle of non-discrimination in employment: Article 5(e)(i-ii) of the Convention against Racial Discrimination, Article 11 of the Convention on the Elimination of Discrimination against Women, Article 25 of the Convention on the Rights of Migrant Workers, and Article 27 of the Convention on the Rights of Persons with Disabilities. Finally, there are some conventions on the prohibition of certain forms of exploitation of child labor. One can recall Articles 32-36 of the Convention on the Rights of the Child, Article 34(3) of the Arab Charter, Articles 15 and 16 of the African Charter on the Rights and Welfare of the Child,[8] as well as some ILO conventions specifically dedicated to the work of children or the prohibition of their exploitation.[9]

---

[7] See above, Sect. 22.1.

[8] African Charter on the Rights and Welfare of the Child, 1 July 1990.

[9] See, e.g., ILO Convention No. 138 concerning Minimum Age for Admission to Employment (1973); and ILO Convention No. 182 concerning the Prohibition and Immediate Action for the Elimination of the Worst Forms of Child Labour (1999).

23.1.2 Content of the Right

The right to work in general and the specific worker protection rights that flow from the former are, in principle, neither non-derogable in time of emergency nor absolute in nature But this does not apply to the prohibition of forced labor[10] and the prohibition of exploitation of certain forms of child labor.

With regard to the content of these rights, it is not possible here to go into the substance of the many detailed and specific rights of workers provided for in the treaty norms. I will therefore limit myself to a few words on the right to work in general, especially in the light of Article 6 of the Covenant on Economic, Social and Cultural Rights, which is the most important norm in this area.

The right to work, within the meaning of Article 6, is to be understood, in the first place, in close connection with the right to free choice of employment. In other words, paragraph 1 of Article is not intended to give every person the right to obtain work or even the right to obtain employment from the State; but, more simply, the right to choose or accept work freely, from among various possible offers, without interference from the State; and the right to choose a certain type of work in order to earn a living.[11] According to the Committee on Economic, Social and Cultural Rights, Article 6 also establishes the right not to be unfairly deprived of work.[12] What is more, this right may be restricted on the basis of Article 4 of the Covenant.

However, paragraph 2 of Article 6 is more ambitious, because, as mentioned, in order to ensure the full realization of the right to work, States undertake to take a series of measures. But these are mostly "progressive" obligations[13] and sometimes only political and non-binding commitments.[14] After all, the same Committee on Economic, Social and Cultural Rights recognizes:

> [. . .] the existence of structural and other obstacles arising from international factors beyond the control of States which hinder the full enjoyment of article 6 in many States parties.[15]

The question is partly different in relation to Article 7 of the Covenant, which deals with the right to fair and favorable working conditions, and which has, as seen above, a more precise content. Also on this provision there is a General Comment by the Committee on Economic, Social and Cultural Rights,[16] which serves to clarify the various components of this right, such as remuneration, safe and healthy working conditions, equal opportunities for promotion at work, rest, holidays and working time limits.

---

[10]See above, Sect. 16.1.

[11]CteeESCR, General Comment No. 18, 6 February 2006, paras. 2, 4 and 6.

[12]*Ibidem*, paras. 4 and 6.

[13]*Ibidem*, para. 19.

[14]*Ibidem*, paras. 38–47.

[15]*Ibidem*, para. 5.

[16]CteeESCR, General Comment No. 23, 27 April 2016.

The European Social Charter also deserves some mention. As already noted, it contains very detailed norms on workers' rights. In this regard, it should be emphasized that the European Committee of Social Rights has recently been developing an interesting practice, which shows that some of these rights are judicially enforceable and impose immediate obligations on States.[17]

23.1.3 Obligations

Once again, State obligations of a different nature correspond to the right to work and the specific rights of workers.

Many of the obligations described above, as said, are typical "progressive" obligations. The right to work in general, provided for in Article 6 of the Covenant on Economic, Social and Cultural Rights, is explicitly formulated in this sense. In fact, it speaks of "steps to be taken by a State Party [...] to achieve the full realization of this right". However, States also have negative obligations: for example, the prohibition by the State or public bodies to impose on people work that is not freely accepted. There are also positive and immediate obligations, both of result and of due diligence. An example of the former is the State obligation to eliminate any discriminatory labor laws or practices. An example of the latter is the State's obligation to prevent violations of workers' rights by third parties.

Finally, there are also certain political and programmatic commitments on the part of the States, which cannot be considered as true legal obligations. For example, the undertaking of States, contained in Article 6(2) of the Covenant on Economic, Social and Cultural Rights, to develop policies to ensure economic, social and cultural development and full productive employment.

23.2 Right to Property

23.2.1 Norms

The right to respect for private property has an important place in Western tradition and in the famous human rights declarations of the seventeenth and eighteenth centuries.[18] However, its affirmation in international human rights law has been more controversial, due to conflicting opinions about the importance of this right among Western countries on the one hand, and socialist and developing countries on the other.

---

[17] See, e.g., ECteeSR, *Finnish Society of Social Rights v. Finland*, Decision of 8 September 2016; *Confederazione Generale Italiana del Lavoro (CGIL) v. Italy*.

[18] See, for example, the English Bill of Rights of 13 February 1689, the Virginia Declaration of Rights of 12 June 1776, the American Declaration of Independence of 4 July 1776, the French Declaration of the Rights of the Man and of the Citizen of 26 August 1789.

This diversity of opinion had already manifested itself, in the first half of the twentieth century, in relation to the protection of aliens' property and, in particular, the investments of foreign companies in developing countries. In international law, the problem had arisen in particular with regard to the practice of nationalization, which had begun after the end of the First World War and had been vigorously resumed after the Second World War. For a long time these groups of States have debated and supported very different views on the question of the legitimacy of the nationalization of foreign property and the extent, timing and modalities of compensation. In extreme synthesis, industrialized countries were in favor of the maximum protection of foreign investments, and therefore, of the existence of certain limits of international legitimacy for nationalizations and the right to a "prompt, adequate and effective" compensation. On the contrary, developing countries supported the absolute freedom of the territorial State to nationalize foreign property and contested the Western rules concerning compensation. These differences about the subject of foreign investments have, however, diminished in more recent times.[19]

The ideological contrast between States, regarding the importance of the right to property, has also produced an impact on international human rights law, as can also be seen from the comparison between the 1948 Universal Declaration and the 1966 UN Covenants. In fact, the Universal Declaration, mainly inspired by Western conceptions, recognizes the right to property in Article 17, which is formulated as follows:

1. Everyone has the right to own property alone as well as in association with others.
2. No one shall be arbitrarily deprived of his property.

On the contrary, the two Covenants, influenced to a large extent by the human rights conceptions of socialist countries and a group of developing countries,[20] do not contain any provision establishing the right to property. However, the drafters of the Covenants reached a sort of compromise between the different opinions, since the Covenants contain certain rules that are indirectly relevant to the protection of property.[21] For example, both Covenants provide that property cannot be a ground for discrimination,[22] and that peoples have the right to dispose of their natural wealth and resources.[23] Furthermore, Article 11 of the Covenant on Economic, Social and Cultural Rights establishes, inter alia, the prohibition for States to destroy, in certain circumstances, land or housing or to uproot people from certain of their properties. Finally, in the Covenant on Civil and Political Rights, implicit protection of property derives from the rights to an effective domestic remedy and to a fair trial,[24] which

[19]See, for all, Conforti (2018), pp. 250–252.

[20]See above, Sects. 8.1.1 and 10.4.1.

[21]See Weissbrodt and de la Vega (2007), p. 91.

[22]CCPR, Art. 2(1); CESCR, Art. 2(2).

[23]CCPR, Art. 1(2); CESCR, Art. 1(2).

[24]CCPR, Arts. 2(3) and 14.

require States to judge the legitimacy of certain confiscations or expropriations of property. Indeed, the Human Rights Committee has had the opportunity to decide on a number of cases affecting the right to property.

However, it should be noted that this very cautious stance on the right to property, contained in the two Covenants, has not been followed by the majority of human rights treaties. Indeed, the main regional treaties explicitly recognize this right. Very important is Article 1 of Protocol No. 1 to the European Convention on Human Rights, which states that:

> Every natural or legal person is entitled to the peaceful enjoyment of his possessions. No one shall be deprived of his possessions except in the public interest and subject to the conditions provided for by law and by the general principles of international law.
> The preceding provisions shall not, however, in any way impair the right of a State to enforce such laws as it deems necessary to control the use of property in accordance with the general interest or to secure the payment of taxes or other contributions or penalties.

Article 21 of the American Convention and Article 17 of the EU Charter of Fundamental Rights are formulated in a very similar way. Article 14 of the African Charter and Article 31 of the Arab Charter also recognize the right to property, albeit with more concise provisions.

There are also norms on property rights in many sectoral human rights treaties. Some of these treaties contain provisions on non-discrimination in the right to property: Article 5(d)(v) of the Convention against Racial Discrimination, Articles 15(2) and 16(1)(h) of the Convention on Elimination of Discrimination against Women, and Article 12(5) of the Convention on the Rights of Persons with Disabilities. Other treaties protect the right to property of certain vulnerable persons: for example, the Geneva Convention relating to the Status of Refugees (Arts. 13 and 14), the Convention on the Rights of Migrant Workers (Art. 15), the Convention relating to the Status of Stateless Persons,[25] and ILO Convention No. 169 relating to Indigenous and Tribal Peoples.[26]

Finally, the right to property is also protected by international humanitarian law and international criminal law. Indeed, the Geneva Conventions of 1949 and the Additional Protocols of 1977 protect personal property and financial resources of prisoners[27] and internees,[28] prohibit the pillage and destruction of movable and immovable property in militarily occupied territories,[29] and protect property of a civil nature or essential to the civilian population.[30] The Statute of the International Criminal Court considers "extensive destruction and appropriation of property, not

[25]Convention Relating to the Status of Stateless Persons, New York, 28 September 1954.

[26]Indigenous and Tribal Peoples Convention (ILO No. 169), 27 June 1989, Artt. 13 and 14.

[27]GC III, Art. 18.

[28]GC IV, Art. 97.

[29]GC IV, Arts. 33 and 53, and AP II, Art. 4(2)(g).

[30]AP I, Arts. 51–54.

justified by military necessity and carried out unlawfully and wantonly" as a war crime.[31]

23.2.2 Content of the Right

The right to property is derogable in time of emergency and is not absolute. In fact, the above mentioned conventional norms usually provide for the possibility of restrictions by the State for reasons of public or general interest. In order to better clarify the content of this right, reference should be made in particular to the European Convention on Human Rights and the EU law.

Article 1 of Protocol No. 1 to the European Convention contains a particularly important provision because of the extensive case-law developed over time by the Strasbourg monitoring bodies. Those bodies have stated on several occasions that Article 1, in its three sentences, contains *three different but related rules*:[32] (*a*) the first rule is of a general nature and lays down the principle of protection of the property ("peaceful enjoyment of . . . possessions") of every natural or legal person; (*b*) the second rule concerns the deprivation of property and the conditions to which it is subject; (*c*) the third rule recognizes the power of the State to control and regulate the use of property in the general interest.

According to the European Court of Human Rights, the second and third rules relate to particular situations of interference with the general principle of property protection and must therefore be interpreted in the light of that principle.[33] Moreover the Court, when an interference in the enjoyment of property does not entail deprivation of it nor can it be regarded as a control in "the use of property", usually examines whether the case can be considered as generic interference in the enjoyment of the possessions within the meaning of the first general rule, which then works as a closure hypothesis.[34]

As regards the concept of "possessions" used in Article 1, the Strasbourg bodies interpreted that concept "autonomously" with respect to the domestic laws of the States Parties, and also very extensively,[35] equating it with a sufficiently significant "substantial interest" or "patrimonial interest".[36] The concept of "possessions" therefore includes movable and immovable property, but also intellectual property

[31]Rome Statute, Art. 8(2)(a)(iv). See also Art. 8(2)(b)(xiii), which considers as a war crime "destroying or seizing the enemy's property unless such destruction or seizure be imperatively demanded by the necessities of war".

[32]ECtHR, *Béláné Nagy v. Hungary*, para. 72.

[33]See, e.g., ECtHR, *Sporrong and Lönnroth v. Sweden*, para. 61; *Beyeler v. Italy*, para. 98; *Depalle v. France*, para. 77; *Jahn and Others v. Germany*, para. 79; *Chinnici v. Italy (no. 2)*, para. 29.

[34]Zagrebelski et al. (2016), p. 350.

[35]ECtHR, *Iatridis v. Greece*, para. 54; *Beyeler v. Italy*, para. 100.

[36]ECtHR, *Bozcaada Kimisis and Others v. Turkey*, paras. 41 and 50.

and other rights and interests of a patrimonial nature, such as credits,[37] trademarks,[38] patents,[39] radio broadcasting concessions,[40] town-planning permits,[41] as well as other rights and interests of a patrimonial nature. For the purposes of Article 1, the interpreter must also consider as "possessions" the legitimate expectations of obtaining the effective enjoyment of them, provided these expectations are sufficiently based on internal law or jurisprudence.[42] But, except what just said, Article 1 covers only existing and not future possessions, unless they have already been acquired on the basis of secure credit.

In relation to the second rule of Article 1, there is the problem of defining the concept of "deprivation" of property. This notion refers to the loss of a right to property or other rights *in rem* not only formally but also *de facto*. For example, expropriation and nationalization are measures that deprive the owner of property, as is the destruction of property. A "deprivation" can be justified if it cumulatively satisfies three criteria: (*a*) it is in conformity with the law of the State concerned;[43] (*b*) it is in accordance with international law; (*c*) it has been carried out in the public interest.[44]

The requirement of conformity with State law (the so-called legality criterion) is similar to that laid down in various provisions of the European Convention on Human Rights, and means that the deprivation must be based on existing norms that are accessible, precise and predictable.[45] The requirement of compliance with international law (which concerns in particular the obligation of fair compensation in the case of nationalization) applies, according to the Strasbourg bodies, only to deprivations of property of foreign citizens.[46] Finally, for the requirement of public interest, a margin of appreciation is usually granted to the State, related to the consideration of its political, social or economic interests; but in any case, the public

---

[37]ECtHR, *Pressos Compania Naviera S.A. and Others v. Belgium*, paras. 30-31.

[38]ECtHR, *Anheuser-Busch Inc. v. Portugal*, para. 78.

[39]ECmHR, *Smith Kline and French Laboratories Ltd v. The Netherlands*.

[40]ECtHR, *Centro Europa 7 s.r.l. and Di Stefano v. Italy*, paras. 171–179.

[41]ECtHR, *Pine Valley Developments Ltd and Others v. Ireland*, para. 51.

[42]ECtHR, *Fabris v. France*, paras. 49–52; *Kopecký v. Slovakia*, paras. 45–52.

[43]In the *Sharxhi* case, according to the European Court the taking and demolition of a building in violation of domestic law automatically amounts to a violation of the ECHR and thus "makes it unnecessary to ascertain whether a fair balance was struck between the demands of the general interest of the community and the requirements of the protection of the individual's fundamental rights". See ECtHR, *Sharxhi and Others v. Albania*, para. 174.

[44]In the *Scordino* case, the European Court condemned Italy for infringement of Article 1 following the expropriation of certain land belonging to the applicants. This expropriation was lawful and not arbitrary, but the compensation received by the applicants had been lower than the actual market value without apparent public interest reasons. The Court therefore held that the applicants had suffered "a disproportionate and excessive burden which cannot be justified by a legitimate aim in the public interest pursued by the authorities". See ECtHR, *Scordino and Others v. Italy (no. 1)*, Judgment of 29 March 2006, paras. 99–104.

[45]See Focarelli (2013), p. 231.

[46]ECtHR *James and Others v. UK*, paras. 58-66; *Lithgow and Others v. UK*, paras. 111-119.

interest must be balanced, according to the principle of proportionality, with the individual right to property.

The third rule of Article 1 of the Protocol concerns, as mentioned above, the power of the State to regulate and control the use of property in the general interest or to ensure the payment of taxes, contributions or penalties. The European Court considers that those State measures, which do not result in the loss of property for the owner, must be considered as interventions regulating the use of the property and falling within the scope of this rule.[47] Examples of such measures are the lack of authorization to build on certain land, the imposition of town planning restrictions, the revocation of licenses or concessions, the seizure of obscene publications, the temporary seizure of the property of defendants, and certain confiscation measures.[48] Measures aimed at regulating the use of property are legitimate if they respect three conditions: (*a*) they comply with a legal requirement; (*b*) they are aimed at protecting a general interest; (*c*) they are necessary and proportionate to this objective.

Also in EU law the right to property has been the subject of interesting case-law by the European Court of Justice. According to the Court, the right to property forms part of the general principles of Community law (now EU law). This right was then incorporated into Article 17 of the EU Charter of Fundamental Rights. Article 17 should be read in conjunction with Article 16, which establishes the freedom to conduct a business, and with Article 15, which deals with the freedom to choose an occupation and the right to engage in work. The three freedoms have, in fact, been jointly listed by the European Court of Justice among the fundamental rights of the Community legal order.

However, the Court held that the exercise of the right to property is not absolute, but may be restricted by the European Institutions, for objectives of general interest pursued by the Community (now the EU), as well as in a proportionate manner and in respect of the right itself. In this regard, the Court of Justice, since the *Nold* case,[49] has stated:

> If rights of ownership are protected by the constitutional laws of all the member states and if similar guarantees are given in respect of their right freely to choose and practice their trade or profession, the rights thereby guaranteed, far from constituting unfettered prerogatives, must be viewed in the light of the social function of the property and activities protected thereunder. For this reason, rights of this nature are protected by law subject always to limitations laid down in accordance with the public interest. Within the Community legal order it likewise seems legitimate that these rights should, if necessary, be subject to certain limits justified by the overall objectives pursued by the Community, on condition that the substance of these rights is left untouched.[50]

---

[47] See Zagrebelski et al. (2016), p. 352.

[48] See the case-law of the European Court of Human Rights cited by Zagrebelski et al. (2016), p. 352, footnotes 25–29, and Focarelli (2013), p. 232.

[49] ECJ, *Nold, Kohlen- und Baustoffgroßhandlung*. The applicant Nold, a German limited partnership, claimed that the sales rules of Ruhrkohle AG and their application infringed the right to property and that the exclusion of the company from the coal trade amounted to expropriation.

[50] *Ibidem*, para. 14.

More recently, in the well-known *Kadi* judgment of 2008,[51] the European Court of Justice held that the general interest goal of combating threats to international peace and security posed by terrorist acts justified, in principle, restrictions on the right to property arising from the freezing of funds and other economic resources of persons identified by the Security Council or the UN Sanctions Committee as being affiliated to terrorist organizations. However, the Court then found that these restrictions were not legitimate because they were adopted without allowing the persons concerned to present their case to the competent authorities.[52]

More generally, as has been pointed out in doctrine,[53] the Court of Justice has maintained a restrictive approach to the right to property when this right was in conflict with general EU interests relating to the creation of the internal market, while it has interpreted this right more extensively when it came to the fore as a complementary element to the realization of Community freedoms, such as, for example, freedom of establishment.

Finally, outside the European system for the protection of human rights, it is worth noting that the right to property of ancestral lands by indigenous peoples has become increasingly important. I will come back to this later.[54] Here it is sufficient to say that the Inter-American Court has included this right within the scope of Article 21 of the American Convention and that this interpretive approach has also been taken up by the Human Rights Committee and the supervisory bodies of the African system.

23.2.3 Obligations

The right to property corresponds, first of all, to negative obligations of States, which must refrain from interfering in the enjoyment of people's property, except in cases where such interference is expressly permitted by the relevant treaty norms.

But effective protection of the right to property also entails a number of positive and immediate obligations on States. For example, the State must take the appropriate measures of prevention and repression to ensure that the right is also protected in relations between private individuals. This implies, among other things, the adoption of norms (primary, secondary and tertiary) for the protection of property; and also norms that are suitable for making the enforcement of judgments or insolvency proceedings effective.[55] An obligation on the part of the State to intervene, in order to protect the property of a private individual, may also arise in the event of omission

---

[51]ECJ, *Kadi*, Judgment of 3 September 2008.

[52]See also, for subsequent developments of the affair, EGC, *Kadi*; ECJ, *European Commission and Others v. Kadi*.

[53]Zagrebelsky et al. (2016), p. 363.

[54]See below, Sect. 25.2.

[55]See ECtHR, *Fuklev v. Ukraine*, paras. 89–93; *Scollo v. Italy*, para. 44.

by other public authorities, for example in the case of illegal occupation of property.[56]

References

Conforti B (Iovane M ed) (2018) Diritto internazionale, 11th edn. Editoriale Scientifica, Napoli
Focarelli C (2013) La persona umana nel diritto internazionale. Il Mulino, Bologna
Pustorino P (2019) Lezioni di tutela internazionale dei diritti umani. Cacucci, Bari
Weissbrodt D, de la Vega C (2007) International Human Rights Law. An Introduction. University of Pennsylvania Press, Philadelphia
Zagrebelsky V, Chenal R, Tomasi L (2016) Manuale dei diritti fondamentali in Europa. Il Mulino, Bologna

[56]See ECtHR, *Casa di Cura Valle Fiorita Srl v. Italy*, paras. 46–60.

Protection of Freedom of Movement 24

Human rights aimed at protecting people's freedom of movement[1] play an important role in the context of those rights that have the function of protecting the main aspects of individuals' private, social and public life. Indeed, it can be said that their importance has gradually grown and has now become very significant in contemporary society, characterized by great movements, individual and collective, of people. From the point of view of human rights, there are two conceptual aspects to take into consideration. The first, which concerns individual and collective movements, is that the freedom of movement of people deserves protection because it is an important component of their personal development. The second aspect, which concerns collective movements in particular, is that migrants, asylum seekers, refugees and displaced persons are vulnerable individuals who need security and require special protection.

This explains why international human rights law has, since its inception, been concerned with the freedom of movement of people. Indeed, the Universal Declaration, in its Article 13, enshrines this freedom in broad terms, because it refers to *all persons*.[2] In fact, Article 13 proclaims:

1. Everyone has the right to freedom of movement and residence within the borders of each state.
2. Everyone has the right to leave any country, including his own, and to return to his country.

However, in the light of successive developments in the international human rights regime, a distinction must be made between the freedoms of movement of citizens in their own State, which are widely recognized, and the movement rights of

[1]In the practice and doctrine one sometimes speaks of "freedom of movement" and sometimes of "freedom of circulation" (for example in the Italian language). I will use the first term.

[2]However, it should be noted that, according to Art. 13(2) of the Declaration, the right of a person to return to his or her country is implicitly attributed to citizens only.

R. Pisillo Mazzeschi, *International Human Rights Law*,
https://doi.org/10.1007/978-3-030-77032-7_24

aliens, which are much more restricted. There are also aliens who are subject to a special protection regime: these are asylum seekers, refugees and other internationally protected migrants. These different categories of persons should therefore be kept separate: (*a*) citizens; (*b*) aliens (in general); (*c*) asylum seekers; (*d*) refugees; (*e*) other internationally protected migrants.

24.1 Freedom of Movement of Citizens

24.1.1 Norms

It follows from the human rights treaty regime that citizens have: (*a*) the right to move and reside in their own State; (*b*) the right to leave the territory of their State; (*c*) the right to return to it; (*d*) the right not to be expelled from the territory of their State (which implicitly derives from the right to move and reside).

The Covenant on Civil and Political Rights, taking over and clarifying Article 13 of the Universal Declaration, recognizes these rights of citizens. Moreover, some of them (movement and residence) are also extended to all persons legally present in the territory and others (the right to leave) to each person. In fact, Article 12 of the Covenant states that:

> 1. Everyone lawfully within the territory of a State shall, within that territory, have the right to liberty of movement and freedom to choose his residence. 2. Everyone shall be free to leave any country, including his own. 3. The above-mentioned rights shall not be subject to any restrictions except those which are provided by law, are necessary to protect national security, public order (*ordre public*), public health or morals or the rights and freedoms of others, and are consistent with the other rights recognized in the present Covenant. 4. No one shall be arbitrarily deprived of the right to enter his own country.

As can be seen, some of the rights guaranteed by the Covenant may be subject to restrictions and limitations, which are necessary for reasons of national security, public order, public health or morality, and respect for the rights of others. However, such restrictions, according to the practice of the Human Rights Committee, must be proportionate.[3]

Regional human rights treaties contain substantially similar rules, even if not identical to those of Article 12 of the Covenant. But note that Protocol No. 4 to the European Convention (Arts. 2 and 3) and the American Convention (Art. 22(1-5)) are more complete because, after recognizing the three rights of movement that are provided for in the Covenant, they also explicitly add the right for citizens *not to be expelled*, either by individual or collective measures, from the territory of their State. On the other hand, the African Charter (Art. 12(1-2)) and the Arab Charter (Arts. 26 and 27) conform almost entirely to Article 12 of the above-mentioned Covenant.

[3]See, e.g., HRCtee, *Peltonen v. Finland*, para. 8.4; *González del Río v. Peru*, para. 5.3. See also ECtHR, *Popoviciu v. Romania*, para. 89.

Finally, the EU Charter of Fundamental Rights has a rather special character because it reflects the general principles of the European Union and the *acquis communautaire* on the free movement of persons. Article 45 of the Charter establishes: (*a*) freedom of movement and residence for every citizen of the Union within the territory of the Member States; (*b*) the possibility of guaranteeing, in accordance with the Treaties, freedom of movement and residence to nationals of third States legally resident in the territory of a Member State.

24.1.2 Content of the Freedoms

The freedom of movement of citizens, as we have seen, actually includes *four specific rights*, the content of which should be examined separately. Before this, it must be premised that this freedom, in its various components, can be derogated in time of emergency and is not absolute in nature. The restrictions and limitations are those traditionally found in other human rights that are not absolute in character. But an exception must be made for the right of citizens not to be expelled from their own country, which does not allow restrictions or limits.

Turning now to the various specific rights, it should be noted that *the right of movement and residence within the borders of one's own State* was the subject of interpretation by the Human Rights Committee in its General Comment No. 27. According to the Committee:

> Everyone lawfully within the territory of a State enjoys, within that territory, the right to move freely and to choose his or her place of residence [. . .] The right to move freely relates to the whole territory of the State [. . .] The enjoyment of this right must not be made dependent of any particular purpose or reason for the person wanting to move or stay in a place [. . .] The State party must ensure that the rights guaranteed in article 12 are protected not only from public but also from private interference.[4]

The right of citizens to freely choose their residence also includes the right to remain in the chosen residence; and thus guarantees protection against the practice of forced displacement and relocation of people. Forced relocation of people may also constitute a violation of international humanitarian law if it occurs during periods of armed conflict.[5]

As for *the right to leave the territory of one's own State*, it constitutes a historically very ancient human right, which dates back as far as the *Magna Charta* of 1215 and has been taken up by many subsequent legal acts. The Human Rights Committee has stated on this right:

> Since international travel usually requires appropriate documents, in particular a passport, the right to leave a country must include the right to obtain the necessary travel documents.

[4]HRCtee, General Comment No. 27, 2 November 1999, para. 4.

[5]See GC IV, Art. 49; AP II, Art. 17(1).

> The issuing of passports is normally incumbent on the State of nationality of the individual.[6]

Also *the right to enter or re-enter one's own State* has been clarified by the Human Rights Committee:

> The right of a person to enter his or her country recognizes the special relationship of a person to that country [. . .] It implies the right to remain in one's own country. It includes not only the right to return after having left one's own country; it may also entitle a person to come to the country for the first time if he or she was born outside the country [. . .] The right to return is of the utmost importance for refugees seeking voluntary repatriation.[7]

Finally, citizens also have *the right not to be expelled from the territory of their State*. As already noted, this right, implicit in the right of free movement and residence, is, anyway, expressly provided for in some treaties. In particular, Article 3(1) of Protocol No. 4 to the European Convention on Human Rights states that:

> No one shall be expelled, by means either of an individual or of a collective measure, from the territory of the State of which he is a national.

Similar terms are used in Article 22(5) of the American Convention:

> No one can be expelled from the territory of the state of which he is a national [. . .].

The term "expulsion" is used in a broad sense to include both administrative and judicial expulsion measures as well as measures of deportation and *refoulement*.

24.1.3 Obligations

The obligations of States corresponding to the above rights are, as usual, of various kinds. Most of them are configured as negative obligations; but there are also positive and immediate obligations, both of result and of due diligence. An example of the former is the State's obligation to issue the necessary travel documents to its citizens who want to leave their country. An example of the latter is the State's obligation to protect the right of movement of citizens from interference by other individuals.

---

[6] HRCtee, General Comment No. 27, 2 November 1999, para. 9.

[7] *Ibidem*, para. 19.

24.2 Rights of Movement of Aliens

Let me now address the human rights of movement of aliens, making it clear that I intend to refer to *all aliens* (including migrants), without considering, for the time being, certain categories of aliens subject to a special protection regime, such as asylum seekers, refugees, and other internationally protected migrants, which I will deal with later.[8]

Another preliminary clarification is necessary. I will only examine here the rights of movement of aliens.[9] But it is clear that this does not exhaust the subject of the human rights of aliens, since *all aliens* (and all migrants), as human beings, are, in principle, addressees of *all* international human rights norms.[10] However, it should be recognized that this last statement of principle must be mitigated, since, in reality, many of the human rights of aliens are subject to legitimate exceptions or legal restrictions by States or to the margin of appreciation of the same. Moreover, other human rights, in theory applicable to aliens, in fact find obstacles and difficulties of a practical nature to their effective implementation.[11] Nevertheless, there can be no doubt that "fundamental" human rights are applicable to all aliens and migrants *without any restrictions due to their status*.[12]

When examining the rights of movement of aliens, a distinction will be made between the norms governing: (*a*) their entry into a State; (*b*) their stay; (*c*) their expulsion from that State.

24.2.1 Admission and Entry into the Country

Under general international law, each State is free to regulate the admission or entry of aliens into its territory. This is based on the principle of territorial sovereignty, which implies the freedom of the State to establish its own immigration policy.[13] Therefore, foreigners do not have any right to enter the territory of a State, unless that State has taken on treaty obligations in this area with other States, for example through the so-called treaties on establishment. This freedom of States is also confirmed by international case-law.[14] Note that even the 1990 UN Convention on

---

[8]See below, Sects. 24.3, 24.4 and 24.5.

[9]The literature on this subject is immense. Among the most recent works see Calamia et al. (2012).

[10]See *Declaration on Human Rights of Individuals Who are not Nationals of the Country in which They Live*, GA Res. 40/144 of 13 December 1985, esp. Artt. 5–9. Cf. anche Weissbrodt (2000), p. 5.

[11]See Pisillo Mazzeschi (2011), pp. 556–558 and 565–569.

[12]*Ibidem*, pp. 558–565.

[13]See, for all, Conforti (2015), p. 249.

[14]See, e.g., ECtHR, *T.I. v. UK*, according to which the States Parties to the European Convention "have the right, as a matter of well-established international law and subject to their treaty obligations [. . .] to control the entry, residence and expulsion of aliens".

the Rights of Migrant Workers does not place any obligations on States Parties to allow the entry of migrant workers from other States Parties.

Therefore, the regulatory discipline in this area is left, to a large extent, to international treaty regimes, among which the European Union law stands out, and is entrusted, above all, to the domestic law of each State.

However, in my opinion, *two exceptions* to the general regime of freedom of States can be identified in general international law; that is, two customary norms which impose on the State the obligation, in certain exceptional circumstances, not to reject aliens (including migrants) who wish to enter its territory or the areas subject to its "jurisdiction", and to give them *temporary* admission and reception.

The first exception is the customary norm on the *obligation of rescue at sea.* This norm was formed and consolidated during the first half of twentieth century.[15] It requires States, through the masters of their ships, whether public or private, to assist any person found at sea in distress and to proceed as quickly as possible to rescue them. This refers to *any human being* in danger, regardless of nationality and whether he or she is a legal, irregular or illegal migrant. This norm has also been reaffirmed and clarified in the 1982 UN Convention on the Law of the Sea (Art. 98)[16] and in various treaties concluded in the framework of the IMO, such as the 1974 London Convention for the Safety of Life at Sea (SOLAS)[17] and the 1979 Hamburg Convention on Maritime Search and Rescue (SAR).[18] It should be noted that an amendment to the SAR Convention provides for the obligation to land rescued persons in a "place of safety".[19]

In reality, as mentioned above, the obligation of rescue at sea (which is an *erga omnes* obligation of the States) does not mean that the State carrying out the rescue must grant the alien a real and proper legitimate entry into its territory or on its ships or in other spaces under its control; rather it has the more limited effect of granting the alien in danger a *de facto*, albeit *temporary*, admission and reception in such spaces. It is, anyhow, a limit to the general freedom of the State to reject foreigners from its territory.

The norm on the obligation of rescue at sea, in my view, has taken root as an autonomous norm in customary international law. Furthermore, it is closely and

---

[15]See, recently, Starita (2019), pp. 5–47, esp. pp. 7–17.

[16]United Nations Convention on the Law of the Sea, Montego Bay, 10 December 1982, Art. 98: "1. Every State shall require the master of a ship flying its flag, in so far as he can do so without serious danger to the ship, the crew or the passengers: (a) to render assistance to any person found at sea in danger of being lost; (b) to proceed with all possible speed to the rescue of persons in distress, if informed of their need of assistance, in so far as such action may reasonably be expected of him [. . .]".

[17]International Convention for the Safety of Life at Sea, 1 November 1974.

[18]International Convention on Maritime Search and Rescue, 27 April 1979. Cf. also IMO, Resolution MSC 167(78), Guidelines on the Treatment of Persons Rescued At Sea.

[19]Adoption of Amendments to the International Convention on Maritime Search and Rescue, 1979, as Amended, MSC Res. 155(78), 78th sess, Agenda Item 26, IMO Doc MSC78/26/Add.1 annex 5 (4 June 2004, adopted 20 May 2004).

functionally linked to the right to life, since the obligation to rescue at sea logically derives from the fundamental obligation of States to protect the right to life of people through positive preventive measures. It is clear, for example, that if a State does not provide aid to vessels with migrants on board who are in danger of death, it is committing a violation of its obligation to protect the right to life. Unfortunately, it must be noted, with regret, that the Italian Government has recently, on several occasions, failed to comply with its obligation to provide rescue at sea, and has even issued decrees in contravention of that obligation.[20] One can mention the well-known *Hirsi*,[21] *Diciotti*,[22] *Sea Watch 3*[23] and *Gregoretti*[24] cases.

The second exception, to the general regime of freedom of States on the admission of aliens, is the so-called principle of *non-refoulement*, which I have already mentioned in connection with the right to life and the prohibition of torture.[25] The content of this principle, which must be interpreted *extensively* in contemporary international law, should now be clarified. The principle obliges States not to reject aliens (including, of course, migrants) to a country where there is a grave risk that they may suffer *serious violations of fundamental human rights*. Again, the prohibition of *refoulement* does not mean that the State must grant legitimate entry to areas subject to its sovereignty or control;[26] it only implies a *de facto* and *temporary* admission and reception of the alien.

In order to justify the extensive interpretation of the principle of *non-refoulement*, its historical development should be briefly explained. This principle has gradually affirmed itself over time by a sort of accumulation or integration between *three different norms*. The first norm is that provided for in Article 33 of the 1951 Geneva Convention relating to the Status of Refugees, which prohibits States from expelling or returning a refugee "in any manner whatsoever" to the frontiers of territories where "his life or freedom would be threatened on account of his race, religion, nationality, membership of a particular social group or political opinion", with the

[20]See Decree Law no. 113 of 4 October 2018 and Decree Law no. 53 of 14 June 2019.

[21]ECtHR, *Hirsi Jamaa and Others v. Italy*. For a comment, see Liguori (2012) and Lenzerini (2012).

[22]On the case of the ship *Diciotti*, see Trib. Catania, Ministerial Offences Section, Report of 7 December 2018.

[23]On the case of the ship *Sea Watch 3*, see ECtHR, *Rackete and Others v. Italy*; Trib. Agrigento (GIP), *Rackete*, Order of 2 July 2019. For comments, see Gradoni and Pasquet (2019) and De Sena and Starita (2019).

[24]On the case of the ship *Gregoretti*, see Trib. Catania, Ministerial Offences Section, Report of 28 November 2019.

[25]See above, Sects. 14.1.3.1 and 14.2.3.1.

[26]It is not clear whether the operation of the principle of *non-refoulement* should be ensured even when the applicant is in the embassy of a foreign State to which he has requested diplomatic asylum. On this issue, see Pustorino (2020), pp. 197–198, who cites the 2018 Inter-American Court's advisory opinion on asylum.

exception set out in paragraph 2.[27] Therefore, the principle here protects only refugees and only against the dangers arising from the specific grounds of discrimination listed in the Geneva Convention.

The second norm is the prohibition of torture and inhuman or degrading treatment or punishment. This norm, as already seen,[28] has been interpreted, in the practice of the human rights supervisory bodies, as meaning that a State may not expel an alien to a country where there is a serious risk that he may be subjected to torture or inhuman or degrading treatment or punishment.[29] Therefore, the prohibition of *refoulement* has been extended, from a subjective point of view, to all aliens and, from an objective point of view, to the dangers of being subjected to torture or other inhuman treatment.

Finally, the third norm is that which protects the human right to life. This norm has been interpreted, in the practice, as meaning that a State cannot expel a foreigner to a country where he or she is in serious danger of suffering attacks on his or her life, consisting not only in acts of violence but also in situations such as the absolute lack of health services.[30]

In essence, in my view, there has been integration over time between the three norms and their implementation practice. As a result of this integration, there has been, firstly, a widening of the sphere of those entitled to *non-refoulement*. This right, originally intended only for refugees, now applies to all aliens. Secondly, there has also been a broadening of the grounds for *non-refoulement*. Protection not only operates because of the danger of serious threats motivated by specific grounds for discrimination, but has also extended to the danger of being subjected to torture or inhuman or degrading treatment and the danger of being deprived of life. It should be added that recent practice tends to further broaden the grounds for *non-refoulement*: some treaties, for example, have extended the protection of the principle to those who flee situations of generalized violence or armed conflict in their country or even climate-induced threats.[31]

Ultimately, based on these developments in international practice, I believe that today the principle of *non-refoulement* has expanded its protection to all dangers of serious violations of "fundamental" human rights. Furthermore, there is now a widespread opinion that the principle, with such a broad content, has become part of customary international law and has also the character of *jus cogens*.[32]

---

[27]That is, when there are reasonable grounds to believe that the refugee constitutes a danger to the security of the State of refuge or to its community.

[28]See above, Sect. 14.1.3.1.

[29]For an extensive overview of the ECtHR's case law see ECtHR, *J.K. and Others v. Sweden*, para 78 ff. and *F.G. v. Sweden*, para. 111.

[30]See above, Sect. 14.1.3.1. For "exceptional cases" of application of the *non-refoulement* principle see, inter alia, ECtHR, *Paposhvili v. Belgium*, para. 183.

[31]HRCtee, *Teitiota v. New Zeland.*

[32]See, for all, Lenzerini (2009a), pp. 378–389.

24.2.2 Stay and Residence

The international legal regime for the residence of aliens is simpler than that for their entry. Aliens legally present on the territory of a State have the right to move freely within the territory of that State and the right to choose their residence. These two rights, which are already implicit in Article 13(1) of the Universal Declaration, are then expressly set out in Article 12(1) of the Covenant on Civil and Political Rights, Article 2(1) of Protocol No. 4 to the European Convention, Article 22(1) of the American Convention, Article 12(1) of the African Charter, and Article 26(1) of the Arab Charter. These provisions can be considered to reflect general international law. However, these rights are subject to limits and restrictions by the territorial State. This is clear from all the above-mentioned treaties.[33] For example, the territorial State may impose on an alien, for reasons of security or public order, an obligation to dwell, i.e. not to leave the territory of the municipality of habitual residence without authorization.

A special legal regime is provided for in the Convention on the Rights of Migrant Workers. The notion of "migrant worker" is very broad, since, according to Article 2 (1) of the Convention:

> The term 'migrant worker' refers to a person who is to be engaged, is engaged or has been engaged in a remunerated activity in a State of which he or she is not a national.

Then the Convention sets out in great detail the rights of migrant workers and their families, and also provides for certain rights for workers not legally resident in the territorial State. Among other things, it stipulates that the rights of movement of these persons are subject to fewer restrictions than the rights of other foreigners (Art. 39). However, the Convention has had a limited number of ratifications and reflects only a small part of customary international law.

24.2.3 Limits to Expulsion and Other Removal Measures

The concept of "expulsion" of aliens by a State is rather generic and is normally used to incorporate, in a comprehensive concept, three more specific types of State removal measures, which are called "expulsion" (in the strict legal meaning), "deportation" and "extradition".[34] I will use, for simplicity, the generic term. The legal regime relating to the removal of aliens is also subject, for the most part, to the principle of State sovereignty. Therefore, each State is, in principle, free to remove

---

[33] See, e.g., CCPR, Art. 12(3).

[34] Usually, "expulsion" means a legal measure (judicial or administrative) requiring a person to leave the territory of a State; "deportation" means the forced execution of an expulsion; "extradition" means the surrender of a person, accused or convicted of an offence, from one State to another, at the request of the second State.

aliens from its territory. However, the limits set by customary norms of international human rights law have a greater impact in this area.

Firstly, there are *procedural limits* to expulsion. An alien, if legally present on the territory of a State, may be expelled only following a decision based on law; and he must be allowed to oppose and defend himself before a competent authority. These two conditions are clear from Article 13 of the Covenant on Civil and Political Rights, according to which:

> An alien lawfully in the territory of a State Party to the present Covenant may be expelled therefrom only in pursuance of a decision reached in accordance with law and shall, except where compelling reasons of national security otherwise require, be allowed to submit the reasons against his expulsion and to have his case reviewed by, and be represented for the purpose before, the competent authority or a person or persons especially designated by the competent authority.

Similar norms, although sometimes more concise, are contained in Article 1(1) of Protocol No. 7 to the European Convention, Article 22(6) of the American Convention, Article 12(4) of the African Charter, Article 26(2) of the Arab Charter, and Article 22(1), (2), (3) and (4) of the Convention on the Rights of Migrant Workers. However, these procedural limits are not always absolute, as States may derogate from them on grounds of public order or national security or similar.

Secondly, *collective expulsions are prohibited.* This prohibition is explicitly provided for in Article 4 of Protocol No. 4 to the European Convention, Article 22 (9) of the American Convention, Article 12(5) of the African Charter,[35] Article 26 (2) of the Arab Charter, and Article 22(1) of the Convention on the Rights of Migrant Workers. In reality, even in treaties where the prohibition is not explicit, it follows logically from the fact that every expulsion requires, as stated above, an individual decision based on law and the presence of individual guarantees of defense.

Thirdly, the practical arrangements for expulsion or deportation *must not be "outrageous"* to the person concerned; i.e. they must not be carried out with unnecessary or disproportionate use of force.[36]

Fourthly, there is an important limit of a substantive nature, which I have already talked about in relation to the entry of aliens. The principle of *non-refoulement* (despite its name) does not apply today only in the phase of rejection at the borders of aliens, but also at the stage of their expulsion, deportation or extradition. Therefore, there is a ban on expelling foreigners to States where they may suffer serious discrimination, or risk torture or inhumane treatment, or attacks on life or, more generally, risk being victims of serious violations of "fundamental" human rights.[37]

[35]But this provision of the African Charter qualifies as mass expulsions those that are targeted against national, racial, ethnic or religious groups.

[36]See Iran/U.S. Claims Tribunal, *Yeager v. Islamic Republic of Iran.* Cf. also Conforti (2015), p. 249.

[37]Of course, this obligation of the States applies to all persons, both citizens and aliens; but in fact it applies especially to aliens, since the expulsion of citizens is usually excluded in international law and State laws.

Finally, at least within the framework of some conventional human rights systems, there is also a further limit to the freedom of States to expel aliens. In particular, in the European Convention system, the Strasbourg bodies have derived, from the right to respect for private and family life established by Article 8 of the Convention, the obligation of the State not to expel an alien when such expulsion would cause an unjustified and disproportionate *breakup of family unity*.[38] But this limit is not absolute.

24.3 Asylum

Today there is a widespread tendency to confuse the right to asylum with the right to refugee status or to use the term "asylum" in a broad and generic sense, as a container that includes the concept of "refuge" and other forms of international protection of migrants. As we shall see, these confusions are, in part, justified by the historical evolution these legal concepts have undergone in international law, and especially in European Union law. However, in my view, there are still some differences, both historical and conceptual, that make me prefer a *separate treatment* of the right to asylum, the rights of refugees and other forms of international protection of migrants.

That said, it can be noted that asylum (unlike "refuge") is a very old legal institution, which over time has taken on various more specific names (territorial, extraterritorial, political, religious). In a general sense, it means that a State admits to its territory (or to another space under its "jurisdiction" or control) and grants protection to a foreign individual (or stateless person), who seeks such protection against another State. Often the individual tries to escape political persecution by his own nation State; but sometimes he wants to escape other dangers, such as criminal trials, wars, internal conflicts, famine or environmental disasters.

The definition of "asylum", given in 1950 by the *Institut de Droit International*, is very broad. According to the *Institut*, asylum:

> [. . .] means the protection which a State grants on its territory or in some other place within its jurisdiction to an individual who has come to seek it.[39]

It follows from this definition that the concept of asylum is based on two constitutive elements: (*a*) the search for protection by the individual; (*b*) the granting by a State of effective protection in favor of the individual. Such protection by the State presupposes not only the admission, indefinitely, of the alien into its territory, but also, at least in principle, the commitment not to return the individual to the State from which he or she has fled.[40]

---

[38]See, e.g., ECtHR, *Moustaquim v. Belgium*.

[39]IDI, *Asylum in Public International Law*, 43 AIDI, II, 1950, p. 377.

[40]See Lenzerini (2009a), pp. 83–85.

However, it should be noted straight away that the term "right of asylum" has *two completely different meanings*; on the one hand, *the right of a State*, in relation to other States, to grant asylum to a foreign individual; on the other hand, *the right of an individual* to obtain asylum from a State. The first right (which corresponds to the traditional concept of asylum that has dominated for centuries) involves the normal exercise of territorial sovereignty by the State. Therefore, it is common ground that, under customary international law, a State has the sovereign and discretionary right to grant asylum to any individual, except for possible limits with respect to other States arising from international treaties especially in the areas of judicial cooperation and extradition. But I will not deal with this right of asylum, because it does not relate to international human rights law.

On the contrary, I am interested in the human right of the individual to obtain asylum from a State; therefore, from now on, I will speak of the "right to asylum" only in this sense. However, even after having delimited the subject in this way, it should be noted that the human right to asylum has taken on partially different meanings and contents over time, in international law, in State laws and in the law of the European Union.

24.3.1 Norms and Content of the Right

The right of the individual to asylum is included in the Universal Declaration, Article 14 of which states:

1. Everyone has the right to seek and to enjoy in other countries asylum from persecution.
2. This right may not be invoked in the case of prosecutions genuinely arising from non-political crimes or from acts contrary to the purposes and principles of the United Nations.[41]

As can be seen, the Declaration explicitly recognizes the right to asylum, at least the right to political asylum ("asylum from persecution"), as one of the fundamental human rights of the person, even if paragraph 2 of Article 14 sets some limits. However, at the time of the Declaration, this right was conceived more in programmatic terms, as a common goal to be achieved in the future, than as a real positive right of the individual towards the State obligatory for the latter. In fact, if one examines the preparatory work on Article 14, it can be seen that there was strong opposition on the part of several States to including in that provision the right of the individual "to be granted asylum"; and that instead the less demanding formula of the right "to seek and enjoy [...] asylum" was preferred. Moreover, as is well known, the Declaration does not constitute a binding legal act.

Therefore, the question must be asked whether or not subsequent international practice, conventional and otherwise, has confirmed the existence of a human right to asylum, understood, in the broad sense indicated above, as the right of an

[41] See also UDHR, Art. 13(2).

individual persecuted in one State to be admitted indefinitely and also protected in the territory of another State.

In reality, at a universal level, attempts to affirm and consolidate the right to asylum set out in the Universal Declaration have had little success. The two International Covenants of 1966 do not contain any norms on the right to asylum: the Covenant on Civil and Political Rights merely establishes, as already seen, the right to emigrate.[42] Subsequently, in 1967, the UN General Assembly adopted the Declaration on Territorial Asylum[43] in order to implement Article 14 of the Universal Declaration and to better specify the content of the right to asylum. However, the 1967 Declaration is disappointing because it merely recommends States to base their asylum policies on the principles set out in the Declaration itself and reaffirms the discretionary right of each State to judge the conditions for granting asylum. Therefore, this Declaration has in no way contributed to the development of the right to asylum as a human right, since it essentially reaffirmed the traditional concept that the State has a right to grant asylum with respect to other States, but no obligation to grant asylum to the individual.

Subsequently, within the framework of the United Nations, an attempt was made to achieve the adoption of a convention on territorial asylum. A draft had been prepared and the text should have been approved in Geneva in 1977, but it was never adopted. In the following years, the General Assembly took several resolutions calling on States not to obstruct the legal institute of asylum and to cooperate with the activities of the UN High Commissioner for Refugees (UNHCR). But these are merely acts of soft law.

If one looks at regional international human rights acts, one must conclude that the right to asylum has made some, but not very significant, progress. Within the framework of the American States, one can recall the Montevideo Convention on Political Asylum of 1933 (Art. 3),[44] which, however, merely describes the humanitarian nature of asylum. More important is the American Declaration of the Rights and Duties of Man,[45] which, in Article XXVII, proclaims that:

> Every person has the right, in case of pursuit not resulting from ordinary crimes, to seek and receive asylum in foreign territory, in accordance with the laws of each country and with international agreements.

Then, one may mention the 1954 Caracas Convention on Territorial Asylum,[46] which, however, treats asylum as a mere option for States. Instead, the American Convention of Human Rights contains a provision, Article 22(7), which substantially reproduces the content of Article XXVII of the American Declaration, but

---

[42]CCPR, Art. 12(1).

[43]*Declaration on Territorial Asylum*, GA Res. 2312(XXII) of 14 December 1967.

[44]Montevideo Convention on Political Asylum, 26 December 1933.

[45]American Declaration of the Rights and Duties of Man, Ninth International Conference of American States, Bogotá, Colombia, 2 May 1948.

[46]Caracas Convention on Territorial Asylum, 28 March 1954.

expressly limits the right to asylum to persecution for "political offenses or related common crimes". The African Charter (Art. 12(3))[47] contains a provision similar to Article XXVII of the American Declaration.

In truth, these norms differ somewhat from Article 14 of the Universal Declaration, because they do not provide for a right of the individual to "seek and enjoy" asylum, but for a right to "seek and receive" asylum. Therefore, at first sight, they seem to guarantee the individual a right to *obtain* protection, without leaving the State with any discretion in granting it. However, on closer examination, there are many doubts about the recognition of a genuine individual right to asylum *at international level,* because the norms in question expressly refer to the need to regulate this right through the adoption of national norms and the taking into account of relevant international treaties. More specifically, the adoption of national legislation is necessary both to establish the content of the protection granted and to interpret the key concept of "persecution".

As far as the European human rights system is concerned, the balance sheet is not positive either. The European Convention on Human Rights contains no explicit reference to the individual right to asylum, whereas Protocol No. 4 to the Convention only establishes the right to emigrate. Only an extensive and dynamic interpretation of Articles 2 and 3 of the European Convention by the Strasbourg bodies has made it possible to establish certain guarantees for asylum seekers, such as the prohibition of *refoulement.* The Committee of Ministers of the Council of Europe has adopted a number of resolutions on the right of asylum, but these too are merely recommendations. Instead, the argument is different, as we will see, for the law of the European Union.

In conclusion, in order to answer the question asked above, it must be admitted that international practice (*diuturnitas*) and *opinio juris* are not sufficient to demonstrate the existence of a norm of general international law on the right to asylum, understood in the *broad* sense indicated above: that is, the right of an individual persecuted in one State, except for ordinary crimes, to seek and receive indefinite admission and protection in another State. It is likely that the broad and vague content of the right to asylum has also made it difficult to transpose it into customary law. In other words, it must be concluded that the right of the individual "to enjoy in other countries asylum from persecution", proclaimed by the Universal Declaration, has not acquired a precise, complete and binding content in international law.

However, this negative conclusion must be partially corrected in three respects. The first aspect relates to a *limited part of the content* of the right to asylum; that is, to some more specific and limited rights than the right to asylum in its entirety.[48] These rights allow every foreign individual to obtain a kind of *provisional and temporary* asylum from persecution in certain circumstances. I am referring to the principle of *non-refoulement* and the principle prohibiting extradition for political crimes. I have already talked about the first principle. The second principle has also become

[47]The Arab Charter (Art. 28) provides only for the right to "seek" asylum.

[48]See Pisillo Mazzeschi (1999a), pp. 700–701.

increasingly established in international treaty practice; and this has probably helped to form a customary norm. This norm, too, obliges States to grant a kind of provisional and temporary asylum to persons persecuted for political reasons.

The second aspect concerns the *domestic legal systems* of States. Many States have adopted constitutional or legislative provisions that grant asylum to aliens, or at least to aliens subject to political persecution. In this way, the content of the right to asylum has sometimes been clarified, compared to its very indeterminate content under international law. The Italian Constitution, for example, in Article 10, paragraph 3, states that:

> Lo straniero, al quale sia impedito nel suo paese l'effettivo esercizio delle libertà democratiche garantite dalla Costituzione italiana, ha diritto d'asilo nel territorio della Repubblica, secondo le condizioni stabilite dalla legge.[49]

As can be seen, this norm contains a broad formula, which guarantees asylum to the foreigner on the grounds that he comes from a country that denies fundamental freedoms, even if he is not personally persecuted.[50] In fact, initially, Italian case-law had supported the opinion that the Constitution directly attributes to the foreigner, who is in such conditions, a real subjective right to obtain asylum, which can be invoked before the ordinary courts.[51] However, later on, this opinion has been abandoned, and the most recent jurisprudence interprets Article 10, paragraph 3, of the Constitution as a mere reference to the forms of migrant protection that have been implemented in Italy through the three legal notions of refugee protection, subsidiary protection and humanitarian protection.[52]

To give another example, the French Constitution, in its Preamble, states that:

> [. . .] tout homme persécuté en raison de son action en faveur de la liberté a droit d'asile sur les territoires de la République.[53]

However, since the right to asylum, which is conferred by domestic legal systems, has a different content from one State to another, it cannot be considered that these systems have done much to clarify the content of the right to asylum also at the level of international law.

The third aspect is the most important. It concerns the phenomenon whereby the international legal regime of asylum has gradually been integrated and supplemented

---

[49]"A foreigner who is prevented in his country from effectively exercising the democratic freedoms guaranteed by the Italian Constitution has the right of asylum in the territory of the Republic, under the conditions established by law" (my translation).

[50]See Favilli (2013), p. 75.

[51]Italian Court of Cassation, *Allen v. Min. Int.* Judgment No. 4674/1997.

[52]See, e.g., Italian Constitutional Court, Judgment of 20 June 2019, No. 194; Italian Court of Cassation, *Min. Int. v. Yarbo Musa*. On the topic see also Lenzerini (2009b).

[53]"[. . .] every man persecuted because of his action in favor of liberty has the right to asylum in the territories of the Republic" (my translation).

by the international legal regime of refugees. I will deal with the latter regime later.[54] But it is worth noting right now that international refugee law, since the 1951 Geneva Convention and the 1967 Protocol, has shown considerable expansive force in its content and in its personal and material scope, so much so that it has largely *absorbed* the legal regime of asylum.[55] This should come as no surprise. In fact, it is true that, originally, the legal regulation of the right to asylum and that of refugees had many differences, of historical origin and legal basis, nature and content.[56] However, the two disciplines share the same general purpose and the same practical effects; that is, the protection of the host State in favor of aliens subject to persecution. This explains the progressive *convergence* between the two juridical regimes and the fact that the normative discipline of refugees, from the beginning more detailed and complete, also because of its conventional origin, has generated a process tending to give a more precise (but also more limited) content to the discipline of asylum and has then ended up, to a large extent, replacing it.

This normative evolution has occurred, even more clearly, in European Union law. Within this law, the concept of asylum is used with *two different meanings*, creating a certain confusion of terminology. In a *broad and a-technical sense*, the notion of asylum is used, in the so-called asylum policy, with the generic meaning of protection granted to those who flee their country and require shelter and reception.[57] This meaning of "asylum" comes close to that used by international law. On the contrary, in a *strict and technical-legal sense*, the concept of asylum refers to a specific component of the above-mentioned policy, which includes three regulatory areas: (*a*) norms on asylum; (*b*) norms on subsidiary protection; (*c*) norms on temporary protection.[58] In addition (and this point is important), the EU norms on asylum in the strict sense of the term *refer, in fact, to those on refugee protection* laid down in the 1951 Geneva Convention.[59]

Therefore, in EU law, the phenomenon of absorption of the concept of asylum seeker into that of refugee has been fully realized. As has been noted,[60] this has also been the case at terminology level, since, in current language, those who apply for refugee status are usually said to be "seeking asylum". This development of EU law is also confirmed by the EU Charter of Fundamental Rights, whose Article 18 (entitled *Right to asylum*) states:

> The right to asylum shall be guaranteed with due respect for the norms of the Geneva Convention of 28 July 1951 and the Protocol of 31 January 1967 relating to the status of

---

[54]See below, Sect. 24.4.

[55]See Conforti (2015), p. 251; Lenzerini (2009a), p. 173.

[56]See Lenzerini (2009a), p. 145 ff., esp. pp. 166–174.

[57]See, for example, TEU, Art. 3(2), which lists, among the fundamental objectives of the EU, that of providing an area of freedom, security and justice, in which appropriate measures are ensured "with regard to [. . .] asylum [. . .]".

[58]See TFEU, Art. 78.

[59]Lenzerini (2009a), p. 120.

[60]Conforti (2015), p. 251.

> refugees and in accordance with the Treaty on the European Union and the Treaty on the Functioning of the European Union [...].

As can be seen, the Charter links the individual right to asylum in the EU system to the persecution cases laid down in the Geneva Convention, thus neglecting the broader scope of the institution of asylum in international law.

24.3.2 Obligations

It has been concluded above that there is no general norm of international law on the right to asylum, understood as the right of an individual persecuted in one State to be admitted, received and protected indefinitely in another State. Nor are there any conventional norms that effectively guarantee this individual right.[61] As a result, one cannot even speak of real obligations of States regarding the right to asylum.

However, I have argued that there are at least two more specific and circumscribed rights that derive from the right to asylum: the right of the asylum seeker to *non-refoulement* and his or her right not to be extradited for political reasons. These specific rights correspond to true obligations of States. I have already talked about the negative obligation relating to the prohibition of *refoulement*.[62] The State's obligation not to extradite the asylum seeker is also a negative obligation.

24.4 Rights of Refugees

24.4.1 Norms

The international regime for the protection of refugees is primarily and universally established by the Geneva Convention relating to the Status of Refugees of 28 July 1951 and the subsequent Protocol of 31 January 1967. As already mentioned, this conventional system has much developed over time its subjective and objective scope of application.[63] At the regional level, one should recall the 1969 Convention governing the Specific Aspects of Refugee Problems in Africa, the 1984 Cartagena Declaration on Refugees,[64] and the 1994 Arab Convention on the status of refugees.[65]

[61] I have emphasized above (Sect. 24.3.1) the limits of Art. 22(7) of the American Convention and of Art. 12(3) of the African Charter.

[62] See above, Sects. 14.1.3.1, 14.2.3.1 and 24.2.1.

[63] OAU Convention governing the Specific Aspects of Refugee Problems in Africa, Addis-Ababa, 10 September1969.

[64] Cartagena Declaration on Refugees, 22 November 1984.

[65] Arab Convention on Regulating Status of Refugees in the Arab Countries, adopted by the Arab League in 1994, but not yet in force.

But also very important is the refugee protection regime established within the European Union, which is very complex, and on which I have already made some comments. The aim of this regime is to establish uniform norms for the EU Member States to supplement and strengthen the Geneva Convention system.[66] The main components of this regime are: Article 3(2) of the Treaty on European Union (TEU), Articles 77–80 of the Treaty on the Functioning of the European Union (TFEU), Articles 18 and 19(2) of the EU Charter of Fundamental Rights, the so-called Dublin system currently governed by Regulation No. 604/2013, and finally Directives Nos. 2011/95, 2013/32 and 2013/33.

24.4.2 Content of the Rights

The 1951 Geneva Convention, in Article 1, defines as a refugee any person who:

> [. . .] owing to well-founded fear of being persecuted for reasons of race, religion, nationality, membership of a particular social group or political opinion, is outside the country of his nationality and is unable, or owing to such fear, is unwilling to avail himself of the protection of that country; or who, not having a nationality and being outside the country of his former habitual residence as a result of such events, is unable or, owing to such fear, is unwilling to return to it.

The Convention, because it focused on refugees who had originated from events during the Second World War in Europe, also contained geographical and temporal limitations in its definition of "refugees".[67] However, most States Parties to the Convention subsequently ratified the 1967 Protocol, which removed these limitations.

Therefore, the refugee must meet four requirements: (*a*) he must be outside his country of origin (or habitual residence if he is stateless); (*b*) he cannot or does not wish to avail himself of the protection of that State; (*c*) he must have a well-founded fear of persecution; (*d*) persecution must be based on five specific reasons, listed in Article 1.

The first requirement is easy to ascertain: the individual must have crossed a national border to be considered a refugee. Therefore, "internally displaced persons" cannot be qualified as refugees.

The second requirement is that of the "breaking" of the relationship between the refugee and his State and therefore of the protection of the latter towards the former. This "breaking" can depend on the will of the State, which, for example, takes away the citizenship of the individual or, more often, on the will of the individual, who refuses to return to his country for fear of persecution.

The third requirement is more complex and comprises two elements. The element of "well-founded fear" requires a subjective state of mind, but also objective reasons

[66]See Di Filippo (2012), pp. 242–243.

[67]The Convention originally applied to events prior to 1 January 1951. Cf. CSR, Art. 1(A)(2).

that can justify such fear. For example, the individual may bring evidence about past persecution suffered by him in his own country or even about persecution suffered in his own country by individuals who have the same characteristics or belong to the same group as him. In the domestic jurisprudence of the States, sometimes the restrictive standard of "clear probability of persecution" and sometimes the more flexible standard of "good reason to fear persecution" has been requested as evidence of "well-founded fear".[68] The other element of the third requirement is that of "persecution". The *UNHCR Handbook on Procedures and Criteria for Determining Refugee Status* maintains that:

> [...] there is no universally accepted definition of 'persecution', and various attempts to formulate such a definition have met with little success. From Article 33 of the 1951 Convention, it may be inferred that a threat to life or freedom on account of race, religion, nationality, political opinion or membership of a particular social group is always persecution. Other serious violations of human rights – for the same reasons – would also constitute persecution.

Therefore, persecution certainly includes arbitrary deprivation of life, torture, and arbitrary detention. But, according to some doctrine and jurisprudence,[69] other serious violations of human rights may also constitute "persecution". Persecution usually comes from the State or State authorities; however, in the practice of many States, individuals persecuted by other private individuals are also recognized as refugees when the State of origin is unable to protect them.[70]

Finally, the fourth requirement for refugee status is that the persecution must be based on one or more of the five reasons specified in the Convention: race, religion, nationality, political opinion, or membership of a particular social group. With regard to persecution on the grounds of race, reference should be made to the definition of racial discrimination contained in Article 1 of the UN Convention against Racial Discrimination.[71] The UNHCR Handbook has defined persecution on the grounds of religion in the following terms:

> Persecution for 'reasons of religion' may assume various forms, e.g. prohibition of membership of a religious community, of worship in private or in public, of religious instruction, or serious measure of discrimination imposed on persons because they practice their religion or belong to a particular religious community [...].

Persecution based on nationality, political opinions or membership of particular social groups has been defined quite precisely by international and internal case-law.

According to the Geneva Convention and the Protocol, refugees, once they have been granted refugee status, enjoy a detailed set of rights, including the right not to be discriminated against (Art. 3), to practice their religion (Art. 4), to have their

---

[68] See Weissbrodt and de la Vega (2007), p. 75 and the case-law cited therein.

[69] *Ibidem*, pp. 76–78 and the case-law cited therein.

[70] See Kälin and Künzli (2019), pp. 545–546.

[71] See above, Sects. 10.4.2.3 and 18.2.

personal status governed by their country of domicile (Art. 12), to association (Art. 15), and to access to the courts (Art. 16). Moreover, they have the right to favorable treatment (and in any case not less than that granted to other foreigners) with regard to their property (Art. 13), their work activities (Arts. 17–19), housing (Art. 21), and public education (Art. 22).

But the most important, and best known, norm is that of Article 33 of the Convention, which establishes the principle of *non-refoulement*, about which I have already spoken several times. It is worth repeating here that Article 33 established this principle in a restrictive manner, because it was limited to the dangers arising from the five grounds for discrimination mentioned above. But it has then been interpreted in an evolutionary manner in practice, and therefore now applies to all cases in which the refugee[72] risks being subjected to serious violations of fundamental human rights in the country to which he could be sent back. However, Article 33 provides an exception when the refugee can reasonably be considered a danger to the security of the host State or when, having been convicted of a very serious crime, he constitutes a danger to the community of that State (Article 33(2)).

Turning now to the content of the regional treaty norms on refugee protection, it should be noted that these norms tend to adopt a broader notion of refugee than that of the Geneva Convention and its Protocol. In particular, the Convention governing the Specific Aspects of Refugee Problems in Africa takes over the definition of refugee adopted by the Geneva Convention and the Protocol, but adds that the term "refugee" will also apply:

> [. . .] to every person who, owing to external aggression, occupation, foreign domination or events seriously disturbing public order in either part or the whole of his country of origin or nationality, is compelled to leave his place of habitual residence in order to seek refuge in another place outside his country of origin or nationality.[73]

Even in the Inter-American system, there is a similar trend. The 1984 Cartagena Declaration on Refugees recommends extending the concept of refugee under the Geneva Convention to include as refugees:

> [. . .] persons who have fled their country because their lives, safety or freedom have been threatened by generalized violence, foreign aggression, internal conflicts, massive violation of human rights or other circumstances which have seriously disturbed public order.[74]

---

[72] And, more generally, the alien.

[73] OAU Convention governing the Specific Aspects of Refugee Problems in Africa, Art. 1(2).

[74] Cartagena Declaration on Refugees, Colloquium on the International Protection of Refugees in Central America, Mexico and Panama, 22 November 1984, para. III(3). See also San José Declaration on Refugees and Displaced Persons, 1994.

The same approach has been adopted by other regional systems: Article 1(2) of the above-mentioned Arab Convention on the status of refugees can be cited.[75]

Finally, it is worth describing, albeit in a very concise manner, the content of the legal regime for refugees that has developed within the framework of the European Union. As already mentioned, in EU law it is customary to speak of norms on the right to asylum, but they actually refer, as a framework regime, to the refugee protection system of the Geneva Convention; and then they are realized and specified in more detail, as rules of a subsidiary and complementary nature to the system of that Convention. This is clear from the aforementioned Article 18 of the EU Charter of Fundamental Rights and Article 78(1) of the Treaty on the Functioning of the European Union (TFEU), according to which:

> The Union shall develop a common policy on asylum, subsidiary protection and temporary protection aimed at offering an appropriate status to any third-country national in need of international protection and ensuring respect for the principle of non-refoulement. This policy must be in accordance with the Geneva Convention of 28 July 1951 and the Protocol of 31 January 1967 relating to the status of refugees and other relevant treaties.

That said, it should be remembered that EU legislation has been created over time, moving from a phase based mainly on intergovernmental cooperation between Member States to a progressive "communitarization" of the subject. At present, it is based on Article 3(2) TEU and Articles 77–80 TFEU. Of particular importance is Article 78 TFEU, which, after having set out, in paragraph 1, the objectives of the common European policy on asylum, provides, in paragraph 2, that, in order to achieve those objectives, the European Parliament and the Council adopt a series of measures. These include, inter alia: (*a*) a uniform status as regards asylum for nationals of third countries; (*b*) common procedures for obtaining and losing that status; (*c*) criteria and mechanisms for determining the Member State responsible for examining the asylum application; (*d*) norms on reception conditions for asylum seekers.

In fact, there are four main aspects of the common asylum system in the European Union, in logical order. The first concerns the determination of the *State responsible for examining the asylum application*. It is governed by the so-called Dublin system, originally regulated by the 1990 Dublin Convention[76] and the Convention implementing the Schengen Agreement, then by Regulation No. 343/2003 (so-called "Dublin II")[77] and now by Regulation No. 604/2013 (so-called "Dublin

[75] But this Convention is not in force.

[76] Dublin Convention determining the State responsible for examining applications for asylum lodged in one of the Member States of the European Communities, 15 June 1990.

[77] Council Regulation (EC) No 343/2003 of 18 February 2003 establishing the criteria and mechanisms for determining the Member State responsible for examining an asylum application lodged in one of the Member States by a third-country national.

III"),[78] which replaced the previous one. This system, as is well known, provides that responsibility for examining the asylum application rests with a single Member State, identified on the basis of certain criteria that are applied in successive order.[79] If the application is accepted, protection is effective only in that Member State; if it is rejected, it cannot be resubmitted in another Member State. A critical aspect of the Dublin system is that it does not solve the problem that certain countries, such as the Mediterranean ones, are subject to greater migratory pressure than other EU countries.[80] For this reason, a revision of this system has been under discussion for a long time, but so far it has been impossible to achieve it.

The second aspect concerns the *procedures* used by EU Member States for the recognition and withdrawal of refugee status: it is now governed by Directive No. 2013/32,[81] which replaced Directive No. 2005/85.[82] This Directive is very important because it concerns a matter that is not covered by the Geneva Convention system. In summary, Directive No. 2013/32 regulates, in a very detailed manner, the fundamental aspects of the procedures for determining the requirements for refugee status[83] and the guarantees to be afforded to applicants at each stage of the procedure. The fairness and adequacy of these procedures is very important, because otherwise there may be excessive obstacles for applicants for refuge and the danger that they will be unlawfully rejected.

The third aspect, and here the most important one, concerns the norms on *refugee status* and the *content of the protection* granted to refugees. This matter is mainly regulated by Directive No. 2011/95,[84] which replaced the previous Directive No. 2004/83.[85] The purpose of these harmonization norms is to supplement and extend the minimum protection regime for refugees established by the Geneva

[78]Regulation (EU) No 604/2013 of the European Parliament and of the Council of 26 June 2013 establishing the criteria and mechanisms for determining the Member State responsible for examining an application for international protection lodged in one of the Member States by a third-country national or a stateless person.

[79]The State where certain family members have already received refuge, or the State which has already issued the applicant with a residence permit or visa, or the State into which the person first entered, legally or irregularly.

[80]See Di Filippo (2012), p. 250.

[81]Directive 2013/32/EU of the European Parliament and of the Council of 26 June 2013 on common procedures for granting and withdrawing international protection.

[82]Council Directive 2005/85/EC of 1 December 2005 on minimum standards on procedures in Member States for granting and withdrawing refugee status.

[83]Or for subsidiary protection status.

[84]Directive 2011/95/EU of the European Parliament and of the Council of 13 December 2011 on standards for the qualification of third country nationals or stateless persons as beneficiaries of international protection, for a uniform status for refugees or for persons eligible for subsidiary protection and for the content of the protection granted.

[85]Council Directive 2004/83/EC of 29 April 2004 on minimum standards for the qualification and status of third country nationals or stateless persons as refugees or as persons who otherwise need international protection and the content of the protection granted.

Convention.[86] Firstly, the Directive lays down the qualifications for being considered a refugee and adopts an evolutionary interpretation of the notion provided for by the Geneva system, clarifying some controversial concepts relating both to the fear of being persecuted[87] and to the reasons for persecution.[88] However, it does not incorporate the tendency of other regional systems to extend refugee status to people fleeing situations of generalized violence, conflict, natural disasters or massive human rights violations. Secondly, the Directive brings some improvements to refugee's rights compared to those provided by the Geneva Convention.[89]

The fourth aspect of the EU common asylum system concerns the *reception* of applicants for refugee status. It is governed by Directive No. 2013/33,[90] which replaced Directive No. 2003/9.[91] The aim is to harmonize the reception conditions for applicants in all Member States. The Directive contains, inter alia, a number of guarantees for persons who are detained and norms in favor of vulnerable persons.

Finally, it is worth recalling the EU Charter of Fundamental Rights, which, in Article 18, guarantees the right to asylum and, in Article 19(2), reaffirms the principle of *non-refoulement* in favor of all individuals.

24.4.3 Obligations

It has been seen that the international and the European Union refugee protection regimes are very complex, because they include a multitude of norms and rights concerning refugees. As a result, the obligations of States are also manifold and have different characteristics. It is not possible here to dwell on these obligations, but they can be easily deduced from the content of the above-mentioned rights. It should at least be noted that many of these obligations are positive and immediate (both of result and of due diligence). Moreover, the obligations contained in the above-mentioned EU Directives have the particular characteristics that distinguish these acts.

---

[86]See Di Filippo (2012), pp. 244–245.

[87]See Arts. 5–8 of the Directive.

[88]See Arts. 9–10 of the Directive.

[89]See Arts. 20–35 of the Directive.

[90]Directive 2013/33/EU of the European Parliament and of the Council of 26 June 2013 laying down standards for the reception of applicants for international protection.

[91]Council Directive 2003/9/EC of 27 January 2003 laying down minimum standards for the reception of asylum seekers.

24.5 Rights of Other Internationally Protected Migrants

It is now worthwhile to briefly examine the human rights that belong to individuals who, although not entitled to seek asylum or refugee status, are forced to leave their homes and places of residence to seek reception and protection elsewhere. These individuals can be defined as "forced migrants". However, a distinction must be made between two different situations: (*a*) that of those who leave their own country to seek protection in another country (a situation similar to that of refugees and asylum seekers); (*b*) that of those who seek reception in another, safer place within their own country (so-called "internally displaced persons").

In the first situation, various legal forms of protection for these migrants can be identified, particularly in European Union and State law: (*a*) "subsidiary" protection; (*b*) "temporary" protection; (*c*) "humanitarian" or "special" protection.

24.5.1 "Subsidiary" Protection

In the common asylum system of the European Union, there is a normative discipline on the so-called "subsidiary" protection. In the language of the EU, it constitutes a part, together with the regulation on refugees, of the overall regime of the so-called "international protection". In reality, the aim of subsidiary protection is to ensure a range of rights for those migrants who cannot obtain refugee status, but who have fled their country and seek protection from an EU country. Subsidiary protection is mainly regulated by the above-mentioned Directive No. 2011/95, which sets out the *qualifications* for such protection and the status and content of the protection; but also by Directive No. 2013/32 on common *procedures* and Directive No. 2013/33 on standards for *reception*.[92]

The beneficiary of subsidiary protection is a third country national, or a stateless person, who does not qualify as a refugee, but in respect of whom there are reasonable grounds to believe that he or she would face a real risk of suffering serious harm if returned to his or her country of origin or usual residence.[93] Serious harm can be, alternatively: (*a*) the sentence or execution of the death penalty; (*b*) torture or other inhuman or degrading treatment or punishment; (*c*) a serious and individual threat to the life or to the person of a civilian resulting from indiscriminate violence in situations of internal or international armed conflict.[94]

[92] In fact, as mentioned above, these three directives deal jointly (both with common and separate rules) with the two forms of international protection.

[93] See Art. 2(f) of Directive 2011/95.

[94] See Art. 15 of Directive 2011/95.

24.5.2 "Temporary" Protection

Still in the framework of EU law, another regime of protection of forced migrants, called "temporary" protection, is foreseen. It provides for a lower level of protection for beneficiaries than subsidiary protection. Temporary protection is governed by Directive No. 2001/55[95] and concerns situations of mass influx of displaced persons who cannot return to their country of origin.[96] Displaced persons are defined, in Article 2, as:

> [. . .] third-country nationals or stateless persons who have had to leave their country or region of origin, or have been evacuated [. . .] and are unable to return in safe and durable conditions because of the situation prevailing in that country [. . .] in particular: (i) persons who have fled areas of armed conflict or endemic violence; (ii) persons at serious risk of, or who have been the victims of, systematic or generalised violations of their human rights [. . .].

In essence, the aim of temporary protection is to establish a procedure of an exceptional nature, which can provide immediate and temporary protection to displaced persons.[97] Displaced persons are entitled to a fairly basic form of reception by the Member States for a period of one year, with the possibility of extension for a maximum period of a further year.[98] Temporary protection is without prejudice to the granting of refugee status under the Geneva Convention.[99] However, as has been noted,[100] this form of protection has the disadvantage that it is not a mechanism that operates on an ongoing basis, but whose activation requires a Council decision taken, on a case-by-case basis, in relation to a specific situation. It is therefore a procedure of limited effectiveness.

24.5.3 "Humanitarian" or "Special" Protection

The temporary protection regime of Directive No. 2001/55, which has just been described, should not be confused with the Italian legislation which provides for *temporary residence permits* for humanitarian reasons, and which has long been referred to as "humanitarian" protection and recently as "special" protection.

However, it should be pointed out that this legislation has changed a great deal over time. Legislative Decree No. 286/1998 had established, in Article 5(6), that the

[95]Council Directive 2001/55/EC of 20 July 2001 on minimum standards for giving temporary protection in the event of a mass influx of displaced persons and on measures promoting a balance of efforts between Member States in receiving such persons and bearing the consequences thereof.

[96]See Arts. 1 and 2 of Directive 2001/55.

[97]See Art. 2(a) of Directive 2001/55.

[98]Art. 4 of Directive 2001/55.

[99]Art. 3(1) of Directive 2001/55.

[100]Di Filippo (2012), p. 246.

refusal or revocation of a residence permit could not be adopted if there were "serious reasons, in particular of a humanitarian nature or resulting from constitutional or international obligations of the Italian State".[101] Subsequently, the Legislative Decree No. 25/2008, in Article 32, had provided that:

> In cases in which it does not grant the application for international protection and considers that there may be serious humanitarian reasons, the Territorial Commission shall forward the documents to the police commissioner [Questore] for the possible issue of a residence permit pursuant to Article 5(6) of Legislative Decree No 286 of 25 July 1998.[102]

In addition, Legislative Decree No. 286/1998 had introduced another form of "humanitarian" protection of an exceptional nature, by providing that the President of the Council of Ministers might adopt a decree introducing temporary protection measures for serious humanitarian needs during conflicts, natural disasters or other very serious events occurring in third countries. In the past, a temporary protection regime on such a basis has been adopted in certain circumstances in Italy.[103]

In reality, humanitarian protection is intended to be a form of protection for forced migrants that is *residual* in nature but very useful compared to the three international protection schemes provided for by EU law (asylum, subsidiary protection and temporary protection). However, in 2018, the Italian Government had practically abolished the institute of humanitarian protection, by introducing a strict typing of cases (renamed "special cases") in which temporary residence permits could be issued for humanitarian reasons and establishing very restrictive requirements for the individuals concerned.[104]

Finally and rightly, in 2020 the Italian Government has once again amended the relevant legislation, reintroducing the concept of humanitarian protection, albeit under the different name of "special protection".[105]

24.5.4 Internally Displaced Persons

As already mentioned, the situation of "internally displaced persons" concerns individuals who are forced to leave and abandon their homes and places of residence, but who remain within their own country. Therefore, unlike the asylum seekers, refugees and other forced migrants described above, they do not flee their country to seek protection in another country.

---

[101] My translation.

[102] My translation.

[103] See Favilli (2013), p. 83.

[104] See Law Decree No. 113/2018, converted into Law No. 132 of 1 December 2018.

[105] See Law Decree No. 130/2020, converted into Law No. 173 of 18 December 2020.

In reality, there is no specific international legal regime for internally displaced persons[106] other than the one provided for in the 2009 Kampala Convention.[107] These people, remaining in the State of their nationality, can invoke all the human rights that are due to other citizens, as well as, in situations of armed conflict, the same norms of international humanitarian law. However, their situation as displaced persons makes them particularly vulnerable; and makes certain human rights of special importance to them from a practical point of view.

To meet this situation, the United Nations has taken a number of initiatives. In 1992 a UN Secretary General's Representative for internally displaced persons was established. Then, in 1998, the *Guiding Principles on Internal Displacement*,[108] an act of soft law, was adopted; which was later approved by the *World Summit*.[109] These principles provide for a rather precise definition of the concept of internally displaced persons. These are individuals:

> [...] who have been forced or obliged to flee or to leave their homes or places of habitual residence, in particular as a result of or in order to avoid the effects of armed conflict, situations of generalized violence, violations of human rights or natural or human-made disasters, and who have not crossed an internationally recognized State border.

Among the human rights that are most relevant to internally displaced persons are: (*a*) the prohibition of forced displacement; (*b*) the prohibition of discrimination; (*c*) freedom of movement; (*d*) subsistence rights, such as the right to food, water, housing and health care; (*e*) the right to return to their homes when the emergency has been overcome or, alternatively, the right to integrate elsewhere.

References

Calamia AM, Di Filippo M, Gestri M (eds) (2012) Immigrazione, Diritto e Diritti: profili internazionalistici ed europei. Cedam, Padova

Conforti B (2015) Diritto internazionale, 10th edn. Editoriale Scientifica, Napoli

De Sena P, Starita M (2019) Navigare fra istanze 'Stato-centriche' e 'cosmopolitiche': il caso 'Sea Watch' in una prospettiva conflittuale. SIDIBlog, 14 July 2019

Di Filippo M (2012) L'ammissione di cittadini stranieri. In: Calamia AM, Di Filippo M, Gestri M (eds) Immigrazione, Diritto e Diritti: profili internazionalistici ed europei. Cedam, Padova, pp 81–126

Favilli C (2013) Migration law in Italy. Kluwer, Alphen aan den Rijn

Gradoni L, Pasquet L (2019) Lisistrata a Lampedusa: una riflessione sul caso Sea Watch 3. SIDIBlog, 6 July 2019

[106] On this topic see Kälin and Künzli (2019), pp. 538–543.

[107] African Union Convention for the Protection and Assistance of Internally Displaced Persons in Africa (Kampala Convention), 23 October 2009.

[108] UN Doc. E/CN.4/1998/53/Add.2 (Annex).

[109] 2005 *World Summit Outcome*, GA Res. A/Res/60/1 (2005), para. 132, and subsequent resolutions by the UN General Assembly, including Resolution 72/182 (2017), para. 7, and by the HRC, including Resolution 32/11 (2016), para 4.

Kälin W, Künzli J (2019) The law of international human rights protection, 2nd edn. OUP, Oxford-New York

Lenzerini F (2009a) Asilo e diritti umani. L'evoluzione del diritto d'asilo nel diritto internazionale. Giuffrè, Milano

Lenzerini F (2009b) The evolution of Italian jurisprudence concerning the relationship between the constitutional right of asylum and the recognition of refugee status. Ital Yearb Int Law 19:139–156

Lenzerini F (2012) Il principio del *non-refoulement* dopo la sentenza *Hirsi* della Corte europea dei diritti dell'uomo. RDI 95:721–761

Liguori A (2012) La Corte europea dei diritti dell'uomo condanna l'Italia per i respingimenti verso la Libia del 2009: il caso *Hirsi*. RDI 95:415–443

Pisillo Mazzeschi R (1999a) Il diritto di asilo 50 anni dopo la Dichiarazione universale dei diritti dell'uomo. Riv int dir uomo 12:694–703

Pisillo Mazzeschi R (2011) The relationship between human rights and the rights of aliens and immigrants. In: Fastenrath U et al (eds) From bilateralism to community interest: essays in honour of Judge Bruno Simma. OUP, Oxford, pp 552–573

Pustorino P (2020) Lezioni di tutela internazionale dei diritti umani, 2nd edn. Cacucci, Bari

Starita M (2019) Il dovere di soccorso in mare e il diritto di obbedire al diritto (internazionale) del comandante della nave privata. DUDI 13:5–47

Weissbrodt D (2000) Prevention of discrimination: the rights of non-citizens: final Report of the Special Rapporteur. UN Doc. E/CN.4/Sub.2/2003/23 and Add.1, 25 May 2000

Weissbrodt D, de la Vega C (2007) International human rights law. An introduction. University of Pennsylvania Press, Philadelphia

25 Collective Human Rights and Political Objectives of the International Community

The individualistic character of human rights is an original imprint of human rights theory, which is influenced by a strongly Western approach, and this character still remains dominant in the overall legal regime of the matter. However, over time, especially because of the impact of the concept of human rights in developing countries,[1] this character has somewhat diminished and the idea of the importance of collective human rights has grown; that is, the idea that the scope of human rights should be extended to certain communities, or groups of persons, such as peoples, minorities and indigenous peoples. This new conception is important, because it enriches the value and the universal reach of human rights; but it has so far achieved only partial success in the international community as a whole.[2]

The first, and most important, success of this conception has been the rapid consolidation, in international law, of the principle of self-determination of peoples, which I have already discussed.[3]

Therefore, in this chapter, I will first turn my attention to the human rights of minorities and indigenous peoples. Afterwards, I will address the question of whether other collective human rights have become established in international law. In this regard, today there is often talk of certain rights of peoples, other than self-determination, which would become affirmed in international law in the framework of third and fourth generation human rights. However, in my view, as it will be seen, most of these rights are still in a phase of progressive development and do not yet seem to be the subject of binding international norms, but only of commitments or political objectives of the international community.

Finally, I will mention the phenomenon for which certain human rights are emerging in international law in which the individual dimension is strongly linked

---

[1] See above, Sects. 8.1.1 and 10.3.

[2] For a different view see Pustorino (2020), p. 23, who believes that the individualistic approach to human rights is completely outdated in today's reality.

[3] See above, Chap. 19.

R. Pisillo Mazzeschi, *International Human Rights Law*,
https://doi.org/10.1007/978-3-030-77032-7_25

to the public or collective dimension. It seems to me that this is happening in matters of security (right to human security) and the environment (right to a healthy environment).

25.1 Rights of Minorities

The international protection of minorities, starting from the sixteenth and seventeenth centuries and then especially after the First World War, was one of the aspects that anticipated the phenomenon of the general protection of human rights, even though the aims of the treaties on minorities were motivated more by political reasons for stability in Europe than by humanitarian reasons.[4] After the Second World War, the protection of minorities found its place within the more modern framework of international protection of human rights; but, to tell the truth, it has not had a very significant development.

The reason for this is that States are reluctant to grant many rights to minorities, fearing that this might further their secessionist aspirations, which obviously run counter to State sovereignty. Consider also the large number of religious, ethnic, linguistic, cultural and other minorities present in the States of the international community; and the fact that many of these minorities historically aspire to secession.

One might wonder why such a hostile attitude on the part of States has not been manifested towards peoples with regard to the right of self-determination. There are two main reasons for this. First, the movement for the self-determination of peoples has found a strong push, not postponable for political and historical reasons, by the process of decolonization. Secondly, the self-determination of peoples essentially concerns their right to free themselves from a foreign domination achieved illegally and by force (or from an illegitimate apartheid regime).[5] Therefore, it does not undermine the sovereignty of the great generality of States acting legitimately; or in any case, it does not conflict with State sovereignty to the same extent as secessionist aspirations on the part of minorities.

25.1.1 Norms

It should first of all be noted that the UN Charter, while containing a number of provisions on non-autonomous territories and the international system of trusteeship of certain territories, does not contain norms explicitly aimed at the protection of minorities. Moreover, the Universal Declaration also contains no provisions on the protection of minorities, and this exclusion is very significant.

---

[4]See above, Sect. 1.2.9.

[5]See above, Chap. 19.

It is only with the Covenant on Civil and Political Rights of 1966 that a norm on minority rights emerges in international human rights law. It is contained in Article 27, which reads:

> In those States in which ethnic, religious or linguistic minorities exist, persons belonging to such minorities shall not be denied the right, in community with the other members of their group, to enjoy their own culture, to profess and practice their own religion, or to use their own language.

This is a very important provision, because it is the only norm on minorities contained in a general and universal human rights treaty. However, it should be emphasized from the outset that Article 27 speaks of "persons belonging to such minorities" rather than "minorities". I will return to this point later.

Among the sectorial treaties, and always of a universal nature, one can mention the Convention on the Rights of the Child, which contains a provision (Art. 30) very similar to that of the Covenant, with the sole addition of a reference to persons of indigenous origin.[6] Subsequently, on a universal level, the UN General Assembly adopted, in 1992, the Declaration on the Rights of Persons Belonging to National or Ethnic, Religious and Linguistic Minorities.[7]

On the European continent, the most important legal instrument is the Framework Convention for the Protection of National Minorities,[8] adopted by the Council of Europe in 1995. This Convention, of which I have already spoken,[9] contains many principles on the rights of minorities, such as non-discrimination; the promotion of cultural, religious and linguistic traditions; freedom of assembly, association, expression, thought, conscience and religion; access to the media; linguistic rights; rights to participate in public life, etc. However, as already said, this Convention lays down general principles rather than detailed norms and it is doubtful whether the rights given to minorities actually correspond to precise and immediate obligations of the States Parties. Furthermore, the Council of Europe had already adopted, in 1992, the European Charter for Regional or Minority Languages,[10] which seeks to promote multilingualism. It should be remembered that the OSCE also approved certain documents on the protection of minorities and, in 1992, set up a High Commissioner for National Minorities.[11]

---

[6]CRC, Art. 30: "In those States in which ethnic, religious or linguistic minorities exist, a child belonging to such a minority or who is indigenous shall not be denied the right, in community with other members of his or her group, to enjoy his or her own culture, to profess and practice his or her religion, or to use his or her language".

[7]Declaration on the Rights of Persons Belonging to National or Ethnic, Religious and Linguistic Minorities, GA Res. 47/135 of 18 December 1992.

[8]Framework Convention for the Protection of National Minorities of 1 February 1995 (FCPNM).

[9]See above, Sect. 11.1.3.3.

[10]European Charter for Regional or Minority Languages of 5 November 1992 (ECML). See above, Sect. 11.1.3.2.

[11]High Commissioner on National Minorities, *www.osce.org/hcnm*.

In the Inter-American human rights system, there are no specific treaties on the protection of minorities; but some provisions of the American Declaration on the Rights and Duties of Man[12] and of the American Convention of Human Rights[13] may offer indirect protection to minorities. Indeed, the case-law of the Inter-American Court has addressed some important aspects in relation to minorities, such as the responsibility of the State for enforced disappearances or violations of the right to life or property rights of minority groups or for violations of the right to a nationality.[14]

In Africa, too, certain provisions of the African Charter have been used to protect minorities. For example, the African Commission, in the *Amnesty International v. Sudan* case, applied Article 8 of the Charter,[15] on the free choice of religion, to protect the Catholic minority in Sudan and to declare that this State had committed violations, because non-Muslim citizens did not have the right to pray or build their places of worship and had also been subjected to mistreatment, arbitrary detention and other abuses.

25.1.2 Content of the Rights

Turning now to the content of minority rights, three main problems can be identified: (*a*) the definition of the concept of "minority"; (*b*) the question of individual or collective ownership of the rights granted; (*c*) the main rights granted to minorities.

The first problem is very important and also affects the controversial relationship between the notion of "minority" and that of "people". As has been said about the self-determination of peoples, the concept of "people", according to the prevailing view, is inspired by the idea of *demos*.[16] Instead, the concept of "minority" expresses the idea of *éthnos*, that is, a group of people, which stands out because it has in common race, religion, language, culture and traditions, and is united in a bond of mutual solidarity. However, this general idea of "minority" is not sufficient to give rise to a precise legal concept. In fact, in international law, especially within the framework of the United Nations, numerous attempts have been made to arrive at an exact definition of the notion of "minority", but without certain results.

Furthermore, the Covenant on Civil and Political Rights and the Convention on the Rights of the Child do not specify what they mean by minorities. The European Framework Convention has also failed to define the concept of minorities, although

---

[12]See, e.g., American Declaration of the Rights and Duties of Man, Arts. II, III, IV, VIII, XII, XX, XXI, XXII.

[13]See, e.g., ACHR, Arts. 12, 13, 15, 16, 22, 23, 24.

[14]See, e.g., IACtHR, *Aloeboetoe et al. v. Suriname (Merits)*, Judgment of 4 December 1991; *Aloeboetoe et al. v. Suriname (Reparations)*, Judgment of 10 September 1993; *Case of the Girls Yean and Bosico v. Dominican Republic*. See also, below, Sect. 25.2, on the rights of indigenous peoples.

[15]ACmHPR, *Amnesty International and Others v. Sudan*, paras. 72–76.

[16]That is, a group of people belonging to a certain territorial entity. See above, Sect. 19.1.2.

it expressly deals with national minorities. One definition that has gained much consensus is the one proposed by F. Capotorti in his report to the UN, published in 1979, according to which a minority is:

> [. . .] a group numerically inferior to the rest of the population of a State, in a non-dominant position, whose members – being nationals of the State – possess ethnic, religious or linguistic characteristics differing from those of the rest of the population, and show, if only implicitly, a sense of solidarity directed towards preserving their culture, traditions, religion or language.[17]

The elements present in this definition, and in other similar ones that have been subsequently proposed in doctrine,[18] are the following: (*a*) the minority dimension of the group compared to the majority of the population of a State; (*b*) the non-dominant position of the group; (*c*) the nationality of the members of the group; (*d*) an identity established on the basis of ethnic, linguistic, religious or cultural criteria (objective requirement); (*e*) the willingness of the members of the group to preserve these characteristics and to maintain a feeling of mutual solidarity (subjective requirement). As can be seen, there are as many as five requirements, all of which must be present, and which therefore end up giving a rather restrictive definition of the legal notion of "minority". However, it should be stressed that the Human Rights Committee tends to broaden this definition, because it has sometimes extended the protection of Article 27 of the Covenant also to members of minorities who are citizens of States other than the one in question or who are stateless.[19]

The second problem, perhaps the most crucial, concerns individual or collective ownership of the rights granted to minorities. Indeed, international law has always shown a tendency *not to recognize minorities as collective entities*, but rather to grant rights exclusively to individuals belonging to minorities (the so-called *individualistic* approach to the question of minorities).[20] In other words, members of minorities enjoy a number of *individual* human rights, such as, above all, the right to non-discrimination and the right to maintain their cultural, religious and linguistic traditions. Furthermore, in line with this approach, international law does not recognize minorities as holders of the most classic and important collective human right; that is, the right to external self-determination.[21] The reason for this clearly lies, as has already been said, in the interests of States to defend their sovereignty and territorial integrity.

This individualistic tendency is revealed by Article 27 of the Covenant on Civil and Political Rights, which is the most important norm at the level of universal

---

[17]Capotorti (1979), para. 568.

[18]See, among others, Deschênes (1985), para. 181; Thornberry (1991), p. 6 ff.; Capotorti (1992), pp. 107–109; Pocar (1998), pp. 36–37; Tancredi (2001), p. 625 ff., esp. p. 636; Pustorino (2006), pp. 259–263; Castellino (2014), pp. 34–36.

[19]HRCtee, General Comment No. 23, 8 April 1994, para. 5.2.

[20]See, among others, Meijknecht (2001), p. 171.

[21]See Tancredi (2001), pp. 229 and 628.

international law. In fact, according to the dominant interpretation, and that seems correct to me, Article 27 limits itself to recognizing *individual rights*; that is, cultural, religious and linguistic rights, which belong to individual members of the minority, and not collective rights of the minority as such.[22] This means, in essence, that the provision does not add much to the traditional and general prohibition of discrimination between human beings on ethnic, cultural, religious and linguistic grounds. Moreover, Article 27 is formulated more in terms of negative obligations (of non-interference) than positive obligations of States. The obvious shortcoming of this approach lies in the fact that it fails to address the structural disadvantages suffered by minorities and the difficulty of responding to certain collective demands of minorities, such as having their own schools in their own language, proportional representation in administrative and political bodies, recognition of their language as an official language, establishment of their places of worship, etc. The Convention on the Rights of the Child and the 1992 UN Declaration also adopt the same *individualistic* approach.

More complex is the interpretation, on this point, of the European Framework Convention for the Protection of National Minorities. According to some authors,[23] this Convention would protect, at least in part, the *collective* human rights of minorities. According to others,[24] however, this Convention also gives rights to individual members of the minority and not to the minority as such. In my view, this second opinion is more convincing, also according to a literal interpretation, since almost all the provisions of the Convention are directed at "persons belonging to national minorities".

Finally, the individualistic approach to the issue of minorities is reinforced by the fact that minorities as collective entities do not usually have the procedural standing to bring complaints before international human rights monitoring bodies.[25]

The third problem, mentioned above, concerns the substantive content of the rights granted to minorities. Firstly, persons belonging to minorities have the right not to be discriminated against because of their status. Therefore, the general prohibition of discrimination operates for such persons as a framework principle, which always includes, among the prohibited grounds for discrimination, language,

[22] On the other hand, according to a different view, Article 27 does not exclude certain collective rights, since it provides that individuals belonging to minorities may enjoy the rights provided for "in common with the other members of their group". Cf. Kälin and Künzli (2019), p. 369. But it does not seem to me that this specification of Article 27 is really intended to recognize rights to minorities as such. The Human Rights Committee also recognizes that the rights protected by Article 27 are individual rights; but it adds that: "they depend in turn on the ability of the minority group to maintain its culture, language and religion. Accordingly, positive measures by States may also be necessary to protect the identity of a minority [. . .]". (HRCtee, General Comment No. 23, para. 6.2).

[23] Kälin and Künzli (2019), pp. 370–371.

[24] Focarelli (2013), p. 239.

[25] In addition, minorities have difficulty complying with the frequent condition of admissibility of appeals constituted by the status of victim of the violation. See, e.g., ECtHR, *Noack and Others v. Germany*. Cf. also Pustorino (2020), p. 236.

religion, national origin or other conditions. This framework principle is reaffirmed and specified, in relation to minorities, in the conventional norms examined above. Secondly, these norms establish a more specific set of rights aimed at protecting the cultural, linguistic and religious identity of persons belonging to minorities. However, the implementation of these rights is, to a large extent, left to the national law of the States.

25.1.3 Obligations

The issue of the obligations of States, corresponding to the rights of minorities, can be dealt with very briefly. With regard to the prohibition of discrimination against members of minorities, I can refer to what I already said above about the general prohibition of discrimination.[26]

As for the obligations of States corresponding to the various specific rights of members of minorities, they include negative obligations (e.g. to allow freedom of assembly, association, expression, religion)[27] and, above all, positive obligations. But, as noted, many of the positive obligations under existing international instruments are not sufficiently precise and complete and thus require implementation measures in national law.[28]

25.2 Rights of Indigenous Peoples

Since the 1980s, the need to address the problem of discrimination against indigenous peoples and to create an ad hoc legal system of protection for them has been progressively affirmed in international law. Indigenous peoples are the "original inhabitants" of a territory; that is, the descendants of the population of a territory who lived there before the now dominant population took control of that territory as a result of immigration and/or conquest.[29] Moreover, they usually live in tribes or communities governed by very different customs or traditions, socially, culturally and economically, from those of the dominant population in the territory.[30]

Indigenous peoples do not usually aim at secession from the State in which they live; rather, they aspire to forms of self-government, the right to use their "ancestral" lands and natural resources, and the right to maintain their cultural identity. These

[26] See above, Sect. 18.1.3.

[27] See, e.g., FCPNM, Art. 7.

[28] Perhaps the right to property of ancestral lands, by members of indigenous peoples and members of common minorities who are assimilated to these peoples, can be regarded as sufficiently precise and complete, at least in the practice of the Human Rights Committee on Article 27 of the Covenant.

[29] For a list of factors recognized as relevant for the identification of a community as indigenous, see ACtHPR, *African Commission on Human and Peoples' Rights v. Kenya*, para. 107.

[30] See Martinez Cobo (1983), paras. 379 and 381; Id. (1986), p. 29; Focarelli (2013), pp. 241–242. See also Lenzerini (ed.) (2008).

claims, initially opposed by the vast majority of States, have more recently found greater acceptance, so much so that, in 2007, the UN General Assembly even approved with a large majority the Declaration on the Rights of Indigenous Peoples,[31] which, albeit as a non-binding document, incorporates most of their aspirations.

25.2.1 Norms

In a distant historical period, from the sixteenth to the seventeenth century, indigenous peoples made agreements with colonial powers; but their nature as international treaties has almost always been challenged by domestic courts and international arbitrators and courts.[32] Turning to international human rights law, the relevant norms are few and they are, in essence: (*a*) the 1957 ILO Convention No. 107 on Indigenous and Tribal Populations,[33] which has, however, been replaced almost entirely by the 1989 ILO Convention No. 169 on Indigenous and Tribal Peoples;[34] (*b*) the above mentioned Article 27 of the Covenant on Civil and Political Rights; (*c*) the UN Declaration of 2007.

The ILO Convention No. 169 contains a definition of "indigenous peoples" and a number of rights which States Parties undertake to grant them. In particular, the Convention provides that States Parties are obliged to recognize and protect the values and customs of indigenous peoples;[35] to consult them when adopting legislative or administrative measures that may affect them;[36] to respect the historical and cultural relationship of indigenous peoples with their lands;[37] and to protect certain rights of theirs concerning work, social security and welfare.[38] In reality, the ILO Convention has been ratified by a small number of States; however, since almost all Latin American countries are parties to it, this treaty has significant regional relevance.

As for Article 27 of the Covenant on Civil and Political Rights, which, as already seen, protects all ethnic, religious or linguistic minorities, it certainly applies to indigenous peoples.[39] However, it has already been said that this provision has important limitations, because it protects the *individual* rights of members of minorities, rather than minorities as collective entities. This individualistic approach

[31] *Declaration on the Rights of Indigenous Peoples*, GA Res. 61/295, 13 September 2007.

[32] See Focarelli (2013), p. 243, also for more specific references.

[33] Indigenous and Tribal Populations Convention (ILO No. 107), 26 June 1957.

[34] Indigenous and Tribal Peoples Convention (ILO No. 169), 26 June 1989.

[35] *Ibidem*, Art. 5.

[36] *Ibidem*, Art. 6.

[37] *Ibidem*, Arts. 7, 13–19.

[38] *Ibidem*, Arts. 20–25.

[39] See, e.g., HRCtee, General Comment No. 23, 8 April 1994, para. 3.2; *Lovelace v. Canada*, para. 14; *Kitok v. Sweden*, paras. 6.3 and 9.2.

in Article 27, which is already defective in itself for all minorities, is even more inadequate with regard to indigenous peoples, who require, above all, collective protection for their historical and cultural identity and for the enjoyment of their lands and natural resources.

For these reasons, the 2007 UN Declaration is particularly important. Despite its non-legally binding nature, it indicates that a consensus is gradually developing within the international community on the need to recognize that indigenous peoples are holders, *also as collective entities*, of certain human rights.

25.2.2 Content of the Rights

I have given above a descriptive definition of the concept of "indigenous peoples", which is based on historical and sociological elements. However, a legal notion must be more precise and must also establish the relationship between the notion of "indigenous peoples" and the notions of "minorities" and "peoples" under international law.[40] In fact, the definitions of "indigenous peoples" contained in ILO Conventions No. 107 and No. 169 appear rather deficient. And also the UN Declaration on the Rights of Indigenous Peoples of 2007 has renounced to provide a precise legal definition, since, according to its Article 33(1), it refers to the so-called criterion of "self-identification" by the indigenous peoples themselves.[41] A definition should therefore be drawn up in the light of all international acts and practice relating to indigenous peoples.

At a first summary examination, the legal concept of "indigenous peoples" lends itself to being framed within the more general concept of "minorities", since it coincides for the most part with the idea of *éthnos* and is almost always characterized by the constitutive elements of the concept of "minority".[42] Following this approach, one could argue that "indigenous peoples" constitute *sui generis minorities*, since they are characterized by two distinctive and additional elements: (*a*) the oldest historical origin of the territorial settlement of "indigenous peoples" with respect to "common" minorities; (*b*) the particular importance of the territorial factor and the

[40]See Pisillo Mazzeschi (2016), pp. 459–465.

[41]*Declaration on the Rights of Indigenous Peoples*, Art. 33(1): "Indigenous peoples have the right to determine their own identity or membership in accordance with their own customs and traditions [...]".

[42]As seen above, these elements are: (*a*) the minority dimension of the group in relation to the majority of the population of a State; (*b*) the non-dominant position of the group; (*c*) the nationality of the members of the group; (*d*) an identity established on the basis of ethnic, linguistic, religious or cultural criteria (objective requirement); (*e*) the willingness of the members of the group to preserve these characteristics and to maintain a feeling of mutual solidarity (subjective element). In indigenous peoples, the only element that is sometimes (but rarely) missing is the numerical inferiority of the indigenous population over the majority of the State's population.

functional relationship between the control of the territory and natural resources by the indigenous people and the maintenance of their cultural identity.[43]

However, the classification of the concept of "indigenous people" in that of "minority", albeit with *sui generis* minority status, is not convincing; what is more, it has always been rejected by the indigenous peoples themselves, who were, and are, aware that this classification has considerable disadvantages from a legal and "regulatory policy" point of view. In fact, indigenous peoples have always avoided remaining "bound" to the weak international legal regime of minorities and have instead sought, with great tenacity, to obtain a different and more favorable legal status; in particular more based on the protection of their *collective* human rights.

And in reality, there are various elements of recent practice that show a tendency to assimilate the concept of "indigenous people" to the more general concept of "people". First of all, the very affirmation, on the juridical level, of the terminology "indigenous peoples" cannot be without meaning. Second, Article 2 of the 2007 UN Declaration explicitly states that indigenous peoples are "equal to all other peoples". Third, the majority doctrine also considers that indigenous peoples should be considered as a category of "peoples" under international law, even if they would enjoy fewer rights than the peoples subject to colonial domination, conquest or occupation by force or an apartheid regime. In particular, they would not have the right to "external" self-determination.[44]

However, in my view, even the (almost total) assimilation of indigenous peoples to "peoples" under international law is not entirely convincing, both because of the structural characteristics of indigenous peoples and because "external" self-determination lies at the heart of the affirmation of peoples' international rights.

Therefore, I believe that indigenous peoples have many characteristics in common with minorities, but also some characteristics in common with peoples, which go beyond the simple terminology. On the whole, it seems to me that international law considers indigenous peoples as a *tertium genus* with respect to minorities and peoples: a *tertium genus* that enjoys a "special" and intermediate legal status compared to those of the other two groups. In essence, indigenous peoples enjoy all the rights due to minorities; but in addition, as *special minorities* for historical-political reasons, they enjoy *further* rights, which are typical and exclusive of indigenous peoples (those linked to a strong cultural identity and the historical use of natural resources). Finally, they also enjoy *some* of the rights of peoples, albeit in a lesser and weaker form than peoples; that is, they have the right to "internal" self-determination and not the right to "external" self-determination.

This conclusion is confirmed by the examination of the single rights that are granted to indigenous peoples by the 2007 UN Declaration. I limit myself here to a summary of these rights. Firstly, members of indigenous peoples have the non-discrimination rights that all minorities have. Secondly, indigenous peoples,

[43]See Pustorino (2006), p. 261.

[44]See above, Sect. 19.1.2.

also as collective entities, have many specific rights concerning their cultural identity. Thirdly, they have certain *collective rights* that protect their ownership or possession of land, water and other natural resources historically held or used by them. These rights also differ from those of "common" minorities. Finally, indigenous peoples also have the right to "internal" self-determination, understood as a form of local self-government. However, this right does not seem to have an autonomous and unlimited character; rather, it appears to be closely and functionally linked to indigenous peoples' rights of cultural identity. In other words, the territorial State's obligation to grant forms of local self-government to indigenous peoples may be proportionate to the aim of protecting their cultural identity.

In conclusion, it seems to me that the political-diplomatic strategy of the indigenous peoples, aimed at obtaining a more favorable legal regime than that, rather weak, of "common" minorities, and in some respects similar to that of the peoples, has been successful overall. In the UN Declaration of 2007 they obtained three important objectives: (*a*) a special juridical regime, based on the human rights due to "common" minorities, but integrated and enriched by further rights concerning their own cultural identity and natural resources; (*b*) the right of "internal" self-determination, albeit with certain limits; (*c*) the ownership, also as collective entities, of certain human rights.

It is clear that the UN Declaration has no binding character; but the three aspects mentioned above are being confirmed in the practice of international human rights monitoring bodies. One can mention, for example, the judgments of the Inter-American Court of Human Rights in the cases of the *Awas Tingni*, *Yakye Axa*, *Moiwana, Sawhoyamaxa*, and *Kuna*[45] communities; as well as some cases of the Human Rights Committee.[46] Therefore it can be argued that a process of creating customary international law norms is developing on these issues. In particular, this concerns the specific rights of indigenous peoples linked to their cultural identity and those protecting their possession of land, water and other natural resources. But it does not seem to me that this process has yet been concluded.[47]

25.2.3 Obligations

The conclusions reached above show that, at least in already established general international law, the legally binding obligations of States towards indigenous

[45]See, e.g., IACtHR, *Mayagna (Sumo) Awas Tingni Community v. Nicaragua (Merits)*, paras. 116–127, 142–155; *Yakye Axa Indigenous Community v. Paraguay (Merits)*, paras. 123–156; *Moiwana Community v. Suriname (Merits)*, paras. 125–135; *Sawhoyamaxa Indigenous Community v. Paraguay*, paras. 116–144; *Saramaka People v. Suriname*, paras. 87–96, 133–137 and 147; *Kuna and Emberá Indigenous Peoples v. Panama*, paras. 111–124.

[46]See, e.g., HRCtee, *Länsman (Jouni) et al. v. Finland*, paras. 10.4 and 10.5; *Mahuika et al. v. New Zealand*, para. 9.5; *Poma Poma v. Peru.*

[47]For a different view, see ILA Resolution No. 5/2012, *Rights of Indigenous Peoples*, 75th Conference of the ILA, Sofia, 26–30 August 2012.

peoples are, in large part, those that exist towards "common" minorities.[48] I therefore refer to what I already said about these obligations.[49]

25.3 Other Collective Human Rights?

The question now has to be asked whether there are any collective human rights, in the international legal order, other than those already examined. As has been mentioned, today there is often a tendency to talk about certain new rights, which would belong to peoples (sometimes even together with individuals), and which are framed in the human rights of the third or fourth generation. Usually mentioned are the rights to development, natural resources, peace, democracy and good governance.[50] These rights, which have been promoted and then supported at international level especially by developing countries, are mainly contained in non-binding international acts, such as resolutions or declarations of international organizations or conferences; but some of them are also provided for in treaties, such as the African Charter and the Arab Charter.

However, one should wonder whether they are true binding rights, to which legal obligations of States or other entities correspond, or whether they should be classified as commitments or political objectives undertaken by States or by the international community as a whole.[51] Another theory argues that, at least in some cases, these are only social factors, the presence of which in a given State favors the internal realization of human rights by that State.[52]

Indeed, these rights seem, at first sight, to possess certain common characteristics, which lead to doubts about their mandatory legal nature:[53] (*a*) they are almost always provided for by non-binding international acts; (*b*) they do not appear to be supported by those *diuturnitas* and *opinio juris* which are required for the formation of customary norms, nor by that general consensus of the whole international community which is required for the creation of general principles of international law; (*c*) there is uncertainty as to whether the holders of these rights are peoples or individuals or even other entities; (*d*) there are also doubts as to whether States are really the bearers of the obligations corresponding to the rights; (*e*) finally (and above all), the content of the rights in question is often so vague and indefinite that it is doubtful whether it is really normative in character.

---

[48]The argument can be different, and more complex, as we have seen, within the framework of certain conventional systems of human rights protection, such as the Inter-American and African systems.

[49]See above, Sect. 25.1.3.

[50]On this subject see especially Tomuschat (2014), pp. 149–164.

[51]See above, Sect. 8.2.4.

[52]For this theory see Tomuschat (2014), pp. 155–161, in relation to democracy, good governance and human security.

[53]*Ibidem*, pp. 152–154. See also Pisillo Mazzeschi (2008), pp. 302–310.

That said, it is true that each of these rights has its own specificity and could be studied independently and in depth with respect to the others. However, for my purposes, a summary examination of them can be attempted, for the sole aim of verifying whether, and if so to what extent, each of these rights actually has the above characteristics, and what overall conclusions can be drawn about their legal nature. As we shall see, the conclusions are similar (though not identical) for all of these rights.

25.3.1 Right to Development

The right to development has been affirmed in a number of resolutions of the (former) Commission on Human Rights and the UN General Assembly. In particular, the 1986 GA Declaration on the Right to Development[54] defines it as an inalienable human right. But this definition has generated much skepticism on the part of many Western States. Subsequent attempts by the Commission on Human Rights to clarify the content of this right have been unsuccessful. However, it should be noted that the right to development is also laid down in the African Charter on Human and Peoples' Rights,[55] which is a binding instrument, and in the ASEAN Human Rights Declaration.[56]

As for the holders of the right, according to the GA Declaration of 1986, they are both peoples and individuals; whereas the African Charter considers it only a right of peoples. But it is not clear, particularly in the UN documents, whether the notion of "people" is used in a strict sense, to oppose the people to the State-government, or whether it is used in an emphatic sense, to actually mean "State". In other words, it is not clear whether these international acts are intended to affirm that peoples have a right to development vis-à-vis their own governments (and one would then be in the field of human rights), or that poorer States have a right to development vis-à-vis richer States or the international community as a whole. Therefore, there is also uncertainty as to who the real bearers of the possible obligation to ensure development are.

Finally, as far as the content of the right to development is concerned, it is too vague and generic to produce binding legal effects. The 1986 GA Declaration proclaims:

> The right to development is an inalienable human right by virtue of which every human person and all peoples are entitled to participate in, contribute to, and enjoy economic, social,

---

[54] *UN Declaration on the Right to Development*, GA Res. 41/128, 4 December 1986.

[55] ACHPR, Art. 22: "1. All peoples shall have the right to their economic, social and cultural development with due regard to their freedom and identity and in the equal enjoyment of the common heritage of mankind. 2. States shall have the duty, individually or collectively, to ensure the exercise of the right to development".

[56] ASEAN Human Rights Declaration, paras. 35–37.

cultural and political development, in which all human rights and fundamental freedoms can be fully realized.[57]

It is clear that, in these terms, the right to development appears not as a real binding right, but rather as a broad political objective that States and the international community as a whole must give themselves in order to advance the cause of human rights. But neither the means, nor the resources, nor the legal limits that States or the international community must respect in order to achieve this objective are indicated. Moreover, development depends on an extensive and complex set of factors, many of which are beyond the control of individual States.[58]

Therefore, at present and at the *universal* level, it is not possible to speak of true obligations of States to guarantee development, but only of non-binding political goals. However, as we shall see,[59] in the framework of some *regional* systems of human rights protection, there are signs that go in the direction of giving some normative content to the right to development.

25.3.2 Right to Natural Resources

The right to wealth and natural resources lends itself to considerations similar to those just made for the right to development. It was first affirmed in the 1962 UN General Assembly Declaration on Permanent Sovereignty over Natural Resources[60] and then in the Charter of Economic Rights and Duties of States,[61] where, however, it is configured as a right of States and not of peoples or individuals. Instead, in the African Charter,[62] the right to wealth and natural resources is attributed to peoples, States and individuals (but for the latter only in cases of expropriation of their property). Therefore there is uncertainty about the possible holders of the right.

As for the content of the right to natural resources, it is very vague and indeterminate. Actually, as has been noted in doctrine,[63] the right of States and peoples to dispose freely of their wealth and natural resources does not add much to the content of the traditional right of States to territorial sovereignty. If anything, it has the merit, of an exquisitely political nature, of directing the regulatory discipline on the treatment of aliens' property and investments in favor of weaker States.

Therefore, also in this case, one cannot speak of a real human right to natural resources; but rather, of a political objective assumed especially by the international

---

[57] *UN Declaration on the Right to Development*, Art. 1(1).

[58] Tomuschat (2014), p. 153.

[59] See below, Sect. 25.3.6.

[60] *Permanent Sovereignty over Natural Resources*, GA Res. 1803 (XVII), 14 December 1962, Art. 1.

[61] *Charter of Economic Rights and Duties of States*, GA Res. 3281 (XXIX), 12 December 1974. Cf. esp. Arts. 2 and 7.

[62] ACHPR, Art. 21.

[63] See Conforti (2018), p. 208.

community, under the push of the movement promoted by the developing countries for the so-called New International Economic Order.[64] However, this movement, after initial success, has rather faded over time. Nevertheless, again, more encouraging indications are coming from some regional human rights systems.[65]

25.3.3 Right to Peace

The right to peace was first proclaimed by the Commission on Human Rights in 1976 and then by the UN General Assembly in a Declaration of 1978[66] and a subsequent one in 1984;[67] but many States abstained during the vote. Some more recent resolutions of the General Assembly were also adopted with many votes against and several abstentions.[68] However, it can be noted that the right to peace is enshrined in the African Charter.[69]

As for the holders of the right, the 1978 General Assembly Declaration mentions nations and individuals, while the 1984 Declaration and the African Charter speak only of peoples. Here too, therefore, there is considerable uncertainty about the holders of the right and the bearers of the corresponding obligations.

Finally, coming to the content of the right to peace, it is, if possible, even more vague and indefinite than the rights to development and to natural resources. As has rightly been noted,[70] the main purpose of the United Nations system, and one of the fundamental purposes of the entire international legal order, is to ensure international peace and security; and the effectiveness of such systems is not enhanced by the mere recognition of a human right to peace for the benefit of individuals, peoples and nations.

25.3.4 Right to Democracy

The human right to democracy is not expressly mentioned in the main human rights acts and treaties of a general nature, which prefer to contain norms on the rights to participate in political and public life.[71] It has already been seen, in fact, that Article 21 of the Universal Declaration states that everyone "has the right to take part in the

---

[64]On the New International Economic Order see the classic work of Bedjaoui (1979).

[65]See below, Sect. 25.3.6.

[66]GA Res. 33/73, 15 December 1978.

[67]GA Res. 39/11, 12 November 1984.

[68]GA Res. 57/216, 18 December 2002; GA Res. 60/163, 16 December 2005.

[69]ACHPR, Art. 23 (1): "All peoples shall have the right to national and international peace and security [. . .]".

[70]Tomuschat (2014), p. 153.

[71]See above, Sect. 22.2.

government of his country" (para. 1) and that "the will of the people shall be the basis of the authority of government" (para. 3).

Article 25 of the Covenant on Civil and Political Rights resumes the first statement of the Universal Declaration. But, as has been noted,[72] the word "democracy" is not used. The reference to a democratic society appears only in certain clauses restricting guaranteed rights, as a limit to such restrictions.[73] For example, in Article 21 of the Covenant, on freedom of assembly, it is stated that restrictions on this freedom can only be imposed if they are in accordance with the law and *necessary in a democratic society*. Similar clauses are contained in the provisions on freedom of association and fair trial.[74] The European Convention on Human Rights also contains many provisions with similar content. On the other hand, the two UN Covenants contain a provision on the right of peoples to self-determination; but this right should not be interpreted as equivalent to the right to democracy.[75]

However, a different approach to the issue of democracy has been developing within the United Nations since the late 1990s.[76] The Commission on Human Rights affirmed the right to democracy in two resolutions, in 1999 and 2000.[77] The Commission insisted on the close relationship between democratic governance and the protection of human rights.[78] These concepts were taken up by the General Assembly, particularly in its Resolution 55/96 of 2000,[79] on which, however, many States abstained. Subsequently, other resolutions of the General Assembly were adopted, which defined democracy as a "universal value", but also used more general and flexible language, stating, for example, that there is no single model of democracy in the world. A more secure legal basis for the right to democracy can be found on the European continent, within the systems of the European Convention on Human Rights,[80] the European Union[81] and the OSCE.[82]

In the face of these uncertain regulatory elements, the doctrine is divided on the question of the human right to democracy and three positions can be identified, in extreme synthesis. According to a first, more "optimistic" theory,[83] "a general norm that attributes to all individuals under the jurisdiction of a State the right to

[72]Tomuschat (2014), p. 155.

[73]See above, Sect. 4.4.2.

[74]According to Art. 14 of the CCPR, "The press and the public may be excluded from all or part of a trial for reasons of morals, public order [. . .] or national security in a democratic society [. . .]".

[75]See above, Sect. 19.1.3.

[76]See Tomuschat (2014), pp. 156–157.

[77]CmHR, Res. 1999/57, 27 April 1999; Res. 2000/47, 25 April 2000.

[78]See CmHR, Res. 1999/57, para. 1: "[. . .] democracy fosters the full realization of all human rights, and vice versa".

[79]GA Res.55/96, 4 December 2000.

[80]See above, Sect. 22.2.1.

[81]See TEU, Preamble and Arts. 2, 10(1), 21.

[82]See Charter of Paris for a New Europe, Paris, 19–21 November 1990.

[83]Cassese (2003–2004), vol. II, pp. 110–112.

democratic government"[84] is emerging in international law. This norm ends up coinciding with the right of peoples to "internal" self-determination. However, this concept of democracy would include only some aspects of the general model of democracy; namely "a representative government, based on free and impartial elections; respect for human rights; the rule of law".[85] In any case, the right to democracy would not yet have crystallized definitively as a right recognized to all individuals living within a State.

On the contrary, on the basis of a second, more "pessimistic" theory,[86] the right to "internal" self-determination, from a legal point of view, cannot be interpreted as a right to democracy. That is, it must be excluded that "international law requires that all governments in the world enjoy the consent of the majority of their subjects and are freely chosen by them".[87] There is a tendency of the majority of States in favor of the democratic legitimation of governments; but there are still many countries that do not follow this tendency and there is "no serious and generalized fight against undemocratic countries".[88]

There is, finally, a third theory, intermediate and more articulated,[89] which tends to see democracy above all from the point of view of social factors and the context of the institutions that promote the realization of human rights. From this perspective, it can be observed that human rights of political participation already existed in the various treaties on human rights, but that the action taken, over the last twenty years, by the United Nations, the Council of Europe, the OSCE, the European Union[90] and other international bodies, has added an important political dimension. Now democracy is recognized as the only legitimate form of government,[91] even if the concept of democracy has not been well defined and has remained rather generic. On the other hand, some resolutions of the UN General Assembly, adopted only by majority vote, call for "a democratic and equitable international order"; and therefore pose the difficult problem of a democratization of the international community itself and a redistribution of political power at the global level.[92]

As can be seen, the issue is very complex and cannot be further explored here. It seems to me, restricting the question to the human right of individuals and peoples to democratic government, that there are no theoretical difficulties in conceiving individuals and peoples as holders of that right and the State/government as the bearer of the corresponding obligation. However, over and above the individual rights of political participation expressly provided for in human rights treaties and

---

[84] *Ibidem*, p. 110 (my translation).

[85] *Ibidem*, p. 111 (my translation).

[86] Conforti (2018), pp. 29–30.

[87] *Ibidem*, p. 29 (my translation).

[88] *Ibidem* (my translation).

[89] Tomuschat (2014), pp. 155–158.

[90] For democratic principles within the framework of the European Union, see Starita (2011).

[91] Tomuschat (2014), p. 156.

[92] *Ibidem*, p. 157.

their guarantees,[93] it is not clear what legal means individuals and peoples currently have, *in international law*, to assert a broader right to democracy, conceived in all its components, vis-à-vis their own State.

It therefore seems to me that, in the concrete reality of international practice and in the light of the actually existing State institutions, one cannot speak of a right to democracy as a true and binding human right, but rather as a general political objective that the States and the entire international community must give themselves in order to advance the cause of human rights. Furthermore, one can also agree with the idea that the affirmation and consolidation of the democratic principle within the States constitutes a general framework that favors and promotes respect for human rights.[94]

25.3.5 Right to Good Governance

Not very different considerations apply to the human right to good governance, which appears to be a further development of the democratic principle. The concept underlying the principle of good governance is that the full enjoyment of human rights depends not only on an apparatus of democratic government, but also on the concrete behavior of the bodies and institutions governing the State: transparency, professionalism and accountability of these bodies, participation of civil society and adherence to the rule of law.

In these terms, the principle of good governance has been developed mainly by some international economic organizations, such as the World Bank,[95] the International Monetary Fund (IMF), and the African Development Bank. This principle was then taken up by the Commission on Human Rights and then also included in the *United Nations Millennium Declaration*[96] and the *World Summit Outcome*.[97] The principle has also found its place in EU law.[98]

In my view, even this principle must be understood not as a real human right, but as a guiding principle of a political nature, aimed at promoting a structure of government that is genuinely capable of ensuring the enjoyment of all human rights.

---

[93]See above, Chap. 22.

[94]For this view see Tomuschat (2014), p. 155.

[95]See World Bank, *Governance: The World Bank Experience*, Washington, 1994. The World Bank has described the principle of good governance as follows: "Good governance is epitomized by predictable, open, and enlightened policy-making [. . .], a bureaucracy imbued with a professional ethos; an executive arm of government accountable for its actions; and a strong civil society participating in public affairs; and all behaving under the rule of law" (*ibidem*, p. vii).

[96]GA Res. 55/2, 8 September 2000, para. 13.

[97]GA Res. 60/1, 16 September 2005, paras. 11, 21, 39.

[98]See, e.g., TFEU, Art. 15; EUCh, Art. 41.

25.3.6 Conclusions

In conclusion, the collective rights described above[99] present uncertainties as to their juridical basis, the holders of the rights, the bearers of the obligations, and especially as to their legally binding content. These uncertainties, in my view, do not depend on defects in the formulation of these rights in the relevant international acts, but rather on shortcomings in their nature and in that of the possible corresponding obligations. In fact, these are not rights that the State can effectively guarantee through its own negative obligations, or positive and immediate obligations, nor through obligations "of progressive realization".

Actually, in my opinion, these are not real human rights to which legally binding obligations of States can correspond; but rather general objectives of improvement and progress of both the State-apparatus and the State-community and, above all, of the entire international community. Their realization creates general situations and conditions (development, full use of resources, peace, democracy, good governance) that are favorable, and sometimes even necessary, for the full enjoyment of all human rights. But the international acts relating to these objectives dictate neither the legal constraints, nor the means, nor the resources for the attainment of these far-reaching and long-term objectives, which remain within the discretion of States and which are also, in certain respects, beyond the control of States and of the international community as a whole.

Therefore, in relation to these objectives, one should generally speak, in the present time, of political goals and programs that are not mandatory for individual States and the international community.

However, this negative conclusion must be downsized, if one places oneself in the perspective of certain conventional human rights systems, particularly the African system, which is favored by the fact that the African Charter expressly provides for some of these collective rights. In fact, both the Commission and the African Court have at times held States responsible for violations of these rights, especially the right to development and the right to natural resources,[100] and have attributed entitlement to these rights both to the population of a State and to specific ethnic groups considered as indigenous peoples.[101] Consider also the extensive interpretation of the right to property and the right to natural wealth and resources of indigenous peoples and other ethnic minorities that is developing within the Inter-American human rights system.[102] Therefore, in these regional systems, the right to development and the right to natural resources have acquired a certain normative

---

[99]See above, Sect. 25.3.

[100]See, e.g., ACmHPR, *SERAC and CESR v. Nigeria*, paras. 53–58; *Centre for Minority Rights Development and Minority Rights Group v. Kenya*, paras. 277–298; *Sudan Human Rights Organisation & Centre on Housing Rights and Evictions (COHRE) v. Sudan*, paras. 217–224; ACtHPR, *African Commission on Human and Peoples' Rights v. Kenya*, paras. 201–211.

[101]See Cadin (2019), pp. 194–202.

[102]See above, Sect. 25.2.

content. Moreover, as has also been noted by some authors,[103] these rights can to a certain extent reinforce the content of other human rights, such as the right to property or the subsistence rights.

Finally, it cannot be excluded that, over time, others of the aforementioned general objectives may also take the form of more precise and specific commitments, and thus produce genuine rights and obligations. For example, the democratic principle and that of good governance could, over time, give rise to the right of individuals and groups of individuals to demand respect for the rule of law from the State.[104]

25.4 Human Rights Between Individual and Collective Interests

There is frequent talk today of certain human rights, which cannot be properly defined as "collective", because they are mainly intended to protect individuals; but they also protect broader public or collective interests, which can (or should) be claimed by associations, committees or other groups of persons. In other words, in these cases, individualistic interests in the protection of human rights are strongly intertwined with public interests. This is particularly the case with regard to security and environmental protection.

25.4.1 Right to Human Security

Since the 1990s, the concept of the "right to human security"[105] has gradually emerged, particularly within the United Nations. This concept has gained international notoriety thanks to the *United Nations Development Programme* (UNDP), which, in a 1993 report,[106] criticized the traditional idea that security should be conceived only as the military security of States; and stated that "security should be reinterpreted as security for people, not security for land".[107]

Subsequently, the UNDP, in other reports, developed the new concept of human security, arguing, in summary, that security concerns not only States, but also individuals and groups of individuals; and that it must deal not only with defense against armed conflict, but also with other dangers to persons, such as hunger, disease, poverty, attacks on physical security and freedom, and other forms of oppression of people; and this in the general perspective of the freedom of people

[103] See, e.g., Pustorino (2020), p. 223.

[104] See Cassese (2003–2004), vol. II, p. 111.

[105] Pisillo Mazzeschi (2017) and the doctrine cited therein, pp. 353–354, footnotes 1 and 2.

[106] UNDP, *Human Development Report 1993*, New York, 1993.

[107] *Ibidem*, p. 1.

from fear and from need. More specifically, the UNDP, in a 1994 report,[108] speaks of economic, sanitary, environmental, personal, community and political security.[109]

This innovative concept of human security has had an influence both on a group of States[110] and non-governmental organizations, which have set up the so-called *Human Security Network*,[111] and on the United Nations, where ad hoc committees and commissions have been established,[112] reports by the Secretary-General have been submitted[113] and resolutions adopted by the General Assembly.[114] In essence, the concept of human security has ended up acquiring an important role in the foreign policy of a group of States,[115] in debates and resolutions within the United Nations, among international policy-makers, and in doctrinal debate. The new concept has achieved the aim of broadening the traditional concept, which was only pertinent to the military security of States.

However, moving from the field of politics to the field of law, the problem with the concept of human security is that it has a very broad, vague and indeterminate content; it is therefore difficult to give it a precise definition, especially for the purposes of its use in the field of human rights. On this point there are various doctrinal theories.

According to a first approach,[116] human security would not be an autonomous legal notion that intends to influence existing law, but only a guide for certain operational political choices of States. In essence, it would be only a political concept and not also a legal one.

On the contrary, according to a second approach, there would be a link between human security and human rights, and therefore one could speak of a real right of individuals and groups of individuals to human security. However, within this doctrinal approach, different theories coexist on how to define the content of this

[108]UNDP, *Human Development Report 1994*, New York, 1994, esp. pp. 23–25.

[109]These definitions mean: freedom from poverty, access to care and protection from disease, protection against pollution, physical protection against torture, war and other crimes, the right to maintain cultural traditions, and freedom from political oppression.

[110]Among the main promoters of the concept are the Governments of Canada, Norway, Switzerland and Japan.

[111]The first meeting of the Human Security Network was held in Lysoen, Norway, in 1999. Since then there have been several other meetings of the group.

[112]The Commission on Human Security was established in 2001. Subsequently, in 2004, the High-level Panel on Threats, Challenges and Change presented the document *A More Secure World: Our Shared Responsibility*. See also the document *2005 World Summit Outcome*, GA Res. 60/1, 16 September 2005.

[113]See, e.g., Secretary General, *Human Security*, UN Doc. A/64/701, 8 March 2010; UN Doc. A/66/763, *Follow-up to General Assembly resolution 64/291 on human security*, 5 April 2012; UN Doc. A/68/685, *Follow-up to General Assembly resolution 66/290 on human security*, 23 December 2013.

[114]See, e.g., GA Res. 66/290, 10 September 2012.

[115]Some States (Canada and Norway) have adopted the concept of "human security" as a guideline for their foreign policy.

[116]See, e.g., Ryngaert and Noortmann (2014).

right. Some authors[117] argue that the right to human security may serve in the future as a unifying principle of various norms in the areas of human rights, humanitarian law, refugee law and international criminal law. Other writers[118] argue that the right to human security would not add anything to existing human rights, but would have the function of pushing States and international institutions towards the common unifying objective of the full enjoyment of human rights. Finally, other authors[119] believe that this concept is linked, in essence, only to those human rights that relate to the basic needs of the person.

In my view, human security cannot be considered as a separate and autonomous human right in itself, and such as to impose on States immediate or even "progressive" obligations. Its content is too vague, complex and indeterminate to be capable of giving individuals, or groups of individuals, true rights to be asserted against States. Human security appears rather as a kind of "container", which includes within it a wide range of *specific human rights*, which pursue the common purpose of protecting the security of individuals and groups of individuals: in particular, the right to life, the prohibition of torture and inhuman or degrading treatment, the prohibition of slavery, the right to liberty and physical security of persons, and the subsistence rights.

Therefore, if the concept of human security has not created a new autonomous human right, what is its legal value? At the present time, it seems to me that, from a human rights perspective, it should be conceived as a *general political objective* of the States and of the international community as a whole, aimed at unifying and strengthening the effective implementation of all of the above specific human rights strictly related to the security of people.

However, the consensus that has been achieved so far within the United Nations on this concept suggests that, if the recognition and acceptance of the international community is consolidated in the future, it can develop and become a general principle of international law operating in the field of human rights and humanitarian law.[120] The human security principle could be useful to: (*a*) guide the interpretation of certain specific norms on human rights and humanitarian law which are included in the principle; (*b*) give systematic coherence to these norms; (*c*) promote their progressive development.

[117] Sunga (2009), esp. p. 143.

[118] Tomuschat (2014), pp. 159–161.

[119] Focarelli (2013), p. 54.

[120] I intend to refer to those general principles of international law that derive, for a process of abstraction or induction, from existing customary norms (those on fundamental human rights mentioned above). See above, Sect. 3.3.

25.4.2 Right to a Healthy Environment

The existence of a human right to a healthy environment[121] is highly controversial, especially because of the scarcity of normative sources on it and the vagueness of its content.

As regards the first aspect, most human rights treaties and acts of a general character do not provide for the human right to a healthy environment. In fact, the Universal Declaration, the two International Covenants, the European Convention, the American Convention and the European Social Charter make no mention of this right. The same conclusion can be drawn from the most important sectorial human rights treaties. Nor do I believe that the various provisions contained in these treaties, which aim to protect the health or, more generally, adequate standards of living of people,[122] can be interpreted as indirect or implicit references to the right to a healthy environment.

This silence on the environment on the part of the main international human rights instruments can be explained by several reasons.[123] The most obvious reason is that these instruments were prepared at a time in history when the normative field of international environmental law had not yet developed, let alone the idea that environmental protection should be considered as a value pertaining to the dignity of the human person and also a collective value for humanity. Another important reason is that international environmental law has developed, especially in the early years, as a typically interstate law, i.e. through a series of treaties that only regulate relations between States. This interstate character was hardly reconcilable with the human rights legal regime, based on relations between States and individuals; and this created a sort of "barrier" between the field of international environmental law and that of the protection of human rights.

Indeed, the right to a healthy environment, in its connotation of human right, has long been affirmed especially in non-binding legal acts. Among the main ones, I can mention the 1972 Stockholm Declaration,[124] the UN General Assembly's resolutions 37/7 of 1982 and 45/94 of 1990,[125] the 1992 Rio Declaration on Environment and Development,[126] the Final Declaration of the 2020 World Summit

[121]The literature dealing with the human right to a healthy environment is extensive. I limit myself to mentioning: Boyle and Anderson (1996); Castellaneta (2000); Francioni (2010); Anton and Shelton (2011). See also, recently, Rossi (2019).

[122]On these provisions see above, Sects. 15.1, 15.2, 15.3 and 15.4.

[123]See Rossi (2019), pp. 159–160.

[124]*Declaration of the United Nations Conference on the Human Environment*, Stockholm 1972, A/CONF. 48/14/Rev. 1 and Corr.1. Cf. Principle 1: "Man has the fundamental right to freedom, equality and adequate conditions of life, in an environment of a quality that permits a life of dignity and well-being [. . .]".

[125]GA Res. 37/7, *World Charter for Nature*, 28 October 1982; GA Res. 45/94, 14 December 1990, para. 1.

[126]*Rio Declaration on Environment and Development*, 14 December 1992. See esp. Principles 1 and 10.

for Sustainable Development and the 2030 Agenda for Sustainable Development,[127] the ASEAN Declaration on Human Rights adopted in 2012.[128] But some of these acts, as has been noted,[129] adopt cautious formulas, insisting on the concept of sustainable development[130] and the commitments of States to protect the environment rather than the rights of individuals.

However, in a different direction, some important aspects should be emphasized. Firstly, there are some regional human rights treaties, adopted since the 1980s, which explicitly provide for the right to a healthy environment. The 1981 African Charter, in Article 24, states that:

> All peoples shall have the right to a general satisfactory environment favorable to their development.

The 1998 San Salvador Protocol, in Article 11, reads:

> 1. Everyone shall have the right to live in a healthy environment [. . .]
> 2. The States parties shall promote the protection, preservation, and improvement of the environment.

The 2004 Arab Charter also contains a provision (Art. 38) that contemplates the right of every person to a healthy environment. More specific treaties include the Aarhus Convention on access to information, public participation in decision-making and access to justice in environmental matters (Art. 1)[131] and the Escazú Regional Agreement on access to information, public participation and justice in environmental matters in Latin America and the Caribbean (Art. 4).[132]

A second aspect to be noted is that, in recent decades, the recognition of a human right to a healthy environment has occurred in many State legal systems, often at the level of constitutional norms. This fact could have an impact on the formation of a principle generally recognized by civilized nations *in foro domestico*.[133]

A third and even more important aspect is the practice of international human rights monitoring bodies.[134] As is well known, in the system of the European Convention on Human Rights, despite the lack of a provision on the right to a healthy environment, the Strasbourg bodies have extensively interpreted other rights expressly recognized, especially the right to private and family life, and have derived

---

[127] *Johannesburg Declaration of the World Summit on Sustainable Development*, 4 September 2002, para. 1; *Transforming Our World: The 2030 Agenda for Sustainable Development*, GA Res.70/1, 25 September 2015.

[128] *ASEAN Human Rights Declaration*, 19 November 2012, Principle 28(f).

[129] Tomuschat (2014), p. 151.

[130] For this approach see, especially, the Rio and Johannesburg Declarations and the 2030 Agenda.

[131] Convention on Access to Information, Public Participation in Decision-making and Access to Justice in Environmental Matters, Aarhus, 25 June 1998.

[132] Regional Agreement on Access to Information, Public Participation and Access to Justice in Environmental Matters in Latin America and the Caribbean, 4 March 2018.

[133] See above, Sect. 3.2.

[134] On this practice see Pavoni (2013).

from them a protection for the human right to a healthy environment, mainly in its procedural dimension. The latter is realized above all in the right of individuals to be informed by the State about activities that are seriously polluting or dangerous for the environment.[135] However, in the framework of the European Convention, the right to a healthy environment has maintained a predominantly individualistic dimension, with few openings towards the "collectivization" of cases relating to environmental disputes. This is also due to the fact that associations and other collective bodies have limits of access to the Strasbourg Court.

This has not happened in other regional human rights systems. In the Inter-American system, the situation is complex, because the human right to a healthy environment is intertwined, in somewhat contradictory ways, with the rights of indigenous peoples, especially those related to their traditional lands and natural resources. Sometimes the protection of the environment, for example through protected ecological areas, has come into conflict with the property rights of indigenous peoples; but, more often, the approach according to which the right to property constitutes a powerful ally of environmental protection has prevailed.[136] In any case, in the Inter-American system, the intertwining of individual and public interests in a healthy environment is more evident than in the European Convention.

Moreover, there have also been some interesting recent developments in the Inter-American system. First, mention should be made of an important advisory opinion on the relationship between environment and human rights, adopted by the Inter-American Court of Human Rights in 2017.[137] The opinion deals with the obligations of States with regard to the protection of the environment, in relation to the right to life and the right to human treatment provided for in Articles 4 and 5 of the American Convention. The Court has affirmed the existence of an autonomous human right to a healthy environment,[138] based on Article 11 of the San Salvador Protocol and Article 26 of the American Convention, and has also clarified the obligations on environmental protection arising from Articles 4 and 5 of that Convention. Secondly, the Inter-American Court has issued an important ruling in 2020 on the right to a healthy environment, in the case of the *Communities of the Lhaka Honrat Association*.[139] The Court said that States have not only an obligation to respect the environment, but also to ensure that obligation through measures to prevent violations. According to the Court:

> This obligation extends to the 'private sphere' in order to avoid 'third parties violating the protected rights', and 'encompasses all those legal, political, administrative and cultural measures that promote the safeguard of human rights' [...] at times, the States have the

[135]See, e.g., ECtHR, *López Ostra v. Spain*; *Hatton and Others v. UK*, Judgment of 8 July 2003; *Fadeyeva v. Russia*; *Hardy and Maile v. UK*; *Cordella and Others v. Italy*. For further examples see Pavoni (2013), pp. 32–47 and 121–132.

[136]Pavoni (2013), p. 70.

[137]IACtHR, *The Environment and Human Rights*.

[138]*Ibidem*, paras. 59 and 62–63.

[139]IACtHR, *Indigenous Communities of the Lhaka Honrat Association v. Argentina*.

> obligation to establish adequate mechanisms to monitor and supervise certain activities in order to ensure human rights, protecting them from actions of public entities and also private individuals.[140]

Moreover, the Court added that:

> [. . .] it should be stressed that the principle of prevention of environmental harm forms part of customary international law [. . .] Based on the duty of prevention, the Court has pointed out that 'States are bound to use all the means at their disposal to avoid activities under its jurisdiction causing significant harm to the environment'.[141]

The practice developed within the African human rights system, although not extensive, is even more favorable to the collective dimension of the right to a healthy environment.[142] Of course, this is facilitated by the fact that the African Charter provides for numerous human rights of a collective nature and that the provision on the right to a healthy environment (Art. 24) is addressed to peoples. In any case, this practice plays an important role in the process of progressive affirmation of the human right to a healthy environment. The famous *SERAC* decision of the African Court[143] and the *SERAP* decision of the ECOWAS Court[144] deserve to be highlighted.

Finally, it is worth noting one last aspect. It is true that international environmental law has mainly developed at interstate level. But today it is made up of a very large number of treaties that establish precise and detailed obligations between the contracting States in terms of environmental protection, prevention of pollution and reparation of environmental damage. In my view, it cannot be excluded that *some* of these obligations, although they are primarily interstate obligations, may be *interpreted* as obligations which are *also* addressed to individuals and are likely to create rights in their favor. Think, for example, of certain obligations of information or certain obligations of reparation for transboundary environmental damage. In other words, over time, there has been a necessary and logical convergence, in the name of protecting the environment as a goal for the whole of humanity, between the area of international environmental law and that of human rights. This convergence leads to a dilution of the old separation between the two areas. In this way, those individual rights that may be derived from international environmental law treaties can serve to clarify the content of the human right to a healthy environment.

In conclusion, from the point of view of normative sources, it seems to me that the old shortcomings regarding the right to a healthy environment contained in the less

---

[140] *Ibidem*, para. 207.

[141] *Ibidem*, para. 208.

[142] See Pavoni (2013), pp. 96–107.

[143] ACmHPR, *Social and Economic Rights Action Center and Other (SERAC) v. Nigeria.*

[144] CCJ, *The Registered Trustees of the Socio-Economic Rights and Accountability Project (SERAP) v. Nigeria & UBEC.*

recent human rights treaties can now be overcome by means of the elements that I have highlighted so far.

There remains the problem of the *content* of the right to a healthy environment,[145] which is still considered by many to be too vague and indefinite to meet the requirements for the recognition of a new right under the international human rights regime.[146] The UN General Assembly itself, establishing guidelines for States for the creation of new regulatory instruments on human rights, has established, inter alia, as requirements, that each new norm must:

> (a) Be consistent with the existing body of international human rights law [...]
> (c) Be sufficiently precise to give rise to identifiable and practicable rights and obligations.[147]

In my opinion, the requirement for the precision of the norm is correct. However, on closer inspection, if one looks at the whole system of international human rights law, one notices that the requirement that the content of the norm be precise is not always strictly respected. In this book it has been seen that the degree of precision of the human rights content is not uniform at all, on the contrary, it is very variable. There are some rights that have a precise and well circumscribed content, others that have a broader content, still others with such extensive and complex content that they can be considered as "containers" of more specific rights. Of course, there is also a limit, beyond which the excessive vagueness and indeterminacy of the content of a right leads to the exclusion that it is a real legal right and to classify it as a mere political and non-binding objective.

In the light of these premises, it seems to me that the right to a healthy environment, although it has maintained for some time a vague and indeterminate character, has, over time, gone through an evolutionary process, especially by virtue of the practice mentioned above, which has gradually ended up specifying its normative content. This is also the opinion of the Special Rapporteur, appointed by the Human Rights Council[148] to study the human rights obligations relating to the enjoyment of a healthy environment. In fact, he has stated that:

> [T]he time has come for the United Nations to formally recognize the human right to a safe, clean, healthy and sustainable environment.[149]

The right to a healthy environment can be understood, *broadly*, as the right of individuals and groups of individuals to obtain that States use and preserve the

---

[145] Rossi (2019), pp. 178–179.

[146] See, e.g., Tomuschat (2014), pp. 151–154.

[147] GA Res. 41/120, *Setting international standards in the field of human rights*, 4 December 1986, para. 4 (a) and (c).

[148] HRC, *Human rights and the environment*, A/HRC/RES/19/10, 19 April 2012.

[149] See GA, *Human rights obligations relating to the enjoyment of a safe, clean, healthy and sustainable environment*, 19 July 2018 (A/73/188), para. 37.

environment in the best possible way,[150] based on standards that have been established especially in the extensive practice of conventional environmental law. It seems to me that mainly State obligations "of progressive realization" correspond to this general right to a healthy environment; and that in these obligations the balance between the duties of the States relating to the environment and their "available means and resources" is very important, but also difficult.[151]

However, one can perhaps also identify more specific rights to which immediate State obligations correspond: for example, the obligation to prevent with due diligence significant environmental damage, the obligation to repress the relative violations, and the obligation to give reparation to victims. These obligations are strengthened and clarified when they are functionally linked to other obligations of States arising from other human rights, such as especially the right to life. The recent statements contained in General Comment No. 36 of the Human Rights Committee are important in this regard.[152]

Finally, other immediate State obligations may arise from some procedural rights of individuals, which are also very specific, such as, for example, their right to be informed about certain potentially polluting activities and to participate in certain environmental risk assessment procedures.

References

Anton DK, Shelton D (2011) Environmental protection and human rights. CUP, Cambridge

Bedjaoui M (1979) Towards a new international economic order. Holmes & Meier Publishers, New York-London

Boyle AE, Anderson MR (eds) (1996) Human rights approaches to environmental protection. Clarendon Press, Oxford

Cadin R (2019) Profili ricostruttivi e linee evolutive del diritto internazionale dello sviluppo. Giappichelli, Torino

Capotorti F (1979) Study on the rights of persons belonging to ethnic, religious and linguistic minorities. UN Doc. E/CN.4/Sub.2/384/Rev.1

Capotorti F (1992) Il regime delle minoranze nel sistema delle Nazioni Unite e secondo l'art. 27 del Patto sui diritti civili e politici. Riv int dir uomo: 102–112

Cassese A (Gaeta P ed) (2003–2004) Diritto internazionale, Vol. I: I lineamenti, Vol. II: Problemi della comunità internazionale. Il Mulino, Bologna

Castellaneta M (2000) L'individuo e la protezione dell'ambiente nel diritto internazionale. RDI 83:913–964

Castellino J (2014) International law and self-determination: peoples, indigenous peoples, and minorities. In: Walter C, Von Ungern-Sternberg A, Abushov K (eds) Self-determination and secession in international law. OUP, Oxford, pp 27–44

Conforti B (Iovane M ed) (2018) Diritto internazionale, 11th edn. Editoriale Scientifica, Napoli

[150]See Rossi (2019), pp. 179–181.

[151]See above, Sect. 8.2.3.

[152]HRCtee, General Comment No. 36, 3 September 2019, para. 62: "The obligations of States parties under international environmental law should thus inform the content of article 6 of the Covenant, and the obligation of States parties to respect and ensure the right to life should also inform their relevant obligations under international environmental law".

Deschênes J (1985) Proposal concerning a definition of the term "minority". UN Doc. E/CN.4/Sub.2/31
Focarelli C (2013) La persona umana nel diritto internazionale. Il Mulino, Bologna
Francioni F (2010) International human rights in an environmental horizon. Eur J Int Law 21:41–55
Kälin W, Künzli J (2019) The law of international human rights protection, 2nd edn. OUP, Oxford-New York
Lenzerini F (ed) (2008) Reparations for indigenous peoples: international and comparative perspectives. OUP, Oxford
Martinez Cobo J (1983) Study of the problem of discrimination against indigenous populations, conclusions, proposals and recommendations. UN Doc. E/CN.4/Sub.2/1983/21/ Add.8, 30 September 1983
Martinez Cobo J (1986) Study of the problem of discrimination against indigenous populations. UN Doc. E/CN.4/Sub.2/1986/7 and Add. 1-4
Meijknecht A (2001) Towards international personality: the position of minorities and indigenous peoples in international law. Intersentia, Antwerpen-Groningen-Oxford
Pavoni R (2013) Interesse pubblico e diritti individuali nella giurisprudenza ambientale della Corte europea dei diritti umani. Editoriale Scientifica, Napoli
Pisillo Mazzeschi R (2008) Responsabilité de l'État pour violation des obligations positives relatives aux droits de l'homme. RC 333:175–506
Pisillo Mazzeschi R (2016) Popoli indigeni. In: Enciclopedia di Bioetica e Scienza Giuridica, Parte giuridica, ESI, Napoli, pp 459–473
Pisillo Mazzeschi R (2017) Sicurezza umana e diritto internazionale. In: Triggiani E et al (eds) Dialoghi con Ugo Villani, vol I. Cacucci, Bari, pp 353–362
Pocar F (1998) Note sulla giurisprudenza del Comitato dei diritti dell'uomo in materia di minoranze. In: Bartole S, Olivetti Rason N, Pegoraro L (eds) La tutela giuridica delle minoranze. Cedam, Padova, pp 31–39
Pustorino P (2006) Questioni in materia di tutela delle minoranze nel diritto internazionale ed europeo. Studi integr eur 1:259–279
Pustorino P (2020) Lezioni di tutela internazionale dei diritti umani, 2nd edn. Cacucci, Bari
Rossi V (2019) Il riconoscimento del diritto universale a un ambiente sano: questioni aperte e percorsi evolutivi. In: Cataldi G (ed) I diritti umani a settant'anni dalla Dichiarazione universale delle Nazioni Unite, vol I. Editoriale Scientifica, Napoli, pp 157–189
Ryngaert C, Noortmann M (2014) Human security and international law: the challenge of non-state actors. In: Ryngaert C et al (eds) Human security and international law: the challenge of non-state actors. Intersentia, Cambridge, pp 1–11
Starita M (2011) I principi democratici nel diritto dell'Unione Europea. Giappichelli, Torino
Sunga LS (2009) The concept of human security: does it add anything of value to international legal theory or practice? In: Frick ML, Oberprantacher A (eds) Power and justice in international relations: interdisciplinary approaches to global challeges. Ashgate, Farham, pp 131–146
Tancredi A (2001) La secessione nel diritto internazionale. Cedam, Padova
Thornberry P (1991) International law and the rights of minorities. Clarendon Press, Oxford
Tomuschat C (2014) Human rights: between idealism and realism, 3rd edn. OUP, Oxford

1. Websites

- African Commission on Human and Peoples' Rights
  https://www.achpr.org
- African Court on Human and Peoples' Rights
  https://www.achpr.org/afchpr/
- Committee Against Torture
  https://www.ohchr.org/en/hrbodies/cat/pages/catindex.aspx
- Committee on Economic, Social and Cultural Rights
  https://www.ohchr.org/en/hrbodies/cescr/pages/cescrindex.aspx
- Committee on Enforced Disappearances
  https://www.ohchr.org/en/hrbodies/ced/pages/cedindex.aspx
- Committee on Migrant Workers
  https://www.ohchr.org/en/hrbodies/cmw/pages/cmwindex.aspx
- Committee on the Elimination of Discrimination against Women
  https://www.ohchr.org/en/hrbodies/cedaw/pages/cedawindex.aspx
- Committee on the Elimination of Racial Discrimination
  https://www.ohchr.org/en/hrbodies/cerd/pages/cerdindex.aspx
- Committee on the Rights of Persons with Disabilities
  https://www.ohchr.org/en/hrbodies/crpd/pages/crpdindex.aspx
- Committee on the Rights of the Child
  https://www.ohchr.org/en/hrbodies/crc/pages/crcindex.aspx
- Economic and Social Council
  https://www.un.org/ecosoc/en/home
- ECOWAS Community Court of Justice
  http://prod.courtecowas.org/
- European Commission of Human Rights
  https://www.refworld.org/publisher/COECOMMHR.html
- European Committee of Social Rights
  https://www.coe.int/en/web/european-social-charter/european-committee-of-social-rights
- European Court of Human Rights
  https://echr.coe.int/Pages/home.aspx?p=home
  https://hudoc.echr.coe.int/eng

R. Pisillo Mazzeschi, *International Human Rights Law*,
https://doi.org/10.1007/978-3-030-77032-7

- European Court of Justice
  https://curia.europa.eu/jcms/jcms/j_6/en/
- European General Court
  https://curia.europa.eu/jcms/jcms/p1_217427/en/
- General Assembly of the United Nations
  https://www.un.org/en/ga/
- Human Rights Committee
  https://www.ohchr.org/en/hrbodies/ccpr/pages/ccprindex.aspx
- Human Rights Council
  https://www.ohchr.org/en/hrbodies/hrc/pages/home.aspx
- Inter-American Commission on Human Rights
  http://www.oas.org/en/iachr/
- Inter-American Court of Human Rights
  https://www.corteidh.or.cr/index.cfm?lang=en
- International Arbitral Tribunals (*RIAA*)
  https://legal.un.org/riaa/
- International Court of Justice
  https://www.icj-cij.org/en
- International Criminal Court
  https://www.icc-cpi.int/
- International Criminal Tribunal for Rwanda
  https://unictr.irmct.org/
- International Criminal Tribunal for the Former Yugoslavia
  https://www.icty.org/
- International Law Commission
  https://legal.un.org/ilc/
- International Military Tribunal of Nuremberg
  https://avalon.law.yale.edu/subject_menus/imt.asp
- Permanent Court of Arbitration
  https://pca-cpa.org/
- Permanent Court of International Justice
  https://www.icj-cij.org/en/pcij
- Security Council of the United Nations
  https://www.un.org/securitycouncil/
- Special Tribunal for Lebanon
  https://www.stl-tsl.org/en

2. Table of Cases

Permanent Court of International Justice (PCIJ)

- *Mavrommatis Palestine Concessions Case (Jurisdiction) (Greece v. United Kingdom)*, Judgment of 30 August 1924

International Court of Justice (ICJ)

- *Accordance with International Law of the Unilateral Declaration of Independence in respect of Kosovo*, Advisory Opinion of 22 July 2010
- *Application of the Convention on the Prevention and Punishment of the Crime of Genocide (Bosnia and Herzegovina v. Yugoslavia), Preliminary Objections*, Judgment of 11 July 1996
- *Application of the Convention on the Prevention and Punishment of the Crime of Genocide (Bosnia and Herzegovina v. Serbia and Montenegro)*, Judgment of 26 February 2007
- *Application of the Convention on the Prevention and Punishment of the Crime of Genocide (Croatia v. Serbia)*, Judgment of 3 February 2015
- *Application of the Convention on the Prevention and Punishment of the Crime of Genocide (The Gambia v. Myanmar)*, Order of 23 January 2020
- *Application of the International Convention for the Suppression of the Financing of Terrorism and of the International Convention on the Elimination of All Forms of Racial Discrimination (Ukraine v. Russian Federation), Preliminary Objections*, Judgment of 8 November 2019
- *Application of the International Convention on the Elimination of All Forms of Racial Discrimination (Georgia v. Russian Federation)*, Request for the Indication of Provisional Measures, Order of 15 October 2008
- *Application of the International Convention on the Elimination of All Forms of Racial Discrimination (Georgia v. Russian Federation)*, Judgment of 1 April 2011
- *Armed Activities on the Territory of the Congo (Democratic Republic of the Congo v. Uganda)*, Judgment of 19 December 2005

R. Pisillo Mazzeschi, *International Human Rights Law*,
https://doi.org/10.1007/978-3-030-77032-7

- *Armed Activities on the Territory of the Congo (New Application: 2002) (Democratic Republic of the Congo v. Rwanda)*, Judgment of 3 February 2006
- *Arrest Warrant of 11 April 2000 (Democratic Republic of the Congo v. Belgium)*, Judgment of 14 February 2002
- *Avena and Other Mexican Nationals (Mexico v. United States of America)*, Judgment of 31 March 2004
- *Barcelona Traction, Light and Power Company, Limited (New Application: 1962) (Belgium v. Spain), Second Phase*, Judgment of 5 February 1970
- *Corfu Channel Case (The United Kingdom v. Albania), Merits*, Judgment of 9 April 1949
- *East Timor (Portugal v. Australia)*, Judgment of 30 June 1995
- *Gabčikovo-Nagymaros Project (Hungary v. Slovakia)*, Judgment of 25 September 1997
- *Jadhav Case (India v. Pakistan)*, Judgment of 17 July 2019
- *Jurisdictional Immunities of the State (Germany v. Italy: Greece Intervening)*, Judgment of 3 February 2012
- *LaGrand (Germany v. United States of America), Merits*, Judgment of 27 June 2001
- *Legal Consequences for States of the Continued Presence of South Africa in Namibia (South West Africa) notwithstanding Security Council Resolution 276 (1970)*, Advisory Opinion of 21 June 1971
- *Legal Consequences of the Construction of a Wall in the Occupied Palestinian Territory*, Advisory Opinion of 9 July 2004
- *Legal Consequences of the Separation of the Chagos Archipelago from Mauritius in 1965*, Advisory Opinion of 25 February 2019
- *Legality of the Threat or Use of Nuclear Weapons*, Advisory Opinion of 8 July 1996
- *Legality of Use of Force (Serbia and Montenegro v. Belgium, Canada, France, Germany, Italy, The Netherlands, Portugal and The United Kingdom)*, Judgments of 15 December 2004
- *Military and Paramilitary Activities in and against Nicaragua (Nicaragua v. United States), Jurisdiction and Admissibility*, Judgment of 26 November 1984
- *Military and Paramilitary Activities in and against Nicaragua (Nicaragua v. United States), Merits*, Judgment of 27 June 1986
- *Questions relating to the Obligation to Prosecute or Extradite (Belgium v. Senegal)*, Judgment of 20 July 2012
- *Pulp Mills on the River Uruguay (Argentina v. Uruguay)*, Judgment of 20 April 2010
- *Reservations to the Convention on the Prevention and Punishment of the Crime of Genocide*, Advisory Opinion of 28 May 1951
- *United States Diplomatic and Consular Staff in Tehran (United States v. Iran), Merits*, Judgment of 24 May 1980
- *Western Sahara*, Advisory Opinion of 16 October 1975

Iran-United States Claims Tribunal (IUSCT)

- *Yeager v. Islamic Republic of Iran*, Decision of 2 November 1987, 17 *Reports* 92

Other Arbitration Tribunals

- *Alabama claims of the United States of America v. Great Britain*, Award of 14 September 1872, in De Martens (1975), pp. 698-775; Moore (1898), pp. 495-682

Human Rights Committee (HRCtee)

- *A v. Australia*, Communication No. 560/1993, Views of 3 April 1997
- *Ackla v. Togo*, Communication No. 505/1992, Views of 25 March 1996
- *Alzery v. Sweden*, Communication No. 1416/2005, Views of 25 October 2006
- *A. S. v. Nepal*, Communication No. 2077/2011, Views of 6 November 2015
- *Aumeeruddy-Cziffra et al. v. Mauritius*, Communication No. 035/1978, Views of 9 April 1981
- *Baban et al. v. Australia*, Communication No. 1014/2001, Views of 6 August 2003
- *Basongo Bondonga v. Democratic Republic of the Congo*, Communication No. 1483/ 2006, Views of 30 July 2009
- *Baumgarten v. Germany*, Communication No. 960/2000, Views of 19 September 2003
- *Bautista de Arellana v. Colombia*, Communication No. 563/1993, Views of 27 October 1995
- *Bwalya v. Zambia*, Communication No. 314/1988, Views of 14 July 1993
- *C. v. Australia*, Communication No. 900/1999, Views of 28 October 2002
- *Celiberti de Casariego v. Uruguay*, Communication No. 56/1979, Views of 29 July 1981
- *Chongwe v. Zambia*, Communication No. 821/1998, Views of 25 October 2000
- *Coeriel and Aurik v. The Netherlands*, Communication No. 453/1991, Views of 31 October 1994
- *Kaba v. Canada*, Communication No. 1465/2006, Views of 25 March 2010
- *Karker v. France*, Communication No. 833/1998, Views of 26 October 2000
- *El Ghar v. Libyan Arab Jamahiriya*, Communication No. 1107/2002, Views of 2 November 2004
- *Faure v. Australia*, Communication No. 1036/2001, Views of 31 October 2005
- *González del Rio v. Peru*, Communication No. 263/1987, Views of 28 October 1992
- *Gordon C. Van Duzen v. Canada*, Communication No. 50/1979, Views of 7 April 1982
- *Grioua v. Algeria*, Communication No. 1327/2004, Views of 10 July 2007
- *Gueye et al. v. France*, Communication No. 196/1985, Views of 3 April 1989

- *Hinostroza Solís v. Peru*, Communication No. 1016/2001, Views of 27 March 2006
- *Huamán v. Peru*, Communication No. 1153/2003, Views of 24 October 2005
- *Hudoyberganova v. Uzbekistan*, Communication No. 931/2000, Views of 5 November 2004
- *Jacobs v. Belgium*, Communication No. 943/2000, Views of 7 July 2004
- *Judge v. Canada*, Communication No. 829/1998, Views of 5 August 2003
- *Kall v. Poland*, Communication No. 552/1993, Views of 14 July 1997
- *Kennedy v. Trinidad and Tobago*, Communication No. 845/1999, Views of 26 March 2002
- *Kitok v. Sweden*, Communication No. 197/1985, Views of 27 July 1988
- *Kivenmaa v. Finland*, Communication No. 412/1990, Views of 31 March 1994
- *Korneenko et al. v. Belarus*, Communication No. 1274/2004, Views of 31 October 2006
- *Lansman (Ilmari) et al. v. Finland*, Communication No. 511/1992, Views of 26 October1994
- *Länsman (Jouni) et al. v. Finland*, Communication No. 671/1995, Views of 30 October 1996
- *Laureano Atachahua v. Peru*, Communication No. 540/1993, Views of 25 March 1996
- *L.T.K. v. Finland*, Communication No. 185/1984, Inadmissibility decision of 9 July 1985
- *Leirvåg et al. v. Norway*, Communication No. 1155/2003, Views of 3 November 2004
- *Lopez Burgos v. Uruguay*, Communication No. 52/1979, Views of 29 July 1981
- *Love et al. v. Australia*, Communication No. 983/2001, Views of 25 March 2003
- *Lovelace v. Canada*, Communication No. 024/1977, Views of 30 July 1981
- *Maksudov and Others v. Kyrgyzstan and Uzbekistan*, Communications Nos. 1461/2006, 1462/2006, 1476/2006, 1477/2006, Views of 16 July 2008
- *Marshall et al. and the Mikmaq tribal society v. Canada*, Communication No. 205/1986, Views of 4 November 1991
- *Matkarim Aminov v. Turkmenistan*, Communication No. 2220/2012, Views of 14 July 2016
- *Mahuika et al. v. New Zealand*, Communication No. 547/1993, Views of 27 October 2000
- *Mojica v. Dominican Republic*, Communication No. 449/1991, Views of 15 July 1994
- *Ng v. Canada*, Communication No. 469/1991, Views of 5 November 1993
- *Peltonen v. Finland*, Communication No. 492/1992, Views of 21 July 1994
- *Pereira Montero v. Uruguay*, Communication No. 106/1981, Views of 31 March 1983
- *Poma Poma v. Peru*, Communication No. 1457/2006, Views of 27 March 2009
- *Q v. Denmark*, Communication No. 2001/2010, Views of 1 April 2015
- *Queenan v. Canada*, Communication No. 1379/2005, Decision on admissibility of 26 July 2005

- *Radosevic v. Germany*, Communication No. 1292/2004, Decision on admissibility of 22 July 2005
- *Rodríguez v. Uruguay*, Communication No. 322/1988, Views of 19 July 1994
- *Rouse v. The Philippines*, Communication No. 1089/2002, Views of 25 July 2005
- *Sarma v. Sri Lanka*, Communication No. 950/2000, Views of 16 July 2003
- *Sayadi and Vinck v. Belgium*, Communication No. 1472/2006, Views of 22 October 2008
- *Singh Bhinder v. Canada*, Communication No. 208/1986, Views of 9 November 1989
- *Suarez de Guerrero v. Colombia*, Communication No. 45/1979, Views of 31 March 1982
- *Teitiota v. New Zealand*, Communication No. 2728/2016, Views of 7 January 2020
- *Teran Jijon v. Ecuador*, Communication No. 277/1988, Views of 26 March 1992
- *V.D.A. v. Argentina*, Communication No. 1608/2007, Views of 29 March 2011
- *Wallmann and Others v. Austria*, Communication No. 1002/2001, Views of 1 April 2004
- *Warsame v. Canada*, Communication 1959/2010, Views of 21 July 2011
- *Yevdokimov and Rezanov v. Russia*, Communication No. 1410/2005, Views of 21 March 2011
- *Zalesskaya v. Belarus*, Communication No. 1604/2007, Views of 28 March 2011

Committee Against Torture (CteeAT)

- *M. Qani Halimi-Nedzibi v. Austria*, Communication No. 8/1991, Views of 18 November 1993

Committee on the Elimination of Discrimination Against Women (CteeEDAW)

- *J. I. v. Finland*, Communication No. 103/2016, Views of 5 March 2018
- *The Vienna Intervention Centre against Domestic Violence v. Austria*, Communication No. 6/2005, Views of 6 August 2007

Committee on the Elimination of Racial Discrimination (CteeERD)

- *Dawas and Shava v. Denmark*, Communication No. 46/2009, Opinion of 6 March 2012
- *Hagan v. Australia*, Communication No. 26/2002, Opinion of 20 March 2003
- *Qatar v. The United Arab Emirates* (Jurisdiction), Decision of 27 August 2019
- *Qatar v. The United Arab Emirates* (Admissibility), Decision of 27 August 2019
- *Qatar v. Kingdom of Saudi Arabia* (Jurisdiction), Decision of 27 August 2019

- *Qatar v. Kingdom of Saudi Arabia* (Admissibility), Decision of 27 August 2019
- *Saada Mohamad Adan v. Denmark*, Communication No. 43/2008, Opinion of 13 August 2010
- *State of Palestine v. Israel* (Jurisdiction), Decision of 12 December 219, Parts I, II and III

European Commission of Human Rights (ECmHR)

- *Arrowsmith v. The United Kingdom*, Decision of 16 May 1977.
- *Austria v. Italy*, Decision of 11 January 1961
- *France, Norway, Denmark, Sweden and The Netherlands v. Turkey*, Report of 7 December 1985
- *H. v. Norway*, Decision of 19 May 1992
- *Iversen v. Norway*, Decision of 17 December 1963
- *Lawless v. Ireland*, Report of 12 April 1960
- *Smith Kline and French Laboratories Ltd v. The Netherlands*, Decision of 4 October 1990
- *W.P. v. The United Kingdom*, Decision of 13 May 1980
- *X v. Federal Republic of Germany*, Decision of 5 July 1977
- *X v. Federal Republic of Germany*, Decision of 10 March 1981

European Court of Human Rights (ECtHR)

- *A. v. The United Kingdom*, Judgment of 23 September 1998
- *A. and Others v. The United Kingdom*, Grand Chamber, Judgment of 19 February 2009
- *Adolf v. Austria*, Judgment of 26 March 1982
- *Ahmed and Others v. The United Kingdom*, Judgment of 2 September 1998
- *Airey v. Ireland*, Judgment of 9 October 1979
- *Akdivar and Others v. Turkey*, Grand Chamber, Judgment of 16 September 1996
- *Akkoç v. Turkey*, Judgment of 10 October 2000
- *Aksoy v. Turkey*, Judgment of 18 December 1996
- *Aktaş v. Turkey*, Judgment of 24 April 2003
- *Al-Adsani v. The United Kingdom*, Grand Chamber, Judgment of 21 November 2001
- *Al-Dulimi and Montana Management Inc. v. Switzerland*, Judgment of 21 June 2016
- *Alexandridis v. Greece*, Judgment of 21 February 2008
- *Alikaj and Others v. Italy*, Judgment of 29 March 2011
- *Al-Jedda v. The United Kingdom*, Grand Chamber, Judgment of 7 July 2011
- *Al-Saadoon and Mufdhi v. The United Kingdom*, Decision of 30 June 2009
- *Al-Saadoon and Mufdhi v. The United Kingdom*, Judgment of 2 March 2010
- *Al-Skeini and Others v. The United Kingdom*, Judgment of 7 July 2011

- *Andronicou and Constantinou v. Cyprus*, Judgment of 9 October 1997
- *Anguelova v. Bulgaria*, Judgment of 13 June 2002
- *Anheuser-Busch Inc. v. Portugal*, Judgment of 11 January 2007
- *A.P., Garçon and Nicot v. France*. Judgment of 6 April 2017
- *Assenov and Others v. Bulgaria*, Judgment of 28 October 1998
- *Avotiņš v. Latvia*, Grand Chamber, Judgment of 23 May 2016
- *Avsar v. Turkey*, Judgment of 10 July 2001
- *Aydin v. Turkey*, Judgment of 25 September 1997
- *Babar Ahmad and Others v. The United Kingdom*, Decision of 8 July 2010
- *B. v. The United Kingdom*, Judgment of 8 July 1987
- *Banković and Others v. Belgium and 16 Other States*, Grand Chamber, Admissibility Decision of 12 December 2001
- *Bayatyan v. Armenia*, Judgment of 7 July 2011
- *Beer and Regan v. Federal Republic of Germany*, Grand Chamber, Judgment of 18 February 1999
- *Beizaras and Levickas v. Lithuania*, Judgment of 14 January 2020
- *Béláné Nagy v. Hungary*, Grand Chamber, Judgment of 13 December 2016
- *Belgian Linguistic Case (Case relating to certain aspects of the laws on the use of languages in education in Belgium v. Belgium), Merits*, Judgment of 23 July 1968
- *Belilos v. Switzerland*, Judgment of 29 April 1988
- *Beyeler v. Italy*, Grand Chamber, Judgment of 5 January 2000
- *Bosphorus Hava Yolları Turizm ve Ticaret Anonim Şirketi v. Ireland*, Grand Chamber, Judgment of 30 June 2005
- *Bozcaada Kimisis Teodoku Rum Ortodoks Kilisesi Vakfı v. Turkey*, Judgment of 3 March 2009
- *Brannigan and McBride v. The United Kingdom*, Judgment of 26 May 1993
- *Buckley v. The United Kingdom*, Judgment of 25 September 1996
- *Budayeva and Others v. Russia*, Judgment of 29 September 2008
- *Burghartz v. Switzerland*, Judgment of 22 February 1994
- *Buscarini and Others v. San Marino*, Grand Chamber, Judgment of 18 February 1999
- *C.N. v. The United Kingdom*, Judgment of 19 October 2012
- *Çakici v. Turkey*, Judgment of 8 July 1999
- *Calvelli and Ciglio v. Italy*, Grand Chamber, Judgment of 17 January 2002
- *Campbell and Cosans v. The United Kingdom*, Judgment of 25 February 1982
- *Cara-Damiani v. Italy*, Judgment of 7 February 2012
- *Casa di Cura Valle Fiorita S.r.l. v. Italy*, Judgment of 13 December 2018
- *Casado Coca v. Spain*, Judgment of 24 February 1994
- *Case of United Communist Party of Turkey and Others v. Turkey*, Judgment of 30 January 1998
- *Catan and Others v. Moldova and Russia*, Grand Chamber, Judgment of 19 October 2012
- *Cengiz and Others v. Turkey*, Judgment of 1 December 2015,
- *Centro Europa 7 s.r.l. and Di Stefano v. Italy*, Judgment of 7 June 2012
- *Cestaro v. Italy*, Judgment of 7 April 2015

- *Chahal v. UK*, Judgment of 15 November 1996
- *Chapman v. Belgium*, Decision of 5 March 2013
- *Chinnici v. Italy (no. 2)*, Judgment of 14 April 2015
- *Chiragov and Others v. Armenia*, Grand Chamber, Judgment of 16 June 2015
- *Chitos v. Greece*, Judgment of 4 June 2015
- *Chovancik v. Slovakia*, Judgment of 17 June 2003
- *Chowdury and Others v. Greece*, Judgment of 30 March 2017
- *Connors v. The United Kingdom*, Judgment of 27 May 2004
- *Contrada v. Italy (n.3)*, Judgment of 14 April 2015
- *Cordella and Others v. Italy*, Judgment of 24 January 2019
- *Cyprus v. Turkey*, Grand Chamber, Judgment of 10 May 2001
- *De Haes and Gijsels v. Belgium*, Judgment of 24 February 1997
- *Depalle v. France*, Grand Chamber, Judgment of 29 March 2010
- *De Tommaso v. Italy*, Judgment of 23 February 2017
- *Dink v. Turkey*, Judgment of 14 September 2010
- *D.H. and Others v. Czech Republic*, Grand Chamber, Judgment of 13 November 2007
- *D.J. v. Croatia*, Judgment of 24 July 2012
- *Djavit An v. Turkey*, Judgment of 20 February 2003
- *Drėlingas v. Lithuania*, Judgment of 9 September 2019
- *Dubowska and Skup v. Poland*, Decision of 18 April 1997
- *Dudgeon v. The United Kingdom*, Judgment of 22 October 1991
- *Ebrahimian v. France*, Judgment of 26 November 2015
- *Edwards v. The United Kingdom*, Judgment of 16 December 1992
- *Edwards Paul and Audrey v. The United Kingdom*, Judgment of 14 March 2002
- *El-Masri v. The Former Yugoslav Republic of Macedonia*, Grand Chamber, Judgment of 13 December 2012
- *Engel and Others v. The Netherlands*, Judgment of 8 June 1976
- *Ergi v. Turkey*, Judgment of 28 July 1998
- *Fabris v. France*, Grand Chamber, Judgment of 7 February 2013
- *Fadeyeva v. Russia*, Judgment of 9 June 2005
- *F.G. v. Sweden*, Grand Chamber, Judgment of 23 March 2016
- *Filip v. Romania*, Judgment of 14 December 2006
- *Finogenov and Others v. Russia*, Judgment of 4 June 2012
- *France, Norway, Denmark, Sweden, Netherlands v. Turkey*, Decision of 6 December 1983
- *Fretté v. France*, Judgment of 26 February 2002
- *Frumkin v. Russia*, Judgment 5 January 2016
- *Fuklev v. Ukraine*, Judgment of 7 June 2002
- *Gaskin v. The United Kingdom*, Judgment of 7 July 1989
- *Gentilhomme, Schaff-Benhadji and Zerouki v. France*, Judgment of 14 May 2002
- *Gitonas and Others v. Greece*, Judgment of 1 July 1997
- *Giuliani and Gaggio v. Italy*, Grand Chamber, Judgment of 24 March 2011
- *G. N. and Others v. Italy*, Judgment of 1 December 2009
- *Golder v. The United Kingdom*, Judgment of 21 February 1975

- *Gongadze v. Ukraine*, Judgment of 8 November 2005
- *Goodwin v. The United Kingdom*, Grand Chamber, Judgment of 27 March 1996
- *Goodwin Christine v. The United Kingdom*, Grand Chamber, Judgment of 11 July 2002
- *Grande Stevens and Others v. Italy*, Judgment of 4 March 2014
- *Graziani-Weiss v. Austria*, Judgment of 18 October 2011
- *Greek Case – Denmark v. Greece, Norway v. Greece, Sweden v. Greece, Netherlands v. Greece*, Report of 5 November 1969
- *Grzelak v. Poland*, Judgment of 15 June 2010
- *Guillot v. France*, Judgment of 24 October 1996
- *Güleç v. Turkey*, Judgment of 27 July 1998
- *Gustafsson v. Sweden*, Grand Chamber, Judgment of 25 April 1996
- *Haas v. Switzerland*, Judgment of 20 January 2011
- *Hadjianastassiou v. Greece*, Judgment of 16 December 1992
- *Handyside v. The United Kingdom*, Judgment of 7 December 1976
- *Hardy and Maile v. The United Kingdom*, Judgment of 14 February 2012
- *Harkins and Edwards v. The United Kingdom*, Judgment of 17 January 2012
- *Hasan and Eylem Zengin v. Turkey*, Judgment of 9 October 2007
- *Hassan v. The United Kingdom*, Grand Chamber, Judgment of 16 September 2014
- *Hatton and Others v. The United Kingdom*, Judgment of 8 July 2003
- *Herczegfalvy v. Austria*, Judgment of 24 September 1992
- *Hirsi Jamaa and Others v. Italy*, Grand Chamber, Judgment of 23 February 2012
- *Hirst v. The United Kingdom (No. 2)*, Judgment of 6 October 2005
- *Iatridis v. Greece*, Grand Chamber, Judgment of 25 March 1999
- *Ilaşcu and Others v. Moldova and Russia*, Grand Chamber, Judgment of 8 July 2004
- *Ilhan v. Turkey*, Grand Chamber, Judgment of 27 June 2000
- *Informationsverein Lentia and Others v. Austria*, Judgment of 24 November 1993
- *Ireland v. The United Kingdom*, Judgment of 18 January 1978
- *Isayeva v. Russia*, Judgment of 24 February 2005
- *Isayeva, Yusupova and Bazayeva v. Russia*, Judgment of 24 February 2005
- *Issa and Others v. Turkey*, Judgment of 16 November 2004
- *Jahn and Others v. Germany*, Grand Chamber, Judgment of 30 June 2005
- *Jalloh v. Germany*, Grand Chamber, Judgment of 11 July 2006
- *Jaloud v. The Netherlands*, Grand Chamber, Judgment of 20 November 2014
- *James and Others v. The United Kingdom*, Judgment of 21 February 1986
- *Janowski v. Poland*, Grand Chamber, Judgment of 21 January 1999
- *Jecker v. Switzerland*, Judgment of 6 October 2020
- *Jersild v. Denmark*, Grand Chamber, Judgment of 23 September 1994
- *J.K. and Others v. Sweden*, Grand Chamber, Judgment of 23 August 2016
- *Jones and Others v. The United Kingdom*, Judgment of 14 January 2014
- *Kafkaris v. Cyprus*, Grand Chamber, Judgment of 12 February 2008
- *Kasymakhunov and Saybatalov v. Russia*, Judgment of 14 March 2013
- *Kaya v. Turkey*, Judgment of 19 February 1998

- *Khatsiyeva and Others v. Russia*, Judgment of 17 January 2008
- *Khlaifia and Others v. Italy*, Grand Chamber, Judgment of 15 December 2016
- *Keenan v. The United Kingdom*, Judgment of 3 April 2001
- *Kelly and Others v. The United Kingdom*, Judgment of 4 May 2001
- *Kılıç v. Turkey*, Judgment of 28 March 2000
- *Kjeldsen, Busk Madsen and Pedersen v. Denmark*, Judgment of 7 December 1976
- *Klass and Others v. Germany*, Judgment of 6 September 1978
- *Klausecker v. Germany*, Decision of 6 January 2015
- *Koch v. Germany*, Judgment of 19 July 2012
- *Kokkinakis v. Greece*, Judgment of 25 May 1993
- *König v. Germany*, Judgment of 28 June 1978
- *Kononov v. Latvia*, Judgment of 17 May 2010
- *Kopecký v. Slovakia*, Grand Chamber, Judgment of 28 September 2004
- *Konečný v. Czech Republic*, Judgment of 26 October 2004
- *Köse and 93 Others v. Turkey*, Decision of 24 January 2006
- *Kruslin v. France*, Judgment of 24 April 1990
- *Kurt v. Turkey*, Judgment of 25 May 1998
- *L.C.B. v. The United Kingdom*, Judgment of 9 June 1998
- *Labita v. Italy*, Grand Chamber, Judgment of 6 April 2000
- *Lachiri v. Belgium*, 18 September 2018
- *Lambert and Others v. France*, Grand Chamber, Judgment of 5 June 2015
- *Lautsi v. Italy*, Judgment of 3 November 2009
- *Lautsi and Others v. Italy*, Grand Chamber, Judgment of 18 March 2011
- *Lawless v. Ireland (No. 3)*, Judgment of 1 July 1961
- *Leela Forderkreis E.V. and Others v. Germany*, Judgment of 6 November 2008
- *Leyla Şahin v. Turkey*, Grand Chamber, Judgment of 10 November 2005
- *Lingens v. Austria*, Judgment of 8 July 1986
- *Lithgow and Others v. The United Kingdom*, Judgment of 8 July 1986
- *Loizidou v. Turkey (preliminary objections)*, Grand Chamber, Judgment of 23 March 1995
- *Loizidou v. Turkey (merits)*, Grand Chamber, Judgment of 18 December 1996
- *Loizidou v. Turkey (Article 50)*, Grand Chamber, Judgment of 28 July 1998
- *Lopes de Sousa Fernandes v. Portugal*, Grand Chamber, Judgment of 19 December 2017
- *López Ostra v. Spain*, Judgment of 9 December 1994
- *López Ribalda and Others v. Spain*, Grand Chamber, Judgment of 17 October 2019
- *M.C. v. Bulgaria*, Judgment of 4 December 2003
- *M.S.S. v. Belgium and Greece*, Grand Chamber, Judgment of 21 January 2011
- *Mahmut Kaya v. Turkey*, Judgment of 28 March 2000
- *Makaratzis v. Greece*, Grand Chamber, Judgment of 20 December 2004
- *Maktouf and Damjanović v. Bosnia and Herzegovina*, Grand Chamber, Judgment of 18 July 2013
- *Marckx v. Belgium*, Judgment of 13 June 1979

- *Markt Intern Verlag GmbH and Klaus Beermann v. Germany*, Judgment of 20 November 1989
- *Maslova and Nalbandov v. Russia*, Judgment of 24 January 2008
- *Mastromatteo v. Italy*, Grand Chamber, Judgment of 24 October 2002
- *Mathieu-Molin and Clerfayt v. Belgium*, Judgment of 2 March 1987
- *Matter v. Slovakia*, Judgment of 5 July 1999
- *Matthews v. The United Kingdom*, Grand Chamber, Judgment of 18 February 1999
- *McCann and Others v. The United Kingdom*, Grand Chamber, Judgment of 27 September 1995
- *Medvedyev and Others v. France*, Grand Chamber, Judgment of 29 March 2010
- *Members of the Gldani Congregation of the Jehovah's Witnesses v. Georgia*, Judgment of 3 May 2007
- *Michaud v. France*, Judgment of 6 December 2012
- *Mikayil Mammadov v. Azerbaijan*, Judgment of 22 May 2014
- *Miller v. United Kingdom*, Decision of 25 July 2019
- *Moldovan and Others v. Romania (No. 2)*, Judgment of 12 July 2005
- *Moustaquim v. Belgium*, Judgment of 18 February 1991
- *Müller and Others v. Switzerland*, Judgment of 24 May 1988
- *Nachova and Others v. Bulgaria*, Judgment of 26 February 2004
- *Nachova and Others v. Bulgaria*, Grand Chamber, Judgment of 6 July 2005
- *Nada v. Switzerland*, Grand Chamber, Judgment of 12 September 2012
- *Naït-Liman v. Switzerland*, Grand Chamber, Judgment of 15 March 2018
- *Naletilić v. Croatia*, Decision of 4 May 2000
- *NA. v. The United Kingdom*, Judgment of 17 July 2008
- *Nasr and Ghali v. Italy*, Judgment of 23 February 2016
- *N.B. v. Slovakia*, Judgment of 12 June 2012
- *Nikolova and Velichkova v. Bulgaria*, Judgment of 20 December 2007
- *Noack and Others v. Germany*, Judgment of 25 May 2020
- *Norris v. Ireland*, Judgment of 26 October 1988
- *Oberschlick v. Austria*, Judgment of 23 May 1991
- *Obote v. Russia*, Judgment of 19 November 2019
- *Öcalan v. Turkey*, Judgment of 12 March 2003
- *Öcalan v. Turkey*, Grand Chamber, Judgment of 12 May 2005
- *Öcalan v. Turkey (n. 2)*, Judgment of 18 March 2014
- *Oğur v. Turkey*, Grand Chamber, Judgment of 20 May 1999
- *Öneryildiz v. Turkey*, Judgment of 30 November 2004
- *Open Door and Dublin Well Woman v. Ireland*, Judgment of 29 October 1992
- *Osman v. The United Kingdom*, Grand Chamber, Judgment of 28 October 1998
- *Otto-Preminger-Institut v. Austria*, Judgment of 20 September 1994
- *Ouranio Toxo v. Greece*, Judgment of 20 October 2005
- *Öztürk v. Germany*, Judgment of 21 February 1984
- *P. and S. v. Poland*, Judgment of 30 October 2012
- *Panaitescu v. Romania*, Judgment of 10 April 2012
- *Paposhvili v. Belgium.* Grand Chamber, Judgment of 13 December 2016

- *Perinçek v. Switzerland*, Grand Chamber, Judgment of 15 October 2015
- *Perk and Others v. Turkey*, Judgment of 28 March 2006
- *Perna v. Italy*, Grand Chamber, Judgment of 6 May 2003
- *Pierre-Bloch v. France*, Judgment of 21 October 1997
- *Pine Valley Developments Ltd and Others v. Ireland*, Judgment of 29 November 1991
- *Pla and Puncernau v. Andorra*, Judgment of 13 July 2004
- *Paposhvili v. Belgium*, Grand Chamber, Judgment of 13 December 2016
- *Popoviciu v. Romania*, Judgment of 1 March 2016
- *Pressos Compania Naviera S.A. and Others v. Belgium*, Judgment of 20 November 1995
- *Pretty v. The United Kingdom*, Judgment of 29 April 2002
- *Provenzano v. Italy*, Judgment of 25 October 2018
- *Rackete and Others v. Italy*, Decision (on interim measures) of 25 June 2019
- *R.R. v. Poland*, Judgment of 26 May 2011
- *Ramsahai and Others v. The Netherlands*, Grand Chamber, Judgment of 15 May 2007
- *Rantsev v. Cyprus and Russia*, Judgment of 7 January 2010
- *Refah Partisi (the Welfare Party) and others v. Turkey*, Grand Chamber, Judgment of 13 February 2003
- *Renolde v. France*, Judgment of 16 October 2008
- *Rivière v. France*, Judgment of 11 July 2006
- *Saadi v. Italy*, Grand Chamber, Judgment of 28 February 2008
- *Sadak and Others v. Turkey (No. 2)*, Judgment of 11 June 2002
- *Şahin v. Turkey*, Grand Chamber, Judgment of 10 November 2005
- *Sakik and Others v. Turkey*, Judgment of 26 November 1997
- *Saoud v. France*, Judgment of 9 October 2007
- *Sciacca v. Italy*, Judgment of 11 January 2005
- *Scollo v. Italy*, Judgment of 28 September 1995
- *Scoppola v. Italy (no. 3)*, Grand Chamber, Judgment of 22 May 2012
- *Scordino and Others v. Italy (no. 1)*, Decision of 27 March 2003
- *Scordino and Others v. Italy (no. 1)*, Grand Chamber, Judgment of 29 March 2006
- *Seguin v. France*, Decision of 7 March 2000
- *Selmouni v. France*, Grand Chamber, Judgment of 28 July 1999
- *Sharxhi and Others v. Albania*, Judgment of 11 January 2018
- *Sigurjónsson v. Iceland*, Judgment of 30 June 1993
- *Siliadin v. France*, Judgment of 26 July 2005
- *Sinan Işik v. Turkey*, Judgment of 2 February 2010
- *Soering v. The United Kingdom*, Judgment of 7 July 1989
- *Sørensen and Rasmussen v. Denmark*, Grand Chamber, Judgment of 11 January 2006
- *Sporrong and Lönnroth v. Sweden*, Judgment of 23 September 1982
- *Stafford v. The United Kingdom*, Grand Chamber, Judgment of 28 May 2002

- *Stec and Others v. The United Kingdom*, Grand Chamber, Judgment of 12 April 2006
- *Stichting Mothers of Srebrenica and Others v. The Netherlands*, Decision of 11 June 2013
- *Streletz, Kessler and Krenk v. Germany*, Grand Chamber, Judgment of 22 March 2001
- *Sulejmanovic v. Italy*, Judgment of 16 July 2009
- *Sunday Times v. The United Kingdom (No. 1)*, Judgment of 26 April 1979
- *Tagayeva and Others v. Russia*, Judgment of 18 September 2017
- *Taranenko v. Russia*, Judgment of 15 May 2014
- *T.I. v. The United Kingdom*, Judgment of 7 March 2000
- *Thlimmenos v. Greece*, Grand Chamber, Judgment of 6 April 2000
- *Thorgeir Thorgeirson v. Island*, Judgment of 25 June 1992
- *Torreggiani and Others v. Italy*, Judgment of 8 January 2013
- *Trijonis v. Lithuania*, Decision of 17 March 2005
- *Trijonis v. Lithuania*, Judgment of 15 December 2005
- *Tyrer v. The United Kingdom*, Judgment of 25 April 1978
- *Tysiąc v. Poland*, Judgment of 27 March 2007
- *Vallianatos and Others v. Greece*, Grand Chamber, Judgment of 7 November 2013
- *Vasiliauskas v. Lithuania*, Grand Chamber, Judgment of 20 October 2015
- *V.C. v. Slovakia*, Judgment of 8 November 2011
- *Velikova v. Bulgaria*, Judgment of 18 May 2000
- *VgT Verein gegen Tierfrabriken v. Switzerland*, Judgment of 28 June 2001
- *Vilvarajah and Others v. The United Kingdom*, Judgment of 30 October 1991
- *Vinter and Others v. The United Kingdom*, Grand Chamber, Judgment of 9 July 2013
- *Vo v. France*, Grand Chamber, Judgment of 8 July 2004
- *Vukota-Bojić v. Switzerland*, Judgment of 18 October 2016
- *Waite and Kennedy v. Germany*, Grand Chamber, Judgment of 18 February 1999
- *Weber v. Switzerland*, Judgment of 22 May 1990
- *Wemhoff v. Germany*, Judgment of 27 June 1968
- *Williamson v. Germany*, Decision of 31 January 2019
- *Wingrove v. The United Kingdom*, Judgment of 25 November 1996
- *X and Y v. The Netherlands*, Judgment of 26 March 1985
- *X, Y and Z v. The United Kingdom*, Grand Chamber, Judgment of 22 April 1997
- *Yaşa v. Turkey*, Judgment of 2 September 1998
- *Young, James and Webster v. The United Kingdom*, Judgment of 13 August 1981
- *Z and Others v. The United Kingdom*, Grand Chamber, Judgment of 10 May 2001
- *Zana v. Turkey*, Grand Chamber, Judgment of 25 November 1997
- *Zdanoka v. Latvia*, Judgment of 17 June 2004
- *Zdanoka v. Latvia*, Grand Chamber, Judgment of 16 March 2006

European Committee of Social Rights (ECteeSR)

- *Confederazione Generale Italiana del Lavoro (CGIL) v. Italy*, Complaint No. 91/2013, Decision of 12 October 2015
- *Finnish Society of Social Rights v. Finland*, Complaint No. 88/2012, Decision of 9 September 2014
- *Finnish Society of Social Rights v. Finland*, Complaint No. 106/2014, Decision on admissibility and the merits of 8 September 2016
- *International Federation of Human Rights Leagues (FIDH) v. France*, Complaint No. 14/2003, Decision of 8 September 2004

European Court of Justice (ECJ)

- *Accession by the Community to the European Convention for the Protection of Human Rights and Fundamental Freedoms*, Opinion 2/94 of 28 March 1996
- *Brüstle v. Greenpeace eV*, Case C-34/1018, Judgment of 18 October 2011
- *European Commission and Others v. Kadi*, Joined Cases C-584/10 P, C-593/10 P and C-595/10 P, Judgment of 18 July 2013
- *Hauer v. Land Rheinland-Pfalz*, Case C-44/79, Judgment of 13 December 1979
- *Internationale Handelsgesellschaft mbH v. Einfuhr– und Vorratsstelle für Getreide und –Futtermittel*, Case 11/70, Judgment of 17 December 1970
- *Kadi and Al Barakaat International Foundation v. Council and Commission*, Joined Cases C-402/05 P and C-415/05 P, Judgment of 3 September 2008
- *Meryem Demirel v. Stadt Schwäbisch Gmünd*, Case C-12/86, Judgment of 30 September 1987
- *Nold, Kohlen– und Baustoffgroßhandlung v. Commission*, Case 4-73, Judgment of 14 May 1974
- *Stauder v. City of Ulm – Sozialamt*, Case 29/69, Judgment of 12 November 1969
- *Stork & Cie v. High Authority of the European Coal and Steel Community*, Case 1/58, Judgment of 4 February 1959
- *The Society for the Protection of Unborn Children Ireland Ltd v. Stephen Grogan and Others*, Case C-159/90, Judgment of 4 October 1991
- *Wachauf v. Bundesamt für Ernährung und Forstwirtschaft*, Case C-5/88, Judgment of 13 July 1989

Court of First Instance (CFI) (now European General Court) (EGC))

- *Kadi v. Council and Commission*, Case T-315/01, CFI Judgment of 21 September 2005
- *Kadi v. European Commission*, Case T-85/09, EGC Judgment of 30 September 2010
- *Yusuf and Al Barakaat International Foundation v. Council and Commission*, Case T-306/01, CFI Judgment of 21 September 2005

Inter-American Commission on Human Rights (IACmHR)

- *Baby Boy Case (Christian S. White and Gary K. Potter v. United States)*, Case 2141, Report No. 23/81 of 6 March 1981
- *Coard et al. v. United States*, Case 10.951, Report No. 109/99 of 29 September 1999
- *Ecuador v. Colombia (Inter-state Petition IP-02 Admissibility Franklin Guillermo Aisalla Molina)*, Report No. 112/10, Decision on admissibility of 21 October 2010
- *Garay Hermosilla et al. v. Chile*, Case 10.843, Report No. 36/96 of 15 October 1996
- *"Haitian Interdiction" (Haitian Center for Human Rights et al. v. United States)*, Case 10.675, Report No. 28/93, Decision on admissibility of 13 October 1993
- *"Haitian Interdiction" (Haitian Center for Human Rights et al. v. United States)*, Case 10.675, Report No. 51/96, Decision on the merits of 13 March 1997
- *Raquel Martín de Mejía v. Peru*, Case 10.970, Report No. 5/96 of 1 March 1996
- *Romer Morales Zegarra et al. v. Peru*, Cases 10.827 and 11.984, Report No. 57/99 of 13 April 1999
- *Salas and Others v. United States*, Case 10.573, Report No. 31/93, Decision on admissibility of 14 October 1993

Inter-American Court of Human Rights (IACtHR)

- *Aloeboetoe et al. v. Suriname (Merits)*, Judgment of 4 December 1991
- *Aloeboetoe et al. v. Suriname (Reparations)*, Judgment of 10 September 1993
- *Almonacid Arellano et al. v. Chile*, Judgment of 26 September 2006
- *Artavia Murillo et al. ("In vitro fertilization") v. Costa Rica*, Judgment of 28 November 2012
- *Azul Rojas Marín et al. v. Peru*, Judgment of 12 March 2020
- *Bámaca-Velásquez v. Guatemala (Reparations)*, Judgment of 22 February 2002
- *Barrios Altos v. Peru (Merits)*, Judgment of 14 March 2001
- *Barrios Altos v. Peru (Reparations)*, Judgment of 30 November 2001
- *Bueno Alves v. Argentina*, Judgment of 11 May 2007
- *Caballero Delgado and Santana v. Colombia*, Judgment of 8 December 1995
- *Caesar v. Trinidad and Tobago*, Judgment of 11 March 2005
- *Cantoral Benavides v. Peru (Merits)*, Judgment of 18 August 2000
- *Cantoral Benavides v. Peru (Reparations)*, Judgment of 3 December 2001
- *Case of the Girls Yean and Bosico v. Dominican Republic*, Judgment of 8 September 2005
- *Case of the Santo Domingo Massacre v. Colombia*. Judgment of 30 November 2012
- *Castillo Petruzzi et al. v. Peru*, Judgment of 30 May 1999
- *Claude-Reyes et al. v. Chile*, Judgment of 19 September 2006

- *Gender identity, and equality and non-discrimination with regard to same-sex couples*, Advisory Opinion of 24 November 2017
- *Godínez Cruz v. Honduras (Merits)*, Judgment of 20 January 1989
- *Goiburú et al. v. Paraguay (Merits)*, Judgment of 22 September 2006
- *González et al. ("Cotton Field") v. Mexico*, Judgment of 16 November 2009
- *Habeas Corpus in Emergency Situations (Arts. 27(2), 25(1) and 7(6) American Convention on Human Rights)*, Advisory Opinion of 30 January 1987
- *Heliodoro Portugal v. Panama*, Judgment of 12 August 2008
- *Hilaire v. Trinidad and Tobago (Preliminary Exceptions)*, Judgment of 1 September 2001
- *Hilaire, Constantine and Benjamin et al. v. Trinidad and Tobago*, Judgment of 21 June 2002
- *Indigenous Communities of the Lhaka Honhat (Our Land) Association v. Argentina*, Judgment of 6 February 2020
- *Ituango Massacres v. Colombia*, Judgment of 1 July 2006
- *Ivcher Bronstein v. Peru*, Judgment of 24 September 1999
- *Juan Humberto Sánchez v. Honduras*, Judgment of 7 June 2003
- *Judicial Guarantees in States of Emergency (Arts. 27(2), 25 and (8) American Convention on Human Rights)*, Advisory Opinion of 6 October 1987
- *"Juvenile Reeducation Institute" v. Paraguay*, Judgment of 2 September 2004
- *Kuna Indigenous People of Madungandí and the Emberá Indigenous People of Bayano and their members v. Panama*, Judgment of 14 October 2014
- *López Soto et al. v. Venezuela*, Judgment of 26 September 2018
- *Maritza Urrutia v. Guatemala*, Judgment of 27 November 2003
- *Masacre de las Dos Erres v. Guatemala*, Judgment of 24 November 2009
- *Mayagna (Sumo) Awas Tingni Community v. Nicaragua (Merits)*, Judgment of 31 August 2001
- *Miguel Castro Castro Prison v. Peru*, Judgment of 25 November 2006
- *Moiwana Community v. Suriname (Merits)*, Judgment of 15 June 2005
- *Montero Aranguren et al. (Detention Center of Catia) v. Venezuela*, Judgment of 5 July 2006
- *Neira Alegría et al. v. Peru (Merits)*, Judgment of 19 January 1995
- *Olmedo Bustos et al. ("The Last Temptation of Christ") v. Chile*, Judgment of 5 February 2001
- *Paniagua Morales and Others ("White Van") v. Guatemala*, Judgment of 8 March 1998
- *Proposed Amendments of the Naturalization Provisions of the Constitution of Costa Rica*, Advisory Opinion of 19 January 1984
- *Saramaka People v. Suriname*, Judgment of 28 November 2007
- *Sawhoyamaxa Indigenous Community v. Paraguay*, Judgment of 29 March 2006
- *States of Emergency*, Advisory Opinion of 30 January 1987
- *The Environment and Human Rights (State obligations in relation to the environment in the context of the protection and guarantee of the rights to life and to personal integrity – interpretation and scope of Articles 4(1) and 5(1) of the*

American Convention on Human Rights), Advisory Opinion of 15 November 2017
- *The institution of asylum, and its recognition as a human right under the Inter-American System of Protection (interpretation and scope of Articles 5, 22(7) and 28(8) in relation to Article 1(1) of the American Convention on Human Rights)*, Advisory Opinion of 30 May 2018
- *The Right to Information on Consular Assistance in the Framework of the Guarantees of the Due Process of Law*, Advisory Opinion of 1 October 1999
- *The "Street Children" (Villagrán Morales et al.) v. Guatemala (Merits)*, Judgment of 19 November 1999
- *The "Street Children" (Villagrán Morales et al.) v. Guatemala (Reparations)*, Judgment of 26 May 2001
- *Tibi v. Ecuador*, Judgment of 7 September 2004
- *Trujillo-Oroza v. Bolivia (Reparations)*, Judgment of 27 February 2002
- *Vargas Areco v. Paraguay*, Judgment of 26 September 2006
- *Velásquez Rodríguez v. Honduras (Merits)*, Judgment of 29 July 1988
- *Ximenes Lopes v. Brazil*, Judgment of 4 July 2006
- *Yakye Axa Indigenous Community v. Paraguay (Merits)*, Judgment of 17 June 2005

African Commission on Human and Peoples' Rights (ACmHPR)

- *Amnesty International, Comité Loosli Bachelard, Lawyers' Committee for Human Rights, Association of Members of the Episcopal Conference of East Africa v. Sudan*, Communications Nos. 48/1990-50/1991-52/1991-89/1993, Decision of 15 November 1999
- *Centre for Minority Rights Development (Kenya) and Minority Rights Group (on behalf of Endorois Welfare Council) v. Kenya*, Communication No. 276/03, Decision of 11-25 November 2009
- *Curtis Francis Doebbler v. Sudan*, Communication No. 236/00, Decision of 4 May 2003
- *Free Legal Assistance Group, Lawyers' Committee for Human Rights, Union Interafricaine des Droits de l'Homme, Les Témoins de Jehovah v. The Democratic Republic of Congo*, Communications Nos. 25/89-47/90-56/91-100/93, Decision of 4 April 1996
- *Garreth Anver Prince v. South Africa*, Communication No. 255/02, Decision of 7 December 2004
- *Institute for Human Rights and Development in Africa (on behalf of Sierra Leonean refugees in Guinea) v. Guinea*, Communication No. 249/02, Decision of 7 December 2004
- *Malawi African Association, Amnesty International and Others v. Mauritania*, Communications Nos. 54/91-61/91-96/93-98/93-164/97-196/97-210/98, Decision of 11 May 2000

- *Purohit and Moore v. Gambia*, Communication No. 241/01, Decision of 29 May 2003
- *Social and Economic Rights Action Center (SERAC) and Center for Economic and Social Rights (CESR) v. Nigeria ("Ogoniland")*, Communication No. 155/96, Decision of 27 October 2001
- *Sudan Human Rights Organisation and Centre on Housing Rights and Evictions (COHRE) v. Sudan*, Communications Nos. 279/03-296/05, Decision of 13-27 May 2009
- *Zimbabwe Human Rights NGO Forum v. Zimbabwe*, Communication No. 245/02, Decision of 15 May 2006

African Court on Human and Peoples' Rights (ACtHPR)

- *African Commission on Human and Peoples' Rights v. Republic of Kenya*, Judgment of 26 May 2017
- *APDF & IHRDA (Association pour le progrès et la défense ders droits des femmes maliennes and the Institute for Human Rights and Developments in Africa) v. Republic of Mali*, Judgment of 11 May 2018

ECOWAS Community Court of Justice (CCJ)

- *Hadijatou Mani Koraou v. Niger*, Judgment of 27 October 2008
- *The Registered Trustees of the Socio-Economic Rights and Accountability Project (SERAP) v. Nigeria & UBEC*, Judgment of 30 November 2010

International Military Tribunal of Nuremberg (IMT)

- *The United States et al. v. Göring et al.*, Judgment of 1 October 1946, in *Trial of the Major War Criminals before the International Military Tribunal, Nuremberg, 14 November 1945-1 October 1946*, vol. I, Nuremberg, 1947, pp. 1-367; rep. in *AJIL*, vol. 41, 1947, pp. 172-333
- *The United States v. Wilhelm von Leeb et al. (High Command Case)*, Judgment of 27 October 1948, in *Trials of the War Criminals Before the Nuremberg Military Tribunals under Control Law No. 1, Nuremberg, October 1946-April 1949*, vol. IX, Washington, 1950, pp. 462-697

International Criminal Tribunal for the Former Yugoslavia (ICTY)

- *Delalić (Prosecutor v. Delacić et al.)*, Trial Chamber, Case No. IT-96-21-T, Judgment of 16 November 1998

- *Delalić (Prosecutor v. Delacić et al.)*, Appeals Chamber, Case No. IT-96-21-A, Judgment of 20 February 2001
- *Furundžija (Prosecutor v. Anto Furundžija)*, Trial Chamber, Case No. T-95-17/1-T, Judgment of 10 December 1998
- *Jelisić (Prosecutor v. Jelisić)*, Trial Chamber, Case No. IT-95-10-T, Judgment of 14 December 1999.
- *Jelisić (Prosecutor v. Jelisić)*, Appeals Chamber, Case No. IT-95-10-A, Judgment of 5 July 2001.
- *Krstić (Prosecutor v. Krstić, 'Srebrenica')*, Appeals Chamber, Case No. IT-98-33-A, Judgment of 19 April 2004
- *Kunarac (Prosecutor v. Kunarac et al.)*, Trial Chamber, Case No. IT-96-23&23/1-T, Judgment of 22 February 2001
- *Kunarac (Prosecutor v. Kunarac et al.)*, Appeals Chamber, Case No. IT-96-23&23/1-A, Judgment of 12 June 2002
- *Kvočka (Prosecutor v. Kvočka et al.)*, Trial Chamber, Case No. IT-98-30/1-T, Judgment of 2 November 2001
- *Kvočka (Prosecutor v. Kvočka et al.)*, Appeals Chamber, Case No. IT-98-30/1-A, Judgment of 28 February 2005
- *Mladić (Prosecutor v. Ratko Mladić)*, Trial Chamber I, Case No. IT-09-92-T, Judgment of 22 November 2017
- *Tadić (Prosecutor v. Dusko Tadić)*, Appeals Chamber, Case No. IT-94-1-AR72, Decision on the Defence Motion for Interlocutory Appeal on Jurisdiction, Decision of 2 October 1995
- *Tadić (Prosecutor v. Dusko Tadić)*, Appeals Chamber, Case No. IT-94-1-A, Judgment of 15 July 1999

International Criminal Tribunal for Rwanda (ICTR)

- *Akayesu (The Prosecutor v. Jean-Paul Akayesu)*, Chamber I, Case No. ICTR-96-4-T, Judgment of 2 September 1998
- *Akayesu (The Prosecutor v. Jean-Paul Akayesu)*, Case No. ICTR-96-4, Judgment of 1 June 2001
- *Kayishema et al. (The Prosecutor v. Clément Kayishema et al.)*, Appeals Chamber, Case No. ICTR-95-1-A, Judgment of 1 June 2001

Special Tribunal for Lebanon (STL)

- *El Sayed (In the matter of El Sayed)*, Case No. CH/PRES/2010/01, Order of 15 April 2010

National Courts

Canada

Supreme Court

- *Kazemi Estate v. Islamic Republic of Iran*, Judgment of 10 October 2014, [2014] 3 SCR 176
- *Re Secession of Quebec (Reference by the Governor in Council concerning Certain Questions relating to the Secession of Quebec from Canada)*, Advisory Opinion of 20 August 1998, [1998] 2 SCR 217
- *Suresh v. Canada (Minister of Citizenship and Immigration)*, Judgment of 1 November 2002, [2002] 1 S.C.R. 3

France

Court of Cassation (Cour de Cassation, Chambre Criminelle)

- *Gaddafi*, Judgment of 13 March 2001, *RGDIP*, vol. 105, 2001, p. 473.

Germany

Federal Constitutional Court (Bundesverfassungsgericht)

- "*Solange I*", Order of 29 May 1974, BVerfGE 37, 271

Greece

Supreme Court

- *Margellos and Others v. Federal Republic of Germany*, Judgment of 17 September 2002, *ILR*, vol. 129, 2007, p. 533

Italy

Constitutional Court

- *Frontini*, Judgment of 18 December 1973, n. 183, *www.cortecostituzionale.it*
- Order of 8 April 2013, n. 69, *www.cortecostituzionale.it*
- Judgment of 22 October 2014, n. 238, *www.cortecostituzionale.it*
- Judgment of 20 June 2019, n.194, *www.cortecostituzionale.it*

Supreme Court of Cassation

- *Allen c. Min. Int.*, Judgment of 26 May 1997, n. 4674, *RDI*, vol. 80, 1997, p. 844
- *Boyisele Kumayo c. Min. Int.*, Judgment of 17 December 1999, n. 907, *http://pluris-cedam.utetgiuridica.it*

- *Ferrini c. Repubblica Federale di Germania*, Judgment of 11 March 2004, n. 5004, *RDI*, vol. 87, 2004, p. 539
- *Medero et al. (Abu Omar* case*)*, Judgment of 25 September 2014, n. 39788, *www.cortedicassazione.it*
- *Milde*, Judgment of 13 January 2009, n. 1072, *RDI*, vol. 92, 2009, p. 618
- *Min. Int. c. Yarbo Musa*, Judgment of 23 February 2018, n. 4455, *www.cortedicassa zione.it*
- *Nasr et al. (Abu Omar* case*)*, Judgment of 19 September 2012, n. 46340, *www.penale contemporaneo.it*
- *Toldo c. Repubblica Federale Tedesca, Republica Italiana*, Judgment of 28 September 2020, n. 20442. *www.cortedicassazione.it*

Court of Appeal of Milan

- *Abu Omar et al.*, Judgment of 12 February 2013 n. 6709, *www.penalecontemporaneo.it*
- *Courtney et al.* (*Abu Omar* case), Judgment of 15 December 2010, n. 3688, *www.penalecontemporaneo.it*

Court of Agrigento (GIP Office)

- *Rackete* (*Sea Watch 3* case), Order of 2 July 2019, *Giur. pen.*, 4 luglio 2019

Court of Catania (Ministerial Offences Section)

- *Diciotti* case, Report of 7 December 2018 (deposited on 22 January 2019) *www.penalecontemporaneo.it*
- *Gregoretti* case, Report of 28 November 2019 (deposited on 12 December 2019) *www.giurisprudenzapenale.com/wp-content/uploads/2020/02/*

Netherlands

Supreme Court (Hoge Raad)

- *State of the Netherlands v. Mustafić et al.*, Judgment of 6 September 2013 *www.rechtspraak.nl/Organisatie/Hoge-Raad/Supreme-court/*

The Hague Court of Appeal

- *Mehida Mustafić-Mujić et al. v. The Netherlands*, Judgment of 5 July 2011 *http://uitspraken-rechtspraak.nl/inziendocument?id=ECLI:NL:GHSGR:2011:BR53886*

Poland

Supreme Court

- *Natoniewski v. The Federal Republic of Germany and The Federal Chancellery for Payment*, Judgment of 29 October 2010, *Pol.YBIL*, vol. 30, 2010, p. 299

United Kingdom

House of Lords

- *Al-Skeini and Others v. Secretary of State for Defence*, Judgment of 13 June 2007, [2007] UKHL 26
- *Jones and Mitchell v. Ministry of Interior Al-Mamlaka Al-Arabiya AS Saudiya (the Kingdom of Saudi Arabia) and Others*, Judgment of 14 June 2006, [2006] UKHL 26
- *"Pinochet I" (Regina v. Bartle and the Commissioner of Police for the Metropolis and Other, Ex Parte Pinochet* and *Regina v. Evans and Another and the Commissioner of Police for the Metropolis and Others, Ex Parte Pinochet)*, Judgment of 25 November 1998, *ILR*, vol. 119, 2002, p. 51
- *"Pinochet II" (Regina v. Bow Street Metropolitan Stipendiary Magistrate, Ex Parte Pinochet Ugarte (No. 2))*, Judgment of 15 January 1999, [1999] UKHL 1
- *"Pinochet III" (Regina v. Bartle and the Commissioner of Police for the Metropolis and Others, Ex Parte Pinochet; Regina v. Evans and Another and the Commissioner of Police for the Metropolis and Others, Ex Parte Pinochet)*, Judgment of 24 March 1999, *ILR*, vol. 119, 2002, p. 135

High Court of Justice

- *Al-Skeini and Others v. Secretary of State for Defence*, Judgment of 14 December 2004, [2004] EWHC 2911 Admin
- *Serdar Mohammed v. Ministry of Defence*, Judgment of 2 May 2014, [2014] EWHC 1369 (QB)

Court of Appeal (Civil Division)

- *Al-Skeini and Others v. Secretary of State for Defence*, Judgment of 21 December 2005, [2005] EWCA Civ 1609

United States of America

Supreme Court

- *In re Yamashita*, Judgment of 4 February 1946, 327 U.S. 1 (1946)

3. Table of Treaty-Bodies' Comments and Recommendations

Human Rights Committee (HRCtee)

a) Concluding Observations

- Concluding Observations: *Chile*, 30 March 1999
- Concluding Observations: *Guatemala*, 27 August 2001
- Concluding Observations: *Iraq*, 30-31 October 1991
- Concluding Observations: *Israel*, 18 August 1998
- Concluding Observations: *Israel*, 21 August 2003
- Concluding Observations: *Netherlands*, 27 August 2001
- Concluding Observations: *Poland*, 23 November 2016
- Concluding Observations: *Suriname*, 4 May 2004
- Concluding Observations: *Yemen*, 12 August 2002

b) General Comments

- General Comment No. 6: *Article 6 (The right to life)*, 30 April 1982
- General Comment No. 8: *Article 9 (Right to liberty and security of persons)*, 30 June 1982
- General Comment No. 18: *Non-discrimination*, 10 November 1989
- General Comment No. 20: *Prohibition of torture, or other cruel, inhuman or degrading treatment or punishment, Article 7*, 10 March 1992
- General Comment No. 22: *The right to freedom of thought, conscience and religion (Article 18)*, 30 July 1993
- General Comment No. 23: *Rights of minorities (Article 27)*, 8 April 1994
- General Comment No. 24: *Issues relating to reservations made upon ratification or accession to the Covenant or the Optional Protocols thereto, or in relation to declarations under article 41 of the Covenant*, 4 November 1994
- General Comment No. 25: *The right to participate in public affairs, voting rights and the right to equal access to public service (Article 25)*, 12 July 1996
- General Comment No. 26: *Continuity of obligations*, 8 December 1997
- General Comment No. 27: *Freedom of movement (Article 12)*, 2 November 1999
- General Comment No. 28: *Article 3 (The equality of rights between men and women)*, 29 March 2000

R. Pisillo Mazzeschi, *International Human Rights Law*,
https://doi.org/10.1007/978-3-030-77032-7

- General Comment No. 29: *States of emergency (Article 4)*, 31 August 2001
- General Comment No. 31: *Nature of the general legal obligation imposed on States parties to the Covenant*, 26 May 2004
- General Comment No. 32: *Article 14: Right to equality before courts and tribunals and to a fair trial*, 23 August 2007
- General Comment No. 34: *Article 19: Freedoms of opinion and expression*, 12 September 2011
- General Comment No. 35: *Article 9 (Liberty and security of person)*, 23 October 2014
- General Comment No. 36: *Article 6 (the right to life)*, 3 September 2019
- General Comment No. 37: *Article 21 (right of peaceful assembly)*, 17 September 2020

Committee on Economic, Social and Cultural Rights (CteeESCR)

a) Concluding Observations

- Concluding Observations: *Israel*, 23 May 2003

b) General Comments

- General Comment No. 3: *The nature of States parties' obligations (art. 2, para. 1, of the Covenant)*, 14 December 1990
- General Comment No. 4: *The right to adequate housing (art. 11 (1) of the Covenant)*, 13 December 1991
- General Comment No. 7: *The right to adequate housing (art. 11 (1) of the Covenant): Forced evictions*, 16 May 1997
- General Comment No. 11: *Plans of action for primary education (article 14 of the International Covenant on Economic, Social and Cultural Rights)*, 10 May 1999
- General Comment No. 12: *The right to adequate food (art. 11)*, 12 May 1999
- General Comment No. 13: *The right to education (article 13 of the Covenant)*, 8 December 1999
- General Comment No. 14: *The right to the highest attainable standard of health (article 12 of the International Covenant on Economic, Social and Cultural Rights)*, 11 August 2000
- General Comment No. 15: *The right to water (arts. 11 and 12 of the International Covenant on Economic, Social and Cultural Rights)*, 20 January 2003
- General Comment No. 17: *The right of everyone to benefit from the protection of the moral and material interests resulting from any scientific, literary or artistic production of which he or she is the author (article 15, paragraph 1(c), of the Covenant)*, 12 January 2006
- General Comment No. 18: *The right to work (art. 6 of the International Covenant on Economic, Social and Cultural Rights)*, 6 February 2006
- General Comment No. 23: *The right to just and favorable conditions of work (article 7 of the International Covenant on Economic, Social and Cultural Rights)*, 27 April 2016

Committee on the Elimination of Racial Discrimination (CteeERD)

Recommendations

- General Recommendation No. VIII *concerning the interpretation and application of article 1, paragraphs 1 and 4 of the Convention*, 38th Session (1990)

Committee Against Torture (CteeAT)

General Comments

- General Comment No. 4 (2017) *on the implementation of article 3 of the Convention in the context of article 22*, 4 September 2018

Selective Bibliography

Abi-Saab G (1985) Reflexions on the contemporary processes of developing international law. Ninth Gilberto Amado Memorial Lecture presented at the International Law Commission, 25 June 1985

Abi-Saab G (1987) Cours général de droit international public. RC 207:1–464

Abi-Saab G (1988) Entangled treaty and custom. In: Dinstein Y (ed) International law at a time of perplexity: essays in Honour of Shabtai Rosenne. Nijhoff, Dordrecht, p 717 ff

Acconci P (2001) Tutela della salute e diritto internazionale. Cedam, Padova

Ackerly B (2008) Universal Human Rights in a world of difference. Cambridge University Press, Cambridge

Addo MK (ed) (2006) International law of Human Rights. Ashgate, Aldershot

Ago R (1938) La regola del previo esaurimento dei ricorsi interni in tema di responsabilità internazionale. Archivio di diritto pubblico, Padova, p 178 ff

Ago R (1939) Le delit international. RC 68:415–554

Ago R (1977) Sixième rapport sur la responsabilité des Etats. ACDI 1977(II-1)

Aja Agwu F (2014) The African Court of Justice and Human Rights: the future of international criminal justice in Africa. Africa Rev 6:30–43

Alexidze L (1981) Legal Nature of *Jus Cogens* in contemporary international law. RC 172:221–270

Alexy R (2000) On the structure of legal principles. Ratio Juris 13:294–304

Alexy R (2002) A theory of constitutional rights. Oxford University Press, Oxford

Alston P (1987) Out of the abyss; the challenges confronting the new UN Committee on economic, social and cultural rights. Hum Rights Q 9:332–381

Alston P, Goodman R (2013) International human rights. The successor to international human rights in context: law, politics and morals. Text and materials. Oxford University Press, Oxford

Anaya J (2004) Indigenous peoples in International Law, 2nd edn. Oxford University Press, Oxford

Anton DK, Shelton D (2011) Environmental protection and Human Rights. Cambridge University Press, Cambridge

Ascensio H, Decaux E, Pellet A (eds) (2012) Droit international pénal, 2nd edn. Pedone, Paris

Balboni M (ed) (2017) The European Convention on Human Rights and the principle of non-discrimination. Editoriale Scientifica, Napoli

Barret JQ (2010) Raphael Lemkin and 'Genocide' at Nuremberg, 1945-1946. In: Safferling CM, Conze EA (eds) The Genocide Convention sixty years after its adoption. Asser Press, The Hague, pp 35–54

Bartolini G (2009) Riparazione per violazione dei diritti umani e ordinamento internazionale. Jovene, Napoli

Bassiouni MC (1990) A functional approach to 'General principles of international law'. Mich J Int Law 11:768–818

Baxi U (2012) The future of human rights. Oxford University Press, New York

Baxter R (1965-66) Multilateral treaties as evidence of customary international law. Br Yearb Int L 41:275–300

R. Pisillo Mazzeschi, *International Human Rights Law*,
https://doi.org/10.1007/978-3-030-77032-7

Baxter R (1970) Treaties and custom. RC 129:27–105
Bedjaoui M (1979) Towards a new international economic order. Holmes & Meier Publishers, New York
Benvenisti E (2008) The conception of international law as a legal system. German Yearb Int Law 50:393–405
Benvenisti E (2012) The International Law of Occupation. Oxford University Press, Oxford
Benvenisti E (2018) The margin of appreciation, subsidiarity and global challenges to democracy. J Int Disp Settlement 9:240–253
Besson S (2012) The extra-territoriality of the European Convention on Human Rights. Why human rights depend on jurisdiction and what jurisdiction amounts to. Leiden J Int Law 25:857–884
Besson S (2020a) Due diligence and extraterritorial human rights obligations – mind the gap! ESIL Reflections 9:1–9
Besson S (2020b) La *due diligence* en droit international. RC 409:153–398
Bestagno F (2003) Diritti umani e impunità. Obblighi positivi degli Stati in materia penale. Vita e Pensiero, Milano
Bestagno F (ed) (2009) I diritti economici, sociali e culturali. Promozione e tutela nella comunità internazionale. Vita e Pensiero, Milano
Bianchi A (1997) Overcoming the Hurdle of State Immunity in the domestic enforcement of international human rights. In: Conforti B, Francioni F (eds) Enforcing international human rights in domestic courts. Nijhoff, The Hague, pp 405–439
Bianchi A (1999) Immunity versus human rights: the *Pinochet* case. Eur J Int Law 10:237–277
Bianchi A (2004) L'immunité des états et les violations graves des droits de l'homme: la fonction de l'interprète dans la détermination du droit international. RGDIP 108:63–101
Bianchi A (2008) Human Rights and the magic of *Jus Cogens*. Eur J Int Law 19:491–508
Boerefijn I (2009) Impact on the law of treaty reservations. In: Kamminga MT, Scheinin M (eds) The impact of human rights law on general international law. Oxford University Press, Oxford, pp 63–97
Bonetti P (2005) Terrorismo e stranieri nel diritto italiano. Disciplina legislativa e profili costituzionali. I parte. L'applicazione agli stranieri delle norme comuni sul terrorismo. Diritto, immigrazione e cittadinanza 3:13–41
Bourgeois H, Wouters J (2018) Methods of identification of international custom: a new role for *Opinio Juris*? In: Pisillo Mazzeschi R, De Sena P (eds) Global justice, human rights and the modernization of international law. Springer, Cham, pp 69–111
Boyle A (2014) Soft law in international law-making. In: Evans MD (ed) International law, 4th edn. Oxford University Press, Oxford, p 118 ff
Boyle AE, Anderson MR (eds) (1996) Human rights approaches to environmental protection. Clarendon Press, Oxford
Brownlie I (1998) The rule of law in international affairs. Nijhoff, The Hague
Brownlie I (2008) Principles of public international law, 7th edn. Oxford University Press, Oxford
Buergenthal T, Shelton D, Stewart DP (2004) International Human Rights in a nutshell, 3rd edn (2nd rep). West Group, St. Paul
Bufalini A (2013) La natura del divieto di detenzione arbitraria secondo il *Working Group on Arbitrary Detention* del Consiglio dei diritti umani. DUDI 7:525–531
Buscemi M (2020) Illeciti delle Nazioni Unite e tutela dell'individuo. Editoriale Scientifica, Napoli
Cadin R (2019) Profili ricostruttivi e linee evolutive del diritto internazionale dello sviluppo. Giappichelli, Torino
Calamia AM, Di Filippo M, Gestri M (eds) (2012) Immigrazione, Diritto e Diritti: profili internazionalistici ed europei. Cedam, Padova
Caligiuri A, Cataldi G, Napoletano N (eds) (2010) La tutela dei diritti umani in Europa: tra sovranità statale e ordinamenti sovranazionali. Cedam, Padova
Campiglio C (1995) Il principio di reciprocità nel diritto dei trattati. Cedam, Padova
Cançado Trindade AA (2005) International law for humankind: towards a New *Jus Gentium*. General course on public international law. RC 316:9–440, RC 317: 9-332

Cançado Trindade AA (2012) Le droit international pour la personne humaine. Pédone, Paris
Cannizzaro E (2000) Il principio della proporzionalità nell'ordinamento internazionale. Giuffrè, Milano
Cannizzaro E (2012) Diritto internazionale. Giappichelli, Torino
Cannone A (2018) Violazioni di carattere sistemico e Convenzione europea dei diritti dell'uomo. Cacucci, Bari
Capotorti F (1979) Study on the rights of persons belonging to ethnic, religious and linguistic minorities. UN Doc. E/CN.4/Sub.2/384/Rev.1
Capotorti F (1992) Il regime delle minoranze nel sistema delle Nazioni Unite e secondo l'art. 27 del Patto sui diritti civili e politici. Riv int dir uomo:102–112
Carli E (2019) La Politica di Sicurezza e di Difesa Comune dell'Unione europea. Profili di responsabilità internazionale. Giappichelli, Torino
Carpanelli E (2013) *Extraordinary renditions* e diritti umani: alcune riflessioni sul caso *Abu Omar*. DUDI 7:315–330
Carrillo Salcedo JA (1997) Reflections on the existence of a hierarchy of norms in international law. Eur J Int Law 8:583–595
Cassella S (ed) (2018) Le standard de *due diligence* et la responsabilité internationale, Société Française pour le Droit International, Journée d'etudes du Mans. Pedone, Paris
Cassese A (1984) Il diritto internazionale nel mondo contemporaneo. Il Mulino, Bologna
Cassese A (1995) Self-determination of peoples. A legal reappraisal. Cambridge University Press, Cambridge
Cassese A (1999) *Ex iniura ius oritur*: are we moving towards international legitimation of forcible humanitarian countermeasures in the world community? Eur J Int Law:23–30
Cassese A (2000) The Martens Clause: half a loaf or simply pie in the sky? Eur J Int Law 11:187–216
Cassese A (2003) International criminal law. Oxford University Press, Oxford
Cassese A (Gaeta P ed) (2003-2004) Diritto internazionale, Vol. I: I lineamenti, Vol. II: Problemi della comunità internazionale. Il Mulino, Bologna
Cassese A (2004) I diritti umani nel mondo contemporaneo. Laterza, Bari
Cassese A (2005) Lineamenti di diritto internazionale penale: Vol. I. Diritto sostanziale. Il Mulino, Bologna
Cassese A (Gaeta P ed) (2006) Diritto internazionale. Il Mulino, Bologna
Cassese A (2008) International criminal law, 2nd edn. Oxford University Press, Oxford
Cassese A (2012) A plea for a global community grounded in a core of human rights. In: Cassese A (ed) Realizing Utopia. The future of international law. Oxford University Press, Oxford, pp 136–144
Cassese A (Gaeta P ed) (2013) Diritto internazionale, 2nd edn. Il Mulino, Bologna
Cassese A, Gaeta P (2008) Le sfide attuali del diritto internazionale. Il Mulino, Bologna
Castellaneta M (2000) L'individuo e la protezione dell'ambiente nel diritto internazionale. RDI 83:913–964
Castellino J (2014) International law and self-determination: peoples, indigenous peoples, and minorities. In: Walter C, Von Ungern-Sternberg A, Abushov K (eds) Self-determination and secession in international law. Oxford University Press, Oxford, pp 27–44
Cataldi G (2006) Le deroghe ai diritti umani in stato di emergenza. In: Pineschi L (ed) La tutela internazionale dei diritti umani. Norme, garanzie, prassi. Giuffrè, Milano, pp 752–772
Cataldi G (2007) Diritti inderogabili. In: Flores M, Groppi T, Pisillo Mazzeschi R (eds) Diritti Umani. Cultura dei diritti e dignità della persona nell'epoca della globalizzazione: Dizionario, vol I. Utet, Torino, pp 382–385
Cataldi G (2012) Articolo 15. In: Bartole S, De Sena P, Zagrebelsky V (eds) Commentario breve alla Convenzione europea per la salvaguardia del diritti dell'uomo e delle libertà fondamentali. Cedam/Kluwer, Padova, pp 555–564
Cataldi G (2019) Sulla recente prassi in materia di comunicazioni di deroga alla Convenzione europea dei diritti dell'uomo. In: Sicilianos LA et al (eds) Regards croisés sur la protection

nationale et internationale des droits de l'homme, Liber Amicorum Guido Raimondi. Wolf Legal Publishers, Tilburg
Charney JI (1993) Universal international law. Am J Int Law 87:529–551
Chowdhury AR, Bhuiyan JH (eds) (2010) An introduction of International Human Rights Law. Brill, Leiden
Citroni G, Scovazzi T (2013) La tutela internazionale dei diritti umani, Parte III del Corso di diritto internazionale (Scovazzi T ed). Giuffrè, Milano
Clapham A (1993) Human Rights in the private sphere. Clarendon Press, Oxford
Clapham A (2006) Human Rights obligations of non-state actors. Oxford University Press, Oxford
Clapham A, Kamminga M (eds) (2004) Extraterrritorial application of Human Rights treaties. Intersentia, Antwerp
Cohen–Jonathan G, Flauss J (eds) (2005) Les ONG et le droit international des droits de l'homme. Bruylant, Bruxelles
Combacau J (1986) Le droit international: bric-à-brac ou système? Archives de philosophie du droit 31:85–105
Combacau J, Sur S (2006) Droit international public, 7th edn. LGDJ, Paris
Conforti B (1976) Appunti dalle lezioni di diritto internazionale. Editoriale Scientifica, Napoli
Conforti B (2006) Diritto internazionale, 7th edn. Editoriale Scientifica, Napoli
Conforti B (2007) Unité et fragmentation du droit international: glissez, mortels, n'appuyé pas. RGDIP 111:5–18
Conforti B (2015) Diritto internazionale, 10th edn. Editoriale Scientifica, Napoli
Conforti B (Iovane M ed) (2018) Diritto internazionale, 11th edn. Editoriale Scientifica, Napoli
Cornelisse G (2010) Immigration detention and human rights. Rethinking territorial sovereignty. Nijhoff, Leiden
Craven M (2000) Legal differentiation and the concept of the human rights treaty in international law. Eur J Int Law 11:489–519
Crawford J (1993) Democracy and international law. Br Yearb Int L 63:113–133
Crawford J (2002) The ILC's articles on responsibility of states for internationally wrongful acts: a retrospect. Am J Int Law 96:874–890
Crawford J (2006) The creation of states in international law, 2nd edn. Clarendon Press, Oxford
Crawford J (2013) Change, order, change: the course of international law. General course on public international law. RC 365:9–389
D'Amato A (1971) The concept of custom in international law. Cornell University Press, Ithaca
D'Argent P (2005) Le droit de la responsabilité internationale complété? Examen des principes fondamentaux et directives concernant le droit à un recours et à la réparation des victimes de violations flagrantes du droit international des droits de l'homme et de violations graves du droit international humanitaire. AFDI 51:27–55
D'Aspremont J (2011) Formalism and the sources of international law. Oxford University Press, Oxford
Daniele L (2014) Diritto dell'Unione europea. Sistema istituzionale-Ordinamento-Tutela giurisdizionale-Competenze, 5th edn. Giuffré, Milano
Davis H (2013) Human Rights law directions. Oxford University Press, Oxford
de Frouville O (2004) L'intangibilité des droits de l'homme en droit international. Pedone, Paris
De Martens GF (1875) Nouveau Recueil Général de Traités, Tome XX. Gottingue (Klaus reprint 1975)
De Schutter O (2010) International human rights law. cases, materials, commentary. Cambridge University Press, Cambridge
De Sena P (2002) La nozione di giurisdizione statale nei trattati sui diritti dell'uomo. Giappichelli, Torino
De Sena P (2004) Esigenze di sicurezza nazionale e tutela dei diritti dell'uomo nella recente prassi europea. In: Boschiero N (ed) Ordine internazionale e valori etici, VIII Convegno della SIDI (Verona, 2003). Editoriale Scientifica, Napoli, pp 195–268

De Sena P (2016) Proportionality and Human Rights in international law: some . . . 'Utilitarian' reflections. RDI 99:1009–1025
De Sena P, De Vittor F (2005) State immunity and human rights: the Italian Supreme Court Decision on the *Ferrini* case. Eur J Int Law 16:89–116
De Sena P, Saccucci A (2007) Diritti fondamentali. In: Flores M, Groppi T, Pisillo Mazzeschi R (eds) Diritti Umani. Cultura dei diritti e dignità della persona nell'epoca della globalizzazione: Dizionario, vol I. Utet, Torino, pp 376–382
De Sena P, Starita M (2019) Navigare fra istanze 'Stato-centriche' e 'cosmopolitiche': il caso 'Sea Watch' in una prospettiva conflittuale. SIDIBlog, 14 July 2019
De Wet E (2004) The prohibition of torture as an international norm of jus cogens and its implications for national and customary law. Eur J Int Law:97–121
De Wet E, Vidmar J (eds) (2012) Hierarchy in international law: the place of human rights. Oxford University Press, Oxford
Decaux E, de Frouville O (2016) Droit international public, 10th edn. Dalloz, Paris
Deschênes J (1985) Proposal concerning a definition of the term "minority". UN Doc. E/CN.4/Sub. 2/31
Di Filippo M (2012) L'ammissione di cittadini stranieri. In: Calamia AM, Di Filippo M, Gestri M (eds) Immigrazione, Diritto e Diritti: profili internazionalistici ed europei. Cedam, Padova, pp 81–126
Di Stasi A (2010) Diritti umani e sicurezza regionale. Il sistema europeo. Editoriale Scientifica, Napoli
Di Stasi A (ed) (2016) CEDU e ordinamento italiano. La giurisprudenza della Corte europea dei diritti dell'uomo e l'impatto nell'ordinamento interno (2010-2015). Kluwer/Cedam, Milano
Di Stasi A (ed) (2020) CEDU e ordinamento italiano. La giurisprudenza della Corte europea dei diritti dell'uomo e l'impatto nell'ordinamento interno (2016-2020), 2nd edn. Kluwer/CEDAM, Milano
Di Stefano A, Sapienza R (eds) (2012) La tutela dei diritti umani e il diritto internazionale. Editoriale Scientifica, Napoli
Dinstein Y (2006) The interaction between customary international law and treaties. RC 322:243–428
Dipla H (1994) La responsabilité de l'Etat pour violation des droits de l'homme: problèmes d'imputation. Pédone, Paris
Dominicé C (2013) La societé internationale à la recherche de son équilibre. Cours général de droit international public. RC 370:9–392
Doswald-Beck L (2011) Human rights in time of conflict and terrorism. Oxford University Press, Oxford
Dupuy P-M (2002) L'unité de l'ordre juridique international. Cours général de droit international public. RC 297:9–490
Dupuy P-M (2018) From a community of states towards a universal community? In: Pisillo Mazzeschi R, De Sena P (eds) Global justice, human rights and the modernization of international law. Springer, Cham, pp 47–66
Dupuy P-M, Kerbrat Y (2020) Droit international public, 15th edn. Dalloz, Paris
Dworkin R (1967) The model of rules. Univ Chic Law Rev 35:14–46
Dworkin R (1977) Taking rights seriously. Cambridge University Press, Cambridge
Edel F (2010) L'interdiction de la discrimination par la Convention européenne des droits de l'homme. Les Editions du Conseil de l'Europe, Strasbourg
Eide A (1984) The international human rights system. In: Eide A et al (eds) Food as a human right. The United Nations University, Tokyo, pp 152–161
Ergec R (1987) Les droits de l'homme à l'épreuve des circonstances exceptionnelles. Etude sur l'article 15 de la Convention européenne des droits de l'homme. Bruylant, Bruxelles
Ergec R (2006) Protection européenne et internationale des droits de l'homme. Bruylant, Bruxelles
Falk R (2014) Humanitarian intervention and legitimacy wars: seeking peace and justice in the 21th century. Routledge, Abington

Favilli C (ed) (2011) Procedure e garanzie del diritto di asilo. Cedam/Kluwer, Milano
Favilli C (2013) Migration law in Italy. Kluwer, Alphen aan den Rijn
Favuzza F (2018) Security detention in times of armed conflict: the relevance of international human rights law. Kluwer/Cedam, Milano
Ferrari Bravo L (2002) Lezioni di diritto internazionale, 4th edn. Editoriale Scientifica, Napoli
Focarelli C (2001) Equo processo e Convenzione europea dei diritti dell'uomo. Contributo alla determinazione dell'ambito di applicazione dell'art.6 della Convenzione. Cedam, Padova
Focarelli C (2008) Lezioni di diritto internazionale, vol I. Cedam, Padova
Focarelli C (2012–2013) Diritto internazionale, vol I, 2nd edn. Cedam, Padova
Focarelli C (2013) La persona umana nel diritto internazionale. Il Mulino, Bologna
Focarelli C (2015) Trattato di diritto internazionale. Utet/Kluwer, Torino-Milano
Focarelli C (2017) Diritto internazionale, 4th edn. Kluwer/Cedam, Milano
Focarelli C (2019) Diritto internazionale, 5th edn. Kluwer/Cedam, Milano
Forlati S (2005) Diritto dei trattati e responsabilità internazionale. Giuffrè, Milano
Forman L (2016) Can minimum core obligations survive a reasonableness standard of review under the optional protocol to the International Covenant on Economic, Social and Cultural Rights? Ottawa Law Rev 47:557–576
Forman L et al (2016) Conceptualising minimum core obligations under the right to health: How should we define and implement the 'morality of the depths'. Int J Hum Rights 20:531–548
Forsythe DP (2012) Human Rights in international relations. Cambridge University Press, Cambridge
Franchi M, Viarengo I (2016) Tutela internazionale dei diritti umani. Casi e materiali. Giappichelli, Torino
Francioni F (2007) The right of access to justice under customary international law. In: Francioni F (ed) Access to justice as a human right. Oxford University Press, Oxford, pp 1–55
Francioni F (2010) International human rights in an environmental horizon. Eur J Int Law 21:41–55
Francioni F (2018) Global justice, equality and social inclusion: what kind of 'modernization' of international law? In: Pisillo Mazzeschi R, De Sena P (eds) Global justice, human rights and the modernization of international law. Springer, Cham, pp 225–238
Francioni F, Scheinin M (eds) (2008) Cultural human rights. Nijhoff, Leiden
Franck TM (1990) The power of legitimacy among Nations. Oxford University Press, New York
Franck TM (1992) The emerging right to democratic governance. Am J Int Law 86:46–91
Freedman R (2013) The United Nations Human Rights Council. A critique and early assessment. Routledge, Abington
Freeman M, Van Ert G (2006) International human rights law: texts, cases and materials. Irwin Law, Toronto
Friedmann WG (1964) The changing structure of international law. Stevens, London
Gaeta P (ed) (2009) The UN genocide convention. A commentary. Oxford University Press, Oxford
Gaja G (1981) *Jus Cogens* beyond the Vienna convention on the law of treaties. RC 172:271–316
Gaja G (1986) Principi del diritto (diritto internazionale). ED XXXV:533–546
Gaja G (2012) General principles of law. EPIL, online edn. Oxford University Press, Oxford
Gaja G (2014) The protection of general interests in the international community. General course on public international law (2011). RC 364:13–185
Gearty C, Douzinas C (eds) (2012) The Cambridge companion to human rights law. Cambridge University Press, Cambridge
Gergen JA (1995–1996) Human rights and the foreign sovereign immunities. Virginia J Int Law 36:765–800
Glanville L (2014) Sovereignty and the responsibility to protect: a new history. University of Chicago Press, Chicago
Gradoni L, Pasquet L (2019) Lisistrata a Lampedusa: una riflessione sul caso Sea Watch 3. SIDIBlog, 6 July 2019
Guastini R (1993) Le fonti del diritto e l'interpretazione. Giuffrè, Milano

Hannikainen L (1988) Peremptory norms (jus cogens) in international law. Historical developments, criteria, present status. Publishing Finnish Lawyers' Company, Helsinki
Hannum H (ed) (2004) Guide to international human rights practice, 4th edn. Transnational Publishers, Ardsley
Hannum H et al (2018) International human rights: problems of law, policy and practice, 6th edn. Wolters Kluwer, New York
Henckaerts JM, Doswald-Beck L (2005) ICRC, Customary international humanitarian law, 3 vols. Cambridge University Press, Cambridge
Henkin L (1989) International law: politics, values and functions. RC 216:9–400
Henkin L (1995) Human rights. EPIL 2:886–893
Henkin L (1995–1996) Human rights and state sovereignty. Georgia J Int Comp Law 25:31–45
Henkin L, Cleveland SH, Helfer LR, Neuman GL, Orentlicher DF (2009) Human rights. Foundation Press, New York
Hennebel L, Tigroudja H (2016) Traité de droit international des droits de l'homme. Pédone, Paris
Hertig Randall M, Hottelier M (eds) (2014) Introduction aux droits de l'homme. Schulthess, Zürich
Higgins R (1976–1977) Derogations under Human Rights treaties. Br Yearb Int L 48:281–319
Hobbes T (1651) In: Shapiro I (ed) Leviathan: or the matter, forme, and power of a commonwealth ecclesiasticall and civill. Yale University Press, New Haven, 2010
Iovane M (2000) La tutela dei valori fondamentali nel diritto internazionale. Editoriale Scientifica, Napoli
Iovane M (2007) Gross violations of human rights. In: Flores M, Groppi T, Pisillo Mazzeschi R (eds) Diritti Umani. Cultura dei diritti e dignità della persona nell'epoca della globalizzazione: Dizionario, vol 1. Utet, Torino, pp 675–680
Iovane M (2008) La participation de la société civile à l'élaboration et à l'application du droit international de l'environnement. RGDIP 112:465–520
Janis MW, Kay RS, Bradley AW (2008) European human rights law: text and materials, 3rd edn. Oxford University Press, Oxford
Jennings RY (1979) Treaties as legislation. In: Wilner GM (ed) Jus et Societas. Essays in tribute to Wolfgang Friedmann. Springer, The Hague, pp 159–168
Joseph S, Schultz J, Castan M (2004) The international covenant on civil and political rights: cases, materials and commentary, 2nd edn. Oxford University Press, Oxford
Kälin W, Künzli J (2009) The law of international human rights protection. Oxford University Press, Oxford
Kälin W, Künzli J (2019) The law of international human rights protection, 2nd edn. Oxford University Press, Oxford
Kamminga MT (2009) Impact on state succession in respect of treaties. In: Kamminga MT, Scheinin M (eds) The impact of human rights law on general international law. Oxford University Press, Oxford, pp 99–109
Kamminga MT, Scheinin M (eds) (2009) The impact of human rights law on general international law. Oxford University Press, Oxford
Kamto M (2002) Une troublante 'Immunité totale' du Ministre des affaires étrangères. RBDI 35:518–530
Kamto M (ed) (2011) La Chartre africaine des droits de l'homme et des peoples. Bruylant, Bruxelles
Keller H, Ulfstein G (eds) (2012) UN Human Rights Treaty bodies: law and legitimacy: studies on human rights conventions. Cambridge University Press, Cambridge
Kelsen H (1966) Principles of international law, 2nd edn. Holt, Rinehart, New York
Kolb R (2001) Théorie du ius cogens international. Essai de relecture d'un concept. PUF, Paris
Kolb R (2002) La structure constitutionnelle du droit international public. Can Yearb Int Law 39:69–115
Kolb R, Scalia D (eds) (2012) Droit international penal: Précis, 2nd edn. Helbing Lichtenhahn, Bâle
Koskenniemi M, Leino P (2002) Fragmentation of international law? Post-modern anxieties. Leiden J Int Law 15:553–579

Krause K, Scheinin M (eds) (2009) International protection of human rights: a textbook. Åbo Akademi University Institute for Human Rights, Turku

Krieg A (2013) Motivations for humanitarian intervention: theoretical and empirical considerations. Springer, Dordrecht

Krieger H, Peters A, Kreuzer L (eds) (2020) Due diligence in the international legal order. Oxford University Press, Oxford

Kulesza J (2016) Due diligence in international law. Brill/Nijhoff, Leiden-Boston

Lattanzi F (1983) Garanzie dei diritti dell'uomo nel diritto internazionale generale. Giuffrè, Milano

Lemkin R (1944) Axis rule in occupied europe: laws of occupation, analysis of government, proposals for redress. Carnegie Endowment for International Peace, Washington, D.C.

Lenzerini F (ed) (2008) Reparations for indigenous peoples: international and comparative perspectives. Oxford University Press, Oxford

Lenzerini F (2009a) Asilo e diritti umani. L'evoluzione del diritto d'asilo nel diritto internazionale. Giuffrè, Milano

Lenzerini F (2009b) The evolution of Italian jurisprudence concerning the relationship between the constitutional right of asylum and the recognition of refugee status. Ital Yearb Int Law 19:139–156

Lenzerini F (2012) Il principio del *non-refoulement* dopo la sentenza *Hirsi* della Corte europea dei diritti dell'uomo. RDI 95:721–761

Lenzerini F (2014) The culturalization of human rights law. Oxford University Press, Oxford

Lerner N (2015) The UN convention on the elimination of all forms of racial discrimination. Brill/ Nijhoff, Leiden

Liguori A (2012) La Corte europea dei diritti dell'uomo condanna l'Italia per i respingimenti verso la Libia del 2009: il caso *Hirsi*. RDI 95:415–443

Lochak D (2009) Les droits de l'homme. La Découverte, Paris

Marchegiani M (2018) Il principio della protezione equivalente come meccanismo di coordinamento tra sistemi giuridici nell'ordinamento internazionale. Editoriale Scientifica, Napoli

Marchesi A (2011) La protezione internazionale dei diritti umani. Nazioni Unite e organizzazioni regionali. Franco Angeli, Milano

Martinez Cobo J (1983) Study of the problem of discrimination against indigenous populations, conclusions, proposals and recommendations. UN Doc. E/CN.4/ Sub.2/1983/21/ Add. 8, 30 September 1983

Martinez Cobo J (1986) Study of the problem of discrimination against indigenous populations. UN Doc. E/CN.4/Sub.2/1986/7 and Add. 1-4

McCorquodale R (ed) (2003) Human rights. Aldershot/Hants, Ashgate

McDonald RSJ (1997) Derogations under Article 15 of the European Convention on Human Rights. Col JTL 36:225–267

McDougal MS (1980) Human Rights and World Public Order: the basic policies of an international law of human dignity. Yale University Press, New Haven

Medina Quiroga C (2016) The American Convention on Human Rights. Crucial rights and their theory and practice, 2nd edn. Intersentia, Cambridge

Meijknecht A (2001) Towards international personality: the position of minorities and indigenous peoples in international law. Intersentia, Antwerpen

Meron T (ed) (1984) Human Rights in international law: legal and policy issues. Clarendon Press, Oxford

Meron T (1986) On a hierarchy of international human rights. Am J Int Law 80:1–23

Meron T (1987) Human rights in internal strife: their international protection. Cambridge University Press, Cambridge

Meron T (1989) Human rights and humanitarian norms as customary law. Clarendon Press, Oxford

Meron T (2003) International law in the age of human rights. General course on public international law. RC 301:9–490

Meron T (2006) The humanization of international law. Nijhoff, Leiden

Milanovic M (2011) Extraterritorial application of human rights treaties: law, principles, and policy. Oxford University Press, Oxford
Moeckli D, Shah S, Sivakumaran S (eds) (2010) International human rights law. Oxford University Press, Oxford
Moore JB (1898) History and digest of the international arbitrations to which the United States has been a party, vol I. G.P.O., Washington
Moriarty B, Massa E (eds) (2012) Human rights law. Oxford University Press, Oxford
Mosler H (1980) The international society as a legal community. Sijthoff, Alphen aan den Rijn
Mowbray A (2004) The development of positive obligations under the European Convention on Human Rights by the European Court of Human Rights. Hart, Oxford
Mullerson R (1993) The continuity and succession of states by reference to the former USSR and Yugoslavia. Int Comp Law Q 42:473–493
Murphy T (2013) Health and human rights. Hart, London
Nigro R (2005) Giurisdizione ed obblighi positivi degli Stati parti della Convenzione europea dei diritti dell'uomo: il caso *Ilaşcu*. RDI 88:413–440
Nigro R (2018) Le immunità giurisdizionali dello Stato e dei suoi organi e l'evoluzione della sovranità nel diritto internazionale. Kluwer/Cedam, Milano
Nowak M (2003) Introduction to the International Human Rights regime. Nijhoff, Leiden
Nowak M, McArthur E (2008) The United Nations Convention against torture: a commentary. Oxford University Press, Oxford
Oberdorff H (2012) Droits de l'homme et libertés fondamentales. LGDJ, Paris
Orakhelashvili A (2006) Peremptory norms in international law. Oxford University Press, Oxford
Orford A (2011) International authority and the responsibility to protect. Cambridge University Press, Cambridge
Padelletti ML (2003) La tutela della proprietà nella Convenzione europea dei diritti dell'uomo. Giuffrè, Milano
Papa MI (2020) La tutela degli interessi collettivi nell'ordinanza sulle misure provvisorie nel caso *Gambia c. Myanmar*. RDI 103:729–755
Parlett K (2011) The individual in the international legal system: continuity and change in international law. Cambridge University Press, Cambridge
Pavoni R (2013) Interesse pubblico e diritti individuali nella giurisprudenza ambientale della Corte europea dei diritti umani. Editoriale Scientifica, Napoli
Pellet A (2000) 'Droits-de-l'hommisme' et droit international. Gilberto Amado Memorial Lecture", 18 July 2000, United Nations
Peters A (2016) Beyond human rights: the legal status of the individual in International Law. Cambridge University Press, Cambridge
Picone P (2005) Obblighi *erga omnes* e codificazione della responsabilità degli Stati. RDI 88:893–954
Picone P (2008) La distinzione fra norme internazionali di jus cogens e norme che producono obblighi erga omnes. RDI 91:5–38
Pineschi L (ed) (2006) La tutela internazionale dei diritti umani. Norme, garanzie, prassi. Giuffrè, Milano
Pisillo Mazzeschi R (1984) Risoluzione e sospensione dei trattati per inadempimento. Giuffrè, Milano
Pisillo Mazzeschi R (1989) "Due Diligence" e responsabilità internazionale degli Stati. Giuffrè, Milano
Pisillo Mazzeschi R (1992) The due diligence rule and the nature of the international responsibility of states. German Yearb Int Law 35:9–51
Pisillo Mazzeschi R (1994a) La dottrina pura del diritto di Kelsen e la realtà del diritto internazionale contemporaneo. Diritto e Cultura IV:43–66
Pisillo Mazzeschi R (1994b) Trattati e consuetudine nella codificazione del diritto internazionale. Com int 49:196–222

Pisillo Mazzeschi R (1999a) Il diritto di asilo 50 anni dopo la Dichiarazione universale dei diritti dell'uomo. Riv int dir uomo 12:694–703

Pisillo Mazzeschi R (1999b) International obligations to provide for reparation claims? In: Randelzhofer A, Tomuschat C (eds) State responsibility and the individual: reparation in instances of grave violations of Human Rights. Nijhoff, The Hague, pp 149–172

Pisillo Mazzeschi R (2003) Reparation claims by individuals for state breaches of humanitarian law and human rights: an overview. J Int Crim Just 1:339–347

Pisillo Mazzeschi R (2004a) The marginal role of the individual in the ILC's articles on state responsibility. Ital Yearb Int Law 14:39–51

Pisillo Mazzeschi R (2004b) The marginal role of the individual in the ILC's articles on state responsibility. Ital Yearb Int Law 14:39–51

Pisillo Mazzeschi R (2008) Responsabilité de l'État pour violation des obligations positives relatives aux droits de l'homme. RC 333:175–506

Pisillo Mazzeschi R (2009) Impact on the law of diplomatic protection. In: Kamminga MT, Scheinin M (eds) The impact of human rights law on general international law. Oxford University Press, Oxford, pp 211–233

Pisillo Mazzeschi R (2011) The relationship between Human Rights and the Rights of aliens and immigrants. In: Fastenrath U et al (eds) From bilateralism to community interest: essays in Honour of Judge Bruno Simma. Oxford University Press, Oxford, pp 552–573

Pisillo Mazzeschi R (2012) Il rapporto fra norme di *ius cogens* e la regola sull'immunità degli Stati: alcune osservazioni critiche sulla sentenza della Corte internazionale di giustizia del 3 febbraio 2012. DUDI 6:310–326

Pisillo Mazzeschi R (2014a) La protezione internazionale dei diritti dell'uomo e il suo impatto sulle concezioni e metodologie della dottrina giuridica internazionalistica. DUDI 8:275–318

Pisillo Mazzeschi R (2014b) Human Rights and the modernization of international law. In: Lenzerini F, Vrdoljak AF (eds) International law for common goods: normative perspectives on Human Rights, culture and nature. Hart, Oxford, pp 89–101

Pisillo Mazzeschi R (2014c) Organi degli Stati stranieri (immunità giurisdizionale degli). ED-Annali VII:735–794

Pisillo Mazzeschi R (2016) Popoli indigeni. In: Enciclopedia di Bioetica e Scienza Giuridica, Parte giuridica. ESI, Napoli, pp 459–473

Pisillo Mazzeschi R (2017) Sicurezza umana e diritto internazionale. In: Triggiani E et al (eds) Dialoghi con Ugo Villani, vol I. Cacucci, Bari, pp 353–362

Pisillo Mazzeschi R (2018a) Le chemin étrange de la due diligence: d'un concept mystérieux à un concept surévalué. In: Cassella S (ed) Le standard de *due diligence* et la responsabilité internationale, SFDI Journée d'etudes du Mans. Pédone, Paris, pp 323–337

Pisillo Mazzeschi R (2018b) Coordination of different principles and values in international law. German Yearb Int Law 61:209–250

Pisillo Mazzeschi R, De Sena P (eds) (2018) Global justice, human rights and the modernization of international law. Springer, Cham

Pisillo Mazzeschi R, Viviani A (2018) General principles of international law: from rules to values? In: Pisillo Mazzeschi R, De Sena P (eds) Global justice, human rights and the modernization of international law. Springer, Cham, pp 113–161

Pocar F (1998) Note sulla giurisprudenza del Comitato dei diritti dell'uomo in materia di minoranze. In: Bartole S, Olivetti Rason N, Pegoraro L (eds) La tutela giuridica delle minoranze. Cedam, Padova, pp 31–39

Provost R (2002) International Human Rights and Humanitarian Law. Cambridge University Press, Cambridge

Pustorino P (1995) Sull'applicabilità diretta e la prevalenza della Convenzione europea dei diritti dell'uomo nell'ordinamento italiano. Riv int dir uomo:23–37

Pustorino P (1998) L'interpretazione della Convenzione europea dei diritti dell'uomo nella prassi della Commissione e della Corte di Strasburgo. Editoriale Scientifica, Napoli

Pustorino P (2006) Questioni in materia di tutela delle minoranze nel diritto internazionale ed europeo. Studi integr eur 1:259–279
Pustorino P (2019) Lezioni di tutela internazionale dei diritti umani. Cacucci, Bari
Pustorino P (2020) Lezioni di tutela internazionale dei diritti umani, 2nd edn. Cacucci, Bari
Ragazzi M (1997) The concept of international obligations Erga Omnes. Oxford University Press, Oxford
Ramcharan BG (2002) The Security Council and the protection of Human Rights. Nijhoff, The Hague
Ramcharan BG (2011) The UN Human Rights Council. Routledge, London
Raz J (1972) Legal principles and the limits of law. Yale Law J 81:823–854
Robert J, Duffar J (2009) Droits de l'homme et libertés fondamentales. LGDJ, Paris
Robertson G (1999) Crimes against humanity: the struggle for global justice. Allen Lane/Penguin Press, London
Robertson AH, Merrils JG (1996) Human rights in the World. An introduction to the study of the international protection of Human Rights, 4th edn. Manchester University Press, Manchester
Rodley NS (1999) The treatment of prisoners in International Law, 2nd edn. Oxford University Press, Oxford
Ronzitti N (1978) La disciplina dello *ius cogens* nella Convenzione di Vienna sul diritto dei trattati. CS XV:243 ff
Ronzitti N (1984) Trattati contrari a norme imperative del diritto internazionale? In: Studi in onore di Giuseppe Sperduti. Giuffrè, Milano, pp 209–272
Ronzitti N (2007) Ius cogens. In: Flores M, Groppi T, Pisillo Mazzeschi R (eds) Diritti Umani. Cultura dei diritti e dignità della persona nell'epoca della globalizzazione: Dizionario, vol II. Utet, Torino, pp 805–808
Ronzitti N (2016) Introduzione al diritto internazionale, 5th edn. Giappichelli, Torino
Rossi V (2019) Il riconoscimento del diritto universale a un ambiente sano: questioni aperte e percorsi evolutivi. In: Cataldi G (ed) I diritti umani a settant'anni dalla Dichiarazione universale delle Nazioni Unite, vol I. Editoriale Scientifica, Napoli, pp 157–189
Russo D (2012) L'efficacia dei trattati sui diritti umani. Giuffrè, Milano
Ryngaert C, Noortmann M (2014) Human security and international law: the challenge of non-state actors. In: Ryngaert C et al (eds) Human security and international law: the challenge of non-state actors. Intersentia, Cambridge, pp 1–11
Saccucci A (2005) Profili di tutela dei diritti umani tra Nazioni Unite e Consiglio d'Europa. Cedam, Padova
Saccucci A (2018) La responsabilità internazionale dello Stato per violazioni strutturali dei diritti umani. Editoriale Scientifica, Napoli
Sands P (2017) La strada verso Est. Guanda, Milano
Sands P, Peel J (eds) (2018) Principles of International environmental law, 4th edn. Cambridge University Press, Cambridge
Scelle G (1934) Précis de Droit des Gens. Principes et systématique, Deuxième partie. Recueil Sirey, Paris
Schachter O (1991) International law in theory and practice. Nijhoff, Dordrecht
Scheinin M (2009) Impact on the law of treaties. In: Kamminga MT, Scheinin M (eds) The Impact of Human Rights law on general international law. Oxford University Press, Oxford, pp 23–36
Scheinin M (2013) Core rights and obligations. In: Shelton D (ed) Oxford handbook of international human rights law. Oxford University Press, Oxford, pp 527–540
Scovazzi T (ed) (2013) Corso di diritto internazionale, Parte III. Giuffrè, Milano
Scovazzi T, Citroni G (2007) The struggle against enforced disappearance and the 2007 United Nations Convention. Nijhoff, Leiden
Seiderman ID (2001) Hierarchy in international law: the human rights dimension. Intersentia, Antwerp
Sen A (2009) The idea of justice. Allen Lane, London

Shabas W (2009) Genocide in International Law. The crime of crimes. Cambridge University Press, Cambridge
Shelton D (2010) Regional protection of Human Rights. Oxford University Press, Oxford
Shelton D (2014a) Advanced introduction to international human rights law. Edward Elgar, Cheltenham
Shelton D (2014b) International law and 'relative normativity'. In: Evans MD (ed) International law, 4th edn. Oxford University Press, Oxford, p 137 ff
Shue H (1980) Basic rights: subsistence, affluence, and US Foreign Policy. Princeton University Press, Princeton
Shue H (1996) Basic rights: subsistence, affluence, and US Foreign Policy, 2nd edn. Princeton University Press, Princeton
Sicilianos LA (1993) The relationship between reprisals and denunciation or suspension of a treaty. Eur J Int Law 4:341–359
Sicilianos LA (2002) The classification of obligations and the multilateral dimension of the relations of international responsibility. Eur J Int Law 13:1127–1145
Sicilianos LA (2012) L'influence des droits de l'homme sur la structure du droit international. RGDIP 116: 5–30 and 241–274
Sieghart P (1983) The international law of human rights. Clarendon Press, Oxford
Simma B (1970) Reflections on Article 60 of the Vienna Convention on the Law of Treaties and its background in general international law. ÖZöR 20:5–81
Simma B (1985) Self-contained regimes. Netherlands Yearb Int Law 16:111–136
Simma B (1993) International Human Rights and general international law: a comparative analysis. In: Collected courses of the academy of European Law, vol. IV, Book 2. EUI, Florence, pp 153–236
Simma B (1994) From bilateralism to community interest in international law. RC 250:217–384
Simma B (2009) Universality of international law from the perspective of a practitioner. Eur J Int Law 20:265–297
Simma B, Alston P (1992) The sources of human rights law: custom, *Jus Cogens*, and general principles. Aust Yearb Int L 12:82–108
Simma B, Paulus AL (1999) The responsibility of individuals for human rights abuses in internal conflicts: a positivist view. Am J Int Law 93:302–316
Simma B, Pulkowski D (2006) Of planets and the universe: self-contained regimes in International Law. Eur J Int Law 17:483–529
Sisay AY (2013) The justiciability of economic, social and cultural rights in the African Regional Human Rights System: theory, practice and prospect. Intersentia, Cambridge
Sommario E (2018) Stati d'emergenza e trattati a tutela dei diritti umani. Giappichelli, Torino
Spencer J, Spencer M (2005) Human Rights. Sweet & Maxwell, London
Ssenyonio M (2009) Economic, social and cultural rights in international law. Hart, Oxford
Starita M (2011) I principi democratici nel diritto dell'Unione Europea. Giappichelli, Torino
Starita M (2019) Il dovere di soccorso in mare e il diritto di obbedire al diritto (internazionale) del comandante della nave privata. DUDI 13:5–47
Steiner HJ, Alston P, Goodman R (2008) International Human Rights in context: law, politics, morals. text and materials, 3rd edn. Oxford University Press, Oxford
Sudre F (1995) Droits intangibles et/ou droits fondamentaux: y a-t-il des droits préeminents dans la Convention européenne des droits de l'homme? In: Liber Amicorum Marc-André Eissen. Bruylant, Bruxelles, pp 381–398
Sudre F (2001) Droit international et européen des droits de l'homme, 5th edn. PUF, Paris
Sudre F (2006) Droit européen et international des droits de l'homme, 8th edn. PUF, Paris
Sudre F (2015) Le droit international et européen des droits de l'homme, 12th edn. PUF, Paris
Sunga LS (2009) The concept of human security: does it add anything of value to international legal theory or practice? In: Frick ML, Oberprantacher A (eds) Power and justice in international relations: interdisciplinary approaches to global challeges. Ashgate, Farham, pp 131–146

Suy E (1983) Droits des traités et droits de l'homme. In: Festschrift für Hermann Mosler. Springer, Berlin, pp 935–947

Svensson-McCarthy AL (1998) The international law of human rights and states of exception. With special reference to the *Travaux Preparatoires* and case-law of the international monitoring organs. Nijhoff, The Hague

Symonides J (ed) (2003) Human Rights: international protection, monitoring, enforcement. Unesco Publishing/Ashgate, Paris

Talmon S (2015) Determining customary international law: the ICJ's methodology between induction, deduction and assertion. Eur J Int Law 26:417–443

Tams C (2005) Enforcing obligations Erga Omnes in international law. Cambridge University Press, Cambridge

Tancredi A (2001) La secessione nel diritto internazionale. Cedam, Padova

Thakur R (2011) The responsibility to protect: norms, laws, and the use of force in International Politics. Routledge, London

Thirlway HWA (1972) International customary law and codification. Sijthoff, Leiden

Thornberry P (1991) International law and the rights of minorities. Clarendon Press, Oxford

Tladi D (2016) First report on peremptory norms of general international law (*jus cogens*). A/CN.4/693, 8 March 2016

Tladi D (2017) Second report on peremptory norms of general international law (*jus cogens*). A/CN.4/706, 16 March 2017

Tladi D (2018) Third report on peremptory norms of general international law (*jus cogens*). A/CN.4/714, 12 February 2018

Tladi D (2019) Fourth report on peremptory norms of general international law (*jus cogens*) A/CN.4/727, 31 January 2019

Tomuschat C (1993) Obligations arising for states without or against their will. RC 241:195–374

Tomuschat C (1999) International law: ensuring the survival of mankind on the eve of a new century. General course on public international law. RC 281:9–438

Tomuschat C (2014) Human Rights: between idealism and realism, 3rd edn. Oxford University Press, Oxford

Tomuschat C (2018) General international law: a new source of international law? In: Pisillo Mazzeschi R, De Sena P (eds) Global justice, human rights and the modernization of International Law. Springer, Cham, pp 185–204

Tomuschat C, Kohen M (eds) (2020) Flexibility in international dispute settlement. Conciliation revisited. Brill/Nijhoff, Leiden/Boston

Tomuschat C, Thouvenin JM (eds) (2006) The fundamental rules of the international legal order. *Jus Cogens* and obligations *Erga Omnes*. Nijhoff, Leiden

Tomuschat C, Pisillo Mazzeschi R, Thurer D (eds) (2016) Conciliation in international law. The OSCE Court of conciliation and arbitration. Brill/Nijhoff, Leiden

Tonolo S, Pascale G (eds) (2020) La Dichiarazoine universale dei diritti umani nel diritto internazionale contemporaneo. Giappichelli, Torino

Treves T (2005) Diritto internazionale. Problemi fondamentali. Giuffrè, Milano

Treves T (2019) The expansion of International Law. General course on public international law (2015). RC 398:9–398

Tunkin GI (1974) Theory of international law (trans: Butler WE). George Allen & Unwin Ltd., London

Ulfstein G, Risini I (2020) Inter-state applications under the European Convention on human rights: strength and challenges. Eur J Int Law Talk! 24 January 2020

Van Alebeek R (2000) The *Pinochet* case: international human rights law on trial. Br Yearb Int L 71:29–70

Van Dijk P, Van Hoof JH, Van Rijn A, Zwaak L (eds) (2006) Theory and practice of the European Convention on Human Rights, 4th edn. Intersentia, Antwerp

Verdross A (1966) *Jus Dispositivum* and *Jus Cogens* in International Law. Am J Int Law 60:55–63

Verdross A (1968) Les principes généraux de droit dans le système des sources du droit international public. In: Guggenheim P (ed) Recueil d'études de droit international en hommage à P. Guggenheim. Georg, Geneva, pp 521–530

Viarengo I (2005) Deroghe e restrizioni alla tutela dei diritti umani nei sistemi internazionali di garanzia. RDI 88:955–996

Villani U (2005) Studi su La protezione internazionale dei diritti umani. Luiss University Press, Roma

Villani U (2015) Dalla Dichiarazione universale alla Convenzione europea dei diritti dell'uomo, 2nd edn. Cacucci, Bari

Villani U (2017) Istituzioni di Diritto dell'Unione europea, 5th edn. Cacucci, Bari

Villani U (2020) Le misure italiane di contrasto al Covid-19 e il rispetto dei diritti umani. Com int 75:165–188

Viviani A (2005) Crimini internazionali e responsabilità dei leader politici e militari. Giuffrè, Milano

Viviani A (2013) L'identità personale nel Sistema della Convenzione europea dei diritti dell'uomo. Editoriale Scientifica, Napoli

Voyiakis E (2003) Access to Court v. State immunity. Int Comp Law Q 52:297–332

Weil P (1983) Towards relative normativity in international law? Am J Int Law 77:413–442

Weil P (1992) Le droit international en quête de son identité. Cours général de droit international public. RC 237:1–369

Weissbrodt D (2000) Prevention of discrimination: the rights of non-citizens: final report of the special rapporteur. UN Doc. E/CN.4/Sub.2/2003/23 and Add.1, 25 May 2000

Weissbrodt D, de la Vega C (2007) International human rights law. An introduction. University of Pennsylvania Press, Philadelphia

Weissbrodt DS, Aolain FN, Newman FC, Fitzpatrick J (eds) (2009) International human rights: law, policy and process. LexisNexis, Newark

Wood M (2013) First report on formation and evidence of customary international law. UN Doc. A/CN.4/663, 17 May 2013

Wouters J, Ryngaert C (2009) Impact on the process of the formation of customary international law. In: Kamminga MT, Scheinin M (eds) The impact of human rights law on general international law. Oxford University Press, Oxford, pp 111–131

Zagrebelsky V, Chenal R, Tomasi L (2016) Manuale dei diritti fondamentali in Europa. Il Mulino, Bologna

Zagrebelsky V, Chenal R, Tomasi L (2019) Manuale dei diritti fondamentali in Europa, 2nd edn. Il Mulino, Bologna

Zanghì C (2013) La protezione internazionale dei diritti dell'uomo, 3rd edn. Giappichelli, Torino

Zanghì C, Panella L (2019) La protezione internazionale dei diritti dell'uomo, 4th edn. Giappichelli, Torino

Zappalà S (2011) La tutela internazionale dei diritti umani. Il Mulino, Bologna

The manufacturer's authorised representative in the EU is Springer Nature Customer Service Centre GmbH, Europaplatz 3, 69115 Heidelberg, Germany. If you have any concerns regarding our products, please contact ProductSafety@springernature.com

Printed and bound by CPI Group (UK) Ltd, Croydon, CR0 4YY
30/09/2026
02225505-0018